Business Law

Tom Harrison BA(Hons), Grad Cert Ed, LLM (London)
John Ellison LLB (Hons), Grad Cert Ed, LLM (Dunelm)
Jim Bedingfield BA(Hons), Grad Cert Ed, Solicitor

The Authors are all Senior Lecturers in Law at New College Durham

Harrison Law Publishing
1997

ISBN 0 907679 92 7

First Edition 1987
  Reprinted 1989,1990
Second Edition 1991
  Reprinted 1992,1993
Third Edition 1994
  Reprinted 1995
Fourth Edition 1997

Cover design by Gerard Callaghan

Illustrations by Moira Page

Published in Great Britain by Harrison Law Publishing in association with
Business Education Publishers Limited
Leighton House 10 Grange Crescent Stockton Road
Sunderland Tyne and Wear SR2 7BN

Tel. 0191 567 4963
Fax. 0191 514 3277

British Cataloguing-in-Publications Data
A catalogue record for this book is available from the British Library

Printed and bound in Great Britain at The Bath Press, Bath

Preface

It is now ten years since the first edition of this textbook was published. In that time most areas of law falling under the collective title of business law have experienced change. In some cases this change has been of marginal impact, but in others change of real substance has emerged, introducing new or amended rights and obligations within the field of business law. This edition reflects a range of recent legal developments that embrace both marginal and substantive change in numerous areas of law including sale of goods and services, contract, tort, intellectual property, employment, business organisations and the European Community.

The dilemma in producing a student textbook of this kind remains that of achieving a balance between proper coverage of the subject for the level of study at which it is aimed, and text which is manageable and accessible. We hope that we have met these dual objectives in this edition. Our aim remains to produce a text which is of use to students embarking on a foundation course in business law and also to serve as a resource for those students going on to study legal options such as corporate law, employment law, commercial law and intellectual property law. Mindful of keeping the content manageable we have reorganised some of the earlier chapters by splitting them up and reordering them. We have also introduced at the beginning of each chapter a glossary of terms aimed at providing a quick guide to the principal concepts and technical expressions covered. We have tried to keep the glossaries as simple and user friendly as accuracy allows, but they should not be seen as a substitute for a legal dictionary. As with previous editions most chapters conclude with assignments designed to confirm the achievements of learning through practical work based problem scenarios.

The book assumes no previous knowledge on the part of the reader. With this in mind the introductory chapters explore the nature of law and the legal system. The overall structure of the text takes the student on a logical journey through the legal environment in which the business community operates, covering in depth the internal and external legal framework of business, including legal relationships, liabilities and the use of business resources.

Above all we hope that readers of the book will find their legal studies enjoyable as well as informative, and that for some it may mark the beginning of a more comprehensive exploration of the law.

For ease of expression the book adopts, in general, the practice of using 'he' for 'he or she', and 'his' for 'his and hers'.

TH

JE

JB

Acknowledgements

Thanks to Paul for his technical assistance, and special thanks to Moira for her patience and her ability to decipher our often woefully handwritten text.

All errors and omissions remain the responsibility of the authors.

The law is stated as at the 1st January 1997.

TH JE JB

Durham, January 1997

Table of Contents

Chapter 5　The Legal Relationships in Business

Chapter 6　Legal Liability in Business

Chapter 7　The Dissolution of Business Organisations

Chapter 8　Contractual Formation

Chapter 9　The Contract: issues of Validity

Chapter 10   The Contract Terms Discharge and Remedies

Chapter 11   Business Contracting

Chapter 12   Consumer Protection: Goods

Chapter 13   Consumer Protection: Services

Chapter 14   Law Relating to the Recruitment of Staff

Table of Cases

A

B

C

D

G

H

I

J

K

L

M

N

O

P

R

S

T

U

V

W

Y

Table of Statutes, Statutory Instruments and Treaties

Legal Terms found in Chapter 1

Actus reus
- conduct prohibited by the criminal law

Adjudicate
- to settle a legal problem by giving judgment

Advocacy
- the activity of pleading a case before a court or tribunal

Civil law
- that part of the law dealing with the personal rights and obligations of individuals and organisations

Criminal law
- a branch of public law describing rules whose breach results in criminal proceedings and punishment

Defendant
- a party against whom a civil claim is brought (also person subject to criminal prosecution, where the term 'accused' is commonly used instead)

Dictum
- statement made by a judge in the course of delivering a judgment at the end of a trial

Doctrine
- general principle of law

Equitable
- literally fair and just, but in a legal sense

Law report
- published report of court proceedings containing the court's judgment

Litigant
- a party involved in civil proceedings

Mens rea
- 'guilty mind', state of mind required for a criminal offence

Plaintiff
- person or organisation bringing a civil action

Chapter 1

An Introduction to Business Law

The Nature and Purpose of Law

The principal objective of a legal system is the establishment of rules designed in the broadest sense to regulate relationships. Human societies are highly complex social structures. Without systems of rules or codes of conduct to control them, such societies have difficulty in maintaining their cohesion, and gradually break up. The interdependence of each member of a community with its other members creates a continuous interaction between individuals and groups and this contact inevitably can lead to occasional disagreement and conflict. In a Western culture like ours, which recognises that people should have the freedom to express their individualism, the realisation of that freedom can result in the infringement of the rights of others. Someone operating a commercial enterprise by selling second hand cars in the street outside his house, or building an extension, or holding regular all night parties may treat these activities as the exercise of basic personal freedoms. They will however give rise to conflict if neighbours resent the street being turned into a used vehicle lot, or find the light to their windows and gardens cut out by the new building, or that they cannot sleep at night for noise. Where interests conflict in this way the law attempts to reconcile differences by referring their solution to established principles and rules which have been developed to clarify individual rights and obligations. The relationships between neighbours are but a small part of the complex pattern of relationships most people are involved in and which the law attempts to regulate.

However the law is not the sole binding agent of our social structure. It is not only legal rules which are responsible for guaranteeing social cohesion. Institutions which create legal rules are merely one facet of the wider institutional structure of our society. Political, economic, commercial, cultural and religious institutions are amongst those located in the broader social fabric and which contribute to what we term our *society*. Their contribution also includes the development of rules. Schools and religious institutions for instance recognise a responsibility for the teaching of ethics and morality, and this reminds us that we should not assume rule making to be the sole prerogative of the law. The rules and codes of conduct developed from our sense of moral justice and our perceptions of fairness and unfairness are important determinants of our behaviour. Like legal rules, moral rules guide our conduct and inform us how we should behave in given circumstances. Rules of this kind are described as *normative*. They indicate how we ought to conduct ourselves.

A major difference between legal and moral rules is seen in the sanctions which apply if they are broken. Breach of legal rules carries a potential formal sanction, proceedings before a court followed by a court order. Breaching the moral code does not of itself trigger any formal consequence; we may however feel personally discredited by how we have behaved and find that others who are aware of our conduct avoid or criticise us. So it may be that our neighbour keeps the noise down at night motivated more by a sense of what is fair and reasonable than through any concern over legal sanctions.

In business, ethical considerations also play a role in informing organisational behaviour, although usually in a more diluted form, for the personality of the individuals making up the organisation has a tendency to be subsumed within the personality of the organisation itself. Cynics may argue that businesses which appear to be guided by ethical standards in their business dealings are simply recognising the value of goodwill and cost of legal sanctions and are thus, in effect, protecting their profits. It has also been argued that businesses are keen to self regulate as a way of avoiding the imposition of legal controls which take away their freedom of action by determining their behaviour for them.

Rules are one of the physical manifestations of the law. They are what it produces, and what students of the law spend much time analysing and understanding. Twining and Miers, in their book, *How to do Things with Rules*, see a rule as *"a general norm guiding conduct or action in a given type of situation."* We have seen that different rule systems exist. Whilst they share common characteristics of this definition, they are also distinguishable from each other. Legal rules, unlike moral rules, represent an official code supported by the state. As we proceed we will be exploring what are the consequences of producing legal rules.

Our study of these legal rules is of course constrained by the particular field of law we are concerned with, business law, and a book devoted to the study of business law focuses specifically on the particular legal relationships that are a product of business activity and the legal rules which have developed around this economic phenomenon. Defining what is meant by business activity is dealt with in some detail later in the book. We can note for the present that essentially businesses are provider organisations, selling goods and services to anyone who requires them. The customers of a business are usually referred to as consumers. They may be other businesses themselves, but they also include of course individuals, *ultimate consumers*, who use the goods and services for their own private benefit. Examining the business world in any detail reveals far more complex legal relationships than the simple neighbour example given above. We discover an environment in which a richly diverse range of transactions are constantly performed; where resources of labour, capital, and land are being acquired and disposed of, various forms of property are being bought and sold, information and advice is given and sought, and decisions are regularly being made which have an impact on the owners, managers and customers of the organisations with which they are associated. In short we are seeing a sophisticated market economy conducting its operations.

At first glance the business environment may appear to have little relevance to anyone other than those who are directly associated with it, such as business managers. In practice the impact of business touches everyone. This is seen clearly when we consider ourselves in our role as consumers, that is as users of products and services. Whether we are buying clothes, household goods, holidays, shares, having the car repaired, opening a bank account, taking a job or renting a flat we participate in a business relationship. It does not always have to be a formal matter, and usually will not be. But all these activities are carried on within a legal framework which, as we shall find, attempts to set out the responsibilities and obligations of the participants.

A starting point for our study is to simplify the types of relationship business organisations are generally engaged in and present them diagrammatically. (See Figure 1.1 on the next page). In this way it is possible to obtain an overview of the business environment .

A business organisation also has an internal dimension to its activities which is equally important to it. Figure 1.2 also on the next page provides a simple illustration of the internal shape a business organisation may demonstrate, and indicating the relationships which exist within it. The example used is that of a registered company.

Even at the superficial level of analysis provided by these models, we can to see that business organisations sit at the centre of a web of relationships which have a strong legal dimension to them. For instance, a business may take decisions on the basis of expert advice provided by a professional advisor in return for payment of a fee or charge. Inaccurate or incomplete advice relied upon by the business may cause it to suffer commercial damage. If this occurs the business may have a legal remedy against the advisor, and will seek to recover any losses it has sustained. Similarly, within the organisation legal relationships exist between managers, owners and staff. Thus, to take one example, directors of a limited company are accountable to the shareholders in general meeting, and can be dismissed from their office by a company resolution in circumstances where they have been guilty of commercial incompetence or malpractice. Exploring the law as it applies to business thus involves examining the legal framework within which all businesses, from the multinational corporations to the one man businesses, pursue their commercial objectives. We have noted that this framework has to do with the relationships their business activity creates. What we must next do is to ascertain more precisely the purposes which underpin legal intervention in business affairs.

The Purpose of a System of Business Law

Complex, affluent, property owning societies develop detailed and sophisticated rules to regulate themselves, and in the United Kingdom as in most modern states almost every aspect of human activity is either directly or indirectly affected by law. These laws seek to achieve different purposes. One major classification in any legal system involves distinguishing between those legal rules which are concerned with private rights and obligations, a branch of law referred to as *civil* law, and those whose primary purpose is the welfare of society generally, and its protection by means of rules that seek to prevent anti-social forms of behaviour, supported by the power to punish those who break them. This is the *criminal* law.

Legal rules in the field of business are designed to fulfil certain primary purposes. These include the remedying of private grievances, the control of anti-social activities and the regulation of harmful activities.

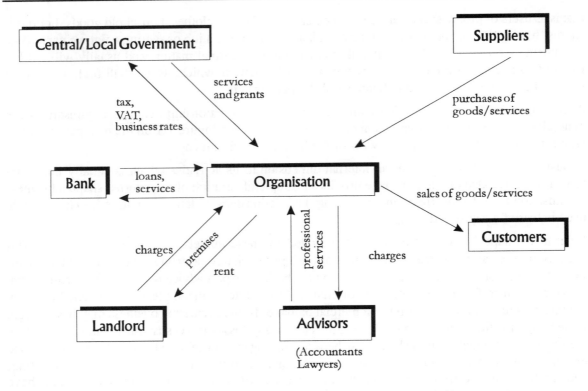

Figure 1.1   The External Dimensions of Business Relationships

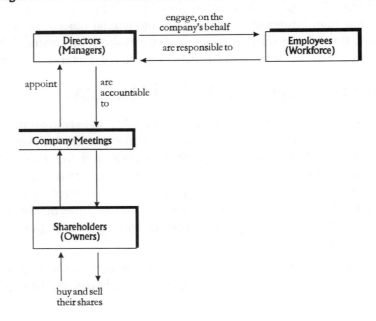

Figure 1.2   The Internal Dimesions of a Business Organisation - the Limited Company

The remedying of private grievances

Various branches of law are concerned with recognising personal rights which can be enforced by means of legal proceedings if they are infringed, or where there is a threat to infringe them. One of these branches is the law of *tort*. It is based upon the existence of a set of obligations referred to as *torts*, or civil wrongs, which have been evolved by the courts as a response to the need for established codes of conduct to protect people from certain types of harm. Tortious obligations are imposed by law, rather than arising by agreement between the parties as is the case with contractual obligations. In effect the law of tort recognises specific legal rights, which entitle anyone for whom those rights have been infringed to sue the wrongdoer for compensation. Examples of torts include those of trespass, nuisance and defamation. The tort of negligence is considered in detail in Chapter 6 on legal liability in business. It is the most important of all the torts which affect business operations. Other business torts such as nuisance and defamation are dealt with in Chapter 17 on business property.

The law of contract is a further example of a branch of law dealing in private rights and obligations. Contractual agreements involve the making of promises which are legally enforceable. A party to a contract therefore has the right to take legal action against the other party to the agreement in the event of that person being in breach of his contractual obligations.

Both the law of contract and the law of tort are crucial to the effective functioning of the business environment. Without the ability to enter into binding agreements businesses would be left fully exposed to the risk of their transactions being unilaterally terminated by the other contracting party. Such vulnerability would seriously undermine business confidence and would hamper economic activity generally, and without the ability to seek compensation and redress for wrongs committed against them businesses could suffer significant economic harm. Consider for instance a situation where a small under-insured business could obtain no compensation following the total destruction of its stock and premises due to negligent repair work carried out to an adjoining gas main by the gas company, or where a supplier of goods has delivered them only to find that the buyer refuses to pay for them.

The control of anti-social activities

This is essentially the task of the criminal law. Whilst it is not possible to prevent crimes from being committed, the presence of penal sanctions, such as imprisonment and fines, which are used to support the criminal code, can act as a deterrent to the commission of an offence.

There is no adequate definition of a crime. Lord Diplock in *Knuller v. Director of Public Prosecutions* 1972 attempted to pin-point the essential differences between civil and criminal law when he said, *"Civil liability is concerned with the relationship of one citizen to another; criminal liability is concerned with the relationship of a citizen to society organised as a state."*

Businesses, like individuals, are subject to the criminal law. Of the wide range of offences that an organisation might commit in the course of its business, the following provide some illustrations:

(a) offences in the field of consumer protection. These are many and varied. They include offences connected with false trade descriptions applied to goods and services, consumer credit arrangements such as engaging in activities requiring a licence but where no licence has been granted, and safety obligations for certain manufactured items, for instance oil heaters and electric blankets, which must meet standards laid down under government regulations;

(b)   offences in the field of employment, such as a contravention of the obligations owed to employees under health and safety legislation;

(c)   offences connected with the operation of registered companies, such as failure to file accounts or the insertion of untrue statements in a prospectus;

(d)   offences in relation to tax liability, such as the making of false returns.

Enforcement of the criminal code is a duty imposed upon a range of agencies. The *Crown Prosecution Service* (the CPS), set up in 1985, is responsible for the prosecution of all criminal offences which have resulted from police investigations. Investigation of potential liability in certain specific fields of the criminal law, and the bringing of prosecutions where appropriate, is placed in the hands of specialised agencies. *Trading Standards Officers* employed by local authorities are responsible for investigation and prosecution of that part of the criminal code dealing with consumer protection, the *Health and Safety Executive* through its inspectorate, deals with criminal aspects of health and safety law, and the *Department of Trade and Industry* has the task of investigating breaches of company legislation where criminal offences are involved. These agencies investigate complaints made to them. They also rely on inspection as a method of systemised investigation.

The regulation of harmful activities

Methods of legal regulation include licensing, registration and inspection. These are useful mechanisms for exercising effective control over a range of activities, which, if uncontrolled, could be physically, economically and socially harmful. As we have noted above powers of inspection, supported by enforcement mechanisms, are granted to factory inspectors working for the Health and Safety Executive. The inspection of work places such as factories and building sites enables inspectors to ascertain whether safety legislation is being complied with, and that employees' physical requirements are thus being met. Certain types of trading practices which are potentially anti-competitive can only be pursued legitimately if the agreements in which they are contained are registered with the Director General of Fair Trading, under the *Restrictive Trade Practices Act* 1976. Even then they are only legally permissible if they are approved by the Restrictive Trade Practices Court. Additionally anyone in the business of providing credit facilities is obliged to register under the Consumer Credit Act 1974 with the Director General of Fair Trading before being legally permitted to lend money. The aim is to eliminate unscrupulous finance dealers from the credit market, overcoming the social problems which arise when poorer members of society borrow at high rates of interest which they are unable to afford, often in an effort to extricate themselves from other debts. And in cases of alleged malpractice in the management of registered companies the Department of Trade and Industry has the power to carry out investigations into the affairs of companies, for instance to establish the true ownership of shares in a company.

The Importance of Law to Business

The legal system affects businesses and individuals alike. Every aspect of business life, from formation and operation to dissolution occurs within an environment of legal regulation. We have seen that many purposes are being served in applying legal regulation to business activity. In broad terms the underlying characteristics of business law may be seen as the dual aims of:

(a) providing a practical and comprehensive framework of legal rules and principles to assist the organisation in its commercial affairs; whilst at the same time

(b) ensuring a sufficient level of protection for the legitimate interests of those who come into direct contact with it. This includes not only members of the public in their capacity as consumers, but also business creditors and the employees and owners of business enterprises.

There appears to be one fundamental and compelling reason why business organisations are likely to seek to comply with the law. If they fail to do so it will cost them money, either directly or indirectly. A business which is in breach of law, whether the civil law or the criminal law, will in most cases suffer from the breach commercially.

The commercial consequences to an organisation which has been found to have broken or otherwise failed to comply with the law includes the possibility of:

- an action for damages against the business, brought by someone seeking financial compensation from it. Such an action may be the result of a breach of contract committed by the business, or be in respect of some form of tortious liability it has incurred. An alternative claim brought against it could be for an injunction restraining it from pursuing a particular course of action;

- a claim that the action of the business is devoid of legal effect because it has failed to follow procedures which bind it. For instance, a limited company cannot act unless it has correctly followed the registration procedures laid down by statute, and has received a certificate of incorporation. Nor can it alter its own constitution, its memorandum and articles of association, unless this is done in accordance with relevant statutory procedures regarding notice periods, the holding of a meeting and the need to secure an appropriate majority of votes cast;

- the loss of an opportunity to take some form of legal action, because the time limit for doing so has passed, for instance bringing a late appeal against an unfavourable planning decision;

- a prosecution brought against it alleging breach of the criminal law, resulting in a fine, or in certain circumstances the seizure of assets;

- the exercise of enforcement action against it for its failure to comply with some legal requirement, for example to take steps to remedy a serious hazard to health, as a result of which its business operations are suspended;

- the bringing of a petition to have the organisation brought to an end. A registered company can for example be wound up compulsorily by its unpaid creditors.

As most commercial enterprises are profit maximisers these outcomes can be seen as interfering in the pursuit of basic organisational aims.

Thus at an organisation level there are sound commercial reasons for keeping properly informed about the law and complying with it as it affects business, apart from any moral or social responsibility for acting within the law. Moreover, legal proceedings often attract public attention and result in adverse publicity to the organisations involved. At a personal level individuals engaged in managing a business may find themselves dismissed and facing civil and/or criminal liability if they are responsible for serious errors of judgment which carry legal consequences, such as negligent or dishonest performance in handling a company's financial affairs.

Developing Legal Knowledge and Skills

Usually it is not possible for people in business to find the time or develop the skills to cope with all the legal demands of operating a business, however there will remain strong reasons for acquiring at least a basic level of legal knowledge and skills and devoting some time to legal issues as and when they arise. This is because:

(a)   many straightforward legal problems can be resolved simply by means of a letter or a telephone call to the other party involved. Legal advice has to be paid for, and in some situations will be both an unnecessary expense, and a time consuming activity;

(b)   certain legal problems require immediate action, for example, what rights the employer has to dismiss an employee against whom an allegation of sexual misconduct has been made; or what rights a buyer has to reject goods delivered late by the seller;

(c)   the daily routine of a business involves frequent encounters with matters of a legal nature, such as examining contracts, signing cheques, negotiating deals and organising the workforce. It would be impractical to seek professional advice regularly in these routine areas;

(d)   many business activities are closely legally regulated, and a working knowledge of them is essential if the business is to function effectively. For example a business providing credit facilities needs to employ staff who are fully aware of the strict legal requirements regulating such transactions;

(e)   when expert advice and assistance is being sought the effectiveness of the process of consultation is assisted if the precise issues can be identified from the outset, and relevant records and materials can be presented at the time. In addition, when the advice is given it will be of little value in the possession of someone who can make no real sense of it;

(f)   managing a business effectively demands a working knowledge of the legal implications not only of what is being decided, but also of the processes by which it is decided. For instance company directors ought to be familiar with the basic principles of the law of company meetings, since it is by means of such meetings that important decision making is achieved.

Obtaining and Using Legal Information

Having established the importance of legal rules and procedures in the running of a business, the next question which emerges is how to obtain and apply relevant legal principles, so that the process of business decision making and practical operation is informed and guided by the legal environment in which it functions. Large organisations employ their own professional advisors. Public companies and local authorities will have departments specialising in legal, financial and other areas of professional work. In such organisations it will be the role of staff in the legal department to deal with the routine legal aspects of the work of the business, and it may be expected of them to produce and distribute to relevant personnel details of legal changes which are likely to have an effect on the way in which the business works. For example, following the introduction of the Health and Safety at Work Act 1974, employers were required to fulfil a number of general duties set out by the Act to ensure the health, safety and welfare of their employees whilst at work. The Act specifically stated that these duties were to include providing staff with any necessary information, instruction, training and supervision. Smaller organisations, whose scale of business operations is insufficient to make the employment of a full time lawyer financially viable will instead rely for their legal needs on the services of a law firm, which will probably be locally based, to deal with legal matters as and when they arise. The nature of such an arrangement makes it unlikely that legal changes affecting the business will always be picked up by their legal advisers and fed into the business in advance of the change. Most of the legal work performed will be as a response to matters which are routinely passed on to the firm, such as the renewal of the business lease, actions for the recovery of debts and financial borrowing by means of the use of a security such as a mortgage or debenture.

In the smallest organisations, such as one man businesses, there may be reluctance to seek legal services at all, unless it is absolutely necessary for the business to do so. Professional advice costs money, and time is taken up in meetings with professional advisors. Whilst this may be a short-sighted view, which can result in the organisation getting itself into greater difficulty in the long term, it is nevertheless the case that some organisations will occasionally try to *go it alone*.

It is clear that the nature of advice and assistance that organisations have need of to operate satisfactorily, is often of a detailed and technical kind which only accountants, lawyers and other professionals are capable of providing. However, it would be quite wrong to assume that in consequence there is little value to be gained from employing staff who have a basic knowledge and appreciation of principles of bookkeeping, or how the principles of the Data Protection Act apply in the workplace. Daily, practical business operations raise a range of issues, many of which, whilst located in areas of technical expertise of which staff have no deep knowledge, can be easily dealt with by people with only a general level of knowledge. There is no reason why a small trading organisation should not be able to cope with most of the contractual disagreements that will arise from time to time between itself and its suppliers and customers in the ordinary course of business.

Whatever method a business uses to obtain legal support, it is obvious that business managers are not doing their jobs properly if they are ignorant of the legal implications inherent in the daily activities carried out by their organisations. How they manage their premises, their staff, their financial affairs and their trading operations should be guided by their business ability, and part of this ability involves recognising the legal implications inherent in pursuing different courses of action. Certainly the failure of management to identify and respond to changes in the law which directly affects the business will prevent it from adapting its operations to accommodate and comply with these changes. How significant such a failure might be can be usefully illustrated by referring to many modern statutes, for example the Consumer Protection Act 1987. This legislative enactment is of considerable importance to any business which is a producer of goods that will ultimately be purchased by consumers. The Act significantly alters the basis of a producer's liability for defective products, and as is the case in respect of many contemporary legal changes, the failure of the organisation to recognise the change and reassess its operational activity in the light of it, can result in the payment of large sums by way of compensation. Legal changes can produce immediate alterations to the extent of an organisation's liabilities, affecting the very heart of its commercial activities. In these circumstances it is essential that information is fed into the organisation to enable appropriate action to be taken. Given the dynamic nature of modern business, the capacity of an organisation to respond to change, of whatever kind, is often crucial to its continued commercial survival.Essentially there are two stages involved in reacting to a legal change; obtaining the relevant information, and applying it.

Obtaining legal information and being able to understand and apply it effectively requires us to examine the various sources of English law.

Sources of English Law

The expression *source of law* carries with it a number of different meanings, but we only need to concentrate on two of them. They are:

- source of law as a way of describing where the law is located, that is where one can obtain legal source materials; and

- source of law in the sense of where the law comes from, in other words who makes it.

These two apparently separate ideas are in practice very closely linked.

Legal source materials

To operate a detailed system of law it is essential that the law be recorded. The effective development of English law as a coherent and uniform body of established rules and principles dates back to the thirteenth century, by which time it was already possible to find comprehensive written accounts of the law. The recording of the law in a written form means that, as far as possible, the ambiguity, inconsistency and lack of precision that comes about when rules are merely passed on by word of mouth is eliminated. In practice, as we shall see, expressing the law by means of the written word is no guarantee of achieving absolute certainty as to meaning, although it does usually seem to achieve a satisfactory and workable framework within which individuals and organisations can conduct their affairs in confidence.

There are two forms of written law:

- the reports of court proceedings in which the judgments delivered by the court contain the statements of principle which express the relevant law; and

- the publication of UK and EC legislation. This includes subordinate legislation, and the various forms of EC legislation.

Both these legal sources are publicly available. Major academic libraries usually hold an extensive range of law reports covering the decisions of all the superior courts, as well as keeping volumes of statutes. In such libraries the statutes are usually held in bound volumes chronologically, the main series being published under the title *Current Law Statutes Annotated*, but also by subject title. Statutes published in this format are under the title Halsburys Statutes, and both these series include annotations, notes, to assist the reader in understanding and applying the law concerned. Individual Acts of Parliament can also be purchased from branches of HMSO.

Various types of Law reports are published. Some concentrate upon specific areas of law, such as local government (*Knights Reports*), whilst others report all the leading cases decided by a particular court or set of courts, whatever the subject matter of the case happens to be. Two major sets of law reports of this kind are the *All England Law Reports*, and the *Weekly Law Reports*. Law reports share at least one common characteristic in that they are published on a chronological basis, so that year by year they build up, volume by volume. Given the large number of annually reported cases there may be two or even three volumes of a particular set of reports covering a single year. In common with any large body of written material, and the English law reports must rank as one of the largest in existence, with approximately half a million decided cases on record, it is essential to have a workable reference system by which a particular decision, or statutory provision for that matter, can be located quickly and simply. The reference system used for law reports uses the case name, followed by a reference to the year, the volume, an abbreviation of the particular series of law report involved, and finally the page reference. Thus a reference to *Smith v. Brown* [1997] 2 WLR 551, would enable a person to easily access the case involving the parties Smith and Brown, whose case is reported in the second volume of the Weekly Law Reports for 1997, at page 551. The table of cases at the beginning of the book includes all the case references for the cases referred to in the text. The corresponding table of statutes lists them all in alphabetical rather than chronological order, but breaks down each statute where appropriate into individual parts, or sections as they are referred to. Usually a section is drafted so that it is further broken down into sub-sections, and maybe further sub-divided into an (a), (b), (c) and so on. It is not uncommon to find that even the (a), (b) or (c) is subdivided into (i), (ii), (iii) etc. Obviously such a way of drafting can make it difficult to understand what the legislature is actually saying without careful attention to detail and examination of how each part of a section relates to the rest of the section, and to the Act itself. For instance the Companies Act 1989 contains provisions dealing with the requirement that at the end of each financial year the directors of a parent company are to produce group accounts representing the financial health of all the companies controlled by the parent company. Section 228 contains certain exemptions. It reads as follows:

"*s.228(1)A company is exempt from the requirement to prepare group accounts if it is itself a subsidiary undertaking and its immediate parent undertaking is established under the law of a member State of the European Economic Community, in the following cases–*

(a)   *where the company is a wholly-owned subsidiary of that parent undertaking;*

(b)   *where that parent undertaking holds more than 50 per cent of the shares in the company and notice requesting the preparation of group accounts has not been served on the company by shareholders holding in aggregate–*

    (i)   *more than half of the remaining shares in the company,, or*

    (ii)   *5 per cent of the total shares in the company.*

Such notice must be served not later than six months after the end of the financial year before that to which it relates."

Here we see an illustration of how detailed statutory provisions can sometimes be. But often they are very straightforward. A little further on in the same Act section 233 sub-section 1, which is expressed in abbreviated written form as S.233(1), states, *"A company's annual accounts shall be approved by the board of directors and signed on behalf of the board by a director of the company."* A provision of this kind expresses a simple idea in a straightforward sentence using clear language.

Law Making Institutions

Until the 1st January 1973 English law was created by two, separate, law making institutions, the courts and Parliament. However in 1973 the United Kingdom became a member of the European Economic Community the effect of which in legal terms was to introduce a new, third, law making source. The impact of this fundamental change has been to say the least considerable, even though there are many areas of activity which remain outside the jurisdiction of the law making bodies of the European Union (EU). Business operations however fall squarely within the remit of the work of the European Union.

To acquire a proper understanding of the law it is necessary to consider the work of the law makers, and examine the methods by which they create the laws we will be considering in our study of business law. In an historical context it was the courts which laid down the original foundations of our law, and so it is appropriate to consider their law making role first. The law making role of Parliament and the EU are examined in the next chapter.

The Courts of England and Wales

For the purpose of the administration of justice in England and Wales two separate court structures exist, one dealing with civil law matters and the other criminal matters. Some courts exercise both a civil and criminal jurisdiction. An example is provided by the Magistrates courts, which are primarily criminal courts but which also exercise a limited but nevertheless important civil jurisdiction in family matters.

An appeals structure gives the parties involved in any form of legal proceedings the opportunity to appeal against the trial court on points of law or fact. The trial court is the court in which the case is first tried, and in which evidence is given on oath to the court by witnesses appearing for the parties involved, to enable the court to establish for the purposes of the case the relevant material facts. The court in which a case is first tried is known as a court of *first instance*. Usually *leave to appeal* must be granted either by the trial court or the appellate court although certain appeals are available as of right.

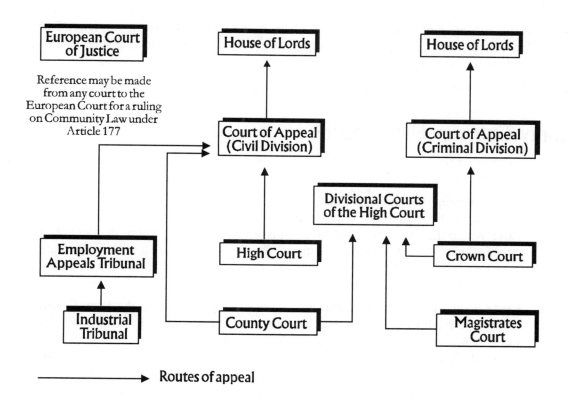

Figure 1.3   Civil and Criminal Courts structure in England and Wales, including Employment Tribunals

The civil courts

In a civil court an action is commenced by a plaintiff who sues the other party, called the *defendant*. If either party takes the case before a higher court on appeal that party is known as the *appellant* and the other as the *respondent*.

Before commencing proceedings the plaintiff must decide whether the case is worth bringing. This is likely to involve a number of considerations including costs, time, the complexity of the action, and the resources of the defendant. We will return to look at these considerations in more detail later in the chapter.

A diagram of the structure of the civil courts is shown in Figure 1.3. Each court has a particular *jurisdiction*, a word which signifies the court's competence to hear a particular action. Civil cases are tried at first instance either before the County Court or before the High Court of Justice. Appeals from either of these courts are heard before the Court of Appeal (Civil Division). The highest appellate court is the House of Lords. A *litigant*, that is a person bringing legal proceedings, is thus faced with the choice of whether to bring the claim in the County Court or the High Court. In respect of some legal disputes, for instance employment disputes, complaints must be made before a tribunal rather than a court.

The procedural aspects of suing in the county court and presenting a complaint before an industrial tribunal are considered in Chapter 3.

County Court or High Court?

The decision whether to bring proceedings in the County Court or the High Court will be based upon a number of factors.

(i) **Convenience**. There are over 400 County Courts in England and Wales. This means they are readily accessible to plaintiffs. A County Court can usually hear those cases where the cause of action arose in its own district, or where the defendant either resides or carries on his business. Thus it is possible that a plaintiff might have the choice of three courts in which to commence proceedings. By contrast the High Court sits in London, and only rarely hears civil cases outside London.

(ii) **Costs**. Court costs are much cheaper in the County Court than the High Court. Bringing a High Court action may involve the payment of additional lawyers, for instance a firm of solicitors acting as the London agents for the local firm who originally handled the case. Lawyers' professional charges, like those of other professionals, vary not only according to the nature of the work involved but also according to where they carry out their work. Legal charges in London and other major cities for example are generally significantly higher than those of lawyers working elsewhere.

(iii) **Quality**. It is very dangerous to make comparisons about the quality or standard of justice as between courts. Sometimes it may be felt that the complexity of a case makes it a more suitable candidate for consideration before a High Court judge than before a circuit judge in a County Court. Equally it may be the case that a plaintiff's lawyer is entirely confident that the case should go before the local County Court. It is worth remembering that the legal complexity of a case is not necessarily related to the amount of the claim involved.

(iv) **Jurisdictional limitations**. As we saw above because of the geographical distribution of County Courts there are jurisdictional rules as to which court can hear the case. No such limitations apply to the High Court. However there are further jurisdictional considerations that need to be borne in mind in the decision about which court should hear the case. These concern the type of action that is being dealt with and the financial value of the claim involved. Over certain kinds of action the County Court has exclusive jurisdiction, such as applications for the renewal of a business lease and in consumer credit cases such as the repossession of goods subject to a hire purchase agreement. With respect to the financial value of a claim, regulations introduced under the Courts and Legal Services Act 1990 have made it possible for the County Courts to deal with many more actions than was previously the case. To cope with the increased workload there are now 72 continuous trial centres. In general, cases with a value of below £25,000 will be heard in the County Court, and with a value of more than £50,000 in the High Court. For those between £25,000 and £50,000 the case will be allocated to either the County Court or the High Court on the basis of financial substance, complexity, importance and the need for the matter to be dealt with as quickly as possible. When a legal claim is brought it is, of course, not always possible to quantify in advance the amount the plaintiff is claiming. A claim for compensation for personal injuries will be for an unspecified sum, or in legal terminology an unliquidated amount, it being left to the court to decide on the evidence the figure which should be awarded. A claim for loss of profits on the other hand can be expressed in a quantified or liquidated form. In the past plaintiffs would often seek to overcome financial allocation requirements by overvaluation of claims. The value to be attached to such claims is now to be the amount in money which the plaintiff could reasonably state the case to be worth to him.

For the purpose of determining small claims, that is those claims not exceeding £3,000, rules made under the County Courts Act 1984 require that the matter must be referred to the arbitration procedure operated by the County Courts. In brief this provides for a relatively informal method for considering the claim, which will usually be heard before a district judge (previously known as a Registrar) rather than a circuit judge, the title given to the senior judge attached to the Court. Although the parties may be legally represented they must normally pay for their own lawyers' fees themselves, whatever the outcome of the case. This is sometimes referred to as the *no costs* regime. Thus a successful plaintiff cannot recover from the defendant the costs of being legally represented.

Most claims can be dealt with under the arbitration procedure if the claim can be quantified in financial terms, and it is not considered that the factual issues are too complex or the point or points of law too difficult. If they are the case is referred to a full trial. A claim for more than £3,000 may be reduced by the party bringing the action to keep the matter within the arbitration procedure. A claim in excess of £3,000 can only be heard within the procedure if both parties agree. The loser will usually bear the costs of the action. This is not the case where the claim is within the £,3000 limit. A sting in the tail for plaintiffs who successfully bring a county court claim estimated as in excess of £3,000, but which is found to be within the small claims jurisdiction, is that such plaintiffs may find that they are not awarded their costs.

The High Court of Justice

The Supreme Court of Judicature is the collective title given to two superior civil courts, the High Court of Justice and the Court of Appeal (Civil Division). These courts sit in London at the Royal Courts of Justice.

The High Court of Justice is for administrative convenience separated into three divisions, each with its own particular jurisdiction. These are the Queen's Bench Division, the Chancery Division and the Family Division. In addition to the cases which are heard in London, High Court cases are also heard at certain centres outside London. These centres are known as High Court and Crown Court Centres, and they include Birmingham, Bristol, Manchester, Leeds and Cardiff.

The Queen's Bench Division hears contractual and tortious actions and any claim not specifically allocated to the other divisions. This makes it the busiest division of the High Court. There is no financial upper limit on its jurisdiction, so it is competent to deal with claims for any amount, though it does not normally try matters which the county court is competent to hear. Two specialised courts within the Queen's Bench Division are the Admiralty Court, which has jurisdiction over shipping matters, and the Commercial Court, which hears only commercial actions and has the advantage for businesses of using a simplified form of procedure. The Queen's Bench Division is headed by the Lord Chief Justice, abbreviated to LCJ.

The Chancery Division has as its nominal head the Lord Chancellor (who is also the head of the Judiciary); however, in practice, the organisation of the work of the court is carried out by the Vice-Chancellor. The jurisdiction of the division includes company law and partnership matters, mortgages, trusts and revenue disputes.

When the High Court deals with a case at first instance exercising what is known as its *original jurisdiction* a single judge is competent to try the case. Such a judge is known by the title 'Mr. Justice' or 'Mrs. Justice' in the case of a woman judge, married or unmarried, so a reference to Smith J is a reference to Justice Smith, a High Court judge.

Each division possesses an appellate jurisdiction which is exercised by three judges (sometimes only two) sitting together, and when it is being exercised the court is known, rather confusingly, as a Divisional Court. The work of the Divisional Courts of the Queen's Bench Division is of considerable importance, and covers the following matters.

- Hearing criminal appeals from Magistrates Courts and the Crown Court by means of a *case stated*. This is a statement of the lower courts' findings of fact which is used by the Divisional Court for redetermining a disputed point of law.

- Hearing civil appeals from certain tribunals.

- Exercising a supervisory jurisdiction over inferior courts and tribunals. This is carried out by means of applications made to the court for the issue of the prerogative orders. These orders provide remedies to protect people and organisations from various forms of injustice. There are three of them; certiorari, prohibition and mandamus.
  Certiorari brings before the court cases from inferior courts and tribunals that have already been decided, or are still being heard, to determine whether the inferior body has exceeded its jurisdiction or denied the rules of natural justice. (An example of these rules is one which provides that both parties in a case must be given the opportunity to be heard.) If such an injustice has occurred the earlier decision will be quashed.
  Prohibition is used to prevent inferior courts, tribunals and other judicial and quasi-judicial bodies from exceeding their jurisdiction.
  Mandamus is a command used to compel performance of a legal duty owed by some

person or body. It may be used against a government department, a local authority, or a tribunal which is unlawfully refusing to hear a case.

The Divisional Courts of Chancery hear appeals on bankruptcy matters from County Courts with bankruptcy jurisdiction.

The Court of Appeal (Civil Division)

Acting in its civil capacity this court has the Master of the Rolls as its president (referred to in written form as MR). Its judges are called Lord Justices of Appeal (referred to as LJ or LJJ in plural), and the quorum of the court is three.

The court can hear appeals from all three divisions of the High Court and appeals from the County Courts. It also deals with appeals from certain tribunals, such as the Employment Appeal Tribunal.

The appeal is dealt with by way of a rehearing, which involves reviewing the case from the transcript of the trial and of the judges' notes. The court may uphold or reverse the whole or any part of the decision of the lower court, alter the damages awarded, or make a different order concerning costs.

The House of Lords

The House of Lords fulfils two functions, for it is not only the upper chamber of Parliament, but also the final appellate court within the United Kingdom. In the exercise of this function it is said to sit as the judicial committee. When it sits as a court its judges are those peers who hold or have held high judicial office. By convention lay peers do not sit. The judges are known as Lords of Appeal in Ordinary or, more commonly, Law Lords, and they are presided over by the Lord Chancellor. Although the quorum of the court is three, usually five judges sit. Majority decisions prevail in cases of disagreement.

The House of Lords hears appeals from the Court of Appeal, but only if that court or the Appeals Committee of the House has granted leave.

The Administration of Justice Act 1969 enables certain appeals from the High Court to be heard by the House of Lords without first passing through the Court of Appeal. This is known as the *leap-frog* procedure, and it is available only where the appeal involves a point of general public importance, for example on a question of the interpretation of a statutory provision, and then only if the parties consent, and if the House of Lords grants leave for the appeal. It has been used only rarely.

The Criminal Courts

The structure of the criminal courts under the criminal justice system within England and Wales is also contained in Figure 1.3. Business organisations are less likely to find themselves involved in legal proceedings within the criminal courts than in the civil courts, and the following account provides merely a brief outline of the way in which criminal cases are dealt with.

In the criminal court proceedings are normally brought in the name of the Crown against the accused (commonly called the defendant). The proceedings are known as prosecutions and if the defendant is found guilty of the offence for which a charge or charges have been brought against him, the defendant is said to be convicted. The court will then determine the appropriate punishment. Most prosecutions are brought by the Crown Prosecution Service, although there are many other agencies involved in the enforcement of the criminal code, including local authorities carrying out duties relating to housing, trading standards, and environmental health, the Inland Revenue, Customs and Excise, the Health and Safety Executive and the RSPCA. The range of agencies involved provides a clear illustration of the extent to which the criminal law infiltrates most aspects of life.

Organisations, just as they may sue or be sued, may *institute* criminal proceedings, such as a theft charge brought by a department store against an alleged shop-lifter, or be *prosecuted* themselves. Corporate bodies, like registered companies, which are regarded as legal persons in their own right, usually incur criminal liability through the acts of their human agents, normally their employees. It is important to appreciate that a corporation will not be responsible for the acts of every employee, but only for the acts of a person, *"…who is in actual control of the operations of a company or part of them and who is not responsible to another person in the company for the manner in which he discharges his duties in the sense of being under his orders."* Lord Reid, in *Tesco Supermarkets Ltd. v. Natrass* 1972.

Corporate liability arising through the misconduct of an employee is said to be *vicarious*, or substituted liability, that is to say liability where the organisation is treated as though the unlawful action of its employee was its own unlawful act. In the case of criminal liability, a corporation is generally only vicariously liable if the offence is one of strict liability, meaning an offence where liability can arise without fault on the part of the wrongdoer. A corporation can also be *directly* liable under the criminal law for any offence except murder. It cannot be convicted of murder as this offence carries a mandatory life sentence, and a corporation cannot be imprisoned. Direct or primary liability for criminal acts has only been recognised by the courts in more modern times.

> In *Lennard's Carrying Company Co. Ltd. v. Asiatic Petroleum Co. Ltd.* 1915, Viscount Haldane remarked that, *"A corporation is an abstraction. It has no mind of its own any more than it has a body of its own; its active and directing will must consequently be sought in the person of somebody who…is really the directing mind and will of the personality of the corporation."* This suggests someone at the very top of the organisation, someone who, in Viscount Haldane's words is the essence of corporation itself since, *"his action is the very action of the company itself."*

It was upon the basis of this line of legal reasoning that the charge of manslaughter was brought against P&O Ferries Ltd. in respect of the 192 deaths resulting from the Zeebrugge disaster in 1987. Although the company was not convicted it is apparent that there is no technical bar to the bringing of a prosecution for *corporate crimes* of this kind. The company escaped conviction when the trial judge, Turner J. directed the jury to find it not guilty. This direction was based upon the failure of the prosecution to show that any of the five senior managers, who were also tried for manslaughter with the company, had the necessary state of mind (the mens rea) to be convicted of manslaughter. Only if at least one of them could be found guilty of the offence could the company be found guilty as well. The judge rejected the argument that the guilt of the company could be established through the collective fault of those responsible for managing it - sometimes referred to as the principle of aggregation. In a well publicised prosecution, *R v. OLL Ltd.* 1994 the requirements identified by Turner J. for the successful prosecution of a company for 'corporate' manslaughter were for the first time met. The company operated an activity centre. Evidence showed that the company routinely employed unqualified instructors. Canoes being used by sixth formers capsized whilst they crossed Lyme Bay. Four of them drowned. They had all been instructed, wrongly, not to inflate their life jackets in the event of a capsize. The managing director of the company, Peter Kite, was convicted of manslaughter and given a three year sentence. His *mens rea* was imputed to the company, which was also convicted of manslaughter and fined £60,000, a sum which allegedly represented its total assets.

The classification of criminal offences

There are various ways which can be used to classify criminal offences. Here we shall note two of them.

Firstly the distinction which is drawn between offences of strict liability, and those requiring a mental element which are said to be fault based. Traditionally a crime consists of two elements, both of which must be proved before a conviction is possible. These elements are the *actus reus* of the offence, and the *mens rea* of the offence. The actus reus consists of the definition of the particular prohibited conduct, which may be either an action or a failure to act. The mens rea, or guilty mind, is the accompanying state of mind which is required for the offence. Words used in the definition of an offence such as *wilfully, knowingly, with intent,* and *permitting* are all concerned with defining particular states of mind. As an illustration the Theft Act 1968 defines theft by stating that, *"A person is guilty of theft if he dishonestly appropriates property belonging to another with the intention of permanently depriving the other of it. "*. Here the words *"dishonestly"* and *"intention"* provide the *mens rea* of the offence.

For reasons of policy some offences do not require a *mens rea*. They are referred to as absolute offences or offences of strict liability and cover cases where the offence is contained in a statute and where effective enforcement would be difficult if *mens rea* were required, for instance in cases of environmental pollution. Even in these cases however the courts will usually imply the existence of a *mens rea* requirement on the grounds that this is what Parliament intended, since, in Lord Reid's words in *Sweet v. Parsley* 1969 *"... there has for centuries been a presumption that Parliament did not intend to make criminals of persons who were in no way blameworthy in what they did."*

Secondly the distinction which is drawn between serious and less serious offences. *Indictable* offences, the most serious, can only be tried before a judge and jury, whilst *summary* offences, the less serious, are dealt with in the Magistrates Courts. Jury trials are conducted in Crown Courts. The seriousness of an offence is obviously associated with its potential threat to society; in crude terms this is measurable by looking at the level of punishment that can be meted out to a person convicted of the offence. Some offences for instance are only punishable by a fine, and these are dealt with by Magistrates Courts. Others will carry the possibility of a prison sentence up to a specified maximum. Magistrates' powers are limited to imposing fines of up to £5,000 and/or sentences of up to 6 months' imprisonment. In many cases where a custodial sentence can be imposed by a Magistrates Court the accused is given the choice of being tried summarily before the Magistrates, or on indictment before the Crown Court. Magistrates Courts hear 98% of all criminal cases.

Law Making by the Courts

We have seen that the two major domestic sources of lawmaking are the courts and the legislature. Whereas the legislature creates law through the introduction of statutes, the law making role of the courts is quite different. Parliament enjoys a virtually unlimited lawmaking capacity. The courts on the other hand are subject to significant restrictions in their role as lawmakers. This is entirely proper since the courts are manned by members of the judiciary, the judges, who are neither elected by the public to this office nor are accountable to the public for the way in which they discharge their responsibilities.

The primary role of the courts, and the various tribunals which supplement the courts system, is the resolution of legal disputes which are brought before them. This process has a history dating back to Norman times.

In order to resolve a dispute it is necessary to have a reference point; some identifiable rule or principle which can be applied in order to solve the problem. One approach is simply to treat each case on its own merits, but such a system would hardly be just for decisions would turn on the character of the individual judge, whose values, prejudices, qualities of analysis and reasoning power would dominate the decision making process. Such a system would be unpredictable and capricious. English law, in common with other law making systems, adopted an approach that sought to achieve a level of certainty and consistency. It did this by means of a process referred to as *stare decisis*, literally *standing by the decision*. Today we talk of the doctrine of judicial precedent. Under the doctrine of judicial precedent, the successor to the stare decisis system, judges when deciding cases must take into account relevant precedents, that is earlier cases based upon materially similar sets of facts. Whether a court is bound to follow an earlier case of a similar kind can be a matter of considerable complexity, however the general rule is that the decisions of higher courts are binding on lower courts within the hierarchical courts structure seen in the diagram in Figure 1.3.

English law became enshrined in the precedent system, and much of our modern law is still found in the decisions of the courts arrived at by resolving the cases brought before them. Not surprisingly this body of law is referred to as case law. It is these cases, or precedents, which make up the contents of the law reports considered earlier in the chapter. The bulk of the law of contract and the law of tort is judge made law, or as it is more usually known, the common law.

In addition to developing and refining the common law, the judges in modern times have played an increasingly important role in the task of interpreting and applying statutory provisions.

The meaning of common law

In its modern usage the expression common law has come to mean law other than that contained in statutory provisions. Common law in this sense means judge made law embodied in case decisions. However, the expression common law is also sometimes used to describe, in a broader sense, the *type* of legal system that operates in England and Wales, a system which has been adopted by countries all over the world and especially those in the Commonwealth.

The common law of England dates back to the Norman Conquest and has its origins in the decisions of the royal judges who attempted to develop and apply principles of law *common* to the whole country. This they did by modifying and adapting rules of Norman law, and rules contained in

Saxon local custom. The development of the common law has involved an evolutionary process extending over hundreds of years. Through the process England and Wales was rewarded with a unified and coherent body of law which remains the foundation upon which significant areas of our law, such as the law of contract and tort are based.

The judgment of the court

Whatever the nature of a case coming before a court the most vital legal aspect of the legal proceedings comes at the end of the trial when judgment is delivered. Whereas certain parts of the judgment will be binding for the future, other parts of the judgment will have merely persuasive authority whenever the case is considered by a future court. These ideas need further explanation.

The binding element of a judgment

When a decision is reached on a dispute before a superior court, the judges will announce their decision by making speeches known as judgments. Within a judgment, the judges will refer to numerous matters, such as the relevant legal principles which are drawn from existing cases or statutes, a review of the facts of the case, their opinion on the relevant law, their actual decision and the reasons for it. For the parties to an action, the matter they are most concerned with is the actual decision, that is who has won the case. The main matter of relevance to the law, however, is the reason for the decision. This is known as the *ratio decidendi* of the case (the reason for deciding). The *ratio* expresses the underlying legal principle relied on in reaching the decision and it is this which constitutes the binding precedent. As we have seen this means that if a lower court in a later case is faced with a similar dispute it will in general be bound to apply the earlier *ratio decidendi*.

The persuasive element of a judgment

All other matters referred to in a judgment are termed *obiter dicta* (things said by the way). The *obiter* forms persuasive precedent and may be taken into account by a court in a later similar case, however the court is not bound to follow it.

The decision of the House of Lords in *Smith v. Stages and Another* 1989 illustrates the distinction between *ratio* and *obiter*. In this case it was necessary to determine the extent to which an employer may be made liable for the actions of his employee, and in particular when an employee can be said to be acting in the course of his employment. The action was brought on behalf of an employee, who as a passenger in the defendant's car, suffered personal injuries as a result of the negligent driving of the defendant, a fellow employee. Despite the fact that the employers neither required nor authorised the journey by car to and from their particular workplace they were joined as second defendants on a claim that they were vicariously liable for the driver's negligence. The House of Lords held that here the employers were vicariously liable for the employee's negligent driving. The court decided that employees who are required to travel to and from non regular workplaces, and are in receipt of wages for doing so, remain within the course of their employment, even if they have a choice as to the mode and time of travel. This statement forms the *ratio* of the judgment and is binding on a lower court if faced with a similar factual situation.

In the course of the judgment however a number of suggestions were made by the House of Lords in relation to the question as to when an employee is acting in the course of his employment during travelling time. The receipt of wages would indicate that an employee was travelling in his employer's time, and acting in the course of his employment. Equally so would an employee travelling in the employer's time between different workplaces. An employee travelling in his employer's time from his ordinary residence to a workplace, other than his regular workplace, to the scene of an emergency such as a fire, accident or mechanical breakdown of plant, would also be acting in the course of his employment. Deviations or interruptions of a journey undertaken in the course of employment unless merely incidental would normally take an employee outside the course of his employment. All of these suggestions are *obiter dicta,* persuasive authority which may or may not be followed by a lower court dealing with a similar case.

Distinguishing

Since the precedent system is based upon the principle of treating like cases alike it follows that a court is not bound to follow an earlier decision if it can be established that the facts of the earlier decision and the instant case are distinguishable; that is the material facts of the two cases are not the same. Of course it is the members of the court in the later case who must decide what constitutes the material facts in the case being heard and in the precedent being cited, in order to declare that the earlier case is distinguishable on its facts. The power to distinguish is a potent tool available to the judiciary. Using it they can attempt to avoid following an earlier decision which they dislike, but the power to distinguish gives rise to a judicial dilemma. Artificially distinguishing a disliked or disapproved case leads to uncertainty if a subsequent court finds itself unable to find any justification for the distinguishing carried out by the earlier court. This dilemma was summed up by Lord Reid in Jones v. Secretary of State for Social Services 1972 when he stated, "... Where an existing decision is disapproved but cannot be overruled courts tend to distinguish it on inadequate grounds. I do not think they act wrongly in so doing, they are adopting the less bad of the only alternatives open to them. But this is bound to lead to uncertainty...".

Overruling and reversing

A court with suitable jurisdiction has the power to declare the decision in a previous case no longer good law. This can be done when there is evidence that the previous court did not accurately interpret the law, or when the later court is of the view that the ratio of the earlier case is no longer sustainable or desirable. Where overruling takes place, the case which has been overruled is considered 'bad law' and does not have to be followed by the present court or any future court.

Reversing occurs when an appeal court overturns the decision of the court below it from which the appeal came. If the appeal court agrees with the lower court's decision it is said to affirm it.

Change and the Law

Legal rules are not made simply for their own sake. They are made because there is a need for them. It may not always be easy to recognise why particular areas of law, or specific legal rules have become necessary. Nor will people always agree that a particular need has been properly established, or that legal rule making is the best way to respond to an identified problem or issue.

However it remains true that all laws originate out of some sense of need for formal regulation or control of a particular situation. We have already seen the variety of purposes these legal rules are designed to fulfil, each purpose being an area of need for rule creation. One way of expressing these ideas is to say that legal rules are an effect rather than a cause.

Although certain fundamental needs are constant, such as food and shelter, others are more variable. Whilst our need for law to regulate human conduct is always present, the form and content of the law varies over time, altering and adapting to take account of the dynamic nature of modern society. We have always had a need for laws to provide for order in society, and the criminal law is the outcome. Crimes have been recognised since earliest times as offences against the well-being of the community, which if allowed to pass unchecked would undermine the fabric of society. Criminal laws have thus been created to protect the individual and property. However whilst crimes such as murder, manslaughter and theft have always been regarded as an essential part of the criminal code, the way we define these crimes today, and the legal penalties that are attached to them are not exactly as they were a hundred years ago, or even thirty years ago. Law evolves as society evolves, and this is entirely appropriate for law is the servant of society rather than its master.

The causes of legal change can be classified under the following broad headings.

- *Social Causes*
  For example to provide tenants with legal protection from unscrupulous landlords who threaten eviction if the tenant refuses to pay unjustifiable rent increases.

- *Economic Causes*
  Within a free market economy trading practices often develop which may be harmful to general economic needs. For example, dominant suppliers who use their market dominance to restrict competition in the supply of such goods are distorting market conditions. Governments may find it necessary to intervene by means of legislation to curb the growth of dominant market suppliers.

- *Political Causes*
  For instance a government may feel it appropriate to introduce legislation to penalise councils who overspend.

- *Technological and Scientific Developments*
  Technological change has from time to time created problems which require legal regulations to control. The growth in the use of computers over the past twenty years as a means of storing personal data, has given rise to concern over the apparent loss of rights of individuals whose lives are recorded in this way and who may have little or no control over the use to which such information is put. Legislation now seeks to provide a measure of security for individuals in this situation.

In practice these change factors usually overlap. For example, the decision to join the European Economic Community was both political and economic. Legally it was achieved by passing the European Communities Act 1972. Potentially it also had social implications, since the Community was pledged to move towards enabling a free movement of labour between the member states, a Europe without barriers. A more specific example of the overlap is provided by various aspects of modern employment legislation. The creation of the right of employees not to be unfairly dismissed by their employers, which is at present contained in the Employment Rights Act 1996, illustrates the use of a legal device (statute) to achieve a social objective (job security), which has political implications (electorally popular) and includes an economic dimension (restriction on employers' freedom to reduce the size of the workforce without good reason).

The protection of the interests of the buying public has produced a spate of legal change over the past two decades. It is a recognition by Parliament that consumers' rights are a matter of national interest and debate, making them a part of the political agenda. Increases in the spending power of the nation, together with technological advances in the production of consumer durables from compact discs to microwave ovens have led to an enormous growth in the demand for goods from consumers, and producers have responded accordingly. As *consumerism* has expanded, and the demand for consumer rights has increased, so the law has been invoked as the means of achieving an appropriate level of consumer protection. Statutory changes have sought to regulate this particular market.

An illuminating illustration of the change process in operation is provided by one facet of modern consumer law. Back in 1893, the Sale of Goods Act was passed as a means of codifying the law of sale. Codification involves bringing all the law in a specific field together in a single statute. It is a way of clarifying the law, and it assists the task of discovering the law on a particular subject if it is primarily contained in a single statute. The rules that were expressed in the Act were based upon the need for a clear legal framework within which trade could be effectively conducted between businesses. At that time the interests of private consumers of goods were given little consideration. One of the provisions of the Act stipulated that in any sale of goods transaction between a buyer and a business seller, the seller would be treated as impliedly promising the buyer that the goods were of a certain standard, known technically as the standard of `merchantable quality'. The seller was however at liberty to exclude this implied promise if he did so clearly, a right eagerly grasped by most sellers, who had no desire to increase their liabilities unnecessarily. At this time the predominant business philosophy was *caveat emptor*, let the buyer beware. It was essentially the buyer's task to satisfy himself that what he was buying was suitable and fit.

By the 1970s it was felt that the interests of private consumers were being largely overridden by the majority of sellers, who simply avoided their legal obligations to provide merchantable goods by the use of contractual clauses excluding liability. This, of course, they were perfectly legally entitled to do, but it was felt that consumers were being treated harshly by being denied the opportunity to reject defective goods, from whose sale the seller had made a profit. In 1973 legislation was introduced which invalidated any attempt by a seller to exclude liability for breach of the merchantable quality provisions in such transactions.

Sellers however continued to exclude, confident that private consumers were largely unaware of their rights, and that in any event attempting to exclude was not unlawful, simply invalid. This subsequently lead to further statutory intervention, so that since 1978 an attempt to exclude liability has constituted a criminal offence, under the Consumer Transactions (Restrictions on Statements) Order. The order has proved an effective deterrent to most traders, and consumer rights have been fully secured in this field.

In 1994 amending legislation, the Sale and Supply of Goods Act, was introduced which replaced the by now rather dated expression *merchantable quality* with the more consumer accessible expression *satisfactory quality*, further evidence that in the late 20th century sale of goods legislation is as much about protection of the interests of the domestic consumer as it is about the interests of the business community, where its origins lie.

One other cause of legal change requires brief mention, that of legal clarity. Legislation is introduced from time to time as an attempt at simply clarifying legal rules, rather than creating new ones. The codified Sale of Goods Act mentioned above provides an example.

Consideration of the various elements of business law reveal just how dynamic our legal system is. This in turn is simply a reflection of a way in which as a society we evolve through change.

Parliament; Europe and Change

There is perhaps an implicit assumption that change is necessarily progressive and beneficial. This may not however be a universally held view. Change can generate conflict. United Kingdom membership of the EU provides us with an excellent and well publicised model of how at national and supranational level such conflict can emerge when there are sharply divergent views over policy matters. Since the EU achieves most of its objectives through the use of legal mechanisms, notable by directives, it has been in the field of law that EU driven changes have from time to time brought the Community and the British government into direct and well publicised conflict. Such was the position in the action brought by the British government against the Commission over the Working Time directive, that was heard before the European Court of Justice in 1996.

The background to the legal action brought by the British government and the events which followed are summarised below.

They began with the issue in 1992 of a European Community draft directive related to Working Time. This directive was originally adopted by the European Commission in July 1990 as part of a package of measures concerned with the implementation of the social action programme. The theme of the directive is that physically demanding and socially disruptive working patterns are dangerous to the health, safety and welfare of the workforce.

The UK approach of leaving matters such as the length of the working week and annual leave to be decided by the parties to an employment contract provides, it is argued, insufficient protection to the weaker party, the employee. Legislating on such matters, as part of the Social Action Programme, has been the focus of profound disagreement between the UK government and the European Commission. The dominant feature of government thinking on employment has been a de-regulatory strategy, directly in conflict with the directive. The government view is that limiting working hours however increases labour costs dramatically. In addition there remains a strong body of opinion in the UK government against the imposition of change by EC institutions in relation to such matters as working hours and also extended rights for part-time workers and a national minimum wage. The UK government disputes the assumption that health and safety concerns justify the imposition of the generalised regulation of the working time for all workers. The view of the Commission is that health and safety at work is an objective which should be achieved at the expense of purely economic considerations.

The revised directive 1/7/91 proposed:

- compulsory rest periods of twelve consecutive hours in each period of twenty four hours;
- one rest day every seven day period;
- a prohibition on overtime by night workers where the work involves special hazards or heavy physical or mental strain;
- regular health checks for night workers;
- maximum working hours;
- minimum periods of annual leave.

In June 1993 the EU's Council of Ministers finalised the most controversial part of the directive, the maximum working week set at forty eight hours per week. The Council of Ministers approved the working time directive by eleven votes to nil with Britain abstaining. The view of the British government, expressed by the Secretary of State for Employment, was that the directive would be a threat to jobs by having an adverse affect on Europe's international competitiveness. The directive provided for implementation of the mandatory forty eight hour week within ten years but allowed only three years to introduce law to protect workers who are asked to work longer hours and do not wish to do so.

The three year deadline under the directive expired on 23 November 1996, and consequently in advance of the deadline the British government sought to challenge the validity of the directive before the European Court of Justice in Luxembourg. What was sought was a ruling that legislation dealing with working hours could not be validly introduced as a health and safety measure, requiring only a qualified majority vote rather than unanimity. Such a ruling would legitimise the refusal of the government to implement the directive. The European Court delivered the judgment on November 12, less than two weeks before the expiry date. It found against the government. By then it was too late for appropriate legislation to be introduced to implement the directive, leaving the government open to the possibility of action for damages being brought against it.

The influences and pressures which lead to legal change come from many sources. They range from the development of government policies and the impact of the work of the European Commission at one end of the spectrum, to the campaigns of individuals and groups, usually highlighting specific concerns, at the other. Legislative change is essentially internally driven through the workings of the Parliamentary system. At the beginning of the Parliamentary calendar the Queen's Speech outlines the legislative programme the government wishes to promote for that year. Since the government commands an overall Parliamentary majority in the Commons it can expect to convert it's proposals into law. Individual M.P's also have the right to promote their own legislative proposals through the devise of the private members bill. Most of the Parliamentary timetable is made over to the passage of government sponsored legislation, and some time, albeit very limited, is available for the debating of private members bills. However whilst legislation is predominately the result of internal pressure for new law (from Parliament itself and from Europe) legislation sometimes emerges from external pressure for legal change from campaigners who have been particularly successful in the strategies they have used. The abolition of the poll tax in favour of the council tax is a striking example.

Law Reform Agencies

Each years spate of new statutes adds to the bulk and the complexity of our law. New statutes may repeal or make amendments to existing law in addition to introducing new provisions. Nor is it only legislation whose volume continually expands, for each year the courts generate a substantial number of new precedents too. This growth puts enormous pressure on the civil and criminal justice systems, and makes demands for effective law reform. Surprisingly, law reform, in the sense of reform as a method of improving the law, was not a matter managed in a systematic and continuous manner, until the introduction in 1965 of the *Law Commission*, which was set up by the Law Commissions Act of that year. The Commission consists of a chairman and four commissioners who work for the Commission full-time. Under the Act, the Commission's remit includes keeping *"under review all the law... with a view to its systematic development and reform, including in particular the codification of such law, the elimination of anomalies, the repeal of obsolete and unnecessary enactments and generally the simplification and modernisation of the law"*. In the 1994 Annual Report of the Commission its chairman, Mr Justice Brooke, summed this up by saying, *"The Commission's only purpose in life is to make the law simple, fairer and cheaper to use."*

Usual practice is to publish a working paper, to encourage discussion and debate and the making of recommendations. Subsequently a final report embodying a draft bill to achieve the proposed legal changes is published.

Many of the recommendations contained in the Commission's reports have been implemented by subsequent legislation. Later chapters contain a number of examples, including the Minors Contracts Act 1987, the Law of Property (Miscellaneous Provisions) Act 1989, and the Sale and Supply of Goods Act 1994.

Other reform agencies operate only on a part-time or ad hoc basis. They include the Criminal Law Revision Committee, and various Royal Commissions which are used from time to time to consider legal questions of wide public importance.

Legal Terms found in Chapter 2

Bill	• draft legislation
Binding precedent	• a precedent which has to be followed by a lower court dealing with a similar case
Codification	• bring law together in a formal code
Consolidation	• bring a number of statutes together into one statute
Delegated legislation	• law produced by individuals and organisations granted the power by Parliament
Directive	• a type of EC law which is in effect an instruction to member states to pass a law giving effect to the rules set out in the directive by a given date
European Community	• an organisation of 15 European member states which share policy and law making powers in certain defined areas of activity
European Union	• an organisation of 15 European member states which consists of the European Community and two other elements or pillars. These are common policies on foreign and security policy and on justice and home affairs and are based upon inter governmental co-operation outside the system of binding EC law
Judicial precedent	• a court decision which will act as a guide for future courts and can only be overruled by a higher court
Legislation	• law made by Parliament
Legislature	• formal law making body of a state in the UK Parliament
Persuasive precedent	• a precedent which a court does not have to follow but should take account of in reaching its decision
Qualified majority voting	• a system of voting within the EC Council of Ministers which allows decisions to be taken in certain policy areas without the unanimous agreement of all member states
Regulation (EC)	• type of EC law the text of which directly applies in all member states without the need for further action at national level to bring it into effect
Regulation (UK)	• a form of UK delegated legislation usually contained within a statutory instrument
Subsidiarity	• a principle which determines at which level action should be taken in areas of policy where both the EC and the member sate have power to act
Statute	• an Act of Parliament

Chapter 2

Parliamentary Law Making and European Community Law

The Legislature: Parliament

The legislature, Parliament, sits at Westminster. It consists of a lower house, the Commons, in which M.P.s sit and an upper house, the Lords, which has a non elected membership that includes hereditary and life peers, law Lords and the Archbishop and Bishops of the Church of England. The primary responsibility of Parliament is the enactment of legislation, which in broad terms extends to the granting of consent to the spending of public revenue, and the guardianship of the interests of the nation, which involves controlling the activities of the government when they are believed to conflict with the national interest. This control mechanism relies upon the accountability of Ministers to Parliament. They can be called upon to provide public answers during question time and during debates on proposed legislation. Furthermore they can be summoned to appear before Parliamentary Select Committees for more detailed and rigorous questioning. Undoubtedly the broadcasting on radio and television of Parliamentary proceedings has increased the public awareness of the role of the legislature. Nowadays when the Government faces a severe test during Prime Minister's question time the occasion is built up into a significant media event.

What is legislation?

Technically, legislation is defined as the formulation of law by the Queen in Parliament, thus the Monarch and both Houses are involved in creating it. The Monarch's role is limited to the granting of assent which is a formality and no longer involves the Monarch personally; the real legislative power lies with the two Houses of Parliament of whom the House of Commons is constitutionally the most powerful. During this century two Acts, the Parliament Acts of 1911 and 1949, have reduced the power of the House of Lords. The 1911 Act provides that a money Bill (e.g. the Finance Bill) must be passed through the Lords without amendment, within one month following its passage through the Commons, whilst under the 1949 provisions the Lords are unable to *block* any public

Bill which has passed the Commons in two successive sessions. A Bill is the name given to legislation whilst it proceeds through the various stages which culminate in it becoming an Act after the Royal Assent is given.

A classification of Bills showing their scope is contained in Figure 2.1.

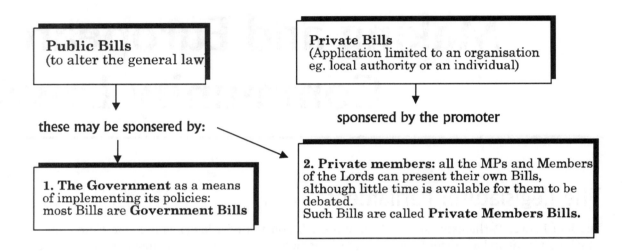

Public Bills
(to alter the general law)

Private Bills
(Application limited to an organisation eg. local authority or an individual)

these may be sponsered by:

sponsered by the promoter

1. The Government as a means of implementing its policies: most Bills are **Government Bills**

2. Private members: all the MPs and Members of the Lords can present their own Bills, although little time is available for them to be debated.
Such Bills are called **Private Members Bills.**

Figure 2.1   The classification of Parliamentary Bills

Something in the region of sixty to eighty Bills become law annually. Creating legislation is the most obvious way in which governments are able to implement their policies, whether they be fiscal, economic or social. The process by which governments arrive at reaching legislative proposals which are put to Parliament is beyond the scope of this book, but it is certainly possible to note some of the most significant factors which influence legislation. These include:

- the reports of Royal Commissions, and other enquiries which are government inspired;

- the activities of pressure and cause groups, such as the RSPCA, and Friends of the Earth;

- UK membership of international organisations, such as the EC. EC policy decisions have a direct impact upon legislative activity in the United Kingdom. For instance the Companies Act 1989 considered in subsequent chapters, was passed as a response to Community requirements;

- public opinion and the media;

- government reports; and

- lobby groups such as local authority associations, trade unions and employees associations.

Before a bill is presented to Parliament many events may have occurred leading to its promotion. One possibility is given in Figure 2.2

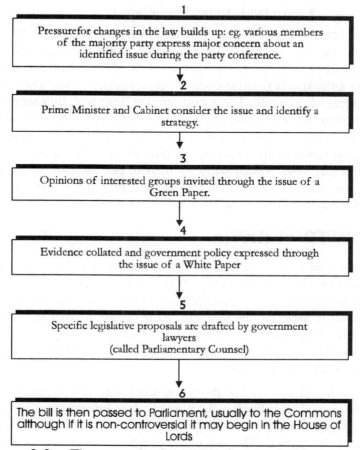

1

Pressure for changes in the law builds up: eg. various members of the majority party express major concern about an identified issue during the party conference.

2

Prime Minister and Cabinet consider the issue and identify a strategy.

3

Opinions of interested groups invited through the issue of a Green Paper.

4

Evidence collated and government policy expressed through the issue of a White Paper

5

Specific legislative proposals are drafted by government lawyers (called Parliamentary Counsel)

6

The bill is then passed to Parliament, usually to the Commons although if it is non-controversial it may begin in the House of Lords

Figure 2.2   The stages leading to the Proposal of Legislation

Delegated or subordinate legislation

It is not possible for Parliament to cope with all the legislative demands placed upon it. One reason is that it lacks time due to its slow procedures; another is that it does not always possess the technical expertise necessary to create detailed rules in specialised fields of knowledge. A further difficulty lies in anticipating, in the legislation being enacted today, what might develop in the future.

Parliament overcomes these inadequacies by delegating law making power to subordinates. These include organisations - local authorities are a prime example - as well as individuals, most notably the various Secretaries of State who head government departments. Thus much of our statute law merely lays down general principles, while specifically granting the power to a Minister, in liaison with his or her department, to *finish the job* by legislatively filling in the details by means of statutory instruments and regulations. Under the Health and Safety at Work Act 1974 the Health and Safety Commission was created and one of its primary functions is to produce health and safety regulations which apply in different work environments. These regulations are brought into force by means of statutory instruments and constitute the main substance of health and safety law. Delegated legislation may also be made under s.2(2) European Communities Act 1972 in order to give effect in the UK to EC directives and other Community obligations.

Without a system of delegated law making effective government could not be carried out in a state as complex as ours, but this does not mean that this method of legislating escapes criticism. Constitutionally the role of Parliament is weakened, as the executive obtains a law making capacity for itself. Moreover delegated legislation does not attract publicity and sometimes the subordinate can legislate on matters of principle. These criticism are dealt with by control mechanisms which seek to maintain a proper balance between effective government on the one hand and accountability on the other. The courts can be resorted to where it is believed that the delegated powers have been exceeded and, if this is established, the action taken by the subordinate will be declared *ultra vires* (beyond the powers) and void. Additionally Parliament has its own *Scrutiny Committee* which examines statutory instruments (one form of delegated legislation) in order to report to Parliament on any matters requiring special attention such as lack of clarity in the instrument.

Statutory Interpretation

When a dispute comes before a court it is the task of the court to hear the evidence, identify the relevant law and apply it. The legal principles which the court has to apply may be common law principles. Often however they will be principles, or rules, which are contained in statutes. Where this is so, the court has to ascertain the meaning of the statute in order to apply it, and sometimes this can cause problems for a court because it discovers that the language of the statute is not entirely clear. The courts take the view that their responsibility is to discern Parliament's will or intention from the legislation under consideration.

In relation to statutes the primary role of the courts and tribunals is to apply the legal rules within them to conflict situations. Inevitably this function involves interpreting the meaning of particular legal rules and so setting precedents which provide guidance to future courts and tribunals as to how these rules should be applied. The task of the courts in interpreting statutory provisions is to attempt to discover Parliament's intention and this should be achieved primarily by examining the specific words of the statute.

An example of a statutory provision may help to illustrate this judicial function. In the Employment Rights Act 1996 there are numerous provisions which confer rights on employees. In particular if a qualified employee believes that he has been dismissed without good reason he may under section 111 present a complaint of unfair dismissal against his employer before an Industrial Tribunal. The Act provides however that there are strict time limits to be complied with, otherwise the right to present a complaint will be lost.

Section 111(2) of the Act states that .... *"an industrial tribunal shall not consider a complaint under this section unless it is presented to the tribunal before the end of the period of three months beginning with the effective date of termination or within such further period as the tribunal considers reasonable in a case where it is satisfied that it was not reasonably practicable for the complaint to be presented before the end of the period of three months."*

The legal rule is stating therefore, in relatively straightforward terms, that if a dismissed employee wants to complain of unfair dismissal before an Industrial Tribunal he must start the proceedings within three months, but if he fails to do so the tribunal still has a discretion to hear the case if it was not reasonably practicable for him to present it within the time limit. If a legal dispute arises over whether an unfair dismissal claim has been presented within the time limits it is the function of the courts and tribunals to attempt to resolve the conflict by applying the exact wording of s.111(2) to the factual situation before it. The subsection requires the Industrial Tribunal therefore to ask itself one or possibly two questions:

1.   Has the complaint been brought within the three months time limit prescribed in the section?

2.   If not, was it reasonably practicable to present the complaint within the time limit?

If the answer to the first question is no and the answer to the second question is yes then the tribunal should not proceed to hear the complaint of unfair dismissal. If the reverse is true however and either the complaint is within the time limits or it was not reasonably practicable to present it in time then the tribunal does have jurisdiction to proceed.

There are many case decisions which over the years have provided guidance to Industrial Tribunals as to the approach to be adopted in addressing these questions. To determine the relevant time period it is necessary to know *"the effective date of termination"* which may be difficult to decide particularly if the complainant is dismissed without being given the notice to which he is entitled.

The specific wording of the section was analysed in *University of Cambridge v. Murray* 1993 where an Industrial Tribunal held that the phrase *"beginning with"* meant that that date forms part of the time period. If the words *"from"* or *"after"* had been used then the three months would be calculated to the corresponding date of the relevant later month or if no corresponding date the last day of the month. As the expression *"beginning with"* is used in section 111(2) however the starting date is a day earlier and so ends with the day before the corresponding date of the later relevant month. If the effective date of termination is the 30th of April therefore the time period expires on the last moment of the 29th July. This case is therefore of great assistance in interpreting the section and provides guidance to future tribunals who are required to apply it.

If a tribunal decide that the complaint was not presented within the time period it would still proceed to hear it if it was not reasonably practicable to present the complaint in time. Parliament has left it to the courts and tribunals therefore to determine the issue of reasonable practicability in any given case. Reasons for late claims brought before tribunals have included postal delays, bad advice from lawyers or civil servants, and obstructive employers. Case decisions made in relation to these reasons provide guidance and in some cases lay down precedents for future cases.

To summarise therefore it is possible to say that the law on time limits for presenting a complaint of unfair dismissal is most certainly contained within s.111(2) of the Employment Rights Act 1996 but also as interpreted in the numerous decisions of our courts and Industrial Tribunals.

The Rules of Interpretation

The courts have a crucial part to play in minimising uncertainty by giving an objective interpretation of statutory provisions. To assist the courts in this process certain rules of interpretation or construction have been developed.

- *The literal rule* Applying this approach a court will give the words of a statute their ordinary natural grammatical meaning, that is they will be applied literally provided there is no ambiguity.

In *R. v. Hinchy* the House of Lords used this approach in a tax case. The defendant had incorrectly completed a tax return for which the penalty under statute was *"treble the tax that ought to be charged"*. This presumably meant three times the excess owed. However the Court construed "tax" to mean the whole tax bill for the year, the difference between £42 and £418.

- *The golden rule* This is used to overcome the problems which occur when the application of the literal rule produces so absurd a result that Parliament could not be taken as having intended it. It simply provides that an interpretation be given which best overcomes the absurdity.

- *The mischief or purposive rule* This rule involves the court in interpreting the statute in accordance with the apparent purpose for which it has been passed, so that its purpose is as far as possible fulfilled. An illustration can be seen in the case of *Mandla v. Dowell Lee* 1983 which involved an alleged offence of discrimination by the headmaster of a school who required of a fee paying Sikh pupil that he remove his turban and cut his hair short to meet the school's uniform regulations. This he refused to do on grounds of his religion. It is an offence to discriminate against a person under the Race Relations Act 1976 *"on grounds of his race, colour, ethnic or national origin"*. The Court of Appeal, on the basis that the statute makes no reference to religion took the view that the action of the school was not discriminatory. The House of Lords took an alternative view, regarding the Act as designed to protect people like Sikhs, and finding that the Sikhs could arguably be regarded as a group identifiable by a common ethnic origin.

In *Knowles v. Liverpool City Council* 1993 a council flagger sued his employer for damages in negligence when he was injured by a flagstone he was handling which broke because it had not been properly cured by the supplier. Under the Employers' Liability (Defective Equipment) Act 1969 an employer may be deemed to be liable in negligence if an employee is injured as a result of defective equipment supplied by a third party. Equipment is defined in the Act as including plant and machinery, vehicles, aircraft and clothing. The issue before the Court of Appeal was whether the definition would cover flagstones which were work materials. The court thought that the term equipment should be interpreted broadly to include the *"materials which an employee is given by his employer to use to do his job. Such a broad approach reflects the general purpose of the legislation and is consistent with the ordinary meaning of the word in the context of an employee carrying out his job"*. As consequence the employer was liable under the Act for the injuries sustained to the employee by defective equipment used in the course of employment.

Other aids to interpretation include certain sub-rules, the most important of which is the ejusdem generis rule which requires that if in a statute, general words are preceded by two or more specific words, the general words should be treated as being of the same kind *(ejusdem generis)* as the specific words. For instance in *Lane v. London Electricity Board* 1955, the words *"shock, burn or other injury"* were used in statutory regulations regarding safety in electrical installations. The plaintiff, who broke his leg as a result of inadequate lighting in an electricity sub-station had not, in the court's opinion, suffered an *"other injury"* since the specific words, if properly construed, suggested injuries arising from direct contact with electricity.

Most statutes also contain an interpretation section which provides specific definitions for words and phrases which are contained in the statute and in addition the Interpretation Act 1978, which is incorporated into many statutes, gives presumptive interpretations to common words and phrases, for instance that the expression *man* when used in a statute should include *woman*. Application of the principle of equal treatment with regard to working conditions, including those governing dismissal, means that men and women shall be guaranteed the same conditions without discrimination on grounds of sex., and vice versa, unless some contrary intention appears. In *Pepper v. Hart* 1993 the House of Lords held that to assist the courts in discovering Parliament's intention in any statute it is permissible to examine statements made in Parliament during the bill's passage. This was done in *R v. Warwickshire County Council* 1993.Parliamentary statements made in the course of debate are published as a record of Parliamentary Proceedings in a document called Hansard.

European Community Law

The process leading up to the present stage of development of the European Community and European Union began with the setting up of the ECSC, the European Coal and Steel Community. This was established in 1951 by a treaty signed in Paris by France, Germany, Italy, Belgium, the Netherlands and Luxembourg, the six original EC members. The Treaty of Paris aimed to promote economic recovery in Europe after the devastation of the Second World War; and to eliminate the possibility of further war between the member states by placing their key industries, coal and steel, under joint control and decision-making.

A process of fuller economic integration between the six member states was set in train by the signing in Rome in 1957 of two treaties establishing the European Economic Community (EEC) and the European Atomic Energy Community (Euratom). In this text we shall refer to the treaty establishing the EEC as the Treaty of Rome 1957. Since the coming into force of the Treaty of European Union in November 1993, the European Economic Community is now known simply as the European Community.

The United Kingdom has been a member of the EC since January 1st 1973, along with Eire and Denmark. In 1981 Greece became the tenth member state, followed by Spain and Portugal in 1986. In 1990 the unification of Germany had the automatic effect of bringing the territory of the former East Germany into the Community which was further enlarged with the accession of Austria, Finland and Sweden at the beginning of 1995. The fifteen member states, with a population of 370 million, now form a single economic region in which goods, services, people and capital can move almost as freely as they do within national boundaries.

As a Member State of the European Community (EC) since January 1st 1973 the United Kingdom is bound by Community Law. In the field of business this is of enormous significance. This is because the European Community is essentially economic in nature and the community objective of the completion of a single European market is based upon the actual harmonisation of laws relating to business and trade between Member States.

Inevitably therefore significant examples of measures which have been adopted and implemented by the UK government as a consequence of European legislation run as a theme throughout any study of business law. Examples can be seen in the fields of:

- company law harmonisation and investor protection;
- consumer rights and consumer protection;
- data protection;
- environmental protection;
- intellectual property rights;
- employment law.

In each of these fields European law has been active in amending and adding to existing UK law, as well as requiring the introduction of new law. For example in employment law the Community has been active in the following areas:

- pregnancy dismissals and maternity leave;
- statutory rights for part-time workers;
- collective redundancy procedures;
- dismissals and detrimental conduct relating to health and safety;
- acquired rights on a business transfer;
- health and safety at work regulations;
- sex discrimination and equal pay.

The framework of Community law is set out in the Treaty of Rome 1957 as amended by the Single European Act of 1986 and the Treaty of European Union signed at Maastricht in 1992 and the institutions of the Community must operate within and give effect to these Treatiest. Later in the chapter the legislative process of the Community Institutions is considered and the means by which Community law becomes incorporated into the domestic law of Members States.

Treaty of Rome 1957

The Treaty of Rome 1957, as amended by the Single European Act and the Treaty of European Union signed at Maastricht, sets out the tasks and objectives of the European Community and defines the policy areas within which the community has competence to legislate.

Article 2 of the Treaty of Rome, as amended, sets out the general aims of the Community *"The Community shall have as its task, by establishing a common market and an economic and monetary union and by implementing the common policies or activities referred to in Articles 3 and 3a, to promote throughout the Community a harmonious and balanced development of economic activities, sustainable and non-inflationary growth respecting the environment, a high degree of convergence of economic performance, a high level of employment and of social protection, the raising of the standard of living and quality of life, and economic and social cohesion and solidarity among Member States. "*

These aims are supplemented by other broad statements of intent set out in the preamble to the treaty, that the member states are determined to lay the foundation of an ever closer union among the peoples of Europe and are resolved by pooling their resources to preserve and strengthen peace and liberty. Together they have been important in providing the impetus for closer European integration and by providing an important statement of principles which are taken into account by the Court of Justice in interpreting the treaties themselves and the laws made under them.

Article 3 sets out the activities which are to be undertaken by the Community in order to fulfil its objectives. Each of the activities is further defined in subsequent articles of the Treaty.

The Single European Act 1986

Although the original Member States had hoped to establish the Common Market fully within twelve years, progress towards that aim was in fact much slower than anticipated. This was a product partly of the conflicting national interests involved and the fact that proposals could be blocked by any member state which thought its vital national interests to be at stake.

One of the principal effects of the Single European Act was to lay down the timetable for the completion of the single European market. A White Paper issued by the Commission in 1985 had identified that 282 proposals for new legislation would need to be introduced in order to complete the internal market. The Single European Act provided that these measures should be adopted by the 31st December 1992 in order to create a single internal market comprising a geographical area without internal frontiers in which there would be a free movement of goods, persons, services and capital. In order to facilitate the adoption of all of the measures necessary to complete the single market within the time limit, the Single European Act provided for qualified majority voting in the Council of Ministers in relation to single market measures.

The Single European Act also extended the Community's competence to legislate by setting out additional objectives in relation to economic and monetary co-operation; the health and safety of workers; economic and social cohesion involving the reduction of differences between various regions in the community and policies to reduce the backwardness of the least favoured regions; research and technological development and environmental protection. It also put onto a formal basis, though outside the framework of Community law, the emerging practice of political co-operation in the sphere of foreign policy.

The Single European Act was implemented in the UK by the European Communities (Amendment) Act 1986 which came into effect on 1st July 1987.

The Treaty on European Union

The Treaty on European Union which was negotiated in Maastricht in November 1991 came into effect at the beginning of November 1993, after completing the difficult process of ratification in each of the member states. It survived a second Danish referendum and challenges to its constitutional validity in the German and UK courts.

The Treaty creates a European Union which has three main elements, often described as *pillars*. The first is the European Community itself, the powers and decision making procedures of which are extended and modified. The second element relates to foreign and security policy, and the third to justice and home affairs. The second and third pillars operate outside of the formal institutional framework of the EC and are based on new inter-governmental arrangements between the member states. As such their decisions do not form part of the body of EC law, which is created by the Council of Ministers acting with the Commission and European Parliament, and are not subject to the jurisdiction of the Court of Justice.

In the present context we are concerned only with the first pillar of the Treaty which provides for closer European integration within the framework of Community law. This part of the Treaty expands the areas of Community activity. Under the Treaty the task of the European Community will be to promote a harmonious and balanced development of economic activities, sustainable and non-inflationary growth respecting the environment, a high degree of convergence of economic performance, a high level of employment and of social protection, the raising of the standard of living and quality of life, and economic and social cohesion and solidarity.

The UK, however, negotiated to opt out of two important parts of the Treaty, the *Social Chapter* and the third stage of economic and monetary union which is the adoption of a single currency. The remainder of the Treaty applies with full effect to the UK.

The Treaty formally extends the legal competence of the EC in a number of areas. In some respects this is simply a confirmation of competence in areas where the Community already takes action, for example its long standing practice of bringing forward consumer protection proposals as single market measures or under broader powers to eliminate distortions in competition. The Treaty on European Union gives or extends EC competence in the following areas:

- Citizenship of the EC
- Transport policy
- Research and technological development
- Culture
- Public health
- Consumer protection
- Trans-European networks in the areas of transport, telecommunication and energy
- Industry
- Education
- Civil protection
- Development co-operation with third world countries
- Environment
- Economic and monetary policy

The Treaty operates, like the Single European Act, by inserting amendments into the Treaty of Rome. The structure which it establishes is contained in Figure 2.3.

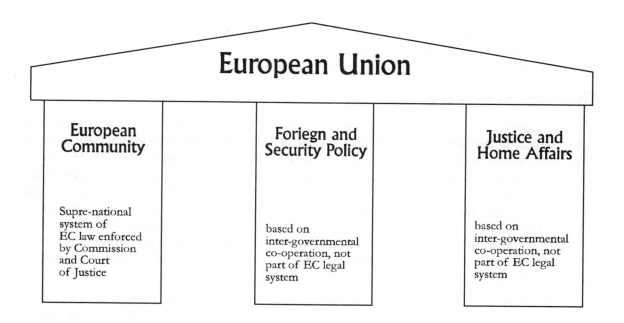

Figure 2.3   Structure of the European Union

The Treaty on European Union makes express provision for the principle of *subsidiarity*. Under this principle the Community will act within the limits of the powers conferred upon it and of the objectives assigned to it. In areas which do not fall within its exclusive competence the Community can take action only if and in so far as the objectives of the proposed action cannot be sufficiently achieved by the member states and can be better achieved by the Community. Thus action should only be taken at EC level where such action if taken at the national or regional level would be inadequate or inappropriate. Any action by the Community must not go beyond what is necessary to achieve the common objectives of the treaties. The principle of subsidiarity is designed to safeguard the residual powers and competences of the member states.

It is clear from an examination of the major EC treaties that the Community has power to legislate over a very broad range of issues which embrace the entire area of business law. It is in practice by far the most important source of new law in this sphere. It should also be appreciated, however, that there are areas of legal regulation which remain exclusively within the domain of national law making powers. These include, for example, major parts of the criminal law, control over the direct taxation of income, family law, the law of inheritance and numerous other important fields of law.

The Community Institutions

The Community Institutions are:

- the Commission
- the Council of Ministers/Council of the European Union
- the European Parliament
- the Court of Justice of the European Communities.

The Commission

The Commission consists of 20 commissioners, two from each of the larger EC states and one from each of the others. They are nominated by their governments and appointed by the unanimous agreements of the governments of the member states for a renewable period of four years. The term of office is increased to five years under the Treaty on European Union which also provides that their appointment shall be subject to the approval of the Parliament. Once appointed they must act with complete independence in the interests of the Community. In the performance of their duties they must neither seek not take instructions from any government or any other body. The main functions of the Commission are to initiate policy and proposals for legislation for ultimate adoption by the Council. It is the executive arm of the EC, with responsibility for ensuring the implementation of agreed policies and managing the community's budget. The Commission President is Jacques Santer.

As *the guardian of the treaties* it must ensure full compliance by member states with Community obligations in accordance with EC law. The Commission has powers to investigate an alleged infringement of the Treaty by a member state and, under article 169, where it considers that the member state has failed to fulfil an EC obligation, the Commission will issue a reasoned opinion on the matter after giving the member state an opportunity to submit its observations. The member state must comply with the reasoned opinion before the deadline stated in it. Where it fails to do so the Commission may refer the matter to the Court of Justice. This procedure is often used where a member state either fails to implement a directive within the given time limit, or implements it incorrectly.

> In *Commission of the European Communities v. United Kingdom of Great Britain and Northern Ireland* 1994 the European Court of Justice ruled against the UK government in two cases brought by the Commission where it was alleged that the UK had failed to properly transpose Directives on collective redundancies and acquired rights. By failing to ensure worker representation in a workplace where there is no recognised trade union the community law obligation to ensure that worker's representatives are informed and consulted on business transfers and collective redundancies had not been complied with. Most of the criticisms were accepted by the UK government and rectified by specific provisions in the Trade Union Reform and Employment Rights Act 1993.

The Commission also has some direct legislative powers which are conferred by the Treaty and others which are delegated to it by the Council. It administers and enforces Community competition policy and has power to impose fines and penalties on organisations or individuals for breach of competition law. In 1992, for example, a fine of 75 million ECU was imposed on Tetra Pak by the Commission for breaches of EC competition law.

The work of the Commision is divided into twenty four Directorates General, each D-G dealing with specific aspects of Community activity and policy under the control of an individual Commisioner. Each Commissioner heads a department, and is known as a Director General (DG). For employment matters there is a Commissioner for Employment, Social Affairs and Education.

The Council of Ministers/Council of the European Union

The *Council of Ministers* is the EC's principal decision making body with the final say on most secondary legislation. The Commission initiates proposals for legislation as the Council does not have power to do this itself. It can, however, request the Commission to submit to it proposals on matters which may be desirable in order to achieve the objectives of the Treaty. The Council consists of one government minister from each member state and its membership varies according to the nature of the matter under discussion. When the Council is discussing the common agricultural policy, for example, the member states are represented by their ministers of agriculture, for transport matters their ministers of transport and so on. The presidency of the Council and therefore of the Community is held by each member state in rotation for a six month term. Towards the end of each term the heads of state will meet for a summit to discuss major current issues and to chart the future course of the Community. When it involves a meeting of the Heads of State the Council is known as the *European Council*.

The Council of Ministers is the one institution which is common both to the European Community and to the Foreign Affairs and Home Affairs pillars of the European Union. Most European Union business is conducted at meetings of the Council of Ministers. Shortly after the coming into force of the Treaty on European Union, the Council of Ministers announced its formal decision to change its name to the Council of the European Union. The other EC institutions, however, have little or no role in the procedures for conducting foreign and home affairs, and it is therefore inaccurate to refer to them as institutions of the European Union. Only the Council has this dual role.

A committee consisting of the permanent representatives of the member states, known as COREPER, is responsible for preparing the work of the Council and for carrying out the tasks assigned to it by the Council. Its permanent staff, who are the ambassadors of the members states to the Community, provide a measure of continuity and organisation to the work of Council.

The UK Parliament has the opportunity to assess the legal and political implications of a proposal for EC legislation before the Council votes on it. This is carried out by the *Scrutiny Committees* of the Commons and the Lords who are given copies of the proposals with an explanatory memorandum. The Scrutiny Committees have power to call for written or oral evidence, consult with government departments, call for a debate and if necessary request that amendments to the proposal be negotiated. Once the Scrutiny Committee has cleared a proposal then the minister is free to accept it in the EC Council of Ministers.

The method of voting used in the Council is of particular importance as the Council is the main legislating body in the community. Clearly if all decisions were taken on the basis of a unanimous vote, each member state would have a veto over every Community decision. On the other hand if some form of majority voting system was used, a member state's interests could be overridden and laws introduced against its wishes.

Article 148 of the Treaty of Rome provides that voting may be by a simple majority, a qualified majority, or on the basis of unanimity. Very few decisions are ever taken by a simple majority. The Treaty originally provided for unanimous voting on all important matters, and envisaged a move towards qualified voting after a defined period of time. This did not happen, however, principally as a result of objections by France. In 1965 the French boycotted Community meetings in protest at the introduction of qualified majority voting. The so-called policy of the empty chair resulted in a crisis for the Community which was finally settled by the adoption of the Luxembourg Accords. Under the Luxembourg Accords a member state has the right to insist on a unanimous vote where it considers that its vital national interests are at stake in the matter under discussion. The Accords are in the nature of a political convention without formal legal standing. They have been used on numerous occasions to justify a veto, sometimes on matters of relative unimportance. The increase in Community membership coupled with the use of the veto in this way meant that progress towards the objectives of the Community was extremely slow. It became increasingly recognised that significant changes were necessary in the decision making procedures of the Community if real and substantial advances were to be made in meeting those objectives.

These changes were made in the Single European Act which introduced qualified majority voting for all measures required to complete the single market, with certain exceptions. These related to approximation of indirect taxes, free movement of persons, and matters affecting the rights of employees, which are still subject to voting by unanimity. Measures related to the health and safety of workers, however, are subject to qualified majority voting procedure.Under the Treaty on European Union qualified majority voting has been extended further, into areas such as consumer protection, health, education and environmental programmes

The European Parliament

Members of the European Parliament, MEPs, are the directly elected representatives of the citizens of the European Union There are a total of 626 MEPs, of which 87 represent British constituencies. The Parliament sits for a five year term and is based partly in Strasbourg and partly in Brussels. Its powers include the right to dismiss the whole of the Commission on a motion of censure by a two-thirds majority. It has no power to dismiss individual commissioners. MEPs can ask oral or written questions of the Council or the Commission, which must be answered. The answers to written questions are published in the Official Journal of the Community. In respect of the Community's budget, the Parliament has a final say over certain items of expenditure, and has the ultimate power to reject the budget as a whole. In terms of law making power, the European Parliament is markedly different from the UK Parliament, having a relatively minor role in the legislative process.

Its powers have been progressively strengthened by the Single European Act and the Treaty on European Union, in response to a fundamental criticism of the lack of democratic accountability of the Community Institutions. This so-called *democratic deficit* has been characterised by a concentration of power in the hands of the unelected Commission, the practice of the Council to take its decisions behind closed doors, the inability of the Parliament to initiate proposals for new legislation, and the limited role of Parliament within the legislative process.

The Treaty on European Union has gone some way towards addressing the democratic deficit, although it may be argued that the criticism remains valid. The increased power of the Parliament is reflected in the three different Community law-making procedures. The *consultation procedure*, under which the Parliament gives its opinion but has little real power, was laid down in the original Treaty of Rome. The *co-operation procedure*, in which it has power to make amendments but not to veto, was introduced by the Single European Act. The *co-decision procedure*, in which it has power to make amendments and a right of veto, is contained in the Treaty on European Union.

The powers of the Parliament have been strengthened in a number of other ways by the Treaty on European Union. Under article 158 the appointment of the Commission and its president is subject to the approval of Parliament.

By virtue of article 138b the Parliament may, acting by a majority of its members, request the Commission to submit a proposal for new legislation where it considers that this is required. The interpretation of this provision is a matter of some debate, in particular the question whether the Commission has a legal duty to carry out the request. If so, the Parliament has in effect a new right to initiate legislation.

Under article 138c the Parliament has power, at the request of a quarter of its members, to set up a temporary Committee of Inquiry to investigate *maladministration* in the implementation of Community law. In addition, article 138e makes provision for the appointment by the Parliament of an *Ombudsman*.

The *Ombudsman*, who must be completely independent in the performance of his duties, will have power to receive complaints from any citizen of the European Union or any person living or doing business in a member state, relating to maladministration in the activities of Community institutions or bodies. He is required to investigate such complaints and to report to the Parliament and the institution or body concerned. The specific powers of the Ombudsman and general conditions governing his duties are to be determined by the Parliament in conjunction within the Commission and the Council

The European Court of Justice

The Court of Justice sits in Luxembourg and is composed of 15 judges who are appointed by the mutual agreement of the member states for renewable periods of six years. They must be persons of absolute independence who are qualified to hold the highest judicial office in their own country or who are legal experts of recognised competence. The court is assisted by nine Advocates-General, who must hold similar qualifications to the judges and are appointed on the same basis. It is the duty of the Advocate-General, acting with complete impartiality and independence, to make reasoned submissions in open court as to the application of Community law to the questions posed in the case before the court. The opinion of the Advocate-General is not binding on the court, which may decide the case in a different way, although this is unusual. There is no equivalent to the Advocate-General within the English legal system.

The Court of Justice has power to hear the following types of case:

- *Actions against member states* Where it appears that a member state has failed to fulfil an obligation under Community law the Commission may take infringement proceedings under article 169. Other member states are also able to bring this type of case, under article 170, provided that they first bring the matter to the attention of the Commission. Prior to the Treaty on European Union the powers of the Court of

Justice in such cases were limited to making a declaration requiring the defaulting member state to take the necessary measures to comply with its judgment. There was no effective sanction, other than political pressure, to enforce compliance. Under the new Treaty, however, a member state may ultimately be fined if it fails to comply with the court's ruling.

- *Actions against community institutions* The Court of Justice has power to review the legality of acts of Community Institutions, or their failure to act. The court may declare void any illegal action, award damages and review decisions.

- *Employment disputes between the Community and its employees* The Court of Justice acts as an industrial tribunal for the employees of Community institutions. Cases of this type account for just under a quarter of its case load.

- *Preliminary rulings under article 177* Any court or tribunal in a member state may request a preliminary ruling from the Court of Justice as to the meaning or interpretation of an aspect of Community law. Such a request may be made where the ruling is required to enable that court or tribunal to give judgment in a case before it. Where there is no appeal from its decision, the court or tribunal must request a preliminary ruling if it considers this necessary to enable it to give judgment. This procedure provides an important bridge between the legal systems of member states and that of the Community. It is designed to ensure that Community law is applied and interpreted in a uniform manner throughout all member states. The function of the Court of Justice is simply to rule on the interpretation of Community law, in the light of which the domestic court or tribunal will decide the case before it.

The Single European Act made provision for a *Court of First Instance of the European Community,* to be attached to the Court of Justice in order to deal with certain categories of case. The need for such a court arises as a result of the growth of the number of cases referred to the Court of Justice, and the likelihood of a continued growth in its workload due to the expansion of the Community itself and to a significant increase in Community legislation related to the completion of the Single Market. It is hoped that the Court of First Instance will reduce the period of time taken to dispose of cases which, before its introduction, averaged 18 months to two years.

The Court of First Instance, established in 1989, has twelve members. They usually act in a judicial capacity, although they are also called upon to undertake the task of Advocate-General. The Court has jurisdiction to hear claims for damages and judicial reviews against Community Institutions, and hear employment cases involving Community employees. There is an appeal on a point of law to the Court of Justice, although a decision of the Court of First Instance on a matter of fact is final. Significantly the Court of First Instance has no jurisdiction to hear cases brought by member states or by Community Institutions, or to deal with references by national courts or tribunals under article 177 for preliminary rulings.

Primacy of Community Law

It is a central feature of Community law that it takes precedence over any conflicting provisions in the national law of member states. This feature has been strongly developed by the Court of Justice in a series of cases as the issue of priority is not addressed directly in the Treaty of Rome. In

VanGend en Loos v Nederlands Administratie der Belastingen 1963 the Court of Justice described the relationship between Community law and domestic law in the following way: *"By creating a community of unlimited duration, having its own institutions, its own personality, its own legal capacity and capacity of representation on the international plain and, more particularly, real powers stemming from a limitation of sovereignty or a transfer of powers from the states to the community, the member states have limited their sovereign rights albeit within limited fields, and have thus created a body of law which binds both their nationals and themselves."*

The principle of supremacy of Community law was clearly affirmed by the Court of Justice in the case of *Costa v ENEL* 1964 in which it held that a provision in the EC Treaty took precedence over a rule in a subsequent Italian statute. The Court relied on the statement in *Van Gend en Loos*, together with the duty imposed by article 5 on each member state to ensure that their obligations under the Treaty are fulfilled, and stated *"The law stemming from the Treaty, an independent source of law, could not, because of its special and original nature, be over-ridden by domestic legal provisions, however framed, without being deprived of its character as Community Law and without the legal basis of the Community itself being called into question."*

The pervasive nature of Community law was described by Lord Denning MR in *Bulmer Ltd. v. Bolinger SA* 1974 in a famous passage. *"When we come to matters with a European element, the Treaty is like an incoming tide. It flows into the estuaries and up the rivers. It cannot be held back. Parliament has decreed that the Treaty is henceforward to be part of our law. It is equal in force to any statute."*

> In *Internationale Handelsgesellachaft mbH* 1970, the Court of Justice, in a case which involved a conflict between an EC regulation and the provisions of the German constitution, decided that the EC rule took precedence. *"The validity of a community instrument or its effect within a member State cannot be affected by allegations that it strikes at either the fundamental rights as formulated in that State's constitution or the principles of a national constitutional structure."*

The significance of these decisions in UK law is underlined by s.3(1) of the European Communities Act 1972, which provides *"For the purposes of all legal proceedings any questions as to the meaning or effect of any of the Treaties, or as to the validity meaning or effect of any community instrument, shall be treated as a question of law and, if not referred to the European Court, be for determination as such in accordance with the principles laid down by and any relevant decision of the European Court."*

This section represents the acceptance by the UK government in the 1972 Act of the principles developed by the Court of Justice in its decisions, including those relating to the supremacy of Community law.

The position of EC law within the English legal system is established by the European Communities Act 1972 which, in s.2(1), gives legal effect to the Community law within the UK. It states *"All such rights, powers, liabilities, obligations and restrictions from time to time created or arising by or under the Treaties, and all such remedies and procedures from time to time provided for by or under the Treaties, as in accordance with the Treaties are without further enactment to be given legal effect or used in the United Kingdom shall be recognised and available in law, and be enforced, allowed and followed accordingly, and the expression "enforceable community right" and similar expressions shall be read as referring to one to which this subsection applies."*

This gives legal force to those provisions in the Treaties and in secondary legislation which are directly applicable. This occurs automatically without the need for further UK legislation. The words from time to time make it clear that future as well as existing Community laws are within the scope of s.2(1). In relation to those Community measures which do not have direct applicability, s.2(2) gives power to make delegated legislation for the purpose of giving them effect within the UK. This power is often used to make Statutory Instruments in order to implement Community directives. The Employment Protection (Part-time Employees) Regulations 1995 were made under s.2(2) to bring the legal position of part-time workers in the UK in line with Europe.

The 1972 Act states that where there is a conflict between domestic law and Community law,the latter will take priority. This is laid down in s.2(4) which provides *"... any enactment passed or to be passed shall be construed and have effect subject to the foregoing provisions of this section."*

The effect of s.2(4) has caused much controversy and debate as to its impact on the unwritten constitution of the UK. This debate centres around the constitutional doctrine of parliamentary supremacy. One of the principal features of this doctrine is that Parliament cannot bind its successors by passing legislation restricting the absolute freedom of a future parliament to repeal or amend existing laws or create new ones. The effect of s.2(4) however is that no future Parliament can validly create legislation which conflicts with Community law.

In *Macarthys Ltd. v. Smith* 1979 Lord Denning MR indicated the view of the UK courts on this issue as follows:

> *"In construing our statute we are entitled to look to the Treaty as an aid to its construction; but not only as an aid but as an overriding force. If on close investigation it should appear that our legislation is deficient or is inconsistent with community law by some oversight of our draughtsmen then it is our bounden duty to give priority to community law. Such is the result of s.2(1) and s.2(4) of the European Communities Act 1972.I pause here, however, to make on observation on a constitutional point. Thus far I have assumed that our Parliament, whenever it passes legislation, intends to fulfil its obligations under the treaty. If the time should come when our Parliament deliberately passes an Act with the intention of repudiating the' Treaty or any provision in it or intentionally of acting inconsistently with it and says so in express terms then I should have thought it would be the duty of our Courts to follow the statute of our parliament."*

In *Macarthys Ltd. v. Smith* 1979 the Court of Appeal was faced with a conflict between the literal interpretation of s.1(2) Equal Pay Act 1970 and article 119 of the Treaty of Rome. Mrs Smith was appointed to the position of stockroom manageress on a salary of £50.00 per week four and a half months after the stockroom manager had left the post. He had been paid a weekly wage of £60.00. Section 1(2)(a)(i) of the Equal Pay Act states that a woman is entitled to equal pay where she is employed on like work with a man in the same employment. The employers argued that as she had never been employed with a man she was not entitled to equal pay. Article 119 requires each member state to maintain the application of the principle that men and women should receive equal pay for equal work. It was argued that this is a directly applicable rule of

Community law creating an enforceable community right in favour of Mrs Smith, which operates regardless of whether she is employed at the same time as a male comparator. The Court of Appeal recognised that EC law takes priority over conflicting national law, but decided to refer a question to the Court of Justice as to the application of article 119 in the circumstances of the case. The Court of Justice found that article 119 was directly applicable and entitled Mrs Smith to equal pay on the facts of the case; and the Court of Appeal accordingly decided in her favour.

Another example of the primacy of community law is provided by the important decision of the House of Lords in *R v. Secretary of State for Employment ex parte Equal Opportunities Commission* 1994. Here their Lordships ruled by a majority of four to one that UK legislation that gives part-time workers (most of whom are women) less protection in relation to unfair dismissal and redundancy than full-time workers (most of whom are men) is indirectly discriminatory and therefore incompatible with European Union Law as to equality between employees.

The issue of supremacy was clearly illustrated in a series of cases known as the Factortame cases. The cases centred around a challenge to the validity of the Merchant Shipping Act 1988. The Act was introduced to prevent fishing companies from one EC state establishing themselves in another and registering their vessels there in order to qualify for part of that state's fishing quota, a practice known as quota-hopping. Spain had not been a member of the EC when a system of fishing quotas designed to conserve fish stocks was introduced. On accession the Spanish did not secure a large allocation of quotas. A number of Spanish fishing companies, including the plaintiff, set up subsidiary companies in the UK and claimed a share of the British quota by re-registering their ships under the British flag. The Merchant Shipping Act 1988 was introduced in order to prevent this from happening. By s.14 of the Act a vessel would only qualify for registration as British if it was owned by a British citizen, domiciled and resident in the UK; or, in the case of a company, if 75% of its shareholders and directors were British citizens, domiciled and resident here. Further, the vessels had to be managed and its operations directed and controlled from the UK. The validity of the Act was challenged by the plaintiff on the grounds that it was inconsistent with a number of articles in the Treaty of Rome. In particular, article 52 guarantees to nationals of one member state the right to take up and pursue activities as self-employed persons in another member state, a right known as freedom of establishment. This right extends to companies under article 58. In addition article 7 prohibits discrimination on the grounds of nationality in relation to areas covered by the Treaty.

In the first case, *Factortame Ltd. v. Secretary of State for Transport* 1989, the applicants sought a judicial review challenging the validity of the 1988 Act. The Divisional Court requested a preliminary ruling from the Court of Justice on the compatibility of the 1988 Act with the relevant provisions of the treaty. As it was likely that the Court of Justice would take up to two years to rule on the issue, the applicants requested the Divisional Court to suspend the provisions of the 1988 Act until the judgment of the Court of Justice was delivered. The Divisional Court granted an interim injunction disapplying the relevant parts of the 1988 Act and restraining the Secretary of State from enforcing them in respect of the applicants until the Court of Justice had given its ruling. The injunction was discharged, however, on appeal to the Court of Appeal whose decision was confirmed by the House of Lords. The Lords accepted that directly effective EC law takes priority over later national legislation on the basis of s.2(4) of the European Communities Act 1972, but held that until a ruling was given by the Court of Justice there was a presumption that the 1988 Act was valid. It further held that English Courts have no jurisdiction to suspend the operation of an Act of Parliament or grant an injunction against the Crown. At the same time, however, the House made a second reference to the Court of Justice requesting a preliminary ruling on the question of whether EC law enabled national courts to grant an interim injunction in these circumstances.

In a separate action the EC Commission took infringement proceedings against the UK in relation to the nationality requirements in section 14 of the Merchant Shipping Act. In *Commission v. UK re Merchant Shipping Rules* 1989 the Court of Justice held that the UK was required to suspend the application of the offending parts of the Act. The decision in this case was given effect by a statutory instrument, the Merchant Shipping Act 1988 (Amendment) Order 1989.

In *Factortame Ltd. v. Secretary of State for Transport (no.2)* 1991 the Court of Justice ruled on the questions which had been referred to it by the House of Lords. It held that a court in a member state must set aside any rules of national law which prevent directly effective Community law from having effect. In the circumstances of the present case the UK courts were therefore required, as a matter of EC law, to set aside the rule of English law that the courts had no jurisdiction to grant an interim injunction disapplying an Act of Parliament. The House of Lords then had to consider, given that it had the power to suspend an Act of Parliament, the circumstances in which it would be appropriate to do so. The House decided that it would only be appropriate to take this exceptional course of action where the challenge to the validity of the Act was so firmly based as to justify the suspension of the provision in question. On the facts it was held that the case made out by the applicants had a strong basis and the offending provisions of the Act should therefore be suspended. The case may be regarded as a major landmark in the development of this area of law in confirming the power of the courts to suspend the operation of an Act of Parliament. Whilst the decision was greeted with surprise from some observers, many regarded it as the logical consequence of the 1972 Act. This view was expressed by Lord Bridge in his judgment *"If the supremacy within the European Community of community law over the national law of member states was not always inherent in the EEC Treaty it was certainly well established in the jurisprudence of the Court of Justice long before the United Kingdom joined the Community. Thus, whatever limitation of its sovereignty Parliament accepted when it enacted the European Communities Act 1972 was entirely voluntary."*

Types of Community Law

The major sources of Community law are *primary* legislation found in the treaties establishing and developing the EC; *secondary* legislation made on an ongoing basis by the Community institutions; judgments of the Court of Justice and unwritten general principles of law. In relation to treaty provisions and secondary legislation it is useful to distinguish between the concepts of *direct applicability* and *direct effect*.

A Community law is said to be directly applicable when it is of a type which is directly incorporated in its entirety into the laws of the members states without the need for further legislative or administrative action on the part of the member state or the Community institutions. Such rules create immediate rights and obligations as between individuals and or organisations and as against member states. These rights or obligations are directly enforceable in the ordinary courts within the member states. Article 189 states that EC regulations are directly applicable. Certain provisions of the treaties have been held to be directly applicable, although they only come within this category where they are:

- clear and unambiguous;
- unconditional;
- precise;
- self-contained - i.e. requiring no further action to put them into effect.

Directly applicable Community laws will automatically take effect within the UK by virtue of s.2(1) of the 1972 Act.

A Community law which is not directly applicable may nonetheless have direct effects in terms of conferring rights upon individuals which may be enforced in the domestic courts. Such provisions usually will not have direct applicability because they are not self-contained, in the sense that they require some action, usually by the member state, in order to implement them. Typically this will apply where directives have not been implemented in full or at all, and the deadline for implementation has passed. In these circumstances the directive may produce direct effects provided it is sufficiently clear, unconditional and precise. One significant limitation on the doctrine of direct effects is that directives are only directly effective as against the state. This is known as *vertical direct effect* and is examined below in the context of the defective implementation of directives.

It may be seen that whilst all directly applicable provisions will have direct effects, the reverse will not be true so that a rule may be directly effective without being directly applicable. Not surprisingly, the two are often confused and even the courts tend to use them interchangeably.

The Treaties

The primary legislation of the EC consists of the European Treaties and associated documents, agreements and protocols. These include:

- The Treaty of Paris 1951, establishing the ECSC;
- The Treaty of Rome 1957;
- The Euratom Treaty 1957;
- The Merger Treaty 1965 which established common institutions for all three communities;
- Treaties of Accession on the admission of new member states to the Community;
- Association agreements with non-members;
- The Single European Act 1986;

- The Treaty on European Union 1992.

Under the UK constitution each new treaty requires an Act of Parliament to give it effect within the national legal system. This was achieved by the European Communities Act in 1972 in relation to the treaties which pre-dated it. Separate legislation has been introduced for each subsequent treaty so that, for example, the European Communities (Amendment) Act 1993 gives effect to the Treaty on European Union.

The European Treaties set out the framework of Community law, create the institutions and lay down the procedures for making secondary legislation on an ongoing basis.

Whilst certain provisions in the treaties lay down broad or vague policies which need to be fleshed out in secondary legislation, the Court of Justice has held that others can be directly applicable. Article 119 of the Treaty of Rome, for example, provides that *"Each member state shall ... maintain the application of the principle that men and women receive equal pay for equal work"*. In *Defrenne v. Sabena* 1976 the Court of Justice held that article 119 imposed on member states *"A duty to bring about a specific result to be mandatorally achieved"* and that it could be relied on in an action between a private individual and her private sector employer. Defrenne, an air hostess, claimed to be entitled to the same pay as a male steward whose duties were identical to hers. It was held that she could rely on article 119 even though it was addressed to the member state and was not framed as a rule giving rights to individuals. In so far as it relates to direct discrimination and equal work it was held to be directly applicable. The case of *Macarthys v. Smith* 1979, discussed above, is a further example of a direct application of article 119.

> In *Barber v. Guardian Royal Exchange* 1990 the Court of Justice applied article 119 in its decision that occupational pension schemes, as opposed to state retirement pension, and the benefits conferred under them on employees, are pay for the purpose of article 119. It is therefore unlawful to discriminate between men and women in relation to them. Mr Barber claimed to be entitled to benefit under his company pension scheme on the same basis as female employees and objected to the fact that he could not receive benefits under the scheme until he reached the age of 65 whereas his female counterparts could benefit at 60. The Court of Justice's decision in his favour caused major changes in many occupational pension schemes to give effect to the equalisation of pension ages and benefits as between men and women.

Many articles of the Treaty have been held to be directly effective, including, for example, article 12 prohibiting member states from introducing new customs duties on imports or exports from other member states, articles 85 and 86 prohibiting anti-competitive practices, article 37(2) on the abolition of customs duties and quantitative restrictions on imports, article 53 on the right of establishment and a number of others.

Secondary Legislation

The Treaties confer significant law making powers on the Institutions of the Community. These powers are limited in that they extend only to areas where the Community has competence to legislate. There are some areas which remain within the exclusive domain of the national sovereignty of the member states. As we have seen, however, the Community's law making competence extents to virtually all aspects of business law.

Article 189 of the Treaty of Rome states *"In order to carry out their task the Council and the Commission shall, in accordance with the provisions of this Treaty, make regulations, issue directives, take decisions, make recommendations or deliver opinions"*. The article goes on to define each of them.

Regulations

A *regulation* has general application. It is binding in its entirety and directly applicable in all member states. Regulations are the equivalent of UK statutes on a community scale. They apply to everyone in all fifteen member states and there is no requirement for action at a national level to bring them into effect. This occurs on the 20th day following their publication in the Official Journal where no other date is specified in them. Council regulation No.295/91, for example, deals with the situation where passengers are denied access to an overbooked scheduled flight for which they have a valid ticket and a confirmed reservation. It establishes common minimum rules applicable in that situation.

Directives

A *directive* shall be binding, as to the result to be achieved, upon each member state to which it is addressed but shall leave to the national authorities the choice of form and methods. Directives are the major instrument for achieving the harmonisation of national laws as between the member states. They operate by setting out the objectives which the proposed new laws must achieve, giving a time limit within which member state governments must achieve them. The resulting law will be in the form of a domestic law within the member state. In the UK directives are implemented either by a new Act of Parliament or by delegated legislation using the enabling powers in s.2(2) of the 1972 Act. The Treaty gives some discretion as to the manner of implementation, provided that the result is achieved. This allows for a certain degree of flexibility, for example, in relation to the consequences for breach of a particular rules which need not be identical in each member state. Breach of the same substantive rule may, for example, give rise to criminal liability in the UK and civil liability in France. There are many examples of directives and their implementation throughout this text, notably in such areas as company law, consumer protection, employment rights and health and safety at work.

Decisions

A *decision* is binding in its entirety upon those to whom it is addressed. They may be addressed to a member state, a business or other organisation or an individual. There is no discretion as to the manner of implementation, and decisions take effect upon notification. They may be used, for example, to enforce Community competition policy.

Recommendations and Opinions

Recommendations and *opinions* are not legally binding or enforceable. They are often addressed to member states and may give a view on a particular matter or set out guidelines to be followed in relation to an issue, sometimes with the implication that if they are not followed proposals for a stronger type of Community law may be made at a later date.

General principles of law

These are an unwritten source of Community law whose existence and validity derive from article 215 which recognises as part of Community law the general principles common to the laws of member states and article 164 which requires the Court of Justice to ensure that in the interpretation and application of this Treaty the law is observed. These provisions enable the Court of Justice to draw from the legal traditions of the member states in developing the jurisprudence of Community law.

Defective Implementation of Directives

Where a member state has failed to implement a directive within the specified time period, or where implementation has taken place in part only, there are a number of possible consequences:

(a) *Infringement proceedings may be taken by the Commission against the member state.* This process is outlined above and ultimately results in a ruling against the member state by the Court of Justice. One problem with this process had been the lack of any power to enforce the judgment of the Court of Justice. Since the coming into effect of the Treaty on European Union however, as we have seen, the Court of Justice has power to fine a member state which fails to comply with a judgment against it.

(b) *A directive may have direct effects in a case involving the state as defendant.* By definition a directive cannot be directly applicable as it requires some action on the part of the member state to give it effect in national law. Where the member state fails to do this, either in whole or in part, the principle of *vertical direct effect* may come into play. This will prevent the member state from using its own wrongful act of failing properly to implement the directive as a defence to a legal action taken by someone who wishes to enforce the rights contained in the directive against it. In order to be directly effective, the rights set out in the directive must be clear, unambiguous, unconditional and precise.

> In *Marshall v. Southampton and South West Hampshire Area Health Authority (Teaching)* 1986, the Health Authority operated a retirement policy for employees under which the normal retirement age was 60 for women and 65 for men. This was consistent with s.6(4) of the Sex Discrimination Act 1975, and in line with state retirement pension ages. An employee's retirement could be postponed by mutual agreement and Miss Marshall continued to work until she was dismissed at age 62. The sole reason given for her dismissal was that she had passed the normal retirement age. She claimed that her dismissal was an unlawful discrimination because men could not be dismissed on grounds of retirement at that age. Her claim was based upon the following articles of the Equal Treatment Directive:
>
> > "*1(1). The purpose of this directive is to put into effect in the member states the principle of equal treatment for men and women as regards access to employment, including promotion, and to vocational training and as regards working conditions...*

2(1). The principle of equal treatment shall mean that there shall be no discrimination whatsoever on grounds of sex either directly, or indirectly by reference in particular to marital or family status.

5(1). Application of the principle of equal treatment with regard to working conditions, including those governing dismissal, means that men and women shall be guaranteed the same conditions without discrimination on grounds of sex."

The Court of Appeal sought a preliminary ruling from the Court of Justice as to whether the retirement policy of the Health Authority constituted discrimination on grounds of sex contrary to the directive; and if so, whether article 5(1) could be relied upon as against a state authority acting in its capacity as employer, in order to avoid the application of s.6(4) of the Sex Discrimination Act 1975.

The Court of Justice ruled that the difference in compulsory retirement ages as between men and women was discriminatory and that article 5(1) was clear, unconditional and sufficiently precise to be directly effective. As the date for implementation had passed, it could be relied upon so as to avoid the application of s.6(4) as against the Health Authority, a public sector organisation *"Where a person involved in legal proceedings is able to rely upon a directive as against the state, he may do so regardless of the capacity in which the latter is acting, whether employer or public authority. In either case it is necessary to prevent the state from taking advantage of its own failure to comply with Community Law".*

The Court of Justice made it clear that directives can only have vertical direct effects in favour of the individual enforceable against the state. They cannot impose obligations on individuals and therefore are not, without full implementation, capable of horizontal direct effect. The *Marshall* case does not, however, make clear exactly which public bodies or manifestations of the state are subject to the rule of vertical direct effect.

In *Foster v. British Gas plc.* 1990, the factual situation was similar to that in Marshall. The sole issue was whether the British Gas Corporation, a nationalised industry, came within the definition of the state for the purposes of the rule. The Court of Justice formulated a broad definition of the state for these purposes. It ruled that the directive could be relied upon in an action for damages against *"... a body, whatever its legal form, which has been made responsible, pursuant to a measure adopted by the state, for providing a public service under the control of the state and has for that purpose special powers beyond those which result from the normal rules applicable in relations between individuals".*

In the light of this definition, the House of Lords held that the British Gas Corporation was part of the state, and the directive could be relied upon in an action for damages against it.

In *Marshall v. Southampton and South West Hampshire Area Health Authority (No.2)* 1993 a further issue arose as to the amount of compensation recoverable from her employers. The Sex Discrimination Act laid down a statutory maximum award of £6250 under s.65(2). Mrs. Marshall claimed that her full loss amounted to £19,405. Relying on the principles of vertical direct effects developed in the earlier case, she argued that the statutory financial limit was inconsistent with article 6 of the Equal Treatment Directive which in effect requires member states to provide an adequate remedy to a complainant who suffers loss as a result of discriminatory treatment. The House of Lords referred the question to the European Court of Justice for a preliminary ruling under article 177. It ruled that the financial limit conflicted with the requirements of article 6 to provide a real and effective remedy which ensured full compensation for the loss or damage actually sustained. The article had vertical direct effect as against the Health Authority, which as a public body is treated as being part of the State, and which was therefore obliged to pay her compensation in full.

In *Karella v. Ministry of Industry, Energy and Technology* 1994 two shareholders in a Greek company, Klostiria Velka AE, successfully challenged action taken by a Greek government authority, the OAE, which affected their company. The OAE had been given powers under Greek legislation to take over the control of a company, and to increase its capital. Using these powers the OAE took control of Klostiria, and increased its capital from 220m drachmas to 4000 m drachmas. The Court of Justice found that these powers were contrary to the second EC Company Law Directive which provides that other than in special circumstances an increase in capital can only be achieved through a resolution of the shareholders.

(c) Member state courts have a duty to interpret national law in the light of the wording and purpose of a relevant directive, not only where the national law in question was introduced in order to give effect to the directive, but also where it pre-dates the directive if no further implementing measure has been introduced and the date for implementation has passed.

In *Marleasing SA v. La Comercial Internacional de Alimentacion SA* 1992 the Court of Justice held that a national court must interpret national law in conformity with an unimplemented directive after the date for its implementation had passed. On the facts this had the effect of disapplying part of the national law which was inconsistent with the directive. The Court of Justice stated *"the obligation of member states under a directive is to achieve its objects, and their duty by virtue of article 5 of the Treaty to take all necessary steps to ensure the fulfilment of that obligation, binds all authorities of member states, including national courts within their jurisdiction. It follows that in applying national law, whether the provisions concerned pre-date or post-date the directive, the national court asked to interpret national law is bound to do so in every way possible in the light of the text and the aim of the directive to achieve the results envisaged by it and thus to comply with article 189 of the Treaty"*.

(d) *A member state may be liable in damages to an individual for any loss suffered as a result of the state's failure to implement a directive.* This important principle was established by the Court of Justice in the case of *Francovich v. Italian State and Bonifaci* 1992. Liability will arise as against a member state which has failed to implement a directive where the following conditions are met:

(a) the result to be achieved by the directive includes the creation of rights in favour of individuals;

(b) the content of those rights are sufficiently defined in the directive; and

(c) the individual's loss is caused by the failure of the state to implement the directive.

In the *Francovich* case, the Italian government had failed to implement directive 80/987 on the protection of employees in the event of the insolvency of their employer. Under the directive it had been required to ensure that a guarantee institution was in place from which employees could claim payments which could not be met by insolvent employers. Francovich was owed 6 million lire which he was unable to recover from his insolvent employer. He sued the Italian government for damages for its failure to comply with the directive and the Court of Justice gave a preliminary ruling on an article 177 reference that the government was liable in damages for its failure to set up the guarantee institution.

The development of the rule that a member state may be liable to pay damages where it has failed properly to implement a directive is significant in a number of ways. Firstly because the rule of vertical direct effect established in the *Marshall* case does not provide a remedy against a private sector defendant. As a result of the *Francovich* decision, a plaintiff who is unable to sue such a defendant may now be able to sue his government for its failure to legislate. On a broader front the decision is significant because it demonstrates the ability and willingness of the Court of Justice to develop creatively the principles of Community law and new mechanisms for ensuring its effectiveness in areas where the Treaties provide little or no guidance.

(e) *Damages for other breaches of community law*. The principle established in the *Francovich* case has now been extended to cover the situation where an individual or organisation suffers loss as a result of national legislation which is contrary to EC law, for example because it is incompatible with a provision of the Treaty of Rome. The member state will be liable in damages where the following conditions are met:

(a) The provision in community law was intended to create rights in favour of individuals;

(b) The breach of community law is a serious breach; and

(c) The loss is directly caused by the member states breach of EC law.

These principles have been established by the European Court of Justice through its decision in a number of cases including *R v. Secretary of State for Transport, ex parte Factortame (No.4)* 1995 and *Brasserie du Pecheur SA v. Federal Republic of Germany* 1996.

In Factortame (No.4), 1995 a further episode in the case of the Spanish fishermen described earlier, damages were claimed against the United Kingdom Government for the losses sustained by the Spanish fishermen prevented from fishing by the rules laid down in the Merchant Shipping Act 1988, which was held by the European Court of Justice in the Factortame (No.3) case to be contrary to article 52 of the Treaty of Rome. In the *Brasserie du Pecheur* case, a French brewery claimed damages against the German Government for losses suffered as a result of the German decision not to allow the French company to sell its beer in Germany on the ground that it did not comply with purity requirements established under German law. This ban had been held by the European Court of Justice to be illegal and contrary to article 30 of the Treaty of Rome. It was held that the member state was liable to the plaintiffs in each case as their losses were caused by national legislation which was contrary to EC law.

Legal Terms found in Chapter 3

Appeal	• asking a higher court to change the decision of a lower court
Appellant	• a person who appeals
Arbitrate	• to settle a dispute without court action by referring it to an arbitrator
Barrister	• lawyer who has capacity to represent a client in any court or tribunal proceedings as an advocate
Cause of action	• reason why a case is brought to court
Civil action	• a case brought by one person (or company) against another alleging a civil wrong
Complainant	• an individual presenting a complaint to a tribunal
Injunction	• court order requiring someone to do something or not to do something
Interlocutory injunction	• temporary injunction
Jurisdiction	• legal powers of a court or tribunal over particular types of disputes
Legal aid	• state funded scheme providing financial assistance for legal claims
Litigate	• to go to law and take an action against another in court
Respondent	• an individual defending a complaint before a tribunal or the party called upon to answer an appeal
Solicitor	• lawyer who is a general practitioner of the law and who has limited rights of audience to represent a client in court proceedings

Chapter 3

The Resolution of Business Disputes

Introduction

This chapter examines the machinery which exists for resolving legal conflict in the business world and considers some of the issues associated with the process of *going to law* over a dispute. While the High Court has an important role to play in hearing civil disputes concerning large sums of money the vast majority of civil legal actions which go to court are dealt with at County Court level. Changes in the jurisdiction of the County Courts, considered in Chapter 1, has increased their workload by passing over to them cases which previously would have been heard before the High Court.

Not all civil disputes however are resolved by means of court proceedings. Many cases are dealt with instead before tribunals. The workload of tribunals has been steadily increasing. Collectively tribunals now handle in the region of six times more work than the High Court and County Court combined. One important field in which they are used is in the handling of employment disputes. These are heard before Industrial Tribunals.

We begin by looking at the organisations and individuals who are available to assist those with a legal problem, then go on to consider the way in which a legal dispute is dealt with both before the County Court and an Industrial Tribunal, finally concluding by considering the use of arbitration as an alternative means of resolving business disputes without having recourse to the courts.

Sources of Legal Advice and Information

Many sources of legal advice and information are available to a trader who has a legal problem. He may be able to research it himself by looking at law books in a library, but more usually he will seek outside help. If he is a member of a trade or professional association or trade union it is probable that he will be able to obtain legal guidance from such a body, particularly if the question is one which is closely associated with the operation or regulation of his business.

In relation to legal enquiries of a general nature, the Citizen's Advice Bureau (CAB) may be able to point the trader in the right direction, or provide the information which he requires. In addition, there are a number of law centres which provide a similar, though more specialist, role in giving legal advice and acting on behalf of clients. Law centres, however, tend to deal with legal problems arising in relation to social issues such as housing, immigration, consumer and employee rights. They do not usually take on the role of advising businessmen in relation to commercial matters.

Lawyers

The most obvious source of advice and legal information is the *solicitor*. Larger business organisations may have their own legal department or in-house solicitor to provide a comprehensive legal service for the business. These permanently employed lawyers will deal with such matters as conveyancing, drawing up contracts, registering intellectual property rights, advising management on day to day legal matters, designing procedures to ensure compliance by the business with its legal requirements and conducting litigation on its behalf.

Smaller business organisations cannot usually justify the expense of a legal department and will use solicitors in private practice to deal with their legal affairs. Solicitors are the general practitioners of the law, although within any particular firm individual solicitors will usually specialise in one or two areas of law. If a businessman refers a legal problem to solicitor and the solicitor requires further specialist help or advice in order to deal with it, the solicitor can obtain the opinion of a *barrister*. The barrister, or counsel, usually specialises in a much narrower field of law than the solicitor. A businessman cannot approach a barrister directly for legal help but must first use a solicitor. The solicitor can refer the matter to a barrister if he feels that it is necessary. The main functions of the barrister are to provide legal opinions, to draw pleadings in preparation for litigation, and to act as an advocate in court. A solicitor cannot always act as an advocate without a barrister because the solicitor has only limited rights of audience before the courts. He is allowed to appear before a Magistrates Court, a County Court and, in certain circumstances, a Crown Court without a barrister. He is unable to appear in the High Court or any of the appeal courts and must use a barrister if he intends to conduct a case in one of these courts.

Communications between a client and a solicitor or barrister are subject to legal professional privilege. This means that the lawyer is duty bound not to disclose the communication to any other party without the authority of the client. In practice the effect of legal professional privilege is that the client can disclose all of the information which is relevant to his legal problem without fear that the information may be used against him at some later stage. The purpose of the rule is to ensure that the client does not hold back information which might be relevant to the legal problem which has arisen. This allows the lawyer to have all of the facts and to make a proper decision as to the course of action which is in the client's best interests.

Legal aid

Under the Legal Aid Scheme an individual may be entitled to receive help with his legal problem. Depending upon his financial circumstances, all or part of the cost of legal help will be paid by the state. This can extend to representation before a court but not before a tribunal. In order to qualify for free legal aid the individual's resources must be very low, both in terms of capital and income. If he is not entitled to free legal aid because he has more than the minimum resources he may still get some help from the legal aid scheme but he will have to make a contribution towards his own costs. If the individual has capital assets or average income, however, he may be caught in the "middle income trap". This is described as a trap because he will be too well off to obtain legal aid but will not be sufficiently well off to be able to afford the costs of litigation himself. He may therefore have to decide not to take legal action in the courts. Even where a prospective litigant satisfies the financial criterion for legal aid the Legal Aid Board will only sanction legal aid if the legal action has some merit and a reasonable prospect of success. It is in these circumstances that an individual consumer is enabled to bring proceedings against a powerful business organisation which may have to incur substantial legal costs in defending the legal action. Legal aid does not extend to all legal actions, for example defamation. In 1990 the McDonalds fast food giant took legal action against two individuals for allegedly distributing a defamatory leaflet about their organisation. The subsequent trial is now, in 1996, in it's second year, and the defendants, Morris and Steel, have had to give up their jobs in order to conduct their own defence to the action as legal aid is not available.

Conditional fee

In July 1995 *conditional fee arrangements*, often referred to as no win no fee arrangements became available for personal injury, insolvency and human rights cases. If the case is won solicitors can charge a success fee of up to double their normal fee. This is to compensate for the risk of not being paid if they lose. The amount of the success fee is reflected by the degree of risk involved. Should the case be lost the plaintiff, under conditional fee arrangements, will have no liability for his own solicitors costs but is still potentially liable for his opponent's costs. This risk for prospective plaintiffs can and should be covered by after-the-event insurance. The Law Society has developed and approved an insurance package called Accident Line Protect, designed to be used in conjunction with conditional fees. At the cost of £85 this insurance cover is however only available where the solicitors are members of the *Law Society's Accident Line Scheme so* guaranteeing that they are experts in personal injury work .The Law Society recommend that the conditional fee charged should not in any event exceed 25% of the damage recovered. There is no doubt that through this scheme many more accident victims particularly those at the workplace, have been encouraged to seek and obtain legal redress, when otherwise they would have been discouraged to do so because of the risk of substantial legal costs. One notable case commenced in September 1996 under conditional fee arrangements is a personal injury claim brought against the tobacco industry. Here solicitors have been prepared to accept the risk of an estimated two million pounds in costs in proceedings which are expected to take two years to get to court.

Suing in the County Court

Before a business takes a decision to sue in the County Court, for example for an outstanding debt, there are a number of matters which must be considered carefully. Probably the most important factor will be that of cost, both in terms of money and in terms of the time and resources which must be invested in legal proceedings. Most of the plaintiff's costs will eventually be payable by the defendant if the plaintiff wins his case. However the plaintiff has a contract with his solicitor and is bound under that contract to pay the solicitor's fees, and disbursements such as court fees, regardless of the outcome of the case. The plaintiff must therefore spend all of this money himself in the hope of later recovering it from the defendant. Even if the plaintiff is successful, he may not be able to obtain an order that the defendant pays all of his legal costs because a defendant can challenge the amount of a successful plaintiff's legal bill. This is done in a *taxation of costs* in which the court will require the defendant to pay only those costs which were reasonably and necessarily incurred by the plaintiff in the action. After a taxation, the plaintiff will usually have to pay some part of his own legal costs. These in effect are deducted from whatever damages he has recovered from the defendant.

Another important consideration, closely associated with the question of costs, is whether the defendant will actually be able to satisfy any judgment which is eventually made against him. If the defendant is a "man of straw", and has no resources, the plaintiff will be wasting his money by pursuing him in the courts. He may end up by having to pay all of his own legal costs and by getting them back from the defendant by instalments of one a month, or by not getting them back at all. For this reason it is essential that the financial circumstances of the potential defendant are investigated before proceedings are issued against him. There is no formal procedure for this type of investigation, so the plaintiff will simply have to conduct it in the best way that he can.

In making the decision to sue someone, a business must also be aware that the legal process is slow. It may take one to four years to obtain judgment against a defendant, depending on the complexity of the case and its particular circumstances. In extreme cases, litigants have suffered mental illness or depression as a result of involvement with litigation. There is recognised mental condition called litigation neurosis. Involvement in litigation over a long period of time is certainly a drain on the resources of the parties in terms of time, money and mental energy.

Publicity is another important factor. Proceedings before the courts are held in public and can be attended by anyone, including the press. Depending on the circumstances, a business may be inviting adverse publicity and a loss of goodwill by taking legal proceedings. If the legal action is being taken against an important customer, the damage to ongoing business relationships can be substantial.

In addition to these factors, it is self evident that the plaintiff must have a sound legal basis for his claim and sufficient evidence to support it. This evidence may be documentary or may be provided by witnesses. In the case of the verbal evidence by witnesses, the credibility of the witnesses will be an important consideration. It may also be necessary to employ expert witnesses if the subject matter of the dispute is technical in nature, for example if it centres around a mechanical or electrical problem.

Negotiation, compromise and settlement

For one or more of the reasons given above, the parties to a dispute will usually try to reach a settlement without the necessity of taking legal proceedings. Negotiations will take place before legal proceedings are issued and will usually continue as an ongoing process right up to the date of the trial. If both parties are prepared to litigate, this is probably an indication that there is some merit in the case that each of them is arguing. If a compromise can be agreed this will probably result in the saving of costs, time and adverse publicity.

County Court Procedure

Once the decision to sue has been taken, the plaintiff must decide in which court to issue proceedings. We considered in Chapter 1 the basis upon which this decision will be made. The procedures in both the County Court and the High Court are broadly similar, although in the High Court the procedure tends to be more complicated. We shall examine County Court procedures only.

Assuming that the case is to be brought in the County Court, the plaintiff must decide which County Court to use. The claim must usually be brought in the district in which the defendant lives or carries on business or in the district in which the cause of action arose (for example where the contract was made).

The procedure for the conduct of the action is laid down in the County Court Rules. These are designed to ensure fairness between the parties. This is achieved by ensuring that the matter in dispute is understood by the parties and by the court, and that neither party is taken by surprise at the trial by the introduction of any new matter which ought to have been disclosed to him before the trial. The rules also give time limits within which procedural steps must be taken by each party. These are designed to ensure that there is no unnecessary delay in the conduct of the case.

The first step which must be taken by the plaintiff is to send a *letter before action* to the defendant. In it the plaintiff will state his claim, invite the defendant to comply with his demands within 7 days, and inform him that court proceedings will be taken if he fails to do so. A letter before action gives the defendant the opportunity to meet the plaintiff's claim without incurring legal costs, or to state any legitimate grounds of defence which are available to him, and which may give rise to negotiations for settlement of the claim. If the plaintiff does not send a letter before action, and the defendant meets his demands as soon as proceedings are issued, the plaintiff will be unable to recover costs from him.

Within a fortnight of sending a letter before action, if there is no positive response to it, the plaintiff may request the court to issue a summons against the defendant. A *default summons* is used whenever the plaintiff is claiming a fixed sum of money. A *fixed date summons* is used either when there is a claim for money which includes an element of damages to be assessed by the court, or a non-money remedy, such as an injunction, the possession of land or the recovery of goods. In this text we shall be examining the procedure which applies to a default summons, because this type of summons is most often used by the businessman. (See Figure 3.1) The procedure for a fixed date summons is broadly similar.

The plaintiff must file a request for the issue of a default summons, together with the summons itself at the County Court office. In addition he must provide two copies of the particulars of claim, one for the court and one for the defendant. In the particulars of claim the plaintiff must specify the legal basis of his claim and remedy which he seeks. He will also include a brief description of the material facts surrounding his claim. The particulars of the claim and summons will be served on the defendant by the court together with forms on which the defendant can either make an admission and a proposal for payment or put forward a defence and/or a counterclaim.

If the defendant fails to respond within 14 days of receiving the summons the plaintiff may request the court to enter judgment against him. The plaintiff has in effect won his case by default, and can enforce the judgment against the defendant if he fails to pay.

On receiving the summons however the defendant may have decided to admit the claim in part or in full, and make an offer to pay the amount due either immediately or by instalments. The majority of County Court actions involve the recovery of debts. If the defendant requests time to pay, he must provide the court with details of his financial circumstances and the exact terms of his proposals

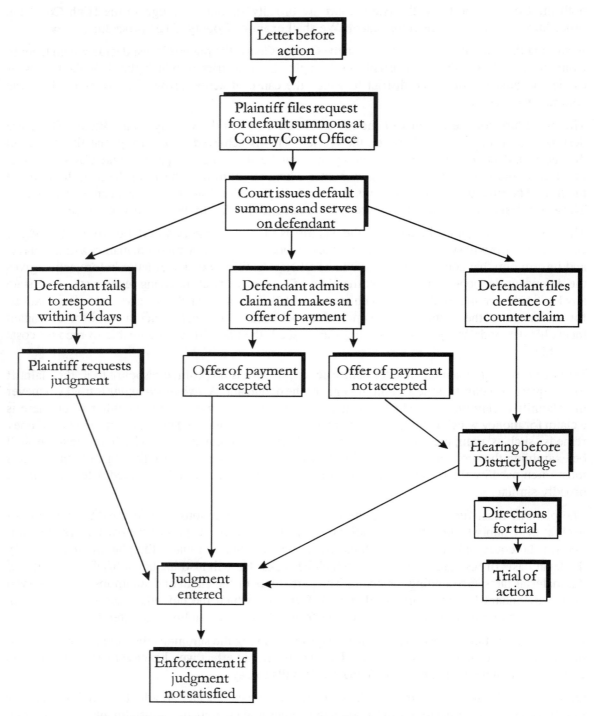

Figure 3.1   Main steps in a default action in the County Court

for payment. These will be forwarded by the court to the plaintiff, who will decide whether or not to accept the offer of payment. If he accepts, judgment will be entered in the terms of the agreement. If the plaintiff does not accept the defendant's proposals, the court will fix a date for a hearing before the district judge for a decision on the terms of payment. The decision of the district judge will be binding on both parties and judgment will be entered.

If the defendant fails to keep up payment, enforcement action may be taken against him by the plaintiff.

If the defendant believes he has a valid defence to the plaintiff's claim, he must file particulars of the defence in the County Court Office within 14 days of receiving the summons, in order to prevent judgment being entered against him in default.

If he feels that he has insufficient information about the plaintiff's claim to set out his defence in full or if he does not have time to prepare a full defence, but still wishes to defend the action, he may lodge a *holding defence* with the court within the time period and give *further and better particulars* of his defence at a later date when he is requested to do so by the plaintiff. A holding defence is simply a statement denying any indebtedness to the plaintiff.

A counterclaim may be made by the defendant at the same time as he lodges his defence with the court. In a counterclaim he is making a separate claim for damages against the plaintiff, which will survive as a separate action if the original claim by the plaintiff is withdrawn. Where circumstances permit, a counterclaim should be made as it provides a useful bargaining tool in negotiations for settlement.

If either of the parties feels that he has insufficient information relating to the claim or defence of the other, he may, within prescribed time, request further and better particulars of the other party's claim or defence. The other party must then supply the information. The County Court Rules make provision for this so that each party may know the exact case which he has to answer, and neither may be taken by surprise at a late stage in the proceedings. In this way the process helps to narrow down the issues and highlight the points of difference between the parties.

Pre-trial review

Once the initial exchange of information about each party's side of the case has taken place, the court will fix a date for a pre-trial review. This will be held in private before the district judge. If the plaintiff fails to attend, the action may be struck out or discontinued on the order of the court. If the defendant does not attend the plaintiff may be able to obtain judgment if he can prove his case.

If both parties are present the district judge will seek to clarify the points at issue, if there is any doubt about them. He may also explore the possibility of a settlement at this stage. If the action is to go to trial, the district judge will give directions to the parties as to the things that they must do in order to prepare the case for trial. Directions given by the district judge at the pre-trial review may include orders that:

(i)   further and better particulars of the claim or the defence must be given;

(ii) each party prepare a list of the documents in their possession relating to the case and give it to the other;

(iii)   each party allow the other to inspect the listed documents, and take copies of them, a process known as *discovery of documents;*

(iv)   the parties try to agree matters which are not disputed, to save the necessity and expense of proving them in court; and

(v)   the parties produce plans, photographs or experts' reports, and agree on their contents if possible.

When the directions given by the district judge at the pre-trial review have been complied with, either party may apply to the court to fix a date for the trial. Once this has been fixed, the court will notify the parties, who must then complete their final preparations.

The trial

Many cases are settled on the doorstep of the courtroom before a trial takes place. This is because the pressure for settlement builds up to a peak when the parties are faced with the reality of a trial. They may be aware of some weakness in their case, or may doubt the ability of a key witness to appear credible and resolute in the face of cross examination. Even at this late stage considerable savings of costs can be made by settling the case.

The proceedings in a County Court trial are conducted in a formal manner. The plaintiff will have to present his evidence first, and any witnesses may be cross examined by the defence, or questioned by the judge. The plaintiff's lawyers can re-examine any of his witnesses, but must confine their questioning to matters already raised by them. Thus they could, for example, clarify any points which may have become confused in cross examination, or emphasise any important points which may have been obscured. Next it is the turn of the defence to present its evidence, and again there may be cross examination and re-examination.

Legal argument may then take place, followed by a summing up of each party's case. The judge will usually deliver judgment at the end of the trial, but may reserve judgment, particularly if there are difficult points of law to consider. If judgment is reserved the parties will have to attend court at a later date when judgment will be given.

As we noted above, the party who loses the case will have to pay the winner's costs, in addition to his own. He can however, challenge the amount of the other party's bill by applying to the court for a taxation of costs. Sometimes before the trial the defendant may make a payment into court. This is a fixed sum that the defendants lawyers have determined. The idea is to avoid a trial in which the defendant may lose, and end up paying damages and full costs. The payment in will be a sum below the amount of damages that the defendant's lawyers predict that the court will order against him. The plaintiff then has a choice; to take the payment in full and final settlement of the claim; or proceed to trial. If he proceeds and is then awarded damages at below or at the same level as the payment in, the defendant only has to pay his own costs incurred up to the date of the payment in, and gets all his costs thereafter from the plaintiff. since the heaviest costs are incurred in the final stages of the trial, the plaintiff who chooses to proceed with the trial incurs a substantial financial risk when a payment in has been made.

An appeal can be made from a decision of the County Court to the Court of Appeal. The appeal may be on a question of law or a question of fact, and must be lodged within specified time limits.

The costs involved in making an appeal will be very high and careful thought should be given before this step is taken.

Enforcement of a Judgment

If judgment is given against a defendant, payment is due immediately unless the court has made an order for payment by instalments or has otherwise postponed payment. If the judgment debtor does not make payment when it is due, steps can be taken to enforce the judgment. There are a number of alternative methods of enforcement, and it will be important to choose a method which will bear fruit having regard to the particular circumstances of the judgment debtor.

To assist in making an informed choice as to the method of enforcement, the party entitled to payment may make an application to the court for an order that the judgment debtor be orally examined before the court as to his means. The order may include provision for the production of books, accounts or other documents. The judgment debtor will be liable to imprisonment if he fails to attend. At the oral examination he will be cross examined on oath, as to his means and resources, by the judge and the applicant. It can be established, for example, whether he has any investments, bank accounts, savings or other assets such as a house or a car; or if he is working, the name and address of his employer and details of his salary and any other source of income. Armed with this information, a decision can be taken as to the most effective method of enforcement. The following are the *principal methods*.

A warrant of execution directs the County Court bailiff to seize any goods belonging to the judgment debtor, and to sell them to raise money to pay the creditor. It will be useful, at the oral examination, to establish what goods belong to the debtor and where they are located, in preparation for the issue of a warrant of execution.

If it has been established that the judgment debtor has regular employment, the plaintiff can apply for an *attachment of earnings order* under the Attachment of Earnings Act 1971. This is in effect a direction to the employer to deduct a specified sum from the debtor's wages each week, and pay it direct to the court, which will forward the money to the plaintiff.

If the plaintiff discovers, at the end of the oral examination, that the debtor is owed money by a third party, he may apply for a *garnishee order*. The effect of the order is to require the third party to pay the money direct to the plaintiff, or at least so much of it as will satisfy the judgment debt and costs. This type of order is particularly useful where, for example, the judgment debtor has money in a bank account or some other similar form of savings.

The plaintiff can apply for a *charging order* on land held by the debtor or on any shares owned by him in a company. This gives him security for the judgment debt which can ultimately be enforced by the sale of the property in question.

A creditor will have grounds to *petition* for the *bankruptcy* of the debtor if a judgment debt of £750 or more remains outstanding after a warrant of execution has been issued but returned unsatisfied. In practice the threat of bankruptcy proceedings is a powerful stimulus to make a defaulting debtor find the money to pay the debt.

Bringing a Claim Before an Industrial Tribunal

Tribunals are an alternative method to the courts used to handle certain types of specific disputes. In general they tend to be quicker, less formal and therefore cheaper than the ordinary courts. The vast majority of individual employment rights and duties are legally enforceable by means of presenting a complaint before an Industrial Tribunal. Originating under the Industrial Training Act 1964 with only a restricted function, the Industrial Tribunal is now the focus for dealing with statutory employment law disputes. Industrial Tribunals have a jurisdiction extending to unfair dismissal, redundancy, employment status and trade union rights all of which are considered later in the book in the context of employing the workforce. In 1995 over 90,000 complaints were presented to Industrial Tribunals which was 15% up on 1994. The Industrial Tribunals (Extensions of Jurisdiction) (England and Wales) Order 1994 provides that Tribunals may also determine wrongful dismissal claims which previously were exclusively heard in the County Court. The Tribunal is composed of three members, a legally qualified chairman and two lay members, one of whom is usually a nominee of an employer's organisation, and the other the nominee of a trade union. Under the Trade Union Reform and Employment Rights Act 1993 certain Industrial Tribunals will be properly constituted with a chairman sitting alone.

Its role has been described as acting as that of "an industrial jury". As such it is the final arbiter on questions of fact. While the aim of conferring jurisdiction on a Tribunal is to encourage decision-making which is both inexpensive and speedy, the reality is that there has been increasing legal complexity introduced into Tribunal proceedings. The procedure of Tribunals is regulated by the Industrial Tribunal (Rules of Procedure) Regulations 1985.

Submitting the claim

It is of crucial importance that a complainant to an Industrial Tribunal presents the claim within the appropriate time limits. In a complaint involving unfair dismissal the claim must be presented within three months of the effective date of the termination of employment. The Tribunal does have a discretion to allow an application out of time where it was not reasonably practicable to present it before the end of the three month period. In practice Tribunals rarely hear applications presented out of time however and in *Swainston v. Hetton Victory Club Ltd*. 1983 the fact that the complainant was only one day late was sufficient for the Tribunal to refuse to hear the complaint.

To present a claim it is usual to complete and submit an Industrial Tribunal 1 (IT1) form to the Regional Office of Industrial Tribunals (ROIT), although the use of that particular form is not a statutory requirement and another form of writing could suffice. Failure to clearly express the nature of the claim and the unlawful act complained of maybe overlooked by the Tribunal which is encouraged to be flexible, particularly when the complainant is unrepresented. The ROIT acknowledges receipt of the IT1 by sending the complainant a form which confirms that copies of the complaint have been sent to the employer and passed on to the Advisory Conciliation and Arbitration Services (ACAS). The form also informs the employee that notice of the hearing will be sent at a future date. The employer (respondent), having received a copy of the IT1 and also a formal notice that the application has been made, has then fourteen days to *enter an appearance*. It is at this stage that the respondent should attempt to clarify the legal position, consider the evidence and, if necessary, apply to the ROIT for an extension of time before entering an appearance. If he requires further clarification of the complainant's grounds for the claim he can make a request for further particulars. Whether or not the respondent wishes to resist the claim, he must complete the notice of appearance and return it to the ROIT. If, in the notice, the respondent fails to provide sufficient particulars of his ground for resisting the claim, he can be required to do so by the Tribunal.

A copy of the notice of appearance is sent to the complainant and to ACAS. It is then in the hands of the ROIT to set a date for the hearing but in practice a postponement can be applied for in writing and is normally granted when requested. It may be that the respondent disputes that the applicant is qualified to bring the claim, perhaps on the ground that the employee has insufficient continuous employment for the purposes of a complaint of unfair dismissal. In these circumstances it is usual to request a preliminary hearing to determine the issue.

Conciliation

One of the functions of ACAS is in relation to conciliation when a complaint is presented alleging that a statutory right has been infringed. The role of a conciliation officer in an unfair dismissal claim for instance, is to endeavour to promote a settlement of the complaint without the dispute having to go before an Industrial Tribunal. The officer is required to promote a settlement if requested to do so by either party or if he feels that he could act with a reasonable prospect of success. For this purpose an officer could seek to promote the reinstatement or re-engagement of a dismissed employee on equitable terms or if this is not practicable, attempt to persuade the employer to agree to make the employee a compensation payment. His function is not to negotiate with the parties but rather to act as a channel of communication through which the parties do their bargaining. The conciliation officer will have considerable experience of this type of conflict and if asked to do so can draw on his experience to give an impartial opinion on the legal position. If a settlement is needed, it is usual for it to be arranged through the conciliation officer. Such a settlement is enforceable in the same way as an award from an Industrial Tribunal, if necessary by action in the county court. In 1995 about 70% of complaints were withdrawn or settled before reaching a Tribunal following conciliation by ACAS.

It is an important feature of employment law that an employee cannot opt out of his statutory rights and previously if a private settlement was reached, which was not approved by an ACAS conciliation officer, either party could still present a complaint to an Industrial Tribunal. Now following the Trade Union Reform and Employment Rights Act 1993 the parties to a dispute can settle without involving ACAS provided the complainant employee had taken independent legal advice. Any sum of money agreed as compensation in a private settlement would however be taken account of in determining a Tribunal award.

While there are a number of exceptions to the general rule, for instance fixed term contracts of employment of one year or more which exclude unfair dismissal rights, it would be prudent to call in a conciliation officer to give his stamp of approval to any private settlement.

Before the hearing

Either party may apply for a *pre-hearing review* to take place, or the Tribunal may arrange an review in the absence of an application. The pre-hearing review is carried out by a the Tribunal Chairman examining the papers, assessing the strength of the claim and deciding whether the respondent's defence has any merit. No evidence from witnesses is heard but the Tribunal may take account of any written applications and the argument of the parties or other representatives. If an opinion is reached that other party's case is particularly weak then the Tribunal may require a deposit and issue a warning that if the party concerned proceeds to a full trial, an order for costs may be made against him. While the Tribunal rarely awards costs, it has a discretion to do so where a party, in bringing the proceedings, has acted frivolously, vexatiously or otherwise unreasonably. By proceeding with a claim after a pre-trial assessment has decided that it is particularly weak, a party would be regarded as acting unreasonably. An employee who brings a claim without any substance with the aim of harassing the employer, acts frivolously or vexatiously and could have costs awarded against him.

In *Ferodo Ltd. v. Bradbury and Mycock* 1990 the purpose of a pre-hearing assessment was referred to by the President of the Employment Appeal Tribunal. *"The industrial members of this court bear in mind the purpose of a pre-hearing assessment namely: to eliminate those cases which have little or no prospect of success, thus to save not only the costs of the respondent employer but also of those representing applicants, who may or may not have received the full picture in their instructions; to identify relevant issues and to discard those issues which are really incapable of being pursued; to shorten the full hearings of originating applications before the tribunal; and lastly, to avoid improper use of industrial tribunal procedures."*

The hearing

An Industrial Tribunal hearing is not conducted with the same degree of formality as a trial in a court of law and the rules of procedure make it clear that a Tribunal may conduct a hearing in a manner most suitable to clarify the issues, without the need to comply strictly to the normal rules relating to the admissibility of evidence. This makes it possible for lay representation which may put the complainant under a disadvantage, particularly if the employer is legally represented. In an attempt to speed up Tribunal proceedings there is no longer a requirement to provide full reasons for a decision except in cases involving discrimination. The reasons must be recorded in a written document signed by the chairman but they could be recorded in a *full* or *summary* form.

In relation to summary reasons, Lord Donaldson MR in the Court of Appeal hearing of *William Hill Organisation Ltd. v. Gavas* 1990 said that *"It is the practice for Industrial Tribunals to give summary reasons and then, if asked, to amplify them as full reasons. It may be convenient to say that, certainly in my experience...we are getting into the position... in which summary reasons have grown and grown until they are scarcely distinguishable from full reasons"*. He went on to suggest that guidance should be given by the Employment Appeal Tribunal to get Tribunals *"back to first principles"* so that the applicant and respondent are given no more than in essence what is the reason for the decision when summary reasons are given.

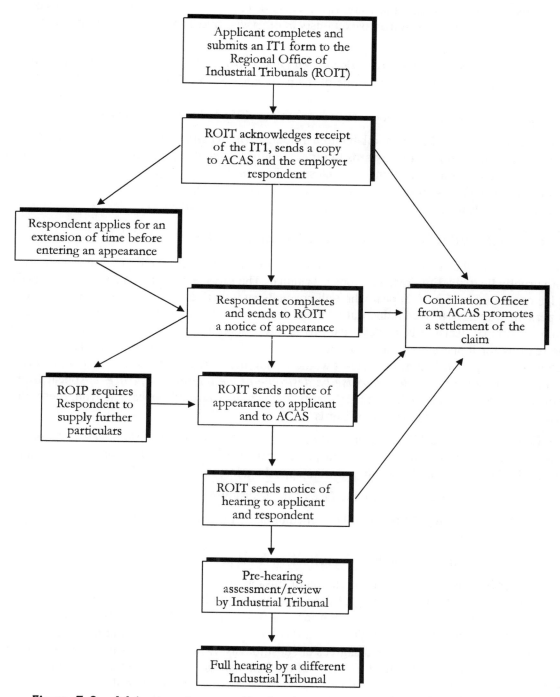

Figure 3.2 **Main steps in an application brought before an Industrial Tribunal**

As a general rule a Tribunal must not award costs or expenses against a party unless it considers that the party has acted frivolously, vexatiously or otherwise unreasonably in bringing or conducting the case.

> In *Port of London Authority v. Payne and Others (No. 2)* 1993 it was held that an order for costs is appropriate where one of the parties has been deliberately untruthful in the presentation of the case. Here the employer had been deliberately untruthful in giving its reasons for dismissal and was ordered to pay 40% of the complainant's costs.

The various remedies that are available to a Tribunal will depend upon the nature of the claim but they range from compensation awards to orders requiring a course of action such as reinstatement, declarations and recommendations. An Industrial Tribunal has no power to enforce its own remedies so that if a mandatory order such as reinstatement is not complied with, it can be reduced to a compensation award and if necessary enforced in the county court.

The Employment Appeal Tribunal (EAT)

An appeal from the Industrial Tribunal on a question of law or a mixed question of law and fact with usually lie to the Employment Appeal Tribunal. The President of the EAT will be a High Court judge or a Lord Justice of Appeal who will normally sit with two lay members drawn from a panel of persons who have proven industrial relations experience. The time limit for submitting an appeal from a Tribunal decision is 42 days and this involves submitting a notice of appeal together with the reasons for it and a copy of the Tribunal decision. Even without the full reasons the EAT can authorise an appeal if it considers that it would lead to the *"more expeditious or economic disposal of any proceedings or would otherwise be desirable in the interests of justice"*. Appeal from the decision of the EAT lies to the ordinary courts, namely the Court of Appeal and from there, in rare cases, an appeal lies to the House of Lords.

The Employment Appeal Tribunal in *East Berkshire Health Authority v. Matadeen* 1992 attempted to resolve the uncertainty in relation to the power of the EAT to overturn a decision of the Industrial Tribunal. The EAT held that it can allow an appeal against the Tribunal decision if:

- there is an error of law on the face of the decision; or
- there is a material finding of fact relied upon by the tribunal which is unsupported by the evidence; or
- there is a finding that the Tribunal's decision is perverse.

An error of law involves a misinterpretation or misapplication of the law. An unsupported finding of fact involves a misunderstanding of the evidence before the Tribunal. Perversity is reaching a decision which is not a permissible option for it is *"a conclusion which offends reason or is one to which no reasonable Industrial Tribunal could reach"*. The EAT cannot therefore simply overturn a Tribunal decision with which it disagrees or substitute its own views of fairness or reasonableness for that of the Industrial Tribunal. The role of the Tribunal as the final arbiter on questions of fact is best illustrated in relation to dealing with complaints of unfair dismissal. Unfair dismissal is covered in depth in Chapter 16.

Arbitration

Arbitration is a means of resolving a dispute without recourse to the courts. An arbitrator is a person to whom both sides of the dispute put their case. He will consider the evidence and make a decision by applying ordinary rules of law to the facts before him. The decision of an arbitrator can be enforced in the courts, if necessary.

The legal framework within which arbitration operates is contained in the Arbitration Act 1950. This deals with matters such as the effect of arbitration agreements, awards, costs and enforcement. The Act does not lay down procedures for the conduct of arbitration, however, as these will vary according to the nature of the dispute and the way in which the parties wish it to be handled. In this respect, as we shall see, arbitration provides a more flexible method of resolving a dispute than proceedings in the ordinary courts.

Arbitration under codes of practice

The Director General of Fair Trading has a duty to encourage trade associations to promote voluntary codes of practice. The aim of these codes is the improvement of standards of service in particular sectors of business; and the laying down of methods for handling complaints about goods or services. Many codes set up low cost independent arbitration schemes for dealing with consumer complaints against traders who are members of the trade association which adopted the code.

Many professional associations sponsor arbitration schemes as a substitute for litigation in relation to complaints against their members.

Arbitration in the County Court

With effect from January 1996 claims for £3000 or less in the County Court, if defended, will automatically be referred to arbitration under the small claims procedure. This is a significant increase in the small claims limit from £1000. The £1000 limit still applies however if the claim is for damages for personal injuries. This dramatic increase in the small claims limit will mean that many more consumer claims will automatically be referred to arbitration. One obvious field of potential conflict surrounds the sale of package holidays where there are often claims for damages of between £1000 and £3000. We shall see later that such contracts usually expressly provide for arbitration as the means of resolving disputes.

Under the small claims procedure the deterrent of being saddled with the opposing party's costs in the event of losing the case does not apply. The Court has only limited power to award costs, for example where the unreasonable conduct of one party causes expense to the other. This no costs rule makes legal representation in small claims arbitration uneconomic.

A County Court arbitration hearing usually takes place in private before an arbitrator without the formalities associated with a full trial. The arbitrator will usually be the County Court district judge but any other suitable person may be appointed if both parties agree. The procedure is designed to encourage people making small claims to handle their own cases without the assistance of a lawyer.

If the amount in dispute exceeds £3000, the matter can still be dealt with as an arbitration if both parties agree or if the court so orders on the application of one of the parties. It is possible to object to the use of arbitration, even for claims under £3000, in any of the following circumstances:

(a)   where the case involves a difficult question of law or an exceptionally complex question of fact;

(b)   where one of the parties is accused of fraud or deliberate dishonesty;

(c)   where the parties both agree that normal court proceedings shall apply;

(d)   where it would be unreasonable for the claim to be heard as an arbitration having regard to its subject matter or the interests of any other person likely to be affected, for example where the decision will, in practice, create a precedent which will be followed in a number of similar cases.

Where a dispute is dealt with by way of arbitration in the County Court, the hearing will usually be informal and strict rules of evidence will not apply. The arbitrator may adopt any method of proceeding which he considers to be convenient, so long as it affords a fair and equal opportunity to each party to present his case. The case could be dealt with by an exchange of documents for example rather than a hearing with the parties present in person.

Arbitration clauses in contracts

Many standard from contracts contain an arbitration clause. This is an agreement to submit any differences or disputes which may arise in relation to the contract to arbitration. An example of such a clause can be found in the standard form contract contained in Chapter 10. Condition 14 of the agreement gives the parties the power to choose arbitration as a means of resolving any dispute. Some standard form contracts contain conditions under which any dispute must be submitted to arbitration. This can be done by adopting the wording of an arbitration clause which was held to be valid in the case of *Scott v. Avery* 1856. Under such a clause the right of action in court only arises after an award has been made by an arbitrator.

Even where there is no arbitration clause in the contract, parties to a dispute can agree at any time to submit the dispute to arbitration. The agreement may be made after the dispute has arisen and any agreement to submit to arbitration operates as a binding contract.

An arbitration agreement comes into being where two or more persons agree that an existing or potential dispute between them shall be resolved in a legally binding way by one or more persons in a judicial manner. Under s. 32 of the Arbitration Act 1950 an arbitration agreement must be in writing. If an arbitrator is appointed under a verbal agreement he will usually invite the parties to enter into a written agreement, in order to bring the arbitration within the 1950 Act. The arbitration agreement may incorporate such matters as the method of appointment of the arbitrator and the procedural rules governing the conduct of the arbitration.

The unique features of arbitration

Where the parties have not laid out in advance any particular procedure, there is a large degree of flexibility in the way in which the arbitration can be concluded. With the agreement of the parties the arbitrator can adopt whatever procedure appears most appropriate. The case may be decided upon documentary evidence alone; or documents and written representations; or a site visit; or the examination of any goods which are at the centre of a dispute. Alternatively there could be a formal hearing of the case with expert witnesses and lawyers in attendance.

In addition to the flexibility of choosing an appropriate procedure, there is flexibility in relation to the location and time of any hearing. The arbitration can be heard at any place which the parties choose. This could, for example, be in a location near the site of the dispute, and take place at the weekend thereby avoiding the loss of working hours.

In a dispute involving matters of a technical nature, an appropriately qualified independent expert could be appointed as arbitrator. This may enable a swifter conclusion to be reached in the case.

Probably the single most important factor in the mind of a businessman who chooses to refer a dispute to arbitration is that the proceedings are totally private. Adverse publicity can therefore be avoided, and so can the public disclosure of confidential information or trade secrets. The advantage of privacy may be lost, however, if there is an appeal against the decision of the arbitrator.

Appeal against the decision of an arbitrator can be made on the grounds either that the proceedings were not conducted fairly, or that the decision contains an error of law. An arbitration award will only be set aside on grounds of unfairness if the arbitrator has failed to comply with the rules of natural justice. These are that he must be, and be seen to be, impartial and unbiased; and that each party to the dispute must be given a fair opportunity to present his own case and to answer the case put forward by his opponent.

One of the parties may suspect that the arbitrator has made an error of law in reaching his decision, but be unable to confirm that suspicion because the arbitrator has not given full reasons for his decision. In such a case that party can apply, under s.1 of the Arbitration Act 1979, to the High Court for an order requiring the arbitrator to give full reasons.

Arbitration is often a less expensive method of resolving business disputes than litigation in the ordinary courts. In some cases, however, where formal procedures are adopted, arbitration may actually be more expensive than litigation. One reason for this is that the cost of the actual hearing must be borne by the parties. This will include, for example, the arbitrator's fee, the cost of accommodation for the hearing, and of recording evidence. In most cases these costs are more than compensated for by the speed with which a case can be dealt with, the informality of procedures and the fact that the arbitrator's award is final and cannot, except in the limited circumstances discussed above, be the subject of an appeal.

One of the disadvantages of arbitration is that an arbitrator, having reached a decision and made an award, in unable to enforce that award. In the event that the award is not complied with, it can only be enforced by taking action in the courts. The agreement to submit a claim to arbitration is a binding contract and failure to comply with an arbitrator's award is a breach of contract which can be the subject of proceedings in the County Court or the High Court. A simple procedure for enforcement is provided for in s.26 of the 1950 Act. Under this the award may be enforced in the same way as a court order with the permission of the High Court. This involves an application to the High Court for the enforcement of the arbitration award. If the court is satisfied that the award is valid it will enter judgment in favour of the successful party. The award can then be enforced in the same way as any other judgment of the court.

Alternative dispute settlement

Alternative ways of resolving legal conflicts without recourse to the courts are becoming an increasingly important feature of dispute settlement. Various schemes, collectively referred to as ADR (alternative dispute resolution) have in recent years been floated. In 1995 the Lord Chief Justice issued a Practice Direction which was concerned with pursuing mechanisms for avoiding cost and delay in court proceedings. The Direction requires solicitors as part of a pre-trial check to identify whether ADR might, *"assist to resolve or narrow the issues in this case"*, and whether the parties have had the opportunity to consider the use of ADR.

In *Lord Woolf's Interim Report* (Woolf Report on Access to Justice 1995), a report which considers ways of improving access to civil justice, emphasis was placed on the value of ADR. One aspect of ADR is the use of *Ombudsmen* in the handling of disputes. The Ombudsman system was originally introduced within the public sector, but has since been extended to a number of industries in the private sector such as insurance, banking, building societies, pensions and estate agencies. Ombudsmen in these sectors can have complaints put to them, without the involvement of lawyers. The service is free. The Ombudsman's findings in relation to a complaint do not have to be acted on by the organisation involved, although they usually are, and in any case the complainants are still free to litigate if they choose to do so. The objective of the Ombudsman system is to provide for independent investigation of a complaint, and its satisfactory resolution on the basis of the Ombudsman's findings of fact.

Assignment To Sue or not to Sue

David Adams and Frank Bartlett are partners in a firm of accountants which carries on business in Dartley, a small market town in the North West. Their work is almost exclusively confined to preparing accounts and advising on tax matters for clients who operate small businesses in the local area. The business has a clientele of between seventy and eighty, providing a turnover of around £390,000. When you bear in mind that the firm has a staff of three employees, an accounting assistant and two secretaries, it is not difficult to appreciate that bad debts are to be avoided at all costs. Unfortunately the firm has had an unpaid bill of £2,340 on its books for the past eighteen months. The bill relates to work done in 1996 for a new client, Andrew Davies, a building merchant in Dartley. Despite three reminders from the firm and a solicitor's letter threatening legal action no payment has yet been received. This is despite the fact that Davies is expanding into bigger premises. Frank Bartlett has also heard on the grapevine that Davies is now using a rival firm of accountants.

Six months ago the accountancy firm purchased a laser printer from Bolton Office Supplies Ltd. for £454. The printer developed a serious fault with it's memory which has rendered it unreliable. The firm sought to reject the machine when the fault was discovered, however the supplier refused to take it back, and offered instead to deliver the printer to the manufacturer for repair under the terms of the manufacturer's guarantee. David Adams wrote to the supplier and rejected this suggestion pointing out that Bolton Office Supplies Ltd. were legally responsible for the defects in the printer. He again demanded a full refund of the purchase price and requested the supplier to take the machine back. The letter was posted three weeks ago and no response has been made by the supplier.

Yesterday Frank Bartlett, the senior partner, received a letter from a firm of solicitors requesting a statutory statement of the reason or reasons for dismissing Sarah Tindley an ex-employee. Sarah had worked as a secretary for the firm for the past eleven years but three weeks ago was summarily dismissed with wages paid in lieu of the three months notice that she was entitled to. The reason for dismissal was that she admitted that she had "borrowed" money from the firm's petty cash to purchase a pair of shoes which were on sale.

Task

In the role of James Morris, a trainee accountant at the firm you are required to prepare an informal report in which you indicate:

1. Whether legal proceedings to recover the debt are worthwhile and the legal process involved in taking county court action for debt recovery.

2. Whether the firm is within its contractual rights to repudiate the contract for the typewriter and if legal proceedings are taken how they differ from the debt action.

3. If Sarah decides to pursue a claim for unfair dismissal indicate the steps which the firm would need to take should they decide to defend the claim.

Legal Terms found in Chapter 4

Articles of Association	• rules concerned with the internal administration of a company
Capital	• funds raised to finance an organisation
Corporation	• an organisation treated as an artificial legal person
Debentures	• written statement acknowledging a company's indebtedness and usually supported by some security
Memorandum of Association	• constitutional document of a company establishing its name, objectives and capital structure
Partnership	• an unicorporated business association often referred to as a 'firm'
Private company	• registered company prohibited from selling its shares to the public
Promoter	• someone involved in setting up a company
Prospectus	• document providing information to the public about a company which is offering its shares
Public company	• registered company able to sell its securities publicly
Quoted company	• company whose securities are traded on the Stock Exchange
Registered company	• a corporate body formed under the registration procedures of the Companies Act 1985
Securities	• investments in a company
Shares	• a unit of company capital which a member can own
Table A	• set of model articles set out in company legislation which company's can adopt
Ultra vires	• legal doctrine expressing the proposition that corporate bodies cannot act outside their powers

Chapter 4

Establishing Business Organisations

Central to the study of business law is examination of the business organisations through which business activity is conducted. We need first to be clear about the meaning of the expression *business organisations*. The problem this raises is that business is an economic rather than a legal concept. Sometimes it becomes necessary to define the meaning of business for legal purposes, but then only in specific situations limited to the context of a particular problem. For instance tax liability may depend upon deciding whether a person who has bought and sold a certain number of cars during the year is trading, and is thus in business as a car dealer. But the answer to such a question would explain little about the nature and quality of businesses in general, even though it would provide a solution to the case in question.

In order then to appreciate fully the law applying to business organisations it is helpful to draw briefly from economics, to summarise what an economist sees as the essential features of a business organisation. Bear in mind that the decision to form a business is a commercial rather than a legal one: those who set up businesses will treat the legal form the business is to take as a secondary rather than a primary consideration. First you decide your business aims and objectives. Then you decide on the form of business appropriate to achieve them. Looking at the general economic background to business organisations is also useful because it helps to explain why substantial parts of business law have evolved, either as an aid to the business community in achieving commercial aims, or as a means of regulating business activities and curbing undesirable commercial practices.

Common Characteristics of Business Organisations

Most business organisations will display the following characteristics.

(a) *They will establish their business aims*. In general organisations are set up for a specific purpose; selling particular products, providing a service, and so on. Successful businesses are those which evolve as the commercial environment changes and new commercial opportunities present themselves;

(b) *The identity of the organisation will be distinct*. It will, for example, be possible to establish who owns the organisation, and who it employs;

(c) *There will be some form of leadership in the organisation.* Leadership will be provided in the form of a system of management within it;

(d) *There will be accountability within the organisation.* The organisation itself will possess accountability. It will be accountable to those who own it, those whom it employs, and those with whom it trades. Similarly those people it employs are legally accountable to the organisation to fulfil their obligations towards it. This idea of legal accountability is fundamental to the principles and practice of English business law.

Business is a broad and loosely defined term. Perhaps it is most generally understood to mean a commercial enterprise which aims to make as much money as possible for its owners, a profit maximiser. Yet there are many other kinds of business. For instance some organisations have scientific, educational, or social goals, and are not primarily concerned with the profit motive in the same way as commercial businesses; examples include charitable organisations such as Oxfam and the National Trust, educational bodies like the GCSE and A level examining boards and BTEC, and a broad spectrum of other bodies such as local chambers of trade, and sports and social clubs. Local authorities are not commercial organisations either, although as incidental activities they may operate profit making ventures such as sports and leisure centres. The expression *business* is however a wide one, and used in some senses would certainly apply to the organisations just mentioned even though they are non-commercial. Sometimes business is used in a general sense to describe the way in which an organisation is run, a *business-like operation*, meaning it is run efficiently. It is also used to characterise the type of organisational activity being carried out, thus someone may loosely describe Greenpeace as being *in the environment business*. For our purposes we will be using business in its commercial sense, looking at organisations which aim to make a profit for their owners, and which are owned privately, rather than by the state.

The Classification of Business Organisations

It is easy to create elaborate charts and diagrams which classify business organisations according to different criteria, but as a starting point a simple diagram showing how these organisations relate to each other is useful. The figure on the next page does so. It distinguishes organisations according to ownership and then breaks down private sector business organisations which form the subject matter of this chapter, into their specific legal categories.

Two features of the figure require special attention. These are the distinctions between:

- corporate and unincorporated bodies; and
- private and public sector organisations.

It is outside the scope of a law textbook to examine the differences between public and private sector organisations in any detail, however it is important to be clear as to the significance of the distinction. Essentially what distinguishes a public sector from a private sector organisation is who owns, and therefore controls it. In the case of the public sector this will be the state; in the private sector it will be private individuals and organisations.

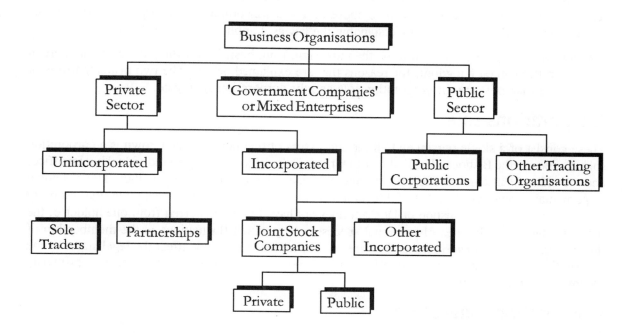

Figure 4.1   General classification of business organisations

Most of the work carried out by organisations in the public sector is not principally concerned with commercial trading, but rather with the provision of public services such as health, education and housing, and the management of a wide range of social welfare benefits such as pensions. The state does however engage in some commercial trading. The Post Office is a state trading organisation; so too is Her Majesty's Stationery Office (HMSO). Much of the law contained in this book is as applicable to these state organisations as to those trading in the private sector.

A further distinguishing feature is the method used to create a public sector organisation. Usually they are created by a specific Act of Parliament, thus local authorities in England and Wales are established under the Local Government Act 1972. The use of an Act of Parliament to create a private sector organisation, whilst not unknown, is most unusual nowadays.

Corporate and Unincorporated Bodies

Under English law all business enterprises can be classified into one of two basic legal forms. They are either *corporate* or *unincorporated* bodies. An unincorporated body is either an individual or (more usually) a group of individuals, who have joined together to pursue a common business purpose. The body and the individuals who compose it are not separate from each other under the law, even though they may trade under a business name, rather than using their own names, thereby creating the appearance that the business is a separate entity. A corporate body, or *corporation*, is also made up of a group of individuals who have joined together for a common purpose, but through the process of legal incorporation they have created an artificial legal person which has a separate legal identity from the members who compose it. The distinction between corporate and non-corporate bodies is fundamental to understanding the law as it applies to organisations.

The corporation has proved itself to be the most significant business for the pursuit of commercial activity in the United Kingdom, for reasons that are explained below. The two primary forms of corporation that exist are the corporation sole and the corporation aggregate.

Corporations sole

These consist of a single person and all the successors of that person. The Crown is a corporation sole. So too are the Bishops. The Bishop of Durham is therefore not only an individual but an office, and the office itself continues to exist despite one bishop being replaced by another. This is known as perpetual succession. It is a useful legal device because it can mean, for example, that property held by the office of the Bishop of Durham does not have to be transferred from one holder of the office to the next. The idea of perpetual succession, by which fluctuations in the membership of the corporation (the *corporators* as they are sometimes known) do not affect the legal status of the corporation is a characteristic of all corporate bodies. Corporations sole are not primarily commercial organisations.

Corporations aggregate

These are by far the most numerous type of corporation, and consist of a number of people who combine to form or constitute the corporation, such as the elected members of a county or district council or the shareholders of a limited company.

Corporations may be created in the following ways:

(a) *by Royal Charter*. Charter, or common law corporations, are rarely created today, although many of the early trading organisations such as the Hudson's Bay Company were created in this way. The charter is granted by the Monarch acting under the royal prerogative upon the advice of the Privy Council. Examples of twentieth century charter corporations include the BBC and the older universities, and professional bodies such as the Institute of Housing;

(b) *by a particular statute*. Here an Act of Parliament creates and grants powers to the corporation. Public corporations such as the Independent Broadcasting Authority have been created in this way, and outside London, the corporate status and powers of all local authorities in England and Wales are contained in the Local Government Act 1972;

(c) *by registration under the Companies Act 1985*. The 1985 Act recognises two basic forms of registered company, public limited companies and private limited companies. In so doing it recognises an important commercial distinction which we shall be exploring later.

The liability of the members of a registered company may be limited either by shares or guarantee, or in rare cases be unlimited. This is provided for by s.1(2) of the Companies Act 1985 which states that a company may be:

(i) limited by *shares,* where the liability of the company members, the shareholders, is limited to any amount as yet unpaid on their shares; or

(ii) limited by *guarantee,* where the members' liability is limited to an amount they have guaranteed to contribute in the event of the company being brought to an end, a process known technically as winding up; or

(iii) *unlimited,* where the members are fully liable for the debts of the company, in the event of it being wound up.

Unlimited companies can only operate as private companies. They are used primarily as service and investment companies. Although the number of public limited companies is relatively small (they are numbered in thousands, whilst private companies are numbered in hundreds of thousands), their commercial importance places them at the heart of the private sector economy. They include the major banks, multinational organisations such as ICI, British Airways and Marks and Spencer, and a range of other household names. Commonly, public companies began life as private companies, becoming sufficiently successful commercially to warrant *going public,* and thus able to offer their shares on the open market.

The types of companies registerable under the Companies Act 1985 are contained in the following figure.

Public Limited Companies	Private Companies
limited by shares	limited by shares
limited by guarantee (with a share capital)	limited by guarantee
	unlimited

Figure 4.2 Types of Registered Companies registerable under the Companies Act 1985

Certain other statutes allow for incorporation by registration, for example working mens' clubs and organisations such as workers' co-operatives, can incorporate by registration under the Industrial and Provident Society Acts 1965-1975. The latter group, which have grown in number over recent years can also be registered as companies limited by guarantee, or alternatively may operate as partnerships.

Statutory registration was first introduced under the Companies Act 1844, to provide a method of which was less expensive and cumbersome than obtaining a charter or sponsoring legislation through Parliament. The system of statutory registration proved immediately popular and helped to provide the capital which the growth of business activity at that time urgently needed. Capital was provided by investors attracted not only by the investment prospects offered by newly formed registered companies but also by the financial protection available through limited liability. The registered company remains just as popular with investors today, and has been further stimulated by the privatisation programme pursued by the Thatcher and Major governments, under which many previously state owned businesses have been sold off to the public, such as Jaguar Cars, British Telecom, British Airways, and the electricity and gas undertakings and parts of British Rail.

Later we will shall look in greater detail at the legal implications of trading as a corporate body, but first we shall consider those business organisations which function as unincorporated bodies, and examine their legal status. The legal status of a business is a matter of considerable importance to its members, not least because it is primarily responsible for describing what their rights and responsibilities are, and hence their relationship to the organisation and towards each other.

The two types of unincorporated businesses we need to consider are the sole trader and the partnership.

Sole Traders

The term *sole trader* is an expression used to describe an individual who is self employed operating a business alone and who has sole responsibility for its management. In practice, of course, sole traders rarely work entirely alone and will usually employ staff to assist them in the operation of the business. There are no specific legal formalities relating to the creation of such businesses. However operating as a sole trader will necessarily involve the owner in buying and selling, employing staff and acquiring business premises. As an employer, a sole trader is subject to the law relating to employment contained in the common law, (that is law defined by the courts) and numerous statutes, (law determined by Parliament), the most important of which is the Employment Rights Act 1996. In addition, as a supplier of goods or services, a sole trader must comply with the law relating to consumer protection, for example the Sale of Goods Act 1979, the Trade Descriptions Act 1968 and the Supply of Goods and Services Act 1982. Some types of business enterprise must also acquire a licence to permit them to operate. For instance a publican requires a licence to sell intoxicating drinks and a turf accountant a betting and gaming licence.

A sole trader's business will normally be financed by the owner himself, which means that the opportunities for raising business capital are necessarily restricted. Whilst the sole owner is entitled to all the profits of the business, he has unlimited liability in relation to its losses and so must bear them personally. The sole trader form of business is therefore most suitable for an individual who wishes to retain absolute control of the sort of business enterprise which requires only a modest amount of financial investment. Obvious examples include retail shops and service trades such as plumbing and hairdressing. Collectively, sole traders provide a valuable service to the community by making a wide range of goods and services available in a personal way, meeting needs which might otherwise be unfulfilled.

The responsibility for decision making in such a business rests with the owner, and there is no individual or group to whom he is made directly accountable. This is very attractive to those who wish to *be their own boss*. Of course there are groups who will be affected by the owner's actions such as the customers or clients, the creditors to whom the business owes money, and especially the employees of the business. Such groups have a valid interest in the decisions made by the sole trader and may ultimately seek to hold him accountable for his actions. An employee may complain that employment rights have been infringed, or a customer that consumer rights have been abused. Accountability is perhaps at its most extreme level in the event of the sole trader becoming insolvent, that is being unable to meet the debts of the business.

Over recent years there has been a substantial increase in the number of one-man businesses being established and this trend has been encouraged by the government by giving grants and offering tax advantages to small businesses. Changes in working practices have resulted in large numbers of skilled and unskilled workers losing their jobs, many receiving lump sum payments as compensation. There is evidence that increasing numbers of such individuals have been willing to use their redundancy payments as initial capital to set up a business in which they will be their own employer.

Partnerships

The other major form of unincorporated business organisation is the partnership. Partnerships are commonly referred to as firms and the Partnership Act 1890 states under s.4 that: *"Persons who have entered into a partnership with one another for the purposes of this Act are called collectively `a firm', and the name under which their business is carried on is called the firm-name"*. There are no detailed legal formalities required when individuals agree to operate a business together and thus form a partnership, and the advantages to a business enterprise of forming a partnership are somewhat similar to those enjoyed by the sole trader. The partners are capable of managing their own firm as they see fit, of sharing the profits and being able to deal directly with their customers or clients.

The partnership provides the compromise of allowing an extension of skill and expertise and the possible influx of additional capital by the introduction of extra partners. This extra potential for capital allows many partnerships to grow to become substantial business enterprises.

Although it has always tended to be overshadowed by the limited company, the partnership remains a significant form of business organisation in the United Kingdom, and is the choice of many people either setting up a new business or modifying an existing one. There are in fact over two million businesses operated either as partnerships or under sole trader arrangements, evidence of their popularity as a business form.

An agreement between two or more persons to form a partnership will constitute a contract but there is no legal requirement as to its specific form. It may be oral, in writing, contained in a deed, or even implied by the law from the surrounding circumstances. The Partnership Act 1890, which contains most of the legal rules relating to partnerships, defines a partnership under s.1 simply as the *"relation which subsists between persons carrying on business in common with a view of profit"*. It follows from this definition that it is possible for a business to be run as a joint venture without the participants ever being aware that their business is in law a partnership. Whilst this may be of no consequence to them for as long as they are able to work together in harmony, in the event of a dispute it is important to them to ascertain whether their relationship constitutes a partnership. If it does the provisions of the 1890 Act will apply, and as we shall see the effect of this statute on the partnership business in terms of the rights and obligations that it lays down is significant.

The main risk in operating a business as a firm is that if the business should get into financial difficulties, the liability of the partners is not limited in any way. The individual members are liable to the extent of their personal wealth to pay off partnership debts, which may result in them losing most of their personal possessions.

Partnership formalities

We have seen that a partnership agreement can be created in many ways. The 1890 Act lays down no formalities. It is of course commercially desirable, and certainly common practice, for partners to execute a deed of partnership, in which they provide for matters such as the capital contribution required from each member of the firm, and how profits and losses are to be divided. If the partners do not agree such details then the rights and duties laid down under the Act will apply to the partnership.

By s.716 Companies Act 1985, a partnership cannot validly consist of more than twenty members. An exception is made however for certain professions, such as accountants and solicitors, who are prevented by statute from practising as limited companies. No restriction is placed upon the size of such firms. Some of the largest firms of lawyers and accountants have in excess of a hundred partners.

Partners may choose any name they please for their firm provided it is not similar to an existing name and therefore not likely to mislead others. However the last name must not be the word *limited* or any abbreviation of it, for this would indicate that the organisation is a company having limited liability. The words *and Co* at the end of the partnership name refers to the fact that there are partners in the firm whose names do not appear in the firm name. When a firm carries on business using a trading name which does not consist of the surnames of all the partners the Business Names Act 1985 requires that their names must appear on their business stationery, and their true names and addresses must be prominently displayed at their business premises in a place to which the public have access. Non-compliance with these provisions is a criminal offence.

The definition of partnership

Earlier we saw that the definition of a partnership under s.1 requires there to be:

- a business;
- carried on in common by its members;
- with a view to making a profit.

Under the Act *"business"* includes every trade, occupation or profession. Although business is a broad term it does imply the carrying on of some form of commercial activity. This may be for a single purpose.

> In *Spicer (Keith) Ltd. v. Mansell* 1970 the Court of Appeal held that two persons who were working together for the purpose of forming a limited company, and had opened a bank account and ordered goods in this connection were not in partnership prior to the incorporation of the company (which in fact was never formed). The reason was that at that time they were preparing for business, rather than operating an existing one.

Further examples of how the courts have approached the question of determining whether a business exists are provided by the following two cases. They in fact involve individuals rather than firms, but they provide a useful illustration of the thin line that often exists between a mere hobby and a business.

In *Eiman v. London Borough of Waltham Forest* 1982 the issue was whether the defendant had been rightly convicted in the Crown Court of the offence of making a demand for unsolicited goods *"in the course of a trade or business"*, contrary to the Unsolicited Goods and Services Act 1971. As a full time employee of the local authority the accused had, as a hobby, composed and published a book of verse. He had then sent out copies of the book to local libraries and made a demand for payment. The High Court held that the Crown Court was entitled to convict the defendant as what had started as a hobby, had become a *"business"* as defined by the Act and therefore the Unsolicited Goods and Services Act did apply. The court found it possible to reach such a conclusion despite the fact that this was an isolated incident without any intention to make a profit.

In *Blakemore v. Bellamy* 1983 the question was whether the accused's spare time activity of buying and selling motor cars through advertisements, contravened the Fair Trading Act 1973, and the Business Advertisements (Disclosure) Order 1977. This is because in the course of a business it is an offence to *"advertise goods for sale"* without making it clear that the goods were sold in the course of a business. Offences under the Trade Descriptions Act, 1968 were also alleged which involved applying false trade descriptions to two of the vehicles in the course of a business. Despite the number of transactions involved, eight in all, the High Court agreed with the magistrates' finding that the defendant's activity was merely a hobby rather than a business. Accordingly the statutory provisions had not been infringed, for the sales were merely private bargains. This was despite the fact that the defendant's objective in making the sales was to achieve gain or reward and as a seller he had clearly demonstrated skill and expertise in the business of buying and selling cars.

The business must be a joint venture, which implies mutual rights and obligations existing between the members of it. There may still be a joint venture even though one (or more) of its members is a *sleeping partner* who does not take an active part in the management of the business but simply contributes capital.

There must be a profit motive underlying the business. It will be a question of fact whether the partners aim to make a profit.

Help in determining when a business may be treated as a partnership is provided by s.2. It states that where a person receives a share in the profits of a business, this will be *prima facie* evidence that he is a partner, although the presumption can be shifted by other conflicting evidence. The section goes on to state a list of situations which do not, of themselves, make a person a partner, namely where a person:

    (i)   receives a debt or other liquidated amount out of the profits of a business, whether or not by instalments;

    (ii)   being a servant or agent is paid out of a share of the profits of the business;

    (iii) being the widow or child of a deceased partner receives an annuity (an annual set payment) out of a portion of the profits of the business in which the deceased was a partner;

(iv) lends money to a person engaged or about to engage in business, on a written contract signed by, or on behalf of the parties to it that the lender shall be repaid either at a rate of interest varying with the profits, or as a share of the profits;

(v)   receives by way of annuity or otherwise a portion of the profits of a business in consideration of the sale by that person of the goodwill of the business.

In *Pratt v. Strick* 1932 a situation of the kind described in (v) above occurred. A doctor sold his medical practice together with its goodwill, on terms that for the following three months he would remain living at the practice, introducing patients, and sharing profits and losses equally with the purchaser. It was held that the practice was the purchaser's as soon as he bought it.

Two further situations are specified by s.2 which it indicates do not automatically give rise to a partnership. Firstly co-ownership of land, even where profits are shared from the use of the land. Secondly the sharing of gross returns even if the people sharing the returns have a common right or interest in the property which is yielding the income. This draws a distinction between returns and profit. A return is the revenue obtained by some business activity, such as the receipts obtained from the sale of a book over a fixed period, whilst the profit is the sum left after deducting costs from revenue. In the example these would include printing and transport costs.

Registered Companies

In our earlier examination of corporations we saw that the registered company limited by shares is a corporate body, an artificial person recognised by the law, which has an identity separate and distinct from the members which compose it. The members of such an organisation are referred to as its shareholders. The limited company is the most common type of business enterprise operated as a corporation.

Thousands of registered limited companies function in the UK between them employing the majority of the nation's workforce and generating about two thirds of the income made by the private sector. Companies can be formed which have only one member. They can also develop into massive multi-national UK registered enterprises which have thousands of shareholders. Such is the diversity of these organisations that it is difficult to generalise on their structure and behaviour but most have been formed with the expectation of future expansion financed by the raising of capital through the issue of shares. As separate legal entities they also give the owners the protection of limited liability and it is this feature more than any other that has contributed to their popularity. Another appealing feature is that ownership can be divorced from management, thus an investor can stake capital in a company without having to be involved in the actual running of it, whilst maintaining control over the managers by means of their accountability in the general meeting.

Limited liability means that where a company is unable to pay its debts its shareholders' legal liability to contribute to the payment of debts is limited to the amount, if any, unpaid on their shares. Thus, if an individual purchases twenty £1 shares in a company and pays 25p on each share (these are called partly paid shares) he is only liable to contribute the amount of the share value remaining unpaid, in this case 20 x 75p, a total of £15.

It is of course only the shareholders whose liability is limited. The company itself is fully liable for its debts, and may be brought to an end through the process of winding-up if it cannot meet them.

Companies can expand and diversify by raising additional capital when it is needed, through the issue of more shares, and hence large scale commercial organisations have evolved with thousands of shareholders holding between them millions of shares. The growth of this form of business enterprise and the recognition of the company as a separate legal entity has however posed many problems and led to many abuses. The law has recognised these difficulties. Various Companies Acts, now consolidated in the Companies Act 1985, have sought to regulate corporate behaviour, bearing in mind not only the interests of the shareholders themselves but also the interests of outsiders who trade with them.

The concept of corporate personality

As an artificial legal person, the registered company has some although not all the powers and responsibilities of a natural person. It is capable of owning property, entering into contracts such as trading contracts and contracts of employment, and of suing or being sued in its own name. But its artificial nature imposes some obvious limitations upon its legal capacity. It cannot generally be held liable for criminal acts, since most crimes involve proving a mental element such as intention or recklessness and a corporation has as such no mind. Nevertheless sometimes the collective intention of the board of directors can be regarded as expressing the will of the corporation. Lord Denning has spoken of the company as having a human body, the employees being the hands that carry out its work while *"others are directors and managers who represent the directing mind and will of the company and control what it does"*. The development of this line of reasoning has enabled companies to be convicted of manslaughter. The issue of corporate criminal liability is explored in Chapter 1.

Since the membership of a company is distinct from the corporate body this means that the company shareholders are separate from their company which has a legal personality of its own. Changes in its membership, including the death or bankruptcy of members, will have no effect upon the company, which may have an almost perpetual life span if there remain investors willing to become or to remain members of it.

> The legal separation of a company from its members was confirmed in the leading case of *Salomon v. Salomon & Co*. 1897. Salomon owned a boot and shoe business. His sons worked in the business and they were anxious to have a stake in it so Salomon formed a registered company with himself as managing director, in which his wife, daughter and each son held a share. The company's nominal capital was £40,000 consisting of 40,000 £1 shares.
>
> The company resolved to purchase the business at a price of £39,000. Salomon had arrived at this figure himself. It was an honest but optimistic valuation of its real worth. The company paid him by allotting him 20,000 £1 shares treated as fully paid, £10,000 worth of debentures (a secured loan repayable before unsecured loans) and the balance in cash. Within a year of trading the company went into insolvent liquidation owing £8,000 to ordinary creditors and having only £6,000 worth of assets. The plaintiff, Mr. Salomon, claimed that as a debenture holder with £10,000 worth of debentures he was a secured creditor and entitled to repayment before the ordinary unsecured creditors.

The unsecured creditors did not agree. The House of Lords held that despite the fact that following the company's formation, Salomon had continued to run the business in the same manner and with the same control as he had done when it was unincorporated, the company formed was a separate person from Salomon himself. When the company was liquidated therefore, and in the absence of any fraud on the creditors and shareholders, Salomon, like any other debenture holder, was a secured creditor and entitled to repayment before ordinary creditors. The court thus upheld the principle that a company has a separate legal existence from its membership even where one individual holds the majority of shares and effectively runs the company as his own. In his leading judgment Lord Macnaghten stated, *"The company is at law a different person altogether from the subscribers to the memorandum; and, though it may be that after incorporation the business is precisely the same as it was before, and the same persons are managers, and the same hands receive the profits, the company is not in law the agent of the subscribers or trustee for them. Nor are the subscribers as members liable, in any shape or form, except to the extent and in the manner provided by the Act."*

Many consequences flow from this basic proposition of company law. For example the company's bank account is quite separate and independent from the account of the majority shareholder.

> In *Underwood Ltd. v. Bank of Liverpool & Martins Ltd.* 1924 it was held that a managing director who held all except one of the shares in his company was acting unlawfully in paying company cheques into his own account, and drawing cheques on the company's account for his own personal benefit.

The application of the Salomon principle makes it possible for a shareholder/director to be convicted on a charge of theft from his own company: *Re: Attorney General's Reference (no. 2 of 1982)* 1984.

A company is also the owner of its own property in which its members have no legal interest, although clearly they have a financial interest.

> In *Macaura v. Northern Assurance Co. Ltd.* 1925 it was held that a majority shareholder has no insurable interest in the company's property. A fire insurance policy over the company's timber estate was therefore invalid as it had been issued in the plaintiff shareholder's name and not the company's name.

Lifting the corporate veil

Both the courts and Parliament have accepted that in some situations it is right and proper to prevent the members from escaping liability by hiding behind the company. The result has been the creation of a number of exceptions to the principle of limited liability. These exceptions seem to be based broadly upon public policy considerations, and many of them are associated with fraudulent practices. If for instance a company is wound up and the court is satisfied that the directors have carried on the business with an intention to defraud the creditors, they may be made personally liable for company's debts.

The common law position

And so, in special cases, the courts are prepared to disregard the separate legal personality of a company because it was formed or used to facilitate the evasion of legal obligations. This is sometimes referred to as lifting the veil of incorporation, meaning that the court is able to look behind the corporate, formal identity of the organisation to the shareholders which make it up. It is a very significant step, since it is effectively denying the protection which the members have sought to obtain by incorporation.

> In *Gilford Motor Co. Ltd. v. Horne* 1933 the defendant had been employed by the plaintiff motor company and had entered into a valid agreement not to solicit the plaintiff's customers or to compete with it for a certain time after leaving the company's employment. Shortly after leaving the employment of the motor company, the defendant formed a new company to carry on a similar business to that of his former employers and sent out circulars to the customers he had previously dealt with whilst working for the old business. In an action to enforce the restraint clause against the new company the court held that as the defendant in fact controlled the new company, its formation was a mere *"cloak or sham"* to enable him to break the restraint clause. Accordingly an injunction was granted against the defendant and against the company he had formed, to enforce the restraint clause.

> Similarly in *Jones v. Lipman* 1962 the defendant agreed to sell land to the plaintiff and then decided not to complete the contract. To avoid the possibility of an order to specific performance to enforce the sale the defendant purchased a majority shareholding in an existing company to which he then sold the land. The plaintiff applied to the court for an order against the defendant and the company to enforce the sale. It was held that the formation of the company was a mere sham to avoid a contract of sale, and specific performance was ordered against the vendor and the company.

The courts are sometimes prepared to lift the veil in order to discover the relationship within groups of companies. It is a common commercial practice for one company to acquire shares in another, often holding sufficient shares to give it total control over the other. In these circumstances the controlling company is referred to as a *holding* company, and the other company its *subsidiary*. In appropriate cases a holding company can be regarded as an agent of its subsidiary, although it is more usual to find the subsidiary acting as an agent for the holding company.

> In *Firestone Tyre & Rubber Co. Ltd. v. Llewellin (Inspector of Taxes)* 1957 the appellant company was a subsidiary of an American company which made and sold branded tyres and had a world-wide organisation. The British subsidiary manufactured and sold tyres in Europe. The House of Lords held that the appellant company was in fact not trading on its own behalf but as agent of the parent company and the parent company was consequently liable to pay United Kingdom income tax.

> In *DHN Food Distributors Ltd. v. Tower Hamlets LBC.* 1976 an arrangement under which two subsidiaries of the holding company were wholly owned by it and had no separate business operations from it, was held by the Court of Appeal to constitute a single corporate body rather than three separate ones. It is difficult to see how this case can be reconciled with the basic principle in *Salomon*.

In *Woolfson v. Strathclyde Regional Council* 1978 the House of Lords, on similar facts came to the opposite conclusion, although it was not prepared to overrule the *DHN* decision.

In *Re: Bugle Press Ltd.* 1961 the company consisted of three shareholders. Two of them, who together had controlling interest, wanted to buy the shares of the third, but he was not willing to sell so the two of them formed a new company which then made a take-over bid for the shares of the first company. Not surprisingly the two shareholders who had formed the new company accepted the bid. The third did not. However since he only held 1/10 of the total shareholding, under what is now s.428 Companies Act 1985, the new company was able to compulsorily acquire the shares. The Court of Appeal however held that this represented an abuse of the section. The minority shareholder was in effect being evicted from the company. The veil of the new company was lifted and, in the words of Harman LJ: this revealed a *"hollow sham"*, for it was *"nothing but a little hut built round"* the majority shareholders.

In some cases the courts have disregarded the separate legal personality of a company and have in the public interest investigated the personal qualities of the shareholders. It is in the public interest that an enemy alien is unable to sue in British courts.

In *Daimler Co. Ltd. v. Continental Tyre and Rubber Co. (Gt. Britain) Ltd.* 1916 the tyre company, which was registered in England, and had its registered office there, sued Daimler for debts incurred before the war with Germany had been declared. Daimler claimed that as all the members of the tyre company except one were German nationals and the directors were German nationals resident in Germany the claim should be struck out because to pay the debt would be to trade with the enemy. The House of Lords held that although the nationality of a company is normally decided by where it is incorporated, in some cases the court has power to consider who was in control of the company's business and assets in order that it might determine its status. Here, those in control of the company were enemy aliens and the action was struck out.

The statutory position

In addition to this common law strategy there are a number of provisions contained in the Companies Act 1985 which have the effect of lifting the veil. They include the following:

(a) a fall in the membership of a public company to below 2, under s.24. In these circumstances if the condition continues for more than six months, the sole shareholder becomes personally liable for the company's debts incurred after that time. Note that to be a member of a company it is only necessary to hold a single share.

(b) Under s.349(4) if an officer of a company or any person on its behalf:

(i) uses the company seal and the company name is not engraved on it;

(ii) issues or authorises the issue of a business letter or signs a negotiable instrument and the company name is not mentioned;

(iii)   issues or authorises the issue of any invoice, receipt or letter of credit of the company and again the company name is not mentioned;

that person shall be personally liable for debts incurred unless they are paid by the company.

In *Penrose v. Martyr* 1858 a bill of exchange was drawn up with the word 'limited' omitted after the company's name and the company secretary who had signed the bill on the company's behalf was held to be personally liable for it.

In *Hendon v. Adelman* 1973 directors of a company whose registered name was L & R Agencies Ltd. signed a cheque on behalf of the company omitting the ampersand between 'L' and 'R'. The bank failed to honour the cheque and the directors were held personally liable on it.

(c)   Under powers granted to the Department of Trade and Industry to investigate the affairs of any company within the same group as one primarily under investigation by a DTI Inspector.S442(1) provides that where there appears to be good reason to do so, the Department may appoint inspectors to investigate and report on the membership of any company in order to determine the true identity of the persons financially interested in its success or failure, or able to control or materially influence its policy.

(d)   Under sections 213 and 214 Insolvency Act 1986. These important provisions are invoked in the course of the winding up of a company. In cases where sections 213 and 214 apply they have the effect of lifting the corporate veil, exposing those who have been engaged in the running of the company to personal liability, and they therefore represent a significant inroad to the principle of limited liability and the separation of the company from its members. Indeed s.214 has been described as one of the most important modifications to the principle of limited liability this century. S.213 deals with cases of fraudulent trading, and s.214 with cases of wrongful trading and both are considered in more depth in the discussion of winding up procedures in Chapter 7.

Classification of Companies

S1 Companies Act 1985 provides that a registered company limited by shares may be either a *public* or a *private* one. The most significant distinction between them is that a public limited company is permitted to advertise publicly to invite investors to take shares in it. A private company cannot advertise its shares in this way. Once purchased, shares in a public company can then be freely disposed of by the shareholder to anyone else who is willing to buy them. By contrast private companies commonly issue shares on terms that if the member wishes to dispose of them they must first be offered to the existing members. Where such rights are available to members they are known as *pre-emption* rights.

Before 1980 all companies were treated as being public ones, unless the company's articles of association contained specific provisions which enabled it to acquire private company status. Legislation passed in 1980, and now contained in the Companies Act 1985, completely reversed this situation, making private companies the residual class. Thus all companies are now treated as though they are private ones, unless certain requirements have been met which allow the company to be registered as a public limited company. This change was introduced to make it easier to define public companies for the purpose of complying with EC company law directives applicable to public companies.

Registration as a public limited company

This can be achieved by satisfying the following requirements:

- (i)   stating both in the company name, and in its memorandum that it is a public company. Thus its name must end in the words *"public limited company"* or the more convenient form *"plc."* The name of a private company will end with the word *"limited"* or *"Ltd."*;

- (ii) registering a memorandum of association which is in the form contained in Table F of the Companies (Tables A to F) Regulations 1985;

- (iii) meeting the requirement of s.11 of the 1985 Act, which states that the company must have an authorised share capital figure of at least £50,000. The memorandum of association always contains a capital clause stating the amount of capital a company can raise by issuing shares, and it is in this clause that the authorised share capital amount appears. At least one quarter of this amount must be paid up before the company can commence trading, or exercise its borrowing powers, and the company must have allotted shares up to the authorised minimum (ss.101 and 107). Consequently a plc. must have at least £12,500 paid up share capital before it starts trading, and be able to call for an additional £37,500 from its members.

An explanation of the terms regarding company capital may be helpful.

The *nominal share capital* is the amount that the company is legally authorised to raise by the issue of shares, the *paid-up share* capital is the amount the company has received from the shares it has issued, and the *uncalled capital* is the amount remaining unpaid by shareholders for the shares they hold; e.g. a company may issue £1 shares but require those to whom they are allotted to pay only 50p per share for the present.

The expression *allotment of shares* describes the notification by the company, usually in the form of a letter, that it has accepted an offer for the shares, and that the new shareholders name will be entered on the register of shareholders.

A registered company which does not meet the three requirements listed above will be treated as a private company. Private companies differ from public companies in a number of respects, and an examination of these differences is a way of gaining an appreciation of the nature of these two forms of registered company. We can carry out the examination by considering the advantages and disadvantages of a private company over a public one.

The advantages of a private company

In contrast to a public company a private company enjoys the following advantages:

- it does not require a minimum level of share capital either to register or to commence trading. Its share capital could legitimately comprise of 1p made up by a single share held by a sole member;

- it can avoid s.89 Companies Act 1985, which provides that ordinary shares issued for cash by the company must first be offered to existing ordinary shareholders in proportion to the nominal value of their existing holdings – a *rights issue*. S.91 provides that s.89 can be excluded by a private company in its articles;

- it has a much greater freedom to issue shares in return for assets other than cash than a public company has (for instance where it purchases property which it pays for by transferring fully paid shares to the vendor);

- the directors have greater freedom in their financial dealings with the company and need not disclose as much information about such dealings in the company accounts as is the case for directors of public companies;

- it can be formed and operated with a single member (see below);

- subject to its size it may be excluded from publishing of some or all of its accounts;

- no special qualifications are required of the company secretary;

- it has power to purchase its own shares, and may do so out of capital;

- it can use procedures to avoid the need to hold meetings and satisfy various other statutory obligations. These procedures were introduced by provisions contained in the Companies Act 1989, designed to make it easier for private companies to comply with the substantial level of statutory regulation imposed upon registered companies. The objective has been to further deregulate the private company, thereby assisting it in the conduct of its business affairs. What the Act does is to permit private companies to *deregulate* themselves by means of the use of two types of resolution, the written resolution and the elective resolution.

The written resolution

By using the written resolution procedure a private company is able to do anything which would otherwise require a resolution of the members in a general meeting of the company. The written resolution must be signed by or on behalf of all the members of the company, who, at the date of the resolution, would be entitled to attend and vote at the meeting which would otherwise have to be held to conduct the business. If their approval is obtained a copy of the proposed resolution has to be sent to the company auditors, who must decide whether it concerns them in their capacity as the auditors. If it does they must then indicate whether they are willing to give it their approval. If they approve it the resolution is effective as if it had been passed in general meeting, but if it is not granted the company must hold a general meeting to conduct the business in the ordinary way. This procedure is not available in certain circumstances e.g. to remove a director, and in other cases there are further formalities which must be complied with.

The elective resolution

An elective resolution can be used by a private company as a means of avoiding a number of formalities that it would otherwise have to observe under company legislation. Such a resolution can dispense with the need to obtain the authority of the members before the company issues shares, the need to lay accounts and reports before the general meeting, the need to hold an annual general meeting, and to reappoint auditors annually. Like the written resolution, the elective resolution requires the unanimous approval of all the company members entitled to attend and vote at a general meeting. There are certain qualifications attached to the use of an elective resolution. For instance if it is used to dispense with the need to hold an annual general meeting, a member may serve written notice on the company no later than three months before the end of the year to which the meeting relates, requiring that it be held. In addition an elective resolution can be revoked by means of an ordinary resolution (which requires a simple majority) passed by the members in general meeting.

The disadvantages of a private company

The only major disadvantage it suffers is that it cannot advertise its securities to the public through the issue of a prospectus or other advertising device. S.170 Financial Services Act 1986 however does enable the Secretary of State to make regulations allowing for purely private advertisements between the issuer and the recipient. This lack of capacity to raise capital through the public issue of shares can really only be regarded as a disadvantage if the growth of the business needs to be financed in this way, when the company faces a choice between remaining privately owned and seeking finance by other means, or of going public and reducing the level of control exercisable by the original members over the new business as new members are brought in. It is worth bearing in mind that in general, company survival is achieved by growth. Such growth may be through the expansion of its core business. Alternatively it may occur through mergers with other companies, or, most commonly, where one company acquires another through a *take-over*. But however growth occurs it must always be financed.

Single Member Companies

The Companies (Single Member Private Limited Companies) Regulations 1992, implementing the Twelfth Company Law Directive, allow for the formation and operation of private limited companies having a *single* member. This amends s.1 CA 1985 which requires a company to have at least two members. Now the rule only applies to public companies. The register of members of a single member company must state that it is such a company, and provide the name and address of the sole member; company resolutions must be evidenced in writing; and any contract between the sole member and the company (unless made in the ordinary course of its business on the usual terms and conditions) must be expressed in writing.

The result of the Regulations is that neither s.24 CA 1985 nor s.122 Insolvency Act 1986 apply any longer to private companies. Under s.24, where company membership falls to one, the sole remaining member can become personally liable for the debts of the company; s.122 enables the court to wind up a company if its membership falls below two.

S.283 CA 1985 is not however affected, so even a single member company must still have two officers, a director and a secretary. Normally the sole member is likely to be the director, and the non-member the secretary.

The meaning of the expression public company

As we have seen a public limited company is one which satisfies certain statutory criteria. However the expression public company is sometimes used in a commercial rather than a legal sense to denote companies whose shares are dealt with on the Stock Exchange; major United Kingdom organisations such as ICI and Marks and Spencer are examples. Technically such companies are *listed* or *market* companies. Not all public limited companies are quoted i.e. listed on the Stock Exchange, but only the largest ones which are able to meet the stringent entry requirements the Stock Exchange demands. Those public limited companies which are not quoted on the Stock Exchange will offer their securities in one of the intermediate securities markets, such as the Unlisted Securities Market (the USM) a *junior league* of the Stock Exchange set up in 1980. The other intermediate securities markets are the Over the Counter Market and the Third Market. Thus public and private companies can be classified by reference to the method by which their shares can be issued. Company financing is considered later in the chapter.

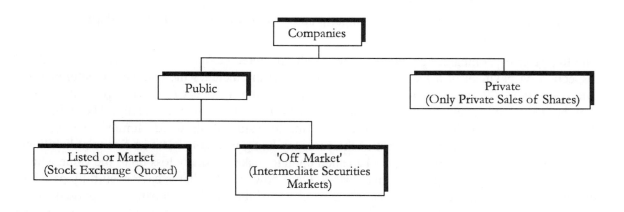

Figure 4.3   Classification of Companies by Market

Formation of a Registered Company

A company is incorporated and so comes into being when the Registrar of Companies issues it with a document called the certificate of incorporation. This certificate is issued following an application by the persons who wish to form the company. They are known as the company's *promoters* and they are considered in more detail a little later. The two main documents which must be included in the application are the *memorandum of association* and the *articles of association*. Once the certificate of incorporation has been granted a private company can commence trading immediately, however a public company must be issued with a further document, a *trading certificate*, before it is authorised to start trading.

The Memorandum of Association

The memorandum of association and the articles of association set out the constitution of a registered company. They are the two major documents within a group of documents to be sent to the Registrar of Companies prior to incorporation. A memorandum is required by the Companies Act 1985 which specifies that it must include the following matters:

(i)   the name of the company with *limited* as the last word in the case of a private company, or *public limited company* in the case of a public company;

(ii)   the situation of the registered office identifying whether the company is situated in England or Scotland;

(iii)   the objects of the company;

(iv)   the liability of the members;

(v)   the nominal capital of the company and its division into numbers of shares and denominations.

The Registrar of Companies maintains a file for all registered companies, which is open to public inspection on payment of a fee. The file for each company includes the company memorandum. The contents of the memorandum are of importance to the members of the company itself (the shareholders), and especially to those who deal with the company commercially. The indication that the company has limited liability shown by the inclusion of the word `limited', serves as a warning to outsiders that in the event of the company being unable to meet its financial liabilities at any time, its shareholders, can only be called upon to make good any loss up to the value which remains unpaid to the company on their shares. Once however the shares have been fully paid the shareholders' financial liability ceases. Of course the liability of the company, as opposed to its members, is not limited in any way and if it is wound up all its assets will be used to meet the claims of the creditors.

Stating the country in which the company is situated determines whether it is an English or Scottish company. Usually a Notice of Situation of Registered Office, giving the company's full address is sent to the Registrar together with the Memorandum. It must, in any event, be sent to him within fourteen days of incorporation of the company. The registered office is important since documents are effectively served on the company by posting or delivering them to this address. Thus a writ (a document used to commence legal proceedings) served on the company will be effectively served if delivered to the registered office.

The *objects clause* sets the contractual limits within which the company can validly operate. The need to state the company's objects may be seen as a protection to shareholders by giving them some reassurance as to the ways in which their capital may be used by the directors. A company, can, however, resolve to alter its objects, and in any event it is usual to draft the objects clause very widely. Furthermore even if a company acts outside its objects clause the transaction will in most cases be binding on it, although the members may seek to censure the authorising directors. This matter is considered in more detail below.

The *liability clause* is a formality which merely states the nature of the shareholders' liability, that is whether it is limited by shares, by guarantee, or unlimited.

The *capital clause* sets out the amount of capital the company is authorised to raise by the issue of shares, and the way in which the shares are to be divided. This amount can be raised by the agreement of the shareholders without difficulty, although a reduction in the share capital, whilst possible, is more of a problem to achieve. It is a basic principle of company law that share capital should be maintained to protect the interests of the company's creditors.

The memorandum concludes with the names and addresses of those people agreeing to take shares in the company on its formation and indicating how many shares each will take. These people are called *subscribers*. The subscribers for the shares in the memorandum will often be appointed as directors. As the statutory minimum membership of a private company is one, a single subscriber to the memorandum will suffice to form the company. The minimum membership for a public company is two. Each subscriber will agree to take a certain number of shares on incorporation of the company, and the subscribers are therefore the first members of the company. Subsequently new members will join the company when it allots shares to them and their names are entered on the register of members which every company must maintain, and which is open to public inspection. Usually the subscribers will have been the promoters – the people engaged in setting up the company.

Company name

Generally a company is free to choose the name it wishes to adopt, although as we have seen the word *limited* for a private company or *plc* for a public company must be inserted at the end of the company name. This is required by s.26 Companies Act 1985. The section also provides that the name cannot be the same as one already held on the index of company names kept by the Registrar. Nor can a name be used which would in the opinion of the Secretary of State constitute a criminal offence or be offensive.

It is a tort for a person to represent his business as that of another and thereby obtain profit from that other's business goodwill. In such circumstances the injured business can claim under the tort of passing off against the business guilty of the deception and recover damages and obtain an injunction, by way of a remedy.

> In *Ewing v. Buttercup Margarine Co. Ltd*. 1917 the plaintiff, who carried on business using the name Buttercup Dairy Co. obtained an injunction against the defendant company on the grounds that the public might be confused as to the identity of the two organisations.

It makes no difference whether the name is real or invented.

> In *Exxon Corporation v. Exxon Insurance Consultants International Ltd.* 1981 the plaintiffs obtained an injunction to prevent the defendants from passing off its goods as the defendant's by the use of the word *Exxon*. The plaintiffs, formerly the Esso Company, had invented the word *Exxon* as a replacement name. They were however unsuccessful in seeking an injunction for breach of copyright. The court held that the word *Exxon* was not an *"original literary work"* under the Copyright Act 1956, since, in the words of Stephenson LJ a *"literary work is something intended to afford either information and instruction or pleasure in the form of literary enjoyment"*.

The objects clause and the ultra vires doctrine

Being a corporate body the registered company can only lawfully do those things which its constitution allows it to do. It is a direct consequence of the artificiality of corporations which, being purely creations of the law, only possess a restricted capacity. As a condition of incorporation every registered company must include a statement in its memorandum which sets out what the company has been formed to do. The scope or extent of this statement, known as the company's *objects clause*, is initially decided by the people setting up the company, its promoters. They will often become the company's first directors following its incorporation.

The details contained in the objects clause provide shareholders with a description of the range of activities their company can legitimately undertake. It is right that, as investors, a company's shareholders should know the purpose for which their financial contribution can be used. A rational investor will want to establish how well the board of directors manages the company, something which can be achieved by looking at the company's trading performance in its particular line of business. An investor may be less willing to put money into an enterprise where the board has a wide freedom under the company's objects clause to pursue diverse commercial activities, some of which may fall well outside their experience as managers. This is particularly likely in the smaller private companies, for whereas the boards handling the affairs of public companies will include executive directors having wide commercial experience, in small private limited companies directors will sometimes have at best only a rudimentary knowledge of business management, and at worst none at all.

If a company acts outside the limits of its permissible activities as expressed in the objects clause it is said to be acting *ultra vires*, that is beyond its powers. At common law an ultra vires transaction has always been treated as a nullity, consequently an ultra vires contract entered into by a company was neither enforceable by it or against it. Even if the other contracting party was unaware that the company was exceeding its powers as expressed in the memorandum this would provide no relief, for under the doctrine of *constructive notice* a person dealing with a company was deemed to be aware of its public documents and hence of any restrictions on the company's capacity contained in them. Nor could the company subsequently ratify in general meeting an ultra vires transaction made on its behalf by the directors. Ratification has the effect of retrospectively validating a transaction, but in the case of an ultra vires contract this is not possible since the contract is a nullity.

> The application of these principles is seen in *Ashbury Railway Carriage Co. Ltd. v. Riche* 1875. The company's objects included the power to manufacture or sell rail rolling stock

and carry on business as mechanical engineers and general contractors. The company purchased a concession to finance the building of a railway in Belgium, but later the directors repudiated the contract. In an action for breach of contract against the company, the House of Lords held that the contract was ultra vires and void from the outset. Lord Cairns expressed the law when he said, *"This contract was entirely beyond the objects in the memorandum ... If it was a contract void at its beginning, it was void because the company could not make the contract".*

When the United Kingdom became a member of the European Community on 1st January, 1973, the European Communities Act 1972, by which entry was effected, in a hurried attempt at providing for some measure of harmonisation between English company law and company law as it applied in the other member states, introduced an important statutory modification to the ultra vires doctrine. This modification which was contained in s.9(1), and was subsequently incorporated unchanged into the Companies Act 1985 as s.35, provided that in favour of a person acting in good faith with a company, any transaction decided on by its directors was deemed to be within the capacity of the company to make. Whilst not eliminating the doctrine of ultra vires s.35 went some way towards reducing its impact. The Companies Act 1989, which more fully implemented the first EC directive on company law, introduced a new s.35 which goes much further towards eliminating ultra vires as it affects the registered company. However the doctrine is still not completely dead.

The present law

The present s.35 states that, *"The validity of an act done by a company shall not be called into question on the ground of lack of capacity by reason on anything in the company's memorandum."* In other words it validates transactions which would otherwise be void on the grounds of breaching the company's constitution as expressed in the memorandum. The section goes on to say that anyone making a transaction with the company is not obliged to check the memorandum to ascertain whether it authorises the transaction. A further provision, s.711A, abolishes the doctrine of constructive notice of matters which would be disclosed by a company search. Previously, as we have seen, a person dealing with a company was in some circumstances deemed to have knowledge of information contained in the public file of the company held at the Companies Registry. This principle no longer applies.

The changes introduced under the Companies Act 1989 do not however completely eliminate the application of ultra vires to registered companies. In this context three matters need to be noted:

(i)   a shareholder still retains the power to seek an injunction to restrain the company from entering into an ultra vires transaction, although this opportunity is lost once the transaction has been made, whether or not it has been carried out;

(ii)   directors are still obliged to act within their company's constitution. S.35(3) says, *"it remains the duty of the directors to observe any limitations on their powers flowing from the company's memorandum"*. The company can now ratify action taken by directors in excess of their powers by means of a special resolution, thus reversing the position in the *Ashbury Railway Carriage* case, and an additional special resolution may be passed to relieve the directors of any liability they may have incurred for breach of duty as a result of exceeding the company's powers;

(iii) as a result of s.109 Companies Act 1989 if a director exceeds his powers and the other party to the contract is a director of the company or the holding company, the company can if it chooses avoid the contract. The section is an attempt at preventing directors defrauding the company using the provisions of the new s.35.

Whilst the powers of a company are found in its memorandum, the rules regulating the way in which these powers should be exercised are usually contained in the articles of association. Articles may, for example, cut down on the general powers enjoyed by directors to make contracts within the company's authorised areas of business, by requiring that transactions involving more than a certain amount of money be approved by the members through an ordinary resolution passed at a meeting of the company. This can give rise to circumstances where an outsider enters into a transaction with a company which its memorandum authorises, but where the company's internal rules have not been complied with. Internal rules contained in a company's articles of association, being contained in its public file, came within the doctrine of constructive notice: the outsider was deemed to be aware of them. What he could not know was whether they had in fact been complied with when a company decision was made.

For instance, he would have no way of discovering whether a resolution *required* to be passed by the company under the articles *had* been passed. As a response to this difficulty the rule in *Royal British Bank v. Turquand* 1856 provided that an outsider was entitled to assume that the necessary rules of internal management had been complied with.

The rule in *Turquands Case* is affected by the Companies Act 1989. It provides that a third party dealing in good faith with a company can treat the company's constitution as imposing no restrictions on the power of the board of directors or persons authorised by them to bind the company. This provision thus supersedes the rule in *Turquands Case*. A third party is assumed to be acting in good faith, unless the contrary can be shown. Knowledge that the directors are acting beyond their powers does not, in itself, amount to bad faith.

Alteration of the objects clause

By virtue of s.4 Companies Act 1985, a company may by means of a special resolution alter its objects clause at any time and for any reason. The alteration is effective so long as no application is made to the court to cancel it within 21 days of the special resolution, and the company sends the Registrar within a further 15 days a copy of the altered memorandum. An application to cancel can be made by the holders of at least 15% of the issued share capital of any class, and the alteration is only effective in these circumstances where the court confirms it. It is relevant here to note in connection with the alteration of objects that a company can now adopt a single object to carry on business as a general commercial company (s.3A). A company formed with such an object will be able to carry on any business or trade, and do anything incidental or conducive to such a business or trade.

The Articles of Association

The articles of association of a registered company must be supplied to the Registrar of Companies prior to incorporation. Like the memorandum of association the articles will then be included in the company's file kept at Companies House in Cardiff.

The articles are concerned with the internal administration of the company, and it is for those setting up the company (its promoters) to determine the rules they consider appropriate for inclusion within the articles. The Companies Act 1985 does however provide a set of model articles which a company can adopt in whole or in part if it wishes. If a company fails to provide a set of articles then the model articles contained in the 1985 Act automatically apply to the company. They are known as *Table A* Articles. Matters which are normally dealt with in the Articles include the appointment and powers of the board of directors, the rules in relation to members' meetings and voting and the types of shares and rights attaching to the share categories.

Other registration documents

In addition to the memorandum and articles of association there are certain other documents which must be supplied to the Registrar prior to incorporation. These include a statutory declaration that all the requirements of the Act have been complied with. Fees must also be paid.

Having examined all the documents filed and ensured that they are in order, the Registrar then issues a certificate under official seal which certifies that the company is incorporated. The certificate is conclusive evidence that all the requirements of the Companies Act 1985 have been complied with and that the company is a company authorised to be registered and duly registered under the Act. A private company can enter into contracts, borrow money, and carry on business immediately on incorporation. However a public limited company registered under the 1985 Act cannot commence business until a certificate is issued by the Registrar that the share capital of the company is not less than the authorised minimum (i.e. £50,000 with at least one-quarter paid up). If more than a year after the incorporation of a public company it has not been issued with such a certificate the Secretary of State may petition the court for the company to be wound up.

Promoters

Promoters are people involved in the setting up of registered companies. The term is a wide one and does not appear to have any special technical meaning. Bowen LJ in *Whaley Bridge v. Green*1880 stated:

> *"The term promoter is a term of business not of law, usefully summing up in a single word a number of business operations familiar to the commercial world by which a company is generally brought into existence".*

The types of operations carried out by promoters include not only the registration of the memorandum and articles but also arrangements for obtaining capital, identifying people suitable to act as directors (head hunting), the negotiation of preliminary agreements and, in the case of a public company, the preparation and issue of a prospectus. Once the company commences business the role of the promoter is at an end. Following the incorporation of the company the promoters will frequently take over its management in the capacity of directors.

Although the activities of promoters are essentially commercial, there are legal consequences attached to the relationship between a promoter, the company that has been set up, and the members taking up shares in it. These consequences all stem from the common law view of a promoter as someone who stands in a fiduciary position towards the company. A considerable body of law has developed around the function of promoter, and this has sought to emphasise the importance of being able to identify who qualifies to be treated as a company promoter.

Who is a promoter?

Although the expression promoter crops up in legislation (it is, for example, used in the Financial Services Act 1986), statute provides us with no definition to work from, and it has been left to the courts to provide a judicial interpretation. As long ago as 1877 Cockburn LJ, in *Twycross v. Grant,* spoke of a promoter as:

> *"one who undertakes to form a company with reference to a given project and to set it going, and who takes the necessary steps to accomplish that purpose."*

Thus a promoter will be:

- anyone giving instructions for preparing and registering a memorandum and set of articles;

- a person who, whilst not actively involved in such activity, is associated with those who are, and the understanding is that he or she will obtain a profit from the setting up of the company;

- anyone involved in pre-trading activities on the company's behalf; for example, by seeking to secure resources such as capital and labour for the prospective company.

It is lawful for one company to be the promoter of another, provided, of course, the promoting company is already in existence. Such promotions will occur where a company decides to form a subsidiary.

Professional people such as solicitors and accountants, who are involved in setting up companies acting on instructions received from their clients, are acting simply as agents and will not, without more, be regarded as promoters themselves.

The definition of a promoter is thus a flexible one, and it is of considerable importance to anyone associated with the process of company formation to identify whether they fall within it. The reason for this is clear. As a company promoter a person becomes subject to the duties and responsibilities imposed by law on such people, which may give rise to financial penalties if they are not met.

The position in law of a promoter

As soon as a person takes steps to set up a company, and with that object in mind, his or her legal duties as a promoter emerge. We noted earlier that these duties are based on a fiduciary relationship with the company about to be formed. This means no profit may be made from the promotion which is not disclosed to the company once it is set up. Undisclosed profit is referred to as *secret profit.* The rule regarding secret profits is a clear indication that the courts view the relationship between a promoter and the company in the same way as the relationship between an agent and a principal, for agents have a duty to their principals to account for any profits they make personally. Such profits are the property of the principal. However, a promoter is not an agent of the company for an obvious reason. A person cannot act as an agent for someone who does not exist and so, until the company is formed, its promoters are acting on behalf of a non-existent principal. The consequences of this position we shall consider shortly. Before doing so we need to explore more fully the consequences of the fiduciary relationship.

The promoter as a fiduciary

The expression *fiduciary* signifies a sort of trusteeship. You may have come across before in other legal contexts. For instance, it appears in the expression *bona fide* meaning good faith, and in *uberrimae fidei* which describes certain types of contracts which are said to be based upon the utmost good faith of the parties making them. Insurance contracts are a good example. As a fiduciary, a promoter has an obligation to disclose fully to the company all relevant matters associated with transactions made between the promoter and the company; in particular, any profit made. There is nothing unlawful in promoters profiting from setting up a company and then selling assets to it. This was exactly what happened in *Salomon's case*, where Salomon set up the new company and then sold his business to it at an inflated price. What is unlawful is the failure to disclose the profit to either an *independent board* or to the existing and any intended shareholders.

Disclosure to an independent board is often impossible since promoters frequently take up office as directors of the newly formed company, especially where private companies are involved. In such circumstances full disclosure must instead be made to the existing shareholders and also, where appropriate, to any intended shareholders. For example, disclosure to intended shareholders could be achieved by information provided in a company prospectus. In this way the promoters will have fulfilled their duty since, in the words of Lindley MR: *"the real truth is disclosed to those who are induced by the promoters to join the company"* – *Lagunas Nitrate Co. v. Lagunas Syndicate* 1899.

The idea underlying this basic principle is that a company has the right to receive a full account of a promoter's interest in any transaction with the company, thus enabling it to arrive at a proper decision whether or not to proceed with the transaction.

Company remedies for breach of promoters duties

A company may have a number of alternative remedies available to it in the event of a promoter being in breach of his fiduciary duty. These are:

Rescission

Rescission is an equitable remedy, which seeks to restore both parties to their pre-contractual positions. It is available in the case of any contract made as a consequence of non-disclosure or misrepresentation. It cannot be used where the company is in liquidation, or where any of the following bars apply:

- The contract has been affirmed, i.e. accepted by the company in knowledge of the breach that has occurred.
- There has been delay in bringing the claim.
- Third party rights have been acquired.
- Substantial restoration of the parties to their pre-contractual position is not possible.

- The court has applied its powers under s.2(2) Misrepresentation Act 1967, to declare the contract subsisting and to award damages in lieu of rescission.

Accounting for any undisclosed profit

Generally, it is not possible for a company to keep the property which is the subject of the transaction and reduce the price paid for it to the extent of the promoter's secret profit. The only circumstance in which this will be possible is where the contract was made by someone acting as an agent of the company at a time when it was formed.

> Making a claim for the promoters' profit can be difficult, as illustrated in *Re: Cape Breton Co.* 1887. Here coal mines were bought by six partners for £5,500. They extracted coal from the mines, but later decided to form a company to conduct these commercial operations. Two of the six partners became directors. The company bought the mines for £42,000 from the vendor, who was one of the six original partners and was acting as a trustee for all of them. The company went into liquidation and a claim was brought for the undisclosed profit made by the two directors, there having been no disclosure to an independent board. Rescission was impossible as the company was in liquidation. The court dismissed the claim for the profit, on the grounds that the mines had not originally been purchased to sell to the company, and therefore had not been bought on its behalf.

Damages

Damages – the award of a sum of money by way of compensation – is not available for breach of fiduciary duty, but may be claimed where the contract has been induced by misrepresentation. This is an indirect means of obtaining damages for breach of duty.

> In *Re: Leeds and Hanley Theatre of Varieties* 1902 an existing company bought two music halls for £24,000 which were then conveyed to a nominee. The intention was to form a new company which would buy the halls. The directors of this new company, after it was formed, issued a prospectus to raise money for the purchase of the halls at a price of £75,000. They did not constitute an independent board. The prospectus made no reference to the promoting company but indicated that the nominee was the vendor. It was held that the promoting company was the real vendor and should have been disclosed. Damages would be awarded representing the difference between the market price and the contract price, i.e. the profit.

Further remedies

Damages may also be available in cases of fraud and, under the rule in *Hedley Byrne v. Heller and Partners* 1964, in cases of negligent misrepresentation, on the grounds that a promoter owes the company a duty of care.

The Insolvency Act 1986 allows for a claim to be brought in a winding up under s.212 where a promoter can be shown to have misapplied property or acted in breach of duty. A promoter will also be liable for loss or damage caused to a subscriber of a company's shares resulting from an untrue statement in the prospectus to which the promoter was a party.

Promoter remuneration

Payment for the work performed by the promoter can be legitimately made by any of the following methods:

(a) by a sale of the promoter's own property to the company for cash, or for fully paid shares at an overvalue of which proper disclosure has been made;

(b) by the promoter being given an option to take up further shares in the company at their nominal (par) value. If the market value of the shares is higher than the par value when the option is exercised, the promoter will make a profit;

(c) by inserting a provision in the articles providing for the payment of a fixed figure to the promoter. This cannot create a binding contract between the company and the promoter. However, it will usually be possible for the promoter to ensure the company makes such a payment and it cannot recover the payment made once it has been made.

Disqualification of promoters

A disqualification order can be made against a promoter by the court under s.1 Company Directors Disqualification Act 1986. This can prohibit him or her from taking part in the promotion of company for up to 15 years. The grounds on which the court can apply the provisions of the Act are considered in Chapter 5.

Pre-Incorporation Contracts

No company can be bound by a contract made on its behalf, or by someone acting as a trustee for it, before it has been incorporated. Such contracts are referred to as *pre-incorporation contracts*. They do not bind it for the simple reason that at the time they are made the company lacks all legal capacity, being for the present non existent. In agency terms anyone purporting to act as the company's agent is acting on behalf of a non-existent principal. The consequences of this proposition of law can be significant for those dealing with the promoters of the company.

> In *Re: English & Colonial Produce Co. Ltd.* 1906 the company was held not to be liable to pay solicitors their fees for work carried out in setting it up. The work had been carried out on the instructions of the promoters, who subsequently became the directors of the company. Similarly the company is unable to sue on such contracts. In *Natal Land v. Pauline Colliery* 1904 the appellant company, Natal Land, entered into an agreement to grant a mining lease to the respondent, Pauline Colliery. The respondent had not, at that time, been incorporated and the agreement was made with a third party acting on the respondent's behalf. The respondent was subsequently incorporated, and discovered coal on the land subject to the lease, at which point the appellant refused to grant the lease. It was held that the respondent could not force the appellant to do so.

Furthermore, it is not possible for a company to *ratify* – that is to adopt – a contract made on its behalf before it was formed. Ratification operates retrospectively and is, therefore, also caught by the fact that the company was not in law a person at the relevant time. However, whilst a company cannot be bound by a pre-incorporation contract, the promoter who is responsible for making the contract can be. In this way the other party may have a remedy. The position is governed by s.36(4) of the Companies Act 1985. The section provides that any contract made by or on behalf of a company as yet unincorporated has the effect of binding the contract maker personally, unless the agreement provides otherwise

> The effect of the section was considered by the Court of Appeal in *Phonogram v. Lane* 1981. The defendant signed an agreement *"for and on behalf of"* the proposed company. However, the company was never formed and the plaintiffs now sought to recover money they had advanced, repayable under the terms of the agreement. They claimed the defendant was personally liable under what is now s.36(4) of the Companies Act 1985. On the defendant's behalf it was claimed that signing as an agent was a way of excluding personal liability. The court disagreed, finding the defendant personally liable. In Lord Denning's words, *"There must be a clear exclusion of personal liability"*.

> The court also suggested a promoter can be made personally liable where the company in question is not as yet even in the process of being formed and both sides are aware the company is not yet in existence.

Novation

Once a company has been incorporated however, it may take up contracts made for it prior to incorporation by means of a process known as *novation*. Novation involves the discharge of the original contract and its replacement with a new one, to which the company is a party. This relieves the promoter of the personal liability which existed under the original pre-incorporation contract. Unlike ratification, novation does not operate retrospectively. It can also be inferred from the conduct of the parties, in other words it does not have to be expressly agreed.

> In *Howard v. Patent Ivory Manufacturing Co.* 1888 a company resolution to adopt a pre-incorporation agreement was held to be sufficient evidence of intention of novation even though the outsider, as the other party to the transaction, was never informed. However, a mistaken belief of the company that it is bound by a pre-incorporation contract is not sufficient to infer novation (*Re: Northumberland Avenue Hotel* 1886).

When a person acts as an agent for an unformed company a very valuable protection for the agent is to include a clause into the agreement stating that personal liability is to cease when the company enters into a fresh contract with the other party on the terms of the original agreement. The clause should further provide for rescission of the original agreement if novation fails to take place. There is, of course, no way a company can be forced to adopt a pre-incorporation contract. In the case of a public limited company, s.117 of the Companies Act 1985 contains an important provision dealing with contracts made by the company after incorporation but before its trading certificate is issued. Such contracts, says the section, are validly made but if the company fails to meet its obligations within 21 days of being asked to do so, its directors become jointly and severally liable to compensate the other party for any loss or damage sustained as a result of its failure to commence business.

Financing the Company

For any company the raising of money for trading purposes is essential to its ability to carry on trade. The capital so acquired is a fundamental resource of the company.

Companies are able to raise the capital in different ways. The methods available and the legal rules and principles associated with them, are examined below. Essentially, this examination focuses upon two ways in which companies acquire capital, namely, through the issue of shares, and by means of borrowing through the issue of debentures. Shares and debentures are often referred to collectively as *company securities*.

Capital

Before examining company securities it may be helpful to say a few words about the expression of capital. In a legal sense, capital is something positive. It is what the company has raised and can use for doing things, to buy business premises for instance, which are then referred to as fixed capital, or to purchase stock, which is referred to as circulating capital. In an accountancy sense, however, capital is something negative, appearing in a balance sheet under the heading of *liabilities*. Thus, to an accountant the money raised by issuing shares – *(share capital;)*, issuing debentures - *(loan capital;)*, as well as, the amount of money owed by the company to its trade creditors, is all regarded as part of the company's indebtedness. This is capital as a *debt*. All these items are owed.

The expression capital is such an important one that it has found its way into a variety of technical terms used in company law. The most important of these terms are:

- *Share capital*
  This is capital raised by the issue of the company's shares, and is often used as a way of distinguishing capital gained in this way, from capital gained through borrowing.

- *Loan capital*
  This is capital acquired by means of borrowing.

- *Nominal (or authorised capital)*
  This expression refers to the value of shares a company is authorised to issue, and it appears in the capital clause of the memorandum of association.

- *Issued capital*
  Usually this term is used to describe the value of capital in the form of shares which have actually been issued to the members.

- *Paid-up capital*
  This is the amount which has been paid to the company by its members for the shares they hold. Companies do not always require immediate payment in full for issued shares. Under s.351 of the Companies Act 1985, if a company makes a reference to share capital on its business stationery or order forms, this must be a reference to its paid up capital.

- *Unpaid capital*
  If shares have been issued which have not been fully paid for, the amount outstanding

is referred to as *unpaid capital*. For example, if 5,000 issued shares have a nominal value (that is a face value, sometimes referred to as *par* value) of £1 each and shareholders have been required to pay only 40 pence per share, then the paid up capital is £2,000 and the unpaid capital is £3,000. Shareholders may be required to pay up the outstanding amount on their shares by the company making a *call* on them to do so. The unpaid amount is the extent of the shareholders' liability to the company.

- *Reserve capital*

  Under s.120 of the Companies Act 1985, a company may, by means of a special resolution, determine that any portion of its unpaid capital shall not be called up except if the company is being brought to an end by being wound up. Such a sum is referred to as *reserve capital*. Once created it is no longer under the control of the company's directors. Consequently, the company cannot charge it, that is, use it as a security (for raising a loan, for example). To do so would be to damage the position of the company's creditors. The only way the special resolution can be revoked is with the consent of the court under a scheme of arrangement. Unlike reserve capital, mere uncalled capital can be charged by the company.

In company law references to capital are usually references to share capital.

Share Capital

We have seen above that issuing shares is one way of financing a company. How far a company is willing to use this method is likely to depend upon many factors. A private company may be willing to issue more shares because existing members are not in a position to invest further in the company, yet do not wish to dilute their control over the running of the company by issuing shares which grant votes to new members. A public company may avoid a share issue if its present investment potential is unlikely to attract the market. An alternative approach is to borrow money, that is raise loan capital, usually by means of the issue of debentures. Again, a company may be reluctant to use this approach, since it will have the effect of tying it down, and at times of high interest rates such borrowings may not be commercially advisable.

Further alternatives used by companies are:

    (a)   to obtain goods and services on credit; for instance, by leasing vehicles or obtaining machinery on hire purchase terms;

    (b)   to retain profits - which simply involves holding back profits made by trading, the effects being borne by the shareholders whose *dividends*, (their return on their investment), will be reduced accordingly.

For the moment, however, we shall concentrate on the use of shares as a way of raising money. In doing so, we need to consider how share capital is raised; and how it can be altered. Before examining these issues however we need to say a little about shares themselves.

Classes of shares

Essentially a share is a unit of company ownership and a shareholder as a stakeholder in the organisation is a company member. Sometimes companies, particularly smaller ones, will issue only one type, or class, of shares. If they do all the shares will carry equal rights. But in larger companies different classes of shares are usually issued with varying rights attaching to them relating such matters as voting, payment of dividends and return of capital on liquidation. The two main types of shares are:

(a) *Preference shares*

The main characteristic of a preference share is that it will carry a preferred fixed dividend. This means that the holder of a preference share is entitled to a fixed amount of dividend, e.g. 6% on the value of each share, before other shareholders are paid any dividend. They are presumed to be cumulative which means that if in any year the company fails to declare a dividend, the shortfall must be made up out of profits of subsequent years. A preference share is therefore a safe investment with fixed interest, no matter how small or large is the company's profit. As far as return of capital on a winding up is concerned, the preference shareholder will rank equally with ordinary shareholders for any payment due, unless the preference shares are made preferential as to capital. Normally, preference shares do not carry voting rights and therefore the preference shareholder has little influence over the company's activities.

(b) *Ordinary shares*

Ordinary shares are often referred to as the *equity share capital* of a company. When a company declares a dividend and the preference shareholders have been paid, the holders of ordinary shares are entitled to the remainder. It follows therefore that an ordinary shareholder in a well-managed company making high profits will receive a good return on his investment and consequently the value of his shares will rise. In this way a share can have a much higher market value than it's face value. Unfortunately, the reverse is also true and they may fall in market value so that ordinary shares inevitably carry a certain risk. This risk is reflected in the amount of control that an ordinary shareholder has over the company's business. While voting rights are not normally attached to preference shares, they are attached to ordinary shares enabling the ordinary shareholder to voice an opinion in a general meeting and vote on major issues involving the running of the company. Ordinary shareholders thus have the capacity to remove directors who have mismanaged the business of the company. An ordinary resolution is required in order to do so.

Where a company's share capital is divided into different classes, statutory provisions apply which limit the ability of the company to alter the rights attached to the classes of shares. S.125 provides that the written consent of three quarters in *value* of the shares of the class or alternatively their approval by way of an extraordinary resolution of a meeting of the shareholders of that class is needed for an alteration to be validly made. Even then a 15% or more dissenting group of shareholders of that class have 21 days in which to challenge the variations before the court (s.127).

Raising share capital

Private companies and public companies

One of the fundamental differences between private and public companies lies in their ability to raise share capital. Public companies usually seek to raise capital, whether through the issue of shares or debentures, by advertising their securities to the public, hence their designation as public companies. Their ability to do so has led to a range of statutory provisions designed to protect the investing public from being misled about the financial condition and future prospects of a business in which prospective investors are considering making an investment. Over the past few years there have been a number of well publicised cases involving public companies which have collapsed causing financial distress to small investors, often retired people, who have little or no chance of recovering their investment. Sometimes the Government has been prepared to provide financial assistance, as in the *Barlow Clowes* case. Large institutional investors, such as pension funds, are of course much better placed to assess the potential and the risks involved in investing in public companies. The general law dealing with investor protection is contained in the Financial Services Act 1986, and statutory references included below are references to the 1986 Act unless stated otherwise.

As to the position of private companies and their ability to raise capital, there are only two significant provisions:

(a)   under s.143, a private company must not apply for its shares to be listed on the Stock Exchange; and

(b)   under s.170, a private company must not issue any advertisement offering its securities, unless the circumstances under which the advertisement is issued are covered by an order made by the Secretary of State for Trade and Industry, exempting the company from the section.

The effect of these two provisions is that, subject to the s.170 exception a private company cannot raise money by selling its securities on the open market. Obviously this limitation restricts the growth of a private company's capital acquired through the issue of its securities, and consequently of limiting the size of its membership. Whereas in a public company the membership will often be measured in thousands, the membership of private companies is inevitably much smaller. Thus, whilst private companies frequently operate under arrangements in which all the members are also directors, in a public company ownership and management is usually found in separate hands.

The development of a company

The investment risks involved make it most unusual for a public company to be formed from scratch and immediately seek to raise capital from the public to finance the new business. Usually, the growth of a company will follow the kind of pattern indicated below.

- A private company is formed, which either establishes a new business or acquires an existing one. Its share capital will be small, and will be contributed by a group of shareholders, who are likely to become the company's directors and managers. Loan capital will come from overdraft arrangements made with banks, which are secured by means of directors' personal guarantees. Most companies do not progress beyond this stage.

- The private company is converted into a public one to enable it to raise more capital from the public and from financial institutions. This move will be motivated by the need to expand and by the ambitions of its owners. Its securities will not be sold on the Stock Exchange, because it is not yet large enough to meet the listing requirements (see below), but instead will be traded in the *intermediate securities markets*, such as the Unlisted Securities Market (USM).

- The company becomes listed on the Stock Exchange. By now it is a very successful commercial organisation. Future expansion will usually be by means of *rights issues* of its shares.

Flotation

Flotation is a term used to describe the process by which a company seeks to raise capital through offering its securities on an established market. A company flotation took place in the example given above, when the company first sought capital by offering its securities in one of the intermediate securities markets. There are a number of these markets, the most important being:

(a) **the Unlisted Securities Market**

This was set up in 1980 by the Stock Exchange to provide a regulated securities market for companies not yet able to meet the full listing conditions to become a company quoted on the Stock Exchange. It is sometimes referred to as the 'junior league' of the Stock Exchange;

(b) **the Over the Counter Market**

This is an alternative to the markets controlled by the Stock Exchange. It is operated by authorised dealers in securities;

(c) **the Third Market**

This was established by the Stock Exchange in 1987 to pick up the securities being dealt with in the Over the Counter Market. Its rules simply require that sponsorship of a member of the Stock Exchange be obtained. Once this has occurred, admission to the market is available.

The legal, as opposed to the commercial, significance of these markets is that the 1986 Act draws an important distinction between *listed securities* – those submitted to the Official List of the Stock Exchange - and those which have not been so admitted – *unlisted securities*.

The legal controls imposed upon both types of securities as part of the process of financial market regulation is one of the objectives of the Financial Services Act.

Securities

There are five methods which may be used by a public company to invite the public to subscribe for, that is to take up, its securities.

(a) *By making a direct invitation to the public.*
This is achieved by the company issuing a prospectus, a document by which the company advertises the securities it wishes to sell. The prospectus is published and distributed to anyone wishing to take a copy. It may appear in newspapers. The privatisation of state-owned industries during the 1980s was handled in this way.

(b) *By means of a rights issue.*
Well established public companies normally raise additional capital by this method. The company sends each of its members a letter informing them they have been provisionally allotted new shares. If the member pays the price for these shares, the *issue price*, he or she is registered as the new holder. Alternatively, the member may sell the right to subscribe on the share market. The price at which the shares will be offered by the company will be below their current open market value, making them a more worthwhile proposition to the existing members. The number of shares provisionally allotted under a rights issue is related to the number of shares being held at the time by the member. Thus one share may be offered for every two presently held. The letter of provisional allotment is treated as a prospectus, since it is not possible to predict who may end up taking the shares, the member or someone buying the right to subscribe from the member.

(c) *By an offer for sale.*
Here the company disposes of the shares through an intermediary, an *issuing house* which buys the shares and then re-sells them at a higher price to the public. The public offer is made by means of a document referred to as an *offer for sale*, which is treated as a prospectus, and for whose contents both the company and the issuing house are responsible. The issuing house is usually a merchant bank. It will provide the company with advice and assistance to ensure that the issue is successful. An offer for sale is the method generally used for a flotation when a company is being launched as a listed or USM company for the first time. One of the requirements of a flotation is that a substantial number of shares are available to be taken up by new rather than existing investors.

(d) *By a placing.*
Here the securities are initially allotted in large *blocks to a limited number of financial institutions, for resale by these institutions* at a profit. Debenture stock is often issued in this way. The expression *placing* is derived from the institutions taking the securities, which are referred to as *places*.

(e) *By an offer by tender.*
This involves the company or an issuing house inviting tenders for fixed numbers of new shares. Usually a specified price is indicated, and the bidders will put in bids above this figure, shares being allotted to the highest bidders.

Whatever method a company uses to issue its securities, the decision made by the potential investor whether or not to take up the company's securities will be dependent upon whether the investor is satisfied, on the basis of the available information, that the investment is a sound one. An investor will generally be looking for a good potential return from the company, some growth over a given period, and the ability to dispose readily of the interest on the market should he or she choose to do so. Investment decisions, indeed the whole system under which a market for company shares can operate effectively, must be based upon a flow of reliable, accurate and up to date information concerning those companies whose securities are publicly available. Investors are interested not only in the current health of the company, but also its trading record and the forecasts of its future prospects and potential. Of course, it is the companies themselves which are best placed to provide this information. Likewise, they are also best placed to manipulate such information, to distort the true picture and mislead the investor by false and inaccurate statements, by half truths and omissions. Not surprisingly, therefore, it has long been the law that certain standards of accuracy must be met in the publication of company prospectuses. The issue of a prospectus, however, is a *one-off* event. If it has done its job the share issue will be fully subscribed. It should be borne in mind that this is not the end of the story as far as the shares themselves are concerned, since over the lifetime of a company they may be bought and sold on numerous occasions.

One further source of information which may be relied upon by the prospective investor is the audited accounts of the company. The extent to which auditors are liable for this information is considered in Chapter 5.

When a company is seeking to issue new new securities it will use a prospectus. If, however, it is a company quoted on the Stock Exchange, the potential investor has the re-assurance of knowing that in order to obtain a Stock Exchange quotation the company has had to meet the demanding listing requirements set out under the Stock Exchange rules. For the company, a Stock Exchange listing means that its securities are being traded on a highly respected and closely controlled market. One effect of this is on the value of the securities themselves. Listing significantly increases their market value.

The control of listed securities

The Stock Exchange is the leading UK securities market. The admission of a company's securities into this market through a Stock Exchange listing, i.e. being *quoted* on the Stock Exchange, increases the market price of the securities because they can readily be bought and sold. Up to 1984 in order to grant a listing the Stock Exchange required to see the draft prospectus before publication, to satisfy itself that the document met the requirements applied to prospectuses under company legislation then current and that it contained the detailed and demanding information required by the Stock Exchange itself. However, the decision regarding a listing was essentially a private matter between the company and the Stock Exchange.

This position was changed in 1984 by the introduction of statutory regulations which gave effect to three European Community Directives. The Directives demanded a much broader system for the regulation of securities markets than existed under UK domestic law on prospectuses. The system is now controlled by the Financial Services Act 1986, Part IV. The effect is that a listing can only take place of the requirements if the so called 'Yellow Book' (The Admission of Securities to Listing) containing the Stock Exchange regulations are met. These regulations are given the force of law under the 1986 Act. The new system of control has two main features:

(a)   the requirements that listing particulars must be published before the securities are listed. The Companies Registry must have a copy of these particulars delivered to it for filing, in effect making the listing particulars a form of prospectus; and

(b)   the imposition of continuing obligations upon the company; for example, to tackle the possibility of directors using inside information to their advantage by buying or selling the company's shares in the period preceding the publication of its results. Admission rules require disclosure of such dealings. Thus admission has the effect of exposing the company to Stock Exchange supervision after the relevant securities have been issued.

Admission to list

The Stock Exchange is allowed a maximum of six months to consider an application, although a decision is normally made in a much shorter time. Application procedures and the conditions to be fulfilled by applicants are contained in the Yellow Book.

Under s.144 it is provided that a transaction involving a listed security is not to be treated as void or voidable solely on the grounds of a breach of listing particulars. However, a claim for damages to recover losses resulting from untrue or misleading statements or the omission of information by the company is not prevented under the section.

Under s.145 the Stock Exchange has the power to suspend a listing. This power is sometimes exercised where take-over rumours are distorting the normal functioning of the market in the company's shares.

Contents of the listing particulars

S.146 requires the company to provide information regarding its *financial condition*. The section defines this as information which investors and their professional advisers would reasonably require in order to make an informed assessment of the company's financial position, its assets and liabilities, its profits and losses, its prospects, and the rights attaching to the securities it is offering.

Less information may be provided to more sophisticated investors.

The Yellow Book contains further requirements.

The effect is that under the listing rules, a company in supplying the Stock Exchange with the listing particulars is really furnishing it with a prospectus.

Supplementary listing particulars

Under s.147 further particulars – *called supplementary particulars* – must be approved by the Stock Exchange and registered with the Registrar of Companies, if any of the following circumstances have occurred:

• there has been a significant change affecting any matter included in the original particulars;

- a new matter has arisen which would have been included in the original particulars if it had been present at the time;

- a significant mistake, i.e. not a trivial change or mistake, has been made in the particulars.

Remedies

S.150 allows *"any person who had acquired any of the securities in question and suffered loss in respect of them"*, the right to claim compensation. The claim may be brought against those responsible for the listing particulars in cases of material mis- statements, material omissions and misleading opinions. The word *'material'* appears to be related to the loss sustained, and a subscriber may thus bring a claim under the section when he or she was not aware of the error, or had not even seen the particulars at all.

The section specifically states that any other civil or criminal liability arising from errors in the listing particulars is not defeated, that is replaced, by it. Consequently, a claim can be brought on grounds of fraud, or in respect of any of the forms of misrepresentation.

Under s.47 criminal liability is imposed upon anyone making false statements in particulars. The section grants the court power to impose a fine and/or up to seven years imprisonment. Civil liability under s.150 is attached to, amongst others, the issuing house and its directors, and anyone expressly taking responsibility for any part of the particulars (s.152).

Defences

S.151 provides that a person who has contravened s.150 shall not be liable if it can be shown:

(a) that he or she had a reasonable belief in the truth of the statements, or that it was reasonable to allow the relevant omission;

(b) that the statement was by an expert and that he or she had a belief in the expert's competence, and of that expert's consent to the inclusion of the statement in the particulars;

(c) when (a) and (b) cannot be established, that the person published a correction or took reasonable steps to have one published and reasonably believed it had been.

The control of unlisted securities

Part V of the Financial Services Act 1986 is designed to replace the provisions regulating prospectuses contained in the Companies Act 1985. At present most offers of unlisted securities are subject to detailed USM (Unlisted Securities Market) regulations, and Part V is simply designed to give these rules statutory force.

Under these arrangements control applies only to *offers of unlisted securities*. Thus there is no provision made for continuing control. The provisions apply largely to the issue of *company prospectuses*, the word *prospectus* being specifically referred to in the relevant sections of the Act. S.160 provides that no advertisement affecting any securities can be made unless a prospectus has been delivered to the Registrar of Companies, or the advertisement is such that no agreement can be entered into as a result of it until a prospectus has been delivered to the Registrar. S.163 specifies the information to be contained in the prospectus. It is the same as that specified in s.146 for listing particulars. S.164 provides for the issue of a supplementary prospectus, a parallel provision to s.147 (see above). Compensation is dealt with under s.166 (paralleling s.150), and defences under s.167 (paralleling s.151). Those responsible for issuing a prospectus are defined in s.168, which is an analogue of s.152.

Exemptions from S.160

The old law on prospectuses required that a prospectus was only needed when an offer was made to the public. This expression caused the courts some difficulty. The position under the 1986 Act is to specify three main areas in which exemption from the need to provide a prospectus in the issue of company securities will apply. These are:

- advertisements of a *private character*. Orders will be made to specify what these are to include, e.g. a rights issue;

- advertisements where investment is a merely incidental aspect of the arrangement; an example would be a scheme under which tenants take shares in the management company which manages their properties;

- offers to professionals in the securities markets.

The securities of private companies

We have seen that private companies cannot offer their securities to the public (s.190). One of the problems this raises is the question of trying to define the expression *offer to the public*, a point referred to above. How widely can a private company offer its shares before it falls foul of s.170? The Department of Trade and Industry has the power to make regulations excepting certain categories of offer from the s.170 provisions.

These categories are:

(a)   advertisements of a private character;

(b)   advertisements which deal with investment only incidentally;

(c)   advertisements addressed to persons who appear to the DTI to be sufficiently expert to understand the risks involved.

Common Law Remedies for Defects in Listing Particulars and Prospectuses

We have seen that the 1986 Act provides compensation for breach of statutory duty in failing to meet the information requirements demanded of listing particulars and prospectuses under its relevant provisions. Nowadays, thorough scrutiny of draft prospectuses by merchant banks and the Stock Exchange generally identifies errors before publication - usually referred to as the *pre-vetting procedure*. The statutory remedies do not in any case apply to securities issued by private companies where individuals have suffered loss as a result of misleading statements. Here the injured party must rely on common law remedies. This involves an examination of the law of misrepresentation.

Misrepresentation

A misrepresentation is a material mis-statement of fact which induces the making of a contract. Misrepresentations may be fraudulent, negligent or innocent. The remedy of misrepresentation is available to the subscriber against the person from whom the shares were acquired, that is either the company itself or an issuing house. If misrepresentation can be established, the injured party may rescind the contract or bring a claim for damages.

Rescission

Rescission is an equitable remedy. Under it the parties are restored to their pre-contractual position. The shareholders name is taken off the register and the company returns to the shareholder any money paid for the shares plus interest. Rescission is available in respect of any of the forms of misrepresentation referred to above, but the problem with it is that the right to rescind is lost if the action is not brought quickly, or if the contract has been affirmed. Usually, in the case of contracts for shares, the right to rescind has been lost before it can be exercised.

The remedy of rescission is only available against the company and not, for example, against its directors. It can only be obtained if the following conditions are met:

(a)   that the company had either actual or constructive knowledge that the contract was made on the basis of the misrepresentation; and

(b)   it was made by someone having authority to act as an agent of the company: *Lynde v Anglo-Italian Hemp Spinning Co* 1896. On this point it should be noted that:

   (i)   a promoter cannot be an agent of the company before its formation;

   (ii)   the person misled may still rescind if the company is aware of the promoter's misrepresentation when the shares are allotted: *Re: Metropolitan Coal Consumer's Association* 1892;

   (iii)   a company will be liable for an experts report concerning it unless the company clearly states it cannot verify the accuracy of the report: *Re: Pacaya Rubber Company* 1914.

Damages

The remedy of damages may be sought at common law in the tort of deceit for fraudulent misrepresentation, and under the principle in *Hedley Byrne v. Heller and Partners* 1964 in the tort of negligence for negligent mis-statements.

In the leading case of *Derry v. Peek* 1889 deceit was defined as, *"a false statement made knowingly, without belief in its truth, or recklessly, careless whether it be true or false"*. It thus covers not only the deliberate lie, but also the statement which the maker thinks might be untrue. Both forms of conduct involve deception. Of course, it is the task of proving this state of mind that is most difficult to establish in bringing a claim. Moreover, a claim can only be brought where:

- the plaintiff was a person intended to rely on the statement; for example, when shares are bought on the open market. A statement made in the prospectus which was published to induce subscriptions for the shares will not give rise to liability, for the method of acquisition is a different one (*Peek v. Gurney* 1873);

- the plaintiff was induced by the statement to take the shares, even if it was only one of the factors that influenced the subscriber (*Edgington v. Fitzmaurice* 1885). When the plaintiff has made independent enquiries and relied on them in arriving at the decision to take shares, the misleading statement is irrelevant.

If a plaintiff is awarded damages, their membership of the company is not terminated. This is based on the principle that capital should not be returned to the company's members, because to do so would be to reduce the fund available to the company's creditors (*Houldsworth v. City of Glasgow Bank* 1880). Such a condition does not apply where the successful claim has been brought against a party other than the company, for instance against a director who authorised the fraudulent statement.

In order to bring a successful action for negligent misrepresentation, under the *Hedley Byrne* principle it will be necessary for the plaintiff to show that the defendant owed him or her a duty of care, which has been broken causing economic loss suffered by the plaintiff. There need not be a contractual relationship between the plaintiff and the defendant. There is some doubt about the application of the principle in a company law context. It is not clear whether company directors or the company itself owes a duty of care to persons subscribing for its securities. Some members of the House of Lords in *Hedley Byrne* felt that such a duty might arise in certain circumstances, such as a rights issue where the offer of securities is being made to existing members. Section 2(1) of the Misrepresentation Act 1967 allows for damages to be claimed in cases of pre-contractual negligent misrepresentations made by one of the contracting parties to the other. Its advantage over the common law remedy is that the burden of proof (i.e. that there was no negligence) lies with the defendant.

Criminal liability

Criminal liability for false statements arises under s.47 Financial Services Act 1986. The section applies to a statement, promise or forecast which is misleading, false or deceptive, where the person making it knows it is misleading, etc., or makes it recklessly.

It is also an offence under s.19 Theft Act 1968 for an officer of a company knowingly to make a statement which is false, misleading or deceptive, with intent to deceive the members or creditors of the company. In the case of a prospectus, s.19 can only apply to a rights issue since the section applies to persons who at the time of the offence were members.

A further example of the use of the criminal code in relation to securities is contained in the statutory rules relating to insider dealing.

Insider Dealing

Shares are commodities which are bought and sold in the market in much the same way as other products. The Stock Exchange is the established market place for this commercial activity. For the Stock Exchange to function as an effective market there has to be confidence that the value of the securities being traded on it reflects their true value. Neither buyers nor sellers of securities will be willing to trade freely if they face the prospect of buying, or selling, for less than the real value of the securities in question. How, then, can a real value be arrived at? The answer is through a process of valuation based upon all the relevant information available at the time. Share values are a reflection of general information regarding national economic performance and the condition of the particular market a company deals in, and specific information about the fitness of the company itself.

Whilst general information is usually available to all market participants, for instance by following the financial press, information specific to the company itself inevitably is held by those who are closest to the company, either because they work for it, or through their association with it as advisors, or as friends or relations of its employees. Such people can gain information about the company before the rest of the market, giving them advance access to the value of its securities, and enabling them to buy or sell advantageously. Such a practice is known as *insider dealing*. In the United Kingdom it is regarded as unethical, as likely to undermine market confidence in the Stock Exchange, and in cases where the insiders are the directors, as a breach of trust.

Legislation was introduced in 1980 making insider dealing a criminal offence. The United Kingdom was the first European country to respond in this way. Financial markets had up to that time regarded it as quite proper for those with access to specific financial information to use it to their own advantage. It was a perk of the job. The new legislation not only removed this perk; it made it a criminal offence, and thus raised one of the continuing arguments about the proper role of business law: is it to facilitate wealth creation or to set standards of business behaviour? In practice it usually seeks to balance these conflicting pressures.

The present law is contained in the Criminal Justice Act 1993, which defines the offence of insider dealing by restricting what an insider can do. Only an individual can commit an offence, not a company. The essence of the offence involves defining insider information, considering how that information may be gained, and restricting its use.

S.56 of the Act treats as insider information, information which:

- relates to particular securities or to a particular issuer of securities (i.e. thus excluding general securities and their issuers);
- is specific or precise;
- has not been made public; and
- if it were made public would be likely to have a significant effect on the price of any securities.

Price-sensitive information is the term used to describe inside information which would be likely to affect significantly the price of securities if it were made public, and such securities are hence termed *price-affected securities*. Information is regarded as publicly available if it has been published for investors or it can be found in public records such as the companies file. It is treated as in the public domain even though it can only be obtained using diligence and expertise or observation, or has been communicated to be a section of the public rather than generally, or has been published outside the UK.

The Act seeks to restrict identified categories of people from making use of inside information by way of dealing in (i.e. buying or selling) price affected securities. Crucial therefore is the way in which the Act describes who these *insiders* are. A person has information as an insider only if they know it is inside information which they have obtained from an inside source. It comes from an inside source if it is obtained by them through their position as a director, employee or shareholder of an issuer of securities, or through their employment office or profession. This latter category is a wide one. Professional advisors, financial journalists, and even staff working for the printer who puts out price sensitive information are swept up by it. All these people are classed as primary insiders.

The legislation also extends to secondary insiders, that is people who either directly or indirectly get the information from a primary insider. For example if a director was to give a friend inside information about the company concerning a possible take-over the friend would become a secondary insider, or tippee i.e. someone who has been tipped off. If however the director had publicly disclosed the information it would no longer be *inside* information, and anyone using it would not consequently be regarded as a secondary insider.

The basic aim of the 1993 legislation is the protection of markets rather than individuals. It creates criminal offences, carrying a maximum of seven years imprisonment, and unlimited fine, which are committed by an insider who deals on a regulated European market in price affected securities, or who encourages another person to deal, or who simply discloses to a person inside information other than in the proper performance of the function of the discloser's employment, office or profession. Only individuals can be prosecuted, not companies, and the decision to prosecute must be made by the Secretary of State or the Director of Public Prosecutions.

The Act does not grant any civil remedy. A director who is in breach may be liable to account to the company for any profit made, as in *Regal (Hastings) Ltd. v. Gulliver* considered earlier but generally in insider dealing cases it will not be the company who is the loser, but rather the market participants deprived of the inside information

The Alteration of Share Capital

The memorandum of association of a company with a share capital has to include a capital clause specifying the amount the company is authorised to raise by the issue of shares. Subsequently the company may wish to make changes to the capital clause, probably to enable it to raise more capital by the issue of new shares. Alteration of share capital is controlled by s.121 CA 1985, which sets out the grounds on which an alteration is permitted. A company may:

(i)   increase its share capital, which may be achieved by means of an ordinary resolution to alter the capital clause, if the articles permit it (Table A does). If they do not then a special resolution is needed to alter them. That same resolution can also be used to authorise the increase;

(ii)   consolidate, or sub-divide shares. Consolidation involves converting a number of individual shares into a single share, whereas sub-dividing occurs where a single share of, say, a £1 nominal value is split into four shares of 25p nominal value. Sub-dividing in this way is useful where the market value of individual shares has become very high, and members wish to have more manageable units, perhaps with a view to selling their shares. A successful private company may be operating on the basis of perhaps only 100 shares with a nominal value of £1, which were issued when the company was first established, but which now have a market value measured in thousands of pounds;

(iii) convert shares into stock, or vice versa. *Stock* is a members holding expressed in money terms. A member may hold £100 worth of stock as an alternative to 100 £1 shares. The stock can be sold in any units the holder wishes, rather than in the case of shares which are fixed units and can only be transferred in that way. Stock is thus more flexible. If articles allow it, fully paid shares can be converted into stock, and stock reconverted into paid up shares of any denomination. Stock cannot be issued directly by a company under English company law, however, so it can only be created through the conversion of shares;

(iv)   cancel unissued shares, thus eliminating the difference between the nominal capital of the company and its issued capital.

An alteration in cases (ii), (iii) and (iv) above is achieved by means of a company resolution. Table A provides than an ordinary resolution is sufficient. Alternatively the unanimous written resolution procedure may be used to achieve any of these alterations.

Capital reduction

It is a basic principle of company law that a company must maintain its share capital. This is essentially to protect the company's creditors, who are entitled to expect that capital will not be returned to the members and that shares will be paid for in full. A creditor may however expect that capital can be lost through business misfortune.

Thus provisions exist:

- to stop capital being watered down as it comes in, through the payment of underwriting commission and the issue of shares at a discount; and

- to stop capital going out of the company by means of various methods whose effect is the dissipation of capital, for instance where the company pays dividends out of capital instead of distributable profits.

The broad aim of the law is to ensure that the financial standing of the company bears some relation to the nominal value of its share capital.

Exceptions to the principle

There are certain particular and general exceptions to the basic principle of capital reduction, where it is lawful for capital to be diminished. Particular exceptions are those under which the court can order a company to purchase its own shares as a remedy for minority shareholders. Thus where there is minority objection to: alteration of articles under s.5 CA 1985; the re-registering of a public company as a private company under s.54; or where the minority have established unfair prejudice under s.459, the court may order the purchase of the shares of the minority by the company.

General exceptions are contained in s.135. This allows a company to reduce the share capital if:

(a)   a special resolution is passed; and

(b)   the articles permit (Table A art 34 does); and

(c)   the court confirms the resolution.

The grounds upon which this statutory power can be exercised are:

- to reduce or extinguish liability on issued shares for unpaid amounts (which is very rare);

- to cancel paid up share capital lost or no longer represented by available assets (i.e. the tidying up of the company books following trading losses/depreciation);

- to pay off paid-up shares in excess of the company's commercial needs (e.g. where it is reducing the scope of its commercial activities).

In *Re: Westburn Sugar Refineries* 1951 it was said that the court should always sanction the reduction unless to do so would be unfair regarding the interests of the creditors, shareholders or the public.

Directors duties on a serious capital loss in a public company

In a public company if its net assets fall to 50% or less of its called up share capital the directors must within 28 days of becoming aware call a meeting of the company to consider the commercial position. There are criminal sanctions for failure to comply.

Purchase by a company of its own shares

Basically such a transaction is unlawful, originally at common law under the *rule in Trevor v. Whitworth* 1887, and now under s.143 CA 1985. If a company buys back its own shares a criminal offence is committed. The company can be fined, and authorising officers may be fined and/or imprisoned. However a purchase is lawful where:

- shares were acquired under a s.135 capital reduction;

- there has been a court order under ss.5, 54 or 459;

- shares have been *forfeited* for non payment (i.e. where the company has expropriated them from a member who has defaulted in making payment);

- there has been a *redemptional purchase* of shares. (see below)

Redeemable shares

Under s.159 a company limited by shares may issue *redeemable* shares if certain conditions are satisfied. These are that:

(i)   such an issue is permitted by the articles;

(ii) some shares have been issued which are not redeemable;

(iii) the redeemable shares are fully paid;

(iv) the shares are redeemed either from distributable profits, or out of the proceeds of a fresh share issue made for the purpose (s.160).

Redeemable shares are those which are capable of being bought back by the company. Under the terms of the issue they may be definitely redeemable, or be redeemable at the option of either the company or the shareholder. When shares are redeemed they are treated as cancelled. The issued share capital is reduced accordingly, but the authorised share capital remains unaltered. Redeemable shares may be issued as either ordinary or preference shares.

Financial assistance for the purchase of a company's shares

The basic rule, contained in s.151, provides that no financial assistance, direct or indirect, may be provided by a company or its subsidiaries for the purpose of acquiring shares in itself. Direct assistance would include a loan; indirect assistance would occur where the company issued a guarantee to support a loan given by a third party. There are however exceptions to the section, and thus financial assistance can be provided:

- to assist in management buy-out schemes;

- where the loan is made in the ordinary course of the company's business, for example where a finance company lends commercially to X, who uses the loan to purchase shares in the company;

- to assist in employee share schemes, by providing loans to employees (including directors);

- to assist employees (other than directors) in taking up shares in the company in the ordinary way.

Other exceptions include:

- the distribution of assets by way of a lawful dividend, or distribution of profits on a winding-up;

- the issue of *bonus* shares. Bonus shares are shares issued to existing members which they do not have to pay for. Usually the issue of such shares is funded by the company capitalising its profits, i.e. using profits to issue more shares;

- the lawful redemption or purchase of shares;

- arrangements and compositions with creditors made under the Insolvency Act 1986.

Consequences of contravention

If the financial assistance rules are broken:

    (i)   the company is liable to a fine and defaulting officers to a fine and/or imprisonment;

    (ii)   the directors will be liable to compensate for any losses on the basis of a breach of trust: *Wallersteiner v. Moir* 1974;

    (iii)   any securities given for providing financial assistance are void: *Selangor United Rubber Co. v. Cradock (No.3)* 1968; and

    (iv)   guarantees similarly provided are unenforceable: *Heald v. O'Connor* 1971.

Under s.155 the rules are relaxed for private companies provided they meet certain conditions, e.g. that the company's net assets are not thereby reduced, or if they are that the financial assistance comes from distributable profits.

Company Borrowing

As a legal person a company can borrow money. The term *loan capital* is applied to the funds the company raises in this way. The level of borrowing, and the procedures to be followed to exercise the power to borrow may be regulated by the memorandum and articles if the company so chooses. If these matters *are* regulated, and the company borrows in breach of them, the lender may still be able to hold the company bound through the application of the internal management rule (the rule in *Turquands Case*) and s.35 Companies Act 1989.

When a company borrows, the lender may require some form of security which the lender can realise in the event of the company defaulting on the loan. This is not a legal requirement, simply commercial common sense. The larger the borrowing, the more likely it is that the lender will demand protection in the event of a default. If security is not taken the lender is an unsecured creditor, and very vulnerable in the event of the company getting into financial difficulties, since secured creditors are able to realise their securities first, often leaving the unsecured creditors with virtually nothing left.

In larger companies there will be plenty of property which can be used as security, such as land and buildings, equipment, stock, together with non tangibles like book debts. In small companies however, with few assets, a lender such as a bank may require individual members to provide personal security. In this way the shareholders/directors of a company in which they are the only members can find that much of the benefit of limited liability is lost to them when they have to put up their homes as a security in relation to their company borrowing.

If a lender to a company takes no security the lender is simply an unsecured creditor, having the capacity to sue the company on the debt (and takes steps to enforce any judgment awarded), or petition as a creditor to have the company wound up if the debt is for £750 or more. A lender who has security is in a much stronger position, since if the company defaults the security can be used to meet the debt.

Debentures

Company borrowing and the term *debenture* are so closely linked it can sometimes be difficult to distinguish between them. The most widely recognised judicial definition of a debenture is that of Chitty J in *Levy v. Abercorris Slate and Slab Co.* 1887 where he said, *"In my opinion a debenture means a document which either creates a debt or acknowledges it and any document which fulfils either of these conditions is a `debenture'. I cannot find any precise legal definition of the term, it is not either in law or commerce a strictly technical term...."* A debenture is thus no more than a written acknowledgement of a debt a company owes. Although debentures are usually secured, they do not have to be. If they are unsecured they are sometimes called *naked* debentures. S.744 Companies Act 1985 does not attempt a definition, but it does allude to the question of security, for it states that a debenture *"includes debenture stock, bonds and any other securities of a company, whether contributing a charge on the assets of the company or not."* A charge involves taking security; the Act indicates that this is not necessary to create a debenture.

Many types of company borrowing arrangements come within the umbrella term debenture. At its simplest it can be merely a written note evidencing a debt, but in its usual commercial sense a debenture is regarded as a document expressing some secured obligation. This security will be in the form of a *charge* on property of the company. This is most important, for a secured debenture holder will normally have the power to appoint a receiver to protect the holders interests if the company defaults in any way, or if the property charged is felt to be in jeopardy.

Debentures are issued in accordance with the articles of the company, and this usually means that their issue will be made following a board resolution. There are three main types of debenture:

- the *single debenture*, where the borrowing is from a single source, such as a merchant bank;

- a *series of debentures*. This occurs for example where the company is raising loan capital from its members. Although each loan is separate usually it is intended that the lenders should rank equally as regards repayment.

- *debenture stock*. This method is used to raise very large sums of money from different lenders at the same time and on the same terms. It is the way public companies raise loan capital on the investment market. The process of issuing debenture stock is not dissimilar to a share issue, however the debenture stock holders are a class of creditors rather than company members. Usually a trust deed is created, under which trustees are appointed to look after the interests of the investors as a class. The trust deed will provide for such matters as meetings of holders of the debenture stock at which votes can be cast, so that their collective views can be ascertained and then represented to the company by the trustees. Usually nowadays all the loans are aggregated into a total fund which is advanced to the company by the trustees. From the company's point of view this is a single loan, but it is made up of loans from different parties and the amount they have contributed determines the amount of debenture stock they hold. The trustees have a contractual relationship with the company. The use of a trust deed is necessary for two reasons. Firstly if the debentures are secured by way of a legal charge, for example where the company has provided land as security, a legal mortgage is created. This is a legal estate in land, and as such cannot be vested in more than four people. Since the company has borrowed from many people the appointment of trustees under the trust deed enables them to hold the land subject to the security as legal owners on behalf of the debenture holders.

Secondly individual lenders may have such a small investment that they would not find it worth their while to take enforcement action if the company defaulted on its obligations, for instance by failing to pay interest. Under the trust deed the entitlements of the individual lenders become the responsibility of the trustees and must be enforced by them. This is a valuable benefit to the lenders.

Although it is not a legal requirement, the company will usually maintain a register of debenture holders. If this is done the debentures so registered are transferable in the way that shares are. Under s.185 a *debenture certificate* must be issued by the company within two months of the allotment or the transfer of debentures or debenture stock.

Charges

A charge is a security interest which the owner of the asset(s), the *chargor* agrees to create in favour of a creditor, the *chargee*. The agreement will provide that the asset charged may be sold by the chargee in the event of default by the chargor. There are two methods used to secure debentures by means of charges, the *fixed charge* and the *floating charge*.

Fixed charges

A fixed or specific charge is like an ordinary mortgage taken out by an individual. It is created by taking out a legal or equitable mortgage on specific property, such as land or equipment. Its advantage is that it attaches to specifically identified assets, and thereafter these assets cannot be disposed of lawfully by the chargor without the chargee's permission. Moreover it should be possible to ascertain the value of the asset at the time the charge is created.

Floating charges

A floating charge also requires the property subject to the charge to be identified, but the charge recognises that the chargor can deal with the property in the ordinary course of business without the permission of chargee. This is referred to sometimes as the *trading power*. A floating charge can only be an equitable charge, but it can apply to company property both present and future.

In *Re: Yorkshire Woolcombers Association Ltd.* 1903 Romer LJ identified three characteristics of the floating charge. He said *"it is a charge on a class of assets of a company present and future; if that class is one which, in the ordinary course of the business of the company, would be changing from time to time; and if you find that by the charge it is contemplated that, until some future step is taken by or on behalf of those interested in the charge, the company may carry on its business in the ordinary way as far as concerns the particular class of assets...."*

Floating charges are used to charge company property of a fluctuating kind which are constantly in use or being turned over in the course of business. Stock in trade is a common example. The company is free to acquire and sell stock subject to the charge, the trading power, unless the charge *crystallises*. Crystallisation results in the floating charge becoming a fixed charge, an event which will occur on any one of a number of grounds. These are where:

(i)   a receiver is appointed;

(ii)   the company goes into liquidation;

(iii)   the company ceases to trade (*Re: Woodroffes (Musical Instruments) Ltd.* 1986), or sells its business (*Re: Real Meat Co. Ltd.* 1996);

(iv)   the debenture enables the charge holder to convert the floating charge into a fixed charge by notice and the notice is given;

(v)   an event identified in the charge document as giving rise to automatic crystallisation has occurred. An example would be if a company creditor seeks to execute a judgment in his favour against the property charged. This last ground has been the subject of considerable controversy, since the crystallisation can occur without either the company or the charge holder being aware of it.

Once crystallisation takes place the directors can no longer deal with the assets charged. Of course it will not be known what the value of the assets actually is until crystallisation has occurred and the charge fixes to the assets in question. Whether a charge is fixed or floating depends upon the substance of the charge; express words identifying it as one or the other are not regarded as totally conclusive. In *Re: Brightlife Ltd.* 1987 Hoffmann J held that a charge over the book debts of a company, expressed as a fixed charge, was in reality a floating charge.

Registration and preferences

Unlike debentures, which do not require registration under statute, charges do require registration. If they are not registered within 21 days of creation the charge is void, and the holder becomes an unsecured creditor (s.395 CA 1985). A charge is also void if it is regarded as a preference.

A *preference* is something a company does or allows to be done which puts a company creditor in a better position in the event of the company going into insolvent liquidation, than they would otherwise have been in. For example if the directors, anticipating imminent company insolvency but intending they will subsequently set up a new business, grant a charge over company land to its principal creditor and trade supplier in the hope the supplier will continue to supply the new company, the charge is likely to be treated as a preference. The intended effect of the charge is to place the supplier before other company creditors, and the charge will consequently be a void one.

The rules on preferences are contained in the Insolvency Act 1986. A floating charge given as a preference within twelve months of commencement of a winding up (or within two years to a connected person) is void. Any other charge given as a preference within six months of winding up commencing (or within two years to a connected person) is also void. A connected person includes a director or shadow director, or an associate of that person or the company itself. This covers a spouse, and relatives of the individual or the spouse, namely parents, siblings, children an uncle, aunt, nephew or niece.

Priority of charges

Sometimes a company may create successive charges over the same property. In these circumstances the general rule is that they rank in order of creation. This means second and subsequent chargees have less valuable security than the first chargee, who can satisfy full liability out of the assets subject of the charge. Furthermore the normal rule is that a fixed charge will rank in priority to a floating charge even if the floating charge was created before it. However if the floating charge contained a prohibition against creating a fixed charge over the same property, and the fixed chargee was aware of this prohibition when he took the charge, his charge will rank after the floating charge. Apart from this one exception the fixed chargee is in a far more secured position than the floating chargee, whose interest is further eroded by certain other creditors who take priority over the floating charge. They are:

(i)   statutory preferential creditors, such as the Inland Revenue, (even though they are unsecured);

(ii)   the claims of a judgment creditor who executed judgment on the property subject to the charge before the charge crystallised;

(iii)   the owner of any property subject to the charge who has the protection of a retention of title clause (a *Romalpa* clause). The use of such clauses is discussed in Chapter 9. The essence of a retention of the title clause is that it enables a seller of goods to retain title in them even when they have passed into the possession of the buyer until the buyer has paid for them in full.

Other Forms of Financing

These include short term loans, such as overdraft arrangements. Additionally, through the use of *factoring* a company may raise money by selling its debts.

The acquisition of assets

A limited company is able to acquire property and property rights in the same way as an individual. As well as purchasing property outright, companies frequently take leased property such as vehicles and land under which they acquire limited rights of ownership. They also obtain goods on credit terms, for example by hiring equipment. The legal considerations applying to such arrangements are examined in detail later in the book.

Assignment   "Its limited liability and all that"

Peter Green's company, Wildblood Records Ltd., was in financial difficulties, and the situation was entirely of Peter's making. As its managing director he had become over ambitious. He decided the company should diversify. Ignoring the objects clause which restricts its commercial activities to music promotion, and its articles, which required all contracts over £100,000 to be approved by the company in a general meeting, Peter negotiated a £250,000 loan with the company's bank Gladstone De La Zouche for the purchase of a restaurant.

The restaurant venture was not a success, and within a few months Peter realised that his company was not going to survive. Concerned about the prospect of being left without a business and the income generated from it he acted quickly. He gave instructions to his friend Sarah Parsons, an accountant, to take all the necessary steps to form a new company, and a few weeks later the new company, Phoenix Music Ltd. received its certificate of incorporation. Peter was appointed as its managing director and took 990 of its 1000 £1 ordinary shares. Sarah took the remaining 10. At the first meeting of the new company it was agreed that it would purchase recording equipment belonging to Peter. Peter valued this equipment at £18,000, and this was the price paid for it by Phoenix. In fact the real market value of the equipment was nearer £7,000, and it has subsequently transpired that some of this equipment was not Peters, but belonged to Wildblood Records.

Wildblood Records has now gone into compulsory liquidation. The liquidator, Mohammed Khan, is particularly interested in the extent of Peter Green's personal liability for the misfortunes of Wildblood Records. His initial view is that the company may be able to avoid the borrowing agreement made with the bank on the grounds that it was unconstitutional, that Peter may be in breach of his duty to the company, that he acted unlawfully in selling the company's property to Phoenix Music Ltd., and that Phoenix is merely a sham. During a telephone conversation Mohammed had with Peter to discuss these issues, Peter angrily remarked *"That's business mate! Its limited liability and all that. You can't touch me."*

Task

You work for Mr Khan, and he has asked you to confirm whether his initial ideas concerning the validity of Peter Green's actions are legally sustainable. Coincidentally, you know Sarah Parsons professionally, and over a drink she has asked for your opinion about any possible breach of promoters duties disclosed in the property transaction between Peter and Phoenix Music Ltd.

Provide Mr Khan and Sarah with the information they are seeking.

Legal Terms found in Chapter 5

Agent	• person empowered to make contracts on behalf of another (the principal)
Auditor	• person responsible for carrying out an annual independent investigation into the financial condition of a registered company
Company secretary	• the senior administrative officer of a registered company
Director	• person responsible for the management of a registered company
Disqualification order	• court order issued against a named person preventing them from acting as a director or company promoter for the duration of the order
Member	• a company shareholder
Pre-emption rights	• an arrangement under which a shareholder wishing to sell his shares must first offer them to existing members
Principal	• person who appoints an agent to act on his behalf for the purpose of making contracts
Rights issue	• an issue of new shares offered first to existing shareholders
Shadow director	• someone effectively controlling the board of directors without sitting on the board
Share certificate	• document issued by a company providing evidence that the person named in it is a shareholder
Shareholder	• person holding shares in a company who enjoys all the rights attached to the shares
Undisclosed principal	• principal who has not been identified by his agent at the time of contracting

Chapter 5

The Legal Relationships in Business

The Nature of Legal Relationships

A legal relationship is one where the parties involved, whether as individuals or organisations, are connected to each other by way of legal rights or legal obligations. Because the relationship is a legally recognised one, rather than say one based upon a moral foundation, it is possible to take appropriate measures such as court proceedings if the relationship is upset or damaged. By way of illustration, a business supplier who sells a defective product to a customer will normally find the customer has enforceable rights enabling him to obtain a remedy against the supplier, for the parties are participating in a *legal* relationship.

The nature of a particular relationship is determined by the way the law regards the connection between the parties to it. Different kinds of relationship generate different sets of rights and obligations (or duties). This is only to be expected for the purposes underlying legal relationships vary enormously. Consider for instance the different purposes which bring together in the form of legal relationships employers and employees, directors and shareholders, sellers and buyers of goods and services, and the partners in a partnership. Anyone engaged in business activity needs to recognise and understand the legal consequences which flow from specific types of business relationship. We can approach the task by considering the legal rights and obligations which attach to the key parties involved in business. A useful starting point is the law of agency, which, as we shall see, provides the legal means by which business enterprises are able to conduct their trading activities.

The Key Parties in Business Relationships

Agents

Definition of agency

The concept of agency is fundamental to the commercial operations of every kind of business organisation. It enables a business to use people to transact, on its behalf, with those with whom it wishes to trade. Agency is therefore a legal mechanism under which a person, called the *principal*, authorises another, the *agent*, to act on the principal's behalf. The object of the relationship is to empower the agent to make contracts with *third parties* on his principal's behalf, so that the principal and the third party become contractually bound. Where this result is achieved the agent then drops out of the picture. Rights and obligations arising out of the contract are now those of the principal and the third party. By exercising his power the agent has altered the principal's legal position. Diagrammatically the relationship can be shown as follows:

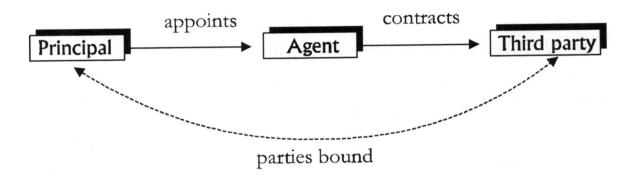

Figure 5.1   The agency relationship

The importance of agency to a business

Were agency arrangements not available to a business it would be obliged to make all its contacts in person. The effect would be to reduce businesses to very small commercial enterprises in which only the proprietor of the business could act on behalf of the business. This would defeat businesses owned by groups of proprietors, such as partnerships, since all the members would need to contact with outsiders collectively. In the case of corporate bodies the result would be even more dramatic. Since a corporation is artificial it can only transact through human agents. Absence of the agency principle would prevent all forms of corporate activity involving trading contracts.

Agency sources

An agency relationship can arise in any of the following ways:

- *Expressly:*
  This occurs where the agent is specifically appointed. Such appointment may be made orally or in writing. An oral arrangement would need to stipulate the scope of the

agency, thus an employer might instruct an employee to negotiate a particular deal for the employer with a named third party, involving perhaps the purchase of some property or the sale of business assets. Alternatively the appointment may be of a more general kind authorising a range of business transactions the agent can make, where perhaps such work is to be the sole or main activity of the employee in question. Written appointment is not a legal requirement unless the agent is to execute deeds on the principals behalf in which case he must be appointed by a deed, granting him what is referred to as a *power of attorney*. The appointment orally or in writing of a director will constitute an express agency, even if the appointment does not stipulate that the director is to act as an agent of the company, since the agency role of company directors is expressed in written form in the articles of association.

- *Impliedly:*

  If the express terms of the appointment fail to specify the full range or precise nature of the appointees role, an agency may be still be recognised by implication. For example appointing a person as a marketing manager, or company secretary will certainly suggest that the employee will have agency powers appropriate or customary to a work role of that kind, either by reference to what previous post holders in that organisation have done, or by reference to the work of someone in that position generally. In addition an express agency appointment will enable the agent to make such contracts which, by implication, are reasonably incidental to the performance of the express agency.

- *By means of apparent authority:*

  Apparent authority is that authority which a third party can reasonably assume the agent to possess, but which the agent in fact has no actual authority to carry out. It can arise where a principal has in some way represented to a third party that the agent has capacity to act on his behalf, and the third party neither knows nor ought reasonably to appreciate that the agent does not in fact have actual authority (i.e. express or implied authority). Such a situation can occur where the principal is aware the agent is making transactions he has no authority to make, but has taken no steps to draw to the third party's attention this absence of authority. In such circumstances the principal will be bound. If however the third party has actual or constructive notice of the absence of real authority of the agent, or if the facts should have aroused suspicion, the third party will not be able to plead apparent authority to hold the principal bound.

In *Reckitt v. Barnett, Pembroke and Slater Ltd.* 1929 the principal had granted the agent wide powers of attorney with the ability to draw cheques "*without restriction*". The agent bought a car for himself, and paid for it with a cheque drawn on the principal's account which he signed as the principals attorney. The principal sought to recover the payment made to the third party. The House of Lords held that the third party was liable, having been put on inquiry by the fact the agent was paying his own debts with his principal's money.

- *By ratification:*

  If an agent carries out an unauthorised act not otherwise binding on the principal, the principal may adopt it retrospectively by means of ratification. Ratification is only possible if the following conditions are satisfied:

(i)   the agent purported to act on the principal's behalf;

(ii)   the principal had full contractual capacity and was named or ascertainable both at the time the agreement was made and when ratification occurred.

In *Kelner v. Baxter* 1866 three people purchased wine for a company which had not yet been formed. On incorporation the company purported to ratify the transaction. It was held it could not do so. As a principal it was not in existence when the contract was made for it, and therefore had no capacity at that time.

In *Keighley, Maxsted & Co. v. Durant* 1901 an agent had authority to buy wheat up to a certain price. He could not purchase at this price, so purchased at a higher price but in his own name. His principal later purported to ratify the transaction, but subsequently failed to take delivery of the wheat, and the seller sued him. The House of Lords held that the principal was not liable. The agents act was unauthorised, and the principal was not disclosed. Ratification was therefore not possible;

(iii) the principal was fully aware of the material facts at the time of ratification, or was willing to ratify whatever the facts may have been.

* *By means of an agency of necessity:*
  This is a special type of agency, which occurs where someone is entrusted with anothers property and has to do something for its preservation. Like apparent authority, agency of necessity involves imposing liability on a principal even though he has not consented to the agents act. The two most significant fields in which such an agency can arise are in the case of:

(i)   the masters of ships, who enjoy wide powers enabling them to sell the cargoes they carry and to purchase necessaries; and

(ii)   carriers on land: *Sims v. Midland Railway* 1913.

The acts of an agent of necessity only bind the principal if:

* there is a genuine emergency;
* it is commercially impracticable to obtain the owners instructions;
* the act in question is carried out in good faith; and
* it is done for the owners benefit.

The type of circumstance where agency of this kind will occur is where perishable goods being transported become subject to the imminent risk of deterioration or harm and it is impossible to obtain the owner's instructions.

In *Great Northern Railway v. Swaffield* 1874, the company successfully claimed against the owner of a horse for the costs of stabling it, when they found no one to receive it when they delivered it to its destination.

Modern communication systems have meant that this type of agency is of much less significance than it was in the past.

Types of agent

Given the importance of agency in commercial operations it is not surprising that many different types of agent are recognised in law. The type of agency indicates the powers the agent in question holds.

- A *universal* agent has unlimited authority to act on his principal's behalf.

- A *general* agent has authority to carry on defined general business activities for his principal e.g. to buy and sell goods of a particular kind.

- A *special* agent is someone carrying out a specific transaction – an example is an agent of necessity.

- An *auctioneer* is employed by an owner of property to sell it at auction. After the fall of the hammer he is also responsible to the buyer. If the principal is not disclosed the auctioneer is personally liable on any contract made. He may also sue on such a contract.

- a *factor* is, quoting Cotton LJ in *Stevens v. Biller* 1883, *"an agent entrusted with the possession of goods for the purpose of sale."* He can sell in his own name, give warranties, and receive payments and give valid receipts. Under the Factors Act 1889 a factor can, as a mercantile agent, pass a good title to goods in his possession in the ordinary course of business, if the third party took them in good faith, even where the factor did not have the owner's authority to sell them. He also has a *lien* on the goods (or the proceeds for their sale) in respect of his charges. This means he can retain the goods as security for payment.

- A *broker* is, like a factor, employed to sell (and buy) goods but unlike a factor does not generally have possession of goods, nor the authority to sell in his own name or the right to a lien regarding his charges. In common with other types of agent however he has implied authority to perform acts usual in his particular business, thus for instance a broker on the London Stock Exchange has implied authority to act in accordance with the customs of that Exchange.

- A *del credere* agent is usually a broker, employed to sell goods but with the special feature that, in return for a payment of commission, the agent *guarantees* to pay the principal the price for the goods in the event of the buyer defaulting.

In *Gabriel (Thomas) and Sons v. Churchill & Sim* 1914 Pickford J described such an agency in the following way. *"Where there is an ascertained or certain sum due from the buyer to the seller and the buyer fails to pay that amount either through insolvency or something that makes it impossible to recover it as in the case of insolvency, the broker has to answer for that default by reason of his having received a del credere commission".*

The Authority of an Agent

We have already seen in our examination of the ways in which an agency relationship can arise that the legal mechanism which gives rise to the agency will provide the means to ascertain the scope of the agent's authority. A principal is only bound where it can be shown that the agent was acting within his authority; once he steps outside this authority the principal is not bound to the third party with whom the agent made the transaction. This simple legal proposition makes it clear why the authority of an agent is the single most important feature of agency law. From it two questions emerge; firstly how is the scope of the agency relationship established; secondly what are the consequences of an agent acting outside his authority? This latter question involves amongst other things a discussion of the duties of an agent and we shall consider it shortly. First let us look at the different types of authority the agent may possess.

- *actual authority*
  Actual or express authority is the specific authority given to the agent by the principal. It may be written or oral. If the instructions given by the principal are ambiguous, then provided the agent acts in a way which represents a reasonable interpretation of the instructions the principal will be bound and the agent will not be liable. (*Weigall & Co. v. Runciman & Co.,* 1916)

- *implied authority*
  An agent has the implied authority to do all those things which can be regarded as necessary for, or incidental to, the carrying out of his express authority. This of course involves examining carefully the terms of the express authority, and what can be reasonably inferred is essentially a matter of construction. An agent instructed to sell property has the implied authority to execute documents transferring title in the property.

- *usual authority*
  Usual authority is simply a limb of the implied authority considered above. An agent has implied authority to do those things which are usual to an agent of that kind. Thus particular types of agent, such as auctioneers and stockbrokers, may be treated as having the authority to do those things usual to their business. This may sometimes require expert evidence to assert what is in fact usual to a particular kind of work. Thus an estate agent employed to find the vendor a purchaser for the property does not have the capacity to sign a contract on the vendor's behalf, but will have such capacity if he has been employed by the vendor to *sell* the property.
  An attempt by the principal to restrict the usual authority of the agent will be ineffective as against a third party who is unaware of it.

In *Watteau v. Fenwick,* 1893, the owner of a public house appointed a person to act as the manager of the premises. The manager took out the licence and his name therefore appeared as licensee over the door. The owner had forbidden the manager to purchase cigars, however he ignored this instruction and bought cigars, on credit, for his own use from a third party. The third party, who had not been paid and was unaware of the restriction, was able to sue the owner for the price. The manager was his agent, and the transaction came within his usual authority.

- *apparent authority*

  Apparent, or ostensible, authority arises where a person represents to a third party that he has authorised an agent to act on his behalf. This may arise by means of a positive act, for instance by the making of an oral statement, or by failure to disabuse the third party of his reasonable belief that the person he is dealing with is an agent with real authority. Both in the case of apparent and usual authority it should be noted that the agent does not have any real authority to do what he has done. Apparent authority is: " ... *merely a form of estoppel and a party cannot call in aid an estoppel unless three ingredients are present (1) representation, (2) a reliance on that representation and (3) an alteration of his position resulting from such reliance.*" Slade J in *Rama Corpn v. Proved Tin and General Investments Ltd.* 1952.

In *Spiro v. Lintern,* 1973, a husband asked his wife to instruct agents to find a buyer for his house. They found a purchaser, and acting on the wife's instructions, signed a contract of sale which they gave to the purchaser. On the strength of this the purchaser instructed a builder to carry out certain repairs to the house. The husband then refused to complete the transaction, arguing that the contract had been made without his authority. The Court of Appeal allowed the purchaser the remedy of specific performance against the husband. He was estopped by his conduct from denying his wife's agency.

The Duties of an Agent

In addition to any obligations expressly agreed to by the agent, he will owe the principal the following duties:

(a)   to exercise due diligence in performing his work, including the use of any special skills associated with his calling.

In *Keppel v. Wheeler,* 1927, an agent employed to sell a block of flats received an offer from a potential purchaser at a lower price than a subsequent offer from another prospective purchaser. The agent then negotiated another transaction under which the second purchaser bought the flats from the first purchaser. The court held the agent liable in damages to the original owners, for he was under a duty to obtain the best price he could;

(b)   to act in good faith and respect the principal's business secrets;

(c)   to avoid placing himself in a position where there is a conflict of interest.

In *Armstrong v. Jackson,* 1917, the plaintiff instructed the defendant to purchase some shares for him. The defendant, a stockbroker, sold the plaintiff his own shares without revealing this to the defendant. The plaintiff was allowed to rescind the contract;

(d)   not to make a secret profit;

(e)   not to delegate, although there are certain expectations to this rule. For example the principal can expressly permit the agent to delegate, and trade usage and custom may also imply such delegation;

(f)   to keep proper accounts.

The Duties of a Principal

These are to pay the agent and to indemnify the agent for acts lawfully carried out and liabilities properly incurred.

Third Party Rights

The rights of a third party with whom the agent has transacted depend upon the nature of the disclosure made by the agent, and the authority the agent holds. Broadly the following observations can be made:

- if the agent acts as an agent for a named principal and within his authority, the third party has rights as against the principal. The principal is liable for the acts of the agent, including wrongful acts committed within the agency such as misrepresentation. In exceptional cases the agent will be personally liable;

- if, acting within his authority, the agent reveals he is an agent but does not reveal the identity of his principal, although the principal is undisclosed he is bound to the third party, and the agent is not personally liable;

- if the agent does not reveal he is an agent, but has acted within this authority, the third party can sue the agent, and the principal when the principal is subsequently disclosed. Similarly they can sue the third party. This is known as the *doctrine of undisclosed principal*;

- if the agent purports to contract on the principal's behalf, but has no authority, the principal will not be liable to the third party, but the third party will be able to claim damages from the agent under the rule in *Collen v. Wright,* 1857 on the grounds of breach of warranty of authority.

The Commercial Agents Regulations 1993

These regulations, which came into effect on the 1st January 1994, implement the EC directive on commercial agents. For the purposes of the regulations commercial agents are agents engaged in transactions involving goods rather than services. A commercial agent can be an individual or a company.

The regulations introduce the following provisions:

- a duty on the part of the agent to comply with the principal's reasonable instructions, and on the part of the principal to provide necessary documentation and information to the agent to enable the agent to carry out his work and to inform the agent when a transaction is not to be executed. These duties are in addition to the common law duties referred to above. They cannot be excluded from any contract but they are clearly not controversial;

- an agent's entitlement to commission where a transaction is concluded either as a result of the agent's action, or where the transaction is made with a previously acquired customer (thus allowing for commission payments on repeat orders). The right to a commission terminates if it is clear that the contract between the principal and the prospective customer will not proceed, provided that this is not due to the fault of the principal;

- regulation of the conclusion and termination of agency contracts. In summary the position is as follows:

    (i) either the principal or the agent can request a signed written contract setting out the terms and conditions of the agency;

    (ii) if a fixed term agency continues beyond the term it is converted to an agreement of indefinite period;

    (iii) the minimum period of notice of termination of the agency is one month for the first year, two months in the second year and three months for the third and all subsequent years;

    (iv) the agent has the right to claim damages as compensation if the agency agreement is terminated. The right arises where the agent terminates it due to the default of the principal, or where age illness or infirmity makes it no longer reasonable for the agent to continue. Compensation is not payable where the principal has terminated on grounds of breach by the agent. A prudent principal is likely to stipulate that the agent must take out insurance against illness at his own expense and for the principal's benefit. It is not clear what the measure of compensation is likely to be.

Business Managers

It is in the field of business management that the practical significance of basic agency principles is most clearly demonstrated. All businesses, irrespective of size, need managers to run them, and by definition a manager will need agency powers to manage. Managers, then, are key figures in the functioning of the legal environment, and careful analysis of their legal role is central to grasping the way in which organisations work.

To understand the role of the business manager we need first to appreciate that English law recognises two quite distinct forms of business enterprise, the registered company, and the partnership. The previous chapter examines the nature of these two organisations in detail. For the purposes of our examination of business managers, which considers their role in the operation of registered companies and of partnerships, we need briefly to note some general points about these two types of organisation.

- a *registered company* is a corporate body, an artificial person in law. It is formed by preparing and presenting to the Registrar of Companies at the Companies Registry in Cardiff a set of documents, the most important of which are the memorandum of association – the company's charter – and the articles of association of the company. This a document regulating such matters as shareholder's rights, the powers of directors, and the holding of meetings. Often a company will adopt the statutory model set of articles, known as Table A. If the registration documents are in order and the registration fees have been paid the Registrar will grant the company a certificate of incorporation. It is now a legal person. In the most common form of company, the company limited by shares, members contribute capital to the company in return for shares in it. Private companies are unable to sell shares publicly; public companies however are allowed to do so. As we shall see, directors manage registered companies on behalf of the company and its members, the shareholders. The principal Act regulating registered companies is the Companies Act 1985, and references below to statutory provisions are references to the 1985 Act unless otherwise specified.

- a *partnership* is a form of unincorporated association whose membership is made up of the individual partners who have joined the business. Unlike company shareholders, whose liability towards the business is limited to the amount, if any, owed on their shares, partners have unlimited liability for the debts of their firm. It is a basic rule of partnership law that all partners have an equal right to participate in its management, and subject to contrary agreement amongst themselves, to contribute equally to losses it makes. Partners manage their business for their own benefit.

Directors as Business Managers

One of the fundamental differences between a limited company and a partnership is found in the management structure. In a partnership, ownership and management are in the same hands, for all partners are entitled to manage the firm and each is an agent of the firm and of the other partners. By contrast, a company is a separate entity which cannot manage itself, but needs people to fulfil this function for it. These people are its directors, and under company legislation all companies must have at least one director. For a public company there must be at least two directors – usually there will be several – and in private companies there are frequently more than the statutory minimum of one.

The function of company directors is crucial to the affairs of the organisation. It needs to be fully grasped to gain any proper understanding of the law relating to company operations. It may help to bear in mind that even in the smallest company there are three distinct components. These are the company *itself,* its *managers* (the directors), and its *owners* or proprietors (the shareholders). A complex legal relationship exists between the three. In a private company with few shareholders, it is common for each shareholder to act also as a director. In larger companies with many members, such an arrangement is not appropriate and consequently ownership and management will not be in the same hands. Public companies invariably appoint as directors people with proven track-records in the management of large organisations, and with commensurately high salaries. In contrast, directors of small private companies may be people with little if any commercial experience. Such experience, whilst clearly of considerable practical importance, is not a legal pre-requisite of directorship.

The following broad observations can be made concerning the relationship between the company, its directors and its shareholders. The directors have certain legal obligations or duties which they owe to the company. They control the company's business affairs and its assets, and in general meeting they are accountable to the company for the way in which they have exercised this control.

They are not accountable to the shareholders as proprietors other than in general meeting. This meeting, has substantial powers and may, for example, be the forum used to remove directors. It is a meeting open to all the membership of the company. Although directors are not answerable to the shareholders as proprietors, directors must, under statute, provide them with a range of information to enable the shareholders to assess how the company is being, and has been operated.

Whilst shareholders are usually responsible for appointing directors, and can remove them, they are not able to tell them how to exercise their powers. At best they can restrict powers available to the directors under the articles, and in respect of some matters it is now necessary for directors to seek approval to act from the general meeting. What this all amounts to is that directors act essentially as agents, not of the shareholders, but of the company itself.

Statutory references below are references to the Companies Act 1985 unless otherwise stated.

Directorship

Definition of a Director

The term director is applied to anyone entrusted with the management of a company who attends board meetings and takes part in their decision-making activities. There must be at least one director for a private company and two for a public one (s.282), but under the articles it is possible to provide for the appointment of more than the statutory minimum, and there is no statutory upper limit. Table A states that unless otherwise determined by ordinary resolution, the number of directors shall not be subject to any maximum but shall not be less than two.

Although the Act defines the term director to include, *"any person occupying the position of director, by whatever name called"* (s.741(1)), this is clearly not a helpful definition because it says nothing about what the nature of what such a position actually involves. Table A is more helpful however. It provides that subject to the provisions of the Act, and the memorandum and articles, and any directions given under the terms of any special resolution, *"the business of the company shall be managed by the directors who may exercise all the powers of the company"*. Thus the role of a director involves managing the company business, and as a consequence of s.741(1), it does not matter whether a person having such responsibility within the company is given the title of director or not. Furthermore, a director could include someone who has not actually been appointed to the board at all, but is acting as if he were a director; a *de facto* director.

This proposition was expressed judicially by Lord Jessel in *Re Forest of Dean Coal Mining Company* 1878 where he stated *"It does not matter much what you call them, so long as you understand what their true position is which is that they are merely commercial men, managing a trading concern for the benefit of themselves and all other shareholders in it"*.

Under the Act a director is an officer of the company; so too is a manager and the company secretary (s.744).

There is no statutory requirement that a director hold shares in the company he is managing.

Shadow Directors

A *shadow director* is a person who gives directions or instructions to the board which the board customarily acts upon. A person acting as a professional adviser to the board, such as a lawyer or an accountant, will not by reason of that capacity alone be regarded as a shadow director. A shadow director is thus someone who is able to exercise influence over the board, even though not formally appointed to sit on it himself. A shadow director could be a majority shareholder who tells the board members how to manage the affairs of the company, but for lack of time or for the avoidance of publicity chooses not to be a member himself. A person does not become a shadow director merely through the act of attempting to assert control. The board must do his bidding.

The possibility of shadow directors being associated with a company is important, since s.741 extends a number of the provisions of the 1985 Act which apply to properly appointed directors, to *de facto* and to shadow directors as well. The relevant provisions are:

*   long-term service contracts;
*   substantial property transactions;
*   loans and similar dealings;
*   interests in contracts made with the company;
*   requirements regarding disclosures to be made in accounts;
*   the rules relating to wrongful trading.

A company is also required to keep a copy of any service contract it has with a shadow director. These contracts are usually held at the company's registered office.

The Company Secretary

Every company must have a secretary, and the secretary has the power to bind the company in any contract of an administrative nature.

> In *Panorama Developments (Guildford) Ltd. v. Fidelis Furnishing Fabrics Ltd.* 1971 the defendant's company secretary hired cars on behalf of the company on the understanding that the cars were being used to meet company customers. In fact he was using them for his own purposes. The court held the company to be bound to pay the hire charges. The transactions were of a kind a company secretary has the power to make, falling within the category of general administrative tasks.

Under Table A, directors have the power to appoint the secretary on such terms as they think fit, and they may also remove the secretary. In a private company the directors can appoint anyone they choose. However, in the case of a public company the directors must be satisfied that the secretary meets the criteria laid down under s.286, namely:

*   appears to the board to have the requisite knowledge and experience to discharge the functions of secretary; and

- possesses one of the qualifications set out under the section. These range from holding a professional qualification as an accountant or lawyer, to having gained the appropriate experience through a previous position held.

Appointment

There are three methods by which a person may be properly appointed as a director. These are:

(i)   under the statement of first directors sent to the Registrar;

(ii)   by being named in the articles;

(iii) under the provisions for appointment laid down in the articles.

One of the forms sent to the Registrar prior to incorporation is the statement of the person(s) to be the first director(s) of the company. S.13(5) says that the person(s) so named is or are deemed to have been appointed as the first director(s). They must, however, have given their consent to act. The appointment of these named people is thus automatic on the granting of the certificate of incorporation.

Often there is a provision in the articles which provides for the appointment of the first directors. If the articles are silent on this point it will be the subscribers who make the appointment. The subscribers are the people named in the memorandum as having agreed to take shares in the company on incorporation.

Whichever means are used to appoint the first directors, that is either the subscribers making the appointment or the articles stipulating who shall act in this capacity, thereafter all subsequent appointments, and also terminations from office, are regulated by the articles.

Broadly, under the standard system contained in Table A, the following arrangements apply:

(i)   at the first annual general meeting after incorporation, all directors must retire. They may, of course, be reappointed at the meeting;

(ii)   at all subsequent annual general meetings one-third of the board must retire. This is referred to as retirement by rotation. Again, there is nothing to prevent a retiring director from being re-elected. Which directors are to retire is determined by length of office, but if they were all appointed at the same time, for instance at the first AGM, then the matter is decided by drawing lots;

(iii) a director retiring by rotation who is not replaced is automatically re-elected, unless it is resolved not to fill the vacancy or a resolution to re-elect the director is lost;

(iv)   any member can by written notice give intention to propose a person for election with that person's written consent;

(v)   *casual vacancies*, those occurring between annual general meetings where a director has died or has resigned during his or her term of office, can be temporarily filled by an appointment made by the existing board. They may also appoint additional directors between AGMs if they wish, for instance to replace a director who cannot attend board meetings through illness. The filling of casual vacancies by the board under the articles saves the need to summon a general meeting to do so. However, anyone appointed in this way must retire at the next annual general meeting of the company enabling the members to vote against such director if they wish to do so;

(vi) in a public company directors must be individually elected unless a resolution has been passed, with no votes cast against it, proposing to vote back the whole board (s.291);

(vii) if the articles appoint a director for life such person is not eligible for re-election under the rotation rules, but can still be removed under the statutory removal provisions contained in s.303, by means of an ordinary resolution. The appointment of a director for life under the articles does not give rise to a *personal* contract between that director and the company, a separate contract would be needed for this. In the case of removal from office of a director who has a service contract with the company, a claim for unfair dismissal may be brought by the director;

(viii) a director may only assign his or her directorship by means of a special resolution (s.308) if the articles permit this;

(ix) a director may appoint an *alternate director,* that is, someone to act as a temporary replacement. The alternate may be another director or some other person. If he is another director it is only the alternate who needs to give his consent, whereas the appointment of a new director requires the consent of the board. Alternate directors have full powers and are liable for their own acts and defaults. They are not agents of the directors who appoint them, and they are not entitled to remuneration. Their appointment can be made and terminated by notice to the board given by the appointing directors.

Persons who cannot be appointed

Table A contains no restrictions on who may be appointed as a director, although articles may be drafted to include particular restrictions. For instance the company may seek to exclude minors from acting as directors, or perhaps another company.

Under statute, a person cannot be a company's sole director and secretary at the same time, nor its sole director and auditor. In addition statute provides that no person shall be appointed as a director of a public company, or of a private company which is the subsidiary of a public company, if at the time of his appointment he has reached the age of 70. This provision may be varied or excluded altogether under the articles, and in any case such a person may be appointed by the members in general meeting by an ordinary resolution of which special notice (of 28 days) has been given.

Under the Company Directors Disqualification Act 1986 it is an offence for an undischarged bankrupt to act as a director without permission of the court. Articles may provide that anyone who has been bankrupt shall not be appointed as a director, and Table A more specifically states that a directors office becomes vacant on his bankruptcy. The 1986 Act also empowers the court to make a disqualification order against a named person. The person named is then prevented for the duration of the order except by leave of the court from:

- being a director of a company;
- being concerned with, or taking part in, directly or indirectly, the promotion, formation or management of a company (s.1).

Grounds for a disqualification order

Under the 1986 Act a number of grounds are identified under which the court may grant a disqualification order. Breach of an order renders the disqualified person liable to criminal proceedings carrying a maximum penalty of six months imprisonment, and it also renders the offender personally liable for the company's debts. These are formidable penalties. The imposition of personal liability, with its effect of lifting the corporate veil, is seen as an appropriate way to deal with someone who has had a disqualification order made against him because he has shown himself not fit to be a director, yet has continued in breach of the order to manage a company.

The grounds include:

(a)   *conviction of an indictable offence (s.2)*

An indictable offence is one which can be tried before a Crown Court, however a s.2 offence may alternatively be dealt with summarily before Magistrates. The Crown Court can on conviction disqualify for up to 15 years, the Magistrates Court up to five years. There is no minimum disqualification period.

One of the most common offences associated with company affairs is fraud. In *R v. Corbin* 1984 the defendant ran a business selling yachts through companies he owned. He was convicted of various fraudulent practices including borrowing from finance companies to buy yachts, falsely stating he had paid a deposit on them. He received two a half years imprisonment and a disqualification order for five years;

(b)   *persistent breaches of company law (s.3)*

Under s.3 the breaches in question involve the failure to provide any return account or documents required to be filed with the Registrar of Companies. There is a presumption that a person has been persistently in default if he has been convicted of a default three times in the past five years. The maximum period for disqualification is five years;

(c)   *fraud, fraudulent trading or breach of duty revealed in a winding up (s.4)*

The court may make an order following the offence of fraudulent trading under s.458 Companies Act 1985, or where the person has otherwise been guilty of any fraud in relation to the company or breach of duty, in his capacity as an officer, liquidator, receiver or manager. The maximum period for disqualification is fifteen years;

(d)   *unfitness (s.6)*

When a company becomes insolvent the person involved in administering the insolvency such as the liquidator or administrative receiver must make a return to the Secretary of State regarding the conduct of the company's directors. On the basis of this information the Secretary of State may apply to the court for a disqualification order against an individual director on the grounds of his unfitness as evidenced in the return. The court must then satisfy itself as to the unfitness before it can make an order. Schedule 1 of the 1986 Act lists the factors to be considered by the court in reaching its decision. In broad terms these factors share a common feature, namely the way the directors have managed the company. The list is a long one, and it includes the following:

(i)   any misfeasance or breach of duty by the director in relation to the company;

(ii)   any misapplication or retention of company money or property by the director;

(iii) the directors responsibility for the company entering into transactions liable to be set aside in a liquidation;

(iv)   the directors failure to keep proper company records, or prepare or file annual company accounts;

(v)   the directors responsibility for the company becoming insolvent;

(vi)   the directors responsibility for any failure by the company to supply goods or services which have already been paid for;

(vii) the directors responsibility for failing to call a creditors meeting in a creditors voluntary winding up;

(viii) any failure by the director to produce a statement of affairs as required in any insolvency proceedings concerning the company.

A disqualification order on grounds of unfitness can only be made if the company is insolvent, which in this context means either that an *administration order* has been made against it, or an *administrative receiver* has been appointed, or at the time of the liquidation its assets are insufficient to pay its debts or other liabilities. An order made on grounds of unfitness must be for a minimum of two years, and may be up to a maximum of fifteen years;

(e)   *matters revealed following a DTI investigation (s.8)*

If the DTI has investigated the affairs of the company and following an inspectors report, or information or documents obtained under powers to require production of documents and enter and search premises (s.447 and s.448 Companies Act 1985 respectively), it appears to the Secretary of State that a disqualification order should be made because a person is unfit to manage or in the public interest, he may apply to the Court. The maximum period for disqualification is fifteen years. This may give rise to a legal challenge against the Secretary of State where the Secretary decides not to proceed with an application. Such was the case in *R v. Secretary of State for Trade and Industry ex parte Lonrho plc* 1992, court proceedings which emerged out of the acrimonious public dispute between Lonrho, under the chairmanship of Tiny Rowland, and the Fayed brothers who had been successful in a take-over bid to acquire Harrods. DTI Inspectors who had criticised the brothers behaviour had not however recommended disqualification, and as a result the Secretary of State decided not to apply to the court for disqualification orders. The challenge against this decision was unsuccessful, the court concluding that it had been arrived at lawfully.

Unfitness under ss6 and 8 relates to management of companies generally rather than unfitness associated with a particular company, even though it will be as a result of specific malpractice that the issue of unfitness will emerge. Consequently disqualification will not be avoided by arguing that a director who is unfit to manage a public company may be fit to manage a private one, a proposition raised, and rejected, in *Re: Poly Peck International plc No.2* 1994. The company had experienced spectacular prosperity under the entrepreneurial direction of Asil Nadir, who held 25% of its shares, but it subsequently suffered an equally spectacular financial collapse. This was allegedly the result of large sums raised by the company from banks and shareholders being passed to subsidiary companies, who did not need it, and who deposited it in banks in the Turkish sector of Cyprus from which it could not be recovered. Facing criminal charges Mr Nadir fled the country. The Secretary of State then sought to commence disqualification proceedings against four remaining directors. This was outside the time limit for an application, which is two years from the date of the insolvency. The court would not waive the time limit. It found the Secretary's case against the remaining directors as *"speculative and very weak"* for they were a minority group on the board, and one of their number, the financial director, had worked hard to secure better financial management.

What should be the duration of a disqualification order?

> In *Re: Sevenoaks Stationers (Retail) Ltd.* 1991 Dillon LJ suggested guidelines for determining the appropriate length of a disqualification under the 1986 Act. Periods of between 10 and 15 years should should be for the most serious cases, such as recidivist directors, periods of between 2 to 5 years should cover the least serious cases, and six to ten years should be appropriate for serious cases not meriting the most severe penalties.

> In *R v. Millard* 1993, a case brought under s.2, a director whose four years of fraudulent trading resulted in losses of £3/4m, was felt by the court to come within the middle category, and an 8 year disqualification was made.

Remuneration

There is no automatic right to payment for a director, but Table A allows for remuneration by way of an ordinary resolution, and grants the right to receive expenses incurred in the discharge of a director's duties (i.e. without the need for a resolution). Such a payment is treated as a gross taxable sum.

It should be remembered in the context of payments to directors that the nature of the relationship between a director and the company will depend upon a variety of factors, not least of which is the size and type of company involved. In some companies with very few members, it is not uncommon to find that each member of the company is also a director. Under such an arrangement the directors may well be satisfied to receive dividends from the company, which they gain in their capacity as members. Another possibility is that the director is someone contributing his or her time to the management of the company on a part-time basis. For instance a person could be a full-time accountant, who also acts as a company director of a company in which he or she holds no shares but receives fees for the advisory or supervisory work involved. Then there are the full-time executives or managers whose directorships are associated with the existence of a contract of employment between themselves and the company. Such a directors are company employees in receipt of a salary. If a director's remuneration is to be by way of payment of fees, the articles must expressly permit such payment. If they do not, the payment of fees is unlawful, even if the members have agreed to it by passing a resolution in general meeting (*Re George Newman & Co.* 1895).

Where a director works under a contract of service, normal principles of employment law will apply. Thus, if the directorship is terminated by the company (under s.303, Companies Act 1985, any director may be removed by the members in general meeting by means of an ordinary resolution), and if the director was working under a contract of service he may:

- bring a claim for wrongful dismissal if he has not been given the necessary notice, or there is still some part of his fixed-term contract unexpired at the time of its termination;

- bring a claim before an industrial tribunal for unfair dismissal, or redundancy. To be eligible to bring such a claim, the employee director must meet the statutory qualification requirements, such as length of service, which are contained in the Employment Rights Act 1996. It may be that the director was required to waive the right to claim for unfair dismissal or redundancy in the event of the contract being terminated or a fixed-term contract not being renewed. Such a waiver of rights is lawful, and precludes a claim from being brought.

Table A grants the board the power to fix the terms of a contract of service with a *service director* as an employee director is called. A director who is not an employee of the company is usually referred to as someone *"holding an office"*. Mere appointment to a directorship, without more, does not give rise to an employer/employee relationship between the company and the director.

There are two important statutory provisions which apply to contracts of service made between companies and their directors. S.318, Companies Act 1985 requires every company to keep a contract of service it has with any director (or director of a subsidiary company), or a memorandum if the contract is an oral one, at either the registered office, the place where the register of members is held, or its principal place of business. The Registrar must be notified of the location of this information, and it must be available for inspection to the members, without charge, for at least two hours per day. Thus members can ascertain the terms under which their directors are employed, and the probable costs involved in removing them.

Some relief is given from these provisions. For work carried out by a director wholly or mainly outside the UK, the company need only keep a memorandum which names the director and notes the duration of the agreement.

S.319 provides a safeguard against possible abuse by directors of their powers to fix their own terms of employment. Any contract for a director's services, even as a self-employed consultant, requires the approval of the company by means of an ordinary resolution in general meeting, unless the contract is one which the company is free to terminate without suffering any penalty within five years of its creation. Approval of any contract coming under s.319 must be sought in advance. Failure to meet s.319 entitles the company to terminate the contract at any time on serving reasonable notice, a term not defined by the Act.

In *James v. Kent & Co. Ltd.* 1950 the plaintiff director had been appointed at a shareholders meeting *"subject to a three year contract with the company"*, however the company solicitor failed to prepare a service agreement, and two years into the contract the company dismissed the plaintiff. In the absence of a written agreement the court was prepared to imply a service contract, and read into it a requirement that it could only be terminated on reasonable notice, which on the facts would be three months notice.

Both sections 318 and 319 apply to shadow directors.

In addition to these provisions, the Act also contains further provisions designed to provide publicity about directors. Thus:

- every company must maintain a register of directors and secretary at its registered office (s.288);

- the annual return sent to the Registrar each year must reproduce this information (s.363);

- changes to this information must be given to the Registrar within 14 days, and receipt of the change published in London Gazette (s.711);

- the company must maintain a register of directors' interests in shares or debentures in it or any other company in the same group;

- the annual accounts must disclose certain specified information regarding the salaries, fees and other payments made to the directors as a group.

Disclosure by Director

A director who is directly or indirectly interested in a contract of the company is required to declare the nature of the interest to the board at the first opportunity, so that the other directors are made aware of it (s.317). This is sometimes referred to as the *self-dealing rule*. Under Table A he may not vote at the meeting of the directors on any matter in which such an interest is held. The purpose of such provisions is to bring into the open any circumstance in which the director faces or is likely to face a conflict of interest. An example would be a situation where a director is a shareholder of another company which is in the process of negotiating a contract with the company of which he is a director. In effect, s.317 imposes a statutory duty of disclosure upon a director. In *Hely-Hutchinson v. Brayhead Ltd.* 1967 the Court of Appeal held that s.317 renders a contract voidable by the company if a director does not declare his interest.

One issue which emerges from s.317 is whether disclosure obligations apply to companies with a single director. The matter was tested in *Neptune (Vehicle Washing Equipment) Ltd. v. Fitzgerald* 1995. The plaintiff company had a sole director, Mr Fitzgerald. The company was later taken over. The new holding company did not appoint a director itself, but it took an active part in its management, and in due course Mr Fitzgerald decided to retire as his services were no longer needed. He caused the plaintiff company to pass a resolution authorising it to make a payment to him of £100,000 as compensation for the termination of his directorship. He retired, the payment was made, and then a new director was appointed to the plaintiff company, who immediately challenged the validity of the payment arguing there had not been formal disclosures of the personal interest of Mr Fitzgerald at a board meeting (of which he was the sole participating director). On its facts the action failed, however the court made clear that as a point of law s.317 does apply to a company with a sole director, with the result that the ordinary meaning of the word *meeting* which demands at least two participants is in these circumstances displaced.

Under s.324, any person who becomes a director of a company and is interested in shares or debentures of the company, or its subsidiary or holding or other subsidiary company must within five days give written notice to the company of these interests. The number of shares, their class and the amount of debentures must be specified. Similar notification must be given where a s.324 interest ceases. The interest of a spouse or infant child is treated as the interest of the director. Information obtained by the company under s.324 is kept in a register of directors' interests which the company must maintain. Contravention of the section is a criminal offence.

Property transactions involving directors

Further recognition of the powerful position enjoyed by directors over the companies they manage is found in the statutory rules which seek to regulate the transactions of directors by which they might gain personal advantage at the expense of the company. These rules can be considered under two heads; substantial property transactions involving directors and loans to directors.

Substantial property transactions involving directors

S.320 makes it unlawful for a company to enter into an arrangement with a director or connected person for the acquisition of a *non-cash asset of the requisite value,* without the prior approval of the company in general meeting.

The meanings of the expressions used in the section require explanation. A *connected person* includes the director's spouse, child or step-child (whilst they are minors); a body corporate with which the director is associated (having at least a 20% holding); a person acting as a partner of the director (or of a partner of someone within the previous categories); and certain types of trustee. The term director includes shadow directors.

A *non-cash asset* does not include a loan, but any other property transaction, for instance, the acquisition by the director from the company of fully paid shares. *Requisite value* means a non-cash asset whose value exceeds £50,000 or 10% or more of the company's net assets taken from the last accounts, subject to a minimum value of £1,000.

Non-compliance renders the agreement avoidable at the option of the company. In other words, it may take steps to end the contract unless:

(a)   restitution is impossible, i.e. because the parties cannot be restored to their pre-contractual positions; or

(b)   the company has been indemnified; or

(c)   third party rights have been acquired; or

(d)   the company affirms the arrangement in general meeting within a reasonable time.

It also renders the director, plus anyone connected with him plus any authorising director, personally liable to account to the company for any direct gain which results, and jointly and severally liable to indemnify the company for any resultant loss.

Liability is, however, avoided where the transaction was with a connected person and the relevant director took all reasonable steps to comply with the section. Relief is also granted to a connected person and the authorising director(s) if they did not know of the contravention at the time of the transaction.

There are certain exceptions from s.320, such as the provision that a transaction of less than £1,000 value need not be disclosed.

The aim of s.320 is to prevent directors purchasing company property at less than its true value, or selling the company their own property at above market value, without the approval of the members. Non-cash assets cover a wide range of property, from the tangible such as land to the non-tangible such as patents and debts.

Loans to directors

In principle, although there are a number of exceptions, a company may not make loans or enter into similar transactions with or for the benefit of a director of the company or of its holding company: s.320. The provisions are complex, and apply mainly to what are called *relevant* companies; that is, public limited companies and private companies which form part of a group containing a public company. The following provides an outline of the law as it applies to loans.

Under s.330(2) no company, whether a relevant one or not, may make a loan to any of its directors or to any director of its holding company, nor enter into any guarantee or provide any security in relation to a loan made by an outsider to one of its directors.

Ss.330(3) and (4), which apply only to relevant companies, extend this prohibition to quasi-loans and credit transactions involving the director or a connected person. A *quasi-loan* arises where a director incurs personal expenditure but the bill is met by the company and the director repays later. For instance, a company might initially pay for a rail season ticket for the director who later recompenses the company, or the company may issue him with a company credit card, enabling the purchase of personal items for which the company is subsequently reimbursed. A *credit transaction* arises where the company acts as the creditor under an arrangement with a director or connected person involving a hire purchase or conditional sale agreement, or a leasing or hiring arrangement involving periodical payments or a deferred payment arrangement. Thus, it would be a credit transaction where a company transferred video equipment it manufactures to a director on the basis that it should be paid for by instalments, or where a company hires out a company car to a director. A relevant company is also prohibited from entering into a guarantee or providing any security in connection with a credit transaction or quasi-loan made by a third party for a director or connected person.

Certain loans are, however, lawful. Under s.332 a quasi-loan not exceeding £5,000 for which the director must reimburse the company within two months is exempted. So too is a loan made by any company to a director for any purpose, which does not exceed £5,000 (s.334). Under s.335 a company which is in the business of providing finance facilities may enter into a credit transaction with a director where the amount is in excess of £5,000, provided this is done in the ordinary course of business and the terms are not more favourable to the director than those that would be offered to another person. Similar provisions apply to moneylending companies (s.338).

Finally, there are exemptions contained in s.337 for companies providing financial assistance to directors in performance of their duties. The company may do anything to provide directors with funds to meet expenditure they incur for company purposes or in performance of their duties. The financial assistance must be either approved by the company in general meeting in advance, or alternatively at the next Annual General Meeting after the assistance has been provided. For a relevant company the section imposes an upper limit of £10,000 on the amount that may be advanced. There is no limit for any other company. If the members do not give their approval, the sum involved must be repaid within six months.

There are both civil and criminal consequences for breach of the loan provisions. S.341 states that a transaction made in breach is voidable at the instance of the company unless restitution is impossible, or the company has been indemnified, or third party rights have arisen. The director and any convicted person will also be personally liable to account for any gain, and indemnify the company for any loss. By s.342 a director of a relevant company who authorises or permits the making by the company of an agreement which contravenes the rules under s.330 commits an offence. The company also commits an offence.

Disclosure of loan transactions

Any transaction coming under s.330, or under any of the exemption provisions of sections 332-338, must be disclosed in notes to the company accounts, and so too any agreement with the company in which the director has a material interest (see section 317 above). The main terms must be identified in the notes; the parties, the terms and so on. Certain transactions are, however, exempt from disclosure, e.g. those not made during the period to which the accounts relate.

The Powers of Directors

In order to understand the significance of directors' powers we need to reflect on the way in which power is divided within a company. What this reveals is two potential power bases; the board of directors, and the members in general meeting. There are certain things which lawfully can only be done by a company in general meeting, for example, alteration of the articles, and alterations to the objects clause. Moreover, it is necessary under the Companies Act to secure the passing of a special resolution, requiring 75% support of the voting shareholders, in order to make certain decisions in general meetings; alteration of the articles and the objects clause are both examples.

Many other matters affecting companies are not required to be decided in general meeting, and can be dealt with by the board of directors as part of the ordinary day-to-day running of the business. It will be recalled that Table A gives directors the power to manage the business of the company and exercise all its powers, that is, carry out the activities expressly or impliedly contained in the objects clause, subject to any restrictions under the Act, the memorandum and articles. The members can however control the activities of the board through any directions issued to the board under the terms of any special resolution they pass. This power-sharing arrangement recognises that a balance must be struck which enables the managers to manage effectively, whilst ensuring that ultimate control is vested in the proprietors of the organisation, the shareholders.

There are various reasons why the division between what the board does, and what the company as a whole must do in general meeting, can be seen sometimes as rather artificial. In the case of very small companies measured in terms of membership, the members may all be directors. Ownership and control is thus in the same hands. In companies having a larger membership, where there is not complete coincidence between those who are members and those who are directors, the question of who does what is sometimes rather stretched. For example, in the case of a share issue, it is the company in general meeting which has the power (under s.121) to pass an ordinary resolution to increase the authorised capital for the purposes of ensuring that it is adequate to cover the issue and to ensure the directors have the necessary authority to issue the shares (s.80). However, the actual issuing of the shares is carried out by the directors themselves.

Despite the power sharing structure which applies to registered companies, real power undoubtedly rests in the hands of the board, partly because of Table A which, as we have seen, grants the board wide management powers, but also because in companies with a large membership, the board members are in close and regular contact with each other. The shareholders are unlikely to maintain such contacts amongst themselves, thus reducing their effectiveness as decision-makers in general meeting. Indeed, in larger companies the management is so firmly placed in the hands of the directors that the only occasion when members are likely to hear from them is when they receive notice of the Annual General Meeting. In such companies there is nothing artificial about the division of power; it is an appropriate practical way of conducting business.

Members' control over the directors

This is achieved in two ways. Firstly, shareholders have the right in certain circumstances to take action on the company's behalf to prevent wrongdoing carried out by or committed against it. On this see *Foss v. Harbottle* 1843 and the various exceptions to it, and also the remedies under s.459 of the Act available where a member has suffered unfair prejudice which are considered later in the chapter. Secondly, the members have powers which they can exercise in general meeting to control the board. These are:

(a)   passing an ordinary resolution under s.303 to remove a director before his or her term of office expires;

(b)   not voting for the re-election of a director when he or she seeks re-election if the company's articles provide for retirement by rotation;

(c)   passing a special resolution to alter the articles to cut down the powers of the directors; and

(d)   passing a special resolution which gives the directors directions on how they should act in relation in a particular matter; in other words, giving them orders in advance.

Delegation of functions

The larger an organisation is, the more valuable it becomes to have the capacity to delegate functions. This helps to avoid the need to hold frequent meetings involving all the managers in order to arrive at decisions which could more appropriately have been taken simply by one of them. In larger companies with boards having many directors on them, the ability to delegate is particularly useful. However, the general principle contained in both the Companies Act 1985 and Table A is that the board should act as a body, taking collective responsibility for its decisions. Article 72 of Table A does, however, allow for delegation of any of the directors' powers (i) to a committee of any one or more directors, or (ii) to a *managing director* or any other director holding executive office (such as a finance director). In exercising the power to delegate, the directors may impose any conditions they see fit, and may alter or revoke the delegation; thus the board has complete control over the terms of the delegation.

Commonly the boards of companies are headed by a managing director who by virtue of delegated powers is able to carry out executive functions alone, without the need to seek the approval of the board as a whole. The mere assumption of the title managing director, however, does not of itself give rise to an act of delegation by the board to that office holder.

Table A also permits the board to employ professional persons and agents to carry out functions which the board itself may carry out.

Beyond those circumstances where the articles allow for delegation, or the members have given their permission, it is well established that directors cannot delegate their powers or functions to others, for the agency principle – *delegatus non potest delegare* – a delegate cannot delegate, applies to them.

The Duties of Directors

The nature of a director's position

The relationship between a company and its directors is unique. They control the company, but cannot treat it as though it were their own, for they owe duties to it. In this broad sense, and in the context of specific duties which directors must carry out, the expression *company* means the corporate body, the members, but, as we shall see, it can sometimes be taken to include the employees and the creditors as well. All these parties, shareholders, employees and creditors have interests in the company and it is the responsibility of the directors to take account of the overall interests of the company, rather than particular sections of it.

A director does not have to be employed by a company to act as its director, thus his position is not necessarily that of an employee or servant. Even if the director is employed under a contract of service, his role as a manager, together with his custodianship of the interests of the company, mean that the duties he must discharge are not limited to those owed by an employee to an employer. Depending upon the particular circumstances he will act as the agent of the company and so will owe an agent's duties, however a director does not enjoy all the rights of an agent, and therefore examination of the law of agency does not provide us with a full account of the director's position either.

In some respects directors are in the position of trustees; they control the company's property and must manage it for the company's benefit. They owe the company a *fiduciary duty*, a duty associated with trusteeship, and must account for any breach of this duty. They are not true trustees, however, since they do not own the company's property. A true trustee must exercise considerable caution in managing the trust, but directors are engaged in commercial activities involving speculation and risk-taking and consequently their liability for the negligent management of the company's business is far less stringent than would be the case for a trustee. Thus, the nature of a director's position draws from a number of legally recognised roles, a clear illustration of the breadth and complexity of the post. It is worth recalling here that a person involved with a company does not need to be designated as a director to fall within the s.741 definition (see earlier) and, therefore may owe the company the same duties as those owed by a properly appointed director.

There have been many judicial statements describing the general nature of directors' duties and Lord Cranworth's remarks in *Aberdeen Railway Co. v Blaikie Bros.* 1854 sum them up: *"The directors are a body to whom is delegated the duty of managing the general affairs of the company. A corporate body can only act by agents, and it is, of course, the duty of those agents to act as best to promote the interests of the corporation whose affairs they are conducting. Such agents have duties of a fiduciary nature towards their principal. And it is a rule of universal application, that no one, having such duties to discharge, shall be allowed to enter into engagements in which he has, or can have, a personal interest conflicting, or which possibly may conflict, with the interests of those whom he is bound to protect."*

To whom are the duties owed?

The shareholders

Directors owe their duties to the company as a whole. This is usually taken to mean the shareholders as a single body, and it will include both present and future shareholders: *Abbey Glen Property Corp. v. Stumborg* 1978. This does not prevent directors from considering the interests of particular sections of shareholders, including themselves, when they make decisions. They do not have to see the company as something distinct from its members. Nor do they, however, owe a general duty to individual shareholders.

In *Percival v. Wright* 1902 the plaintiff, who wished to sell his shares in the company, entered into an agreement to sell them to the members of the board at a valuation he placed on them himself. The transaction went ahead, after which the plaintiff discovered that whilst his negotiations with the board were taking place, a third party was also negotiating a possible take-over of the company. These negotiations were never revealed to the plaintiff by the board, and in the event the take-over negotiations came to nothing. The plaintiff, however, sought to have the sale of his shares to the board set aside on the grounds of non-disclosure. The court held that the sale was binding. The directors were not trustees for individual shareholders who wished to sell their shares to them. They had not dealt unfairly with the plaintiff, since he had approached them and had named his price. Moreover, were the plaintiff to succeed, it would mean that the board should have disclosed to him prematurely the negotiations for the sale of the company which had been taking place, and this might well have damaged the company's interests. Under the Criminal Justice Act 1993, similar conduct on the part of a board could now give rise to criminal liability, although its provisions do not apply to private dealings in shares, and since in *Percival v Wright* the transaction was a private one, it would seem that even today no criminal liability would result.

If directors give advice to shareholders regarding a take-over bid for their company, an injunction may lie to prevent the bid going ahead if there is evidence that the directors have not been honest, as for example, by concealing the information that professional advisers have recommended rejection: *Gething v. Kilner* 1972.

No duty is owed to *individual* shareholders for any loss they have suffered through a fall in the value of their shares resulting from negligent mismanagement, since the loss is the company's. Minority shareholders may however seek relief in such circumstances under s.459, a provision designed to protect minority interests, and which is considered later in the chapter. The basic rights of shareholders to participate in the company's affairs by taking part in company meetings are not affected by fluctuations in share values: *Prudential v. Newman Industries (No.2)* 1982.

Exceptionally, a fiduciary duty may be owed to an individual shareholder on the particular facts of a case, such as those in *Coleman v. Myers* 1977 where the minority shareholders in a small family firm sold their shares to the managing director after he had made misrepresentations to them.

The employees

Under s.309 directors are required to take account of the interests of company employees in general, as well as the interests of the company, in the performance of their functions. Presumably, therefore, it would come within this duty for the directors to adopt a strategy avoiding redundancies, as long as such a strategy also served the interests of the company. The problem for employees lies in their capacity to enforce the section, since it states that the duty is enforceable in the same way as any other fiduciary duty owed to a company by its directors, in other words, by shareholders bringing a claim on behalf of the company within one of the *Foss v Harbottle* exceptions. It would have to be shown that the company had suffered damage to obtain any more than a declaration that the directors had failed to consider the employees' interests, and in any case the employees could only bring such an action if they were also shareholders.

Furthermore the Act deems a company to have the power to provide for its own or a subsidiary's employees or former employees when the company or its subsidiary either ceases to carry on its business or transfers the whole or any part of it. Such power does not need to be exercised in the best interests of the company. This reverses the decision in *Parke v. Daily News Ltd.* 1962 where redundancy payments which the defendant company proposed to pay its staff following the sale of most of its business, were held to be unlawful since, at that time, the law did not require such payments to redundant staff. In consequence, the payments were purely gratuitous, and did not therefore benefit the company.

The creditors

In a solvent company, the duty owed by the directors is a duty owed to the shareholders as a body. They are not responsible to the creditors. In the words of Lord Templeman in *Kuwait Asia Bank v. National Mutual Life* 1991: *"A director does not by reason only of his position as director owe any duty to creditors or trustees for creditors of the company."* If however the company becomes insolvent the interests of the creditors arise. They control the company's assets by means of insolvency procedures (see Chapter 7) and these assets, from a practical position, now belong to them rather than the shareholders.

In *Liquidator of West Mercia Safetywear Ltd. v. Dodd* 1988 the defendant was a director of two companies, West Mercia and A.J. Dodd. Both companies became insolvent. The liquidator of West Mercia brought a claim against the defendant on the basis of his breach of duty to the West Mercia creditors. The liquidator had instructed the directors not to operate the bank account of either company, but despite this instruction the defendant paid £4,000 from West Mercia's account into the other company's account to discharge a debt West Mercia owed it. This benefited the defendant personally, since it reduced his liability on a personal guarantee on the other company's overdraft. The Court of Appeal ordered him personally to repay the West Mercia liquidator.

Specific duties owed

In broad terms, the duties of a director are:

- *fiduciary duties*, arising as a result of the equitable view of directors as quasi-trustees;

- *duties of care and skill*, arising under the common law through the operation of the tort of negligence; and

- *statutory duties*, arising out of the provisions contained in the Companies Act 1985. Since these have already been considered, it is only necessary here to summarise them before examining the non-statutory duties owed.

Statutory duties

These are:

(a)   to notify the company of his or her interest in its shares or debentures or those of an associated company: s.324;

(b)   to disclose for approval at a general meeting any substantial non-cash transaction with the company: ss.320-322;

(c)   to have regard to the interests of the employees: s.309; and

(d)   to disclose personal interests in contracts of the company: s.317.

Fiduciary duties

The fiduciary duties owed by a director can be treated as coming under two headings; firstly the obligation to exercise powers bona fide and for the benefit of the company, and secondly, the obligation to avoid any conflict between their personal interests and those of the company, or as it is sometimes expressed, the duty not to make a *secret profit*. Case law illustrates the application of these duties in practice.

In *Hogg v. Cramphorn Ltd.* 1967 the question of fiduciary duty arose in relation to the issue of shares by the company directors. The share issue was made to trustees to be held for the benefit of company employees. The aim of the board was to fight off a take-over bid. The company made an interest-free loan to the trustees to assist them in the purchase. It was held that the directors were in breach of their fiduciary duty to the company. However, the company members could ratify the decision by simple majority in a general meeting, so long as the new shareholders did not vote. The issue was subsequently ratified.

In *Howard Smith Ltd. v. Ampol Petroleum Ltd*. 1974 directors, acting honestly and within their powers, allotted shares to a company which wanted to make a take-over bid. By doing so, they aimed to prevent two shareholders who between them held 55% of the shares and had indicated they would reject any take-over bid, from being able to do so. It was held that the board had acted improperly. The issue of the shares would be set aside. The proper reason for the issue of shares is the raising of capital, and, *"it must be unconstitutional for directors to use their fiduciary powers over the shares in the company purely for the purpose of destroying an existing majority, or creating a new majority which did not previously exist"*.

Breach of the duty to act bona fide and in the interests of the company will also occur where the directors:

- *issue new shares to themselves, not because the company needs more capital but merely to increase their voting power;*

     In *Piercy v. S. Mills & Co. Ltd*. 1920 the directors used their powers to issue new voting shares to themselves, solely to acquire majority voting power. The court held that the directors had abused their powers and the allotment was declared void.

- *approve a transfer of their own partly-paid shares to escape liability for a call they intend to make;*

     In *Alexander v. Automatic Telephone Co*. 1900 the directors used their position to require all shareholders to pay 3s 6d on each share excluding themselves. The court held that his was a clear abuse of power and the directors were required to pay to the company the same amounts.

- *negotiate a new service agreement between the company and its managing director simply in order to confer additional benefits on him or his dependents;*

     In *Re W and M Roith* 1967 it was held that a new service contract negotiated between a managing director and his company was unlawful as it was solely to make a pension provision for his widow and that no regard had been taken as to whether this was for the benefit of the company.

- *abdicate responsibility for the running of the company and appoint a manager with full powers who is not under the control of the board of directors, or obey the majority shareholder without exercising their own judgment or discretion.*

The following cases illustrate the position regarding the making of a secret profit. In a company law context the term "secret" is somewhat misleading, for a profit remains secret even if it has been disclosed by the director. The profit must be *approved* by the company in general meeting before it becomes lawful.

It is not surprising that a secret profit will arise when a director takes a bribe: *Boston Deep Sea Fishing Co. v. Ansell* 1888. However, a director will also be liable to account for a secret profit even though he could not have profited personally, or even though the company would have suffered no loss.

In *Regal (Hastings) Ltd. v. Gulliver* 1942 Regal owned one cinema, but wished to purchase two others so that it could sell all three together. The company had insufficient capital to buy the two cinemas itself, so it formed a subsidiary, and its directors took sufficient shares in the subsidiary to provide it with the capital to make the purchase. The shares in Regal and the subsidiary were later sold at a profit. The new owners of the Regal company then claimed the profit made by the directors from the sale of their shares in the subsidiary, bringing an action against them in the company name. The House of Lords held that the directors were liable to account, on the grounds that it was through their position as directors of the Regal that they gained the knowledge and opportunity to obtain the shares and make the profit. The decision appears to be rather harsh and to impose a high level of accountability on the directors. It was their money which they put into the subsidiary. They had acted in good faith, and believed they had acted lawfully, and their actions could have been ratified by the company in general meeting. In the later case of *Boardman v. Phipps* 1967 the House of Lords, however, followed its earlier decision in *Regal*.

In *Industrial Development Consultants v. Cooley* 1972 the court arrived at a similar decision on a different set of facts. Here the defendant acted as the managing director of a design company and in this capacity he tried to obtain some work for the company from the Eastern Gas Board. The Board indicated to the defendant that they were not prepared to give his company the work. Realising that he might secure the work for himself, the defendant managed to leave his company on the pretence that he was close to a nervous breakdown. He set up his own company and secured the Gas Board contract. It was held that he must account to his former company for the profit he had made, despite the fact that it was most unlikely the company would ever have obtained the work for itself. Thus it seems a director will remain accountable even where the company has not sustained a loss.

There will be a clear breach of duty where directors negotiate a contract in the company's name, but then take the contract for themselves.

This occurred in *Cook v. Deeks* 1916 where the directors of a company negotiated a construction contract which they took in their names, following which they called a company meeting where they were able to use their 75% shareholding in the company to pass a resolution that the company had no interest in the contract. This was held to constitute a fraud on the minority. It was of no effect, and the directors had to account to the company for the profit they made.

Breach may also occur where a director places himself in a conflict of interest situation.

The case of *Guinness plc v. Saunders* 1990 provides an interesting example. In order to implement its objective of launching a take-over-bid for the Distillers company, the Guinness board appointed a committee comprising of three directors *"with full power and authority"* to settle the terms for the Distillers offer. The three directors were Mr Saunders, Mr Roux and Mr Ward. The committee made an agreement with Mr Ward that Guinness would pay him a sum amounting 0.2% of the ultimate value of a successful bid, for his advice and services. A successful bid was made, and an invoice for £5.2m representing the sum payable to Mr Ward was presented to the committee, and paid by them on behalf of Guinness. When however the full board discovered the payment the company sought to recover the money from Mr Ward. The House of Lords held it was entitled to do so. Under the articles a committee of the board had no power to make such an agreement; only the board could authorise special remuneration to a director. It was a void contract for want of authority. No quantum meruit claim could be based upon an implied contract since the agreement itself was void. Nor was equitable relief available to grant Ward an allowance for his services because he had acted in breach of his fiduciary duty by putting himself in a position where his duty to the company and his personal interests conflicted irreconcilably. In Lord Templemans words the agreement prevented him *"from giving independent and impartial advice to Guinness."* However, in the absence of a firm contract, he was not in breach of the disclosure requirements under s.317.

Duties of care and skill

As we saw earlier, there are common law duties applying to directors, which arise from the obligation of a director not to act negligently in managing the company's affairs. The question is essentially one of identifying the standard of care and skill owed by the particular director towards his or her company.

> The leading case is that of *Re City Equitable Fire Insurance Co.* 1925. Here the company directors had delegated almost all responsibilities of management to the managing director. As a result, the directors failed to recognise a loss of over £1,200,000 from the company's funds, which was caused by the deliberate fraud of the managing director, described by the judge as, *"a daring and unprincipled scoundrel"*. The loss was discovered in the course of the winding-up of the company, and the liquidator successfully sought to make all the other directors liable for their negligence. Romer J. stated the following general propositions of law:
>
> (i)   a director need not show a greater degree of skill than may reasonably be expected of a person with his knowledge and experience;
>
> (ii)   a director need not give continuous attention to the affairs of the company. He is not bound to attend all meetings of the board, although he ought to attend whenever he is reasonably able to do so;
>
> (iii) a director may delegate duties to other officials in the company and trust them to be performed properly so long as there is no reason to doubt or mistrust them.

The judge commented *"It is indeed possible to describe the duties of directors in general terms ... The position of a director of a company carrying on a small retail business is very different from that of a director of a railway company. The duties of a bank director may differ widely from those of an insurance director, and the duties of a director of one insurance company may differ from those of a director of another."*

It is clear, therefore, that the duties of care and skill owed to a company by its directors are of a variable kind. Much higher standards of expertise will be expected of directors who are employed in a professional capacity in executive posts, for example, finance and engineering directors, than of directors who have nor claim to have such professional expertise. Yet even non-executive directors who have experience or qualifications in a field of relevance to the company's affairs may find that high objective standards appropriate to their specialist fields will be expected of them in law, despite their non-executive roles.

This point emerged in the case of *Dorchester Finance Co. Ltd. v. Stebbing* 1989 where the company lost money as a result of the gross negligence of the actions of the company's one executive director. He failed to take out adequate securities on loans made by the company and the company found itself unable to recover the loans made. The two non-executive directors, who had little to do with the company, had signed cheques in blank at the request of the executive director. All three directors had considerable financial experience. The court held the two non-executive directors equally liable with the executive director in damages to the company.

The effect of breach of duty

A director who is in breach of duty is jointly and severally liable with other directors who are similarly liable to make good the loss. He must account for any secret profit made, and in such cases the company is usually able to avoid a contract made with him. In appropriate circumstances the court may grant an injunction.

Relief from breach of duty may occur in the following ways:

- where the company by ordinary resolution waives the breach;

- if the company has indemnified and insured directors against liability for breach, using of any powers available to do so contained in the Companies Acts 1985 and 1989. S.310 of the 1985 Act renders void any provisions in the articles of a company or in any contract it makes which exempts or indemnifies an officer for negligence, breach of duty, breach of trust or default. It is however lawful for articles or a contract term to indemnify a director against liability in defending civil or criminal proceedings against him, where judgment is in his favour or he is acquitted, i.e. meeting any costs incurred by him. S.137 Companies Act 1989 enables a company to insure its directors against liability for their wrongdoing. If it does so there must be disclosure in the directors report;

- if the court has granted relief under the powers available to it under s.727 of the 1985 Act. Relief is available where the director has acted honestly and reasonably and ought in all the circumstances to be excused. The section applies to proceedings brought against a director alleging negligence, default, breach of duty or breach of trust.

In *Re Duomatic* 1969 the court had to consider what would constitute reasonable conduct by a director to obtain relief. The directors in question, without seeking legal advice, had authorised payment of compensation of £4,000 out of company funds to another director who they were unhappy with. He could have been removed by a board vote, but they anticipated he would cause the company trouble if this were done, so offered him the money instead if he would leave. He did. S.312 of the 1985 Act requires such a payment to be disclosed to the members in general meeting and approved by them. These things had not been done. Subsequently the company went into liquidation. The liquidator's claim against the two authorising directors to recover the £4,000 was successful. Moreover, the director in receipt of the payment held it on trust for the company and could be required to repay it. Making a decision like this, *"without a proper exploration of the considerations which contribute, or ought to contribute, to a decision as to what should be done on the company's behalf,"* could not be said to be acting reasonably, said the trial judge, Buckley J.

Auditors

Having looked at the position of directors in some depth we can now consider the role of auditors. The auditing of company accounts is a process by which the company auditors carry out an annual investigation into the financial affairs of the company, so that they can confirm, primarily for the shareholders benefit, that the companies books reflect the actual position of the company's finances.

The relationship between the auditors, shareholders and directors of a company was summarised by Bingham L.J. in *Caparo Industries v. Dickman* 1990:

> *"The members, or shareholders, of the company are its owners. But they are too numerous, and in most cases too unskilled, to undertake the day-to-day management of that which they own. So responsibility for day-to-day management of the company is delegated to directors, The shareholders, despite their overall powers of control, are in most companies for most of the time investors and little more. But it would, of course, be unsatisfactory and open to abuse if the shareholders received no report on the financial stewardship of their investment save from those to who the stewardship had been entrusted. So provision is made for the company in general meeting to appoint an auditor (Companies Act 1985, s.384) whose duty is to investigate and form an opinion on the adequacy of the company's accounting records and returns and the correspondence between the company's accounting records and returns and its accounts (s.237). The auditor has then to report to the company's members (among other things) whether in his opinion the company's accounts give a true and fair view of the company's financial position (s.236). In carrying out his investigation and in forming his opinion the auditor necessarily works very closely with the directors and officers of the company. He receives his remuneration from the company. He naturally, and rightly, regards the company as his client. But he is employed by the company to exercise his professional skills and judgment for the purpose of giving the shareholders an independent report on the reliability of the company's accounts and thus on their investment."*

All registered companies must appoint auditors, unless the company is a dormant one, that is a *"small"* company which has had no *"significant accounting transaction"* since the end of the previous financial year. Appointment is made at each general meeting at which accounts in respect of an accounting reference period are laid. It is thus the members who make the appointment. The first auditors may be appointed by the directors, and casual vacancies may be filled either by the directors, or by the company in general meeting. A private company may now, by means of an elective resolution, opt out of annual appointment arrangements, so that the appointed auditors will continue in office until either side choose to terminate the appointment.

It is clearly important that auditors be both independent from the company, and suitably qualified to perform their functions. Only a registered auditor can carry out company auditing work, and a registered auditor is someone who is regarded as qualified by the Chartered Institutes of Accountants, or the Chartered Association of Certified Accountants, or the Department of Trade and Industry as having the appropriate overseas or other professional qualifications. Education, training and other matters affecting the work of auditors has now been brought under general statutory control. Certain persons are not permitted to act as auditors. These include an officer or servant of the company, a person employed by them, officers and servants of the company's holding or subsidiary companies or persons who have a *connection* with the company. A body corporate may act as an auditor.

A company may remove an auditor by means of an ordinary resolution under s.391. The provisions relating to such a removal are identical to those contained in s.303 for the removal of directors. An auditor may also resign from office, by depositing a notice to that effect at the company's registered office. The resignation is ineffective unless it either states that there are no circumstances connected with the resignation that should be brought to the attention of the members or creditors or alternatively it contains a statement outlining what those circumstances are. If such a statement is made a copy of it must be sent within fourteen days to all members, debenture holders, and every person entitled to receive notices of general meetings of the company. In such cases the auditor may also require the directors to convene an extraordinary general meeting of the company for the purpose of considering the resignation, a very powerful if rarely used threat.

Payment of auditors is determined by the company in general meeting.

Liability of auditors

In *Caparo Industries plc v. Dickman* 1990 the House of Lords was required to consider the extent of an auditor's liability for negligently audited accounts. The auditors in question had verified accounts which showed a pre-tax profit of £1.2m, when the company had in fact sustained a loss of over £400,000. Caparo Industries, who already held shares in the audited company, took more of its shares and later made a take-over bid for it on the strength of the inaccurate accounts. Caparo sued the auditors when the true position was discovered. The action was unsuccessful. The court took the view that auditors of a public limited company owe no duty of care either to a potential investor or to an existing member who takes more shares in the company. To allow otherwise would be to create an unlimited liability on the part of auditors. On the facts there was not a sufficient relationship of proximity between the parties. The audited accounts went into general circulation and might foreseeably have been relied on by strangers for many different purposes. The duty of the auditors was a statutory duty owed to the company as a whole, to enable the members as a body to exercise proper control over it. A duty of care can however arise in cases when auditors have provided accounts with the intention or knowledge that they would be supplied by the company to a particular person or class of people, for example a specific bank, or banks generally, even though the precise purpose for which the accounts will be used is not known by the auditors. On this see the decisions in *Morgan Crucible* 1991 and *James McNaughton* 1991 in Chapter 13.

The Shareholders in a Company

Becoming a shareholder

There are two ways in which a person can become a company member (the words member and shareholder are for all practical purposes interchangeable). These are by subscribing to the company's memorandum, which involves the members name appearing in the subscription clause of the memorandum against the number of shares they agreed to take, or by their name being entered on the register of members under s.22 Companies Act 1985. This is of course the most common method.

The maintenance of this register is a statutory requirement. The register is kept either at the registered office or some other office used for this purpose and it must be available for public inspection. The Act prohibits trusts being entered on the register, so it is only the legal owner of the shares whose name appears. Normally a persons name is included on the register either because they have successfully applied to the company for shares in it, or because an existing shareholder has transferred ownership to them by selling them the shares.

The question of who may become a member is regulated by a combination of the general law and the articles. The articles may wish to exclude certain people from acquiring membership. The shareholders who make up the membership of public and private companies include both individual investors and institutional investors. The latter include organisations such as pension funds. Investors will usually be seeking a return on their investment in the form of dividend payments from the company to them. They will also be looking for the market value of their shares to increase. As we have seen directors manage companies for the benefit of the shareholders whilst auditors advise the shareholders of the financial health of their company. Whilst the principal obligation of shareholders is to pay for their shares, the rights they enjoy and general position they hold within the company is more complex, and we shall now examine it. To begin with it will be useful to consider what holding a share actually means.

Transferring shares

Shares are the shareholders property. They can be transferred at any time to anyone the shareholder chooses. If a number of shares are held some can be transferred and some retained. The articles may however restrict this general right of transfer. The two most common ways in which this will be achieved are by granting the directors power to refuse to register a transfer, and by granting the members pre-emption rights.

When a member wishes to transfer shares the executed *transfer form* together with the share certificate must be sent to the company. On receipt the directors have two months within which to register the transfer and issue the transferee with a share certificate, or notify the transferee that the transfer is refused (s.183). Once the two month deadline has passed a transfer cannot be refused.

If the articles grant the board of directors the discretionary power to refuse a transfer, the fiduciary duty they owe to the company means they must exercise the power in good faith and in what they regard as the company's best interests. Although the courts presume good faith has been present in the decision making (*Tett v. Phoenix Property & Investment Co. Ltd.* 1986), if there is evidence to the contrary the court can order the registration of the transfer to go ahead.

> In *Re: Smith and Fawcett Ltd.* 1942 a company article granted the directors the uncontrolled and absolute discretion to refuse to register any transfer of shares. Smith and Fawcett were the only members of the company. They were also its directors. They held 4001 shares each. Following Fawcetts death, Smith and a co-opted director refused to register the transfer of Fawcett's shares to his son, who was acting as his fathers executor. However Smith offered instead to register 2001 of the shares, and purchase the remaining 2000 shares at a valuation fixed by himself. The sons challenge against the refusal to register all the shares failed. The court could find no evidence of bad faith and was not therefore prepared to intervene. Lord Greene MR observed that small private companies are both commercially and at a personal level closer to partnerships than to public companies, and *"it is to be expected that in the articles of such a company the control of the directors over the membership may be very strict indeed"*.

If the power granted is not an absolute one, but permits refusal on specified grounds, then in the absence of anything to the contrary in the articles the court will compel the directors to specify the ground upon which their refusal is based (*Berry v. Tottenham Hotspur Ltd.* 1935).

Pre-emption rights

If a company issues new shares the interests of existing members may be adversely affected in two ways. Firstly, the balance of power will shift if the shares carry voting rights and they are taken up by new members. Secondly, if the new shares are issued at a price below their real market value, the value of the existing shares will be diluted. S.89 Companies Act 1985 provides protection for existing shareholders by requiring that new equity shares be first offered to existing members so that their proportionate holding in the company can be maintained. This is known as a *rights issue*. There are however a range of exceptions to the statutory obligation. It does not apply for example to shares allotted for a non cash consideration. Moreover shareholders may waive the requirement using a special resolution, and in the case of a private company the right of pre-emption may be excluded by a suitable provision in the company's constitution.

A different form of pre-emption arrangement sometimes found in the articles of a private company is the requirement that if a shareholder wishes to sell his shares they must first be offered to the existing members at a fair value. This has the same effect as a rights issue for it grants the existing members a right of first refusal in respect of company shares which have become available and can be used to prevent the introduction of new members into the company. In very small private companies with perhaps three or four members it can be of great value to retain all the control of the company in the hands of the remaining shareholders when one of their number sells his or her interest. Case-law examples of this form of pre-emption right can be found elsewhere in the chapter.

Shareholders as company controllers

Shareholders collectively own the undertaking of the company. In effect the company is their agent. This agency role is performed by directors appointed by shareholders in company meetings. Directors are accountable to the company for the management of its activities (see Figure 5.2).

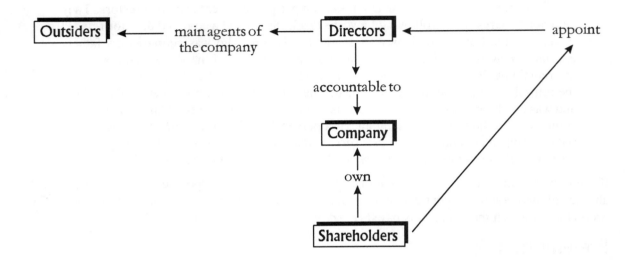

Figure 5.2   Shareholders as company controllers

Share certificates

A *share certificate* is a document issued by a company with provides evidence of title to the shares of the person named on it. It does not have to be issued under the companies seal, but can be issued under the signature of the secretary and a director. S.186 Companies Act 1985 provides that the share certificate is *prima facie* evidence of the title the shareholder has to the shares. This means it is not necessarily conclusive evidence, however the onus is on the person challenging the certificate to prove a defective title.

The share certificate is treated as a representation by the company issuing it that the person named in it was the true owner of the shares at the date the certificate was issued. The company may therefore find itself liable to anyone relying on the information the certificate contains if that information turns out to be untrue.

The application of this principle is well illustrated in the *Re: Bahia & San Francisco Railway Co.* 1868 case. Brokers of a company member, Miss Tritten, transferred her shares to themselves by forging her signature on a share transfer form. They sent the form together with the share certificate they held for her to the company, and it duly issued a new share certificate in their names. They then sold the shares to two innocent parties, whose names were entered on the register of shareholders. Subsequently Miss

Tritten discovered the forgery. The company was obliged to restore her name to the register, and remove the names of the innocent parties from it. They then sued the company. The court held that although the signature on the transfer was a forgery so that the transfer was of no effect, the company was still bound by the representations contained in the new share certificate which erroneously showed the brokers to be the owners of the shares. It was liable to pay the innocent parties damages equal to the value of shares at the time their names were removed from the register.

The effect of forgery needs to be carefully noted. In the *San Francisco Railway* case it was the share transfer which was forged. If someone forges a *share certificate* then the certificate is not issued with the authority of the company and the company is not liable for it. The only exception would be if the forgery has been done by a director of the company, since a director is someone having the authority of the company to issue share certificates.

The Statutory Contract

An important provision for shareholders is s.14 of the Companies Act 1985 which provides that the articles and the memorandum of a company constitute a binding contract between the company and its members. The section has caused some difficulty for the courts in the past, for it has not been clear precisely what the effects of the section are. It states that the company and its members are bound to each other as though each shareholder has covenanted to observe the provisions of the memorandum and articles, the *statutory contract*. It also provides that any money owed by a member to the company is a speciality debt. This means the company has twelve years in which to recover the debt. In the case of debts arising from a simple contract the period would otherwise be six years.

The effect of the articles on shareholders can be summarised as follows:

- *The company is bound to the members in their capacity as members, and they are bound to it in the same way.*

An illustration of this principle is provided by *Salmon v. Quin & Axtens Ltd.* 1909. Here the articles gave directors full management powers, but prevented the directors from purchasing or letting any premises if the managing director dissented. The directors however resolved to deal in premises, despite the dissent of the managing director, and an extraordinary meeting of shareholders affirmed this action by a simple majority. The managing director sought an order from the court that the resolutions were invalid. The Court of Appeal agreed. The resolutions conflicted with the articles, and the company was bound by the articles. It could be restrained from its proposed action.

In *Hickman v. Kent or Romney Marsh Sheepbreeders Association* 1915 the articles of the association stipulated that disputes between itself and its members should be referred to arbitration. The plaintiff, a member, brought court action against the association in relation to a number of matters. It was held that in accordance with the articles these matters must be referred to arbitration.

- *The members are contractually bound to each other, under the terms of the articles.*

Generally it is not possible for an individual member to enforce the contract in his own name against another member, although exceptionally this may be possible if the articles grant him a personal right.

> The position is illustrated in the case of *Rayfield v. Hands* 1960. A clause in the articles of a private company stated, *"Every member who intends to transfer shares shall inform the directors who will take the said shares equally between them at a fair value."* The plaintiff notified the defendant directors of his intention to transfer his shares, however they denied any liability to take and pay for them. The court held they were obliged to do so, firstly because of their binding obligation indicated by the word "will" and secondly because the clause was a term of the contractual relationship between the plaintiff and the directors as company members.

- *The company is only bound to the members in their capacity as members.*

    This proposition of law emerges from the following case.

> In *Eley v. Positive Life Assurance Co Ltd.*, 1876, a provision in the articles of the company stated that the plaintiff should be the company's solicitor for life. He took up shares in the company. Sometime later the company removed him as its solicitor, and he sued the company for breach of contract. The action failed. The court said the statutory contract only granted him rights as a member, and what he was complaining of was breach of an article giving him rights as a legal advisor. Doubts have however been expressed about this decision, for it adds a rider to s.14 which the section does not contain, the phrase, *"in their capacity as members"*.

There is however no problem in using provisions contained in the articles as evidence of the contents of a separate service contract.

> In *Re New British Iron Co Ltd.*, 1898, the articles provided that the directors, all of whom were members, were entitled to remuneration of £1000 p.a.. Their company went into liquidation, and they sought to recover from the liquidator the payment the company owed them for their services. The court held that the article was sufficient evidence of the terms of their contract as to payment, and they were able on this basis to recover the money owing to them.

A further important effect of s.14 results from its assertion that shareholders have entered into *covenants* with the company, for it means that they are bound to the company as if they had made a deed with it. The consequences of this arrangement can be seen in Figure 5.3. As well as resulting in the members being bound to each other, an idea already examined above, the company is bound to people who have become members by purchasing shares from existing shareholders rather than the company itself. Thus legal relationships are created which extend beyond the common law contractual relationship which only exists between the company and those members who have taken shares directly from it. In the figure, Z can enforce his rights as a shareholder against the company, for instance to secure his voting rights, whilst X and Z are bound to each other to the extent that they can enforce personal provisions in the articles. *Rayfield v. Hands* provides an example.

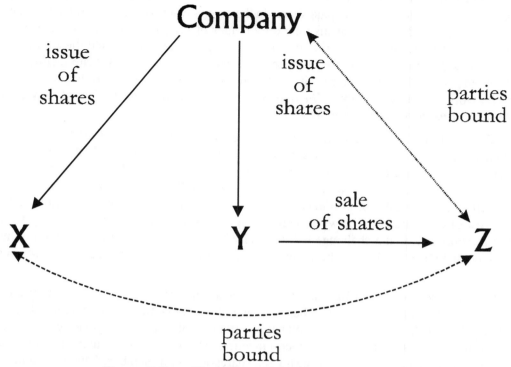

Figure 5.3   The effect of the statutory contract

Alteration of the Articles

Although the constitutional documents of a company make up the terms of the contract between itself and its members, the memorandum and articles are not tablets of stone. The company does have the opportunity to amend them provided it does so lawfully. In the case of the articles they may be altered or added to by means of a special resolution which requires a 75% majority of the members voting in favour of it. No such resolution is necessary if there is unanimous agreement of the members to the proposed alteration. Alterations must however be made *bona fide,* that is in good faith, and for the benefit of the company as a whole. This is an important aspect of the law regulating companies, for as we have just seen articles constitute a contract between the company and its members and identify members' rights, such as the right to vote. Clearly the ability of the company to change the terms of this contract at some future time may have the effect of placing individual members who might be harmed by such changes, in a disadvantageous position. Thus the courts reserve the power to refuse an alteration to the articles which has such an effect, unless there is a benefit to the company as a whole and the alteration has been made in good faith. This principle is best appreciated by looking at some of the caselaw on the subject.

In the leading case, *Allen v. Gold Reefs of West Africa* 1900 the articles of the company which already granted it a *lien* on partly paid shares to cover any liabilities owed to it by a member, were altered by extending the lien to holders of fully paid shares as well. A lien is simply a charge on shares, enabling the company to sell the shares in order to meet the debts owed to it by the members. Here a shareholder who at the time of his death held both fully and partly paid shares in the company and owed the company money for the partly paid shares, was also the only holder of fully paid shares. His executors challenged the alteration on the grounds of bad faith, but the court upheld the alteration. There was no evidence that the company was attempting to discriminate against the deceased personally; it was simply chance that he was the only holder of fully paid shares. In the words of Lord Lindley, *"The altered articles applied to all holders of fully paid shares and made no distinction between them."*

It seems that the test which should be applied is whether the proposal is in the honest opinion of those voting for it, for the benefit of the members. An alteration may be challenged if it is, *"so oppressive as to cast suspicion on the honesty of the persons responsible for it, or so extravagant that no reasonable men could really consider it for the benefit of the company."* (Bankes L.J. in *Shuttleworth v. Cox Bros. & Co. (Maidenhead) Ltd.* 1927). If it can be established that the alteration has the effect of discriminating between members, granting advantages to the majority which are denied to the minority then a challenge will normally be successful, although an alteration may be upheld as bona fide even though the members voting for it are improving their own personal prospects.

In *Greenhalgh v. Arderne Cinemas Ltd.* 1951 the articles of company, which prohibited the transfer of shares to a non member as long as an existing member was willing to pay a fair price for them, were altered to enable a transfer of shares to anyone by means of an ordinary resolution passed in a general meeting. The alteration was made because the majority shareholder wished to transfer his shares to a non member. This was held to be a valid alteration.

The courts will also uphold alterations which cause direct prejudice to individual members, as long as they are shown to be alterations made in good faith, and in the company's interest.

In *Sidebottom v. Kershaw Leese & Co.* 1920 an alteration was made enabling the directors, who were the majority shareholders, to request the transfer to their nominees at a fair value the shares of any member competing with the company's business. The court found this to be a valid and proper alteration for, in the words of Lord Sterndale M R, *"it is for the benefit of the company that they should not be obliged to have amongst them as members, persons who are competing with them in business and who may get knowledge from their membership which would enable them to compete better."*

By way of contrast in *Brown v. British Abrasive Wheel Co.* 1919 a majority of the shareholders (98%) were willing to provide the company with much needed extra capital if they could buy the 2% minority interest. As the minority were unwilling to sell, the majority proposed to alter the articles so as to enable nine-tenths of the shareholders to buy out any other shareholders. The plaintiff, representing the minority, brought an action to restrain the majority. It was held by the court that the alteration would be restrained as it was not for the benefit of the company as a whole but rather for the benefit of the majority shareholding, and was in any case too wide a power and was therefore unlawful as constituting a potential fraud on the members.

In addition the following common law and statutory conditions apply to an alteration:

- • *it must be lawful,* that is not be in conflict with the Act or with the general law;

In *Russell v. Northern Bank Development Corp Ltd.* 1992 an agreement made between the company and its shareholders provided that the capital of the company could not be increased without the consent of all the parties to the agreement. The agreement was expressed to take preference over any conflicting provision in the articles of association. The court held the agreement to be an improper fetter on the powers of a company to increase its share capital, a matter regulated by s.121, and not binding as between the company and its shareholders. In arriving at this conclusion the decision in *Bushell v. Faith* 1969 was cited, in which Russell LJ had observed that a company could not legitimately either by *"its articles or otherwise"* restrict its ability to alter its articles. In the present case the agreement made by the company fell within the expression *or otherwise*.

- • it must not create a conflict between the memorandum and the articles. If this does occur the provisions of the memorandum will prevail for it is the superior document;

- • *it will require the leave of the court in certain circumstances.* These are where a minority of members have applied to the court for the cancellation of an alteration to the objects clause (s.5), where there has been an application for the cancellation of a resolution of a public company to re-register as a private company (s.54), or where a petition has been presented to the court on the ground that the affairs of the company are being conducted in a manner unfairly prejudicial to some part of the membership (s.461);

- • *if it involves an increase in a member's liability it will only be valid if the member has given a written consent (s.16);*

- • *if it affects the rights attached to a particular class of shareholders.* If it does it is subject to the capacity of those disagreeing with the change, who may apply to the court for a cancellation, not exercising this power successfully. This power is available to 15% or more of the holders of the shares who did not give their consent, and it must be exercised within 21 days.

Controlling the company – the powers of the members

A company has two principal sources of control over its affairs. These are the shareholders in general meeting and the directors. The most important matters affecting the company, for example changes in its constitution, rest with the shareholders in general meeting. Decisions reached at such meetings are arrived at through the putting of resolutions, which are then voted on. Generally a simple majority vote is sufficient to carry them, although some matters of special significance require a 75% majority. Since voting power plays such an important role in company matters the type of shares the company has issued is of considerable significance. Some shares, for example ordinary shares, usually carry full voting rights.

However other classes of share, such as preference shares, may carry no voting rights at all and therefore exclude shareholders of that class from effectively influencing the company in its decision making.

Since all public companies and many private companies consist of numerous members it is impractical to operate the company on a daily basis by means of general meetings. The articles will therefore provide for directors to be responsible for the daily running of the company and usually grant them the right to exercise all the powers of the company. They will remain answerable to the members in a general meeting although acts carried out by the directors within the powers delegated to them under the articles cannot be affected by decisions of a general meeting. So, if the directors have acted contrary to the wishes of the members, the ultimate sanction is to dismiss them or to change the articles and so bring in provisions that restrict the powers of the directors. In small companies the directors will often be the principal or only shareholders, so that such considerations will not be relevant.

Meetings

The fundamental principle of accountability of the directors to the members necessarily involves strict regulation of the company's operation. The Companies Act 1985 provides therefore that every company must, in each year, hold an *annual general meeting* and that every member is entitled to notice of this meeting. In addition, the holders of one-tenth or more of paid-up shares with voting rights may at any time compel the directors to call an extra-ordinary general meeting. The articles usually regulate the procedures to be adopted at these meetings, but in any case the minutes of all meetings must be strictly recorded.

Decisions at general meetings are usually taken by ordinary resolution, that is a simple majority of voting members present. For some types of business, usually related to the company's constitution such as the alteration of the articles or objects of the company, a special resolution is necessary which requires a three-quarter majority of voting members. The position is summarised in figure 5.4

Types	Business	When called	Notice
Annual General Meeting *(AGM)*	Declaring dividends Directors' and Auditors' reports, Appointment of Directors	Within 18 months of incorporation then once a year with no more than 15 months between each	At least 21 days Items of ordinary business need not be mentioned in notice
Extraordinary General Meeting *(EGM)*	All business is `special' e.g. alteration to articles, memorandum removal of Directors	Whenever Directors think fit, or if demanded by holders of one tenth or more of paid up shares	At least 14 days. If called by members they must state why they want it

Figure 5.4 Company meetings

Shareholders' rights – majority rule, minority protection

As we have seen the rights enjoyed by a member of a company are primarily contractual, arising from the class of shares acquired and the rights attached to them as specified in the articles. Unlike a partner, who will usually possess the right to take part in the management of the firm, a shareholder will not always be involved in the daily management of the company, unless the organisation has a very small membership and its shareholders are also its directors. Companies' articles usually confer power on directors to operate the business, which they will perform on behalf of the members. The effect of such an arrangement is that ownership and management are separated. Nevertheless, ultimate control of the business is in the hands of the shareholders by the exercise of voting power in the general meeting. Where appropriate they can vote to remove a director.

In any vote which does not produce a unanimous outcome there will be two groups, the majority shareholders and the minority shareholders. In effect it is the majority that make the company decisions. Those who hold 75% or more of the voting shares are the ultimate company controllers. Under company legilsation a three-quarter majority to secure changes to the constitution of the company itself. Thus the majority group can run the company almost as if it were their own. If the minority have a grievance, legally there is little they can do to redress it. The courts have been reluctant to assist minority shareholders who are claiming they have been oppressed or have had their interests prejudiced by the majority. Since it is the majority who rule the company it is not for the court to thwart their actions. If the minority are arguing that the majority have acted in breach of the memorandum or the articles, then it is a wrong which has been done to the company. The proper plaintiff is the company itself, not the minority shareholders. Of course they will find it impossible to pass a resolution that the company sue the majority, for the voting strength of the majority will be sufficient to block such a move. This leaves the minority in a very vulnerable position.

> The case of *Foss v. Harbottle* 1843 laid down as a general principle that the courts will not interfere in the internal management of a company at the insistence of the minority shareholders. Here an action had been brought by the minority alleging that the directors were responsible for losses that had occurred when they sold some of their own land to the company, at what was alleged to be an over valuation. The court held that the action must fail as the proper plaintiff in such circumstances was the company itself. As the action to which the minority shareholders objected could have been ratified by the majority then it was the majority shareholders who should decide whether an action should be brought in the company name. The court saw no merit in interfering in the internal management of a company by passing judgment on its commercial decisions.
>
> In *Pavlides v. Jenson and others* 1956, a company sold an asbestos mine for £182,000 when its real value was close to £1,000,000. A minority shareholder brought an action for damages against three directors who were responsible for the sale and against the company, alleging gross negligence. The court held that the action could not be brought by a minority shareholder because it was the company itself which should decide whether to redress the wrong that had been committed.

Thus the process of incorporation, having invested a company with a separate legal personality, dictates that the company and individual members are separate. If a wrong is committed against the company it is the company, by virtue of a decision made by the board of directors, that should seek redress for it.

The rule in *Foss v. Harbottle* does not however apply to every type of action taken by the majority. In certain situations the court will hear a claim brought by minority shareholders, even though the majority do not wish it. Thus:

- proposed *ultra vires* activities can be restrained, even by a member holding a single share;

- where directors attempt to do something requiring a special resolution which they do not obtain, their action cannot be ratified by an ordinary resolution. Were this to be otherwise, the protection for minorities granted in circumstances where a three-quarters majority is needed would be avoided;

- where a wrong is suffered to a member in his personal capacity, through the action of the directors.

For instance in *Pender v. Lushington* 1877 the company chairman wrongfully refused to accept the votes cast by certain shareholders. The resolution they opposed was in consequence able to be carried. The court held that the company could be restrained from carrying out the proposed resolution;

- when a fraud has been committed against the minority. This does not mean fraud in the criminal sense, rather conduct which is grossly unfair.

An example is provided by *Daniels v. Daniels* 1978.

The company was managed by Mr and Mrs Daniels. They were also the controlling shareholders. In 1970 they agreed to sell land belonging to the company to Mrs Daniels, at a price of £4250. In 1974 she resold the land for £120,000 and minority shareholders brought an action claiming that damages should be payable to the company. The court held that despite no allegation of fraud the action by the individual shareholders should be allowed to proceed. The trial judge, Templeman J, distinguished *Pavlides v. Jensen* on the grounds that the directors there had not benefited from their negligence. He stated *"to put up with foolish directors is one thing; to put up with directors who are so foolish that they make a profit of £115,000 odd at the expense of the company is something entirely different ... a minority shareholder who has no other remedy may sue where directors use their powers, intentionally or unintentionally, fraudulently or negligently, in a manner which benefits them at the expense of the company".*

In addition to the common law, the Companies Act 1985 confers certain statutory rights on minority shareholders.

An important example of this is s.459 which gives a member the right to apply to the court for an order on the ground that the affairs of the company are being or have been conducted in a manner which is unfairly prejudicial to some members (including at least himself), or that any actual or proposed act or omission of the company is or would be prejudicial.

If the case is proved the court may issue an order to:

- regulate the company's affairs for the future;

- require the company to act or refrain from acting in a particular way;

- authorise civil proceedings in the name and on behalf of the company by a person; or

- require the purchase of any member's shares by the company or by other members.

In *Scottish CWS v. Meyer,* 1958, Meyer was a minority shareholder in a manufacturing company which was a subsidiary of the Scottish CWS. The CWS, as holding company, decided to close down the subsidiary, and took steps to cause it to cease trading. As a result Meyer's shares, which had been worth £3.75 each whilst the subsidiary was trading, fell in value to £1. The court ordered the holding company to purchase the shares of the minority members at their original value.

An example of a court order regulating a company's future affairs is seen in *Re H R Harmer Limited* 1959. The company was run by an elderly father acting as chairman and his two sons as directors. The father had voting control. He largely ignored the wishes of the board of directors and ran the business as his own. On an application by the sons as minority shareholders, alleging oppression, the court held that relief should be granted. The father was appointed life president of the company without rights, duties or powers and was ordered not to interfere with the company's affairs.

In *Re Elgindata Ltd.* 1991 the court held that in exceptional cases, serious mismanagement of a company could amount to unfairly prejudicial conduct under s. 459. Generally however the court should be reluctant to arrive at such a finding bearing in mind managerial decision making is matter of commercial judgment and that taking shares in a company carries the risk of their value being tied to the competence of the board of directors.

In *Re a Company, ex p Burr* 1992 Vinelott J discussed the possibility of a s.459 action where the directors continue to run the company despite it operating at a loss and it having no realistic chance of becoming profitable in the future. He said: *"There can be no doubt that if the directors of a company continue to trade when the company is making losses and when it should have been apparent that there was no real prospect that the company would return to profitability, the court may draw the inference that the directors' decision was improperly influenced by their desire to continue in office and in control of the company and to draw remuneration and other benefits for themselves and others connected with them … if that inference is drawn, the court may conclude that the affairs of the company are being conducted in a way which is unfairly prejudicial to the members or the members other than the directors and those who obtain such benefit."*

Non payment of dividends can amount to unfairly prejudicial conduct under s.459.

In *Re: Sam Weller & Sons Ltd.* 1990 the petitioners, who between them held 42.5% of the shares in their family business, complained that the company had not increased its dividend for 37 years, despite its profitability. In 1985 its net profit had been £36,000, but only £2,520 was paid out in dividends. The company was controlled by the petitioner's uncle, Sam Weller, who, together with his sons, continued to receive directors fees and remuneration. Peter Gibson J commented of the petitioners position, *"As their only income from the company is by way of dividend, their interests may be not only prejudiced by the policy of low dividend payments, but unfairly prejudiced."*

In the certain circumstances the remedy under s. 459 will not be available. It cannot be used where:

- the petitioner's complaint is not being made in his capacity as a member.

In *Elder v. Elder & Watson* 1952 the remedy was sought by the applicants for their removal from office as directors and from their loss of employment as company secretary and manager respectively. Their claims failed because the wrong had been done to them in their capacity as officers and employees rather than as members.

- the petitioner is the cause of the harm complained of.

This occurred in *Re R A Noble (Clothing) Ltd.,* 1983. The petitioner's complaint was that he had been excluded from important decision making concerning the company's affairs by his co-director, but his action failed because he had left management in the hands of the co-director and had taken no interest in the business.

The s.459 remedy is often referred to as the *alternative remedy*, since it is an alternative to the more drastic step that minority shareholders can take of bringing the company to an end by petitioning the court to have it compulsorily wound up on just and equitable grounds under s.122 Insolvency Act 1986.

When an action is brought by a minority shareholder it may be in one of two forms. It will be a *derivative* action if the shareholder is suing in the name of the company. If the action is successful the remedy being sought will be awarded to the company. *Daniels v. Daniels* is an example. It will be a representative action if it is brought by a member to enforce a personal right, for instance as in *Pender v. Lushington*.

The Partners of a Firm

The background to the relationship of the partners

Unlike the management arrangements which operate in registered companies, in a partnership every partner is entitled to participate in the management of the business unless the partnership agreement provides otherwise. The partners are managing the business not for others – there are no shareholders , but for themselves. There are obvious problems inherent in attempting to reach the sort of joint decisions which are thus necessary to successfully manage a partnership, and it is not uncommon for partners to disagree. There are also risks involved, both in having unlimited liability, and in the fact that individual partners may be responsible for the acts and defaults of their co-partners. Each partner is an agent of the co-partners and as such has an agent's power to bind the partnership by his acts undertaken within the ordinary course of the business. It is crucial therefore that each partner has trust and confidence in his co-partners, the relationship being one of the utmost good faith. This is sometimes given its latin name and is known as a relationship *uberrimae fidei*. Each partner is therefore under a duty to make a full and frank disclosure to the firm of any matters affecting it that come to the partner's attention.

The power of a partner to bind the other members of the firm by his actions illustrates how important it is that each partner should trust and have confidence in his co-partners, not only in regard to their business ability but also as to their business ethics. In *Helmore v. Smith* 1886 Bacon V-C remarked that, *"mutual confidence is the life-blood"* of the firm, whilst in *Baird's Case* 1870 James LJ stated:

> *"Ordinary partnerships are by the law assumed and presumed to be based upon the mutual trust and confidence of each partner in the skill, knowledge and integrity of every other partner. As between the partners and the outside world (whatever may be their private arrangements between themselves), each partner is the unlimited agent of every other in every matter connected with the partnership business, or which he represents as the partnership business, and not being in its nature beyond the scope of the partnership".*

In the course of business, partnerships enter into transactions with other organisations and individuals and inevitably such transactions are negotiated and executed for the partnership by individual partners, rather than by the firm as a whole. It has already been noted that each partner is an agent of his co-partners. *"In English law a firm as such has no existence; partners carry on business both as principals and as agents for each other within the scope of the partnership business; the firm-name is a mere expression, not a legal entity"*, stated Lord Justice Farwell in *Sadler v. Whiteman* 1910.

As we saw earlier in the chapter, under the law of agency, the person who appoints the agent is called the principal. The principal is bound by contracts made within the agent's actual and apparent authority. If the agent acts within either of these two spheres the contract concluded between the agent and the third party becomes the principal's contract, and hence it is the principal and the third party who become bound to each other. The *actual* authority of an agent is the express power given by the principal. A firm may for instance expressly resolve in a partnership meeting that each partner shall have the power to employ staff. Authority may also arise where the agent's power to make a particular contract or class of contracts can be implied from the conduct of the parties or the circumstances of the case. The apparent, or ostensible authority of an agent is the power which the agent appears to others to hold. Of a partner's apparent authority s.5 Partnership Act, 1890, says:

> *"Every partner is an agent of the firm and his other partners for the purpose of the business of the partnership; and the acts of every partner who does any act for the carrying on in the usual way business of the kind carried on by the firm of which he is a member bind the firm and his partners, unless the partner so acting has in fact no authority to act for the firm in the particular matter, and the person with whom he is dealing either knows that he has not authority, or does not know or believe him to be a partner".*

Whether a particular contract is one carrying on in the usual way business of the kind carried on by the firm is a question of fact.

> In *Mercantile Credit Co. Ltd. v. Garrod* 1962 the court had to decide what would be considered as an act of a *"like kind"* to the business of persons who ran a garage. It was held that the sale of a car to a third party by one of the partners bound the other *partners*. This was despite an agreement between them that provided for the carrying out of repair work, and the letting of garages, but expressly excluded car sales.

A private limitation of the powers of an agent is not an effective way to bring the restriction to the notice of an outsider dealing with the agent, and the law recognises this. But if, for example, a partner has acted as an agent for his firm in the past with a particular third party, and he carries out a further transaction of a similar kind with the third party after the firm has taken away his express authority, the third party can nevertheless hold the firm bound unless he knew at the time of contracting of the partner's lack of authority.

The exact scope of an agent's apparent authority under s.5 has been the subject of much litigation, and the following powers will usually fall within the agent's apparent authority:

in the case of all types of partnership the power to:

- sell the goods or personal property of the firm;
- purchase in the firm's name goods usually or necessarily used in the firm's business;
- receive payments due to the firm;
- employ staff to work for the firm.

in the case of a partnership whose business is the buying and selling of goods (a trading partnership), the following additional powers are within the partner's authority:

- to borrow money for a purpose connected with the business of the firm;
- to deal with payments to and from the firm.

A partnership has no separate legal identity so it is the individual partners who are ultimately accountable for all the firm's debts. Under the Partnership Act every partner is jointly liable with the other partners for all the debts and obligations of the firm incurred whilst being a partner. A legal action by a creditor seeking to recover money owed to him may be brought against any one or more of the firm's partners. However if the judgment obtained in the court does not satisfy the creditor he cannot then sue the remaining partners for having sued one partner, he is precluded from suing the others for the same debt. Nevertheless the creditor, if he had chosen to do so, could have sued the firm in its own name rather than suing an individual partner of the firm. This has the effect of automatically joining all the partners in the action, and means that the judgment will be met out of assets of the firm as a whole and, if necessary, out of the property of the individual partners.

The Act goes on to provide that the firm is liable for the *"wrongful act or omission of any partner"* committed within the ordinary course of the firm's business. The term *wrongful* certainly embraces tortious acts, although it appears that it does not extend to criminal acts.

An exception however occurs in relation to fraudulent acts carried out within the scope of the firm's business.

> In *Hamlyn v. Houston & Co.* 1903 the defendant firm was run by two partners as a grain merchants. One of the partners bribed the clerk of a rival grain merchant, and obtained information from him which enabled the firm to compete at greater advantage. The Court of Appeal held that both partners were liable for this tortious act. Obtaining *information* about rivals was within the general scope of the partners' authority, and therefore it did not matter that the method used to obtain it was unlawful. In the words of Lord Collins, M.R: *"It is too well established by the authorities to be now disputed that a principal may be liable for the fraud or other illegal act committed by his agent within the general scope of the authority given to him, and even the fact that the act of the agent is criminal does not necessarily take it out of the scope of his authority".*

It is no defence for a firm to show that it did not benefit from the unlawful act of its agent.

The House of Lords in *Lloyd v. Grace, Smith & Co.* 1912 held a solicitor's firm liable for the fraud of its managing clerk who induced one of the firm's clients to transfer certain properties into his name. In advising the client the clerk was acting within the scope of his authority, and that alone made the firm liable for his acts.

Although the Act does not apply to criminal matters two points should be noted. Firstly, there may be occasions when one partner may be held vicariously liable for an offence committed by another. Vicarious liability is considered in the next chapter. Secondly, a partner may be a party to an offence committed by another simply because it is in the nature of that partnership that they work together.

In *Parsons v. Barnes* 1973 where two partners worked together in a roof-repairing business, one of them was convicted of an offence under the Trade Descriptions Act 1968, by being present when his co-partner made a false statement to a customer.

If a partner acting within the scope of his apparent authority receives and misapplies the property of a third person while it is in the firm's custody the firm is liable to meet the third person's loss. Similarly when the firm has received property of a third person in the course of its business, and the property has been misapplied by a partner while in the firm's custody, it must make good the loss. The liability of partners for misapplications of property, or wrongs of the firm, is stated by the Act to be *joint* and *several*. This means that if a judgment is obtained by a plaintiff against one partner, this does not operate as bar to bringing a further action against all or any of the others if the judgment remains unsatisfied. Where liability is merely joint this is not possible. Compare liability for debts, which was discussed earlier.

In *Plumer v. Gregory* 1874 two of the partners in a firm consisting of three solicitors accepted on the firm's behalf and subsequently misappropriated money entrusted to them by the plaintiff, a client of the firm. The third member of the firm was unaware of these events, which only came to light after the other partners had died. The plaintiff's action against the remaining partner succeeded, for the firm was liable to make good the loss, and liability of the members was joint and several.

Changes in membership

The membership of a firm will normally alter from time to time. The firm may wish to expand its business by bringing in new partners to provide the benefit of additional capital or fresh expertise. Existing partners may leave the partnership to join a new business, or to retire. A changing membership poses the question of the extent to which incoming and outgoing partners are responsible for the debts and liabilities of the firm. Although partners are responsible for any matters arising during their membership of the firm, incoming partners are not liable for the debts incurred before they joined, nor outgoing partners for those incurred after they leave, provided the retiring partner advertises the fact that he is no longer a member of the firm. This involves sending notice to all customers of the firm while that person was a partner, and advertising the retirement in a publication known as the *London Gazette*. If this is not done a person dealing with the firm after a change in its membership can treat all apparent members of the old firm as still being members of the firm. With regard to existing liabilities the partner may be discharged from them when he retires through the agreement of the new firm and the creditors.

Rights and duties of the partners

Ideally the partnership relationship should be regulated by a comprehensive partnership agreement. If it is not, the provisions of the Partnership Act will apply when the parties are in dispute as to the nature of their duties and are unable to reach agreement amongst themselves. In a business enterprise of this sort, where a member's entire wealth lies at stake, it is clearly of great value to execute a detailed agreement setting out in precise form the powers and responsibilities of the members. For instance it would be prudent for such an agreement to provide grounds for the removal of partners, since the Act makes no such provision. Because the members of the firm have the freedom to make their own agreement, without the statutory controls imposed upon other forms of business organisation, such as the registered company, the partnership stands out as a most flexible form of organisation.

The duties that the Act sets out are based upon a single foundation of fundamental importance to all partnerships, namely that the relationship between the parties is of the utmost good faith.

> This principle can be seen in *Law v. Law* 1905. A partner sold his share in the business to another partner for £21,000, but the purchasing partner failed to disclose to his co-partner certain facts about the partnership assets, of which he alone was aware. When the vendor realised that he had sold his share at below its true value he sought to have the sale set aside. The Court of Appeal held that in such circumstances the sale was voidable, and could be set aside.

A partner is under a duty to his co-partners to render true accounts and full information of all things affecting the partnership. Personal benefits can only be retained with the consent of the other partners.

> In *Bentley v. Craven* 1853 one of the partners in a firm of sugar refiners, who acted as the firm's buyer, was able to purchase a large quantity of sugar at below market price. He resold it to the firm at the true market price. His co-partners were unaware that he was selling on his own account. When they discovered this they sued him for the profit he had made, and were held to be entitled to it. It was a secret profit and belonged to the firm.

A partner is under a duty not to compete with his firm by carrying on another business of the same nature unless the other partners have consented. If a partner is in breach of this duty he must account to the firm for all the profits made and pay them over. If the partnership agreement prohibits the carrying on of a competing business, the court may grant an injunction to stop a partner who disregards the limitation.

Further rights and duties are set out in the Act which states that, in the absence of a contrary agreement:

- all partners are entitled to take part in the management of the partnership business;
- any differences arising as to ordinary matters connected with the partnership business are to be decided by a majority of the partners, but no change can be made in the nature of the partnership business without the consent of all the partners;
- no person may be introduced as a partner without the consent of all existing partners;

- all partners are entitled to share equally in the profits of the business irrespective of the amount of time they have given to it, and must contribute equally towards any losses. The Act does not require the firm to keep books of account, although this will normally be provided for in the partnership agreement, together with specific reference to the proportions of the profit each partner is entitled to. If however there are partnership books they have to be kept at the principal place of business, where every partner is entitled to have access to them for the purpose of inspection and copying;

- if a partner makes a payment or advance beyond the agreed capital contribution he is entitled to interest at 5% p.a.;

- a partner is not entitled to payment of interest on his capital until profits have been ascertained;

- the firm must indemnify a partner in respect of payments made and personal liabilities incurred in the ordinary and proper conduct of the business of the firm, or in or about anything necessarily done for the preservation of the business or property of the firm (e.g. paying an insurance premium);

- a partner is not entitled to remuneration for acting in the partnership business.

In cases where the firm consists of active and sleeping partners the partnership agreement will often provide that as well as taking a share of the profits the active partners shall be entitled to the payment of a salary.

If any of the terms of the partnership agreement are broken, damages will be available as a remedy, and where appropriate an injunction may be granted.

Partnership property

It can be of importance, particularly to the partners themselves, to establish which assets used by the partnership actually belong to the firm itself, rather than to an individual partner. Mere use of property for partnership purposes does not automatically transfer ownership in it to the business.

> In *Miles v. Clarke* 1953 the defendant started up a photography business which involved him in acquiring a lease and photographic equipment. After trading unsuccessfully he was joined by the plaintiff, a free-lance photographer, who brought into the firm his business connection which was of considerable value. The partners traded profitably for some time, on the basis of equal profit sharing. Later, as a result of personal difficulties, it became necessary to wind up the firm. The plaintiff claimed a share in all the assets of the business. The court held that the assets of the business other than the stock-in-trade which had become partnership property, belonged to the particular partner who had brought them in.

The Act provides that all property and rights and interests in property originally brought into the partnership or subsequently acquired by purchase or otherwise on account of the firm, must be held and applied by the partners exclusively for the purpose of the partnership and in accordance with the partnership agreement. Such property is called *partnership property* and will normally be jointly owned by the partners. Because a partner is a co-owner of partnership property, rather than a sole owner of any particular part of the partnership's assets, he may be guilty of theft of partnership property if it can be established that his intention was to permanently deprive the other partners of their share.

Under the Act property bought with money belonging to the firm is deemed to have been bought on account of the firm, unless a contrary intention appears.

Other Key Parties in Business Relationships

Employers and Employees

In any business other than those in which the workforce consists of a single person working as an owner/manager, it will be necessary to employ people to provide the labour and skill the business needs in order to achieve its objectives. Thus most organisations, whether large or small, will be parties to legal relationships by means of which they have secured the labour they demand to function. The law regulating these relationships is examined in Chapters 14, 15 and 16. An understanding of it is fundamental to a grasp of modern business law.

Suppliers and Consumers

Business organisations, whatever their size or shape, share certain common characteristics. As fundamental characteristic is that they all function as suppliers, meeting market needs by the goods and services they provide. To act as suppliers of market needs they necessarily act as consumers themselves. A manufacturer, for example, produces goods by purchasing the materials and components needed to make the goods in question. The manufacturer is a business consumer. All businesses are consumers in a similar way. But there is another type of consumer, sometimes referred to as the *ultimate* consumer, individuals like ourselves who purchase goods and services for private use or consumption.

In the widest sense these two groups, suppliers and consumers, represent the trading activity that makes up the economic activity of the United Kingdom. It is not therefore surprising that comprehensive legal regulation exists in this vital field. Chapters 11, 12 and 13 provide a detailed commentary on the way the law defines the relationship between suppliers and consumers.

Assignment A Family Affair

West Riding Woollens Ltd. is a long established and well regarded company which manufactures high quality woollen garments from its two mills in West Yorkshire. The company was founded in 1913 by John Grisethwaite, and is still controlled by members of the founders family. At present its shares, all of which are ordinary shares carrying voting rights and of which there are 1000 in total, are held by the following shareholders: George Grisethwaite, the founder's son, who is 84 and acts as chairman and managing director, holds 49%; his two sons Ralph and Peter hold 10% each, and so does his daughter Elizabeth. The remaining shares are held by a local businessman Lawrence Stott (8%), a relative of the family by marriage, Grace Clarke (8%), and Walter Thompson, the son of the company's former accountant (5%). The board of directors comprises the Grisethwaite family members.

In the past the business had flourished, but three years ago, at a lively general meeting, the company members voted to alter the objects clause, enabling it to diversify into property development. It was a majority decision, the board members voting in favour, the remaining shareholders against. Since then the value of the company's assets has diminished significantly, largely the non board members feel because of the incompetence of the board in its property development transactions. Last year the company lost £3/4m on the purchase and subsequent resale of a development site which the board had been advised by its accountants to be a potentially high risk commercial property.

Seeing the company's profitability sliding, and aware of the impact on the value of their shares, the minority members criticised the business judgment of the board at the last AGM, held a month ago. They see the chairman, whose style is highly autocratic and who cannot accept criticism, as the author of the company's misfortunes. They understand that he commonly makes decisions without consulting the board, and recently made himself a large profit by selling the company a piece of land which he owned personally. Last week, at a general meeting, the company voted to alter its articles. The alteration provides that the company can, by means of an ordinary resolution, request the sale to the company at a fair market value, the shares of any member holding less than 10% of the ordinary shares of the company, if *"it is in the business interests of the company"* to do so.

You are working at present in a large law firm Leeds whilst deciding whether to train to become a solicitor. The partner you are attached to, Jeremy Lake, specialises in company law matters. Walter Thompson is a client of his, and has arranged an interview with Jeremy as a matter of urgency, to discuss the problems at West Riding Woollens.

Task

Investigate the legal implications of the way in which the board has been running the company and what action, if any, Mr. Thompson can take. Provide a summary of your advice, which should explore all aspects of the company's affairs, for the attention of Mr. Lake.

Assignment   Trouble at Mills

In 1990 Mark Mills, together with his cousin Bryan and an accountant called Peter Marshall, decided to form a company to deal in personal insurance services. The company received its certificate of incorporation at the end of 1990. It was called Mills & Co. (Insurance Services) Ltd. and its premises were in Leeds. Mark and Bryan took up 35% of the shares each, Peter took the remainder. The company objects stated that it could carry on the business of providing *"personal insurance of any kind"*. In 1993 Peter was anxious that his wife should join the company, and each of the existing shareholders agreed to transfer some of their shares to her. As a result she obtained a 25% stake, Mark, Bryan and Peter's shareholding being reduced to 25% each.

Mark was happy with the company structure, since Peter's wife brought to the business considerable commercial expertise, and he received a large sum for the shares he transferred to her. Within a year however, the relationship between the shareholders had deteriorated. In particular Mark felt increasingly isolated. He was anxious that the company expand its insurance business. The other shareholders however were of the view that the company, which was suffering a reduced level of profit, should diversify, and move into the lucrative field of marketing, the area in which Peter's wife had previously worked.

By 1996 Mark had decided to form a separate business to offer a complete range of insurance facilities. He formed a partnership with James Blake-Smith, an old schoolfriend, to carry on the additional business. He did not reveal the existence of this business to his fellow shareholders in Mills & Co. Ltd., assuming that since it was based in Barnsley, a town twenty miles away from the company's place of business in Leeds, it had nothing to do with them. No partnership articles were drawn up. The other members of Mills & Co. Ltd. recently discovered the existence of Mark's new firm. They responded by calling a company meeting, at which, during very stormy business they resolved to alter the company articles to enable it to pursue marketing work, to sell off the company's present business undertaking at a figure well below what Mark believes to be its true value, and to remove him as a director. In addition they are threatening to take away his voting rights. Mark's problems have been compounded by problems in the partnership. He has discovered that James Blake-Smith has been in financial difficulties, and that bankruptcy proceedings have been commenced against him this week. He has also purchased, in a firm's name, an expensive computer system, despite a recent partnership meeting at which it was agreed to defer the expenditure until the next financial year.

In an effort to clarify the legal position in relation to these business difficulties Mark has sought your help., Prior to meeting Mark in a couple of days time, you have decided to analyse the legal position he has found himself in, in order to fully advise him as to the extent of his rights and liabilities.

Task

Draft an outline report which you can give to Mark at your meeting with him, that expresses your considered legal opinion on his present business problems.

Legal Terms found in Chapter 6

Causation
- the notion that a link must be established to show that the harm suffered results from the defendants wrongful act

Contributory negligence
- defence raised in a negligence action where the plaintiff is alleged to have contributed to the harm suffered

Duty of care
- principle of the tort of negligence recognising the circumstances under which one party has a legal responsibility to avoid causing harm to another through carelessness

Fault liability
- liability associated with evidence of blameworthiness

Negligence
- a legal claim for damages based upon the plaintiff establishing that the defendant has caused loss by breach of a duty of care

Occupiers liability
- legal responsibility of someone in control of premises towards those coming onto the premises

Remoteness of damage
- a test for determining whether damage is sufficiently related to a wrongful act to be recoverable

Res ispa loquitur
- rule of evidence under which the plaintiff is relieved from proving the defendant's negligence

Strict liability
- liability imposed without the need to establish fault

Tort
- a civil wrong, the remedy for which is an award of damages or the granting of an injunction

Trespasser
- an entrant onto land without legal authority

Vicarious liability
- the imposition of legal liability upon one person for the unlawful action of another

Visitor
- a person lawfully present on land or premises

Volenti non fit injuria
- tortious defence put forward when a plaintiff has consented to accept the risk of harm

Chapter 6

Legal Liability in Business

The concept of legal liability is the major theme of this chapter, and indeed appears as a theme throughout the book. This is hardly surprising for legal liability is one of the most fundamental of all legal concepts, and we now need to consider the impact it has upon business.

A legal liability arises when someone is under a legal obligation to do or refrain from doing something, and is answerable if they act in breach of such an obligation. Businesses are subject to an extensive range of actual and potential legal liabilities resulting from the performance of their business operations. There are different ways these liabilities can be categorised. If we look at them from the standpoint of the purposes they are designed to meet we come across one of the most well known of all legal categorisations, the division of the law into civil and criminal branches. The distinction between civil and criminal law was discussed in Chapter 1. Essentially, civil law is concerned with private rights and obligations and the remedying of private grievances whereas the criminal law is concerned with the welfare of society generally. Civil law is concerned with compensating victims, criminal law with, amongst other things, the punishment of offenders. Both civil liability and criminal liability arise from the existence of legal rules. In civil law the legal rules which have the greatest impact upon business operations are those involved with contractual and tortious liability.

Criminal liability in business

We have previously seen how business organisations can incur criminal liabilities arising from the way in which they conduct their activities. An unincorporated association cannot be held criminally liable, for the body in question is not a person. Thus in an organisation like a partnership it will be the partners themselves, rather than their firm, who may be found to be criminally liable. The case of *Parsons v. Barnes* 1973 in Chapter 5 illustrates the point.

The position regarding corporate bodies such as registered companies and local authorities is quite different however. Because a corporation is a *person* in law, it follows that it can be held criminally liable. There are in fact two ways in which such liability can be imposed:

- *directly,* where those in control of the company commit an offence in the course of its business, and the company is treated as committing the offence itself on the basis that the state of mind of its controllers constitutes its own state of mind.

    One of the first cases establishing this principle was *R v. ICR Haulage* 1944 in which the company was convicted of the offence of conspiring to defraud, the *mens rea* of the offence - the mental element of it, being provided by the state of mind of its managing director.

There appear to be two limitations placed upon the direct, or primary criminal liability of a corporation. Firstly it will only be liable for the acts or omissions of those at the top of the organisational hierarchy, the officers of the company who in the words of Lord Pearson in *Tesco Supermarkets v. Natrass* 1972 may *"be identified with it, as being or having its directing mind and will ... "*. Secondly it seems that a company will only be liable for the acts of an individual manager or director with whom it is *identified*, making it impossible to aggregate the acts of more than one directing mind to create a corporate offence. The position however is not entirely clear. It does seem though that on the basis of direct or primary liability a corporation could be charged with any offence except those which carry a mandatory prison sentence on a conviction, such as murder.

- *vicariously,* where the company is held liable for the criminal acts of its employees and agents committed within the course of their employment. Usually liability of this kind only occurs where the offence is one of strict liability - that is where no *mens rea* is required. In the *ICR* case mentioned above the company could not have been vicariously liable for the act of another in a crime like conspiracy to defraud.

In *James and Son Ltd. v. Smee* 1955 a driver employed by the company was sent out with a lorry and trailer on a round. During the round he had to disconnect the brakes to the trailer and forgot to reconnect them. It was an offence for anyone to use or cause or permit to be used a vehicle or trailer without an efficient braking system. On appeal by the company against a conviction that it had permitted the trailer to be used Parker J in the Divisional Court said *"before the company can be held guilty of permitting ... it must be proved that some person for whose acts the company is responsible permitted as opposed to committed the offence. There was no such evidence in the present case"*. The *mens rea* of the offence, the permitting, had to be shown to be present in the employee if the company was to be held vicariously liable for what he had done. He had used the vehicle, but not permitted its use.

It seems that there are two circumstances in which a corporation many be criminally vicariously liable under statute. Firstly the statute may make express reference to such liability arising. Examples can be found in the Licensing Act 1964. For instance s.59 of the Act provides that " *... no person shall, except during the permitted hours ... himself or by his servant or agent sell or supply to any person in licensed premises ... any intoxicating liquor, whether to be consumed on or off the premises"*

Secondly liability may arise where a statutory duty supported by criminal sanctions is delegated to an employee. In such circumstances the conduct of the employee will be imputed to the employer.

Fault and strict liability

At common law the basis upon which criminal liability was founded required that the offender not only committed the facts constituting the prohibited conduct, referred to as the *actus reus* of the offence, but also demonstrated an accompanying state of mind suggesting moral culpability or fault. The criminal law has many examples of terms connoting degrees of fault or blameworthiness, words such as *deliberately, recklessly, negligently, wilfully, knowingly, dishonestly, fraudulently* and so on. Such terms are referred to as the *mens rea* of the offence, the guilty mind.

Parliament has seen fit however to introduce many offences under statute, which dispense with the need to prove that the offender was at fault. Usually such offences, which are referred to as *strict* or *absolute* offences, seek to impose liability without fault because it is socially or practically expedient to do so. Many of the minor offences associated with road traffic law are strict liability offences, such as speeding. There are also plentiful examples in the field of consumer protection. For example the Children and Young Persons Act 1937 creates a strict liability offence in relation to the sale of tobacco to children.

> In *St Helens MBC v. Hill* 1991 a shop owner was held liable for the sale of tobacco to a young child even though he was absent from the shop when the sale was made. The court held that the sale must be regarded in the eyes of the law as having been made by the shop owner, and therefore he was liable as though he had sold the cigarettes himself.

As we have seen there is nothing to prevent a business organisation incurring liability for offences where liability is either strict or fault based, although it is more common to find liability arising in relation to the former.

Examples of criminal liability which commonly effect business organisations and which are considered elsewhere in the text are those in fields of:

- consumer protection
- health and safety law
- company law.

Contractual liability in business

A contractual liability arises when two or more parties enter into a contractual relationship with each other. A contract is a legally enforceable agreement. Contract-making is the life blood of business. It is the way businesses trade. Because contract-making is so significant in business operations we need to examine it in some detail, and Chapters 8, 9 and 10 are devoted entirely to the subject of the negotiation and completion of business contracts.

Tortious liability in business

A tort is a civil wrong, and a person or organisation committing a tort is someone who incurs tortious liability. Unlike a contract, where liability depends upon the making of an agreement, in tort liability arises without the need for any agreement between the parties but simply through the operation of the general law.

The civil law recognises a number of distinct areas of tortious liability, each of them resulting from the development of specific torts. Torts are designed to protect people from certain recognised kinds of harm, and to grant them legal remedies if they actually sustain harm as a consequence of a tort being committed against them. Tortious harm covers such areas as:

- the protection of business and personal reputations – *the tort of defamation;*

- the unlawful interference with another's land or personal property – *the tort of trespass;* and

- the unlawful interference with a person's use and enjoyment of land – *the tort of private nuisance.*

The basis upon which liability arises depends upon the specific rules governing each tort. Some torts, for instance, require no proof of fault on the part of the wrongdoer. The tort of *trespass to land* is an example. Another is the tort of *Rylands v. Fletcher,* where strict liability is imposed upon a landowner in respect of any damage caused by the escape of non-natural things brought onto the land. Relying on this tort, strict liability has been imposed for damage caused by escaping water, gas, electricity, germs and even people.

Tortious liability however is normally associated with fault, which involves establishing that the defendant failed to act as a reasonable person would have acted in a particular set of circumstances. Thus in the *tort of negligence*, a defendant who is not shown to be at fault will not incur liability.

> In *Dixon v. London Fire and Civil Defence* 1993 water had leaked from a fire appliance onto the floor of the fire station. The court heard that such leaks were endemic in the fire service and appeared to be insoluble. As a consequence the court held that the fire authority was not in breach of the legal duty of care that it owed to a fire officer who had slipped and fallen as a result of the wet floor.

The tort of negligence is generally regarded as the most important of all the torts, and its impact upon business operations is potentially so significant that we need to look at it in some detail.

Negligence

The Nature of Liability in Negligence

Liability in the tort of negligence arises where foreseeable damage to the plaintiff is caused by the defendant's breach of a legal duty to take care. The tort has wide application and includes liability for losses or injuries suffered at work, on the roads, in dangerous premises, or as a result of medical accidents, professional malpractice or defective products.

A central feature of liability in negligence is that liability is fault-based. A defendant will be liable only if the court is satisfied that he failed to take reasonable care. Negligence provides a mechanism for loss distribution and the apportionment of the risks inherent in activities likely to result in loss or injury. It can be argued that a fault-based system is far from ideal as a means of ensuring fair treatment and proper financial assistance to those who are injured or disabled through no fault of their own. Indeed it has often been said that the law of negligence is like a lottery in which a few successful litigants are handsomely rewarded. Many other claimants are unable to obtain compensation due to lack of evidence of fault, lack of a substantial defendant to pursue or the refusal of the court to impose liability in the circumstances of the case.

One alternative to a system of fault-based liability is the introduction of strict liability for injuries sustained either generally or in particular categories of situation. Under a system of strict liability the injured party should find it much easier to obtain compensation because he will not need to prove a failure to take care on the part of the defendant. Such a system could be financed centrally through taxation, for example an additional tax on petrol to finance a scheme for road accidents. Alternatively it could be funded by compulsory insurance for those who would be exposed to liability, for example medical practitioners in respect of medical accidents. A further alternative is to have a combination of both methods of funding. However the likelihood of the widespread introduction of strict liability for these and other categories of personal injuries in the foreseeable future is remote.

A notable exception is the introduction of strict liability for injuries caused by defective products to the customer in the Consumer Protection Act 1987. The effect of the 1987 Act has been to increase substantially the number of successful claims against manufacturers of defective products. The Act, however, does not impose an obligation on those affected to insure against the liability it creates, nor does it provide an independent source of funds to compensate claimants. It falls upon the individual businessman to make sure that his own insurance arrangements are adequate to cover the additional liability which he is likely to face.

The significance of negligence liability for the businessman

A business is exposed to potential claims in negligence from a number of diverse sources. It is especially vulnerable because, under the rules of vicarious liability examined later, it is liable as an employer for wrongful acts committed by its employees in the course of their work. The prudent business will wish to take steps to minimise the liabilities to which it would otherwise be exposed. There are two things which it can do. First it can try to ensure that the business practices and the systems under which the employees operate are tightly structured and controlled so as to reduce the risk of injury and thereby prevent claims arising. Second it would be well advised to maintain an appropriate range of insurance policies to cover those risks which are most likely to affect the particular type of business it operates.

Types of insurance cover available

Insurance companies usually offer a wide range of policies and will arrange cover to meet the requirements of the individual business. Some types of cover are compulsory and therefore all businesses affected must have them; whilst others, although not compulsory, are such that no prudent businessman would consider it worthwhile to operate without them. Most businesses would be covered by all or most of the following types of policy:

(a) *employers liability* – elsewhere we shall be considering the duty of care owed by the employer at common law to provide a safe system of work, safe equipment and premises and safe fellow employees; and examine the employer's liability in negligence for injury to an employee caused by a breach of any of these duties. Under the Employers Liability (Compulsory Insurance) Act 1969 all employers other than local authorities and nationalised industries are required to insure against the risk of personal injury to their employees. The insurance must be contained in an approved policy which has prescribed contents. The policy must be issued by an authorised insurer.

(b) *motor vehicles* – under the Road Traffic Act 1988 the driver of a motor vehicle is required to be insured against third party personal injury and property risks. Most businesses running motor vehicles, and indeed most other motorists, obtain insurance cover well beyond the minimum laid down by the Act. Additional cover beyond the statutory minimum could include the risks of fire, theft of the vehicle, or full comprehensive cover which would include losses of the insured person's vehicle or property caused by his own fault.

(c) *product liability* – a policy of this type is designed to cover liability for injury or losses caused by defective products manufactured or supplied by the insured in the course of his business. It should cover liabilities arising in contract, negligence or under the Consumer Protection Act 1987.

(d) *public liability* – product liability cover is often included in this type of policy. The policy generally includes loss or injury sustained by a member of the public as a result of the activities of the business, for example liability under the Occupiers Liability Act 1957 for injury to a customer caused by the unsafe state of the business premises, or the organisation's liability in negligence resulting from an accident caused by an employee in failing safely to carry out his duties.

(e) *premises and stock* – this provides insurance against loss of or damage to business property caused by fire, theft or negligence.

(f) *professional indemnity* – a policy of this type covers the insured for claims made against him in respect of professional negligence, for example a claim against an architect for miscalculating the depth of the foundations of a multistorey building or specifying inadequate reinforcements for the structure. In some professions, for example, solicitors, professional indemnity insurance is in effect compulsory because the professional body will refuse to issue a *practising certificate* without evidence of premium payment on an appropriate policy.

(g) *legal expenses insurance* – this is a relative newcomer to the UK insurance market and provides the insured with a full indemnity for legal costs incurred in engaging in legal action in the civil or criminal courts.

Having identified some of the major types of insurance cover available to protect the business from losses which could otherwise be incurred by the business, it is worth pointing out that the levels of cover, in terms of the financial limits on the claims that the insurer would satisfy, are a matter of commercial judgment which will depend on the nature of the business concerned.

Additionally, a business entering into a contract of insurance must disclose all material facts which could affect the insurer's assessment of the risk. It would also be well advised to examine carefully the detailed wording of the policy in order to be certain that it is actually getting the cover which it wants.

Because of the universal use of insurance by businesses, many of the commercial cases litigated before the courts are in reality disputes between insurance companies standing in the shoes of the named plaintiffs and defendants who have often already been paid out by the insurance companies.

Essential Elements of Liability in Negligence

In order to succeed in a claim in negligence the plaintiff will have to prove three things:

    (a)   that the defendant owed him a *legal duty of care*,

    (b)   that *the duty was broken*, and

    (c)   that the defendant's breach of duty resulted in *foreseeable loss or damage* to the plaintiff.

Once the plaintiff has established these elements there are a number of defences available to the defendant. He may try to establish:

- that the plaintiff contributed to his injury by his own negligence - the defence of *contributory negligence*.

- that the plaintiff had voluntarily assumed the risk of injury - a defence based on consent known technically as a *volenti non fit injuria,* or

- that the plaintiff's claim is out of time and therefore *statute-barred* under the Limitation Act 1980 (as amended).

We shall now examine in more detail the elements of liability and the defences available in a negligence claim.

The Duty of Care

The tort of negligence is an area of legal liability which has been developed by the common law through the decisions of judges in individual cases over the centuries. The process is a continuing one and significant developments have taken place in recent years particularly in relation to the question of when a duty of care is owed by a defendant to the plaintiff.

The major milestone in the evolution of the law of negligence was the decision of the House of Lords in *Donoghue v. Stevenson* 1932 in which Lord Atkin laid down general principles which could be applied to any situation in order to determine whether a duty of care is owed. Prior to 1932 there were no legal principles of general application which defined the circumstances in which a person could be liable for loss or injury caused by his carelessness to another.

> The facts of *Donoghue v. Stevenson* 1932 are that the plaintiff's friend bought her a bottle of ginger beer in a cafe. The ginger beer was in an opaque bottle and, after pouring some of it and drinking from her glass, the remainder was poured from the bottle into the glass. This was found to contain the remains of a decomposed snail, the sight of which caused the plaintiff to suffer shock and become ill. As the drink was a gift from her friend, the plaintiff had no contract with the seller. She therefore sued the manufacturer claiming that he owed a duty of care to her to ensure that his product was not contaminated during the process of manufacture. The defendant argued that he owed no legal duty to the plaintiff because there was no contract between them and the case fell outside the existing recognised categories of duty. The House of Lords rejected the defendant's arguments and, by a slim majority of three judges to two, found for the plaintiff.

This case is important for two reasons. First, in the field of product liability, because Lord Atkin's judgment defines the duty of a manufacturer of a product towards a person injured by a defect in the product.

Second, in the context of the development of the law of negligence as a whole, because Lord Atkin in formulating the neighbour principle, laid down a unifying principle of liability for harm caused unintentionally by the defendant. For this reason the decision in *Donoghue* is often regarded as marking the birth of negligence as a tort. In the celebrated passage from his judgment Lord Atkin said *"The rule that you are to love your neighbour becomes in law, you must not injure your neighbour; and the lawyers question, Who is my neighbour? receives a restricted reply. You must take reasonable care to avoid acts or omissions which you can reasonably foresee would be likely to injure your neighbour. Who, then, in law is my neighbour? The answer seems to be - persons who are so closely and directly affected by my act that I ought reasonably to have them in contemplation as being so affected when I am directing my mind to the acts or omissions which are called in question."*

The defendant's duty is a duty to take reasonable care to avoid causing foreseeable harm and it is owed to anyone closely and directly affected by the defendant's conduct. The close relationship necessary between the defendant and plaintiff in order for a duty to exist is often referred to as a *relationship of proximity* between the parties.

> The status of the neighbour principle as a rule of general applicability was underlined by the House of Lords in *Home Office v. Dorset Yacht Co.* 1970. Here the plaintiff's yacht was damaged by borstal trainees who had escaped while on a training exercise on an island. They had been carelessly left unsupervised by their guards. Applying the neighbour principle, it was held that the defendant owed a duty of care to the plaintiff whose yacht had been moored between the island and the mainland, as it was reasonably foreseeable that the trainees might use the yacht as a means of escape. The defendant was vicariously liable for the failure of its employees to supervise the trainees. This breach of duty caused the plaintiff's loss for which the Home Office was liable. In a leading judgment, Lord Reid stated *"Donoghue v. Stevenson may be regarded as a milestone, and the well known passage in Lord Atkin's speech should I think be regarded as a statement of principle. It is not to be treated as if it were a statutory definition. It will require qualification in new circumstances. But I think that the time has come when we can and should say that it ought to apply unless there is some justification or valid explanation for its exclusion."*

Lord Reid's statement implies that there may be cases in which a straight application of the neighbour principle will suggest the existence of a duty of care, but nevertheless the court would refuse to recognise a duty because there are valid justifications for failing to impose liability. The justifications which are used in these circumstances are often referred to as considerations of public policy. We can interpret this expression as meaning reasons based on judicial perceptions of what may or may not be in the best interests of the community at large. It is inevitable that policy issues arise in the course of deciding cases in negligence. This is because Parliament has rarely intervened to influence the direction of legal developments in this field by passing legislation. The judges have, therefore, found it necessary to make decisions on policy issues as part of the process of deciding cases and developing an acceptable coherent and workable body of legal rules.

It should be appreciated that in the majority of claims for personal injuries or damage to property, for example in the field of product liability, there will not be any policy considerations restricting the application of the neighbour principle in order to establish that a duty of care exists. It is in relation to claims for financial loss, for example in the area of professional negligence, that policy considerations - such as the fear of creating open-ended liability - may be taken in to account.

The views expressed by Lord Reid in *Home Office v. Dorset Yacht Co.* 1970 about the significance of the neighbour principle were supported by the House of Lords in *Anns v. London Borough of Merton* 1977. Lord Wilberforce explained the approach which a court should take in determining whether a duty of care exists in any given case *"... the position has now been reached that in order to establish that a duty of care arises in a particular situation, it is not necessary to bring the facts of that situation within those of previous situations in which a duty of care has been held to exist. Rather the question has to be approached in two stages. First, one has to ask whether, as between the alleged wrongdoer and the person who has suffered damage there is a sufficient relationship of proximity or neighbourhood such that, in the reasonable contemplation of the former carelessness on his part may be likely to cause damage to the latter, in which case a prima facie duty of care arises. Secondly, if the first question is answered affirmatively, it is necessary to consider whether there are any considerations which ought to negative, or to reduce or limit the scope of the duty or the class of person to whom it is owed or the damages to which a breach of it may give rise."*

The introduction of Lord Wilberforce's *two-stage* test led to a reassessment of the existence and scope of the duty of care in some situations. Some judges believed that it relieved them of the obligation to follow restrictive pre-1977 precedents and allowed them re-assess those situations having regard only to the two-stage test.

In a number of cases in the 1980's the House of Lords emphasised that the two stage approach to establishing a duty of care laid down in *Anns* was to be applied only to new situations not already the subject of precedent.

One of the first was the decision in *Leigh & Sillavan Ltd. v. Aliakmon Shipping Co. Ltd, The Aliakmon* 1986 where Lord Brandon, delivering a judgment with which the other presiding Law Lords were in complete agreement, expressed the view that the test applied only to novel types of factual situation and that the test was not to be applied where the situation was already covered by pre-1977 precedents. Referring to the two-stage test, Lord Brandon stated that it *"... does not provide, and cannot in my view have been intended by Lord Wilberforce to provide, a universally applicable test of the existence and scope of a duty of care in the law of negligence.."*

The process was taken further in *Curran v. Northern Ireland Co-ownership Housing Association Ltd.* 1987 when Lord Bridge, delivering the single judgment of the House of Lords, stated that the approach adopted in *Anns* "*may be said to represent the high water mark of a trend in the development of the law of negligence by your Lordship's House towards the elevation of the 'neighbourhood' principle ... into one of general application from which a duty of care may always be derived unless there are clear counterveiling considerations to exclude it."*

It is clear that the tide of judicial creativity which rose on the strength of the two-stage test in *Anns*, reached, for a relatively brief period, a high water mark from which it has steadily retreated as a result of a number of decisions both of the House of Lords and the Privy Council over recent years.

The present position can perhaps best be summed up by quoting from the judgment of Lord Bridge in *Caparo Industries plc v. Dickman* 1990:

> *"What emerges is that, in addition to the foreseeability of damage, necessary ingredients in any situation giving rise to a duty of care are that there should exist between the party owing the duty and the party to whom it is owed a relationship characterised by the law as one of `proximity' or 'neighbourhood' and that the situation should be one in which the court considers it fair, just and reasonable that the law should impose a duty of a given scope on the one party for the benefit of the other"..*"

The *Caparo* three stage approach to establishing a duty of care requires a positive response to three questions:

- was the harm caused reasonably foreseeable?

- was there a relationship of proximity between the defendant and the plaintiff?

- in all the circumstances is it just, fair and reasonable to impose a duty of care?

This approach has since been upheld by the Court of Appeal in *Marc Rich & Co. and others v. Bishop Rock Marine Co. Ltd. and others, The Nicholas H* 1994. Here the Court of Appeal held that the three stage approach to establishing a duty of care laid down in *Caparo* should be applied in every case where negligence is alleged. This universal test should be applied to all negligence cases whether the harm alleged is nervous shock, physical harm or purely financial loss. While such a consistant approach to establishing a duty of care is superficially attractive it should be appreciated that there will still be different factors to take account of in determining foreseeability, for example, in relation to physical harm as opposed to psychiatric illness. On a given set of facts one type of harm may be foreseeable, whilst another type may not.

In *Spring v. Guardian Assurance plc* 1994 the Court of Appeal decided that despite the fact that the giver of a reference which was factually incorrect had been negligent, there could be no liability, because a referee owes no duty of care to the subject of the reference. The House of Lords however disagreed. The Law Lords held that an employer can be liable in negligence for failure to take reasonable care in providing a reference for an employee or an ex-employee. This is because there is a proximate relationship between them and it is fair, just and reasonable that the employer should be under such a duty. A further justification for recognising this a duty is that the employer assumes responsibility for the reference and the employee relies on the employer to take reasonable care. It seems that the majority of the judges thought that as references are crucial in the recruitment process it is vital that they are written with reasonable care. It is in the public interest that the referee owes a legal duty of care to the subject of the reference.

The important decision of the House of Lords in *White and another v. Jones and others* 1995 considered the potential liability of defendant solicitors who caused the plaintiff's financial loss as a result of a negligent *omission*. The plaintiffs had originally been cut out of their father's (the testator) will but then reinstated on the testator's instructions to the defendant solicitors. The solicitors had delayed for over six weeks in carrying out the instructions to change the will and unfortunately, in the meanwhile, the testator died.

As there was no contractual relationship between the plaintiffs and the defendants the action for financial loss could only be based on the tort of negligence. The central issue in the dispute was whether a solicitor in drafting a will owes a legal duty of care in the tort of negligence to a potential beneficiary. The High Court thought not. This decision was reversed on appeal and the solicitors then made a final appeal to the House of Lords. By a three to two majority decision their Lordships held that the potential loss to the plaintiffs in these circumstances was reasonably foreseeable and the relationship of a solicitor, called upon to draft a will, and the potential beneficiary, should be brought within the established categories of relationship under which a duty of care arises. This duty of care had been broken by the solicitor's negligence causing financial loss for which the defendants were liable.

Breach of Duty

Once it has been established that the defendant in a given situation owes a duty of care to avoid injury to the plaintiff, the next question which falls to be decided is whether the defendant was in breach of that duty. It should be stressed that these are two separate issues and only after the court is satisfied that a duty exists will it go on to consider the question of breach. A breach of duty is a failure to take reasonable care. This involves a finding of fault on the part of the defendant. In the words of Alderson B. in *Blyth v. Birmingham Waterworks Co.* 1856:

> *"Negligence (in the sense of a breach of duty) is the omission to do something which a reasonable man, guided upon those considerations which ordinarily regulate the conduct of human affairs, would do, or something which a reasonable and prudent man would not do."*

The duty of care is broken when a person fails to do what a reasonable man would do in the same circumstances. The standard of care required of the defendant in a particular case will vary according to the circumstances of the case and the skills which the defendant holds himself out as possessing. Thus a surgeon carrying out out an operation is required to demonstrate the skills and knowledge of a reasonably competent surgeon. On the other hand the degree of care expected of a hospital porter is not so exacting. Whilst the standard of care required of a skilled defendant such as a professional person will be high, the reverse cannot be said to be true. An inexperienced or unskilled defendant will not be able to argue that the standard of care which he is required to demonstrate is correspondingly low.

Thus in *Nettleship v. Weston* 1971 the Court of Appeal held that a learner driver was in breach of her duty of care to the plaintiff, a passenger, for failing to demonstrate the driving skills of a reasonably competent qualified driver, and was liable for the injuries sustained by the plaintiff as a result.

The same principle was applied by the Court of Appeal in *Wilsher v. Essex Area Health Authority* 1986 when it held, by a majority of two judges to one, that inexperience was no defence to an action in negligence against a junior doctor, who would be in breach of his duty of care if he failed to demonstrate the skill of a reasonably competent qualified doctor. On the facts of the case, however, the junior doctor had discharged his duty by asking a more senior colleague to check his work.

In determining whether a duty of care has been broken the court must assess the conduct of the defendant and decide whether he acted reasonably or unreasonably. This assessment allows the judge a large measure of discretion in an individual case, although it could be argued that it also produces some uncertainty in the law. The main factors which the court will take into account in deciding whether there has been a breach of the duty of care are:

- the extent of the risk created by the defendant's conduct - whether the risk was serious or obvious;

- the nature of the harm which is likely to be caused to the plaintiff;

- the practicability and expense of taking steps to minimise the risk;

- the particular circumstances of the case.

A good example of the way in which the courts attempt to balance these factors is provided by the case of *Bolton v. Stone* 1951.

> In *Bolton v. Stone* 1951 the plaintiff was standing on the highway outside her home and was struck by a cricket ball hit by a visiting batsman off the pitch of the local cricket club. She sued the members and committee of the cricket club. The ground had been used for cricket since 1864, well before the surrounding houses were built. Balls were rarely hit out of the ground and onto the highway, perhaps only six times in the previous thirty years, and there was no record of any previous accident. The ball in question had travelled seventy-eight yards before passing over the fence and about twenty-five yards further before hitting the plaintiff. The top of the fence was seven feet about the highway and seventeen feet above the pitch. The House of Lords held that the defendants were not liable because they had taken reasonable care. The chances of such an accident were so slim that the reasonable man would have done no more than the defendants had done to prevent it from happening. In the course of his judgment, Lord Ratcliffe stated *"A breach of duty has taken place if the defendants are guilty of a failure to take reasonable care to prevent the accident. One may phrase it as reasonable care or ordinary care or proper care - all these phrases are to be found in decisions of authority - but the fact remains that, unless there has been something which a reasonable man would blame as falling beneath the standard of conduct that he would set for himself and require of his neighbour, there has been no breach of legal duty. It seems to me in this case that a reasonable man, taking account of the chances against an accident happening, would not have felt himself called upon either to abandon the use of the ground for cricket or to increase the height of his surrounding fences."*

Chapter 15 examines a number of cases involving a breach of the employer's duty of care for the safety of his employees – see for instance *Latimer v. AEC* 1953 and *Paris v. Stepney Borough Council* 1951. Consideration of those cases will further demonstrate the approach of the courts in balancing the factors which are relevant to the question of breach of duty.

Proof of the defendant's breach of duty

The normal rule in a civil case is that the plaintiff must adduce evidence to prove his case on balance of probabilities. It will therefore be the plaintiff's job, in a negligence case, to show that the defendant did not act in a reasonable way. If he is unable to do this his claim will fail.

> In *Wakelin v. London and South Western Railway Co.* 1886 the body of the plaintiff's husband was found near a level crossing on a railway. He had been hit by a train but there was no evidence to suggest what had happened. The accident could have been his own fault or it could have been attributable to the fault of the defendant. As the plaintiff was unable to prove that the defendant acted in an unreasonable manner, her claim failed.

The difficulty involved in proving that a defendant is in breach of the duty of care is illustrated by the legal claims arising from the injuries caused to unborn children by the drug *Thalidomide*. Although legal proceedings were issued in the UK, none of the claims were ever brought before the courts. There were two main legal reasons for this. Firstly because it was not certain that a duty of care could be owed to an unborn child (this has since been established by legislation under the Congenital Disabilities (Civil Liability) Act 1976). Secondly because the plaintiffs would probably have been unable to prove that the defendants had failed to take reasonable care. The drug had undergone extensive testing before it was released onto the market. Although it had not been tested on pregnant women, it is not clear that a reasonable drug manufacturer would have tested a drug of that type - a tranquilliser - for its effect upon the developing child within the womb of the pregnant woman, given the state of scientific knowledge within the pharmaceutical industry at that time. After protracted negotiations an out of court settlement was reached between the parties on terms dictated by the defendants. The levels of agreed compensation were widely regarded as being well below those which might have been awarded at the conclusion of a successful trial. Some observers believe that the defendants would not even have agreed to settle the claims on those terms had it not been for the considerable pressure of public opinion and the efforts of a well organised group of the defendant company's own shareholders on the plaintiffs' behalf.

Res ipsa loquitur

In some cases the plaintiff may be relieved of the burden of proving negligence if the court accepts a plea of *res ipsa loquitur* (the thing speaks for itself). This is a rule of evidence which applies where the plaintiff's injury is one that would not in the ordinary course of events have happened without negligence and there is no satisfactory alternative explanation for the injury other than negligence by the defendant.

The effect of the rule is that the court will infer negligence on the part of the defendant without the need for the plaintiff to pinpoint the cause of the injury or explain how the defendant failed to take reasonable care. The defendant will be liable unless he furnishes evidence to show that his negligence did not cause the plaintiff's loss.

The rule will be of great assistance to the plaintiff where it seems to be obvious that the defendant was negligent but the plaintiff is unable to pinpoint the exact nature of the defendant's breach of duty.

In *Scott v. London and St. Catherine Docks Co*. 1865 a customs officer was injured when six sacks of sugar fell on him as he was passing the defendant's warehouse. The court held that the res ipsa loquitur rule applied and inferred negligence on the part of the defendant which it was unable to disprove. During the course of his judgment, Erle, C.J. stated: *"Where the thing is shown to be under the management of the defendant, or his servants, and the accident is such as, in the ordinary course of things, does not happen if those who have the management use proper care, it affords reasonable evidence, in the absence of explanation by the defendant, that the accident arose from want of care."*

In *Cassidy v. Ministry of Health* 1951, the plaintiff was injured in a surgical operation on his hand. Denning, L.J. asserted that the res ipsa loquitur rule enabled the plaintiff to say, in effect:*"... I went into hospital to be cured of two stiff fingers. I have come out with four stiff fingers, and my hand is useless. That should not have happened if due care had been used. Explain it, if you can."* The defendant was held liable as he was unable to explain how such a result was consistent with the use of reasonable care.

In *Ward v. Tesco Stores* 1976 the plaintiff was injured when she slipped on a pool of yoghurt which had previously been spilled onto the floor of the defendant's supermarket and had not been cleaned up. The Court of Appeal applied the *res ipsa loquitur* rule and the defendant was held liable as it was unable to show that it had taken reasonable care.

Fatal accidents

Where the defendant's breach of duty has resulted in death, legal action may be brought on behalf of the estate of the deceased person under the Law Reform (Miscellaneous Provisions) Acts 1934 and 1970. The dependants of the deceased will have a separate claim under the Fatal Accidents Act 1976 as amended by the Administration of Justice Act 1982.

We shall consider each type of claim in turn:

(a) The personal representatives may pursue any claim which the deceased person would have had if he had survived. Here damages are restricted to items of loss which arose between the injury and the death. The claim could include pain and suffering, loss of earnings and medical expenses, in each case up to the time of death. Funeral expenses are also recoverable but losses or notional losses in respect of the years after the death cannot be claimed in an action by the deceased's personal representatives.

(b) Certain relatives who were financially dependent on the deceased person are entitled to claim against the defendant. These are his spouse, parents, grandparents, children, grandchildren, sisters, brothers, aunts and uncles, and their issue. In addition, any co-habitee who lived with him as husband or wife for at least two years immediately before the death may claim. The aim of the court will be to provide maintenance for those relatives who have lost the financial support which he provided before his death. In order to succeed, the plaintiff must show:

(i)   that he is a relative,

(ii) that there is actionable negligence, and

(iii) that he was a dependant and has suffered financially as a result of the death.

In addition, a claim for a bereavement award for suffering and grief, which is for a fixed sum of £7,500, may be made by the spouse of the deceased or the parents of a child under 18 who is killed.

Resulting Damage

The third essential element of liability in negligence is that the defendant's breach of duty resulted in foreseeable loss or damage to the plaintiff. In reality this involves two separate issues - the issues of *causation* and *remoteness* of damage.

Causation of damage

The causation issue is concerned with the question of cause and effect: was the defendant's breach of duty the operative cause of the plaintiff's loss. The plaintiff's claim will fail if he is unable to prove this link. He must show that but for the defendant's negligence his loss would not have occurred.

> In *Barnett v. Chelsea and Kensington Hospital Management Committee* 1969 the plaintiff's husband was a night watchman, who called at the defendant's hospital in the early hours of the morning complaining of vomiting. He was sent home without being examined and was told to contact his own doctor later that day. He was suffering from arsenic poisoning and died a few hours later. The court held that the defendants were in breach of their duty of care, but the claim failed because the negligence of the hospital had not caused the death. The court accepted on the evidence that even if he had been examined immediately, the plaintiff's husband would still have died from arsenic poisoning.

Remoteness of damage

Where the plaintiff proves that his injuries were caused by the defendant's breach of duty, he can recover damages provided that his injuries were not too remote a consequence of the breach. The law does not necessarily impose liability for all of the consequences of a negligent act. Some damage may be too remote. Only damage which was reasonably foreseeable at the time of the negligent act can be recovered by the plaintiff.

> In *The Wagon Mound* 1961 a large quantity of fuel oil was carelessly spilled by the defendant's employees while a ship was taking on fuel in Sydney Harbour. Some of the oil spread to the plaintiff's wharf where welding operations were taking place. The plaintiff stopped welding temporarily, but recommenced after receiving expert opinion that fuel oil would not ignite when spread on water. Two days later the oil ignited when a drop of molten metal fell onto a piece of waste floating in the oil, causing extensive damage to the plaintiff's wharf. The court found as a fact that it was not reasonably foreseeable that the oil would ignite in these circumstances. It was held that the damage to the wharf was too remote, and the plaintiff's claim failed.

Once it has been established that the type of injury the plaintiff has suffered is foreseeable, then the defendant is potentially liable for all the injury of that type which occurs.

The common law rule that a defendant must *"take the plaintiff as he finds him"* was illustrated in *Page v. Smith* 1995. Here the plaintiff was the victim of a road accident caused by negligent driving. He was physically unhurt but had suffered psychiatric injury from the accident. The plaintiff had suffered from the illness myalgic encephalomyelitis (ME) sporadically for many years and the accident had caused it to become chronic. The Court of Appeal held that even though the plaintiff was directly involved in the accident, nervous shock had to be reasonably foreseeable to establish a duty of care, and in the circumstances of this accident such an injury could not have been foreseen. By a majority however, the House of Lords disagreed. They held that in negligent driving cases, to establish a duty of care it is necessary to show that personal injury of *some kind* was reasonably foreseeable, whether physical or psychiatric. In this case therefore the fact that no physical injury, but rather nervous shock resulted from the accident, did not prevent a legal duty of care being established. The defendant was liable for the full extent of the psychiatric injury on the principle that since the duty of care was established he had to take his victim as he found him.

The plaintiff's damage may be held to be too remote where an unforeseen new independent act, outside the defendant's control, intervenes to break the chain of causation. If the plaintiff's damage is caused by such a *novus actus interveniens* the defendant will not be liable for it. For example an employer's liability for injury suffered by an employee at work will not extend to further injuries received in the course of negligent medical treatment in hospital.

In *Cobb v. Great Western Railway* 1894 the defendant allowed a railway carriage to become overcrowded. As a result the plaintiff's pocket was picked and he lost nearly £100. It was held that the act of the thief was a novus actus interveniens and therefore that the plaintiff's loss was too remote.

Defences to a Negligence Action

Contributory negligence

Where the plaintiff has successfully established all of the elements of a negligence action, but has in some way contributed to his injuries by his own negligence, the defendant may raise the defence of contributory negligence.

Section 1(1) of the Law Reform (Contributory Negligence) Act 1945 provides:

> *"Where any person suffers damage as the result partly of his own fault and partly of the fault of any other person or persons, a claim in respect of that damage shall not be defeated by reason of the fault of the person suffering the damage, but the damages recoverable in respect thereof shall be reduced to such extent as the court thinks just and equitable having regard to the claimant's share in the responsibility for the damage."*

The effect of this provision is simply that the plaintiff's damages will be reduced in direct proportion to the extent to which he is to blame for his injuries.

In *Davies v. Swan Motor Co. (Swansea) Ltd. (third party James)* 1949 the plaintiff's damages were reduced by 20% when he was held to be contributorily negligent. He was riding on the back of a dust lorry contrary to his employer's instructions and was injured when the dust lorry was in collision with a bus.

In *Stapley v. Gypsum Mines* 1953 the plaintiffs were miners who, contrary to specific instructions by their employer, worked under a dangerous roof. They were injured when the roof collapsed and fell in on them. Their damages were reduced by 80% for contributory negligence.

In *Froome v. Butcher* 1976 it was held that the failure to wear a seat belt was contributory negligence and that the appropriate reduction in damages was 25% if the seat belt would have prevented the injury altogether, or 15% if it would merely have reduced the extent of the injury.

In *Sayers v. Harlow UDC* 1958 the plaintiff became locked inside a public lavatory because of the defendant's negligence in failing to maintain the door lock. After failing to attract attention or assistance, she attempted to climb out over the top of the door. In doing so she fell and was injured. It was held that the defendant was liable in negligence, but the plaintiff's damages were reduced by 25% for contributory negligence.

Voluntary assumption of risk (volenti non fit injuria)

This defence, which is universally referred to by its latin name *volenti non fit injuria,* is available to the defendant where the plaintiff freely and voluntarily accepts a risk of which he has full knowledge. In modern times the courts have been reluctant to apply the defence, which has the effect of completely defeating the plaintiff's claim, other than in exceptional circumstances. The reason for this is that the type of behaviour which would come within the defence would also usually amount to contributory negligence. The courts probably take the view that a more just outcome can be achieved by applying the rules of contributory negligence.

In *Smith v. Charles Baker & Sons* 1891 the plaintiff was employed in the excavation of a railway cutting. He was injured by a stone which fell from an overhead crane. He had known that there was an element of risk in working beneath the crane but had not objected to his employer. As a defence to his action for compensation, the employer argued that the plaintiff had voluntarily undertaken the risk of injury. The House of Lords held that the employer was liable. The defence failed because mere knowledge of the risk was not the same as consent to the danger. Lord Herschell stated the volenti rule in the following terms: *"One who has invited or assented to an act being done towards him cannot, when he suffers from it, complain of it as a wrong ... if then, the employer thus fails in his duty towards the employed, I do not think that because (the employee) does not straightaway refuse to continue his service, it is true to say that he is willing that his employer should act thus towards him. I believe it would be contrary to the facts to assert that the plaintiff in this case either invited or assented to the employer's negligence."*

In *Bowater v. Rowley Regis Corporation* 1944 the plaintiff was employed as a carter, and was ordered to take out a particular horse to pull his cart. He protested because the horse was known to be vicious but his protests were in vain. He was injured by the horse and in an action for damages the defendant raised the defence of *volenti non fit injuria*. It was held that the defence was inapplicable because the plaintiff had not genuinely consented to run the risk. In reality he had little choice but to take out the horse.

The defence of *volenti non fit injuria* will not usually be available where the plaintiff has been injured while attempting to rescue someone from a peril created by the defendant's negligence. In these circumstances the rescuer cannot normally be regarded as having freely consented to the risk of injury.

In *Haynes v. Harwood* 1935 for example, a policeman was injured while stopping a runaway horse and cart which endangered the safety of members of the public, including children, in a busy street. It was held that, in the circumstances, he had at least a moral duty to intervene, and his claim for damages succeeded.

By way of contrast in *Cutler v. United Dairies Ltd.* 1933 the plaintiff intervened to stop a runaway horse within a field. It posed no risk of injury to anyone. The plaintiff was unable to recover damages for the injuries which he sustained as the court held that he had voluntarily assumed the risk of injury.

Exclusion of liability for negligence

Under the rules of common law it used to be possible for a defendant to exclude his liability for negligence, either by including an appropriately worded term in a contract, or by displaying a notice to that effect.

In *White v. Blakemore* 1972, for example, the plaintiff's husband, a member of a racing club, stood next to the ropes near a stake watching a race. The wheel of a racing car caught on the rope pulling the stake out of the ground. The stake killed the plaintiff's husband. Notices had been displayed by the defendant in prominent positions excluding all liability for accidents howsoever caused. It was held that the notices were effective to protect the defendant from liability.

Since the introduction of the Unfair Contract Terms Act 1977, however, the scope of the common rules have been considerably cut down. Under s.2 of the 1977 Act liability for death or personal injury caused by negligence cannot be excluded, but that it may be possible to exclude liability for other types of damage or loss. Such an exclusion will only be effective however if the defendant can prove that it is fair and reasonable to allow reliance on it in the circumstances of the case.

Time limits for claims in negligence

The Limitation Act 1980, as amended by the Latent Damage Act 1986, provides that no legal action may be taken in respect of certain types of claim unless proceedings are issued within the limitation period. After this time the claim is said to be statute barred and the court will refuse to entertain it. The limitation period varies according to the legal basis of the claim and the type of injury or damage suffered by the plaintiff.

(a) Personal injuries or death

Personal injury claims in negligence and in contract are subject to a limitation period of three years. Time starts to run either on the date on which the right to sue first arises, or, if later, on the date on which the plaintiff is aware:

    (i)   that he has suffered significant injury,

    (ii)   that this is attributable to the defendant's negligence or breach of contract, and

    (iii) of the identity of the defendant.

Where this formula applies there is no final long term cut off date after which the plaintiff's claim cannot be brought. The plaintiff will usually use this formula when he is suing for injuries which did not manifest themselves at the time of the negligent act. This could apply if, for example, the plaintiff contracted a lung disease through exposure to industrial dust from asbestos or coal, and the disease did not become apparent for a number of years.

(b) Claims other than personal injury

In the case of a claim which does not involve personal injury, for example for property damage or financial loss, the limitation period both in negligence and in contract is six years from the date on which the right to sue first arises. In the case of a negligence claim for this type of loss the Latent Damage Act 1986 enables the plaintiff to commence legal proceedings outside the six year period the 1986 Act does not apply to a contract claim. Under the Act the claim must be made within three years of the date on which the plaintiff became aware:

    (i)   that the damage was significant,

    (ii)   that it was attributable to the negligence of the defendant, and

    (iii) of the identity of the defendant.

Under the 1986 Act, however, the limitation period cannot be extended beyond 15 years of the date of the event which constituted the defendant's breach of duty. As we noted above there is no such *long stop* date beyond which the period for bringing a personal injuries claim cannot be extended.

One of the principal reasons for the introduction of the Latent Damages Act 1986 was to provide an effective remedy for a person in the situation of the plaintiff in the case of *Pirelli v. Oscar Faber*.

> In *Pirelli General Cable Works Ltd. v. Oscar Faber & Partners* 1983 the defendants were consulting engineers who advised the plaintiffs on the design and erection of a large chimney for the boiler at their factory. The design was defective and expert evidence showed that internal cracks had occurred within the chimney before April 1970. The damage was not discovered, however, until 1977 and the plaintiff did not commence legal proceedings until 1978. The House of Lords held that the six year limitation period began to run as soon as the damage occurred and therefore the claim was statute barred. The limitation period had expired even before the plaintiffs knew that they had suffered any damage.

Under the provisions of the 1986 Act the issue of limitation would have been decided in the plaintiff's favour on the facts of the *Pirelli* case. The Act is designed to eliminate this type of injustice.

Business Premises and Liability

Occupiers of business premises whether freeholders or business tenants have duties placed upon them to ensure the safety of all lawful entrants by virtue of the Occupiers Liability Act 1957 and in some cases an obligation to take reasonable care extends to uninvited visitors under the Occupiers Liability Act 1984.

Under the Occupiers Liability Act 1957 an occupier of business premises owes the common duty of care to all his lawful visitors and that is to take such care as in all the circumstances is reasonable to provide for their safety. Notice that the duty is owed by the occupier, the person in control of the premises and he would certainly include the owner in possession or a business tenant or licensee.

> In *Ferguson v. Welsh and others* 1988 an employee, Mr. Ferguson, sustained serious injuries when engaged on demolition work on a site owned by the district council. Having invited and accepted a tender to do the demolition work from Mr. Spence, an approved contractor of the council, the council were unaware that the work had been subcontracted to Mr. Ferguson's employers, the Welsh brothers. This was despite the fact that the original invitation to tender expressly prohibited subcontracting without the council's approval. Mr. Ferguson's claim for damages against his employers, the Welsh brothers, for breach of statutory duty was upheld in the High Court. Whether the council as occupier of the premises owed Mr. Ferguson a duty of care under the 1957 Act was only finally resolved in the House of Lords. Their Lordships held that despite the express prohibition on subcontracts, Mr. Ferguson was nevertheless a lawful visitor of the council. *"The contractor engaged by the council was placed in control of the site for demolition purposes and to one who had no knowledge of the council's policy of prohibiting subcontracts, that would indicate that he was entitled to invite whomsoever he pleased onto the site for the purposes of carrying out the demolition. Moreover having put the contractor into occupation of the premises and thus into a position to invite the subcontractors and their employees onto them for the purpose of demolishing the building, the council must be taken to have invited the appellant in for that purpose so as to create a duty of care."* The House of Lords therefore confirmed that for the purposes of liability there may be different occupiers of the premises. In this case however the council although occupiers were not in breach of the common duty of care when the injury occurred as a result of the unsafe system of work adopted by subcontractors.

The business landlord is regarded as the occupier in relation to parts of the premises which remain under his control, e.g. entrance hall, lifts, forecourt or other common parts. Also if the landlord is under an obligation to repair, he may under s.4 Defective Premises Act 1972 be made liable for injuries that occur as a result of his failure to fulfil a repair obligation. Where the premises are let therefore, both the landlord and the tenant may be regarded as occupier of the premises for different purposes under the Act.

The obligation of the occupier in these circumstances is to take reasonable care in entrusting the work to an independent contractor and to take such steps as he reasonably ought in order to satisfy himself that the contractor was competent and that the work had been done properly. The occupier will have acted reasonably if he selected a reputable organisation to do work on the premises rather than a local handyman.

In *O'Connor v. Swan & Edgar* 1963 the plaintiff was injured by a fall of plaster when she worked as a demonstrator on the first defendant's premises. The fall of plaster was due to the faulty workmanship of the second defendants who had been engaged as contractors to work on the premises. The court held that as the first defendants had acted reasonably in entrusting the work to a reputable contractor then as an occupier he had satisfied the duty of care which was owed. The second defendants however were held liable in the tort of negligence for faulty workmanship.

Following the Unfair Contract Terms Act 1977 it is no longer possible for an occupier of business premises to exclude the common duty of care in relation to his visitors. To fulfil the duty owed it is necessary to ensure that premises are indeed reasonably safe or alternatively ensure that visitors are safe by giving adequate warning of any dangers. The 1957 Act mentions two categories of visitor in particular, children and independent contractors. It says that in relation to child visitors an occupier must be prepared for them to be less careful than adults. This suggests that for instance that an occupier of retail premises to which the public have access will owe a higher standard of care towards children than adults. The requirement of parental control however is a significant factor in establishing liability for injury caused to child visitors.

In *Simkiss v. Rhondda B.C.* 1983 a seven year old suffered injury when she fell 30 or 40 feet after sliding on a blanket down a steep slope owned by the council. The High Court found the council liable for breach of the common duty of care in failing to either ensure that the mountainside was safe for children to play on or alternatively fencing it off. The Court of Appeal took a different view of the matter however and pointing out that adults would have realised that the mountainside must have been an obvious danger, the council was entitled to assume that parents would have warned their children of the danger. In reversing the decision of the High Court, the Court of Appeal stressed that the council's duty of care was not broken by failing to fence the mountain. To require a local authority to fence every natural hazard under its control would impose too onerous a burden.

Not only children but independent contractors are also singled out for mention in the Act. Such persons engaged to carry out specialist work should be aware of the risks inherent in their own trades.

This is reflected in *Roles v. Nathan* 1963 where, despite being warned of the danger, two chimney sweeps carried on working on a boiler and were killed by carbon monoxide poisoning entering from the ventilation system. The employer/occupier was held in the circumstances not to be liable. Lord Denning MR stated that *"when a householder calls in a specialist to deal with a defective installation on his premises he can reasonably expect the specialist to appreciate and guard against the dangers arising from the defect"*.

In *Rae (Geoffrey) v. Mars (UK)* 1990 an experienced surveyor was instructed to survey business premises and given the assistance of a graduate trainee by the defendant to show him round. The surveyor fell and suffered severe injuries when entering a printing ink store, the floor of which was three feet below the level of the door. No warning of the danger had been given by the trainee. In an action for damages under the Occupiers Liability Act 1957 the court held that notwithstanding his specialist expertise the surveyor, like all visitors should have been given a warning of the exceptional nature of the hazard and the occupiers were accordingly in breach of their duty. By failing to switch on his torch however, while entering the store room, the surveyor was also at fault and the damages awarded were reduced by one third to reflect his contributory negligence.

In relation to uninvited visitors it was not until 1972 that the courts finally recognised that in some circumstances an occupier of business premises could be found liable in damages for injuries caused to a child trespasser.

> In *British Railways Board v. Herrington* 1972 British Rail had negligently failed to maintain fencing which ran between their railway track and a park frequently used by children. A six-year old climbed through the fence, wandered onto the track, and suffered severe injury on the electrified rail. The House of Lords held the Board liable in negligence to the child trespasser. The Court stated that, "... *if the presence of the trespasser is known or ought reasonably to be anticipated by the occupier then the occupier has a duty to treat the trespasser with ordinary humanity.*"

It should be noted that the duty owed to a trespasser is a restricted duty and much less than the standard of care owed to a lawful visitor. In addition, the court pointed to the economic resources of the occupier as a factor to determine whether he had acted reasonably. The rule in *British Railways Board v. Herrington* has been applied in later cases.

> In *Pannett v. McGuinness Ltd.* 1972 a demolition contractor was made liable for injuries caused to a five-year old trespasser by an unguarded fire. This was despite the fact that the contractor, aware of the danger, had posted workmen to guard the fire. The fact that the workmen were absent when the injury occurred meant, as far as the injured child was concerned, nothing was done to safeguard him.

In an attempt to clarify the rules relating to the liability of an occupier towards non-visitors, usually trespassers, the Occupiers Liability Act 1984 was passed. The Act replaces the common law, which includes the rules laid down by the House of Lords in Herrington's case, 1972. Surprisingly not all non-visitors are trespassers and in *McGeown v. Northern Ireland Housing Executive* 1994 the House of Lords confirmed that users of a right of way, whether public or private, are not "*visitors*" and as uninvited entrants are only entitled to the protection given by the Occupiers Liability Act 1984.

Under the 1984 Act the occupier will owe a duty to trespassers if:

(a)   he is aware or ought to be of danger; and

(b)   knows or has reasonable grounds to believe that the trespasser is or may be in the vicinity of danger; and

(c)   may reasonably be expected in all the circumstances to offer some protection to the trespasser against the danger.

Having established the existence of a duty the Act goes on to provide that the duty extends to taking such care as in all the circumstances is reasonable to see that the trespasser does not suffer injury by reason of the danger concerned. It is also provided that the duty may in an appropriate case be discharged by warning.

The existence of a duty of care still demands a consideration of *"all the circumstances"* to determine whether the trespasser deserves protection. This may well involve a consideration of the circumstances identified in *Herrington's* case such as the resources of the occupier, the extent of likely harm, the frequency of trespass etc. In addition the 1984 Act has confined itself to personal injury and so the common law is still relevant if the claim involves damage to the property of the trespasser.

Since the Act was passed in 1984 there have been very few cases involving the application of the occupier's duty of care towards trespassers.

> In *Adams v. Southern Electricity Board* 1993 the Court of Appeal held that the board owed a duty of care to a fifteen year old boy who suffered severe injuries when he climbed up a pole-mounted high voltage electrical installation. The board had fitted an anti-climbing device, as required by statute, but at the time of the accident it was in a defective state and the plaintiff had simply climbed over it. While deciding that the board was in breach of its duty of care, as the plaintiff was old enough to appreciate the stupidity of his actions, the amount of damages was reduced by two-thirds to reflect his substantial contributory negligence.

> In *Revill v. Newbery* 1996 the issue of liability was considered in the widely publicised case of a 76 year old defendant who caused injury to a 21 year old burglar when he fired his shotgun through a hole in his allotment shed door. The defendant was in the process of protecting property stored in his shed and had been awoken at night by the plaintiff attempting to break in. Subsequently the plaintiff was convicted of criminal offences and the defendant acquitted, and this case was a civil action for damages for personal injuries caused to the plaintiff trespasser. The claim was based upon common law negligence, the Occupiers Liability Act 1984 and trespass to person. The Court of Appeal confirmed the decision of the High Court that the plaintiff was not barred from succeeding in his claim by the fact that he was a trespasser and engaged in committing a crime at the time he was injured, however his damages should be reduced by two-thirds to reflect his contributory negligence.

The freedom to use premises for business purposes is subject to constraints imposed by both the criminal and civil law. An occupier of land may be restrained by injunction from using his property in such a way as to cause a nuisance to his neighbours, adjoining occupiers or to the public as a whole. Potential liability under statute and common law for activities that constitute a nuisance is dealt with in Chapter 17 on business property.

Vicarious Liability

There are some situations where the law is prepared to impose *vicarious* (substituted) liability on an individual who is not at fault for the commission of the wrongful (tortious) act of another. The best known example of this situation is the common law rule which imposes vicarious liability on employers in respect of torts committed by their employees during the course of their employment. Accordingly, if one employee (Jones) by his negligent act causes harm to a fellow employee Smith then in addition to the possibility of (Smith) pursuing a legal action against Jones he may have the further option of suing his employer who will have become vicariously liable if the negligent act occurred during the course of Jones's employment. The same principle applies equally where the injuries are caused by an employee to some third party. However, while employers have a choice as to whether they insure against the risk of injury to third parties, under the Employer's Liability (Compulsory Insurance) Act 1969, an employer is required to insure himself in respect of injuries caused by his employees to their colleagues.

The imposition of vicarious liability does not require proof of any fault on the employer's part, or any express or implied authorisation to commit the wrongful act. All that must be proved for the purpose of vicarious liability is:

1.   an actionable wrong committed by the worker;

2.   that the worker is an employee;

3.   that the wrongful act occurred during the course of his employment.

What then is the *theoretical* basis for imposing liability in these circumstances? A number of reasons have emerged, such as he who creates and benefits from a situation should assume the risk of liability arising from it. There is also the idea that if an organisation embarks on an enterprise and as a result harm is caused by one member of the organisation, it should be the responsibility of the organisation to compensate for the harm. It is after all the employer who selects and controls the employees who work for him. The employer has the responsibility of training staff and can of course dismiss those whose work is performed incompetently. The practical reason for vicarious liability is of course that if the employee were solely liable he would have to insure himself, and the cost of this would be indirectly borne by the employer in the form of higher wages. Under the present system insurance costs are borne directly by the employer who, as a principle of sound business practice, will normally carry adequate insurance.

To determine an employer's liability it is first necessary to establish the employment status of the worker who is alleged to have committed the wrongful act. This is because the legal position differs dramatically depending on whether the worker is employed as an employee under a contract of service rather than as a self employed contractor under a contract for services. Usually this issue may be settled without argument but in the small proportion of cases where there is doubt the courts are left with the task of identifying the true contractual status of the worker. Obviously the express terms of the contract will be a strong indicator of the parties status but in some cases it is only by examining the substance of the relationship that the true position can be determined.

As a general principle an employer is vicariously liable for the tortious acts of his employees committed during the course of their employment. The phrase *course of employment* has produced numerous interpretations in the courts, but essentially it concerns the question of whether the employee was doing his job at the time of the tortious act. It should be emphasised that an employee will have both express and implied authority to perform work for his employer and while he will normally have no authority to commit torts, he may nevertheless be guilty of a tortious act in the performance of his authorised duties.

> In *Century Insurance Ltd. v. Northern Ireland Road Transport Board* 1942 a tanker driver while delivering petrol at a garage, lit a cigarette and carelessly threw away the lighted match which caused an explosion and considerable damage. His employer was

held to be vicariously liable for his negligence as the employee had acted within the course of his employment. By supervising the unloading, the employee was doing his job, but by smoking he was doing it in a grossly negligent manner.

Even if an employee is carrying out an act outside the basic obligation of his contract of employment, his employer may nevertheless be made vicariously liable if the act is carried out for the benefit of the employer.

In *Kay v. ITW* 1968 the employee injured a colleague when he negligently drove a five ton diesel lorry which was blocking his way. Despite the fact that he was contractually authorised to drive only small vans and trucks, his employer was held to be vicariously liable for his action.

If an employee is doing something of purely personal benefit at the time of the negligent act then he may be regarded, to quote from the colourful language of the Victorian era as *"off on a frolic of his own",* and his employer will not be responsible.

In *Hilton v. Thomas Burton (Rhodes) Ltd.* 1961 the plaintiff's husband was a demolition worker who was killed through the negligent driving of one of his colleagues. The defendant employer denied vicarious liability as, at the time of the accident, the van was being driven from a cafe on an unauthorised break. The court held that although the van had been driven with the permission of the employer, at the time of the incident the driver was not doing that which he was employed to do. Accordingly the employer was not liable for the negligent driving.

The extent to which an express prohibition by the employer will prevent vicarious liability will depend upon the nature of the prohibition. If it merely attempts to instruct the employee how he is to do his job, the employee may still be within the course of his employment for the purposes of vicarious liability.

In *Rose v. Plenty* 1976 a milkman, contrary to an express prohibition, engaged a thirteen year old boy to help him deliver the milk. The boy was subsequently injured by the milkman's negligent driving and sued both the milkman and his employer. The Court of Appeal held that despite the prohibition of the employer, he remained vicariously liable as the milkman had acted within the course of his employment. Scarman L J having considered the prohibition stated that *"There was nothing in the prohibition which defined or limited the sphere of his employment, the sphere of his employment remained precisely the same as before the prohibition was brought to his notice. The sphere was as a roundsman to go the rounds delivering milk, collecting empties and obtaining payment. Contrary to instructions the roundsman chose to do what he was employed to do in an improper way. But the sphere of his employment was in no way affected by his express instructions".*

It seems therefore that only an express prohibition which effectively cuts down the *sphere of employment'* will prevent the establishment of vicarious liability. The fact that contemporary courts seem to favour the idea of a very wide sphere of employment in individual cases, severely limits the opportunity of employers to restrict liability by express instruction. It is only by deciding the authorised parameters of an individual's job, and deciding that the act complained of fell outside these parameters that vicarious liability can be successfully denied.

If the act is done on the employer's premises with the employer's interest in mind, the employer may be made liable provided the act has a close connection with the employee's job.

> In *Compton v. McClure* 1975 the employer was held to be vicariously liable for the negligence of an employee who, when late for work, caused an accident when driving negligently on the factory road.

While it may be reasonable for an employee to use a degree of force in protection of his employer's property, or to keep order, an employee who commits an assault which has no connection with his work will be solely liable for his conduct.

> So in *Warren v. Henleys Ltd.* 1948 the employer was held not to be vicariously liable for a physical attack by a petrol pump attendant on one of his customers. The claim that the attendant was acting within the scope of his employment was rejected, for while the attack developed out of an argument over payment for petrol, it was in reality motivated by an act of private vengeance.

An employer can be vicariously liable for acts of sex or race discrimination committed by employees during the course of employment unless he can show that he took such steps as were reasonably practicable to prevent the employee from committing the act of discrimination.

> In *Bracebridge Engineering v. Derby* 1990 the complainant was the victim of serious sexual harassment by her supervisor which constituted unlawful discrimination. The employer was vicariously liable for the misconduct as at the time the act of sexual harassment took place the perpetrators were supposedly engaged in exercising their disciplinary and supervisory functions and were in the course of their employment.

> In *Tower Boot Co Ltd v. Jones* 1995 the EAT held that racial taunts of fellow workers were not an unauthorised wrongful act connected with employment so as to make the employer vicariously liable. *"The phrase in the course of employment has a well established meaning in law. The nub of the test is whether the unauthorised wrongful act of the servant is so connected with that which he was employed to do as to be a mode of doing it. That has to be judged by reference to all the circumstances of the case. Applying that test to the facts of the present case, the acts complained of, including the deliberate branding with a hot screwdriver and whipping, could not be described by any stretch of the imagination, as an improper mode of performing authorised tasks."*

While such an analysis is rational, adopting this approach means that unless racial harassment is expressly authorised by the employer it seems that he can escape responsibility for it if he is unaware that it is going on. Furthermore such reasoning has not been applied in cases of sexual harassment where the courts and tribunals seem much more likely to find the employer vicariously liable.

To impose liability on an employer for the tortious or criminal acts of an employee under his control, there must be a connection between the act complained of and the circumstances of employment. The fact that employment gives the employee an opportunity to commit the wrongful act is insufficient to impose vicarious liability on the employer.

> In *Heasmans v. Clarity Cleaning Company* 1987 the Court of Appeal found it possible to absolve the defendant cleaning company from liability for the acts of one of their cleaners who, while employed on the plaintiff's premises, used the plaintiff's telephone

to make international telephone calls to the value of £1,411. The mere fact that the cleaner's employment provided the opportunity to fraudulently use the plaintiff's telephone was not itself sufficient to impose liability on the defendant.

In *Irving & Irving v. Post Office* 1987 the complaint of race discrimination was based on the conduct of an employee of the post office who when sorting the mail had written a racially insulting comment on a letter addressed to his neighbours who were of Jamaican origin. The issue before the Court of Appeal was whether the employee was acting in the course of his employment so that the Post Office could be made vicariously liable for the discriminatory act. The employee's act of writing on the mail was clearly unauthorised so the question was whether the act was an unauthorised mode of doing an authorised act. Here the misconduct formed no part of the postman's duties and could not be regarded as an unauthorised way of performing his work. *"An employer is not to be held liable merely because the opportunity to commit the wrongful act had been created by the employee's employment, or because the act in question had been committed during the period of that particular employment".*

The increasing practice of employees contracting out areas of work to contractors and sub contractors has important implications when determining liability for injuries caused due to negligence at the workplace.

In *Sime v. Sutcliffe Catering Scotland Ltd.* 1990 an employee brought a claim alleging negligence by the above catering company when, carrying out her work as a canteen assistant she slipped on some food dropped by a fellow worker and suffered injury. The case was complicated by the fact that the employee was not directly employed by the catering company but by a paper manufacturer, Tullis Russell and Company. Previously the paper manufacturer had contracted out the management of the canteen to the above company, but following pressure from the trade union, had agreed to retain existing canteen staff, including the employee. It was never established whether the worker who had dropped the food was an employee of the catering company or not. The issue therefore was whether the catering company could be held liable vicariously to a worker for the possible negligent act of a worker who they did not employ. The Scottish Court of Session held that responsibility should be with the employer in control. Although not directly employed by the catering company, whether the employer relationship is *"such as to render the company liable for the negligence depends upon whether the substitute employer has sufficient power of control and supervision purely to be regarded as the effective employer at the critical time".* As the *"whole day to day management of the catering operation and staff was undertaken by the catering company and the canteen manager had complete control over the way in which all the canteen workers did their job"*…and *"since one of the employed persons caused the accident by being negligent in dropping food stuff onto the floor and failing to clean it up the company had to accept responsibility for that negligence".* The fault of the injured employee was also recognised and damages were reduced by twenty five percent to reflect her contributory negligence. *"Where a person is working in or near a kitchen where a number of people are working with food or dirty dishes and where it is quite predictable that food might be spilt it is reasonably necessary that a look out be kept for any wet or slippery patches on the floor."*

Generally vicarious liability has been confined to the employer/employee relationship and where contractors are employed, responsibility for their wrongful acts is solely their own. The justification for not extending vicarious liability to employers of contractors, other than in exceptional cases, stems from the fact that the contractor is not subjected to his employer's control in the same way as an employee.

There are then certain legal duties that cannot be delegated, and if the wrongful act of a contractor constitutes a breach of such a duty, owed by an employer to a third party, then the contractor's employer may be made vicariously liable for the default.

> In *Rogers v. Nightriders* 1983 a mini cab firm undertook to provide a hire car to the plaintiff for a journey and did so by engaging a contractor driver. The plaintiff was injured in an accident caused by the negligent maintenance of the mini cab by the contractor. In an action against the mini cab firm the court held that they were not liable as an employer could not be made vicariously liable for their contractor's default. On appeal however, it was held that as the employer had undertaken to provide a vehicle to carry the plaintiff, and since they ought to have foreseen harm to the plaintiff if the vehicle *was defective, they owed a duty of care to the plaintiff to ensure that the vehicle was reasonably fit. Such a duty could not be delegated to a contractor and accordingly the employers were liable for breach of the primary duty that they owed to her.*

This case is a further example of the distinction that must be drawn between vicarious and direct or primary liability previously considered. By providing a negligent contractor, the employer in *Rogers v. Nightriders* had failed to fulfil a direct duty of care he owed to those he could reasonably foresee being affected.

The law imposes numerous duties on an employer in relation to the health and safety of his employees including a duty of care under common law negligence. These duties are considered in some depth in Chapter 15 in the section on health and safety at work.

Assignment The Wandering Child

Fiona Berry and John Cheng are business partners who run a number of travel agency related outlets in Lancashire. One such agency Fiesta Travel is situated in premises in Bolton held on a 21 year lease from North Western Properties Ltd. The lease has now run for six years and despite repeated requests by Fiona, the landlords seem reluctant to fulfil their clear repairing obligation in relation to the plaster work on the ceiling of the main office which is in a dangerous state of disrepair. A further cause for anxiety is the condition of the electrical wiring in the building, which again falls within the landlords responsibility.

Concerned at the time it takes for the landlord to respond to requests to repair, Fiona decided to hire Gerry, a local odd job man, to carry out wiring work in the premises. Coincidently, at the same time, North Western Properties finally responded to the request for repairs to the ceiling by hiring Joplings, a well known building contractor to carry out the work. Because of pressure of work, Joplings decide to sub contract the work to Tom and Jim, a couple of lads who are "quick and cheap and can manage small jobs".

The events of the last two weeks have driven Fiona to despair! The replastering work, while completed in good time, has not been a success. Firstly Jim, in carrying out the replastering work, sustained a violent electric shock when he touched exposed electric cables to a light fitting which Gerry had not properly insulated. Secondly the plaster did not bond properly to the ceiling, and fell on to Sheila, a prospective customer, whilst she was glancing at travel brochures. The plaster fall has caused Sheila head injuries requiring hospital treatment and a period of convalescence.

The icing on the cake was an incident yesterday. Wayne, a six year old on the premises with his parents there to book a holiday, wandered through a door marked *private* apparently in search of toilets. He fell down the steps inside the door leading to the cellar and suffered a broken arm. The stairs were not lit.

Fiona and John feel that they may face potential legal claims for these incidents and fix an appointment with Masters & Milburn a local firm of solicitors to seek legal advice. Despite their problems they don't wish to leave the Bolton Premises.

Task

You are working for Masters and Milburn as part of a work experience programme and have been asked to interview Fiona and John and to follow up the interview with a written report to one of the senior partners Janet Stephenson. You need to include in the report your assessment of the legal position in relation to liability. Your task is to produce the report for Ms Stephenson. The report should clearly state the legal arguments both for and against the likelihood of Fiona and John incurring liability for the injuries to Sheila and Wayne.

Legal Terms found in Chapter 7

Bankruptcy	• personal insolvency
Company dissolution	• striking a company off the register of companies by the Registrar
Compulsory winding up	• winding up by an order of the court
Insolvency	• condition under which the liabilities of a business exceed its assets
Liquidation	• corporate insolvency
Liquidator	• person responsible for managing a company winding up
Official receiver	• an officer attached to all courts with insolvency jurisdiction, employed by the DTI and responsible for insolvency matters
Receiver	• person appointed to take control of specified property of a company
Winding up	• process by which a registered company is brought to an end

Chapter 7

The Dissolution of Business Organisations

Introduction

The life of a business organisation can come to an end for many reasons. It may have achieved what its members required of it, so that it no longer has any useful value. It is not, for instance, unknown for a group of people to form a limited company for the purpose of carrying out a specific business venture, and insert a provision in the company's articles of association making it clear that the business is to last for a fixed period, or that it will expire on the happening of a certain event. A group of businessmen may contribute capital to a company they have formed, with the aim that the company will purchase, renovate and then sell certain industrial premises, or buy and then resell some other substantial asset. The company will end when the sale takes place if its sole purpose was the making of the sale.

A business may also come to an end because the commercial foundations upon which it was based have ceased to exist, or it has become no longer commercially viable to continue. If this occurs there is nothing to prevent the organisation from diversifying if this is acceptable to the members, thus prolonging the life of the business.

An interesting illustration of this process, and the legal consequences which can attach to it, is provided by *Prudential Assurance Co. v. Chatterley-Whitfield Collieries Ltd.* 1949. The colliery company's main business interest was in coal mining, although it had other business interests as well. Following the nationalisation of the coal industry in 1946, the company, in common with other colliery companies, received a large payment by way of compensation. It decided to continue to operate its other business activities, but had more capital than it needed for these, and so it passed a special resolution to repay all its preference shareholders. Under the articles they had the right to priority of repayment of capital in the event of the company being brought to an end. The preference shareholders objected, claiming they would lose the opportunity to share in future profit.

Company legislation strictly controls the power of a company to reduce its capital, in order to protect creditors, shareholders and the public. The court must sanction the reductions, which it will not do if the reduction is not fair and equitable as between different classes of shareholders. The House of Lords nevertheless held that this reduction was fair and equitable on the basis that surplus capital should first be returned to the class of shareholders having priority to repayment in the event of the company being brought to an end.

Most businesses which are terminated however, do not end their own lives out of choice, but because such action has been forced on them by their creditors. This occurs when the creditors lose confidence in the capacity of the organisation to repay them. It is a common feature of commercial life that when a business develops financial ill-health, its creditors will seek to reduce their losses by dissolving the business whilst there are still assets remaining in it.

Thus in considering the law as it affects the dissolution of businesses it is helpful to bear in mind the health of the organisation at the time it is being dissolved. The law, quite understandably, exerts far greater control over businesses which are terminated in circumstances of financial failure, than in cases where they are brought to an end fit and healthy, and nobody will lose money. Dissolution is important to the members of the business, who will be concerned as to what share of the assets they are entitled to, and for much the same reason it will be of concern to the creditors; they will want to know what the assets of the business are, and how they are to be distributed.

The process of dissolution

The process laid down for terminating or dissolving a business depends upon two factors:

- what the type of business is; and
- what its financial condition is.

We have previously seen that business organisations can be classified according to their legal status. Some are corporate bodies, some are unincorporated associations, whilst others are simple one man businesses. By now it should be clear that there are significant differences between these alternative business forms. This is reflected in the procedures for dissolving them. In the case of a limited company the procedure by which it is dissolved is referred to as a *winding-up*. *Bankruptcy* is the term used to describe the process by which an insolvent individual's assets are collected in, converted into money and distributed between his creditors. There is no technical term to describe the process for terminating a partnership. It is simply referred to as dissolution.

Dissolution of a Partnership

When the commercial activity of a partnership ceases so does the business itself, for it is no longer being *"carried on"* as required under the Partnership Act 1890. In such circumstances the partnership will be dissolved, and its assets disposed of to those legally entitled to them. Alternatively, a partnership which is still in operation may be dissolved on any one of a number of different grounds.

Dissolution can occur either with or without the intervention of the court. Under the Partnership Act 1890 a partnership is dissolved *without* the intervention of the court, in any of the following circumstances:

- if it was entered into for a fixed term, when that term expires;

- if it was entered into for a single venture, when that venture has been completed, for example, where the aim of the business is to acquire a single piece of property and resell it;

- if entered into for an undefined time, by any partner giving notice to the other or others of his intention to dissolve the partnership. If such a notice is served then the partnership is dissolved from the date mentioned in the notice as the date of dissolution. If no date has been given, dissolution operates from the time the notice was received, subject to the partnership articles providing for some other date;

- by the death or bankruptcy of any partner. Partnership articles will often provide that in such an event the partnership will continue to be run by the remaining partners. In the case of the death of a partner the articles may provide that the surviving partners will continue to run the business in partnership with the personal representative of the deceased;

- if a partner's share of the business is charged to secure a separate judgment debt, the other partners may dissolve the business;

- by the happening of an event which makes it unlawful for the business of the firm to be carried on, or for the members of the firm to carry it on in partnership. This may occur, for example, where there is a partnership between a British partner and a foreign partner, the business is carried on in the United Kingdom, and war breaks out between the countries of the respective partners.

Dissolution can be granted by *the court* on an application to dissolve, made by a partner, in any of the following cases:

- where a partner is suffering from a mental disorder;

- where a partner other than the partner petitioning:

  (i)   becomes in any way permanently incapable of performing their part of the partnership contract, e.g. through physical illness, or

  (ii) has been guilty of misconduct in business or private life, as in the opinion of the court, bearing in mind the nature of the partnership business, is calculated to be prejudicial to the carrying on of the business, or

  (iii) wilfully or persistently commits a breach of the partnership agreement, or otherwise behaves in a way in matters relating to the partnership business that it is impractical for the other partners to carry on in business with that partner.

Cases on dissolution on these grounds have included a refusal to meet for discussions on business matters, the keeping of erroneous accounts, persistent disagreement between the parties, and in *Anderson v. Anderson* 1857 where a father and son were in partnership together, by the opening by the father of all his son's correspondence;

- where the business of the partnership can only be carried on at a loss;

- if circumstances have arisen which, in the opinion of the court, render it just and equitable that the partnership be dissolved.

In *Re: Yenidje Tobacco Co. Ltd*. 1916 although the company was trading profitably the court held that it was just and equitable to wind it up, on the basis that its two directors had become so hostile towards each other that they would only communicate by means of messages passed to each other via the Secretary, and that this amounted to a position of deadlock. It was pointed out that a private limited company is similar to a partnership, and that had the directors been partners in a partnership, there would have been sufficient grounds for dissolution. Lord Justice Warrington stated *"... I am prepared to say that in a case like the present, where there are only two persons interested, and there are no shareholders other than those two, where there are no means of over-ruling by the action of a general meeting of shareholders the trouble which is occasioned by the quarrels of the two directors and shareholders, the company ought to be wound up if there exists such a ground as would be sufficient for the dissolution of a private partnership at the suit of one of the partners against the other. Such grounds exist in the present case."*

The partnership and bankruptcy

Two distinct insolvency situations may arise which affect the partnership:

- one of the partners is declared personally bankrupt, whilst the remaining partners are personally solvent. This automatically brings the partnership to an end, although a new one may well be formed, without the bankrupt partner. The reason the firm automatically dissolves in such circumstances is because the bankrupt party's share passes to his trustee in bankruptcy, and thus in effect he is withdrawing his contribution and his stake in the business;

- the partnership itself is insolvent. If this is so, all the partners will normally have bankruptcy proceedings brought against them. It should be remembered that since a partnership does not grant limited liability to its members, they become personally liable for the debts which cannot be met by the assets of the firm.

The administration and distribution of assets

If the partnership is dissolved its property is gathered in, and used to pay all debts and liabilities. If after this is done a surplus is left it is distributed between the partners. What they receive will depend upon what their partnership agreement says. If it makes no provision for such a situation, the following rules are laid down by the 1890 Act:

(a)   If there is no loss suffered by the firm, the surplus is used firstly to repay the capital contribution of the partners, and then to the partners in equal shares. Thus if the firm has three partners, A, B, and C, whose respective capital contributions were £2,000, £1,000 and £500, and on dissolution the firm has debts of £3,000 and assets of £8,000, the distribution to the partners will be as follows:

		£
Assets available for distribution		**8,000**
Firm's debts		**3,000**
Surplus assets available for distribution		**5,000**
Repayment of capital contributions	A	**2,000**
	B	**1,000**
	C	**500**
		3,500
Remaining surplus to be equally distributed		**1,500**

The share of net assets taken by each partner will be:
A £2,500 B £1,500 C £1,000

(b) If there are losses these are met in the following order:

(i) out of *profits*;

(ii) out of *capital*;

(iii) by the *partners individually* according to the proportions by which they shared profits.

Using the example of A, B and C above, if the partnership assets on dissolution were £5,000 and the debts £3,000, then assuming profits were shared equally, the distribution to each partner would be as follows:

	£
Assets available for distribution	**5,000**
Firm's debts	**3,000**
Surplus assets available for distribution	**2,000**
Repayment of capital contributions	**3,500**
Shortfall	**1,500**
Losses shared equally	**500**
A receives £2,000 – £500 = £1,500	
B receives £1,000 – £500 = £500	
C receives £ 500 – £500 = £0	

Where there has been a bankruptcy situation with either a partner or the firm itself being adjudicated bankrupt, there will be two groups of creditors; those of the partners personally, and those of the firm itself. It is important therefore that the personal debts and property of the partners can be kept separate from those of the partnership itself.

Dissolution of a Registered Company

We have already seen that the process by which a registered company can be brought to an end is known as a winding up or a liquidation. The process is a detailed and complex one. It is regulated by the Insolvency Act 1986, a statute based upon the report of Sir Kenneth Cork. Shortly before the Royal Assent was granted, the Insolvency Bill as it then was, came back to the House of Lords for approval, where Lord Denning remarked, *"In 1977 Sir Kenneth Cork and his committee entered upon a review of the insolvency law. They sat for five years and heard the most expert evidence. It is the most technical subject you can imagine. Both lawyers and accountants hate it. Most of them know nothing about it."*

The main aspects of it will be examined shortly, but before doing so two points need to be made regarding dissolution. The first is that there are other methods by which a company can be dissolved that do not involve winding up procedures. The second is that where the threat of dissolution is based upon company insolvency, alternatives to the drastic step of terminating the company by winding it up and realising its assets are available to creditors. A creditors composition may be entered into, or an administration order may be made by the court. These points are considered below.

Methods of dissolution

A company is created by incorporation through registration. It can therefore only come to an end when the registration is discharged. Once this happens the contractual relationship between the company and its members, based upon the memorandum and articles of the company, also comes to an end.

A company can be dissolved:

(a)   by proceedings brought by the Attorney-General for cancellation of the registration, on the grounds that the company's objects are illegal.

In *Attorney-General v. Lindi St. Claire (Personal Services) Ltd.* 1980 a lady, Miss St. Claire, formed the defendant company for the purposes of prostitution. The Registrar had granted it a certificate of incorporation, after refusing to register it under various names submitted by Miss St. Claire, including Hookers Ltd., Prostitutes Ltd. and even Lindi St. Claire French Lessons Ltd. The court however granted the cancellation on the grounds that the objects of the company were illegal;

(b)   by an order of the court where the company is transferring its undertaking to another company under a scheme of reconstruction or reorganisation;

(c)   by the Registrar, who under s.652 Companies Act 1985, may strike off the register a company that is defunct. A *defunct* company is one which is no longer carrying on business. The section lays down a procedure to be followed by the Registrar before he can validly exercise the power to remove the company from the register. This has become a very common method of dissolution, for it is cheap and easy;

(d)   by being wound-up, which may be either voluntary or compulsory. The legal provisions relating to company liquidations are contained in the Insolvency Act

1986. The title of this statute is perhaps rather misleading, since it contains provisions which regulate not only companies which are being dissolved on the basis of their insolvency, but also companies which, for a variety of reasons, are being wound up fully able to meet their liabilities.

The process of winding up

Like a partnership, a limited company can be wound up as mentioned above either *voluntarily*, or *compulsorily* by order of the court. The grounds for winding up, whether on a voluntary or compulsory basis, are set out in the Insolvency Act 1986. They recognise that winding up is a step which may become necessary not only in cases of financial instability, but also because the company, which is of course a creature of statute, has failed to comply with the statutory provisions which bind it, or simply because the members no longer wish to trade together. When examining the operation of the limited company it is common to draw an analogy with natural persons. Thus the company is said to be born when its certificate of incorporation is granted, and henceforth its brain, the board of directors, guides its actions and formulates its decisions, which are executed through those it employs. Following this analogy through to its conclusion the process of winding up is akin to the process of administering the estate of a deceased person. Assets are collected and used to satisfy debts owing, after which any property remaining can be distributed to those lawfully entitled to them. In the case of a company this will be to its members. However the process of administering the estate of a deceased person commences with death, whereas winding up is a process which culminates in the dissolution of the company, the administration being completed before the life of the company ends. Statutory references below are to the Insolvency Act 1986 unless stated otherwise.

Terminology

A number of technical expressions are used in liquidation and it is helpful to briefly identify and describe them before proceeding further.

A *petition* is an application to the court requesting the court to exercise its jurisdiction over company liquidations. A petition is presented where the liquidation is compulsory. In such cases the court has a major role to play. This is not so however in voluntary liquidations, where the liquidation is under the control of either the members or the creditors of the company.

A *contributory* is a person liable to contribute to the assets of a company if it is wound up. Existing members whose shares have not been fully paid fall within the definition of a contributory, and so do similarly placed past members, whose shareholding ceased within the year preceding the winding up. However a past member is not liable in respect of any debt contracted after his membership ceased. Nor is he required to make a contribution if the existing members are able to satisfy the contributions required of them.

A *liquidator* is a person appointed to take control of the company, collect its assets, pay its debts, and distribute any surplus to the members according to their rights as shareholders. The liquidator therefore holds a position of great responsibility, and it is important to ensure that only individuals of integrity are qualified to hold such a post. In recent years some disquiet has been felt as a result of company liquidations in which the liquidator has been found to be conducting the winding up for the benefit of directors, rather than the company's creditors. The Insolvency Act 1986 copes with this by requiring that only an *insolvency practitioner*, a term covering liquidators, can act in a winding up. He must be authorised to do so by his own professional body (these include accountancy bodies and the Law Society), or by the Department of Trade and Industry. Certain people are completely excluded. An applicant must be shown to be a fit and proper person, and must provide security, to become an insolvency practitioner.

Liquidators need to be distinguished from receivers. *Receivers* are appointed by the holders of secured debentures, under the terms of the debenture, when the company defaults in making a repayment or commits some other breach. Three types of receiver can be identified; *ordinary receivers* who literally do receive on behalf of the debenture holders, by for example receiving rent from property subject to charge; *receivers and managers*, who are appointed under a floating charge which covers only a part of the company's undertaking and who manage the business of the company to the extent of the assets subject to the charge; and *administrative receivers*. An *administrative receiver* is a receiver appointed under a floating charge which extends to "*the whole or substantially the whole of the company's property*" (s.529). Since floating charges generally do so extend, most appointments are of administrative receivers. Although a company may go into liquidation following the appointment of a receiver this is not an automatic consequence.

The *Official Receiver* is appointed by the Department of Trade, and is concerned both with personal insolvency and with corporate insolvency. Official receivers are attached to courts with insolvency jurisdiction, and they act in the capacity of liquidators in the case of compulsory liquidations, being appointed automatically when a *winding up order* is made, that is when the court issues an order that the company be wound up. The Official Receiver (OR) remains in this office until another liquidator is appointed.

Finally the *London Gazette* is an official publication used to satisfy the requirement of providing public notice of certain legal events, for example, in the case of a liquidation notice of a creditors' meeting.

The Basic Aspects of a Company Liquidation

We have seen that when the process of winding-up has been completed the company will be struck off the register of companies and will cease to exist. Of course no further claims can then be made against it. Consequently for anyone who is connected with the company, whether as an investor, creditor or employee, winding-up is of great significance.

Although statutory winding up provisions are detailed, and sometimes complex, there are basically three aspects to a liquidation:

- who has the ability to institute and control the winding up, and on what grounds;
- what are the legal provisions to be fulfilled during the procedure; and
- in what order are claims made against the company for payment met?

Methods of Winding Up

Under s.73 two methods of winding up are recognised. These are:

(a)   a *voluntary* winding up, which according to s.90 may be either:

(i)   a members' voluntary winding up, or

(ii)   a creditors' voluntary winding up, and

(b)   a winding up by the court, usually referred to as a *compulsory* winding up.

Voluntary winding up is more common than compulsory liquidation. It is a less formal procedure, and is therefore quicker and cheaper.

Voluntary winding up

Shareholders can at any time resolve to end the company. They initiate the procedure by passing a resolution to wind up, either a special resolution if the company is solvent, or, in the case of insolvency, an extraordinary resolution that it cannot continue in business by reason of its liabilities. An ordinary resolution is sufficient where the time period fixed in the articles for the life of the company has passed, or an event stipulated in the articles as giving rise to dissolution has taken place.

Under s.86 when the resolution is passed the liquidation procedure begins. The consequences are that:

- the company ceases to carry on business, other than to enable it to wind up;

- the company's corporate status remains intact until dissolution;

- transfers of shares, and changes in members' rights are void unless sanctioned by the liquidator;

- the directors' powers cease when the liquidator is appointed, although he, or in a creditors' voluntary winding up, they themselves, may permit the directors to continue; and

- if the liquidation is due to insolvency, company employees, who may include directors, will be dismissed. The liquidator may however employ them under a new contract.

Notice of the resolution must be advertised in the *London Gazette* within fourteen days of it being passed. If a majority of the directors within five weeks of the passing of the resolution make a statutory declaration that the company is solvent, then the company members manage the winding up. This includes the appointment of their own liquidator. This is a valuable power for the person appointed will be under their control, rather than the control of the creditors or the court. The court can nevertheless remove a liquidator on the basis of unfitness for office. The declaration of solvency states that the directors have examined the company's affairs and formed the opinion that within a stated period (up to a maximum of twelve months) the company will be able to pay its debts in full. If a declaration of solvency is not made, the winding up is creditors' winding up. A creditors' meeting must be summoned by the company. Details of this meeting must be posted to creditors and members giving them at least seven days notice, and be advertised in the London Gazette and two local newspapers.

The business of the creditors' meeting is to receive from the directors a full statement of the company's affairs, to draw up a list of creditors with estimates of their claims, to appoint a liquidator who will insert a notice in the *London Gazette* notifying other creditors to send in claims and if considered necessary, appoint a liquidation committee.

The liquidation committee cannot consist of more than five people. They will be creditors of company. It is designed to work in conjunction with the liquidator, overseeing the liquidators work, and receiving reports from the liquidator on any matters of concern.

The liquidators' powers in a voluntary winding up

The liquidator has wide powers to act for and in the name of the company, without the need to consult anyone or obtain the sanction of the court.

The liquidator can:

(i)   bring or defend legal proceedings on behalf of the company;

(ii) continue to operate the company's business to the extent necessary to wind it up beneficially;

(iii) issue company documents and use the company seal;

(iv) claim in insolvency proceedings brought by the company against an insolvent estate in which the company has an interest;

(v)   deal with any negotiable instrument issued by or received by the company;

(vi) raise money needed by the company on security of its assets;

(vii) collect in monies due from contributories;

(viii) appoint an agent to carry out work on behalf of the liquidator.

In addition to these powers the liquidator may, in a members' voluntary winding up with the sanction of an extraordinary resolution of the company, or in a creditors' voluntary winding up with the sanction of the court, the liquidation committee or the creditors:

• pay off in full any class of creditors;

• enter into any compromise or arrangement with creditors.

It is possible for a voluntary winding up to be converted into a compulsory winding up, on a petition to the court by a creditor or contributory. This will only be successful if the court is satisfied that it is inappropriate for the winding up to proceed as a voluntary one, for instance where the liquidator is found to have some personal interest in the company he is winding up.

Fraudulent and Wrongful Trading

The concept of *fraudulent trading* is a well known one in company law. It is a crime under the Companies Act 1985, and gives rise to civil liability under the Insolvency Act 1986. Civil liability can only occur when the company is being wound up. If in the course of the liquidation it appears to the liquidator that the company's business has been carried on with intent to defraud creditors or for any fraudulent purpose, the liquidator may apply to the court for an order that any person who has knowingly been a party to such conduct be liable to contribute to the assets of the company. The court can order such a contribution as it thinks proper in the circumstances. In this way the creditors as a whole are compensated in the winding up for any serious wrongdoing committed by the directors, or any other party, in their management of or dealings with the company. The expression *fraudulent* is not defined by statute, however the courts have provided some indication of what must be established.

In *Re William C. Leitch Brass Ltd.* 1932 it was said that a company will be acting fraudulently by incurring debts either knowing it will be unable to meet them when they fall due, or reckless as to whether it will be able to pay them at such time. An important qualification to liability was given in *Re Patrick & Lyon Ltd.* 1933 where it was said that the behaviour of the directors had to demonstrate real moral blame, and it is this feature of fraudulent trading which presents the major limitation upon its effectiveness as a civil remedy. So long as the directors can satisfy the court that, even when the company was in an insolvent situation, they genuinely and honestly believed that the company would be able to meet its debts when they fell due, then it is unlikely that they will be held personally accountable. Clearly the less business competence and experience they possess the easier it will be for them to avoid liability.

It was because of this difficulty in establishing fraudulent trading that the Cork Committee, in the course of examining the reform of the insolvency laws in the early 1980s, recommended the introduction of an additional head of civil liability, which could be established by proving negligence. This recommendation was implemented by the *wrongful trading* provisions contained in s.214 Insolvency Act 1986. Only a director can incur liability for wrongful trading, and as with s.213 action can only be taken by the liquidator of the company. The liquidator needs to establish that the person was at the time a director, that the company had gone into insolvent liquidation, and that at some time before the proceedings to wind up commenced, the person against whom they were being brought knew or ought to have concluded that there was no reasonable prospect that the company would avoid going into insolvent liquidation. If these criteria are met the court may declare the person concerned liable to contribute to the assets of the company. The section is particularly demanding on directors in a number of aspects. Insolvent liquidation means, in the context of s.214, that the assets as realised in the liquidation are insufficient to meet not only the company's debts and other liabilities, but also the costs of the winding up itself, which are generally substantial. The standard of skill expected of the director is based upon two sets of criteria, that is not only the general knowledge, skill and experience which that particular director holds, but also the skill and experience that can be reasonably expected from a reasonably diligent director. The test is an objective rather than a subjective one. Even the defence available under the section operates in a rigorous fashion towards directors. It provides that no order may be made by the court if it is satisfied that the person in question took every step with a view to minimising the potential loss to the company's creditors as he ought to have taken. The expression *every step* is clearly very stringent.

The wrongful trading provisions were applied in *Re Produce Marketing Consortium Ltd.* 1989 where two directors had continued to trade when the accounts showed their company to be insolvent, in the honest but unrealistically optimistic belief that the company's fortunes would change. They were ordered by the court to contribute £75,000 plus interest to the assets of the company.

In *Re Purpoint Ltd.* 1991 the liquidator brought action against a director under both ss212 and 214, to compel contribution from him to the assets of the company. S.212 enables a liquidator, a creditor or a member to petition the court to order repayment or restoration of property obtained by a promoter or director in breach of duty. It is useful because s.214 can only be used when there was a likelihood the company would go into insolvent liquidation, whereas such a requirement does not apply under s.212. Also s.214 is concerned with loss suffered by creditors. S.212 deals with losses caused to the *company*. The court found the director guilty of misfeasance and liable to make a contribution under both sections. The court said his contribution under s.214 should be an amount representing the aggregation of unpaid debts for the period to which the liability under the s.214 order applied.

It seems that s.214 is a more potent weapon in the hands of liquidators than s.213. Establishing fraud is more difficult than establishing negligence, and this together with the rigorous standards demanded by s.214 suggests that wrongful trading is likely to be regarded increasingly by liquidators as a more attractive remedy than fraudulent trading. Even so there may still be reasons why a claim under s.213 may be brought by a liquidator. Orders made under s.213 can be punitive, for example, but perhaps the most significant reason is where a contribution is being sought from someone other than a director, for unlike s.214, s.213 catches anyone 'knowingly' a party to the fraud.

> In *Re Gerald Cooper Chemicals Ltd.* 1978 the court held that a creditor who accepts money from the company knowing it has been procured by carrying on business with the intent to defraud other creditors by the act of paying him, will be liable under s.213. Templeman, J. stated *"A man who warms himself with the fire of fraud cannot complain if he is singed"*.

Compulsory winding up

A compulsory winding up is carried out by the court. This is either the High Court or, if the company's paid up share capital does not exceed £120,000, the County Court in whose district the company has its registered office. Not all County Courts however, possess the necessary insolvency jurisdiction.

Proceedings are commenced by a person presenting a petition to the appropriate court. The petitioner may be the company itself, by resolution, the Secretary of State following an investigation or, in most cases, a creditor.

> In *Re Othery Construction Ltd.* 1966 Lord Buckley stated that if a fully paid up shareholder is to successfully petition to wind up:
>
> *"... he must show either that there will be a surplus available for distribution amongst the shareholders or that the affairs of the company require investigation in respects which are likely to produce such a surplus"*.

Under s.122 a company may be wound up by the court if:

(a)   the company has passed a special resolution requesting it; or

(b)   in the case of a company registered as a public company, the company has been registered for more than a year, but as yet no certificate of ability to commence business has been issued. This certificate, which is issued by the Registrar, can only be obtained when certain financial details have been given to him. The company cannot commence business until the certificate, which is required under s.117 Companies Act 1985, has been issued. Private companies do not require such a certificate and can commence business immediately on incorporation; or

(c)   the company does not commence business in the first year of its incorporation, or suspends business at any time for a whole year. An order will only be granted on this ground if the company has no intention of carrying on business again.

In *Re Middlesbrough Assembly Rooms Co.* 1880 a shareholder petitioned for winding up where the company had suspended trading for over three years, because of a trade depression. The majority shareholders opposed the petition on the basis that the company intended to recommence trading when the economic situation improved. It was held that in the circumstances the petition should be dismissed;

(d)   in the case of a public company if the membership has fallen below two; or

(e)   if the company is unable to pay its debts. This is the ground most commonly relied upon. The company is deemed to be unable to pay its debts if a creditor who is owed a sum exceeding £750 by the company has left a statutory demand for it at the company's registered office, and the demand has remained unpaid for a period of three clear weeks. The £750 figure can be made up by aggregating the debts of different creditors. The company is not however regarded as neglecting the debt if it disputes the payment of it. In such circumstances the petitioner would not be regarded as a creditor. It is also well established law that winding up proceedings are not to be used as a system for debt collection. In *Re a Company ex. p Fin Soft Holding SA* 1991 Harman J regarded the correct test in such cases to be *"is there a substantial dispute as to the debt upon which the petition is allegedly founded?"*. It follows that absence of good faith on the part of the company in disputing payment is irrelevant.

Alternatively the company is deemed unable to pay its debts if:

(i)   execution has been issued on a judgment in favour of a creditor which is returned either wholly or partially unsatisfied; or

(ii)   it is proved to the satisfaction of the court that the company is unable to pay its debts as they fall due.

In *Re a Company* 1986 it was held that a company can be regarded as unable to pay its debts under this ground, where it has funds but persistently fails or neglects to pay its debts unless it is forced to do so. Many companies have a deliberate policy of holding back payment for as long as possible, and for some this may be their means of survival; or

(iii)   where the court is satisfied that taking into account the company's present and future liabilities, the value of its assets is less than the amount of its liabilities; or

(f)   the court is of the opinion that it is just and equitable that the company should be wound up. This ground covers a number of situations. For instance it covers cases where the substratum of the company has been destroyed.

In *Re German Date Coffee Co.* 1882 the company was wound up on the basis that it had become impossible to carry out the main object in the memorandum of association, namely the acquisition and working of a German patent to make coffee from dates, because the patent could not be obtained.

It also extends to circumstances in which the company has been formed for a fraudulent purpose; where the company is a sham, having no business or property; or where the rights of members are being flouted.

In *Loch v. John Blackwood Ltd.* 1924 a director with voting control refused to hold meetings, produce accounts or pay dividends. The court held that the company could be wound up.

In *Ebrahami v. Westbourne Galleries* 1972 two individuals E and N had operated successfully in partnership together for many years. Later they converted the business to a company, with themselves as sole shareholders and directors, and after a time N's son was allowed into the business. This was granted as a favour by the plaintiff, who transferred some of his shares to the son. Unfortunately his generosity was met by N and his son combining their interests to force the plaintiff out of the business. The court granted the plaintiff's application to wind up. Commenting on the expression *"just and equitable"* Lord Wilberforce said:

"The words are a recognition of the fact that a limited company is more than a mere legal entity, with a personality in law of its own; that there is room in company law for the recognition of the fact that behind it, or amongst it, there are individuals, with rights, expectations and obligations ... which are not necessarily submerged in the company structure".

The petition to wind up is presented to the district judge of the court who fixes a time and place for the hearing. The petition must be advertised in the *London Gazette* at least seven clear days (excluding Saturday and Sunday) before the hearing. Rules of Court set out the form in which this advertised information must be provided; if they are not complied with the petitioner may have to meet all the court costs. The aim of the advertisement is to invite interested parties, the company's creditors and contributories, to oppose or support the petition. A person intending to appear at the hearing must give notice of this to the petitioner. After presentation of the petition a provisional liquidator may be appointed who is generally the Official Receiver. In any event when the hearing takes place, and the court makes a winding-up order, the Official Receiver becomes provisional liquidator by statute, and continues as liquidator unless the meeting of the creditors and contributories agree to the appointment of some other liquidator. This person must be an insolvency practitioner. The 1986 Act sets out the liquidator's powers. Essentially his task is to collect and realise the company's assets, including unpaid sums due to the company from contributories for their shares, to settle the lists of creditors and contributories, pay the company's debts in a fixed order, and finally to adjust the rights of the contributories distributing any surplus assets among them. At meetings of creditors and contributories it may be decided to apply to the court to form a committee of inspection. Having fulfilled these responsibilities the liquidator applies to the court for an order that the company be dissolved, and is then released from his or her role. The court has a complete and unfettered discretion as to whether to make an order for winding up. It may as an alternative conditionally or unconditionally adjourn the hearing, make an interim order, or dismiss the petition altogether.

The order of priorities

On dissolution there are likely to be many claims against the assets of the company. Provided the company is solvent this does not create any problems, but if it is insolvent the question which arises is how the shortfall is dealt with. Do all the company's creditors absorb the loss according to the proportion of credit they have provided, or do some creditors rank before others, so that whilst those at the top of the list may be repaid in full, those at the bottom could find themselves with nothing?

The answer is that the Insolvency Act 1986 lays down an order of priorities for the distribution of assets. The relevant provisions are contained in ss.175 and 176, which lays down the following order:

(a)   the costs of winding up (for example the liquidator's fees);

(b)   preferential debts. These include: income tax deducted from the pay of company employees under the PAYE system over the past year; VAT payments owed by the company that have accrued over the past six months; wages and salaries of employees outstanding for the previous four months, up to a present maximum figure of £800 per employee. A director may be a salaried employee, and thus qualify under this head, however a director's fee rather than a salary will not rank as a preferential debt. If assets are sufficient, preferential debts are paid in full. If not, the available assets are distributed rateably between the preferential creditors, and in these circumstances property subject to a floating charge must be applied first in the payment of preferential debts, the holder being entitled only to the balance. Creditors who have the security of a fixed charge over assets of the company are, of course, able to realise the assets charged to meet the company's liability towards them;

(c)   ordinary unsecured debts, such as sums owing to trade creditors. If these cannot be paid in full they are paid rateably amongst the creditors;

(d)   the members according to their rights under the memorandum and articles. It may be that one class of shareholders is entitled to repayment of a certain amount of the surplus before the others, thus preference shareholders may receive repayment of their paid up capital in priority to ordinary shareholders.

Advantages and disadvantages of compulsory winding up

The main advantages of a compulsory winding up over a voluntary winding up are:

(a)   Under s.129 Insolvency Act 1986 a compulsory winding up is deemed to commence when the petition is presented, whilst in a voluntary winding up it commences when the resolution is passed (s.86). The effect is that a compulsory winding up will commence earlier. This can be important since as part of the task of collecting in assets the liquidator can apply to the court to recover assets disposed of by the company within a fixed period before the insolvency, and can seek to have certain transactions set aside where these transactions occurred within a certain date of the insolvency. Going back further into the recent past of the company may mean the recovery of a larger quantity of assets. Examples include:

(i) the setting aside of a transaction made by the company at undervalue within the two years before the winding up has commenced. A transaction at undervalue would cover a gift made by the company at a time it was unable to pay its debts;

(ii) the setting aside of a preference made by the company to a connected person (e.g. a director) within two years of the winding up commencing, or to any other person (e.g. a trade creditor) within six months of the winding up commencing. Again this must have occurred at a time when the company was unable to pay its debts. A preference would occur where the directors, in the knowledge that the company is completely insolvent, settle the debts of just one of the company's creditors, in the expectation that if they subsequently set up a new company the trade creditor will continue to supply them;

(iii) the avoidance of floating charges created by the company within the two years prior to the insolvency if the chargee is a connected person, and one year if the chargee is anyone else.

(b) Wider powers of investigation into the management of the company's affairs, for example where the directors have been acting wrongfully.

The main disadvantages are that a compulsory liquidation will be slower and more expensive. The company will always be the respondent under a compulsory winding up order, and as the 'loser' in the action it will meet both sides' costs, thus reducing the money available for the creditors when the realised assets are finally distributed.

Alternatives to Winding Up

Whilst as we have seen, a company may be dissolved for reasons other than financial difficulty, most dissolutions are the result of a financial crisis. Directors faced with this situation may have the future affairs of the company taken out of their hands in a compulsory or creditors' liquidation, the result of which will be that the life of the company will come to an end, and some creditors at least will be left with their debts unsatisfied. One of the aims of the Insolvency Act 1986 was to provide alternatives to this drastic outcome, which would act as financial rescue packages for companies in difficulty.

(a) Corporate voluntary arrangements – compositions with creditors

These are provided for by ss1–7 Insolvency Act 1986. They enable a company which is insolvent or partially insolvent to follow a procedure which will result in a legally binding arrangement with its creditors. In outline the following stages have to be followed. The directors, or the liquidator if a winding up is in progress, choose an insolvency practitioner to act as a *nominee*, and help them produce proposals to put to the creditors. These may be a composition or a scheme of arrangement for the company i.e. the revision of its financial affairs in some way, such as alterations to class rights, or the extension of time for payment given by debenture notices.

The proposals are reported to the court and a meeting of creditors and shareholders is called both of which must approve them. The outcome is reported to the court. If approved, the proposals bind all the creditors and shareholders having notice of them, under s.5.

(b) Administration orders

One of the problems with a voluntary arrangement is of course the difficulty of obtaining the agreement of large creditors, such as banks. They will want greater control over the organisation of the company's affairs. In such circumstances an administration order may be a useful device. Such an order can be made by the court once it is satisfied that the company is, or is likely to become, unable to pay its debts, and that an administration order would be likely to achieve:

(i)   the survival of the company, and the whole or any part of its undertaking as a going concern; or

(ii)   the approval of a voluntary arrangement (i.e. because of the appointment of an administrator); or

(iii)   a more advantageous realisation of the company's assets than in a winding up.

The company itself, its directors, a creditor or creditors may petition the court for such an order: individual members cannot petition however, in contrast with their power to do so under s.122 to have the company wound-up on just and equitable grounds and under s.459 CA 1985, which enables them to seek relief on the ground of unfair prejudice. If the order is granted the court will appoint an administrator who will be responsible for the management of the affairs, business and property of the company for the duration of the order. This can include the calling of meetings and the appointment and removal of directors. Any winding up petition previously presented must be dismissed on the grant of an administration order. The administrator is empowered to carry on the business of the company generally, including dealing with and disposing of its assets, borrowing, employing agents and so on. He can establish subsidiary companies and transfer the whole or some part of the existing business to them. He can remove directors, and appoint new directors, and call meetings of the members and the creditors. His duties are to control and manage the company's assets and business operations, initially in accordance with directions from the court given in the order, and subsequently in accordance with the proposals he has put forward as to how the purposes stated in the order are to be achieved. The administrator's proposals must be sent to the Registrar of Companies and all the creditors within three months of the administration order being made. A creditors' meeting must then be held to approve the proposals before they can be implemented.

It remains to be seen how much use will be made of the administration order as an alternative to liquidation, however a useful illustration of an order in operation occurred in *Re Consumer & Industrial Press* 1987. The company involved, a small printing and publishing organisation, had only one major asset when it became insolvent, a magazine which it published. An application was made for the appointment of an administrator, so that he could exercise the statutory power to borrow in the company's name in order to continue publishing the magazine. In this way it could be sold as a going concern, rather than it going out of publication and having far less value. The court held that in the interests of the creditors the order should be granted.

Individual Insolvency

Personal insolvency occurs when an individual finds himself in serious financial difficulties and is unable to pay his creditors when debts fall due. If the creditors are unwilling or unable to wait for payment, the debtor may face bankruptcy proceedings under the Insolvency Act 1986. Broadly the purpose of bankruptcy is to ensure a fair distribution of assets to creditors and to allow the debtor to make a fresh start after his discharge.

The law relating to individual insolvency has undergone substantial change in recent years. The procedures under the Bankruptcy Act 1914 have been abolished and replaced with simpler procedures first introduced by the Insolvency Act 1985 and now contained in the Insolvency Act 1986. The new legislation was introduced with two main aims:

(a)   to encourage voluntary arrangements between debtors and creditors; and

(b)   to simplify and update bankruptcy procedures and bring them into line with the procedures applicable to company liquidations.

Under the 1986 Act there are two possible outcomes of individual insolvency: a *voluntary arrangement* or a *bankruptcy order*.

Voluntary arrangements

Where an individual is facing insolvency, he may try to avoid a bankruptcy order by proposing a voluntary arrangement with his creditors. The advantages from the debtor's point of view of such an arrangement are that he avoids the stigma, loss of status and adverse publicity associated with a bankruptcy order, and avoids the disabilities to which an undischarged bankrupt is subject. The benefit of a voluntary arrangement for the creditor is that it should be less expensive, leaving more assets available for payment to him; and it will usually be quicker than bankruptcy procedure, which means that he will be paid sooner. The disadvantage from the creditors point of view is that the supervisor of a voluntary arrangement will not have as many powers as a trustee in bankruptcy, for example to set aside transactions at an undervalue or preferences.

The option of making a voluntary arrangement existed under the old bankruptcy law. Such an arrangement could be made under the Deeds of Arrangement Act 1914. In practice, however, deeds of arrangement are not used to any great extent, mainly because any one creditor, no matter how small the sum owed to him, could petition for bankruptcy if he did not accept the debtor's proposals. He could do this even though all of the other creditors were prepared to accept them. Under the 1986 Act, as we shall see, a dissenting creditor must accept a voluntary arrangement if more than 75% by value of creditors agree to it.

Procedure for making a voluntary arrangement under Part VIII of the Insolvency Act 1986

If a debtor wishes to make a voluntary arrangement he must choose an insolvency practitioner to help him draw up a proposal which can be presented to his creditors. An insolvency practitioner, usually an accountant or a solicitor, must be qualified in relation to insolvency and must be authorised by the Department of Trade to act in that capacity. The insolvency practitioner will have an important role to play in the voluntary arrangement, first as a *nominee* preparing and presenting the proposal; and later as supervisor, implementing the proposal if it is accepted by the creditors.

When the proposal is prepared, and an insolvency practitioner has agreed to act as a nominee, the debtor must apply to the court for an interim order. Once this application is made, the court has power to suspend any legal proceedings against the debtor or his property.

The court will make an interim order if it is satisfied that it would be appropriate to do so, in order to allow the debtor to go ahead and make his proposal. If the court believes that the debtor is not acting in good faith or that the proposal is wholly unrealistic it may refuse to make the order. If an interim order is made, it will last for 14 days unless it is extended by the court. The effect of the order is that no bankruptcy petition can be presented against the debtor and no other legal proceedings may be commenced or continued against him without the court's permission.

Before the interim order expires, the nominee must report to the court stating whether he thinks that a meeting of creditors ought to be summoned to consider the debtor's proposal. To enable the nominee to make his report, the debtor has a duty to deliver a *statement of affairs* to him, together with the details of his proposal.

After receiving the nominee's report, the court will extend the interim order to allow the creditors to consider the debtor's proposal. The nominee must call a *meeting of creditors*. He must inform every creditor of whom he is aware about the meeting.

The purpose of the creditors' meeting is to decide whether or not to accept the debtor's proposals for a voluntary arrangement, either in the form put forward by the debtor or in a modified form.

If the creditors are unable to agree to the proposal, the court can discharge the interim order and normal bankruptcy proceedings will probably follow. If a scheme is approved by over 75% in value of creditors voting at the meeting, the voluntary arrangement will be binding upon all creditors who had notice of the meeting and were entitled to vote.

The voluntary arrangement may be challenged by a dissatisfied creditor who must apply to the court to set it aside within 28 days. His application can be made on the grounds that there was a material irregularity in the calling or conduct of the creditors' meeting; or that the voluntary arrangements unfairly prejudice his interests as a creditor.

The procedure described here is presented diagramatically in Figure 7.1 on the next page.

If the proposal is approved at the creditors meeting, the nominee becomes its *supervisor*. The debtor must hand over his property to the supervisor, who will then carry out the arrangements. During the implementation of the voluntary arrangement by the supervisor, any of the parties, including the debtor, any creditors or the supervisor himself may apply to the court for directions to resolve

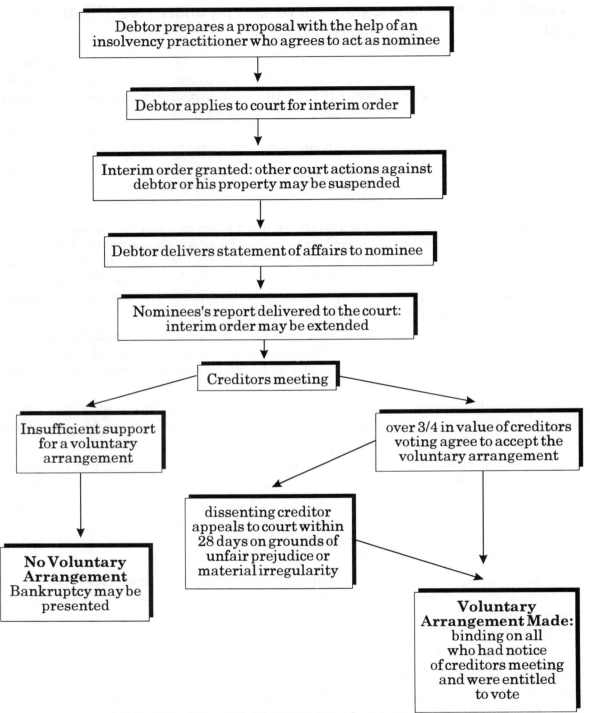

Figure 7.1 Procedure for making a voluntary arrangement

any problems that may arise. When the task of supervision has been completed, the supervisor must notify all creditors and the debtor.

Bankruptcy Orders

A petition for a bankruptcy order may be presented by a creditor, the debtor himself, the supervisor, or a creditor bound by a voluntary arrangement where the debtor has defaulted under the arrangement.

Petition by a creditor

A petition by a creditor must be based on an unpaid debt or debts owed to him by the debtor. The amount owing must be at least £750. In order to commence bankruptcy proceedings, a creditor either must obtain a judgment debt for at least £750 and be unable to enforce it; or he must serve on the debtor a *statutory demand* for payment of the debt (see Figure 7.2). Where a statutory demand is served and the debtor fails to pay within three weeks, the creditor can petition the court for a bankruptcy order. The court can dismiss the creditor's petition if it is satisfied that the debtor is able to pay all of his debts or that he has made an offer to provide security for the payment of the debt or to enter into a voluntary arrangement and the creditor has unreasonably refused to accept his offer.

Petition by the debtor

The sole ground on which a debtor may petition for his own bankruptcy is that he is unable to pay his debts. His petition must be accompanied by a *statement of affairs* setting out details of his assets and liabilities.

Where the debtor's unsecured debts are less than £20,000, his assets are £2,000 or more and he has not been bankrupt or made a voluntary arrangement within the last five years, the court will appoint an insolvency practitioner to investigate the possibility of a voluntary arrangement and prepare a report. If the report is favourable the court will make an interim order with a view to a creditors' meeting and a voluntary arrangement. If the report of the insolvency practitioner indicates that a voluntary arrangement would be unlikely to succeed, the court, if it agrees, will make a bankruptcy order. In these circumstances the order will be by way of a summary administration of the bankrupt's estate.

The advantages of a summary administration are that the procedures are simple and, from the debtor's point of view, he will be discharged from the bankruptcy after two years.

The trustee in bankruptcy

The function of the trustee in bankruptcy is to collect in the assets of the bankrupt and distribute them in accordance with the rules in the Insolvency Act. The order of priority for repayment of debts is similar to that described for the winding-up of companies. All of the bankrupt's property

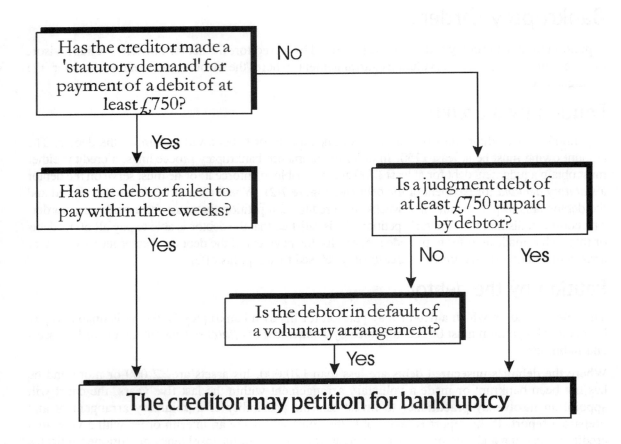

Figure 7.2   Bankruptcy petition by a creditor

vests in the trustee in bankruptcy, with the exception of tools, vehicles and equipment for use by the bankrupt in his employment or business; and such clothing, bedding, furniture and household equipment as are necessary to satisfy the basic domestic needs of the bankrupt and his family.

Any property which is acquired by the bankrupt before he is discharged can be claimed by the trustee. The trustee may also apply to the court for an *income payments order*. Under the terms of such an order part of any income to which the bankrupt is entitled whilst undischarged will be transferred to the trustee for the benefit of the creditors.

Creditors must submit proof of any debts to the trustee in bankruptcy. When the trustee has collected in all the bankrupts property he can declare and distribute a final dividend to creditors. After this has been done he will call a final general meeting of creditors and report on the administration of the estate.

Two further powers of the trustee enable him to apply to the court for an order to overcome certain types of transaction entered into by the bankrupt prior to the presentation of the bankruptcy petition. These are transactions at *an undervalue,* meaning a transaction in which the consideration received by the bankrupt is significantly less than that he has given (or is non existent), and *preferences*, which involves the bankrupt putting a creditor in a better financial position than he would have been in for the purpose of distributing the assets of the bankrupt's estate; in other words advancing the interests of one or more creditors to the disadvantage of others.

Almost identical powers are available to a liquidator in the event of a company winding-up, in cases where prior to the winding up, the company, through its directors, has entered into individual transactions or has given preference to certain of its creditors. Although such activities may be fraudulent, fraud does not need to be established for the court to consider the issue of an order to set aside such transactions.

Duration of bankruptcy

The bankruptcy continues until an individual is discharged from it. If a person is bankrupt for the first time, he will be discharged automatically after three years from the date of the Bankruptcy Order. In a summary administration, as we have seen, discharge will occur after two years. In either case, the period can be extended by the court if the bankrupt has failed to comply with any of his obligations under the Insolvency Act 1986. If the bankrupt has previously been an undischarged bankrupt during the previous fifteen years, he will not automatically be discharged. He must apply to the court for discharge after five years from the making of the bankruptcy order. Where such an application is made, the court may refuse to discharge the bankrupt. It may grant a discharge, either unconditionally or upon condition that he, for example, makes further payments to his creditors.

An undischarged bankrupt is subject to certain legal disabilities. He cannot obtain credit; or become a member of Parliament, a justice of the peace or a councillor.

Discharge from bankruptcy releases the bankrupt from the debts which existed at the commencement of his bankruptcy. A discharge from bankruptcy, however, does not affect his liability for fines imposed by a court for any criminal offence, or the enforcement of any security by a secured creditor.

Choosing the Legal Form for a Business

This chapter and the previous chapters have explored in detail the legal characteristics of the two principal forms of private sector business organisation, the partnership and the registered company. It is clear that the differences between them are significant, not only from a legal standpoint but from a commercial one also. We can conclude our examination of business organisations by examining the basis upon which the decision may be taken whether to operate in partnership or form a registered company, that is whether or not to incorporate.

Partnership or registered company?

There are two circumstances in which the opportunity for choosing the legal form of the business is illusory.

(i)   Sometimes people drift into business relationships rather than discuss and plan them in advance. Perhaps what began as a mere hobby pursued by two friends develops into a money making venture, and they find themselves in a business relationship without any conscious decision on their part. If their relationship satisfies the definition of a partnership contained in s.1 Partnership Act 1890, then the law will regard them as partners. They do not need to have entered into a written agreement. They many not even be aware of their legal status. In law however they are now operating as a firm.

(ii) If professional people, such as accountants, architects, doctors or lawyers seek to carry out their work in combination with co-professionals, the law prevents them from incorporating their business. It is only permissible for them to carry out their work collectively in partnership so the opportunity of incorporating is denied them.

Assuming however that like-minded people are anxious to establish a joint business venture, what factors are likely to influence them in deciding whether or not to incorporate? The following checklist of points covers all the major factors, and illustrates the essential legal and commercial differences between the partnership and the registered company.

Registered companies and partnerships compared

(i)   *Legal status*

A registered company is a corporate body once its certificate of incorporation is granted to it. It is an artificial entity and is required to establish its nationality, a registered office where it can be served with formal notices, and provide itself with a name which it must use for the purpose of conducting business. It is legally separate from its members, who may make contracts with it, for example by selling to it a business previously operated as a partnership or on a sole trader basis.

A partnership is not a corporate body. It is no more than the sum total of the individuals who make it up. Although it must register under the Business Names Act 1985 any name it uses to trade under which does not consist of the surnames of all the partners, this name (e.g. Smith and Co.) does not give it any special persona, although for practical convenience Rules of the Supreme Court enable proceedings by and against the firm to be brought in the firms name.

(ii) *Members' liability*

In a company, the financial liability of the members for any legal liabilities of the business such as trading debts ends when they have fully paid for their shares. There are however particular circumstances where members may still face personal liability, although these are restricted. An example is the potential personal liability of directors who continue to run the company in circumstances where they know or ought to realise the company is unlikely to avoid an insolvent liquidation, and it subsequently goes into an insolvent liquidation (wrongful trading). Essentially however a shareholder has limited liability.

The liability of partners for the debts of a firm is unlimited. If the assets of the firm are insufficient to meet the liability the creditor can look to the personal property of the individual partners. They may have bankruptcy proceedings brought against them. Limited liability is however available in a limited partnership, a special form of partnership which may be established under the provisions of the Limited Partnership Act 1907. There are however very few limited partnerships in operation.

(iii) *Agency*

In a company, mere membership does not of itself invest the shareholder with the power to act as an agent for and on behalf of the company. Agency powers are contained in the articles of association of the company and these powers are the principal agency source. Articles normally grant full powers as agents to the board of directors. In a firm however each partner is an agent of the other partners and of the partnership as a whole (s.5 Partnership Act 1890).

(iv) *Management*

Whereas companies are managed by those granted the power to do so under the articles – the directors of the company, in a firm all the members have the full right to take part in its management. Denial of this right would entitle the aggrieved partner to petition to have the firm dissolved. Thus whilst ownership and management are often in separate hands in the case of a registered company, this is never the position in a firm. Consequently the means available to company members to require directors to account for their actions are of crucial importance, and company law provides that certain decisions, such as alterations to the articles, can only legitimately be carried out at a general meeting of the company where all the membership is entitled to be present.

(v) *Membership*

There is no limit placed on the number of members a registered company may have. New members can join the company with little restriction, although the directors may have the power to refuse a share transfer in some cases. In a firm however a new partner can only join with the consent of all the existing members, emphasising the close commercial relationship of the partners. Moreover normal trading partnerships are restricted to a maximum of twenty partners. There is no limit however placed on the size of a professional partnership. A private company can have a single member but a firm must have two members.

(vi) *Taxation*

A company pays corporation tax on a flat rate basis on its profits. Shareholders are taxed on the dividends the company pays them.

In a partnership partners pay tax on the apportioned profits they receive from the business under Schedule D. This covers earnings from a trade, profession or occupation and enables them to pay tax on a preceding year basis and claim allowances against their tax liability for expenses incurred in their work for the business, e.g. costs of running a car. Tax paid on a preceding year basis means that tax liability for one fiscal year is met by making two equal payments of tax on the 1st January of the following fiscal year, and the 1st July of the next fiscal year, i.e. tax liability of £10,000 for fiscal year 1992/93 paid by instalments of £5,000 on 1st January 1994 and 1st July 1994. From 1997 under self assessment tax rules, tax will be assessed on a current year basis.

(vii) *Borrowing*

Companies, particularly larger ones, have much greater borrowing capability than partnerships. They can raise loan capital by issuing debentures and provide security by way of floating charges, neither of which partnerships can do.

(viii) *Formalities and public inspection*

Whereas a firm can maintain complete secrecy over its affairs (other than providing details of its proprietors where the Business Names Act 1985 applies) a registered company must provide the Registrar of Companies with a wealth of detail about itself on a regular basis. All of this information is held on its file and is available for public inspection. Thus its membership, its annual accounts, and details of the property it has charged, are amongst the long list of details which the Registrar must be provided with. There are also fees to be paid when such documents are delivered e.g. £25 on filing a copy of the annual return, and also of course a considerable internal administration burden for the company in satisfying the extensive information demands of company legislation. Financial penalties can be exacted against companies in default. Moreover company legislation in general is highly prescriptive, demanding particular procedures to be followed, and forms to be used, if a company is to lawfully conduct its affairs.

(ix) *Contractual scope*

Despite the dilution of the ultra vires principle as it applies to registered companies some limited aspects of it remain. A firm on the other hand is not subject to ultra vires.

(x) *Capital*

There are stringent rules controlling the way in which registered companies use capital. In particular it is a general principle of company law that capital investment be maintained and not reduced. A firm however has complete freedom over the way in which it uses its capital.

Assignment The Rise and Fall of John Russell

At the beginning of 1995 the further success of John Russell Ltd as a commercial enterprise seemed assured. The company had been incorporated at the beginning of 1993 out of an existing partnership business, for the purposes, to quote its objects clause of *"carrying on the business of motor vehicle dealers and ancillary activities"*.

The new company quickly established a name for itself, and by the winter of 1994 it felt itself in a strong enough commercial position to proceed with arrangements for the design and construction of expensive and prestigious new sales and office premises on the outskirts of Birmingham. Architects Van Mildert, Clarke, Foster were contracted to carry out the design work, the builders appointed were Western Construction plc, and the office equipment and the computer system was purchased from Zenith Office Supplies Ltd.

The downfall of the company was if anything more dramatic than its rapid growth. It came with the loss of the most lucrative business, fleet car sales. During the first five months of 1995 its three principal fleet customers failed to place new orders as a result of recessionary pressures. John Russell Ltd's three directors, Paul O'Grady, Jim Morgan, and John Russell himself, the managing director, struggled to keep the company afloat.

Still owing large sums on the new premises and advised by their accountants that the business *"would be unlikely to survive beyond the end of the year"* they decided to keep trading in the hope the fleet market would return. In the meantime, with insufficient funds to pay all the creditors, the directors decided to pay their architects charges of £75,000 in full, and to ask the architects to use their influence with the builders, Western Construction, to allow Russells more time to pay the final instalment of the building work, a sum of £400,000, now four months overdue.

The strategy did not work. The builders lost patience and petitioned the court at the end of July 1996 to have the company compulsorily wound up. The petition was granted and Simon Scott was subsequently appointed as liquidator.

You have recently joined the firm of accountants, in which Simon Scott is a partner, as an administrative assistant. In order to give you some experience of company liquidations, and also because he has a heavy workload at present, Simon Scott has asked you to consider a number of aspects of the John Russell liquidation. In particular he would like you to report back to him on the following matters.

1. Whether the payment made to the architects can be recovered for the company's creditors.

2. If any form of personal liability is likely to have been incurred by the directors in their conduct of the operations of John Russell Ltd.

3. Whether the contract the company made to purchase the computer system from Zenith Office Supplies can be avoided. The system purchased is more sophisticated than John Russell Ltd needs, and perhaps falls outside its objects clause. It has been established that Paul O'Grady is also a director of Zenith, although he has never disclosed the fact to the John Russell board.

Task

Advise Simon Scott in writing as to the legal position on the three points referred to above.

Legal Terms found in Chapter 8

Acceptance	• an unconditional assent to all the terms of an offer
Agreement	• essential element of a contract consisting of an offer and an acceptance
Capacity	• requirement that contracting parties be capable of making a binding agreement
Collateral contract	• contract whose existence is based upon another contract
Consensus ad idem	• a meeting of the minds of the contracting parties
Consideration	• the idea that the parties to a contract must exchange promises of value between themselves
Contract	• legally enforceable agreement
Contract of adhesion	• contract under which a party offer terms which are not up for negotiation
Deed	• formal written contract signed by both parties
Freedom of contract	• the notion that parties to a contract should be allowed to make their deal without legal interference
Intention to create legal relations	• legal requirement that a contract can only occur if the parties to an agreement regard it as legally binding
Offer	• an unequivocal undertaking to be bound by an acceptance
Parol contract	• oral contract
Simple contract	• any contract which is not a deed. It can be oral, written or implied

Chapter 8

Establishing Contracts

Contractual Liability

Whenever a contract is made it produces contractual liabilities. The content of such liabilities depends upon the substance of the contract in question, but all contractual liabilities are based upon a simple common element. They involve people entering into agreements consisting of legally enforceable promises exchanged between them. Such promises may be simple or complex; they may be single promises or sets of promises. But in whatever form they emerge contractual promises give rise to contractual liabilities. The result is that if such a promise is not carried out, or is carried out improperly, a legal obligation will have been broken and the injured party may choose to seek a remedy from the contract breaker before the courts.

The remainder of this chapter looks at the issues associated with contractual liabilities, considers how the law defines contracts, how they are made, and what they consist of.

The Contract Defined

A contract is simply a legally enforceable agreement. As it stands this is not a definition which takes us very far, for it raises further questions. We need to establish what the components are of an agreement, and what conditions have to be satisfied in order that an agreement can become legally recognised. Making an agreement does not automatically result in the making of a contract, for there are many other factors that are taken into account before a contract can materialise. For instance the parties to the agreement must have the legal capacity to contract, and there must be evidence that they intend their transactions to be legally binding.

An agreement which does not achieve contractual status will, in consequence, contain undertakings which the parties have exchanged with each other that do not bind them in a legal sense. Non-contractual agreements of this kind may still be honoured by the parties making them our of a sense of moral or social obligation. This serves to reinforce the proposition we have come across elsewhere in the book that the observance rules and principles may be based upon a notion of duty or responsibility which does not always have to be underpinned by legal sanctions. When friends agree to meet in town in the evening for a drink it is most unlikely the law would see the arrangement as legally binding, but we would nevertheless expect them to honour their arrangement because neither would want to let the other down. They would not want to break their promises.

Simple Contracts and Deeds

Contractual arrangements may be expressed in one of two ways. They may be contained within in a simple contract, which is by far the most common form of contract, or they may be contained in the form of a deed.

At common law no restriction is placed upon the way in which a contract can be expressed. The parties are free to make the contract orally, or in writing, or if they wish by using a combination of these methods. In appropriate cases a contract can even be inferred from the conduct of the parties. The term simple contract, suggesting a transaction that does not have to meet special technicalities of form, is therefore used to describe such arrangements.

It may seem surprising that the common law does not insist upon a written contract. It is certainly a commonly held view, although an entirely erroneous one, that something in writing is essential if a contract is to be valid. In fact the only circumstances in which writing is a legal requirement occur where Parliament has intervened to make writing mandatory. We shall consider the main examples shortly. Allowing oral contracts is based upon practical realities. For the majority of day to day transactions written agreements would be cumbersome and time consuming, and simply unnecessary. Nevertheless there are sound reasons why a written contract can be valuable to the parties concerned. The two most obvious reasons are that:

(a)   the writing will stand as evidence of the transaction, should anyone challenge its existence, and

(b)   the task of reducing what has been agreed into writing is likely to help the parties focus more precisely on what each is promising the other. The written document will emerge as one containing all the terms, that is the obligations, that are owed under the agreement. Most of the simple contracts that we make regularly as individual consumers are oral agreements; buying food, petrol, a record or tape, clothes and so on. Those that are commonly expressed in writing include taking a package holiday, buying good on credit, joining a bookclub, employing staff, and opening a bank account. There are of course many more. Sometimes the contract may be part written and part oral. Two companies may for instance enter into an agreement where some of the terms such as price are in writing, but others such as delivery arrangements are left to be orally negotiated. The existence of a contract may also be *inferred* when the facts support it.

In *Brogden v. Metropolitan Railway Co.* 1877 the railway company had been supplied with coal from Brogden for many years. The company was keen to have a formal contract. It drew up a draft agreement, which was sent to Brogden, and was returned by him to the company marked 'approved', although he had inserted a new term to the draft. For the next two years coal was supplied and paid for between the parties in accordance with the draft agreement, although the company never gave notification that it had accepted it. In fact over the two years it lay in a desk drawer. Then a dispute arose between the parties. Brogden alleged there was no contract binding them. The House of Lords disagreed, taking the view that there was a contract, based upon conduct. This occurred when the order was placed for the coal on the terms of the draft agreement, even though it had never been formally accepted. The Lord Chancellor, Lord Cairns, remarked, *"there may be a consensus between the parties far short of a mode of expressing it, and that consensus may be discovered from letters or from other documents of an imperfect and incomplete description".*

Consensus is a concept of considerable importance to the law of contract, and we shall be returning to it at various times later.

Deeds, sometimes referred to as speciality contracts, are formal contracts. Under the Law of Property (Miscellaneous Provisions) Act 1989 a deed must be contained in writing, and be signed by the parties making it, with their signatures being witnessed and attested.

There are relatively few circumstances in which the law demands a deed to give effect to a contract. Under the Law of Property Act 1925 a deed is required to convey, that is transfer legal ownership inland, from one party to another, and to create a lease of more than three years duration.

Whilst most deeds will arise out of agreements between parties who have exchanged promises of value, a deed is valid without the need for consideration to support it. Validity is achieved by the technical form of the document.

Although it was originally necessary for corporate bodies to contract using their corporate seal, the Corporate Bodies Contracts Act 1960 specifies that a corporation can make contracts as though it were an individual, thus there are no longer any special formal requirements attached to corporations and their contract making. It is not uncommon however to find that under their internal rules corporations are obliged for security reasons to use the corporate seal for contracts above a certain financial amount or for contracts of certain kinds.

Contracts where writing is necessary

It was noted earlier that Parliament requires certain contracts to be made in writing. The reasons for demanding a written contract vary. In some cases, the objective is to provide the consumer with a measure of protection which can be achieved by requiring a clear statement of rights and responsibilities to be contained in the written agreement. In other cases it is required in an effort to oblige parties involved in technical transactions, particularly those involving non-tangible property such as shares and copyright, to formally record the making and content of the transaction.

The most important examples include:

(a)   Hire purchase and conditional sale agreements. Under s.65(1) of the Consumer Credit Act 1974 such agreements cannot been forced unless they are properly executed. They become properly executed when a legible document containing all the express terms of the agreement and in the prescribed form is signed by the parties.

(b)   The transfer of shares in a registered company. This is required under s.183 Companies Act 1985, which states that a *"proper instrument of transfer"* must be delivered to the company. The company cannot register the transfer until this is done.

(c)   An assignment of copyright, under s.90 Copyright Designs and Patents Act 1988.

(d)   Cheques, bills of exchange and promissory notes, under the Bills of Exchange Act 1882.

(e)   Contracts for the sale or other disposition of land under the Law of Property (Miscellaneous Provisions) Act 1989. S2(1) of the Act provides that, *"a contract for the sale or other disposition of an interest in land can only be made in writing and only by incorporating all the terms which the parties have expressly agreed in the document or, where contracts are exchanged, in each."* S2(3) provides that, *"the document incorporating the terms... must be signed by or on behalf of each party to the contract."*

Failure to comply with the any of these statutory requirements renders the contract *invalid*.

Contrary to popular belief, apart from merchant seaman and apprentices, there is no legal requirement that a *contract of employment* be in writing. While there are problems associated with identifying the terms of an oral agreement, nevertheless, given the fluid nature of a contract of employment there is no guarantee that a requirement to reduce the original contract to writing would solve all the problems of interpreting its content.

Under s.1 of the Employment Rights Act 1996 there is however a statutory requirement on employers to provide their employees within eight weeks of the commencement of employment with a written statement of the main terms and conditions of employment. This section is considered in some depth in Chapter 14

There remains one type of contract which still only requires written evidence of its existence, rather than a written contract containing it, the contract of guarantee. Such contracts are covered by the Statute of Frauds 1677 (as amended). A contract of guarantee is a *"promise to answer for the debt, default or miscarriage of another person "* and the guarantor's liability arises only upon the failure of the debtor to pay.

Contracts of guarantee operate as *collateral* contracts, that is contracts whose existence is based upon another contract.

Void, Voidable and Unenforceable Contracts

Whilst most contracts are validly created, occasionally they suffer some flaw or impediment which results in them in not being properly established, with the result that the parties do not have full rights of enforcement.

A contract can sometimes will fail in such a fundamental way as to render it *void*. A void contract carries no contractual rights or obligations, so if for instance goods have been transferred under it, ownership in them will not pass and they can be recovered from the person in possession of them. Where services are rendered under a void contract, a reasonable sum is recoverable for the work done, under what is known as the *quantum meruit* rule. Literally quantum meruit means for as much as is deserved.

> *Craven-Ellis v. Canons Ltd.* 1936 provides an illustration. The plaintiff, who had worked for some time as the managing director of the defendant company, had in fact been employed under a deed which was void because he had failed to take up shares in the company as required by the company's articles. The court accepted that he was entitled

to remuneration for the work he had done, despite the absence of a properly executed contract, which deprived him of true contractual claim for payment. Quantum meruit is an equitable remedy.

The term *void contract* is really a contradiction in terms, since if the contract is void there is no legally enforceable agreement amounting to a contract. An example of a void contract is one whose purpose is illegal, such as an agreement to commit a criminal act, or to trade with an enemy alien during time of war.

Sometimes the contract will not be void but merely *voidable*. Where this is so, one of the parties has the option of avoiding the contract, but until the option to avoid is exercised the contract still stands. An example is provided in the case of contracts induced by fraud, where the deceived party can avoid the contract on the grounds of their lack of true consent to the agreement.

Finally, a contract may be *unenforceable*. Where this is so the court is unable to enforce it, if called upon to do so by one of the parties. In other respects however it may possess some effect. For instance if a *collateral* contract such as a guarantee is built upon it the unenforceability will not invalidate the collateral contract. Unenforceability can occur because of a failure to satisfy some technical requirement, such as the need for written evidence to support certain types of contract.

There is of course a significant difference between merely requiring written *evidence* of an agreement, and requiring the *entire contract to* be in writing. In particular the burden of satisfying the former requirement is less onerous than it is to satisfy the latter.

Before exploring the specific rules associated with contracting, let us take an objective view of the contract, looking at it in its operational context to see if we can establish its role and how the law makers have been guided in developing it as a specific body of rules and principles. The first question to consider is why we have a law of contract at all.

Why a law of contract?

The idea of the contract owes its existence to a concept which is central to economics, that of the market. Market activity, the interaction of buyers and sellers of goods and services, has origins going back to the early civilisations and the emergence of the first forms of trading activity within and between societies. One of the conditions necessary for trade to function effectively is the existence within the market place of a code of trading behaviour which provides a framework of rules within which trading parties can transact and to which they are willing to adhere. Without such a framework trading anarchy would prevail, and such a condition would be too uncertain and unstable a climate for individuals and businesses to make investment decisions and financial commitments. In a market free for all where no remedy is obtainable to repair a broken bargain few would have the confidence to trade. The contract has developed as a legal mechanism to provide a formalised set of rules of trading. Modern contract law has increasingly reflected a significant social dimension also. Examples we shall come across later include the limitations placed upon excluding certain types of contractual liability, and the rights of consumers injured as a result of defective manufactured goods, but there are many others. The objectives of social justice can be seen reflected in the protection afforded to employees and tenants within the contract of employment and the tenancy agreement.

The law of contract may thus be regarded in broad terms as a set of rules and principles which

- provides a legal framework offering a measure of trading security;

- seeks to pursue the aims of social justice and to restrict activities which are contrary to public policy;

- sets out the technical means by which parties who wish to make legally enforceable transactions can do so.

Let us now turn to the thinking which has guided the lawmakers in creating and developing the principles and rules which make up this vital body of law. As we shall see the law of contract is founded upon common law principles, having been developed by the courts rather than by Parliament.

The concept of freedom of contract

Contracting parties have never enjoyed unlimited freedom to make whatever deal they choose. Throughout the long development of the English law of contract, which has taken place over many centuries, some restrictions have always existed. No court, for example has ever been prepared to enforce a contract whose purpose is unlawful, such as an agreement to commit a criminal offence. However the extent of contractual regulation has varied over time, reflecting the thinking current at different periods.

Under the capitalist philosophy of the nineteenth century a *laissez-faire* approach to the development of the economy was advocated. This involved leaving the markets for goods and services, as far as reasonably practicable, to regulate themselves. The idea of a free market, which should be left to control itself unhindered by the interventions of the courts or Parliament, helped to reinforce the view that had been influential since the eighteenth century of *freedom of contract*. The advocates of freedom of contract considered that as few restrictions as possible should be placed upon the liberty of individuals to make agreements. The Master of the Rolls, Sir George Jessel, expressed it in the following way in 1875: *"If there is one thing which more than any other public policy requires it is that men of full age and understanding shall have the utmost liberty of contracting and their contracts when entered into freely and voluntarily shall be held sacred and shall be enforced by the courts of justice."*

There appear to be some compelling reasons for supporting this view. Firstly the law of contract is a part of private law, which means that the creation and performance of contracts is the responsibility of parties themselves. It is a basic principle of contract law that contractual rights and obligations only attach to the actual parties entering the contract. (This principle is, it should be added, subject to certain exceptions). Consequently contractual rights and obligations are purely personal. If a contract is broken the only person with the right to a remedy is the injured party; no one else can sue the contract breaker. Secondly it is the parties themselves who are be stable to judge their own contractual needs. If their negotiations are not concluded to their mutual satisfaction then they will not go ahead and complete the contract. If on the other hand they are both in agreement they will be happy to bind themselves formally, and incur contractual obligations. They should be left alone to make the contract that suits them, free from external interference.

The objectives of freedom of contract

The underlying reasons for allowing a wide measure of contractual freedom include:

- *market needs:*
  in the interests of healthy markets the participants in market activity should be allowed to trade unhindered. The able will survive and the weak will flounder. External intervention in this process will tend to weaken rather than strengthen economic performance by the artificial distortion of the bargaining process;

- *personal liberty:*
  interference in contract making is an infringement of individual liberty. In the same way that a person chooses when to marry, or for whom to vote, they should be allowed the freedom to make the contracts of their choosing. If subsequently the choice turns out to be a bad one it is of concern to nobody but the contract maker. The contract is a private, not a public event;

- *knowledge:*
  contracting parties can be assumed to know what they are doing. They can be expected to act in a rational manner and will therefore seek to ensure that the contract they make is the contract they want. Nobody else is better placed to identify contractual wants and needs than the transacting parties themselves.

Closer analysis, however, suggests these factors reflect more a theoretical ideal than the reality of modern contract making. It is important to an understanding of the law of contract to appreciate why the ideas upon which the notion of freedom of contract are based, are in practice largely myths.

The reality of business contracting

The Role of Consent

In a sense we enjoy complete contractual freedom. Individuals and organisations alike are free to choose whether to enter into a contractual relationship. It cannot be forced on them for consent is a precondition of the relationship. But what precisely does consent mean? To answer this question we need to examine how the courts discriminate between those situations where consent is regarded as genuine, and those in which the consent is in reality artificial. Where the consent given to an agreement is not genuine consent there is said to be no *consensus ad idem*, or meeting of the minds of the parties. Circumstances in which the courts will be prepared to consider a claim that the consent is unreal are in cases of misrepresentation, mistake, fraud, duress or undue influence. They are referred to technically as *vitiating elements*. Once established they have the effect of either invalidating the contract in its entirety, in which case the contract is said to be *void*, or of entitling the injured party to escape from the contract if he or she wishes to do so. In such circumstances the contract is said to be *voidable* in the injured favour. To vitiate literally means to make invalid or ineffectual.

The presence of a vitiating factor in an agreement can, as we have seen, defeat the entire contract. By granting relief where consent is a sham because a person has been misled, tricked, coerced or mistaken, the courts are demonstrating that they will look at what the parties believed they were agreeing to when the contract was made. Equally of course, the notion of freedom carries with it responsibility. It is certainly not the role of the courts to repair bad bargains made through lack of prudence. The balance between intervening in an attempt to right legitimate wrongs, whilst leaving the parties to learn from their trading mistakes is not easily achieved. The point is that the courts are prepared in the right circumstances to untie the bond that has been made, thereby protecting parties in a limited way from the consequences that complete freedom of contract would otherwise produce.

Bargaining inequality

A further important element in examining the concept of freedom of contract is the question of bargaining power. True consensus is only possible where the parties meet as bargaining equals. In practice such equality is invariably elusive; it is commonplace to find that there is an inequality of bargaining power so that one party is able to dominate the other. The result is that far from arriving at agreement through a process of negotiation, the contract is a one sided arrangement in which the dominant party presents terms to the weaker party on a take-it-or-leave it basis. Commonly the dominant party will only be prepared to do business on the basis of standard terms designed to provide it with a high level of commercial protection. If the dominant party is a monopoly supplier, like British Gas or British Rail, the consumer is unable to shop around for a better deal or a different set of terms. Even in a reasonably competitive market situation it is often the case that suppliers of goods or services trade on the same or very similar terms, for instance by using a contract designed by the trade association of which they are a member. Contracts arising in this way are sometimes referred to as contracts of *adhesion*, for the weaker party is required to adhere all the terms imposed by the stronger party.

Legal intervention in the market place

To help redress the imbalance of the market place where contract making is concerned Parliament and the courts have been prepared to intervene in appropriate circumstances, to produce a kind of externally manipulated true commercial justice. Thus Parliament has used legislation to bolster the rights of *consumers*, be they businesses or individuals. The range of legislative measures which seek to create a more level playing field for contracting parties is now very extensive. They are considered elsewhere the book, but the most notable examples are the Consumer Credit Act 1974, the Unfair Contract Terms Act 1977, and Sale of Goods Act 1979, the Supply of Goods and Services Act 1982 and the Consumer Protection Act 1987.

The courts have been prepared to intervene in circumstances of exceptional exploitation, drawing on an equitable principle known as *undue influence*.

> A good illustration is provided by the decision of the Court of Appeal in *Lloyds Bank Ltd. v. Bundy* 1975. Here an elderly farmer, who was ill and had little business knowledge, agreed with the bank to guarantee the account of his son's company. The company was in difficulties, and over a period of time the father increased the size of the guarantee, which was secured by a mortgage on his house, so that eventually the mortgage on the property was for more than the property was worth. This arrangement had been made by the father in consultation with the bank manager, upon whom he implicitly relied. The company's debts remained outstanding, and the bank sought to sell

the father's house in order to realise the guarantee. The Court of Appeal unanimously set aside the agreement between the father and the bank. In the course of his judgment Lord Denning MR made the following important observations: *"no bargain will be upset which is the result of the ordinary interplay of forces. There are many hard cases which are caught by this rule ... yet there are exceptions to this general rule ... in which the courts will set aside a contract, or a transfer of property, when the parties have not met on equal terms, when the one is so strong in bargaining power and the other so weak that, as a matter of common fairness, it is not right that the strong should be allowed to push the weak to the wall .... English law gives relief to one who, without independent advice, enters into a contract on terms which are very unfair or transfers property for a consideration which is grossly inadequate ..."*

However the mere fact that one party is weaker than the other is not enough, in itself, to escape the contract. That person must establish that the agreement is unconscionable to obtain equitable relief. In *Barclays Bank plc v. Schwarz* 1995 the defendant, the principal director of a number of property companies, argued before the Court of Appeal that he was not liable to make good debts of over £1/2 m which his companies owed. He had signed personal guarantees in favour of the bank regarding these debts, His defence was his poor understanding of English, something the bank was aware of. It should have explained to him the nature of the documents he was signing. The court rejected these arguments, finding that his weakness in the English language was not a sufficient ground to set aside the guarantees. Illiteracy was not a defence, Simon Brown LJ was not convinced that a man with a number of property companies could argue that *"his understanding of the ... English language, and the nuts and bolts of ordinary commercial life, was so deficient that he could thereby escape the consequences of signing routine legal instruments."*

Anti-competitive practices

Both Parliament and the courts have also been prepared to intervene in cases where the effect of a contract is to act as a restraint of trade. In such situations intervention is prompted not by any concern for individual justice, but rather with the broader considerations of general economic well-being through the maintenance of healthy markets. In the words of Lord McNaghten in *Nordenfelt v. Maxim Nordenfelt Gun & Ammunition Co. Ltd.* 1894 *"The public have an interest in every person 's carrying on his trade freely; so has the individual. All interference with individual liberty of action in trading, and all restraints of trade themselves, if there is nothing more, are contrary to public policy, and are therefore void."*

Many types of restraint of trade are operated. The following are in practice the most common:

- restraints on employment. These usually appear as terms inserted in the contract of employment by the employer, and designed to prevent employees from setting up in competition when they leave the employment;
- agreements between suppliers and retailers under which the retailer agrees to sell only the supplier's goods. The best example of such arrangements can be seen in the practices of the petrol industry. Petrol companies impose *solus agreements upon*

> *petrol stations, requiring them to sell only the petrol and other products of that particular petrol company;*

- price fixing agreements and agreements which seek to restrict or limit supplies of goods.

The essence of a contract in restraint of trade is that it contains an undertaking by one of the parties to restrict that person's freedom of trading action with others in the future. The grounds for legal interference in such arrangements are those of public policy: what the courts and Parliament are seeking to prevent are practices which restrict competition to the detriment of the public. Thus external intervention is thus sometimes necessary to maintain healthy market conditions. Such conditions do not automatically result from leaving the market to regulate itself.

Which law applies?

When contracts are made between parties who are residents or nationals of different countries one question which arises is which body of laws will apply to their agreement. Generally this question does not become important unless a dispute occurs. It may then become apparent that by applying the contractual rules of their respective states different outcomes are obtained. A further issue will be which courts have the jurisdiction to deal with the dispute if it is taken to law. These are important issues, involving consideration not only as to what the law of the different jurisdictions is, but also how effective their different systems of civil justice are. The costs involved in bringing proceedings, the likely duration of those proceedings, and factors of convenience associated with the location of the relevant courts all need to be borne in mind.

As part of the process of legal harmonisation between the member states of the EC, the United Kingdom has incorporated a number of European conventions dealing with contractual conflict of laws in the Contracts (Applicable Law) Act 1990. The major convention which the Act introduces is the Rome Convention. Article 3 provides that the parties to a contract are free to choose which country's law shall govern it. If they have not chosen Article 4 provides that the contract shall be governed by the law of the country with which it is most closely connected, and the presumption is that this will be the country, *"where the party who is to effect the performance which is characteristic of the contract"* has habitual residence or in the case of a business organisation has its central administration. In a contract for the sale of goods between a buyer in France and a seller in England it would be English law which would apply. If however it is clear that in all the circumstances the contract is more closely associated with another country, then the presumption will not apply. Under Article 5, if the contract involves the supply of goods or services to a consumer for a purpose outside his or her trade or profession, the applicable law is that of the country where the consumer habitually resides if, inter alia, *"the supplier received the order from the consumer in that country."*

Although as we have seen the parties can choose which law shall apply to them, even if they do so the Rome Convention indicates that in certain circumstances this will be overridden. One circumstance where this will occur is in the case of a consumer transaction coming within Article 5 above. So if a private consumer in the UK agrees to purchase a motor vehicle from a German motor dealer by placing the order with the German company's agent in London, then even though the contract specifies that German law shall apply to it, the applicable law will be UK law, or at least that part of UK law which, in the words of the convention is *"mandatory"*. Mandatory rules of law are defined as those rules which cannot be ousted under the contract, such as implied conditions under the Sale of Goods Act 1979.

It would seem that with the introduction of the Single Market the application of these rules under the 1990 Act will become of increasing importance to businesses and consumers alike.

Having considered the formalities that are attached to contracting, we now need to look in some depth at the elements involved in forming a valid contract. These elements are represented in Figure 8.1.

The Formation of the Contract

Agreement

To form a contract certain legal requirements must be met. These are that capable parties have entered into an agreement intending to bind themselves legally and have given consideration by exchanging provisions of value. We need to examine these requirements in some detail.

A contract cannot be created without the parties reaching an agreement. The idea of agreement is therefore central to an understanding of the law of contract. There are two basic legal question which arise in respect of all transaction. They are, firstly, whether a legally enforceable agreement has been made, and secondly what the terms are upon which it is based.

The answer to the second question reveals the specific obligations each party owes towards the other which of fundamental importance to them both. It is only by identifying the content and extent of their mutual undertakings that the parties are able to know when they have discharged their responsibilities under the contract, and freed themselves from their legal bond. The two questions are, of course, very closely connected, because it is through the process of reaching their agreement that the parties will expressly fix the terms that are to regulate their contract. In other words, agreements are arrangements to do, or sometimes refrain from doing, specific things, and these specific things are the terms of the contract.

Perhaps most people can rely on instinct or common sense to assess whether they have an agreement or not, but for legal purposes it is not sufficient to rely upon subjective judgments to decide such significant events. If a disputed agreement comes before a court, obviously the court cannot get inside the minds of the parties to discover their actual intentions. At best all that can be achieved is to look at the way they have conducted themselves, examining what they have said and what they have done, in order to decide the matter on the basis of what a reasonable person would assume their intentions to be.

What the courts do is objectively to assess the evidence and then apply established criteria to help resolve contractual disputes. These criteria take the form of fixed and certain rules, which over a long period have been developed and refined by the judiciary and which are used by all courts to determine what constitutes an enforceable agreement. A knowledge and understanding of these rules is of great practical value to individuals and organisations alike.

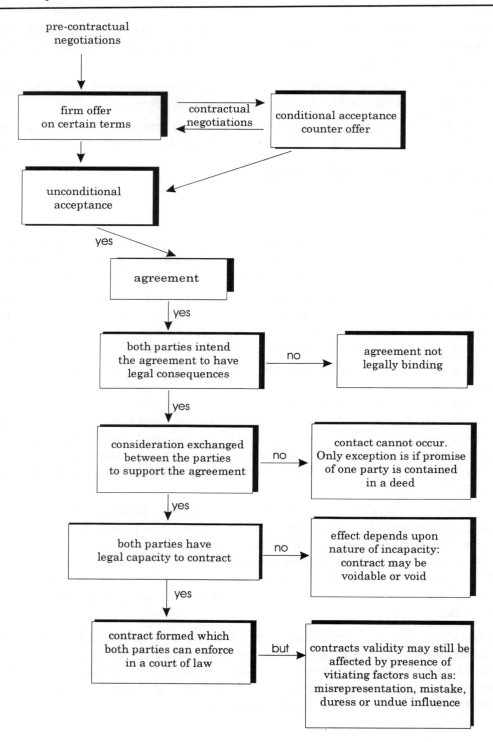

Figure 8.1   Elements in the formation of contract

If an agreement is analysed it will be found to contain two main elements:

(i)   an offer, made by one party to the other; and

(ii)   an acceptance by the other of the terms contained in the offer.

If a court cannot identify the presence of these two components in a transaction, a simple contract will not have materialised, although as we have seen a person can become bound contractually by expressing a promise in the form of a deed without the need for an agreement.

The process of negotiation

The person making an offer is referred to as the *offeror*, and the person to whom it is addressed the *offeree*. In business usually one finds the parties reaching agreement following a period of negotiation. Such negotiations will focus the details of the proposed transaction, and are likely to include matters such as price, specifications concerning the subject matter of the agreement, and the time and place for performing it. Often during these negotiations offers will be made by one party to the other which are rejected, or met by a fresh offer. Either of the parties to the transaction is able to make an offer, not just the one who wishes to sell the goods or services in question or who is the owner or supplier of them.

Examining the negotiating process is important for many reasons. Among them are that:

(i)   it enables us to identify which party made the final offer;

(ii)   it enables us to identify the time at which the contract is made;

(iii)   having established who made the offer we can identify the terms upon which the offer was based, and hence upon which the contract is founded; and

(iv)   during negotiations false statements are sometimes made by one of the parties which induce the other to enter into the contract. These are referred to as *misrepresentations*.

Characteristics of a Valid Offer

To be legally effective an offer must satisfy the following general requirements:

- it must be firmly made;
- it must be communicated;
- its terms must be certain; and
- it must not have terminated.

Firm offer or invitation to treat

The offeror must intend his offer to be unequivocal, so that when acceptance occurs he will be bound. The difficulty that can arise here lies in distinguishing firm offers from statements which do not carry the full legal status of offers. Sometimes what appears to be a firm offer is merely an incentive or encouragement designed by the person making it to encourage the making of offers to him and is certainly not intended to be legally binding. A statement of this kind is known as an *invitation to treat*. It is an indication that the person is willing to do business with anyone who is interested.

In *Pharmaceutical Society of Great Britain v. Boots Cash Chemists (Southern) Ltd.* 1953 one of the shops in the company's chain had been converted into a self-service supermarket. Some of the shelves carried poisons which by statute were required to be sold in the presence of a qualified chemist. The chemist was in attendance at the checkout. The Pharmaceutical Society which had a duty to enforce the statutory provisions claimed that the company was in breach of them. The Society argued that the contract was made at the shelves where there was no pharmacist in attendance. The court however held that the goods displayed on the shelves were merely invitations to treat. The contract was made at the checkout. The customers made the offer when presenting the goods for payment and the offer was accepted by the cashier passing them through the checkout.

No real distinction can be drawn between goods displayed on shelves inside a shop and goods displayed in the window. In *Fisherv. Bell* 1961 a shop keeper was prosecuted for displaying a flick-knife inside his shop window with a price ticket attached. He was found by the court not to have committed the offence of offering for sale an offensive weapon contrary to the Restriction of Offensive Weapons Act 1959. The display was simply an invitation to treat.

Advertisements are also generally regarded as constituting invitations to treat. In *Partridge v. Crittenden* 1968 the Divisional Court of the Queens Bench Division was asked to determine whether an advertisement in a magazine which read, *"Bramblefinch_ cocks,bramblefinch hens 25/- each"*, constituted the offence of offering to sell wild birds contrary to the Protection of Birds Act 1954. The court quashed the conviction against the defendant which had been issued in the Magistrates Court. The advertisement was simply an encouragement to stimulate the market into making offers. Members of the public responding to the advert made the offers, but of course they could not commit an offence since they were offering to buy, not to sell. The defendant should have been charged with the separate offence contained in the Act of selling wild birds.

The legal inference that advertisements will not normally amount to firm offers to sell is helpful to businesses that trade on a mail-order basis. For instance a company that takes out advertising in a newspaper or colour supplement cannot be sure of the demand for its goods that will result. If the advertisement were to constitute an offer, then the response of a member of the public in sending a cheque or postal order to buy the advertised goods would amount to an acceptance. The company could find itself overwhelmed by the demand, and under a legal obligation to supply goods it simply does not have if its stocks are exhausted.

Perhaps the clearest example of an invitation to treat can be seen in an auction sale. This occurs when the auctioneer presents items in the auction, and asks for bids from those who are present, using expressions such as *"how much am I bid for ... ?"* and *"do I see £20?"* The auctioneer is testing demand, and having assessed it will try to increase it and push the price up. The auctioneer is certainly not offering to sell. It is the bids themselves which constitute offers and which the auctioneer is thus able to accept or reject.

As the cases above reveal, it is usually in connection with criminal offences that the question of what constitutes an offer will arise. In relation to auction sales an illustration is provided by *British Car Auctions Ltd. v. Wright* 1972. An unroadworthy car had been sold at auction. The auctioneers were convicted in the Magistrates Court of offering to sell an unroadworthy vehicle, contrary to the Road Traffic Act 1972. In quashing the conviction Widgery LCJ stated: *"The auctioneer when he stands on his rostrum does not make an offer to sell the goods on behalf of the vendor; he stands there making an invitation to those present at the auction themselves to make offers to buy"*.

Further examples of the invitation to treat are advertisements inviting suppliers of goods and services to submit tenders, and prospectuses issued by limited companies inviting members of the public to subscribe for shares.

Tenders

The use of tenders is a common commercial practice. Indeed local authorities are required by the Local Government Act 1972 to contract in this way. Under s.135 a contract made by an authority must comply with its standing orders and these standing orders must include provisions for securing competition and for regulating the manner in which tenders are invited in the case of contracts for the supply of goods or materials or for the execution of works. This is usually satisfied by inviting tenders from contractors on an approved list maintained by the authority. The Local Government Act 1988 imposes particular restrictions on local authorities by requiring that certain activities cannot be carried out by the council's own workforce without first going to competitive tender, which will involve the authority itself in making a written bid for the work. The activities covered by the Act include contracts for the collection of refuse, school and other catering arrangements, ground maintenance and the repair and maintenance of motor vehicles. Under the tendering process a tender is an offer and an invitation to tender is an invitation to treat. It is merely an invitation by an individual or organisation wishing to purchase goods or services to request suppliers to submit a contractual offer in the form of a tender.

In appropriate circumstances however it is possible to treat an invitation to tender as giving rise to a binding contractual obligation. If there is clear evidence from what the parties have said and done that a contractual obligation to consider a particular tender in conjunction with all other tenders meeting the tendering requirements was intended, then the Court will enforce it.

In *Blackpool and Fylde Aero Club v. Blackpool Borough Council* 1990 the local authority owned and managed an airport. The plaintiff flying club had for some years operated pleasure flights from the airport. When the grant of the club's concession came up for renewal the council prepared invitations to tender. These were then sent to the club and six other parties. The forms sent out stated that the council did not bind itself, *"to accept all or any part of any tender"*. The form added, *"No tender which is received after the last date and time specified shall be admitted for consideration."*

The plaintiffs delivered their tender to the council offices before the deadline, however because council staff failed to empty the council letter box when they should have done the council received the tender too late to be considered, and accepted a tender from another tenderer lower in value than the plaintiff's tender. The club sued for damages alleging breach of contract and negligence. The court held that although contracts in such circumstances should not be freely implied, the evidence here was of a clear intention that the council was contractually obliged to consider the plaintiff's tender with the other tenders, or at least that it would be considered if all the others were. The claim for breach of contract was successful. The question of whether the council would have owed the plaintiffs a duty to take reasonable care to consider a tender submitted within the stated time limit, in the absence of an implied contractual obligation to do so, was not decided.

If the invitation to tender stipulates expressly or impliedly that the goods or services will be required, then an acceptance of the tender will create a binding contract. Alternatively, the invitation may stipulate that the goods or services *may* be required, in which case an acceptance of the tender results in a standing offer to supply as and when required. A failure to order by the buyer in such circumstances will not result in a breach of contract.

In *Harvela Investments Ltd. v. Royal Trust Co. of Canada Ltd.* 1985 the House of Lords was required to examine the nature of an invitation to tender in the context of the sale of shares. Royal Trust of Canada was prepared to sell some of its shares, and invited two companies, Harvela and Outerbridge to tender for them. The invitation to do so stipulated that the tender should contain a single offer price, and be sealed i.e. be made privately. It also stated that the highest bid would be accepted. Harvela's bid was $2,175,000. Outerbridge offered $2,100,000 or $101,000 in excess of any other higher bid, whichever was the higher. A bid of this kind is known as a referential bid. The seller informed both parties that the shares had been purchased by Outerbridge, at a price of $2,276,000. Harvela challenged this claim. The court held that on the facts the referential bid by Outerbridge was invalid. It took the view that the presumed intention of the sellers should be deduced from the terms of the invitation read as a whole, and this was then intended to create a fixed bidding scale. In support of this presumed intention were the facts that they had undertaken to accept the highest offer which they had extended to both bidders thus giving them an equal opportunity to purchase the shares. The fact that the sellers insisted on confidentiality in the submission of bids to provoke the best price that each party was prepared to pay was consistent with the presumed intention to create a fixed bidding scale. Accordingly Outerbridge had not been entitled to submit a referential bid and the sellers had not been entitled to accept it. The court ordered the transfer of the shares to Harvela at the price of $2,175,000.

It should be borne in mind that the invitation to treat is not devoid of legal effect. It can give rise to legal liability in the following ways:

- as a statement it can amount to an actionable misrepresentation(see post); and

- it may also give rise to criminal liability under the Trade Descriptions Act 1968, if it constitutes a false trade description, or under the Consumer Protection Act 1987 if it gives a false or misleading indication as to the price of goods or services.

Communicating the offer

The party to whom an offer is directed must be aware of it. An offer will normally be made to a single individual or organisation, however there is nothing to prevent an offer being directed to a specific group of individuals, anyone or more of whom may choose to accept it. For instance a private limited company that is going public may offer some of its shares at favourable rates to the members of its workforce.

It is possible to make an offer to the public generally, in circumstances where the offeror is not able at the time the offer is made to identify who all the possible recipients may be. This long established principle seems to be derived from the willingness of the courts to recognise a contractual obligation on the part of someone offering to pay any member of the public a reward, for example in return for information or for the return of property. It is not uncommon to find banks offering financial incentives for information leading to the conviction of bank robbers by displaying appropriate notices inside the banks. In such circumstances anyone who satisfies the terms of the offer will be entitled to the reward, as long as they were aware of the offer beforehand. A further example can be seen in use of television programmes seeking to solve crimes where financial rewards are sometimes referred to. One of the most celebrated instances of an offer made to the public at large, occurred in *Carlill v. Carbolic Smokeball Co.* 1893 which is considered below.

What constitutes communication is a question of fact for the court.

Certainty of terms

In the event of a dispute between the parties as to the meaning of a term it will ultimately fall to the court to decide the question. The courts will always endeavour to find certainty so that the contract is able to survive wherever possible but if a term is obscure or meaningless then it will fail. This may not prove fatal to the contract if the term constitutes only a minor part of the overall obligations, but where the term is central to the functioning of the contract, uncertainty as to its meaning will defeat the contract as a whole. The following cases illustrate the position.

> In *Loftus v. Roberts* 1902 an agreement provided for the appointment of an actress by another person at a *"West End salary to be mutually agreed between us."* Subsequently the parties were unable to arrive at a salary which satisfied them both. The court held that the contract must fail. Even if it were possible to assess a suitable salary by reference to West End rates of pay, the court could not impose such a figure since the parties had already stated that it had to be mutually agreed, something they had been unable to achieve. What they had was an agreement to agree at a further date. The contract failed.

> In *Scammel v. Ouston* 1941 an agreement for the sale of a van where the balance of the price was to be met *"on hire purchase terms over a period of two years"* also failed. Since there was no previous course of dealing between the parties to enable the court to identify what these "hire purchase" terms might be, the only alternative would have been to treat the terms as standard hire purchase terms. Unfortunately, as the court observed, hire purchase terms are not standardised and identical, but vary from agreement to agreement so that for example different rates of interest can be charged by different companies.

A meaningless term can however often be ignored.

> In *Nicolene Ltd. v. Simmonds* 1953 a contract was made for the sale of 3000 tons of steel bars. The seller later broke the contract. When the buyer sued for damages the seller argued there was no contract between them, relying on a statement in one of the

contractual documents that, *"we are in agreement that the usual conditions of acceptance apply"*. The court, whilst recognising that there are no *"usual conditions of acceptance"*, found that the contract was in every other respect clear as to the obligations of the parties. The meaningless term could be cut out from the rest of the contract. In the course of his judgment Lord Denning MR commented that, *"A clause which is meaningless can often be ignored . . .; whereas a clause which has yet to be agreed may mean there is no contract at all."*

In any contract the price to be paid for goods or services will be a term lying at the heart of the transaction. In the unlikely even that the parties have reached agreement whilst overlooking the question of price altogether how will this affect their agreement? In such circumstances it may still be possible to enforce the agreement. In the case of sales of goods, the Sale of Goods Act 1979 provides under s.8 that if the parties have not agreed price, or arranged a method for fixing price, or previously dealt with each other so that there is a price level in existence, then the buyer is bound to pay a *reasonable* price. This will usually be the market price. A similar rule applies in relation to those contracts which are covered by the Supply of Goods and Services Act 1982. As we saw in *Loftus v. Roberts* the most difficult situation to overcome is one in which an agreement has been made to settle price at a later date.

In *May and Butcher* v. R. 1929 Lord Buckmaster said of this situation, *"It has long been a well-recognised principle of contract law that an agreement between two parties to enter into an agreement in which some critical part of the contract is left undetermined is no contract at all."*

It is an entirely different matter however, if machinery has been agreed which can be used to fix the price, or indeed resolve any other aspect of uncertainty.

In *Sykes (F & G) Wessex v. Fine Fare* 1967 a supplier of chickens undertook to supply a supermarket chain with between 30,000 and 80,000 birds each week over a period of one year. The agreement also provided that for a further four years the supplier would provide chickens in quantities *"as might be agreed"*. The meaning of this expression subsequently led to a dispute between the parties. The court held that since the contract provided for arbitration to settle disagreements, the contract was not void on the basis of the uncertainty of the term as to quantity.

When the sale of land is being negotiated it is usual practice for parties initially to reach an agreement *"subject to contract."* Agreement on a subject to contract basis usually achieves no more than to demonstrate a willingness on the part of the prospective purchaser to proceed towards a formal agreement if his professional advisors make no adverse discoveries concerning the property in question. The technical nature of land transactions makes it extremely unwise for a purchaser to enter into a binding agreement without first making inquiries regarding the property. Thus a purchaser will seek to show the vendor that it is his intention to purchase provided the inquiries that are made prove satisfactory. To achieve this he will make a conditional offer, or a conditional acceptance by using an expression like *subject to contract*. It is well settled that this creates no binding obligation on the parties.

Prior to the Law of Property (Miscellaneous Provisions) Act 1989 the use of the words *"subject to contract"* on all letters and other documents signed by either party or his agent or representative before exchange of contracts was essential, as such documents could otherwise amount to written evidence of the contract under s.40 Law of Property Act 1925. This would enable the other party to sue on the agreement even where no contracts were formally signed or exchanged.

With the introduction of the 1989 Act, however, the rule in s.40 has been repealed and it is no longer possible to enforce an oral contract for the sale of land which is merely evidenced in writing. Rather, under s.2 of the 1989 Act, the contract must be made in writing, signed by the parties and contain all of the express terms in order to be valid.

The offer must not have terminated

If the offer has come to an end in some way before the offeree accepts it, the acceptance is ineffective for there is no longer an offer to accept. However we need to look closely at how offers once made can legally be regarded as at an end. This can occur in the following ways:

(a)   where the offeror has *revoked* the offer; or

(b)   where the offer has *lapsed*; or

(c)   where the offer has been *accepted or met with a counter offer*.

Where the offeror has revoked the offer

Revoking, or withdrawing, the offer is permissible at any time before the offeree has accepted it, and the revocation can be effective even if it is not communicated directly by the offeror, provided it is communicated through some reliable channel. However, like an offer, a revocation will only be effective when it is actually communicated by being brought to the attention of the offeree. The following cases illustrate these points.

> In *Dickinson v. Dodds* 1876 an offer to sell some houses was expressed to remain open until 9 a. m. on Friday . The offeree however learnt from a reliable third party on Thursday that the offeror had negotiated a sale to another purchaser. This was held to be sufficient to amount to a revocation.

> In *Byrne & Co. v. Leon Van Tienhoven & Co.* 1880 an offer to sell tin plate was received by the offeree on 11 October, and immediately accepted by telegram. The offeror however had posted a revocation which the offeree received on 20 October. It was held the revocation was only effective when actually received, and was therefore too late.

Does actual receipt mean physical delivery to the business premises of the offeree or must it in addition be opened and read? The House of Lords has suggested that it will be effective even if it has not been opened, provided that it would have been opened, *"if the ordinary course of business was followed"*. This comment the course of the court's judgment made in *Eagleshill Ltd. v. J Needham (Builders)Ltd.* 1972 indicates that a business which for whatever reason fails to promptly deal with its mail may nonetheless find itself bound by the contents of any letters of revocation it has received.

If the offeror seeks to revoke an offer made to the public generally, although there is no decided case on the point, it is likely that the revocation can be effected by using the same publicity as that afforded to the original offer. For instance if a new supermarket which is to open next week advertised in the local paper that the first twenty customers taking goods to the checkout on opening day would receive a free bottle of champagne, then a further advertisement in the same paper informing the public that no champagne will be available should be a sufficient act of revocation, despite doing little to promote business goodwill.

Sometimes an offeror may seek to revoke the offer after the offeree has started to perform the act required by the offeror, but has not yet completed it. It seems that such a revocation will not be effective on the grounds that the offer carries with it an implied undertaking that it will remain open until the offeror has been given a reasonable opportunity to complete, and that in any event once the offer starts to carry out the work this will constitute acceptance of the offer which cannot thereafter be revoked.

Where the offer has lapsed

When an offer is made it will not remain open indefinitely, but will lapse. This occurs automatically in the following circumstances:

(a)   after a stated time limit for which the offer was to be held open has passed; or if there is no such time limit, after a reasonable time;

In *Ramsgate Victoria Hotel Co. Ltd. v. Montefiore* 1866 the defendant offered by letter on 8 June to buy shares in the company, and was allotted the shares on 23 November. It was held that the defendant was entitle to refuse the shares on the grounds that his offer had lapsed before the company had made the allotment. Clearly the market value of shares can fluctuate widely over a period of six months;

(b)   if the situation on which it was based has fundamentally changed, for instance if the property which has been offered for sale has been destroyed by fire or has been stolen, before acceptance occurs;

(d)   where the offeror has died, provided this is known to the offeree before acceptance. If the offeree is unaware of the offeror's death the latter's estate will be bound by the contract.

An offeror is not obliged to keep the offer open for any particular length of time, unless some separate contract has been entered into between the parties to achieve this. So if A is interested in buying goods from B, and B promises to hold open the offer to sell A the goods at a particular price for a fixed period of time, this promise is only binding if A has given a valuable promise in return –probably by agreeing to pay B for the benefit of the offer being kept open.

Characteristics of a Valid Acceptance

Acceptance is defined as the unconditional assent to all the terms of the offer. It must therefore be unequivocal. We have already seen that a conditional acceptance will occur when a potential purchaser of land agrees to buy it subject to contract. This is acceptance subject to happening of a future event which may or may not occur, and is not therefore binding.

The following points provide an indication of how to determine whether an acceptance is valid.

It must be unconditional

It is not uncommon to find people believing that they have accepted the offer, when in fact they have made a fresh offer themselves by accepting on conditions. The general position regarding the need for unconditional assent is as follows:

(a) a conditional acceptance will constitute a *counter offer*. Thus a conditional acceptance does not complete the transaction but rather continues the negotiations;

(b) a counter offer both rejects and extinguishes an original offer.

In *Hyde v. Wrench* 1840 the defendant offered his farm to the plaintiff for £1,000. The plaintiff replied offering £950. The defendant subsequently rejected this, so the plaintiff purported to accept the original £1,000 offer. It was held that there was no contract since the original offer had been extinguished by the counter offer. Although expressed as an acceptance, it was in fact a fresh offer;

(c) any alteration to the terms of the offer will render the acceptance invalid.

In *Northland Airlines Ltd. v. Dennis Ferranti Meters Ltd.* 1970 a case which concerned negotiations for the purchase of an aircraft by Northland from Ferranti, a telegram from Ferranti stated, *"confirming sale to you – aircraft – £27, 000. Winnipeg. Please remit £5,000 for account of . . ."* to which Northland replied by telegram, *"This is to confirm your cable and my purchase – aircraft on terms set out in your cable. Price £27, 000 delivered Winnipeg. £5, 000 forwarded to your bank in trust for your account pending delivery. Balance payable on delivery. Please confirm delivery to be made 30 days within this date."* This was held by the Court of Appeal to be a counter offer, for it contained new terms, namely provisions regarding delivery, and payment of the deposit in trust rather than outright.

(d) in commercial dealings between parties each trading on their standard terms, the terms which apply to the contract will often be those belonging to the party who fired the last shot. This situation has become known as the *battle of the forms*.

In *Butler Machine Tool Co. v. Ex-Cell-O Corporation (England)Ltd.* 1979 the plaintiffs offered to sell a machine tool to the defendants in a quotation. The quotation contained a price variation clause, which by means of a specific formula enabled the plaintiffs to raise the quoted price between contract and delivery if their own costs rose. The defendants ordered the goods but on their own standard terms which did not include a price variation clause. The plaintiffs, on receipt of the order form, signed and returned an acknowledgement slip which it contained.

The plaintiff's costs rose considerably between contract and delivery and they sought to apply the price variation clause. The defendants disputed that it was part of the contract. The Court of Appeal treated the defendant's order as a counter offer, and the return of the acknowledgement slip as the plaintiff's acceptance consequently the contract between them did not contain the price variation clause.

Communicating the acceptance

The offeror is free to stipulate the method by which acceptance maybe made. If however no stipulation is given, anything that achieves communication will suffice; words, writing or conduct. Where it is clear that the offeror demands a particular method of acceptance then no other method will be effective. In most cases however, the offeror is likely to do little more than to give a general indication of the form of acceptance to be used. Where this occurs but the offeree adopts a different method of acceptance which is as quick or quicker than the specified method, the acceptance will be effective, since the offeror will have suffered no disadvantage.

> Consequently the Court of Appeal in *Yates Building Co. v. R J Pulleyn & Son (York)* 1976 held that an acceptance by means of ordinary post was effective, despite the offeror directing that registered post or recorded delivery should be used.

Since contractual communications require positive action silence can never amount to an effective acceptance of the offer. This holds true even if the parties have, in advance, agreed such an arrangement. For instance, if following an interview, an employer says to the interviewee that the job is his or hers if they hear nothing from the employer in the next five days, the interviewee agrees this arrangement, and the five days elapse without word from the employer, a binding contract will not have come into existence. What the law requires is some positive act.

> In *Felthouse v. Bindley*1862 an uncle wrote to his nephew offering to buy the nephew's horse for £30.15s. and stating *"If I hear no more about him I shall consider the horse mine at that price"*. The nephew gave instructions to the defendant, an auctioneer, not to sell the horse as he intended it for his uncle. The defendant inadvertently sold the horse, and the uncle sued him in the tort of conversion. The court held that action must fail. Ownership in the horse had not passed from the nephew to the uncle for there was not a contract between them. Actual communication of acceptance never occurred.

The existence of this common law principle did not in the past act as a disincentive to curb the practice of inertia selling, and it was not until the passing of the Unsolicited Goods and Services Act 1971 (as amended) that the practice was effectively controlled. Inertia selling involves sending goods by post to recipients who have not requested them. Usually an accompanying letter will indicate that if the goods are not wanted they should be returned, but that if the recipient retains possession of them beyond a stated period (usually between seven and twenty one days) this will be treated as acceptance, and payment should then be made. Prior to 1971 this type of 'hardsell' was widespread: it is an example of the way in which the less scrupulous take advantage of the public's absence of legal knowledge and awareness. The 1971 Act provides that the recipient of such unsolicited goods can treat them as an unconditional gift after six months have elapsed. The period is reduced to thirty days if the recipient serves notice on the sender asking that that goods be collected and the sender fails to repossess them.

There are two circumstances in which acceptance can operate without communication occurring at the same time, firstly in cases where the post is used to create the contract and secondly where the nature of the offer makes formal notification of acceptance unrealistic.

Transactions using the post

Transactions effected by means of correspondence in the form of letters, fax's, email, invoices, quotations and share applications are obviously very common forms of commercial activity. Business organisations need to keep records of their commercial activities, and the use of written correspondence is an effective way of achieving this.

Where the post is used there is of course the period whilst the letter is in transit when the person to whom it is addressed is unaware of its contents. Whereas an offer or revocation of an offer made by post is effective only when it is received by the party to whom it is sent, in the case of an *acceptance* by post the courts have laid down a rule that the letter is effective at the time and place of posting, provided it was correctly addressed and pre-paid. This remarkable rule, which is completely at odds with he normal requirements regarding communication, applies even if the letter of acceptance is lost or destroyed in the post.

The parties are free to vary these rules if they wish to do so, and it may be prudent for an offeror to stipulate that an acceptance in writing which is posted to him shall not be effective until it is actually received. It is common to find terms in standard form business contracts to this effect, and the courts seem willing to infer a variation of the post rules whenever possible.

In *Holwell Securities Ltd. v. Hughes* 1974 an option (offer)provided that it should be exercisable *"by notice in writing"*.The court held that this requirement effectively excluded the postal rule and that actual receipt of the letter of acceptance was necessary to conclude a contract.

The consequences of the post rules can thus be remarkable. In *Household Fire Insurance Co. v. Grant* 1879 the defendant applied for 100 shares in the plaintiff company. The company received his application form, and the company secretary in consequence completed and posted a letter of allotment to the defendant, and entered his name on the register of shareholders. The letter never arrived. Sometime later the company went into liquidation, and the liquidator claimed the payment outstanding on the shares from the defendant. By a majority the Court of Appeal held that the defendant was liable for this sum. The shares became his when the letter of allotment was posted, even though he never received it and was therefore unaware that he had become a shareholder.

Formal acceptance unrealistic

Sometimes the circumstances of the offer are such that the courts will regard conduct which occurs without the knowledge of the offeror as a sufficient method of acceptance. Although in a sense this is not the same as silence, from the offeror's point of view it amounts to the same thing, since if the offeree does not have to make contact with the offeror, the offeror remains in the dark. Where an offer has been made to the public at large the courts may take the view that the offeror could not possibly have expected to receive an acceptance from every person who has decided to take up the offer. This would be a commercial nonsense.

In *Carlill v. Carbolic Smokeball Co.* 1893 the defendant company advertised a medical preparation they manufactured, and claimed in the advertisement that they would pay £100 reward to anybody who contracted *"the increasing epidemic of influenza"* after purchasing and using the product as directed. The advertisement added that _£1000 was deposited with the Alliance Bank *"showing our sincerity in the matter"* The plaintiff purchased a smokeball, used it as directed, then caught influenza. She sued for her £100 reward. The court held that the advertisement constituted a firm offer intended to be legally binding since the bank deposit indicated an intention to meet claims, the offer could be made to the public at large, and acceptance of the offer in such circumstances could be implied by the conduct of those like the plaintiff, who performed the stated conditions. In consequence the company were held liable.

It is only when the parties have reached an agreement which satisfies the common law requirements relating to offer and acceptance that a contract can be said to have been made. One of the traditional views of contracting sees the contract in terms of a meeting of minds or *consensus ad idem*, however an examination of the law relating to agreement reveals that sometimes a binding agreement can occur where the minds of the parties are not entirely at one. This situation can be seen most clearly in the next chapter, which considers the effect of circumstances where consent to the agreement is not a true consent. Sometimes, however, even the presence of a consensus between the parties will not be enough for an agreement to be treated as legally valid if the fundamental principles of offer and acceptance have not been met.

In *Gibson v. Manchester City Council*1979 the parties were engaged in negotiations for the sale of a council house to the plaintiff, a council tenant. The plaintiff, having completed a request for information, received a letter from the council saying it might be prepared to sell the house to him for £2,180 freehold and that if he wished to make a formal application to purchase he should return the application form. This the tenant did. He left the purchase price blank because he was unsure whether the price given by the council had taken into account defects in the path of the property. A further letter from the council confirmed that defects in the path had been taken into account in fixing the price. In interpreting the above correspondence a majority of the Court of Appeal held that a contract of sale had indeed been entered into. Lord Denning M R put forward the view that in such circumstances there was no need to look for a strict offer and acceptance rather, *"you should look at the correspondence as a whole and at the conduct of the parties and see therefrom whether the parties have come to an agreement on everything that was material"*.This decision was later reversed following a further appeal to the House of Lords in 1979. The Law Lords adopted the more traditional approach by analysing each piece of correspondence, and held that no firm offer had been made or accepted by the council. The words that the council *"may be prepared to sell"* only amounted to an invitation to treat and thus no contract of sale had resulted.

It is clear in Gibson that whilst no contract actually resulted from their negotiations, both sides were, at least initially, willing to contract over the sale of the property. There are other authorities by way of contrast which suggest that under suitable conditions a contract may arise where there is clearly no consensus between the parties, but where logic or common-sense seems to demand that the court read one into the situation.

In *Clarke v. Dunraven*1897 the parties were yacht owners who entered their vessels for a yacht club regatta. Each owner who took part in the regatta undertook in a letter sent to the yacht club to obey its rules. These included an obligation to pay *"all damages"* caused by fouling another vessel. Whilst preparing for a race Clarke's yacht, the Satanita, fouled Dunraven's vessel, which sank. Under statute Clarke was liable to pay only limited damages of £8 per ton of the registered tonnage of the vessel, however Dunraven claimed the existence of a contract between the parties, on the terms of the club rules, and sought to recover full damages. The House of Lords accepted his argument that a contract existed, even though the parties had not dealt contractually with each other. Lord Herschell stated *"The effect of their entering for the race, and undertaking to be bound by the rules to the knowledge of each other … is to indicate a liability on the part of the one to the other … to create a contractual obligation to discharge that liability."*

The Court of Appeal reviewed the question of contractual formation in *G Percy Trentham Ltd. v. Archital Luxfer Ltd.* 1993. The plaintiffs were the main contractors engaged in a building contract, and they had negotiated with the defendants a sub-contract under which the defendants were to supply and fit architectural furniture such as(doors and windows). The sub-contract was satisfactorily performed, but a dispute arose when the plaintiffs, who were obliged to make a penalty payment under the main contract, sought a contribution from the defendants. The defendant's response was that no contract had ever been concluded between the parties. Telephone calls had been made and letters exchanged but no discernible offer and acceptance could be identified. As a result it was not possible to determine whose standard terms of trading applied to the agreement.

The Court of Appeal held that a contract had been made between the parties. In carrying out the work the defendants had agreed to an offer from the plaintiffs. Steyn LJ took the view that the test to determine whether a contract has been formed is an objective one, and in this case one should look to *"the reasonable expectations of sensible businessmen"* rather than the *"subjective and unexpressed mental reservations of the parties."* Although the usual mechanism of contractual formation is offer and acceptance in some circumstances this is not necessary. The instant case was an example, which concerned *"a contract alleged to have come into existence during and as a result of performance."* The contract was an executed one (i.e. had been carried out) making it very difficult to argue lack of intention to create legal relations, or invalidly based upon uncertainty of terms. *"If a contract comes into existence during and as a result of performance of the transaction,"* said his Lordship, *"it will frequently be possible to hold that the contract impliedly and retrospectively covers pre-contractual performance."*

Consideration

Under English law the simple contract has always been seen in terms of a bargain struck between the parties. The bargain is arrived at by negotiations and concluded when a definite and certain offer has been made which has been met with an unequivocal acceptance. Millions of transactions of this kind are made each day.

Making an agreement, as we have seen, involves giving undertakings or promises. The offeror makes a promise, and indicates what the offeree must do in return. For instance the seller of goods undertakes to transfer ownership in the goods, and specifies the price to be paid by the buyer for acquiring ownership. Similarly an employer indicates the type of work the employee will be required to perform, and promises certain wage rate or salary for doing it. The idea of a contract as an exchange of promises is fundamental to an understanding of the simple contract. We have already encountered a basic definition of a contract as being a legally enforceable agreement. There are others however. A definition provided by Sir Frederick Pollock, a leading legal writer, described the contract as *"a promise or a set of promises which the law will enforce"*. Pollock was seeing the *agreement* of original first definition as something always made up of promises.

Bilateral and unilateral contracts

When promises have been exchanged the contract is said to be *bilateral*. This is the most common type of arrangement. For instance, if a partnership offers a person a place in the business if they are prepared to contribute £5,000 to the capital of the business, and the prospective partner undertakes to do so the contract is a bilateral one. If however the offeror, rather than requiring a promise in return requires of the offeree some other act, then the contract is said to be *unilateral*. An example of a unilateral contract occurs where a company promises to make payment or provide goods to any of its customers who collect a certain number of tokens from buying the company's products. Petrol companies frequently use this type of device to compete with their rivals, so that by the time a customer has purchased a specific quantity of petrol they become entitled to items such as glasses or cutlery. The customer has made no promise to the garage, but is certainly entitled to the advertised items if he satisfies the requirements stipulated by the petrol company to qualify for the *gifts*.

Executory and executed consideration

Consideration, and hence the contract itself, is said to be *executory* where the promises that have been made are to be performed in the future. An example is an agreement in which the seller promises to deliver goods next week, and the buyer agrees to pay for them on delivery. Consideration is said to be executed where in return for a promise the offeree provides the required consideration which also acts as acceptance of the offer. This would occur, for instance, in the case of a member of the public who provides the Post Office with information that leads to the conviction of those responsible for an armed robbery at a sub-post office, where the Post Office has offered a reward for such information.

An agreement in which the consideration exchanged is entirely executory is fully enforceable, although legal action for breach of contract can only be commenced after the date for performance has passed, or if before this time one of the parties has made clear that they will not perform their obligations when they fall due. This referred to as *anticipatory breach* of contract. Where a contract is entirely executory, legal action on it may prove difficult to sustain if there is no written evidence and the other party disputes the existence of the alleged agreement.

There are a number of important principles which clarify the nature of consideration and which need to be examined.

Consideration is required to support all simple contracts

In the absence of valid consideration passing between the parties the general rule is the agreement they have made will be of no legal effect. If however their agreement is expressed in the form of a deed, the absence of a valuable promise made by the promisee to the promisor does not invalidate the contract. If a person executes a deed under which he promises to make a payment or transfer property to someone else a future date, the promise will bind him, and be enforceable by the promisee, despite the absence of any consideration provided by that person.

Consideration need not be adequate but must have some value

The word *adequate* in this context means equal to the promise given. The principle of adequacy of consideration has developed to cope with contractual disputes in which one of the parties is arguing that the contract is bad because the value of the consideration provided by the other party is not the economic equivalent of the value of the promise given in return.

The courts are not prepared to defeat an agreement merely on the grounds that one of the parties has, in effect, made a bad bargain. Bad bargains are a fact of commercial life. A deal that is struck where one of the parties has entered it in haste, or without proper enquiry, or has been swayed by convincing salesmanship, may be bitterly regretted subsequently, but it is certainly not possible in such circumstances to escape liability on the grounds that *"I gave more than I got"*.Consequently there is no relief for the business or the individual who is at the receiving end of a hard bargain.

> The case of *Haigh v. Brooks* 1839 provides a useful illustration of the idea of the bargain taken to its most extreme position. The plaintiffs were owed large sums of money by a third party, and the defendant agreed to guarantee these debts. He later asked the plaintiffs if they would cancel the guarantee. This they agreed to, provided that in return the defendant would pay off certain debts they owed. He agreed, and the guarantee was returned to him. On examination the defendant discovered that because the written guarantee failed to meet certain statutory requirements it was unenforceable, and indeed always had been. He refused to pay the debts on the grounds that all he had received in return was a worthless piece of paper. The court held that the agreement was binding. Even though the guarantee was legally invalid the defendant had received what he bargained for – his release from the supposed liability. Lord Chief Justice Denman remarked, *"The plaintiffs were induced by the defendant's promise to part with something they might have kept, and the defendant obtained what he desired by means of that promise"*.

> Similarly in *Mountford v. Scott* 1975 the defendant made an agreement with the plaintiff, granting the plaintiff an option to purchase the defendant's house for £10,000 within six months. The plaintiff paid £1 for the option, and later sought to exercise it. The value of the defendant's property had risen by this time and he refused to sell. The court was prepared to grant an order for specific performance, compelling the defendant to transfer the property for the agreed price. It was for the defendant to fix the value of the option. Some consideration was provided and this was enough. The trial judge commented: *"It is only necessary, as I see it, that the option should have been validly created"*.

However apparently insignificant the consideration may be, as long as it has some discernible value it will be valid.

> In *Chappell and Co. Ltd. v. Nestlé. Ltd* 1960 the defendants, as part of a sales promotion, offered a record at a reduced price if their chocolate bar wrappers accompanied the

payment. The plaintiffs held the copyright in the record, and argued that the royalties they were entitled to should be assessed on the price of the record plus the value of the wrappers, which the defendants in fact simply threw away when they had been received. The House of Lords agreed with the plaintiffs, seeing the subsequent disposal of the wrappers as irrelevant, since each wrapper in reality represented the profit on the sale of a bar of chocolate, and was therefore part of the consideration.

Adequacy is not determined solely by economic criteria. It is enough that the promise is a promise to refrain from doing something which the promisor is legally entitled to do. It may be a promise not to take legal proceedings, or not to exercise a legal right such as aright of way. Even where the promise is related to a positive act the act may have little to do with anything capable of economic valuation, yet still be good consideration in the eyes of the law. A parent may undertake to pay a sum of money to a son or daughter in the event of them marrying, or graduating, and the marriage or graduation will be valid consideration in these circumstances.

Moreover it is not necessary that the promisor should obtain direct personal benefit from the consideration provided by the promisee. Thus a parent's promise to a son or daughter to pay them £10,000 to help them set up in business is enforceable if the business is established, whether or not the parent has a financial stake in it.

> The case of *Shadwell v. Shadwell* 1860 illustrates how the courts will accept as valuable consideration promises which cannot be valued purely economically. Here an uncle promised to pay his nephew a yearly sum in consideration of the nephew getting married. The nephew married, but the annuity fell into arrears. On his uncle's death the nephew brought action against the executors of the estate. They were held bound since, *inter alia*, the nephew's marriage was something of interest to the uncle.

The question of whether a forbearance will operate as adequate consideration may sometimes concern those engaged in business and commercial activity. Suppose the owner of the only retail travel agency in a small town is approached by a larger company, with a number of agencies in the area. The owner is told that in consideration of the payment of £30,000 by him to the company, it will not set up a competing business in the town. Would this be a valid agreement? In *Thorne v. Motor Trade Association* 1937 Lord Atkin, commented, *"it appears to me that if a man may lawfully, in the furtherance of business interests, do acts which will seriously injure another in his business he may also lawfully, if he is still acting in the furtherance of his business interests, invite that other to pay him a sum of money as an alternative to doing the injurious acts"*.

Consideration must be sufficient

Consideration is treated as insufficient, and therefore incapable of supporting a contract, when it involves the promisor undertaking to do something he is already obliged to do legally. The rationale is that since the promisor is bound to carry out the promise anyway, there can be no true bargain in using performance of this promise to support another contract. Consideration is insufficient therefore in the following circumstances:

- Where the promisor has an existing contractual obligation to carry out the promise offered as consideration.

In *Stilk v. Myrick* 1809 a promise by a ships captain to pay sailors an additional sum for working the ship on the return voyage as unenforceable, even though they had to work harder due to the desertion of two crew members. The court found that their existing contracts bound them to work the ship home in such circumstances, thus they had provided no new consideration to support the promise of extra wages.

In dramatically changed circumstances it may be possible to show a fresh contract has been negotiated.

In *Hartley v. Ponsonby* 1857, a ships crew was so depleted that the ship was dangerous to work. In these circumstances the promise of the captain to pay extra wages was held to be enforceable.

In *Williams v. Roffey Bros. & Nicholls (Contractors) Ltd.* 1990 the defendants had a contract with a housing association for the refurbishment of a number of flats. They subcontracted the joinery work to the plaintiff. After performing most of his obligations under the contract the plaintiff found himself in financial difficulties, for the agreed price of £20,000 was too low. The defendants were anxious for their contract with the housing association to be completed by the agreed date, since under a penalty clause they would suffer financially for late completion. The defendants met the plaintiff and agreed to pay him an additional £10,300 for completion of the joinery work. He then carried out most of the remaining work, but refused to finish it when the defendants indicated that they would not pay him the additional agreed sum. They argued that he was under a contractual obligation to carry out the work arising from the original contract. He had given no new consideration for the promise of extra payment.

The Court of Appeal held that the new agreement was binding on the defendants. By promising the extra money they had received a benefit, namely the avoidance of a penalty payment, or alternatively the need to employ another sub-contractor. This benefit was consideration to support the new agreement even though the plaintiff was not required to any more work than he had originally undertaken. The court approved the decision in *Stilk v. Myrick* , however on its facts the Williams case seems to suggest that the courts are now prepared to take a more liberal approach in their willingness to recognise a fresh contract and what can be properly regarded as good consideration.

Of further relevance to the question of how to assess sufficiency is the old common law principle that payment of a lesser amount to a creditor than the full debt cannot discharge the debtor from liability for the full amount even though the creditor agrees it, and accepts the lesser amount. This is known as the rule in *Pinnel's Case* 1602, a rule subsequently confirmed by the House of Lords in *Foakes v. Beer* 1884. It is based upon the view that there can be no real bargain in a person agreeing to accept a lesser sum than they are legally entitled to. But if the varied agreement contains an additional element, such a promise to pay the reduced sum earlier than the date on which the full debt is due, then provided the creditor agrees it, this will be binding. It may be of considerable commercial advantage to receive a smaller amount immediately than have to wait for the full sum, where, for example, the creditor is experiencing cash flow problems.

In addition to early payment of a reduced amount if agreed by the creditor, there are certain other exceptions to the rule in Pinnel's case. They include:

(i)   Substituted performance. This arises where the creditor accepts some other form of consideration instead of money, such as the delivery of goods. Alternatively payment of a lesser sum together with an additional element, such as a promise to repair the creditor's car, would suffice.

(ii)   Payment of a lesser sum where the debtor is disputing the value of the work that has been performed, and the creditor accepts the reduced amount. The reason why the creditor is bound by such an arrangement is that if the dispute were to be resolved by court action, the court might determine the value of the work performed as worth even less than the debtor has offered to pay, hence accepting the reduced sum may be seen as a new bargain.

(iii)   When the *equitable doctrine of promissory estoppel* applies.

- Where the promisor has a public obligation to carry out the act.

Performance of a public duty as a means of furnishing considerations is insufficient to support the contract.

This is demonstrated in the case of *Collins v. Godefroy* 1831. The plaintiff had received a *subpoena* (a court order) to give evidence in court. He then agreed with the defendant to give the evidence in return for his expenses. The court held that there was no contract for the payment of expenses, as the promise of payment was not support by sufficient consideration. The plaintiff was under an existing duty to give evidence.

However if the promisor performs some act beyond the public duty, this will operate as valid consideration.

In *Harris v. Sheffield United F C* 1987 the football club challenged its contractual liability to pay for the policing of its football ground during home matches. It was held that the contract between itself and the police authority was valid. The number of officers provided was in excess of those who would have been provided had the police simply been fulfilling their public obligation to keep the peace and prevent disorder.

Consideration must be Legal

If it is illegal the whole contract will be invalidated.

There are two classes of illegal contract, those existing under the common law and those made illegal by Parliament. Illegality at common law arises in cases where the contract is regarded as being contrary to public policy, for example contracts involving sexual immorality, contracts involving the commission of crime and contracts associated with corruption in public life. In these cases it is the moral wrongdoing associated with them that has lead the judiciary to regard the nature of the promises being exchanged between the parties as unlawful and thus unenforceable. Amongst those contracts rendered illegal by Parliament are agreements made between the suppliers of goods to refuse to sell to retailers who are not prepared to comply with minimum resale price arrangements (s.1 Resale Prices Act 1976). Such arrangements, by means of which retailers are effectively blacklisted, are regarded by Parliaments as morally reprehensible, and thus illegal. It is however the case that both Parliament and the judiciary also recognise further classes of contracts which whilst not unlawful, are nonetheless void and unenforceable because their effects are regarded as undesirable for social or economic reasons. Contracts falling within this category are not therefore tainted by being regarded as morally reprehensible. They include contracts in restraint of trade. The question of illegality and public policy is considered further in the next chapter. It should be noted that attempting to enter into an illegal contract may itself give rise to criminal liability.

Consideration must not be past

A party to contract cannot use a past act as a basis for consideration. Therefore, if one party performs an act for another, and only receives a promise of payment after the act is complete, the past act would be past consideration. What is required is that the promise of one of the parties to the alleged contract is given in response to the promise of the other. If an act is carried out with no promise of reward having been made, it will be treated as purely gratuitous.

> In *Roscorla v. Thomas* 1842 the seller of a horse, after the buyer had purchased it, promised the buyer that it was sound and free from vice. It was not, and the buyer sued the seller on the promise. The action failed. The promise was supported by no new consideration. There are three exceptions to the rule:

(a)   where the work has been performed in circumstances which carry an implication of a promise to pay.

> In *Re Casey's Patents, Stewart v. Casey* 1892 the joint owners of a patent agreed with Casey that he should manage and publicise their invention. Two years later they promised him a third share in the patent, as *"consideration of your services as manager"*. The court rejected the view that this promise was supported by past consideration from Casey. The request to him to render his services carried an implied promise to pay for them. The promise of a third share was simply the fixing of the price.

> By way of contrast in *Re Magrath* 1934 Durham County Council agreed with its treasurer in 1931 to pay him an additional £700, representing extra work he had carried out between 1920 and 1925, but which had not been recognised in his salary. The payment was successfully challenged as being unlawful, for it was not supported by consideration, thus making the payment a gratuity to the treasurer. The payment of gratuities to council officers is illegal. Council members who had voted for the payment were surcharged. Lord Maugham stated: *"It is, I think, clear that the local authority cannot out of public money's give gratuities to their officers and servants over and above their fixed salaries and wages... Different considerations might well apply to a case where the officer or servant was asked to perform extra services in respect of a specified job or undertaking, on the understanding that as soon as the work was complete the authority would determine the amount of his special remuneration";*

(b)   where a debt, which has become unrecoverable by operation of the limitation period (i.e. statute barred) is revived by a subsequent acknowledgement of it by the debtor, which is made in writing. In such circumstances the Limitation Act 1980 states that no consideration of any kind need be sought to enforce the debt;

Only the parties to the agreement who have provided each other with consideration can sue on the contract. A person who has provided no consideration does not have the right to sue on the contract, for that person is not a party to it. This principle, known as *privity of contract*, is examined later.

Intention to Create Legal Relations

A valid agreement supported by consideration may still fail as a contract

unless it is able to satisfy a further legal test, namely that the parties intended their agreement to have legal consequences. In many agreements it is obvious from the context that it was never in the contemplation of the parties to bind themselves legally. How then can a court discriminate between those arrangements where the parties did intend their agreement to be legally enforceable, and those where this was not the intention? To answer this question the court will look at all the available evidence, and in particular whether the parties have expressly indicated their intention. For instance committing an agreement into written form may suggest a more formal type of relationship.

Common law presumptions regarding intention

At common law certain presumptions regarding intention are applied by the courts. If the subject matter of the agreement is of a social or domestic kind, where the context of the agreement or the relationship between the parties is such as to suggest an absence of full legal commitment, then the courts will presume there was no intention to create a contract. This does not mean, for example, that it is impossible for members of the same family to contract each with the other, and certainly many families are participants in joint business ventures such as partnerships which are founded on a contractual relationship. Rather it is simply a requirement of the common law that there is clear evidence of such an intention. This must be sufficient to rebut the presumption that the parties did not intend to contract.

> Thus in *Snelling v. John G. Snelling Ltd.* 1972 the court had to identify the nature of an agreement between the plaintiff and his two brothers, who together were all directors of the defendant company. Each of them had provided loans to the company, and when they took a further loan from a finance company the brothers agreed not to reduce their own loan until the amount borrowed from the finance company had been repaid. By a separate agreement made between the three of them they undertook that if any of them resigned voluntarily as a director before repayment to the finance company had been made, repayment of the loan to the defendant company would be forfeited. The plaintiff voluntarily resigned and sued the company for the return of his money. The court held that the agreement between the brothers was intended to create legal rights, not least because it had emerged out of strong disagreements between the brothers.

Commercial transactions - honour clauses and letters of comfort

In commercial transactions the courts will presume an intention that they are intended to be legally binding. Indeed whenever there is a business dimension to the agreement the only way to prevent the judicial presumption from operating is to indicate clearly that the agreement is *not* intended to be a contract. The inclusion of the phrase *"binding in honour"* on a football coupon was held by the court in *Jones v. Vernons Pools Ltd.* 1938 to amount to clear evidence that there was no intention to create a contract.

In *Rose and Frank Co. v. Crompton Bros* 1923 a written agreement entered into by two commercial organisations included the following clause *"This arrangement is not entered into, nor is this memorandum written, as a formal or legal agreement... but... is only a definite expression and record of the purpose and intention of the ... parties concerned, to which they each honourably pledge themselves"*. This clause, the court held, was sufficient evidence to overturn the presumption that the commercial agreement was intended to be legally binding.

Since *honour clauses* have the effect of making an otherwise legally enforceable agreement unenforceable by means of court action, they need to be treated with some care. There may appear to be sound reasons for their use in the right circumstances, but the inability to bring a claim for breach of the terms of the agreement before the courts does have the effect of leaving the parties commercially vulnerable. Suppose such a term is included in an agreement between the sole supplier of a particular type of goods and a customer who makes his profits form reselling these goods. The customer has no legal protection against the supplier unilaterally determining the agreement, leaving the customer with orders that cannot be met and the task of finding a new type of business. Of course the supplier may be left with a large quantity of goods he will have to find new outlets for. This may be difficult or even impossible at short notice, however he will be unable to recover his losses by legal action.

A particular commercial practice which can sometimes give rise to questions of contractual intention is the use of the so called *letter of comfort*. These are letters which are designed to provide commercial reassurance, and their use is illustrated in the following case.

In *Kleinwort Benson Ltd. v. Malaysia Mining Corporation Bhd* 1989 the plaintiff bank agreed to make loan facilities of up to £10M available to a subsidiary company owned by the defendants. The defendants were not prepared to give the bank a formal guarantee to cover the loan facility to the subsidiary, MMC Metals Ltd., however they wrote to the bank stating, *"It is our policy to ensure that the business (of MMC Metals) is at all times in a position to meet its liabilities to you...,"* and, *"We confirm that we will not reduce our current financial interest in MMC Metals Ltd."*.

Subsequently MMC Metals, a tin dealer, went into liquidation following the collapse of the world tin market. The bank looked to the defendants to make good the loss suffered by it on the loans it had made to MMC. The Court of Appeal held that on the facts the defendants letter did not give rise to a binding contract, for on a proper construction of it, it showed no intention to create a legal relationship. In particular the use of the expression "policy" indicated that the defendants were making it clear they were not to be legally bound. Companies are free to change their policies, and often do. The parties were trading equals, and the bank ought to have been aware of the implications of being offered a letter of comfort rather than a letter of guarantee.

Clauses ousting the courts jurisdiction and arbitration clauses

Whilst a term contained in an agreement which attempts entirely to exclude the court's jurisdiction will be void on the grounds that its effect would be to prevent a court from even determining the preliminary issue of the nature of the agreement itself, it is quite legitimate to insert an arbitration clause into the contract. Arbitration clauses are a common feature of business agreements providing a dispute solving mechanism which is generally cheaper, quicker and more private than court proceedings. The rights of consumers under agreements they have made which contain arbitration clauses are now protected under the Consumer Arbitration Agreements Act 1988. The Act is designed to deal with contracts where an arbitration clause is being used by a business as a mechanism for preventing a dispute from being heard before the courts, so that the consumer is bound to follow arbitration arrangements which may well be weighted against him. The Act provides that where a consumer has entered into a contract which provides for future differences between the parties to be referred to arbitration, the arbitration arrangements cannot be enforced against him unless, under s.1:

(a)   he has consented in writing after the difference has occurred to the use of the arbitration; or

(b)   he has submitted to the arbitration; or

(c)   the court has made an order under s.4. This enables the court to determine that the consumer will not suffer a detriment to his interests by having the difference determined by the arbitration arrangements rather than by court proceedings.

The court must consider all relevant matters, including the availability of legal aid.

For the purposes of the Act, a consumer is someone who enters into the contract without either making the contract in the course of a business or holding himself out as doing so. The other party must have made the contract in the course of a business, and if the contract is a sale of goods transaction the goods must be of a type ordinarily supplied for private use or consumption.

Collective agreements

Contractual intention is also of significance in relation to collective agreements, A *collective agreement* is one between trade unions and employers' organisations by which an agreement or arrangement is made about matters such as terms and conditions of employment. It is estimated that as many as 14 million employees within the United Kingdom are employed under contracts which are regulated in part by collective agreements. The Trade Union and Labour Relations (Consolidation) Act 1992 provides that a collective agreement is presumed not to have been intended by the parties to be a legally enforceable contract unless the agreement is in writing and contains a statement that the parties intend it to be legally enforceable. Often the statutory statement of the particulars of the employment which the employer is legally obliged to give the employee will make express reference to a collective agreement in operation within the particular employment sector involved, and this will have the effect of incorporating it into the individual contract of employment. Once this has occurred changes in the contract of employment created by re-negotiation of the collective agreement will automatically vary the individual employee's contractual relationship with the employer.(see Chapters 14 and 15)

Capacity to contract

Capacity is an expression that describes a person's ability to do something. In legal terms it covers the ability to make contracts, commit torts and commit crimes.

The general rule under English law is that anyone can bind themselves by a contract, as long as it is not illegal, or void for public policy. There are however exceptions to the rule. The most significant are contracts made by corporations and contracts made by minors.

Corporations

The nature of corporate bodies is dealt with in Chapter 4. Corporations are regarded as legal persons in their own right, thus enabling then to make contracts, commit torts (and some crimes), and hold land. Since they enjoy legal rights and are subject to legal obligations they can sue, and be sued, in respect of these rights and obligations. Whilst corporations are created in different ways, for example by registration in the case of limited companies and by specific statute in the case of state corporations, they share certain common characteristics, and as far as their capacity is concerned they are all subject to the principle of *ultra vires,* although in the case of registered companies the Companies Act 1989 has severely limited the scope of the ultra vires doctrine.

The Doctrine of ultra vires

A corporation must be formed with stated objectives. These are located in the documents which create the organisation: its charter, the statute which establishes it or its memorandum and articles of association. If the corporation acts outside these objectives it is said to be acting *ultra vires* - beyond its powers - and at common law it cannot be bound. It lacks the capacity to do anything that its stated objectives do not authorise. Equally all activities falling within these objectives can be validly achieved, for they are *intra vires* - within the powers. Other than in the case of a registered company, no action can be brought to enforce a contract which is ultra vires a corporation: if there is any liability it will rest with those who have authorised or carried out the ultra vires activity. The issue of ultra vires will emerge either where a corporation is using it as a defence in circumstances where it is refusing to perform its contractual obligations, or where a challenge is being brought against the corporation by someone with a legal interest in doing so, in an attempt at preventing the corporation from carrying out an alleged ultra vires act.

> In *Attorney General v. Fulham Corporation* 1921 the corporation had power by statute to operate wash-houses where its inhabitants could wash their own clothes. The corporation established a municipal laundry, acting under these statutory powers, where the washing work could be carried out by employed staff. A ratepayer challenged the legality of this action, and through the Attorney General proceedings were brought against the corporation. The court held that the statutory powers did not extend to the running of a laundry, and therefore the activity was ultra vires. An injunction was granted restraining the corporation from running it.

Limitations upon the ultra vires doctrine

Although the ultra vires doctrine is still of great importance in some spheres, notably the activities of central and local government, its impact on registered companies is no longer as significant as it used to be. This is because:

(i)   the courts are prepared to recognise objects clauses which are broadly drafted (see Bell Houses), and Statute now permits companies to register objects clauses permitting general commercial activities;

(ii)   the courts interpret objects clauses less strictly than they did in the past;

In *Re: New Finance and Mortgage Co.* 1975 the company's objects allowed it to carry on business as *"financiers, capitalists, concessionaires, bankers, commercial agents, mortgage brokers, financial agents and advisers, exporters and importers of goods and merchandise of all kinds and merchants generally"*. The company ran a filling station business, which owed Total £24,000 for the petrol. The business went in to liquidation. The liquidator claimed the business was an ultra vires activity, and refused to meet the payment. The court held the words *"and merchants generally"* to cover the running of a petrol filling station business, and thus that Total's claim was good;

(iii)   the courts imply powers necessary for a company to achieve its stated objects.

In *Deuchar v. Gas Light and Coke Co.* 1925 the defendant company's main object was making and selling gas and the conversion of residual products into a marketable state. One residual product was napthalene which the company converted into beta-napthol which it sold commercially. The conversion required caustic soda, which the company originally bought from another company, however it realised that it would be cost effective to manufacture the soda itself. This it started to do. Deuchar was the secretary of the company which had previously supplied the soda. It was aggrieved at the loss of its business with the defendant company, but had no means available to challenge the ending of the business relationship with the defendant company. Instead Deuchar bought shares in the company, and then sought an injunction, in his capacity as a member, to prevent the manufacture of the caustic soda which he claimed was ultra vires. The House of Lords held the activity to be intra vires on the grounds that the company had implied power manufacture the products which were reasonably incidental to its express powers of converting residual products into a marketable state;

(iv)   the Companies Act 1989 has come close to completely removing the availability of an ultra vires defence for a company in the face of a claim brought by a creditor. The Act has introduced a new s.35 into the Companies Act 1985. This topic is thoroughly considered in Chapter 4. Since the common law position on ultra vires (points (i) to (iii) above) is now so liberal, very few commercial transactions made by companies are likely to be ultra vires, and thus the impact of 1989 Act is far less significant than it might seem.

Ultra vires and local authorities

We have already seen that the same basic principles apply to local authorities as to registered companies. Local authorities are statutory bodies under the Local Government Act 1972 and the objects which such corporations may legitimately pursue must be ascertained from the Act itself. Over the years however, the ultra vires doctrine has not been applied rigidly to local authorities and the courts have consistently held that local authorities may not only do things for which there is express or implied authority, but also whatever is reasonably incidental to the doing of those things.

> Thus in *Attorney General v. Smethwick Corporation* 1932 a resolution was passed by the corporation for the establishment of a printing and stationery works which would meet all the printing requirements of the authority. An action was brought by the Attorney General on behalf of a ratepayer on the grounds that the proposal was ultra vires. The court held that the formation of this department was reasonably incidental or consequential upon the carrying out of the corporation's statutory duties and was not therefore ultra vires.

This common law rule was reflected in the general power to contract conferred on local authorities by virtue of s.111 Local Government Act 1972. This section provides that authorities are empowered to do anything (whether or not involving the expenditure, borrowing or lending of money or the acquisition or disposal of any property or rights) which is calculated to facilitate, or is conducive or incidental to, the discharge of any of their functions. Provided therefore that the activity carried on is related to the particular functions of the council in question it seems that it can be justified. This general power to contract conferred on local authorities is of course supplemented by a multiplicity of specific powers from various statutes. The Local Authority (Goods and Services) Act 1970 for instance, enables an authority to contract with other public bodies for the supply of goods and services.

> In *Hazell v. Hammersmith and Fulham LBC* 1991 the local authority had during the period 1987 to 1989 engaged in speculative financial activities using a capital market fund set up by the Director of Finance for the authority. The activities involved an attempt at making gains through financial transactions on the London capital and money markets through taking advantage of favourable interest rate movements sums of over £100M were involved. If these transactions involved proper management of the Council's funds then under s.111 they would be lawful, but if they constituted the carrying on of a business they would be ultra vires and unlawful. The Court of Appeal held that interest rate risk management could be regarded as coming within the Council's implied powers, although it would be unlawful to engage in purely speculative trading transactions. The House of Lords however reversed this decision. It held that a local authority has no specific statutory power to enter into interest rate swap transactions of the kind made by Hammersmith, and said that these transactions were not saved by s.111 as they were not incidental or conducive to, nor did they facilitate the discharge of the council's borrowing functions. In addition although the council in question was incorporated by royal charter granting it the powers of a natural person this did not enable it to exercise any greater powers than any other local authority since it was still essentially a statutory corporation established under the London Government Act 1963.

Minors

The law has always sought to protect minors from the consequences of making transactions detrimental to themselves. The aim has been to provide them with some protection from their lack of commercial experience, whilst at the same time recognising circumstances where it is appropriate that they should be fully accountable for the agreements they make. The result is a mixture of common law and statutory rules which seek to achieve a balance between these conflicting objectives. The expression *minor* refers to anyone under the age of eighteen, this being the age of majority under the Family Law Reform Act 1969. There are three categories of contracts which may be entered into by a minor. They are:

(a)   Valid contracts, which include beneficial contracts of employment, and contracts for necessaries. A beneficial contract of employment is one which is substantially for the minor's benefit. Benefit is invariably taken to mean that the contract must include some element of training or education, although this can usually be easily established. The court will set aside a contract of employment which viewed overall is not beneficial.

In *De Francesco v. Barnum* 1890 a minor's contract of apprenticeship provided that she was to be totally at the disposal of her principal, who had no obligation to pay her. The court held the contract to be invalid, since its terms were harsh and onerous.

In *Roberts v. Gray* 1913 the defendant, a minor, with a view to becoming a professional billiards player, had entered an agreement with the plaintiff, himself a leading professional, to accompany the plaintiff on a world tour. The plaintiff spent time and money organising the tour, but following a dispute the defendant refused to go. The plaintiff sought damages of £6000 for breach of contract. The Court of Appeal held that the contract was for the defendant's benefit, being in the nature of a course of instruction in the game of billiards. The plaintiff was awarded £1500 damages.

Necessaries are defined in s.3 Sale of Goods Act 1979 as *"goods suitable to the condition in life of the minor ... and to his actual requirements at the time of sale and delivery."* This is a subjective test of the minors needs, found by reference to his economic and social status.

(b)   Voidable contracts, which bind the minor until he repudiates them. Repudiation is the expression used to describe the act of rejecting a contract. Repudiation must occur before reaching majority or within a reasonable time thereafter. If a repudiation has not taken place after this time the contract becomes valid. Contracts falling within this category are those of a long term nature, such as non-beneficial contracts of employment, contracts for a lease, contracts to take shares in a company, and partnership agreements.

(c)   Contracts of what have been described as a *negatively voidable* kind, that is contracts which the minor can enforce to a certain extent, but which cannot be enforced against him. As a general principle contracts that do not come within the previous two categories fall within this one. In particular it includes contracts for non-necessary goods, and contracts in which the minor has set up in business as a trader.

The lowering of the age of majority in 1969, together with the reluctance of many organisations such as travel companies to deal with minors has meant that the law as it affects negatively voidable contracts is probably no longer of much significance.

Assignment Are we Agreed?

You work as a legal assistant in the legal department of Anglo-Swedish Metal Industries plc. On returning from your summer holiday you find two files in your in-tray, accompanied by a memorandum from your superior, Jane West, one of the company's lawyers, which states, "Please respond to the letters contained in the attached files. See me if you have any difficulties."

The first file contains the following letter from a solicitor:

> I represent Miss Sally Goldwell. I understand from my client that she was interviewed for a clerical post with your company. Following the interview she was asked if she would be willing to accept the post, and she indicated that she would. A week later, on 10th September 199X, she received a formal offer of the post from your company's Personnel Officer. She was asked to reply in writing within five days. She was ill at the time and arranged for a friend to notify you of her acceptance by phone. Her friend telephoned sometime after 7 pm on 13th September 199X. This was a Friday, and her friend had to leave a message on the Personnel Department's answerphone. I gather that the Personnel Department closes from 4.30pm on Friday, until 8.30 the following Monday, and that the message only reached the Personnel Officer at midday on Monday 16th September. He had that morning telephoned another interviewee to offer her the job, which she accepted. My client subsequently heard from you that the post was no longer available for her.
>
> I am of the opinion that a contract exists between my client and yourselves, in respect of which you are in breach. I look forward to your prompt response.
>
> Yours faithfully,
>
> Roger Major

The second file contained the following letter from one of the company's suppliers, Humberside Steels Ltd.:

> We refer to our offer to supply you with 40 tonnes reinforced steel bars, to which you responded with an order (68747/5/NX) for the goods to be delivered to you on 1st May. We replied immediately informing you that due to circumstances beyond our control delivery would be on the 24th May. We heard nothing from

you, and delivered the goods on 24th May, only to find that you rejected them on the basis that they had not been ordered. We are at a loss to understand your action, particularly as we have often varied the delivery date with you in this way in the past, without complaint by you.

We should be grateful therefore to receive your remittance in due course.

Yours faithfully

James Leach pp

Humberside Steels Ltd.

Tasks

1. In the form of a memorandum to your superior, Jane West, indicate any weaknesses you have been able to identify regarding the company's legal position in respect of the two claims.

2. Draft replies to each of the letters, in which you state the legal basis upon which the company challenges the contractual claims they make.

Assignment   The Brothers

Tim and Anthony O'Brien are brothers who set up together in business as builders some years ago. The business was based in Dagenham where they both lived. In 1985 Tim married and moved some miles away to Colchester. As as a result the business was dissolved, each brother re-establishing a business in his own right. Tim was more successful than Anthony, who was not such a good businessman. Anthony acquired a reputation as a bad credit risk, and found it increasingly difficult to find suppliers who were prepared to deliver building materials without payment in advance. He told Tim about the problem.

Tim's main supplier was a company called Anglian Associated Materials Ltd. Tim knew the managing director well, since they both belonged to the local golf club and were District Councillors together. Tim mentioned his brother's problem to Charlie, the managing director, and Charlie agreed to supply Anthony. "Obviously I'll see you all right Charlie, if anything goes wrong", responded Tim.

Earlier this year Anthony placed an order with Charlie's company for £4,000 worth of timber, and £8,000 of scaffolding. Due to acute cashflow problems he subsequently found himself unable to pay the full debt when it was demanded, and contacted Charlie direct to discuss the matter. Charlie reluctantly agreed to accept £2,000 for the timber, but insisted the scaffolding had to be paid for in full. Charlie then approached Tim, reminding him of his earlier promise, and requesting him to meet the outstanding £2,000 debt. Tim subsequently replied by letter as follows:

> Dear Charlie,
>
> I have been advised that I have no legal liability regarding payment of the outstanding amount of my brothers indebtedness to your company. However, in recognition of our friendship and all the help you have given me in the past I am prepared to make a payment of £1000 towards the bill.
>
> Yours sincerely,
>
> *Tim O'Brien*
>
> Tim O'Brien

Later that week Tim wrote again:

> Dear Charlie,
>
> I understand that my brother's business is in credit again. In the circumstances I feel I must withdraw my offer to you, and suggest that you pursue him for the outstanding amount.
>
> Yours sincerely,
>
> *Tim O'Brien*
>
> Tim O'Brien

Task

As an administrative assistant to the Company Secretary of Anglian Associated Materials Ltd. you often deal with legal problems involving facing the company, and Charlie, the managing director, has asked you to consider whether the company has a legitimate claim for payment against either of the brothers.

Draft an informal report for the managing director in which you indicate the company's legal position in the matter.

Legal Terms found in Chapter 9

Bilateral mistaken	• mistaken belief of both the parties to the contract
Duress	• use of threats to force someone into making a contract
Economic duress	• using improper economic pressure to induce a contract
Misrepresentation	• remedy available to a person induced into making a contract by a false statement
Mistake	• legal principle under which a contract is treated as at an end though the mistaken belief of either or both the parties
Public policy	• concept guiding judicial decision making based on consideration of the public interest
Representation	• statement which induces the making of a contract
Solus agreement	• contracted arrangement binding one party exclusively to another under a supply agreement
Undue influence	• unlawful pressure put on someone which prevents them from acting independently when they make a contract
Unilateral mistake	• mistaken belief of one of the parties to the contract

Chapter 9

The Contract: Issues of Validity

Introduction

In the last chapter the fundamental issues considered were how and when a contract is made. It might be supposed that no further contractual issues are likely thereafter to emerge. The parties to the agreement, having met the basic legal requirements and formed their contract, will simply carry out their respective responsibilities to their mutual satisfaction and performance will have been completed. This is indeed what usually happens. The contract is made and performed. Each side is satisfied. The transaction is completed.

But contracts do not always run so smoothly. They can go wrong, sometimes for technical reasons and sometimes for practical reasons. Among the more common claims that are asserted are:

- that the contract is not binding because there was not true consent given to it. Such a possibility was mentioned in the discussion of freedom of contract. It may be alleged that the contract was induced by the making of false statements, or that one or even both parties were mistaken in reaching their agreement. A further possibility is an allegation that one side exerted unfair influence over the other, or perhaps even made threats against the other;

- that the contract is invalid because its purpose is something contrary to the public interest, for instance because it imposes an unreasonable restraint upon trading freedom;

- that some event has occurred which has brought the contract to an end, without performance having been completed.

- that the obligations arising under the contract have not been performed either partially or in total, so that there has been a breach of contract;

Of these various possibilities the most frequent are claims of breach of contract. Whatever the nature of the claim may be, however, it will always involve the innocent party seeking some remedy; perhaps financial compensation in the form of damages, or a court order to prevent a threatened breach of contract or enforcing the performance of the contract.

Validity

Sometimes what appears superficially to be a properly constituted contract, proves on closer examination to be one containing a defect which was present when the agreement was made. Certain defects of this kind the law recognises as sufficiently serious to invalidate the contract either partially or wholly. Such defects are referred to as *vitiating* factors, and they occur in circumstances of misrepresentation, mistake, duress and undue influence. To vitiate means to invalidate.

Misrepresentation

Before arriving at a contractual agreement the parties will often be involved in a process of negotiation. Negotiations can range over any issues which the parties think are relevant to the protection of their interests, but they are certainly likely to cover questions of payment, when and how the contract is to be performed, and what terms will be attached to it. The aim of negotiating is both to obtain information and to drive a good bargain, and negotiating skills are a valuable commodity in most areas of commercial and industrial life. Not all contracts are preceded by negotiations however, and as a general rule the more marked the imbalance in trading strength between the parties the less likely will be serious negotiation of terms and conditions. Thus transactions between large organisations on one side, and small organisations or private consumers on the other tend to be characterised by the dominant party presenting the weaker party with a set of terms which are not open to discussion but have to be accepted in their entirety if a contract is to be made.

The nature of representations

Statements made during the bargaining process may become a part of the contract itself, that is, they may become *terms* of the contract and give rise to an action for breach of contract if they prove untrue. But in many cases there will be no intention by the maker of the statement that the statement should be absorbed into the contract at all. It will be made merely to induce the other party to make the contract. Statements of this sort are known as *representations*. If a representation is untrue for any reason it may constitute a *misrepresentation*, and as such it will be actionable. The injured party (*the misrepresentee*) will base a claim not on breach of contract, but on the law applicable to misrepresentation. The reason is that the misrepresentation, whilst influential in the creation of the contract, has not been *incorporated* as a part of it. The contract itself has not been broken, but rather an assertion that was made in advance of it. It may however be possible to satisfy the court that in the particular circumstances a representation has become a contractual term, and in that event the action brought will be a contractual one. The important distinction between representations and terms is considered in more detail later.

A representation is a statement or assertion of fact made by one party to the other before or at a time of the contract, which has the effect of inducing the other to enter into a contract. The statement can be in any form. It can be in writing, such as a company prospectus containing details of the company's trading activities, or it can be spoken, or be implied from conduct. The definition enables us to distinguish a number of statements whose form or content excludes them from being treated as representations.

Statements of opinion

It frequently occurs that during the negotiation process statements are given which are based upon the opinion of the person making them. Since the representation must be one of fact, a statement expressed as an opinion cannot become a representation. It can be a difficult task to discriminate between what is, or can be fairly regarded as an issue of fact rather than opinion. The following cases illustrate the judicial approach to this question.

In *Bisset v. Wilkinson* 1927 the vendor of some land in New Zealand told the purchaser that the land would carry his 1,000 sheep. The purchaser was aware that the vendor had no experience of sheep farming, and also that the land had never carried sheep, but he went ahead and bought the land, only to find that it was too poor to support that number of animals. He brought an action against the vendor for rescission, i.e. cancellation of the contract. His action failed. The court considered that the purchaser was not justified in treating the vendor's statement about the carrying capacity of the land as anything more than an expression of opinion. It would have been different if the vendor had been a sheep farmer himself, for then he would have been in a position to give accurate information.

In *Esso Petroleum Co. Ltd. v. Mardon.* 1976 Mardon took a tenancy of a filling station owned by Esso, having been given a forecast by an experienced Esso sales representative of the quantity of petrol the station could be expected to sell annually. This quantity was never reached during the four years Mardon remained as tenant, and the business ran at a loss. The Court of Appeal decided that the company had made a misrepresentation, since the sales representative's knowledge of such matters made the forecast a statement of fact rather than opinion, and the sales representative was acting in the capacity of an agent of the company. Mardon's claim for damages was successful. The misrepresentation was regarded as a negligent one, and the court also took the view that the representation amounted to a contractual warranty, that is a contractual promise. In his leading judgment Lord Denning MR commented: *"it was a forecast made by a party, Esso who had special knowledge and skill. It was the yardstick by which they measured the worth of a filling station. They knew the facts. They knew the traffic in the town. They knew the throughput of a comparable station. They had much experience and expertise at their disposal. They were in a much better position than Mr. Mardon to make a forecast. It seems to me that if such a person makes a forecast – intending that the other should act on it and he does act on it – it can well be interpreted as a warranty that the forecast is sound and reliable in this sense that they made it with reasonable care and skill. That warranty was broken. Most negligently Esso made a fatal error in the forecast they stated to Mr. Mardon, and on which he took the tenancy. For this they are made liable in damages"*.

Clearly it is not possible to avoid liability for a statement which is expressed as, or is subsequently claimed to be an opinion, when the knowledge and experience of the representor in the matter is far greater than that of the representee.

Advertising and sales boasts

Although there is no rule of law which prevents such statements from amounting to representations, they will be seen as no more than sales boasts, provided they are not capable of substantial verification. They do not attract any legal consequences. They are regarded simply as the over inflated belief of the seller in seeking to promote the product. Examples include the holiday tour company's, *holiday of a lifetime,* and the carpet company's *We cannot be equalled for price and quality.* However to advertise that *interest free credit is available on all items bought this month,* or that a motor vehicle has returned *31 m.p.g. at a constant 75 m.p.h* are clearly statements of fact. If untrue they give rise to a criminal offence under the Trade Descriptions Act 1968 as well as amounting to misrepresentations. In respect of descriptions applied to *properties* the Property Misdescription Act 1991 has introduced stringent controls over the language that may be used in their sale. The Act is examined in Chapter 13.

Statements of law

A false statement of law cannot constitute a misrepresentation. This principle is based upon the general legal proposition that ignorance of the law does not excuse an otherwise unlawful act. The assumption is that the representee knows the law, and cannot therefore rely upon a plea that he relied upon inaccurate statements of law. Of course it would be quite different if these statements were being made by his legal adviser, upon whom he is placing reliance.

Distinguishing statements of law from statements of fact can in some cases be a difficult task. A single statement may be one of mixed law and fact. For example, to make a statement that a person is a *tenant* is both a statement of law, since the expression tenant carries a technical meaning which may or may not be accurate in this instance, and a statement of fact; either the individual is or is not a tenant. If a point of law is arrived at from a statement of the facts, then it seems the statement can be treated as one of law. An example would be a comment that, *"since this contract was made by post it became binding when the acceptance was sent"*. Sometimes a statement may involve distinguishing between law, opinion and fact.

> In *Smith v. Land and House Property Corporation* 1884 in a contract for the sale of an hotel the seller stated that it was leased to *"a most desirable tenant"*. In fact the tenant was far from desirable and the purchaser attempted to terminate the contract on the grounds of misrepresentation. The court held that the statement was not one of law, for its principal observation was not the evidence of the person being a tenant, but rather that the tenant was a person who had qualities of value to the purchaser.

Statements of future intention

A statement of future intention is not a statement of fact and is therefore not actionable. This is not so however where the statement of future intention conceals the present state of mind of the misrepresentor, which may constitute a fact.

> In *Edgington v. Fitzmaurice* 1885 the directors of a company invited a loan from the public to finance expansion. However their real intention was to use the money raised to pay off debts. This statement of intention was held to be a statement of fact which was false and actionable. Bowen LJ in the course of his judgment, remarked *"The state of a*

man's mind is as much a state of fact as the state of his digestion. It is true that it is difficult to prove what the state of man's mind at a particular time is, but if it can be ascertained it is as much a fact as anything else. A misrepresentation as to the state of a man's mind is, therefore, a misstatement of fact".

Silence

It might be assumed that a representation cannot arise where no statements of fact are made. However, although generally a non-disclosure cannot amount to a representation, there are some important exceptions to this rule. In contracts *uberrimae fidei* (of the utmost good faith) duties of full disclosure are imposed.

The obligation of disclosure under such contracts is based on the nature of this particular class of agreement. They are in general contracts where one party alone has full knowledge of all material facts. Insurance contracts and contracts for the sale of shares through the issue of a prospectus are examples of *contracts uberrimae fidei*. If full disclosure is not made in such cases the injured party can rescind the contract. Thus before entering into an insurance agreement the party seeking cover must disclose all facts which are material to the nature of the risk which is to be insured. In the case of a company issuing a prospectus, the Financial Services Act 1986 s.162 requires that the document must contain information prescribed under rules made by the Secretary for Trade and Industry (for instance the financial record of the company and details of contracts it has entered into.) A general duty of disclosure is laid down in s.163 which covers any information potential investors, or their professional advisers, would reasonably require in order to make an informed assessment of (a) the company's financial position and (b) the rights attaching to the shares to be issued. In determining what information comes within the general duty to disclose, the following matters are required by statute to be considered.:

(i)   the nature of the shares and who issued them;

(ii) the nature of those who are likely to acquire them;

(iii) the fact that certain matters (i.e. of an investment nature) may reasonably be expected to be known by the professional advisers likely to be consulted by the acquirers of shares; and

(iv) information available to investors or their professional advisers under statute.

In contracts for the sale of land the vendor is under an obligation to disclose any defects in his title, that is in his *ownership* of the property, although the obligation does not apply to defects in the property *itself*, for instance dry rot or damp.

In relation to a contract of employment there is no duty on a job applicatant to volunteer information which is not requested during the recruitment process, including the completion of an application form.

In *Walton v. TAC Construction Materials Ltd.* 1981 the complainant was dismissed after working for thirteen and a half months when the employer discovered that he was a heroin addict. During a medical inspection prior to employment the employee had answered *"none"* when asked to give details of serious illnesses, and failed to reveal that he was injecting himself with heroin. While the tribunal decided that it was fair to dismiss him because of the deception *"it could not be said that there is any duty on the employee in the ordinary case, though there may be exceptions, to volunteer information about himself otherwise than in response to a direct question"*.

If a statement is true when made but becomes untrue before the contract is concluded, the representor will be under a duty to disclose this alteration to the other party.

> In *With v. O'Flanagan* 1936 the purchaser of a doctor's practice was able to rescind the contract because, despite being told accurately during negotiations that the annual income of the practice was £2,000, he was not informed prior to the sale, which took place some months later, that the income of the practice had fallen sharply because of an illness which prevented the doctor from working.

The Financial Services Act 1986, also deals with this possibility in relation to the issue of a prospectus. It requires the issue of a supplementary prospectus if a *"significant change"* occurs or a *"significant new matter"* arises after the issue of the original prospectus and whilst the offer for shares is still open.

Inducement

The representation must induce the person to enter into the contract. There can be no inducement in cases where the other party is unaware of the representation or does not believe the statement, or has relied on his own skill and judgement. In such cases no action will lie in misrepresentation.

> In *Attwood v. Small* 1838 during the course of negotiations for the sale of a mine, the vendor made exaggerated statements of its capacity. The buyers subsequently appointed their own experts to investigate the mine, and the agents reported back to the buyers that the vendor's statements were true. As a result the buyers purchased the mine, only to discover that the statements were inaccurate. It was held that the buyers had no remedy in misrepresentation. They placed reliance upon their own independent investigation.

No test of reasonableness is applied to an inducement so a claim is not prevented by evidence that a reasonable person would not have been induced by the statement, *Museprime Properties Ltd. v. Adhill Properties Ltd.* 1990, provided the belief in the statement is genuine.

The representation need not be the sole or major inducement. It will be enough that it had a material affect upon the person's mind, in their decision to reach an agreement.

> In *Gran Gelato Ltd. v. Richcliff (Group) Ltd.* 1992 the plaintiffs took a basement and ground shop premises by way of an underlease from the defendants for a term of ten years. The plaintiffs paid a £30,000 premium for the property, and spent about £100,000 on alterations and improvements. The property was to be used for the purpose of making and selling Italian ice cream. The underlease had been created out of two head leases, clauses in which enabled the head landlord to terminate the leases on giving twelve months notice. A clause of this kind is known as a break clause. Before taking the underlease the plaintiff's solicitors *inquiries before lease* asked the defendant's solicitors if there were, *"any ... rights affecting the superior leasehold titles which would ... in anyway inhibit the enjoyment of the property by the Tenant..."*. The answer given was *"Not to the Lessors' knowledge."* The head landlord subsequently exercised the right to

terminate under the break clause. The plaintiffs still had four and a half years of their underlease to run. The court held that the defendants were guilty of negligent misrepresentation and liable in damages. The defendants had intended that the plaintiffs should rely upon and act on the statement made, and could not complain when it was trusted by the plaintiffs. The defendants could not therefore claim contributory negligence on the part of the plaintiffs. Furthermore, although on the facts the defendant's solicitors owed no duty of care to the plaintiffs, special situations could arise said the court, where a duty of care could be implied into dealings between a vendor's solicitor and a purchaser.

Types of misrepresentation

Actions for breach of contract and misrepresentation differ in an important respect. If a term of a contract is broken it is irrelevant to consider the state of mind of the contract breaker in establishing the existence and extent of liability. If however a mere representation has proved to be untrue and has become a misrepresentation, the effect this has on the liability of the misrepresentor depends on the state of mind accompanying it.

A misrepresentation may be made *innocently*, *negligently* or *fraudulently*.

A misrepresentation is *innocent* if the person making it had reasonable grounds for believing it to be true, and negligent where there was a lack of reasonable care taken to determine the accuracy of the statement. In contrast, a *fraudulent* misrepresentation is a representation which a person makes knowing it to be untrue, or believing it to be false, or which is made recklessly where the person making it does not care whether it is true or false. Thus it is a representation which is not honestly believed by the person making it, or where there has been complete disregard for the truth.

> Fraudulent misrepresentation was considered in the leading case of *Derry v. Peek* 1889. Under a private Act of Parliament a company was granted power to operate horse-drawn trams, and could run steam powered trams with the Board of Trades' consent. This the directors applied for, and in the belief that the consent would be granted, they went ahead and offered shares to the public through a prospectus that stated the company had power to run trams by steam. Shares were taken up. The consent was not given, and in consequence the company was wound up, many investors losing their money. Action was brought against the directors in the tort of *deceit*. The House of Lords defined a fraudulent misrepresentation as stated above, and having found that the directors believed the consent was simply a formality, held that the tort had not been committed. The directors were inaccurate but not dishonest, and inaccuracy without more is not fraud. They were not liable to pay damages.

At common law it has been possible since 1964 to claim damages in the tort of negligence for a *negligent* misrepresentation under the principle laid down in *Hedley Byrne v. Heller* 1964. This important case is considered extensively in Chapters 6 and 13 and all we need do here is briefly note the main aspects of the decision. *Hedley Byrne* provides that where there is a special relationship between the person making a statement and the recipient of it, a duty of reasonable care is owed in making it. If the duty is broken damages will be available, representing the loss suffered. The special relationship concept is central to the decision. The quality of this relationship was referred to by Lord Morris when he stated:

> *"Where in a sphere in which a person is so placed that others could reasonably rely on his judgment or his skill or on his ability to make careful inquiry, a person takes it on himself to give information or advice to, or allows his information or advice to be passed on to another, who, as he knows or should know, will place reliance on it then a duty of care will arise".*

The reliance placed on the statement by the recipient of it must be reasonable. In *Hedley Byrne* itself, a disclaimer of liability was enough to prevent reliance on a financial reference that had been given by a bank to a third party being reasonable (the effect being to render the whole decision *obiter*). Following the decision in *Esso Petroleum v. Mardon* 1976 the *Hedley Byrne* principle has been extended to apply to pre-contractual relationships, in addition to the non contractual relationships of the kind that appeared in *Hedley Byrne*.

Remedies available for misrepresentation

A variety of remedies are available to the misrepresentee. They include common law and equitable remedies, and the remedies available under the Misrepresentation Act 1967. At common law, as we have seen, damages are available in the tort of deceit for fraudulent misrepresentation, and in the tort of negligence for negligent misrepresentation. In equity *rescission* is available in any case of misrepresentation. It is a remedy which seeks to put the parties back to their pre-contractual position. If this cannot be achieved, for instance where the subject matter of the contract has been altered, lost, or sold to a third party, rescission is not available. Nor can it be claimed if it would be inequitable to grant it. Thus if a person in full knowledge of the misrepresentation *affirms* the contract, so indicating that that he intends to continue, the right to rescind will be lost. Affirmation can occur through delay in bringing an action.

> In *Leaf v. International Galleries* 1959 the plaintiff bought from the defendants a picture described as a Constable, but was unable to rescind the contract some five years later when he discovered on trying to re-sell it that it was not a Constable after all. The plaintiff also argued, unsuccessfully, that the contract was affected by mistake. It can be of advantage to a plaintiff to plead alternative legal arguments in this way, for if one proposition fails the other might succeed, and clearly a plaintiff would not choose to bring two separate actions, or even more, if the matter can be dealt with in one trial.

Unlike the common law remedy of damages, which are available as of right once liability has been established, rescission, being an equitable remedy, is discretionary. The court exercises this discretion in accordance with certain principles, referred to as *equitable maxims*. Essentially these principles are concerned with ensuring that in awarding equitable relief the court should be satisfied not only that the plaintiff has acted fairly, but also that the defendant will not be unfairly treated if the remedy sought by the plaintiff is granted. This is the justification for the restrictions on the granting of rescission which have previously been referred to.

> The question of the measure of common law damages available to an injured party induced into making a contract through fraudulent misrepresentation was considered in *Doyle v. Olby (Ironmongers) Ltd.* 1969. The plaintiff purchased an ironmongers business from the defendants, following negotiations with members of the Olby family. On taking over the business he discovered that a number of false statements had been made to him.

In particular he had been told that all the trade of the business was over the counter, when in fact half the trade was wholesale, and involved employing a representative to visit the customers, something the plaintiff had not planned for nor could afford. He claimed damages for fraud and conspiracy against the defendant company and members of the family. At first instance the trial judge awarded damages on a contractual basis, as though the reference to trade being entirely retail was a contractual term. The result was that the plaintiff could recover only foreseeable damages under the rule in *Hadley v. Baxendale* (see Chapter 10). Such damages amounted to £1,500.

The Court of Appeal took a different view however. Lord Denning MR observed: *"The object of damages is to put the plaintiff in as good a position, as far as money can do it, as if the promise had been performed. In fraud, the defendant has been guilty of a deliberate wrong by inducing the plaintiff to act to his detriment .... In contract, the damages are limited to what may reasonably be supposed to have been in the contemplation of the parties. In fraud, they are not so limited. The defendant is bound to make reparation for all the actual damage directly flowing from the fraudulent inducement."*

By applying this approach the plaintiff was awarded £5,500 damages.

In *Smith New Court Securities Ltd. v. Scrimgeour Vickers (Asset Management) Ltd.* 1994, the plaintiffs made a successful bid for shares in the company called FIS Ltd. They paid 82.5 pence per share. There were two factors regarding price which they were unaware of when they made their bid. Firstly a fraudulent misrepresentation had been made to them on behalf of the defendants, that other parties were putting in competing bids. This was a fabrication. Had the plaintiffs known the truth the real market value of the shares would have been 78 pence. Secondly FIS Ltd. had suffered a massive fraud committed against it by an unconnected third party which at the time of the bid had not become common knowledge. If the market had been aware of the fraud it would have reduced the share price to 44 pence The question for the Court of Appeal was the measure of damages available to the plaintiffs. The court concluded that damages should be assessed by reference to the general knowledge of the market at the time the transaction occurred. The unrelated fraud was not common knowledge when the bid was made consequently the price the plaintiffs would have paid if the defendants had not made their misrepresentation was 78 pence instead of 82.5 pence per share. They were awarded £1,176,010 damages. This was a major blow to them for the trial judge had treated the measure of damages as the difference between 82.5 pence and 44 pence a share, and awarded them £10,764,005 damages.

Under statute, damages are available under the Misrepresentation Act 1967 in respect of negligent and innocent misrepresentation. Under s.2(1) damages are available for negligent misrepresentation. It is a defence for the maker of the statement to show that up to the time of the contract he believed that the statement was true and that there was reasonable cause to believe this. Obviously such a belief will depend upon the steps taken by representor to verify the statement. There is an important difference between a claim brought for negligent misrepresentation under s.2(1) and a claim founded in the tort of negligence, which is that the burden of proof lies with the misrepresentor under s.2(1), but with the misrepresentee in the tort of negligence.

Under s.2(2), where a misrepresentation is a purely innocent one, damages may be awarded; however, the section requires that the party seeking relief must ask the court to rescind the contract. If the court is satisfied that grounds for rescission exist it may award damages instead, if it is of the opinion that it would be equitable to do so. The aim of this provision is apparently to cover cases where the misrepresentation is of a minor nature and so give the court the discretion to award damages, whilst leaving the contract intact.

The following diagram illustrates the remedies available for the different types of misrepresentation.

	Fraudulent misrepresentation	**Negligent misrepresentation**	**Innocent misrepresentation**
At Common Law	Damages in the tort of deceit	Damages in the tort of negligence under the rule in Hedley Byrne v. Heller (1964), if a special relationship exists.	
In Equity	Rescission (and damages). If the contract is executory the fraud is a defence if the misrepresentor brings action for specific performance	Rescission	Rescission
Under the Misrepresentation Act 1967		In addition to recission, or, at the court's discretion instead of rescission, damages under s.2(1) if as a result of the misrepresentation the innocent party has suffered loss. If the defendant can prove that up to the time of the contract he believed, with reasonable cause, that his statements were true, this will be a defence.	If the grounds for rescission exist, the court, in its discretion, may award damages instead under s.2(2).

Figure 9.1   Remedies for Misrepresentation

Under s.2 of the Act a person may not avoid liability in respect of claims brought under ss.2(1) and (2), unless the court, in its discretion, considers that reliance on a provision seeking to avoid such liability is fair and reasonable in the circumstances of the case. The case of *Howard Marine v. Ogden* 1978 provides an illustration of a claim brought under s.2(1), and the use of an exemption clause coming within s.3. The section exposes such a clause to a test of reasonableness.

The facts of *Howard Marine & Dredging Co. Ltd. v. Ogden & Sons (Excavations) Ltd.* 1978 were as follows. Ogdens agreed to hire two sea going barges from Howards, for the purpose of dumping earth at sea. Howards quoted a price in a letter to Ogdens, stating the cubic capacity of each vessel. At a later meeting Ogdens enquired of Howards representative what the carrying capacity of the vessels was in tonnes. The representative stated this to be about 1,600 tonnes. He made the statement honestly, based upon his recollection of the tonnage specified in Lloyds Register in London, which he had previously examined. He had also seen the shipping documents for the two vessels, which indicated the tonnage as 1,195 tonnes per vessel. This was in fact the correct figure, but all the representative remembered at the time of his statement was the Lloyds entry, which unusually was incorrect. The lack of carrying capacity held up Ogden's work, and they refused to pay the hire charges. Howards withdrew the barges, and sued for damages. Ogdens counterclaimed, seeking damages under s.2(1) Misrepresentation Act 1967. The agreement between the parties, referred to technically where a vessel is being hired as a charter party, contained the following exemption clause: *"Charterers acceptance of handing over the vessel shall be conclusive that (it is) in all respects fit for the intended and contemplated use by the Charterers and in every other way satisfactory to them."*

By a majority the Court of Appeal held that Howards were in breach of s.2(1), and they could not rely on the exemption clause. Accordingly Ogdens could recover damages representing their losses. Bridge LJ stated: *"In the course of negotiations leading to a contract the 1967 Act imposes an absolute obligation not to state facts which the representor cannot prove he had reasonable grounds to believe."* On the facts the representative was found by the court not to have established this *reasonable ground*, for he had overlooked the disparity in tonnage between the shipping documents and the Register, recalling only the latter document with its inaccurate information.

On the issue of the exemption clause the court held that since its effect was to seek to exempt for negligent misrepresentation it was not a reasonable clause, and thus reliance on it was not fair and reasonable.

In cases of this kind, whilst the courts task is to apply the law to the facts, this will often involve issues of legal discretion. The courts are guided in their exercise of such discretion by recognising the commercial reality of the situation. In his dissenting judgment Lord Denning MR commented of the exemption, *"The parties here were commercial concerns and were of equal bargaining power. The clause was not foisted by one on the other in a standard printed form. It was contained in all the drafts which passed between them, and it was no doubt given close consideration by both sides . . . It is a clause common in charter party's of this kind . . . it is specially applicable in cases where the contractor has the opportunity of checking the position for himself. It tells him that he should do so; and that he should not rely on any information given beforehand, for it may be inaccurate. Thus it provides a valuable safeguard against the consequences of innocent misrepresentation."*

The general legal position regarding liability for false statements is summarised in Figure 9.2 on the following page.

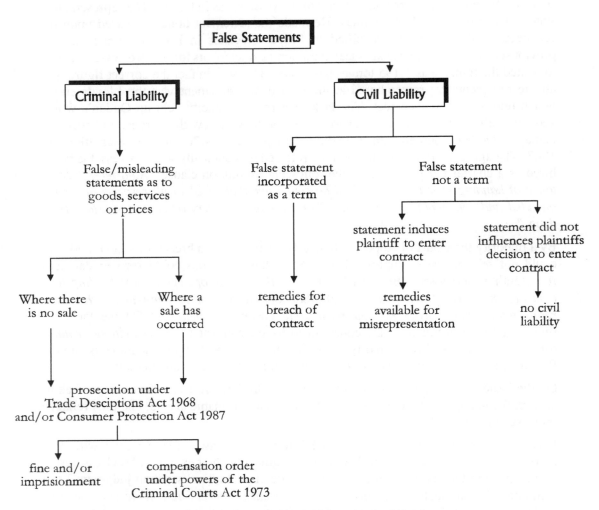

Figure 9.2 Liability for False Statement

Mistake

The courts have always been reticent about treating mistake as a ground for the avoidance of contractual liabilities. Previously we have seen that a contract will remain valid despite its proving to be economically disadvantageous to one of the parties because of what is, in effect, a mistake as to the value or quality of the subject matter. Provided the parties have made their deal openly and voluntarily the courts will enforce it. *Haigh v. Brooks* 1839 provides a very useful illustration (see Chapter 8). In contracts for goods the common law traditionally has taken the view it is the buyers responsibility to ensure the transaction is worth making. This is summed up in the expression *caveat emptor* (let the buyer beware). Modern consumer legislation, notably the Sale of Goods Act 1979 (as amended) readjusts this responsibility by imposing obligations on sellers regarding the quality, suitability and description of the products they sell. However these obligations attach only to business sellers, for the legislation is designed to prevent business from sheltering behind the *caveat emptor* rule. In private sales, where it is assumed the parties can bargain as equals, caveat emptor still applies. If someone buys a car privately, and subsequently finds they have paid well above the market price, or the car is much heavier on petrol than they anticipated, or is simply not a very good vehicle, the law does not give them any remedy against the seller. They must live with their error of judgment. Of course if their error was engineered by the seller making false statements about the vehicle the situation is different, for in these circumstances a misrepresentation claim will lie. It can sometimes be difficult to distinguish between mistake and misrepresentation, and they often overlap, but they do involve different principles of liability. Part of the confusion lies in the terminology itself. A misrepresentation involves mistaken belief, because the representee has gone ahead with the contract believing certain statements to be true when they are not true. The essence of misrepresentation is that the false statement simply induces the transaction, but it does not become a part of it. Where a person is seeking a remedy on the grounds of contractual mistake, the argument being put forward is that the substance of the contract itself is tainted by the mistake, and the remedy is a contractual one. This is not merely an exercise in semantics. The differences are significant. For example the level of damages awarded may vary as between a misrepresentation and a mistake.

The following types of mistake will not effect the validity of a contract:

- A mistake of law.

- An error of judgment about the value of the subject matter of the contract, unless a misrepresentation was made.

- A mistake about the meaning of a trade term. In *Harrison & Jones Ltd. v. Bunten & Lancaster Ltd.* 1953 a buyer purchased 100 bales of *Sree brand* kapok from the seller. Both parties believed that this type of kapok was pure, but when the buyer discovered that Sree brand was a mixture of different types of kapok he claimed that the contract was void for mistake. The court, however, held that the contract was valid, being unaffected by the mistake.

- A mistake about ability to perform the contract within a certain time, e.g. in a building contract.

Despite this wide range of mistake situations which are ignored in law, there are still some instances in which the mistake is regarded as so fundamental to the transaction that the courts will take account of it. Such mistakes are known as *operative* mistakes, and they render the contract void. The following is an outline of the types of operative mistakes which are recognised.

Mistake about the nature of a signed document

We are brought up on words of warning about care in signing documents, and with good reason for the law does not permit a person to escape liability from a document they have signed simply because they have not read it, or have read but not understood it. A defence, known as *non est factum* (not my deed), is available if all the following conditions can be satisfied:

(i) that the document signed is fundamentally or radically different from the one the signatory believed it to be;

(ii) that the signatory exercised reasonable care in signing the document;

(iii) that fraud was used to induce the signature.

Collectively these factors are very demanding, and the defence is thus rarely successful.

> In *Saunders v. Anglia Building Society* 1974 the House of Lords indicated the narrow limits of the defence of non est factum. The facts were that a 78 year old widow had signed a document which a Mr. Lee had told her was a deed of gift of her house to her nephew. She did not read the document as her glasses were broken when she signed it. The document in fact transferred her property to Lee, who subsequently mortgaged the property to a building society. The widow now sought to recover the deeds, pleading non est factum. The action failed. The document had been signed with carelessness, and furthermore it was not substantially different from the one she believed she was signing: they were both assignments of property.

There will sometimes be grounds other than mistake on which a person who has signed a contractual document can rely to avoid the contract. For example, in the case of consumer credit agreements such as hire-purchase agreements, the Consumer Credit Act 1974 grants a five-day period after the agreement is made within which the debtor can cancel the agreement, provided it was signed somewhere other than on the creditor's premises. Signing a contract which is void at law, such as an illegal contract, will incur no contractual liability at all.

Mistake as to the identity of the other party

Mistake of this kind is usually *unilateral*, where only one of the parties is mistaken about the identity of the other party to the contract. When this occurs the contract will be void only if the mistaken party can show that the question of identity was material to the making of the contract, and that the other part knew or ought to have known of the mistake. The majority of cases in which this type of mistake occur involve fraud, so the requirement of knowledge of the mistake will have been satisfied, bearing the mistaken party with the difficult task of trying to show that he would not have made the contract if the true identity of the other party had been known.

> In *Cundy v. Lindsay & Co.* 1878 the respondents, a firm of linen manufacturers in Belfast, received an order for 250 dozen handkerchiefs from a rogue called Blenkarn whose address was 38 Wood Street, Cheapside. He signed the order to make it appear that it had come from a firm called Blenkiron and Company who traded at 123 Wood Street, Cheapside. The respondents knew Blenkiron and Company to be a reputable firm, and therefore sent the goods, together with an invoice headed Blenkiron and Company, to 37 Wood Street. Blenkarn then sold the goods to the appellant, who was unaware of the fraud. Lindsay & Company were held to be entitled to the goods since their contract with Blenkarn was void. His existence was entirely unknown to them; they intended to deal only with Blenkiron and Company.

If the parties deal face to face, mistake about identity will be far more difficult to establish. In a shop, for instance, the shopkeeper presumably intends a contract with the person on the other side of the counter, irrespective of what the person calls himself.

> In *Phillips v. Brooks* 1919 a fraudster called North entered a jeweller's shop where he represented himself to be a gentleman called Sir George Bullough. He purchased a ring for £450, for which he gave the jeweller a worthless cheque. The following day North

sold the ring to a firm of pawn brokers. On discovering his loss later, the jeweller traced the ring to the pawnbrokers and sought to recover it from them, alleging that his original contract with North was void for mistake. The court disagreed, since the parties had dealt face to face. The contract was, however, voidable on the grounds of fraud. Unfortunately, this did not help the jeweller, as he had not taken steps to avoid the contract until after the ring had been purchased by the pawnbroker, who now had a good title (i.e. legal ownership) to it.

The expression voidable contract was considered in the previous chapter. A voidable contract, such as one induced by fraud, gives the fraudulent party ownership of the goods until the innocent party takes action to avoid the contract, for example by informing the police of the loss. If before the contract has been avoided the rogue has sold the goods to a third party who buys in good faith and is unaware of the fraud, that third party becomes the owner of the goods, and the original owner cannot reclaim them. This was the position that Phillips the jeweller found himself in.

An example of the limited extent to which a unilateral mistake may affect the validity of a contract is provided by *Centrovincial Estates plc v. Merchant Investors Assurance Co. Ltd.* 1983 a case involving a business tenancy between the plaintiffs, the landlords, and the defendants who were the tenants. The issue concerned the fixing of a new rent, under a rent review clause in the lease. The mistake in question was made by solicitors acting for the plaintiffs who wrote to the defendants on June 22 1982 asking them to agree to a new rent of £65,000 per annum to operate from the rent review date. The defendants were happy to agree to the new rent by letter the following day, for the figure suggested was a reduction of over £3,000 per annum on the current rent. The plaintiff's solicitors, when they discovered the error a few days later attempted to persuade the defendants to accept the true figure of £126,000 per annum. The plaintiffs claimed the mistake had prevented any *consensus ad idem* between the parties. The Court of Appeal, applying strict contract law, held that acceptance of an unambiguous offer resulted in a contract. The mere assertion of a mistake, of which the offeree was unaware, did not affect the contract's validity.

Bilateral mistakes

The instances of mistake considered so far have concerned mistakes made by just one of the parties, unilateral mistakes. In cases of bilateral mistake however both the parties are mistaken, either about the same thing, *common* mistake, or about something different, *mutual* mistake.

Mutual mistake

Where a mutual mistake occurs the parties are at cross purposes, and in cases of fundamental error arguably there can be no contract in existence anyway, on grounds of the uncertainty of their agreement. Thus if one company agrees to sell a machine to another, and the description of it is so vague that the seller believes he is selling an entirely different machine to the one the buyer believes he is buying, there is no effective agreement within the process of offer and acceptance. The approach applied by the courts in these circumstances is an objective one.

In *Raffles v. Wichelhaus* 1864 the buyer purchased a cargo of cotton from the seller, to arrive *"ex Peerless from Bombay"*. Remarkably there were two ships named Peerless sailing from Bombay, one in October which the buyer had in mind and one in December which the seller had in mind. The court held that no contract had been entered into. Viewed objectively the facts denied the existence of an offer and an acceptance for there was no *consensus ad idem*.

Common mistake

An example of a common mistake occurred in *Couturier v. Hastie* 1856. A contract was made for the sale of some wheat which at the time was being carried on board a ship. Unknown to both parties, when they made the agreement the wheat had already been sold by the ship's captain because during the voyage it had started to overheat. The court held the contract to be void, since it was a contract of impossibility.

There are some significant exceptions to this type of claim. At common law relief from a contract affected by a common mistake will not be available where the mistake:

(a)   occurs after the contract is made. In *Amalgamated Investment & Property Co. Ltd. v. John Walker & Sons Ltd.* 1976 the defendants sold the plaintiffs a warehouse for £1.7m. The defendants knew the plaintiffs intended to redevelop the site, and both knew planning permission would be necessary. Contracts were exchanged on 25 September. On 26 September the defendants were informed by the Department of the Environment that the building had become 'listed'. This made development consent most unlikely, and without it the property was worth £200,000. The plaintiffs sought to rescind the contract. The Court of Appeal rejected the claim. There was no mistake in the minds of the parties when the contracts were exchanged sufficient to set the contract aside;

(b)   is as to quality. An example of a mistake about quality is seen in *Leaf v. International Galleries* 1950 where the purchaser believed he was buying a work by Constable only to discover later that Constable was not the artist. The mistake was not operative, since the purchaser had received under the contract what he had bargained for, namely the painting.

A further illustration occurred in *Bell v. Lever Bros. Ltd.* 1932. Bell, who was the managing director of a company controlled by Lever Bros. Ltd., became redundant as a result of company amalgamations, and Lever Bros. Ltd. paid him, £30,000 as compensation for his loss of office. It was subsequently discovered that as managing director he had committed serious breaches of duty by secret trading and could have been summarily dismissed without compensation. Although Bell had not revealed his misconduct to the company before he received the compensation, he was not acting fraudulently because he was unaware that what he had done rendered him liable to dismissal without compensation. The company sought to recover the compensation it had paid to him on the grounds of mistake. The House of Lords decided that it could not do so, since the company had paid the compensation in the belief that Bell was an employee who had carried out his duties in a proper way.

The company was therefore mistaken about the quality of its employee, which was insufficient to give rise to an operative mistake.

The doctrine of common mistake was reviewed by the court in *Associated Japanese Bank (International) Ltd. v. Credit Du Nord SA* 1988. The facts of the case were that an individual, Bennett, purported to sell specified items of machinery to the plaintiff bank, which the bank then leased back to him. Under the transaction Bennett received approximately £1 million. The plaintiff bank required Bennett to provide a guarantee from another bank, and this he obtained from the defendants. The machinery was non-existent. Bennett disappeared with the money, and the plaintiffs claimed under the guarantee against the defendants. The defendants argued that (a) the guarantee was subject to an express or implied condition that the machinery existed, or alternatively (b) that the guarantee was void from the outset on the grounds of the mistaken belief of both parties that the machinery existed. The plaintiff's claim failed. On the facts the judge, Steyn J took the view that the guarantee agreement included an express condition that the machinery existed. Even if it had not, he was of the view that it would contain an implied term to this effect for a reasonable man would regard this as so obvious as hardly to require saying. The guarantee was also void from the outset for the mistake, at common law. The judge summarised the common law approach to mistake as follows:

(i)   the courts should seek to uphold rather than defeat apparent contracts;

(ii)   the rules regarding mistake are designed to deal with the effect of exceptional circumstances upon apparent contracts;

(iii) the mistake must concern existing facts at the time of the contract, and both sides must substantially share the mistake;

(iv)   the mistake must render the subject matter of the contract essentially and radically different from what was in the minds of the parties; and

(v)   there must be reasonable grounds for the belief of both parties.

Remedies

At common law

The effect of an operative mistake at common law is to render the contract void *ab initio* - from the outset. The true owner is thus entitled to the return of goods, or damages, from whoever is in wrongful possession.

In equity

The position in equity is different however, for equity recognises certain types of operative mistake which the common law does not grant relief for, in particular in cases involving mistake as to quality. The following cases illustrate the position.

In *Solle v. Butcher* 1950 the parties entered into a lease in the mistaken belief that, due to substantial improvements carried out to it, the flat being let was not subject to rent control legislation. The tenant had been paying rent at the agreed rate of £250 p.a. when it was discovered that the flat was in fact subject to rent control. This meant that the maximum rent which could lawfully be charged was £140 p.a. However if the landlord had served a statutory notice on the tenant before the lease had been executed, he would have been entitled legitimately to charge £250 p.a., the extra amount representing the value to the tenant of the improvements. The tenant claimed the overpayment of rent. The landlord counterclaimed for possession. The Court of Appeal found itself unable to grant relief at common law for the mistake was one of quality. However exercising its equitable jurisdiction the court allowed the lease to be rescinded on condition that a new lease on the same terms at the higher rent be offered to the tenant, the new lease enabling the landlord to serve the relevant notice on the tenant.

In *Magee v. Pennine Insurance Co. Ltd.* 1969 a proposal for insurance of a motor car had been incorrectly completed without the insured's knowledge. Following a crash, a claim was made and the insurance company agreed to pay £385 which the insured was willing to accept. On discovery of the material inaccuracy in the policy however, the company withdrew their offer of payment and the insured sued them to obtain it. The Court of Appeal held that under the common law the common mistaken belief that the policy was valid was inoperative and the contract of the insurance was valid. In equity however the agreement to pay £385 would be set aside as there had been a fundamental misapprehension, and the party seeking to rescind was not at fault.

Rectification

Where parties to a contract have executed a written document which contains errors, the equitable remedy of rectification may enable the court to rectify the document so that it accords with the parties true agreement. For rectification to operate there must be:

(i)   agreement on the particular aspect in question;

(ii)   which is certain and unchanged at the time the agreement is put in writing; and

(iii) the writing must fail to express the agreement.

In *Craddock Bros. v. Hunt* 1923 an oral agreement for the sale of a house expressly excluded an adjoining yard and yet the later written agreement and conveyance included the yard. The court ordered a rectification of the documents in order to express the parties true original intention.

The equitable remedy of rectification cannot however be used where one party has made a miscalculation and the written agreement does not express his real intention.

In *Riverplate Properties v. Paul* 1975 the plaintiffs granted a long lease of a maisonette to the defendant and had intended that the lessee should pay half the cost of exterior and structural repairs that were required. The lease however put the entire burden on the plaintiff. The defendant believed that she was not responsible for those repairs and the plaintiff's claimed for rectification or rescission of the lease. The court held that a unilateral mistake of this kind could have no impact on the terms of the lease agreed by the parties. There was no justification for equity to disrupt the transaction actually entered into and the mistake was inoperative. The error in failing to include a suitable term in the lease was soley the plaintiffs.

Duress and Undue Influence

At common law coercing a person into making a contract by means of actual or threatened violence to them is referred to as *duress,* and if it can be proved the contract is treated, not surprisingly, as void. Because of its narrow limits the plea of duress is an extremely unusual one, although it was raised in a case that was heard by the Privy Council in 1976.

> *Barton v. Armstong* 1976 involved death threats made by Armstrong against Barton, designed to force Barton to purchase Armstrong's shares in a company of which they were both major shareholders. There was evidence that Barton regarded the acquisition as a satisfactory business arrangement in any event. He subsequently sought to have the deed by which he purchased Armstrong's shares declared void. By a majority the court held the agreement to be void. The minority view however was that the claim should fail, because it seemed that although Barton took the threats seriously, the real reason for making the purchase was commercial.

Equity however goes much further than the common law. The doctrine of *undue influence* which it has developed recognises more subtle forms of improper pressure that are sometimes relied on to create agreements. Where undue influence is shown to have occurred equity will allow the innocent party the opportunity to rescind the contract. In certain relationships a presumption of undue influence arises, for example in fiduciary relationships, and in those where one person is in a position of dominance over the other. Parent and child, solicitor and client, doctor and patient, and trustee and beneficiary are classic illustrations. The dominant party who attempts to uphold a transaction entered into in such a relationship must rebut the presumption of undue influence by showing that he has not abused his position in any way. Evidence that the innocent party has taken independent advice will go a long way to achieving this and saving the contract.

> In *Lancashire Loans v. Black* 1934 the Court of Appeal recognised that the presumption of undue influence between a parent and a child can transcend the child marrying and leaving home. Here a married daughter, without independent advice, had contracted to pay off part of her mother's debts. The court held that the transaction could be set aside as the daughter had not exercised her free will but acted under the influence of her mother.

The courts are still prepared to recognise new relationships where the doctrine can be applied, for example an influential secretary companion and his elderly employee in *Re Craig* 1971, and a banker who sought to obtain a benefit from his customer in *Lloyds Bank v. Bundy* 1975.

> In *Barclays Bank plc v. O'Brien* 1993 Mr. O'Brien, who was a shareholder in a manufacturing company, wanted to increase the overdraft available to the company from its bank, Barclays. The bank agreed to an overdraft facility of £135,000. The O'Brien's matrimonial home, jointly owned by Mr. & Mrs. O'Brien, was used as security for the loan, and the O'Briens executed a legal charge in favour of the bank. The bank did not advise Mrs. O'Brien as to the effect of the charge; nor did she read the documents she signed. Her husband had told her merely that the charge was to secure £60,000, and would last for only a short time. The company's debts increased, and the bank sought

to enforce its security. The House of Lords unanimously held that Mrs. O'Brien was entitled to set aside the legal charge on the matrimonial home. The court restated the law applying in surety cases involving marriage partners and cohabitees. In a case such as this, where the spouse placed trust and confidence in the principal debtor (the husband) and acted as surety on the basis of a misrepresentation or through undue influence, the legal position would be as follows. If the surrounding circumstances were such as to put the creditor on inquiry, for instance where on the face of it the transaction was not to the wife's benefit, then the creditor should take reasonable steps to establish that her consent had been properly obtained. This could be done by discussing the matter with her privately, warning her of the risks, and suggesting she take independent legal advice. A creditor put on inquiry, who failed to take such reasonable steps would take the security subject to the equitable rights of the wife to have it set aside, for the creditor would have constructive notice of those rights.

There have been a number of subsequent cases which have explored the implications of the *O'Brien* decision. Essentially they have all involved questions of what the duty of a bank is taking into account its knowledge or its potential knowledge of misrepresentation or undue influence occurring between the parties to the relationship.

In modern times the courts have demonstrated an increased willingness to see the principles underlying duress and undue influence as elements in a broader principle of law which Lord Denning referred to in *Lloyds Bank v. Bundy* 1975 as *inequality of bargaining power*. It may be useful to refer to his judgment, which is contained in the previous chapter.

> In *Clifford Davies Management Ltd. v. WEA Records Ltd.* 1975 this inequality approach was clearly demonstrated. Two composer members of a pop group (Fleetwood Mac) had entered into an agreement with their manager to assign the copyright in all their work to him for a period of ten years. In return they received a very small financial consideration and his promise to use his best endeavours to publish the work they composed. The Court of Appeal found that on the basis of bargaining inequality the contract could be set aside at the option of the composers. The factors cited by the court that pointed to the inequality were: the overall unfairness of a ten year tie, supported by vague consideration offered in return by the manager; the conflict of interest arising from the manager acting as the business adviser to the composers, whilst at the same time representing his own company's interests in negotiating with them; and the absence of any independent advice available to the composers, and their reliance upon the manager, who exerted undue influence over them.

Further development of this approach has lead to the recognition of *economic duress*. Economic duress is a plea based upon a claim that the weaker party gave their consent to the agreement as a result of improper commercial influence or pressure put on them. The following cases illustrate situations in which the courts have been prepared to recognise economic duress as a ground for contractual relief.

> In *Universe Tankships Inc. of Monrovia v. International Transport Workers' Federation* 1982 a ship, the Universe Sentinal, owned by Universe Tankships, was blacked by a union, the ITWF, which refused to make tugs available to assist in docking at Milford

Haven. The ship was blacked because it was sailing under a flag of convenience. Following negotiations between the parties, the ITWF agreed to lift the restriction in return for an undertaking from Universe Tankships to improve crew pay and conditions on the vessel and make a contribution to an ITWF fund - The Seafarers' International Welfare Protection and Assistance Fund. The company later sought to recover their $6480 contribution, and the House of Lords held they were entitled to its return, since it had been paid under economic duress. The agreement was voidable.

In *Atlas Express v. Kafco (Importers and Distributors)* 1989 the defendants were a small company involved in the import and distribution of basketware. They sold a quantity of their goods to Woolworths, and agreed with the plaintiffs, a national road carrier, for deliveries to be made by the plaintiffs. The plaintiffs depot manager quoted a price for deliveries based upon his guess as to how many cartons of goods would be carried on each load. In the event he overestimated how many cartons would be required to be carried on each load, and now refused to proceed with the contract unless the defendants agreed to a minimum payment for each load of £440, in substitution for the original arrangement of £1.10 per carton. Anxious to ensure the goods were delivered on time, and unable in the circumstances to find an alternative carrier, the defendants agreed to the new arrangement, but later refused to pay. The plaintiff's claim for breach of contract failed. The court took the view that the plaintiff's threat to break the contract together with their knowledge of the defendants dependency on them represented a clear example of economic duress.

The Effect of Public Policy on Contracts

Although contracts are part of the private law, this does not make contracting the exclusive domain of the parties themselves, granting them the freedom to make whatever type of contract they choose. At common law certain types of contract are regarded as *illegal* on the basis that they are contrary to public policy, and additional forms of illegality have been recognised by Parliament.

Public policy is a vague but important term which has never been clearly defined. In *Esso Petroleum Company v. Harpers Garage (Stourport) Ltd.* 1967. Lord Pearce in the House of Lords referred to it as an *"unruly horse"*. The legal writer Pollock has seen it as *"a principle of judicial legislation or interpretation founded on the current needs of the community."* This appears to mean that it is concerned with the public good, rather than for example with what is politically appropriate. Questions of public policy involve the court in applying economic, moral and other criteria to the contract in question to decide whether it is desirable in the general public interest. By these means the courts have held many types of contract to be illegal including contracts to commit criminal and tortious acts, contracts for trading with the enemy in times of war, and contracts which oust the jurisdiction of the courts.

The effects of declaring a contract illegal vary. Sometimes a party who is unaware of the illegality will be allowed to sue on the contract, but where the parties are fully informed of the illegal nature of the transaction the court will deny them any remedy.

In *Foster v. Driscoll* 1927 a group of people entered into a partnership agreement in England, the object of which was to smuggle a ship-load of whisky into the USA. This was a violation of the prohibition laws then in force in the USA, so the partnership was illegal on the grounds of public policy, and it was held that no action could be brought in respect of any matter arising out of the agreement.

The decision in *Bowmakers v. Barnet Instruments* 1945 established the principle that a person can recover property transferred under an illegal transaction as long as they do not have to rely on the illegality to establish the right to the property. The *Bowmakers* principle was applied by the House of Lords in *Tinsley v. Milligan* 1993. The two parties purchased a house using money supplied by them both, however the house was put into the sole name of the appellant, to enable the respondent, Milligan, to make false social security claims. Later, after the parties had a disagreement, the respondent claimed a share in the house, arguing it was held on a resulting trust for her by the appellant. The appellant said that since the original arrangement had been made to further an illegal purpose, social security fraud, the claim should fail. The court said the proper test was whether the respondent had to rely on the illegality to support her claim. On the facts she did not need to do so. By contributing to the purchase price a presumption of a resulting trust in her favour was established. The appellant could only use the illegality to defeat the presumption. By a majority of 3 to 2 the court found in the respondent's favour. (Note: a trust occurs where one person holds property for the benefit of another).

An example of illegality arising in relation to a contract of employment arises when the parties to the contract agree not to make deductions of tax and National Insurance contributions from the wage or salary. Even if the employee merely passively acquiesces in the fraud the contract is still illegal and any subsequent claim based upon it cannot stand as a consequence. The position is different however if the employees subsequent claim is not contractual in nature. In *Leighton v. Michael and Another* 1996 the EAT held that a claim of sex discrimination based on sexual harassment could still be made despite the fact that the complainants contract of employment was illegal.

Contracts in Restraint of Trade

One aspect of common law illegality of particular application within the sphere of business and commerce involves contracts regarded as being in restraint of trade. This area of law is of sufficient importance that some types of restraints contained in a contract are regulated by statute. The essence of such a contract is that it contains an undertaking which restricts the future freedom of one of the parties to trade with others who are outside the contract. Because the doctrine of restraint of trade is guided by considerations of public policy, the categories of contract to which it applies alter as economic and social conditions change. Examination of the law regarding restraints reveals that essentially what the courts and Parliament see to prevent are practices which restrict competition to the detriment of the public. A balance however has to be struck between the public interest on the one hand, and the commercial interests of businesses on the other. It is recognised that a restraint will not be legitimate if it goes further than is reasonably necessary to grant a business a proper level of commercial protection.

For convenience restraints are considered below under two headings:

- restraints controlled at common law; and
- restraints controlled by statute.

Restraints at common law

The leading authority here is the decision of the House of Lords in the *Nordenfelt* case.

> In *Nordenfelt v. Maxim Nordenfelt Guns and Ammunition Co. Ltd.* 1894 the seller of a gun and ammunition manufacturing business agreed with the buyer not to manufacture guns or ammunition anywhere in the world, or compete in any way, for a period of twenty five years. Although the undertaking not to compete in any way was considered unreasonable by the court as being too wide, it was severed from the rest of the restraint, which was considered to be a reasonable protection for the buyer. The seller, who was an inventor, had a world-wide reputation in the field of munitions, and this helped to explain the length and geographical extent of the restraint clause. In the course of his judgment Lord MacNaghten laid down the following principle: *"The public have an interest in every person's carrying out his trade freely; so has the individual. All interference with individual liberty of action in trading, and all restraints of trade themselves, if there is nothing more, are contrary to public policy, and therefore void".*

> This is a *prima facie* presumption i.e. one made on first sight. It can be rebutted where the restraint can be shown to be reasonable. The onus will however be on the restrainer to establish the reasonableness.

Restraints take many forms, but among the more important are the following:

- Restraints on employment. These are imposed by employers as a device to prevent employees from setting up in competition when they leave the employment.

- Restraints on the sale of a business. It is standard commercial practice to impose a restraint on the vendor of a business to protect the business goodwill the vendor has sold to the purchaser.

- Agreements between suppliers and retailers under which the retailer agrees to sell only the supplier's goods. Most cases have involved *solus* agreements under which petrol stations have agreed to sell only the petrol and other products of a particular petrol company.

- Price fixing agreements and agreements which seek to regulate or limit supplies of goods. Such agreements are regulated by statute.

Whilst there is a presumption that a contract in restraint of trade is void, if the restraint can be shown to be reasonable both in the interest of the parties to it and of the public generally, then it will be treated as valid and will survive. How this balance is achieved in practice is best examined by looking at some of the extensive case law on the subject.

Restraints on Employment

An express term found in many contracts of employment, particularly those in the private sector, is a clause which purports to restrict the freedom of the employee, on the termination of employment, from engaging in a competing business or working for a competitor for a specified period. Provided such a clause is inserted to protect a genuine *proprietary interest* of the employer and is reasonable in extent, the express restraint will be valid and enforceable. Thus the presumption that a restraint clause is invalid can be overcome if the court is satisfied:

(a)   the employer has a genuine proprietary interest worthy of protection such as clientele, confidential information, or trade connection; and

(b)   the restraint clause is drafted in such a way that it is no wider than is reasonably necessary to achieve the desired objective.

However if the court is satisfied that the real purpose of the restraint clause is simply to prevent healthy competition then it will be declared void and of no legal effect.

In *Strange v. Mann* 1965 the manager of a bookmakers agreed not to engage in a similar business to that of his employer within a twelve mile radius of his place of work on the termination of his employment. In an action to enforce the clause, the court held that as the bookmaker had little or no influence over the firm's clientele and in fact communicated with them mainly by telephone, the employer had no valid interest to protect. The primary aim of the clause was simply to prevent competition and it was declared void.

A distinction needs to be drawn between an attempt by an employer to prevent his ex-employee revealing trade secrets or lists of clients to competitors, and the attempt to simply prevent an ex-employee putting into practice the knowledge, skills and abilities acquired during his period of employment. The former is protectable, the latter is not.

In *Herbert Morris Ltd. v. Saxelby* 1916 a seven year restraint on the employee was held to be void as being simply an attempt to prevent the employee making use of the technical skill and knowledge which he acquired with his employer if he took up employment with a rival firm. The acquired skills and knowledge were not owned by the employer.

In *Forster and Sons v. Suggett* 1918, on the other hand, a covenant which was aimed at preventing the defendant divulging a secret glass making process to any rival organisation in the United Kingdom, was held to be valid and enforceable. The process was one in which the owner had a proprietary interest.

Having identified a proprietary interest worthy of protection, the next step is to analyse the restraint clause to discover whether it is reasonable in the circumstances. Factors taken into account by the court are the area of the restraint, the length of time it is to run and the nature of the work which the employer is attempting to restrain. The wording of the clause is therefore crucial, for if it is too extensive in the geographical area of protection, or of excessive duration, or it prevents working in fields which present no threat, it will be unenforceable. Each case turns on its own facts and all the circumstances are considered. There is a wealth of caselaw on the subject.

In *Fitch v. Dewes* 1921 a lifetime restraint on a solicitor's clerk from working for another solicitor within a radius of seven miles of Tamworth Town Hall was held to be valid. The House of Lords felt that the modest area of the restraint, which covered the area from which the employer relied for his clientele, offset and justified a lifetime restraint.

In *Commercial Plastics v. Vincent* 1965 the defendant was employed as a plastics technologist to co-ordinate research and development in the production of thin PVC calendering. In that role he had access to secret information so that it was a condition of his contract of employment that he would not seek employment with any of the plaintiff's competitors in the calendering field for one year after leaving employment. The Court of Appeal held that in the circumstances the restraint clause was drafted in such a way that it purported to protect the employer on a world-wide basis when, in fact, the company did not require protection outside the United Kingdom. Accordingly the condition was unreasonable and consequently void and unenforceable.

A different attitude to restraint clauses is illustrated by the decision of the Court of Appeal in *Littlewoods Organisation v. Harris* 1978. Here the defendant was employed as a director by Littlewoods, a large company which competed with Great Universal Stores Ltd. for the major share of the mail order business in the United Kingdom. As a consequence, the defendant agreed in his contract of employment that he would not, for a period of twelve months after its termination, enter into a contract of employment with Great Universal Stores Ltd. or any subsidiary company. Littlewoods, by such a restraint clause was seeking to protect confidential information of which the defendant was aware, relating to the preparation of their mail order catalogue. As Great Universal Stores operated all over the world it was argued that the restraint clause was wider than reasonably necessary to protect Littlewood's interest in the UK. A majority of the court held however that restraint clauses should be interpreted bearing in mind their object and intention. As a matter of proper construction, the clause was intended to relate to the UK mail order business only and was therefore valid and enforceable.

Crucial then to the validity of the clause is the requirement that it should not be excessive. The restraint should go no further than to limit the activities of the employee having regard to the clients the employee will have had dealings with and the business locations in which the employee has been placed by the employer. It would, for example, be unreasonable for an employer to attempt to prevent competition in geographical locations into which it has not yet penetrated.

In *Greer v. Sketchley Ltd.* 1979 the restraint clause purported to prevent the employer competing nation-wide when in fact the employer's business was limited to the Midlands and London. The argument that an employer is entitled to seek protection in geographical areas in which he intends to expand was rejected.

In *WAC Ltd. v. Whillock* 1990 the Scottish Court of Session emphasised that restrictive covenants must be construed fairly and it is *"the duty of the Court to give effect to them as they are expressed and not to correct their errors or to supply their omissions"*. Here the clause in question specifically prevented any ex-company shareholders from carrying on business in competition with the company for two years. The clause did not impose any restriction on the right of an employee to be a director or employee of another company which carried on business in competition, and so it could not prevent the employee/shareholder from becoming a director of a competing company.

If a restraint clause is drafted in such a way that it is reasonable in extent, then provided it does not offend the public interest it will be binding and can be enforced by means of an injunction. In practice such injunctions are rarely granted for the very presence of the clause acts as a sufficient deterrent.

In *Lawrence David Ltd. v. Ashton* 1989 the Court of Appeal emphasised that the decision whether or not to grant an *interlocutory* (temporary) injunction to enforce a restraint of trade clause should be taken in accordance with the principles laid down in *American Cyanamid Company. v. Ethicon Ltd.* 1975 (see later). In restraint of trade cases, the most relevant criterion is whether or not an employer would have any real prospect of succeeding in a claim for a permanent injunction at the trial.

There have also been a few exceptional cases where the courts have determined that part of a restraint clause is unreasonable but other separate parts of the clause are reasonable and would be valid and enforceable. In such circumstances, rather than declare the whole clause to be void and unenforceable, the courts have severed the unreasonable part of the contract and, provided that what remains has been able to stand alone, have declared it to be valid and enforceable.

In *Scorer v. Seymour-Jones* 1966 an employee of an estate agent who had offices in Kingsbridge and Dartmouth had entered into a contract not to carry on a business similar to that of his employer for a period of three years after leaving the employment, within a five mile radius of the Kingsbridge office. When he left his employer he set up in business as an estate agent within five miles of the Kingsbridge office, and his employer sought an injunction to restrain him from doing so. The injunction was granted by the court. The geographical area of the restraint was reasonable in the case of the Kingsbridge office, although there was no justification for the restraint regarding the Dartmouth office, since the employee had not worked there; however, it could be severed from the valid part of the contract.

In *Lucas T & Company v. Mitchell* 1974 the defendant salesman contracted that he should not for one year after the determination of his employment solicit orders within his trading area from present customers and those whom his employer supplied during the previous twelve months, and deal in the same or similar goods to those that he sold. In an action for breach of contract, the court found that the two obligations were severable so that the second clause against dealing was unreasonable and void but the first clause not to solicit orders was valid and enforceable.

In *Living Design (Home Improvements) Ltd v. Davidson* 1994 the employer attempted to restrain a promotions manager's employment activities for period of six months on the termination of her employment *"however that comes about whether lawful or not"*. The contract also attempted to deal with the possibility of the restraint being found unreasonable and void by providing for the unlawful content to be severed from the agreement. Such clauses the Court of Session held were in themselves unreasonable and would not be enforced. A wrongful dismissal in breach of contract will always have impact on the validity of a restraint clause. Also it is for the courts to determine the extent to which severance is applicable. *"The court should not strike out words where to do so would alter the scope and intention of the agreement. Moreover, in the case of a covenant by an employee, there should be severance only if the enforceable part is clearly severable and, even then, only where what it struck out is of trivial importance or technical and not part of the main import and substance of the clause."*

Sometimes an employment restraint will be in the form of a tie to operate during the subsistence of the employment arrangement, rather than to commence at the end of it.

> This was the position in *Watson v. Prager* 1991. The plaintiff, a boxer, entered into a contract in 1987 with the defendant, better known as the boxing promoter, Mickey Duff. The contract provided for the defendant to act as the plaintiff's manager for three years. The defendant had an option to extend the period for a further three years if the plaintiff won a title. He did so in 1987, taking the Commonwealth Middleweight championship. The defendant then exercised his option to extend the management contract. The plaintiff's claim was that the extended contract was an unreasonable restraint, because the defendant in his capacity as a promoter could arrange a fight for the plaintiff, and in his capacity as a personal manager require the plaintiff to take part in it. This was a conflict of interest, since the defendant's responsibility towards the career interests of the plaintiff could conflict with his personal financial interest in a promotion. The court agreed. The test for a restraint is what could happen within the scope of it. The fact that under this contract a conflict had not yet occurred, and indeed might never occur, was not relevant to the validity of the restraint.

The kind of tie occurring in *Watson v. Prager* is standard practice in the music industry where recording contracts between musicians and their recording companies generally bind the parties to each other for many years, frequently resulting in well publicised disputes when companies refuse to release their artists from the recording deal that had been signed. The musicians argue that these ties restrict their artistic freedom or complain that their companies do not sufficiently promote them. Lawyers for the musicians rely on the claim that long tie clauses are an unreasonable restraint and that the agreements containing them are frequently tainted by undue influence, the argument used in *Clifford Davis v. WEA* 1975 considered earlier in the chapter.

> In these cases a crucial question will be whether the agreement has been signed after taking independent specialist advice. If it has a court will be far less likely to declare the agreement invalid. Such was the position in *Panayoitou v. Sony Music Entertainment (UK) Ltd.* 1994 where George Michael unsuccessfully sought to extricate himself from a 15 year deal with Sony. His original contract with the company gave him the opportunity to renegotiate it, and he had used this option to secure superior terms for himself. These terms were renegotiated for him by specialist lawyers. A clause in the renegotiated contract said, *"I am not a minor and I have taken legal advice in relation to this agreement prior to entering into the same."* On this evidence the court was not prepared to declare the agreement invalid.

Restraints on the sale of a business

When a business is sold the buyer will probably seek some form of protection to prevent the seller from setting up in competition. The *Nordenfelt* case referred to above provides an illustration of the type of clause which can be used. Restraints that are imposed in such cases are more likely to survive than those imposed on employees, since the buyer and seller of a business will usually be negotiating on an equal footing, and will be legally represented. Even so, if the clause is too wide it will fail.

In *British Reinforced Concrete Engineering Co. Ltd. v. Schelff* 1921 the defendant, who operated a business selling road reinforcements in the UK, sold his business to the plaintiff. In the contract of sale the seller agreed not to compete for a specified period in the *"sale or manufacture of road reinforcements"* in the UK. The defendant took employment in the same type of business working for a competitor, and the plaintiff sued to enforce the restraint clause. The court held that had the clause been confined to *sales* it would have been valid, but to include the manufacture of reinforcements made the restraint wider than was necessary, and therefore void.

There is no rule of law which prevents a supplier and a dealer from entering into an agreement under which the supplier is to be the retailer's sole supplier, but the duration of such an agreement must not be of unreasonable length, or the restraint will be void as being against the public interest. Such arrangements are known as *solus* agreements.

In *Esso Petroleum Co. Ltd. v. Harpers Garage (Stourport) Ltd.* 1968 Harpers Garage entered into a *solus agreement* with Esso for the supply of Esso petroleum to two garages owned by Harpers. They received a discount from Esso for agreeing for take only Esso petroleum and for undertaking to keep the two garages open at all reasonable hours. The House of Lords held that the restraint which tied one garage to the agreement for four years and five months was valid, but the restraint which tied the other garage to take only Esso petroleum for twenty one years, in return for a £7000 loan to assist in the purchase and improvement of the garage, was too long and therefore invalid.

Restraints regulated by statute

Successive governments have used legislation to curb market practices which are considered to be anti-competitive and therefore contrary to the public interest. In a sense this gives rise to a curious situation in which the government attempts to limit trading freedom to make agreements which reduce competition, whilst at the same time encouraging a free market in which the stronger organisations inevitably seek to eliminate their competitors. Legislation in this field seeks to find a balance between these conflicting forces.

The first piece of modern legislation was the Monopolies and Trade Practices Act 1948, which created the body now known as the Monopolies and Mergers Commission. The Commission's main responsibility is to act as a watch-dog enquiring into possible *monopoly* situations and reporting its findings to the government for possible further action. The Fair Trading Act 1973 established the Office of the Director-General of Fair Trading. The Director-General was given authority to refer to the Commission possible areas where market concentration could be detrimental to the public interest, and was also given authority to assist the Commission in its investigation of such situations.

The 1973 Act:

(a)   defines both a monopoly situation and a merger situation, and

(b)   grants investigatory powers to the Secretary of State for Trade and Industry to issue orders to deal with monopolies and mergers.

Under the 1973 Act a monopoly/merger situation exists in either of the following circumstances:

(i) a single enterprise has (or through a merger, is likely to have) control of 25% of an individual market (a monopoly share) or

(ii) if the total assets of the *target company* (the company to be taken over) exceed £30M. This figure represents the book value of the assets, less provision for matters such as depreciation.

The Monopolies and Mergers Commission is technically independent of the government. It has a statutory duty to *"investigate and report on any question...with respect to the existence of a monopoly situation...or with respect to the creation of a merger situation.."* Both the Secretary of State and the Director-General of Fair Trading can report matters to the Commission for investigation.

In its report the Commission will decide if either of the above circumstances exist and, if so, whether or not there are any factors which could justify the government in allowing them to continue. There are many instances of industries in which a single company has at least a twenty five percent market share and the fact that they have not been referred to the Commission reflects the belief of successive governments that competition in these industries is not harmful. If a referral is made, the Commission will consider whether or not the merger or the level of concentration operates in the public interest. To decide this, the Commission must bear in mind factors such as:

- the need to promote effective competition within the UK:
- the need to protect consumers' interests regarding the price and variety of goods:
- the need to minimise the costs of production;
- the need to develop new techniques and products;
- the need to ensure unrestricted entry for new competitors into existing markets; and
- the need to ensure a balanced distribution of industry and employment within the UK.

If the Commission's report indicates areas of concern, the Secretary of State for Trade and Industry on behalf of the government has the following options open to him. He may by order:

(a) require the transfer of property from one organisation to another;

(b) require the adjustment of contracts;

(c) require the reallocation of shares in an organisation;

(d) prohibit a merger taking place.

The above orders are enforceable by court action through an injunction, that is a court order prohibiting or requiring specified action.

The process described above is illustrated in Figure 9.3 on the next page.

Legal Control of Anti-Competitive Practices

In order to make sense of the legislation designed to control trading practices regarded as anti-competitive, it is necessary to identify the parties involved in operating them, as well as the nature of the restraints the legislation targets.

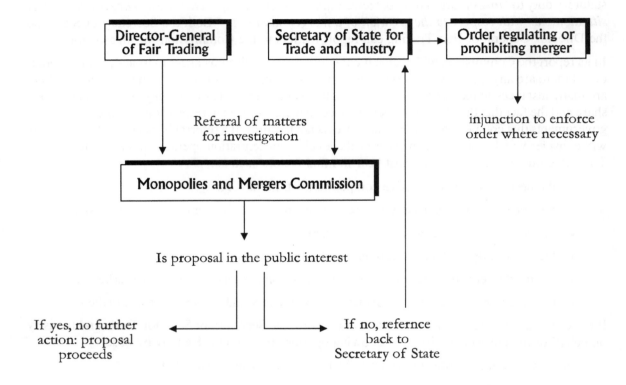

Figure 9.3   Referral to the Monopolies and Mergers Commission

Restraints in the form of restrictive trade practices are commonly operated within agreements made between suppliers, and between suppliers and their distributors and retailers.

Agreements between suppliers

Suppliers often form agreements or associations with other suppliers in the same industry with the aim of manipulating the market. This may occur by:

- limiting the supply of goods or services;

- fixing standard prices;
- standardising contractual terms of sale;
- purchasing raw materials through a *common pool* at an agreed price.

Agreements between suppliers and distributors or retailers

Suppliers who are dominant in a market may enter into agreements with distributors or retailers under which a minimum price is set for the *resale* of the supplier's products. Commonly these agreements may also restrict the distributor who may be required to stock exclusively the supplier's products. In return the retailer may be granted sole dealership over the product in a particular area, and substantial discounts on the supplier's standard price.

Examples of other restrictive practices include:

Full line Forcing. This involves a supplier requiring a distributor or retailer who wishes to stock the supplier's major product, to carry the full range of his products. For example, a shopkeeper wishing to sell a major brand of baked beans may be required to carry the full range of the supplier's tinned products.

Tie-in sales. This is a less extreme form of the same arrangement, in which the sale of one product is tied to the sale of others. Thus, a purchaser of a certain type of photocopier may also have to enter into a service agreement with the supplier to purchase all photocopying paper from him.

Reciprocal trading. This involves organisations agreeing to purchase each other's products exclusively. Thus other competitor's products cannot be purchased where such an agreement is in force.

Long term contracts. Here a distributor agrees to carry the supplier's products exclusively for a long period and therefore effectively restricts competitors from entering the market.

The practices described above are all examples of the means by which dominant suppliers may exert pressure on distributors or retailers. The ultimate sanction which may be used against distributors or retailers who fail to agree to such practices is a withdrawal of supplies.

The use of anti-competitive trading practices is of course not confined solely to the United Kingdom. Anti-competitive arrangements operate throughout the European Union, threatening the economic objectives of the member states. Community law designed to make unlawful prescribed activities plays a major role in the maintenance of healthy European markets, and domestic anti-competition law echoes it.

EC Competition Law – Articles 85 and 86 of the Treaty of Rome

These two Articles are the principal provisions of Community Law designed to control restrictive practices operated by enterprises engaged in economic or commercial activities. They of course apply directly to the UK, and create rights and obligations which take precedence over those provided for under domestic law.

Article 85

This prohibits trading practices which may affect trade between Member States and whose object or effect is *"the prevention restriction or distortion of competition"* within the Community. In particular it specifically prohibits practices which:

- directly or indirectly fix purchase or selling prices or any other trading conditions;
- limit or control production, markets, technical development, or investment;
- share markets or sources of supply;
- apply dissimilar conditions to equivalent transactions with other trading parties, thereby placing them at a competitive disadvantage; and;
- make the conclusion of contracts subject to acceptance by other parties of supplementary obligations which have no connection with the subject of such contracts.

Matters falling within the prohibitions of the Article are automatically void, however the provisions may be declared inapplicable in the case of a trading arrangement *"which contributes to improving the production or distribution of goods or to promoting technical or economic progress while allowing consumers a fair share of the resulting benefit."*

If a trading agreement infringes Article 85 the consequences are that:

(i) the restrictive part of the agreement is void and unenforceable in the national courts of the Member States. The void provisions may however be severable from the rest of the agreement;

(ii) the Commission may order the parties to end the infringement, and it has the power to impose a daily fine to enforce its order;

(iii) the parties are individually liable to fines for the breach itself. The fine may be up to a maximum of one million ECU's or 10% of the turnover of the business from the preceding business year, whichever is the greater; and

(iv) third parties may be able to recover losses sustained as a result of the prohibited agreement against the parties concerned in the national courts. This occurred in the *Garden Cottage Foods* case considered below.

The Commission has the power to grant exemption from Article 85 for individual agreements. Broadly these are agreements whose anti-competitive disadvantages are outweighed by their economic and social advantages. The Commission can also issue block exemptions.

Examples of the infringement of Article 85 have occurred under cartel arrangements and in exclusive distribution agreements. Under a cartel, companies engaged in similar commercial activities collude with each other in the fixing of prices.

In the *Dyestuffs Cartel* 1969, for instance, following information received from trade users of dyestuffs by the Commission, it carried out an investigation which revealed that the ten leading manufacturers of dyestuffs had over a period of four years raised their prices uniformly and virtually simultaneously on their manufactured goods. The companies were fined.

A celebrated exclusive distribution agreement which infringed Article 85, *Consten and Grundig* 1966, was considered by the European Court of Justice. Grundig had established throughout the Community exclusive distributorship arrangements. In France, its exclusive distribution agreement was made with Consten. Consten agreed with Grundig not to sell Grundig products other than in France, and was granted by Grundig the right to register the Grundig trademark as its own French trademark. Subsequently, when another company imported into France Grundig products, Consten responded by bringing proceedings against the importer for breach of trademark. The European Court of Justice held that the trademark agreement was a prohibited agreement under Article 85, and therefore void. Its objective was to prevent third parties importing Grundig products into France, and this was a restrictive trade practice.

Decisions of the European Court of Justice have established that agreements coming within Article 85 will not be treated as prohibited unless it can be shown that the agreement has an "appreciable" effect on trade and competition between Member States in relation to the relevant market concerned. What is an appreciable effect is a question of fact in each case: *Suiker Unie v. EC Commission* 1975.

Article 86

This provides that *"Any abuse by one or more undertakings of a dominant position within the Common Market or in a substantial part of it shall be prohibited as incompatible with the Common Market in so far as it may affect trade between Member States. Such abuse may, in particular, consist in:*

(a) *directly or indirectly imposing unfair purchase or selling prices or other unfair trading conditions;*

(b) *limiting production, markets or technical development to the prejudice of consumers;*

(c) *applying dissimilar conditions to equivalent transactions with other trading parties, thereby placing them at a competitive disadvantage;*

(d) *making the conclusion of contracts subject to acceptance by other parties of supplementary obligations which …. have no connection with the subject of such contracts."*

Essentially for Article 86 to be infringed there must be (i) a dominant position held, (ii) an abuse of that position, and (iii) an effect on the trade between Member States resulting from that abuse.

Dominance involves possessing the power to impede effective competition with the relevant market. Usually dominance will be associated with the market share held by a particular business.

In *Europemballage and Continental Can v. Commission* 1973 the Commission took the view that Continental Can, an American company, was in a dominant market position which it had abused, as a result of it acquiring firstly a German company which was the largest German producer of metal packaging (tin cans, etc.), and then acquiring a majority shareholding in a Dutch company, which was the main producer of such packaging in the Benelux Countries. The court recognised that the effect was to have largely eliminated competition in relation to such products in the North Western area of the EC, thus infringing Article 86, although on technical grounds the Commission's claim failed, for it had not sufficiently precisely defined the market being abused.

In *Garden Cottage Foods Ltd. v. Milk Marketing Board* 1983 the appellant company alleged breach of Article 86 by the Board. The facts were that the company's business involved it purchasing butter from the Board which it then resold in bulk to purchasers in the UK and Europe, at a profit. A problem that the company had involving the packaging of its butter led the Board to withdraw its direct supplying arrangements with the company. This was despite the problem having been apparently overcome. Instead the Board said the company must purchase from independent distributors nominated by the Board. These distributors were in fact competitors of the company. It would have to pay more for the butter and as a result could no longer remain in business, since it could not maintain a competitive price. In the Court of Appeal an interlocutory injunction was granted against the Board, requiring it to continue to maintain normal supplies until the trial of the Article 86 application. The House of Lords held however that such an injunction cannot lie where the evidence shows that on a trial of the action damages would be an adequate remedy and the defendant would be able to meet the payment (the principle in *American Cyanamid v. Ethicon Ltd.* 1975) . This was clearly the case here. The loss of the company's butter business was purely financial. The injunction was withdrawn, the court taking the view that the eventual claim would be for damages. It is not altogether clear however whether infringement of Article 86 does enable an English Court to award damages.

The significant powers of the Commission in the enforcement of Articles 85 and 86 is graphically shown in the *Tetra Pak* case in 1992. Tetra Pak is a world leader in liquid food packaging, having a market share of between 80%-90%. The Commission investigated the market practices of the company and established infringement of Article 86. The infringements were based upon a range of abuses, in particular onerous tying conditions attached to the sale of the company's machinery, excessively priced and lengthy leasing arrangements, and draconian penalty clauses in the event of contractual breaches. The company had previously been found to have abused its market position in 1991. In the present case the company was fined 75 million ECU's (over £85m), and the various abuses were ordered to be ended.

UK competition legislation

The Competition Act 1980 echoes the language of EC competition legislation. Under the Act trade practices, other than those registrable under the Restrictive Trade Practices Act 1976, (see below) which *"involve a course of conduct which has, and is intended to have the effects of restricting, distorting or preventing competition in connection with the production, supply and acquisition of goods and the securing of services in the UK"* are treated as "anti-competitive practices". Whereas EC legislation deals with competition within the broad geographical area of the Community, the 1980 Act is obviously restricted to UK markets.

A detailed investigation procedure is set out under the 1980 Act and is shown in the figure on the next page (Figure 9.4). Essentially all the alleged anti-competitive practices are subject to preliminary investigation by the Director General of Fair Trading. If the practice is proven to be anti-competitive, action can be taken by the Secretary for Trade and Industry.

Particular practices by individual organisations may now be investigated and if necessary prevented without the need to investigate the industry as a whole. However, only large organisations are brought under scrutiny, that is companies with a turnover of more than £5m or more than a 25% share of their particular market.

Unlike the Restrictive Trade Practices Act 1976 there is no presumption under the 1980 Act that an agreement referred to the Commission operates against the public interest. In determining this question of public interest, the Commission simply takes into account all matters which appear to it to be relevant in the particular circumstances. For example, a manufacturer may offer its products to a supermarket at much bigger discounts than it offers to corner shops. The practice of offering such discounts could be referred to the Commission as being anti-competitive in that the number of corner shops is likely to be reduced because of the practice. The Commission in deciding the question of public interest, would have to balance the advantage to the consumer of obtaining lower-priced products against the convenience of the consumer of local shopping.

Having reached a conclusion on a reference, the Commission must then report to the Secretary of State for Trade who has the power, by order, to declare an anti-competitive practice unlawful if the offender refuses to refrain from that type of conduct. The Act expressly excludes restrictive practices already registrable under the Restrictive Trade Practices Act 1976 to prevent an overlap of proceedings.

The types of practice which may be investigated by the Director-General of Fair Trading under the 1980 Act include the giving of specific discounts, rebates and allowances, full-line forcing, tie-in sales, reciprocal trading and long-term contracts.

The Restrictive Trade Practices Act 1976

It was mentioned above that the Competition Act 1980 does not apply to agreements registered under the Restrictive Trade Practices Act 1976. Under this Act, duties are imposed on the Director-General of Fair Trading. He is required to compile and maintain a register of restrictive agreements, and also to bring such agreements before the Restrictive Practices Court, which has the function of deciding whether they are contrary to the public interest. The types of agreement registrable under the Restrictive Trade Practices Act are those made by suppliers of goods which lead to a restriction relating to:

- the price charged for goods;
- the terms and conditions of supply of goods;
- the quantities or description of goods to be supplied;
- the process of manufacture to be applied to any goods;
- those who may obtain the goods;
- the area in which the goods may be obtained.

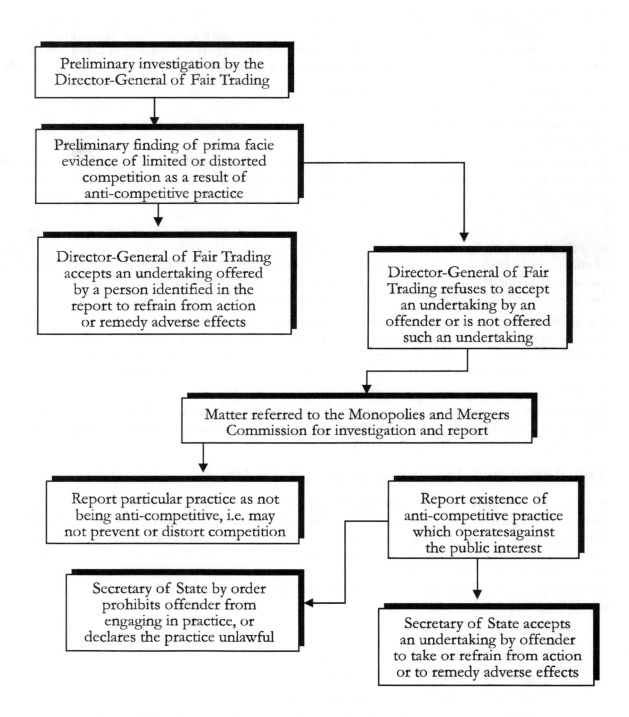

Figure 9.4   Investigation procedure under the Competition Act 1980

A registrable agreement is presumed to be contrary to public policy and it is for this reason the Director-General of Fair Trading must bring such agreements before the Restrictive Practices Court. If the parties can satisfy the court that the agreement does not harm the public interest then it may be declared valid. To assist the parties there are eight grounds, called the *eight gateways,* set out in the Act. If they can establish any one of the gateways then the agreement will be treated as a valid one.

The gateways seek to:

(i)   protect the public against injury;

(ii)   counteract restrictive measures taken by anyone not a party to the agreement;

(iii) enable the parties to negotiate fair terms with a monopolistic supplier or customer.

In fact, relatively few agreements have been approved by the court, indicating the tough line that it has taken with regard to restrictive practices.

> In *Re: Chemist Federation Agreement* 1958 an agreement by the Federation to limit the sale of patent medicines to the public, allowing their sale only by qualified pharmacists, was declared void. The court was unimpressed by the argument that the restriction was necessary to protect the public against injury in view of the potentially dangerous nature of the goods being sold.

> The agreement itself does not need to be legally enforceable. In one case an arrangement between a group of contractors to delay submitting their individual tenders until they had met to discuss each others tenders was held to constitute a restrictive trading agreement (*Re: Installations at Exeter Hospital Agreement* 1970).

The Resale Prices Act 1976

One of the most fundamental aspects of competition between retailers is that they should have the ability to charge whatever price they wish. Yet one of the most widely used restrictive agreements was the practice by dominant suppliers of imposing standard prices for their goods on all their retail outlets. These *resale price maintenance* agreements were forced on distributors and retailers by suppliers, who could always threaten to withhold supplies to ensure compliance. Such agreements were originally controlled by legislation in 1964, their regulation now being contained in the Resale Prices Act 1976. Under this Act it is unlawful for suppliers to make agreements to withhold supplies from, or supply on less favourable terms to, distributors who do not observe resale price conditions. As with other restrictive practices, the Restrictive Practices Court has power to grant exemption on one or other of the grounds specified in the Act upon an application made by the Director-General of Fair Trading.

Up to 1993 there were two fields in which the court had granted exemption orders under the Act, books and medicines. In 1993 the exemption for books was removed, leaving now only medicines as the only exemption. In *Re: Medicaments Reference (No. 2)* 1971 the court found that ending resale price maintenance would cause a substantial reduction in the varieties of medicines available to the public, in the number of retail chemists, and in the services provided by pharmacies. At the time of writing this, remaining exemption is due to be challenged by the Safeway Supermarket chain.

Apart from this single exemption it is *prima facie* unlawful for a manufacturer to withhold supplies in an attempt to enforce a minimum resale price. Such a refusal to supply goods could, however, be justified if the producer shows that the dealer in question has, within the preceding 12 months, been selling the same or similar goods as a loss leader, that is selling at a retail price below wholesale cost in order to attract custom for that and other products.

In *Oxford Printing Ltd. v. Letraset Ltd.* 1970 the defendants withheld supplies from the plaintiffs, who had cut the price of the defendant's products and also used them to promote the sales of a competitor's product. Such withholding of supplies was held to be lawful in the circumstances.

At common law the difficulty of directly enforcing a resale price maintenance agreement can be seen in *Dunlop Pneumatic Tyre Co. Ltd. v. Selfridge and Co. Ltd.* 1915.

Here Dunlops sold tyres to a wholesaler on terms that he should resell them only at list price. The terms of the sale included the following provisions:

"Price Maintenance agreement is to be entered into by trade purchasers of Dunlop Motor Tyres

We will not alter or remove or in any way tamper with any of the manufacture marks or numbers on Dunlop covers or tubes.

We will not sell or offer any Dunlop motor tyres, covers or tubes to any private customers or to any co-operative society at prices below those mentioned in the said price list current at the time of sale, nor give to any such customer or society any cash or other discounts, or advantages reducing the same. We will not sell or offer any Dunlop motor tyres, covers or tubes to any other person, firm or company at prices less than those mentioned in the said price list.

We agree to pay to the Dunlop Pneumatic Tyre Co. Ltd., the sum of £5 for each and every tyre, cover or tube sold or offered in breach of this agreement, as and by way of liquidated damages and not as a penalty, but without prejudice to any other rights or remedies you or the Dunlop Pneumatic Tyre Co. Ltd., may have hereunder."

The wholesaler sold some of the tyres to Selfridges, who also agreed not to sell at below Dunlop's list price. However they subsequently did so and Dunlop sought an injunction against them and damages. The House of Lords held that the action must fail, since there was no privity of contract between Selfridges and Dunlop, in other words the parties were not contractually bound to each other. Dunlop's contract was with the wholesaler not Selfridges.

Privity of Contract

The doctrine of privity of contract has already been referred to in the context of the principles applying to contractual consideration, and its effect can be far reaching as the *Dunlop case* above shows. The doctrine arises out of the contractual principle that consideration must move from the promisee, so that as a general rule the legal effects of a contract apply only to the contracting parties. A company shareholder for example is unable to take the benefit of a contract made by the company in the sense of obtaining personal rights under it, for the company and the shareholder are separate persons. Similarly a purchaser of a new vehicle who discovers faults in it has contractual rights against the garage which sold it, but not against the manufacturer. The manufacturer was not *privy* or party to the contract. It would be different if the manufacturer had issued a guarantee which the customer completed and returned when the vehicle was purchased. This would constitute a collateral contract between the manufacturer and the purchaser. If however the faults were the cause of physical injury to the purchaser a remedy could be sought outside contract law under the Consumer Protection Act 1977, and at common law a duty of care is owed by the manufacturer to an ultimate consumer that is independent of any contractual relationship between them.

There are a number of exceptions to the doctrine of privity of contract, where a person who has not provided consideration under a contract and is therefore a *stranger* to it may nevertheless possess legal rights and obligations. They include the following:

- Contracts made by an agent acting within his authority, but contracting on his principals behalf without indicating to the other party that he is an agent. In such circumstances the *doctrine of undisclosed principal* allows the principal to step in and sue, or be sued, on the contract.

- Where there has been an *assignment* of contractual rights, such as the right to a debt, the assignee can sue the original debtor under s.136 Law of Property Act 1925. If the creditor fails to notify the debtor that the assignment has been made, the debtor can validly discharge the debt by payment to the creditor rather than the assignee.

- Under s.11 Married Womens' Property Act 1882 the parties who benefit under a life policy if they are a surviving spouse and/or children of the insured can sue the insurance company on the policy.

- Under the Road Traffic Act 1988, which enables a person driving a vehicle with the owners consent to cover under the owners insurance policy in certain circumstances. It also permits recovery of compensation to a third party injured by a driver in respect of the drivers compulsory third party risks cover.

- In respect of *restrictive covenants* imposed upon land where subsequent purchasers will be bound to observe the covenant.

- Under the Resale Prices Act 1976 where the Restrictive Practices Court has exempted a resale price maintenance agreement, resale price maintenance conditions imposed by a seller will bind anyone obtaining the goods with a view to resale, if they have notice of the restriction.

Beyond these exceptions it seems that common law developments to reduce the impact of the privity principle are unlikely.

Lord Denning attempted to do so in *Jackson v. Horizon Holidays* 1975. The plaintiff had booked a months holiday in Ceylon staying in an hotel. The defendant's brochure described the hotel facilities. These included a swimming pool, a mini-golf course and a hairdressing salon. The hotel in fact had none of these facilities and its food was poor. The Court of Appeal granted the plaintiff damages of £1,100. This represented not only his loss, but also that of his family who accompanied him, even though they were not parties to the contract. The court said that the plaintiff had made the contract partly for their benefit. The House of Lords in *Woodar v. Wimpey* 1980 criticised the *Jackson* decision. They rejected the view put forward in Jackson that there is any rule of English law enabling a contract made with A for the benefit of B, to entitle A to sue for damages suffered by B which B could have recovered if the contract had been made with him. Mr. Jackson's damages, said their Lordships, were increased because he not only suffered discomfort and disappointment personally, but witnessed his family similarly distressed.

In *Foster v. Silvermere Golf and Equestrian Centre* 1981 Dillon J referred to this restriction of English contract law enabling only the parties to the contract to recover for their personal losses as *"a blot on our law and most unjust,* and further judicial criticism has more recently come from Steyn LJ who in *Darlington BC v. Wiltshire Northern Ltd.* 1995 said that there are no *"logical or policy reasons why the law should deny effectiveness to a contract for the benefit of a third party when that is the expressed intention of the parties. Moreover often the parties, particularly third parties, organise their affairs on the faith of the contract. They rely on the contract. It is therefore unjust to deny effectiveness to such a contract..."*

In the *Darlington* case the council was involved in the construction of a recreation centre. For financial reasons the deal involved the council in arranging for a finance company to carry out the building work. The council would pay the finance company on completion of the work. To this end the finance company contracted with the defendants for the work to be carried out. The intention was to assign the rights of the finance company under the construction contract to the council when the building was complete. This was duly done. Problems arose however when alleged major defects in the building were discovered. Could the council claim against the construction company, with whom it had no contract? The court had no difficulty in recognising that it could, since it had always been understood that the building was being constructed for the council.

Assignment The Premises

Midlands & Northern Property Holdings plc is a company whose business involves the development of industrial and commercial sites for sale and for letting. R & C Enterprises Ltd., a small company based in Northampton, had been seeking commercial premises for some time when one of its directors became aware of an industrial unit that Midlands & Northern had available on a small development just outside town. Following a site visit and a meeting between the director and the representative of the property company, the director, Tom Armstrong raised with the rest of his board the possibility of taking a ten year lease of the premises, which Midlands & Northern were offering.

The company's main business is in coachworks, which involves it building and fitting different types of bodywork to lorry bases. Whilst the existing site was adequate for this work, the company had decided to diversify and use its skills and expertise in the construction of mobile buildings for schools and building sites. It was for this purpose that the new premises were required. Following a further meeting with the representative from Midlands & Northern, a number of questions were raised by Tom Armstrong. In particular he wanted to know if planning permission would be granted to use the premises in the way anticipated by the company; whether the large hard surfaced area to the rear of the site was included in the lease; and whether the premises were suitable for the anticipated use. The representative wrote in reply; *"I can assure you that planning consent for the change of use of the premises will be forthcoming, following a conversation I have had with the Chief Planning Officer of the local authority. I can confirm that the premises include the hard area referred to by you. I would add that the premises are entirely suited to the business operations planned by you, and that I see no reason why the business should not operate profitably."*

R & C Enterprises Ltd. leased the premises. A month after doing so planning consent for their proposed change was refused. The lease granted to them makes no reference to the hard area to the rear of the premises, which is now being used by an adjoining owner, and the vehicular access to the premises is about to be cut off for months for major works of repair and improvement to be carried out by sub-contractors acting for Midlands & Northern. You work for R & C Enterprises, and Tom Armstrong has asked you to produce a report for him, which he is anxious to establish whether it is possible to terminate the lease. He has also given you a letter received from Midlands & Northern which states that due to an error by the company surveyor in correctly measuring the internal dimensions of the premises, the quarterly rental being charged is £1,000 less than it should be. The letter adds, *"you were aware that the rental of the premises was based upon the number of square meters of floor space in the factory site, since this was discussed by us during negotiations"*. Tom is wondering how to respond to the letter.

Task

Produce a report requested by Tom Armstrong, and draft a reply to the letter from Midlands & Northern, for Mr. Armstrong's approval, which rejects their claim, and contains a statement of the legal grounds for doing so.

Legal Terms found in Chapter 10

Conditions	• major terms which allow for repudiation and damages if broken
Damages	• contractual remedy under which a monetary award is made
Discharge of contract	• bringing a contract to an end
Estoppel	• rule of evidence under which a person is prevented from denying the truth of a previous statement of fact
Exclusion clauses	• contract terms seeking to eliminate specified or general contractual liabilities
Express Terms	• contractual regulations expressly agreed orally or in writing by the parties to a contract
Frustration	• principle under which a contract, whose performance cannot be achieved through no fault of the parties, is treated as discharged
Implied terms	• contractual obligations which are implied into a contract by operation of the common law or statute
Injunction	• court order ordering or restraining some course of action
Interlocutory injunction	• temporary injunction
Liquidated damages	• claim for damages where the amount being sought has been quantified
Quantum meruit	• 'as much as he has deserved'
Rescind	• to annul or cancel for instance a contract
Restitutio in integrum	• returning everything to the state as it was before
Specific performance	• equitable remedy under which the court orders a contracting party to carry out their promises
Terms	• the contractual undertakings of the parties
Unliquidated damages	• claim for damages where the amount is not quantified
Warranties	• minor terms which if broken enable only a claim for damages to be brought

The Contract: Terms Discharge and Remedies

Contract Terms

The terms of a contract are the obligations owed by the parties to each other under it. All contracts contain terms. In transactions involving large sums of money, or where the agreement is of a complex or technical nature, the terms are likely to be numerous and detailed. By inserting terms into the contract the parties will be trying to clarify their mutual obligations. They will be attempting to define the nature and scope of the contract, and will try to anticipate eventualities which may possibly emerge after the contract has been made but before it has been carried out. Thus they may make provision for such contingencies as shortages of labour or materials. Different types of contract obviously reflect different sets of terms appropriate to the nature and purpose of the agreement. For example if the contract involves the construction of a building its terms will seek to identify clearly the specifications involved. On the other hand the granting of a lease or tenancy will concentrate on matters such as who has responsibility for carrying out repairs, and how the property should be used. It is not only large organisations which are involved in detailed and technical contracts; even small organisations will encounter documents such as leases when they set up in a business and seek accommodation. Clearly not all contracts contain detailed terms. In the simplest contracts terms will be single promises made by each party to the other. In more complex agreements however the contract may run into many pages of detailed obligations. An extensive set of contract terms is set out in Chapter 11.

The classification of terms

The terms of a contract vary in importance. Sometimes the contract itself will say how much importance is attached to a certain term, while in other cases it may be left to the court to decide the question because the parties to the contract have not made it clear. The value that is attached to each term is of great significance because it determines what the consequences will be if the particular term is broken.

Major terms are called *conditions*. A condition is a term which is said to go to the root of the contract, and where performance is essential to the contract. If it is broken the innocent party has the right to treat the contract as repudiated and to refuse to perform his or her obligations under it. In addition the injured party may sue for damages.

Minor terms are called *warranties*. They are terms which are said to be collateral to the main purpose of the contract. In consequence, if a warranty is broken the contract still stands, and the innocent party does not have the right to treat the contract as being at an end, merely the right to damages.

Where breach of a condition occurs the injured party is not bound to repudiate the contract. As an alternative the injured party can elect to treat the contract as subsisting, treating the breach of condition as if it were a warranty. The obligation that has been broken is then referred to as an *ex post facto* warranty, and only damages will be available. There may be sound commercial reasons for treating a breach of condition as one of warranty, and letting the contract stand. The innocent party may realise that if the contract is repudiated it will be difficult to obtain an alternative supplier of the goods and services in question, or undue delay and inconvenience will be caused if the goods have to be disassembled, removed from the premises and returned to the supplier.

> Two similar cases illustrate the distinction between conditions and warranties. In *Bettini v. Gye* 1876 the plaintiff, an opera singer agreed in writing to sing in various concerts and operas over a period of three and a half months, and to be present at rehearsals for at least six days before the engagements were due to begin. Due to illness he arrived with only two days of rehearsals left, and as a result the defendant terminated the agreement. Looking at the contract as a whole, the court decided that the rehearsal clause was not a condition, but merely a warranty, for which damages alone was the remedy. The contract had been wrongfully terminated and the plaintiff could counter-claim for damages.

> In *Poussard v. Spiers and Pond* 1876 an opera singer was unable to take part in the first week of performances due to illness. In the meantime the management had engaged a substitute and refused the original singer the part when she arrived. They were held to be entitled to do so, for her non-attendance at the performances was a breach of a vital term of the contract.

Sometimes it is impossible to say whether a term is a condition or a warranty when it is first created because it will be so broadly framed that it could be broken in a major respect or a minor respect, and therefore it is only possible to say after the event what effect the particular breach should have on the contract. Such terms are referred to as *innominate*, meaning intermediate terms.

> The position is illustrated in *Hong Kong Fir Shipping Co. Ltd. v. Kawasaki Kaisen Kaisha Ltd.* 1962. Here a ship was chartered on terms that stated what it would be *"in every way fitted for ordinary cargo service"*. Inefficient engine-room staff and old engines contributed to a number of breakdowns so that during the first seven months of the charter the ship was only able to be at sea for eight and a half weeks. The charterers repudiated the contract. The Court of Appeal decided that this particular breach did not entitle the charterers to repudiate. Diplock J stated that the terms in the contract were not really either a condition or a warranty but rather *"an undertaking, one breach of which may give rise to an event which relieves the charterer of further performance ... if he so elects and another breach of which may not give rise to such an event but entitle him only ... to damages."*

A further illustration is provided by the case of *Cehave NV v. Bremer Handelsgesell-schaft, mbh, The Hansa Nord* 1975. A term in a contract under which the defendants agreed to sell citrus pulp pellets to the plaintiffs stipulated *"shipment to be made in good condition"*. Delivery was by consignments. When delivery of one of the consignments was made, out of the 3293 tons supplied 1260 tons were found to be damaged. The market price for such goods had fallen at this time, and the buyers used the damaged goods as an opportunity for repudiating the whole contract on grounds of breach of condition. In fact they later bought exactly the same cargo at well below half the original contract price from a third party who had obtained it from the original sellers. They then used it to make cattle food which was exactly what they had bought it for in the first place. The Court of Appeal held the term to be an intermediate one, and damages rather than repudiation was an appropriate remedy. Lord Denning commented *"if a small portion of the whole cargo was not in good condition and arrived a little unsound, it should be met by a price allowance. The buyer should not have the right to reject the whole cargo unless it was serious or substantial."* In the later case of *Bunge Corporation, New York v. Tradax Export SA Panama* 1981 the House of Lords emphasised that parties cannot artificially create intermediate terms. Whether a term is to be regarded as intermediate is a matter of construction.

Terms and conditions of employment

While *terms* of employment contain the mutual rights and obligations of the parties *conditions* of employment refer to matters over which the employer alone has control and which are subject to unilateral change. A contractual term could include a condition of employment which would entitle an employer to require the employee's compliance without his consent.

In *White v. Reflecting Road Studs Ltd.* 1991 a term in the employee's contract provided that *"the company reserves the right when determined by requirements of operational efficiency to transfer employees to alternative work and it is a condition of employment that they are willing to do so when requested"*. This meant that the employee could be lawfully transferred from one department to another without his consent.

It is common practice in many spheres of employment for the employer to issue work rules by printing notices or handing out rule books. Such rule books often contain instructions as to time-keeping, meal breaks, disciplinary offences and grievance procedures, sickness and pension rights, job descriptions, and the employer's safety policy. Although there is still some doubt as to the legal status of work rules, the present view is that such documents are unlikely to contain contractual terms. One school of thought is that work rules should be regarded as *conditions* rather than *terms* of employment, and as such they should be subject to unilateral change by the employer. For example, while the number of hours worked would normally be the subject of express agreement and constitute a contractual *term,* instructions as to when these hours should be worked will normally be contained in a rule book and as a *condition* be liable to unilateral change.

In *Dryden v. Greater Glasgow Health Board* 1992 the Employment Appeal Tribunal decided that an employer was entitled to introduce a rule imposing a smoking ban at the workplace and the staff had no implied right to smoke. *"An employer is entitled to make rules for the conduct of employees in their place of work within the scope of the contract"*.

Where, however, a rule book is given or referred to by the employer at the time the contract of employment is formed, the fact that the employee has agreed that it is to be part of the contract and acknowledges that fact by his signature would more than likely give the rule book contractual effect. Certainly there is case law authority which suggests that by posting a notice of the fact that the rule book is to have contractual effect, an employer would ensure that these rules become incorporated into individual contracts of employment.

How terms originate

The examples of terms that have so far been considered are those which have been expressly agreed between the parties. There are however two additional sources of contract terms, the courts and Parliament. Both these law making institutions are responsible for inserting terms into contracts, independent of the wishes of the parties involved. The broad justification for doing so appears to be the desire to enable the contract to *function*, and in appropriate cases to achieve a level of *protection* for consumers of goods and services. Terms may thus be express or implied.

Express terms

These are the terms which have been specifically detailed and agreed upon by the parties. The parties are free to classify them in advance as being conditions or warranties if they so wish. If they fail to do so it will be for the court to decide how significant a particular breach is by looking at the term in relation to the contract as a whole. Even where the contract itself classifies a term or terms, the court still reserves the right to construe the meaning of the term by looking at the contract as a whole.

> In *L Schuler AG v. Wickham Machine Tool Sales* 1973 the appellant company, a German organisation, by an agreement, granted sole selling rights over their panel presses in England, to the respondents Wickham. The agreement provided that Wickham's representatives should visit six named firms every week for the purpose of seeking orders. Clause 7(6) indicated the status of this particular obligation stating that *"it shall be a condition of this agreement"*. On certain occasions Wickham's employees failed to satisfy the requirement, and Schulers responded to this by claiming that they could repudiate the contract, arguing that a single failure would be sufficient to constitute a breach. The House of Lords rejected this argument. Such a construction was so unreasonable that the parties could not have intended it.

As we saw in the previous chapter some statements made prior to contract will constitute representations. Sometimes a representation will actually become a term of the contract. This being so, if the term is broken the innocent party will be able to bring an action for breach of contract, rather than for misrepresentation. It is often difficult to determine whether a representation has in fact become a term where there has been no express incorporation of it, and the courts will take into consideration a number of factors. For instance, a representation will be presumed not to have become a term if a formal written contract is executed after the representation and does not contain it. There is, however, one main test to be applied: whether the person making the statement was promising its accuracy. If so, the statement will become a contractual term.

How difficult it can be to draw a distinction between representations and terms is illustrated by *Oscar Chess Ltd. v. Williams* 1957. The defendant wished to take a new car on hire-purchase terms from the from the plaintiffs, who were car dealers. In part exchange he offered them his own car, which was described in the log book as a 1948 Morris. He confirmed the vehicle to be a 1948 model, honestly believing this to be so, and received £290 part-exchange allowance. Eight months later the plaintiffs discovered that the car was a 1939 model, for which only £175 should have been allowed. They sued the defendant for the difference, i.e. £115. The Court of Appeal decided by a majority that the defendant's statement about the age of the car was not a term of the contract. Lord Denning made the point that, *"as motor dealers, the plaintiffs could without difficulty have checked the true age of the car with the manufacturers by giving them the engine chassis numbers."*

If the parties to a contract of employment have included their respective rights and obligations under it in a signed document called the contract of employment, then this document will contain the express terms of the agreement. In many cases however the express term of a contract of employment can only be determined by establishing the content and status of the various documents transferred during the *recruitment* process and what the parties orally agreed at the inteview. Express terms will be found in the statutory statement of the main term and conditions of employment, a job application form and in rare cases even a job advertisement.

In *Holliday Concrete v. Wood* 1979 a job advertisement indicated that a fifteen month contract was available and this was held to be the period of employment.

In *Joseph Steinfeld v. Reypert* 1979 the fact that a post was advertised as *"sales manager"* indicated the contractual status of the successful applicant.

In the event of conflict between the writing and what was orally agreed the written statements will normally have priority. However the express terms are decided by discovering the intention of the parties to the contract and it could be the case that an oral promise has more significance because of the importance attached to it.

In *Hawker Siddely Power Engineering Ltd. v. Rump* 1979 the complainant was employed as a heavy goods vehicle driver in 1973 and signed a contract of employment which stated that he would be liable to travel all over the country. The obligation was confirmed in a later statement of terms and conditions of employment issued in 1976 and signed by the complainant. In fact the complainant had made it clear when he took the job that because of his wife's illness he would not travel outside the south of England. This had been orally agreed by the manager when the contract was signed. In 1978 the complainant refused to obey an instruction to travel to Scotland. This led to his dismissal. One issue before the tribunal was whether he was contractually obliged to do so. The tribunal thought not deciding that the promise to work only in the south was an oral contractual term. Here *"there was a direct promise by the employers which must have become part of the contract of employment because it was following upon the promise that the employee signed the contract"*. Even the subsequent written statement which included a mobility clause signed by the employer was insufficient to exclude the oral term previously agreed, for the employee *"had no notice that the oral term that he had secured was going to form no part of his new contract. The mere putting in front of him a document and invitation for him to sign it could not be held to be a variation by agreement so as to exclude the important oral term which he had previously secured".*

Terms implied by the courts

It is not the task of the courts to insert new terms into contracts, but rather to interpret those that already exist. But they will sometimes imply a term to give a contract *business efficacy*. The rationale underlying such an approach is that since the parties clearly intended to create a binding agreement, they must have intended to include terms to make the contract function.

In *The Moorcock* 1889 a term was implied by the court in a contract between a ship owner and a firm of wharfingers. The contract was to use their wharf on the Thames for the discharging and loading of his vessel, the Moorcock. He was going to pay a charge for the use of the cranes alongside the wharf. While the vessel was moored there she was damaged when the tide ebbed and she came to rest on a ridge of hard ground. The Court of Appeal held that the wharfingers were liable for breach of an implied term that the mooring was safe for the vessel. *"In business transactions such as this,"* said Bowen LJ, *"what the law desires to effect by implication is to give such business efficacy to the transaction as must have been intended at all events by both parties who are business-men."*

In *Irwin v. Liverpool City Council* 1977 the defendant council let a flat in an upper floor of a block of flats to the plaintiff tenant. A term was implied by the court into a tenancy agreement between the plaintiff and the defendant council to the effect that the defendants had an obligation to keep in repair the stairs and the lift in the block of flats which they owned, thus ensuring that the plaintiff could gain access to his property.

In *Baylis v. Barnett* 1988 the plaintiff lent the defendant a sum of money. The defendant knew this involved the plaintiff in borrowing the money from a bank. Although the parties did not discuss the question of interest the court held there was an implied term that the defendant would indemnify the plaintiff for any interest he owed to the bank.

Two fields in which the courts have been active in implying terms are in the employment relationship, and in the landlord and tenant relationship. Thus at common law there are certain fundamental obligations owed by the employer to the employee and vice versa, which are implied by the courts. For instance the *employee* owes a duty of good faith to the employer at common law, whilst the *employer* has an obligation to provide for the employee's safety.

In *Woods v. W H Car Services Ltd.* 1982 the court acknowledged that in every employment contract there is an implied term of great importance, that of trust and confidence between the parties. Such a term requires that employers *"will not without reasonable and proper cause, conduct themselves in a manner calculated or likely to destroy the relationship of trust and confidence between employer and employee".*

In the landlord and tenant relationship the common law imposes an obligation upon the tenant not to commit *waste*, i.e. (*physical harm*), to the premises being occupied, and upon the landlord to provide the tenant with quiet enjoyment, that is not to interfere with the tenant's occupation of the premises. Parliament has also legislated to insert terms into certain categories of contract, primarily with the view to protecting the weaker party from exploitation by the stronger.

Statutory implied terms

Parliament has been particularly active during the post-war period in the use of legislation to introduce specific terms into certain types of contractual agreement. Statutory implied terms are now many and varied and, being statutory, the obligations they impose tend to be detailed. In many cases statutory terms are implied as a legislative attempt to counter-balance the inequalities that exist in a particular bargaining situation. In other cases statutory terms can be seen as a vehicle for effecting profound social and economic change, such as the insertion of the *equality clause* in contracts of employment. Yet again, there are those statutory terms which simply represent a codification of judicially recognised mercantile custom, for example those within the Sale of Goods Act 1979. Detailed examples of statutory implied terms can be found in Chapter 11.

Exclusion Clauses

Legal liability can arise in a variety of different ways, for example through misrepresentation, breach of contract or negligence. One way of trying to reduce or extinguish this liability is by the use of exclusion or limitation clauses. An *exclusion clause* in a contract is an express term which attempts to exempt one party from all liability for failure to perform some part of the contract.

An example of an exclusion clause in a contract for the supply of goods is: *"the seller hereby excludes all liability for breach of any express or implied condition, term or warranty"*. A *limitation clause* on the other hand is slightly different for it aims to *reduce* rather than extinguish the liability. These clauses may be drafted to place an overall financial limit on the liability of one party for breach of contract, or to limit liability to the replacement of goods supplied, or to deprive the other of a particular remedy for the breach. In this text we will be dealing with the legal principles which apply both to the exclusion and limitation of liability, but, for convenience, we will refer to exclusion only which can be taken to mean total or partial exclusion of liability.

The principle of freedom of contract permits the use of exclusion clauses. The courts however have developed a number of common law principles designed to rob such clauses of effect in certain circumstances. These principles were developed because the courts recognised that the use of exclusion clauses could result in unfairness to one of the contracting parties. Judicial controls were developed largely by the application of existing principles of contract law and are necessarily limited in scope. It was not until the 1970's that legislation was introduced. The Unfair Contract Terms Act 1977 now provides a comprehensive set of rules which regulate both the use of exclusion clauses in contracts and the use of non-contractual notices. These rules have been supplemented by the Unfair Terms in Consumer Contracts Regulations 1994 which were introduced to give effect to the 1993 European Council Directive on Unfair Terms in Consumer Contracts. The Regulations do not alter the operation of the 1977 Act, which remains unchanged, but provide an additional set of rules designed to strengthen consumer protection in this area.

In determining the validity of an exclusion clause, several legal principles have to be applied. The first step is to make sure that legal liability of one type or another would arise if the exclusion were not present. Next the common law rules of incorporation and interpretation (discussed below) must be applied. If the exclusion survives the application of the common law rules, we must then apply the provisions of the 1977 Act and the 1994 Regulations are then applied. Figure 10.1 summarises these steps in diagrammatic form.

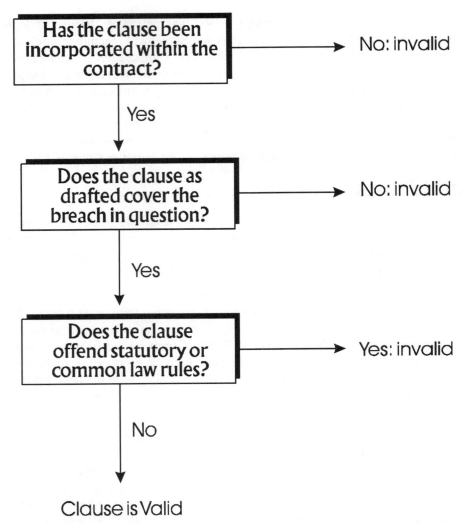

Figure 10.1   Legal Control over exclusion and restriction of contractual liability

Incorporation – is the term part of the contract?

Signed documents

Where a person has signed a document containing an exclusion clause he will be bound by the terms contained in the document whether or not he has read or understood them. The only exceptions to this rule are where the signature is induced by fraud or misrepresentation. Otherwise the exclusion clause will automatically be part of the contract.

In *L'Estrange v. Graucob* 1934 the plaintiff, who was the proprietress of a cafe, bought a vending machine under the terms of a sales agreement which she signed without reading. The contract contained a clause excluding the seller's liability, among other things, for breach of the implied terms under the Sale of Goods Act. The vending machine was defective. The Court of Appeal held that the plaintiff had no remedy against the seller because she was bound by the terms of the exclusion clause in the document which she had signed.

In *Spriggs v. Sotheby Parke Bernet and Co. Ltd.* 1984 the plaintiff deposited a diamond with Sotheby's to be auctioned. He signed a document, without reading it, and put it straight into his wallet. The document contained details of the agreement and a declaration in bold type immediately above the space for the plaintiff's signature. The declaration stated *"I have read and agree to the instructions for sale as detailed on the reverse of this form"*. On the reverse of the form there was an exclusion clause. It was held that the clause had been validly incorporated into the contract.

Where the contents of a document have been misrepresented before it is signed, an exclusion clause in the document will be uneffective to the extent of the misrepresentative effect of the clause.

In *Curtis v. Chemical Cleaning and Dyeing Co.* 1951 the plaintiff took a wedding dress to the defendant company for cleaning. An assistant asked her to sign a receipt, and before she signed she was told that the effect of her signature was to exclude the cleaner's liability for damage to any beads or sequins on the dress. In the process of cleaning the dress was stained, although no damage was done to the beads and sequins. In fact the signed receipt had excluded the defendants' liability for any damage to the dress *"howsoever caused"*. The Court of Appeal held that the defendants were liable for the damage to the dress and could not rely on the full exclusion clause because they had misrepresented its effect to the plaintiff.

Unsigned documents

Where the term is contained in an unsigned document, or displayed on a notice, it will be effective only if the person relying on it took reasonable steps to bring it to the attention of the other party, and where the document or notice might reasonably be regarded as likely to contain contractual terms.

In *Chapelton v. Barry U.D.C.* 1940 the plaintiff hired a deck chair from the defendant for use on a beach. He paid an attendant and was given a ticket in return. He was injured when the chair collapsed as he sat down on it. There was an exclusion clause printed on the back of the ticket which the plaintiff had not read. The Court of Appeal held that the ticket was merely a receipt and not the sort of contractual document which a reasonable person might have expected to contain contractual terms. The exclusion clause was therefore ineffective and the defendants were liable.

Where a term is particularly onerous or unusual, then even if it has been incorporated within a contractual document, the party seeking to enforce it must nevertheless show that it has fairly and adequately been drawn to the other party's attention.

In *Interfoto Picture Library Ltd. v. Stiletto Visual Programmes Ltd.* 1988 the defendants, who were advertising agents, required photographs for a 1950's presentation. The plaintiffs, in response to the defendant's request, sent 47 transparencies with a delivery note which clearly stated that they were to be returned in 14 days. In the small print on the back of the delivery note, condition 2 stated *"a holding fee of £5 plus VAT per day will be charged for each transparency which is retained by you for longer than the said period of 14 days"*. The defendants did not use the transparencies, put them to one side, and forgot about them for a further two weeks. The plaintiffs sent an invoice for £3,783.50 for the holding fee. The Court of Appeal held that, although the contract was made upon the terms in the delivery note, condition 2 was not part of the contract. The term was highly onerous, extortionate and unreasonable and could not be relied upon as it had not been sufficiently brought to the defendants' attention.

Before leaving this case it should be noted that condition 2 was not in fact an exclusion clause, and that whilst the principle laid down by the Court of Appeal applies to such clauses, the court's decision may be interpreted as having a wider application which extends to any onerous or unusual terms in an unsigned contract.

Terms introduced after the contract is made

An exclusion clause will not be effective unless it is adequately brought to the attention of the other party before the contract is made. It must be part of the contractual offer, and the rules of offer and acceptance can be used to determine whether the clause is actually part of the contract.

In *Olley v. Marlborough Court Hotel Ltd.* 1949 the plaintiff booked into an hotel and paid for the room in advance. She went up to her hotel room where there was a notice which stated *"The proprietors will not hold themselves responsible for articles lost or stolen unless handed to the Manageress for safe custody"*. The plaintiff left her fur coat in the room and it was stolen. The Court of Appeal held that the defendant was not entitled to rely on the exclusion clause as it was not a term of the contract. The contract was concluded at the reception desk and the plaintiff had no notice of the clause at that stage.

In *Thornton v. Shoe Lane Parking* 1971 the plaintiff drove into a car park which he had not used before. At the entrance there was a machine which issued a ticket to him before raising a barrier to allow entry. On the back of the ticket there was a statement that it was issued subject to terms and conditions displayed within the car park. One of these conditions purported to exclude the defendant's liability for injury to customers howsoever caused. The plaintiff was injured by the defendant's negligence when he came to collect his car. The Court of Appeal held that the exclusion clause was ineffective because it had been introduced after the contract was concluded. Lord Denning analysed the process of contract formation in the following way. *"The customer pays his money and gets a ticket. He cannot refuse it. He cannot get his money back. He may protest to the machine, even swear at it; but it will remain unmoved. He is committed beyond recall. He was committed at the very moment when he put his money into the machine: the contract was concluded at that time. It can be translated into offer and acceptance in this way. The offer is made when the proprietor of the machine holds it out as being ready to receive the money. The acceptance takes place when the customer puts his money into the slot. The terms of the offer are contained in the notice placed on or near the machine stating what is offered for the money. The customer is bound by these terms as long as they are sufficiently brought to his notice beforehand, but not otherwise. He is not bound by the terms printed on the ticket, if they differ from the notice, because the ticket comes too late. The contract has already been made".*

Where there is a previous course of dealing between the parties the court may be prepared to recognise the incorporation of an exclusion clause into a contract even though it was not specifically referred to at the time the contract was made. This will occur where the past dealings between the parties have consistently been made on the same terms and with the exclusion clause.

In *Spurling v. Bradshaw* 1956 the plaintiffs were warehousemen who had dealt with the defendant for many years and always on the plaintiff's standard contractual terms. These terms excluded the plaintiff's liability for *"negligence, wrongful act of default"*. The defendant delivered eight barrels of orange juice to the plaintiff for storage and a few days later received an acknowledgement which referred to the standard terms of contract. When the defendant came to collect the barrels they were found to be empty. He refused to pay the storage charges and the plaintiff sued. It was held that the exclusion clause, although on this occasion introduced after the contract was made, was part of the contract. This was because the parties had regularly dealt with each other in the past and had done so consistently on the same contractual terms. The defendant was therefore well aware of these terms when he deposited the goods. The exclusion of liability was valid and the plaintiff's claim for storage charges succeeded.

Overriding oral promises

An exclusion clause may be overridden by a later statement by the seller to the buyer.

In *Harling v. Eddy* 1951 the plaintiff bought a heifer at a cattle auction. One of the auctioneer's printed conditions of sale stated that no warranty was given in respect of any animal sold. When the heifer was put up for sale little interest was shown and no bids were made until the auctioneer said *"there is nothing wrong with her. I will guarantee her in every respect and I will take her back if she is not what I say she is"*. The plaintiff bought the animal which died of tuberculosis four months later. It was held by the Court of Appeal that the verbal statement overrode the exclusion clause in the printed conditions, and the plaintiff's claim succeeded.

Interpretation and drafting of exclusion clauses

An exclusion clause must be drafted carefully. It must be clear and unambiguous, and it must cover the liability which has arisen. The former rule that an exclusion clause will be interpreted narrowly against the party seeking to rely on it, known as the *contra proferentem* rule, has been relaxed in the interpretation of commercial contracts between businessmen. Under the 1994 Unfair Terms in Consumer Contracts Regulations the supplier in a consumer contract must ensure that any written contract term is expressed in *plain intelligible language*. Regulation 6 provides that the interpretation most favourable to the consumer will be followed where there is any doubt about the meaning of a written term.

In any event the need to express contractual terms clearly is very important. This is especially so when the term is an attempt by one of the parties to exclude liability. As Scrutton LJ pointed out in *Alison (J Gordon) Ltd. v. Wallsend Shipway and Engineering Co. Ltd.* 1927 *"if a person is under a legal liability and wishes to get rid of it, he can only do so by using clear words."*

> In *Andrews Ltd. v. Singer and Co. Ltd.* 1934 the plaintiff agreed in writing to buy a *new Singer car*. The contract contained a clause which excluded the defendant's liability for breach of *"all conditions, warranties and liabilities implied by statute, common law or otherwise."* The car delivered to the plaintiff had in fact done a considerable number of miles. It was held that the seller was in breach of an express condition that the car would be new. He could not therefore rely on an exclusion of implied terms, and was liable to the plaintiff.

> In *Baldry v. Marshall* 1925 the plaintiff told the defendant that he required a car suitable for touring. The defendant was a car dealer and, on his recommendation, the plaintiff bought a Bugatti from him. The written contract of sale excluded the seller's liability for breach of any *"guarantee or warranty, statutory or otherwise"*. The car proved unsuitable for touring. It was held that the seller was in breach of the implied condition under s.14 of the Sale of Goods Act that the car would be suitable for a purpose made known to the seller. The exclusion clause was ineffective because it excluded only guarantees or warranties and did not exclude liability for breach of a condition of the contract.

Exclusion clauses are sometimes introduced by words which indicate that the party imposing them will take all reasonable care or will make every effort to perform his obligations. This type of wording may be interpreted by the courts as imposing a pre-condition for the operation of the exclusion clause. If the party relying on the clause does not fulfil the pre-condition he cannot take the benefit of the exclusion.

> In *B & S Contracts Ltd. v. Victor Green Publications Ltd.* 1984 the plaintiffs were contractors who traded on standard terms which excluded their liability for non-performance which resulted from industrial action by their workforce. The exclusion clause began with the words *"Every effort will be made to carry out the contract, but..."* The Court of Appeal held that the contractors were obliged to take reasonable steps to perform the contract before they could rely on the exclusion clause. They failed to prove that they had done this and were therefore unable to rely on the exclusion clause.

The approach of the courts to the interpretation of exclusion clauses has changed since the introduction of the statutory controls contained in the Unfair Contract Terms Act 1977. Before the 1977 Act the courts had few means of invalidating exclusion clauses in contracts and, because of the potential injustice which they caused, were prepared to interpret such clauses in a hostile manner. Judges would sometimes place a strained meaning on the words of the clause in order to deprive it of effect. However since the introduction of the 1977 Act, the capacity to parties to use unfair exclusion clauses has been reduced greatly and the courts are now able to adopt a less hostile approach in interpreting their wording.

In *Photo Productions Ltd. v. Securicor Transport Ltd.* 1980 the defendant contracted to provide security services, including night patrols, at the plaintiff's factory. While on patrol one of the defendant's employees deliberately lit a small fire which got out of control and destroyed the factory and its contents. The contract, which was on Securicor's standard terms, contained the following condition *"Under no circumstances shall the company (Securicor) be responsible for any injurious act or default by any employee of the company unless such act or default could have been foreseen and avoided by the exercise of due diligence on the part of the company as his employer; nor, in any event, shall the company be held responsible for; (a) any loss suffered by the customer through burglary, theft, fire or any other cause, except insofar as such loss is solely attributable to the negligence of the company's employees acting within the course of their employment..."*The House of Lords held that the exclusion clause was effective. It was clear and unambiguous and it covered the breach of contract complained of. Lord Diplock stated: *"in commercial contracts negotiated between businessmen capable of looking after their own interests and of deciding how risks inherent in the performance of various kinds of contract can be most economically borne (generally by insurance) it is, in my view, wrong to place a strained interpretation on words in an exclusion clause..."*

Figure 10.2 on the following page identifies the numerous statutes and statutory instruments which exercise control over exclusion clauses. At the heart of this legislation is the Unfair Contract Terms Act 1997.

The Unfair Contract Terms Act 1977

The Unfair Contract Terms Act 1977 is the first attempt by Parliament to deal with exclusion and limitation of liability in a comprehensive way. There are provisions in the Act which control attempts to exclude or limit liability in relation to negligence, contractual obligations, indemnities, guarantees, implied terms in contracts to supply goods and misrepresentation. For the purposes of the 1977 Act, exclusion or restriction of liability is widely defined so as to include:

- making enforcement of a remedy subject to restrictive conditions, for example a requirement that notice of loss or damage must be given within a specified time or in a specified manner;

- excluding or restricting any right or remedy, for example taking away the right to reject goods for breach of condition and confining the buyer's remedy to damages only;

- restricting the liability, for example to a maximum amount recoverable;

- restricting the time within which the remedy may be claimed, for example by specifying that no claim may be made more than 28 days after the date of the contract; and

- preventing liability arising in the first place, for example by including a term which provides that the seller does not give any warranty or undertaking that the goods are fit for any purpose.

Legislation	Controls
Misrepresentation Act 1967 section 3	contract terms restricting liability for misrepresentation invalidated unless shown to be reasonable.
Defective Premises Act 1972 section 6(3)	invalidates contract terms restricting liability in connection with the provision of an unfit dwelling.
Consumer Credit Act 1974	invalidates contract terms taking away consumer protection in agreements by the Act.
Unfair Contract Terms Act 1977 whole Act	prohibits or applies a test of reasonableness to exclusion of liability for: - negligence - supply of services - occupiers liability - breach of contract generally - breach of statutory implied terms in contracts for the sale or supply of goods.
Consumer Transactions (Restrictions on Statements) (Amendment) Order 1978	creates criminal liability for using invalid exclusion clauses purporting to take away the consumers statutory rights in contracts for the sale or supply of goods.
Consumer Protection Act 1987 sections 7 and 41	invalidates exclusion of strict liability for injuries caused by defective products prohibits exclusion of liability for breach of statutory consumer safety duties.
Unfair Terms in Consumer Contracts Regulations 1994	- requires the use of plain English in written consumer contracts - reinpowers the Director General of Fair Trading to challenge the use of unfair terms draw up for general use - invalidates unfair contract terms in standard form contracts between a business supplier and a consumer involving the supply of goods or services.

Figure 10.2 Control of exclusion clauses by legislation

The Act only applies to a *business liability*. This is defined as liability for breach of obligations arising from things done in the course of a business or from the occupation of premises used for business purposes. The meaning of the term *business* is discussed elsewhere. For the purposes of this Act it includes a profession, and the activities of any government department or local or public authority. The Act provides varying degrees of protection against exclusion clauses and notices. Some are totally invalidated, others are subjected to a test of reasonableness, and there are others to which the Act does not apply at all.

Exclusion clauses to which the Act does not apply

The Act does not apply in the following situations, where in consequence the exclusion will be subject only to the common law rules discussed above:

(a) where the liability in question is not a business liability, for example liability arising from the defective state of a private house;

(b) where the situation falls outside the wording of a particular section of the Act. A verbal contract in which neither party deals as a consumer is, for example, outside the scope of s.3;

(c) where the Act specifically states that it does not apply. Schedule 1 tells us that the Act, in whole or in part, does not extend to the following types of contract:

    (i) insurance contracts

    (ii) contracts involving land

    (iii) contracts dealing with intellectual property

    (iv) contracts relating to the formation or dissolution of business organisations

    (v) contracts involving the creation or transfer of securities

    (vi) in relation to contracts of employment, except in favour of the employee.

The reasonableness test

Where the Act subjects an exclusion clause to the *reasonableness* test, the burden of proving that the contract term or notice is reasonable lies with the party seeking to rely on the exclusion. The test in relation to a contract term is that the term shall have been a fair and reasonable one to be included in the contract, having regard to the circumstances which were or should have been known to the parties at the time when the contract was made. In relation to a non-contractual notice the test is whether it would be fair and reasonable to allow reliance on it, having regard to all the circumstances at the time when the liability arose. An example of a non-contractual notice would be a notice displayed at the entrance to a public park.

Schedule 2 of the Act lays down guidelines which the court can take into account in determining whether a contract term satisfies the requirement of reasonableness.

Exclusion of liability for negligence

In dealing with exclusion of liability for negligence, the Act defines the term *negligence* to cover the following:

(a)   contractual negligence, or the breach of any duty to use reasonable skill and care in the performance of a contract,

(b)   common law negligence, for example under the rule in *Donoghue v. Stevenson* 1932 discussed in Chapter 5, and

(c)   liability for breach of the common duty of care, owed to visitors by an occupier of premises, under the Occupier's Liability Act 1957.

Section 2 of the 1977 Act provides:

"(1)   A person cannot by reference to any contract term or to a notice given to persons generally or to particular persons exclude or restrict his liability for death or personal injury resulting from negligence.

(2)   In the case of other loss or damage, a person cannot so exclude or restrict his liability for negligence except insofar as the term or notice satisfies the requirement of reasonableness".

This gives us two important basic rules. First that it is not possible to exclude liability for death or personal injury resulting from negligence. The case of *White v. Blackmore* 1972 gives an example of a notice which, before the Act, effectively excluded negligence liability for death or personal injury. Such a notice is now invalid. The plaintiff in that case would have succeeded had the Act been in force at the time of the negligent act. Furthermore in *Thornton v. Shoe Lane Parking* 1971 discussed above, the exclusion of liability for personal injury would have been wholly ineffective under the 1977 Act, if it had actually been part of the contract.

The second rule is that liability for loss or damage other than death or personal injury cannot be excluded unless the exclusion is reasonable. This would apply, for example, to clauses which excluded liability for damage to property or financial loss caused by negligence. Under this provision the exclusion clauses in cases like *Spurling v. Bradshaw* 1956 and *Olley v. Marlborough Court Hotel* 1949 would be subject to the reasonableness test. In Chapter 13 there are a number of examples of cases in which the reasonableness test has been applied, for example *Smith v. Eric S. Bush* 1989, *Stevenson v. Nationwide Building Society* 1984 and *Harris v. Wyre Forest District Council* 1989.

In *Spriggs v. Sotheby Parke Bernet and Co. Ltd.* 1984, considered earlier in the chapter, the plaintiff, who was a businessman, deposited a diamond with Sotheby's to be auctioned. He signed a document which, among other things, excluded Sotheby's liability for negligence. He was given the opportunity to insure the diamond but did not do so. Whilst the diamond was on view prior to the auction, it was stolen despite the defendant's fairly comprehensive security system. The plaintiff sued for negligence and the defendants relied on the exclusion clause. Under s.2(2) the clause is only valid if the defendant can show that it is reasonable. The court held that the clause in this case was reasonable and valid. The plaintiff was a successful and experienced businessman and no doubt was used to contracts containing exclusion clauses. He could not be regarded as having unequal bargaining power. The risk was one which could have been covered by insurance but the plaintiff turned down the opportunity to take this precaution.

In *Phillips Products v. Hampstead Plant Hire* 1983 the defendant hired out a JCB to the plaintiffs under a standard term agreement. They supplied the driver but excluded any liability in negligence for his acts. Whilst he was working under the plaintiffs' direction, the driver damaged their factory through his own negligence. It was held that the exclusion clause was unreasonable and invalid. This was because the hire was for a short period and the plaintiffs had little opportunity to insure. They did not select, nor effectively controlled the driver. Moreover their experience of such hiring arrangements was very limited.

An exclusion of liability for negligence is sometimes contained in a *guarantee* given by a manufacturer or distributor of goods. Such a guarantee will usually offer to repair or replace faulty goods such as televisions, washing machines and other electrical goods, free of charge within a specified time period commencing with the date of purchase; and will often be subject to stated exceptions, for example that the defect is not due to misuse, accidental damage or attempted repair by an unqualified person. In some cases, however, a guarantee may attempt to do more than qualify the benefit which it gives. It may purport to take away other rights of the consumer which are independent of the guarantee, such as the right to sue the manufacturer in the tort of negligence. This could be done by supplying a postcard with the goods which the consumer is asked to fill in and send to the manufacturer within a specified time in order to 'preserve his rights under the guarantee'. The postcard would then refer to the rights under the guarantee and contain an exclusion clause limiting the consumer's other rights.

In relation to exclusion clauses in guarantees, s.5(1) provides:

> *"In the case of goods of a type ordinarily supplied for private use or consumption, where loss or damage:*
>
> *(a)   arises from the goods proving defective while in consumer use; and*
>
> *(b)   results from the negligence of a person concerned in the manufacture or distribution of the goods, liability for the loss or damage cannot be excluded or restricted by reference to any contract term or notice contained in or operating by reference to a guarantee of the goods".*

For these purposes the goods are *"in consumer use"* when a person is using them or has them in his possession for use, otherwise than exclusively for the purposes of a business; and a *"guarantee"* includes anything in writing which contains some promise or assurance (however worded or presented) that defects will be made good by repair, replacement, financial compensation or otherwise. This section does not apply where the guarantee is given by the seller as part of the contract of sale with the buyer. In such a case other provisions of the Act would apply. Figure 10.3 on the next page illustrates the effect of s.2 of the Act.

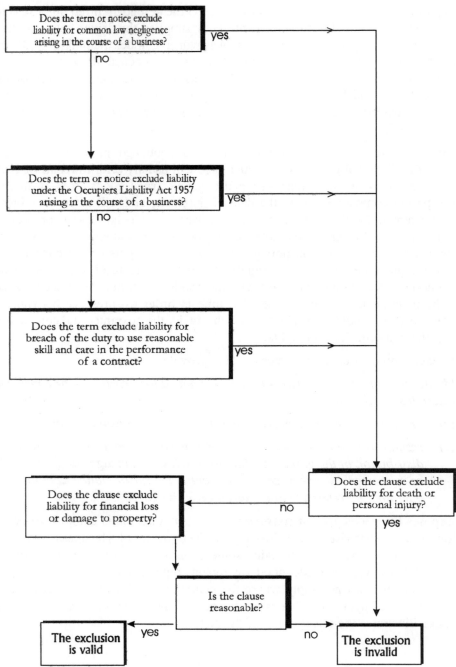

Figure 10.3   Exclusion of Liability for Negligence
Section 2 Unfair Contract Terms Act 1977

Exclusion of liability for breach of contract

Section 3 of the Act applies where one of the parties to a contract deals as a consumer, or where the contract is made on written standard terms of business. In either of these situations, the section subjects to the test of reasonableness any term in which the other party:

"(a) when himself in breach of contract, excludes or restricts any liability of his in respect of the breach; or

(b) claims to be entitled -

    (i) to render a contractual performance substantially different from that which was reasonably expected from him, or

    (ii) in respect of the whole or any part of his contractual obligation, to render no performance at all".

This section is extremely wide in its application covering all types of business contract, and all manner of exclusion or limitation of liability clauses. In the case of contracts for the supply of goods, even tighter controls are applied under the provisions of s.6 and s.7, examined below. Many of the exclusion clauses considered in previous cases, such as *Curtis v. Chemical Cleaning and Dyeing Company* 1951, *Olley v. Marlborough Court Hotel* 1949 and *Photo Productions Ltd. v. Securicor Transport Ltd.* 1980 would be caught by s.3.

In addition to straightforward exclusion clauses, the section applies to contract terms in which one party claims to be entitled to give *substituted performance*, for example in a holiday contract where the travel operator reserves the right to change the destination. It also applies to contract terms in which one party claims to be entitled to render no performance at all.

The application of s.3 can be seen in the following cases involving contracts for the development and printing of photographs.

In *Woodman v. Photo Trade Processing Ltd.* 1981 the plaintiff sent a reel of film of wedding photographs to the defendant for processing. The film was lost by the defendant. The contract contained the following clause *"all photographic materials are accepted on the basis that their value does not exceed the cost of the material itself. Responsibility is limited to the replacement of the films. No liability will be accepted consequential or otherwise, however caused"*. In considering the reasonableness of this clause, the Judge referred to the Code of Practice for the Photographic Industry, which had been approved by the Office of Fair Trading. This code recognised the possibility of a two tier system of trade, the lowest tier of which would be a cheaper service with full exclusion of liability; and the other would be a more expensive service with the processors accepting a greater degree of liability. The Judge concluded that this approach, which had not been adopted by the defendant, would be both reasonable and practicable. On that basis the court held that the defendants had not proved that their arrangements were reasonable and they were held liable.

In *Warren v. Truprint Ltd.* 1986 photographs of the plaintiff's silver wedding were sent to the defendant for processing. They also were lost and the defendant sought to rely on an exclusion clause printed on their envelope. This limited their liability to the cost of unexposed films plus a refund of the processing charge and postage. The clause went on to say that *"we will undertake further liability at a supplementary charge. Written details on request"*. The court held that this was not sufficient to make the clause reasonable under the 1977 Act. A reasonable clause would, plainly and clearly, set out the alternative with details of the cost to the consumer. The plaintiff's claim succeeded and he was awarded £50 damages.

Section 4 provides that a person dealing as a consumer cannot by reference to any contract term be made to indemnify another person for liability for breach of contract or negligence unless the indemnity term satisfies the reasonableness test. This is a further restriction on the effective transfer of liability by the use of an indirect exclusion clause.

The combined effect of s.3 and s.4 of the Act is summarised in Figure 10.4 on the following page.

The effect of the Act upon exclusion of the implied terms in contracts for the sale and supply of goods is considered in the next chapter.

Unfair Terms in Consumer Contracts Regulations 1994

These regulations came into force on 1st July 1995 and were introduced to implement the directive on Unfair Terms in Consumer Contracts (93/13/EEC) adopted by the EC Council of Ministers on the 5th April 1993. The Regulations cover a wide variety of contract terms within a broad range of different types of contract. There are, however, a number of exceptions. These are contracts of employment, contracts relating to the creation and operation of companies or partnerships and contracts dealing with succession rights or rights under family law. Whilst the latter are outside the scope of EC legislative competence, the former are regulated by a number of other Community laws.

The Regulations apply when a seller or supplier of goods or services, acting in the course of a business, makes a contract with a consumer. The expression *consumer* in this context covers any natural person purchasing goods or services other than for business purposes.

The Regulations introduce three major changes to the present law on unfair contract terms by:

- invalidating any terms in consumer contracts which are unfair and which have not been individually negotiated;

- requiring that plain English is used when consumer contracts are drawn up in writing; and

- providing a mechanism for preventing the continued use of unfair terms by allowing the Director General of Fair Trading to challenge particular contract terms before the courts.

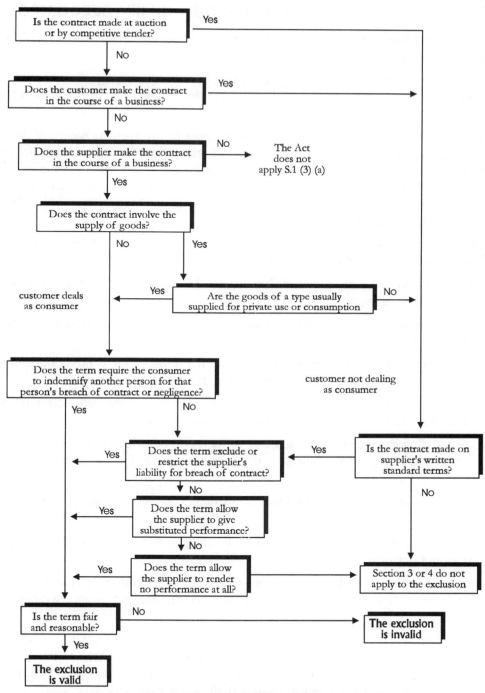

Figure 10.4   Exclusion of Liability in Contract Section 3 and
Section 4 Unfair Contract of Terms Act 1977

Unfair terms which have not been individually negotiated

A term in a standard form contract between a business supplier and a consumer will be held to be unfair, under reg. 4(1) where:

> *"...contrary to the requirement of good faith the term causes a significant imbalance in the parties' rights and obligations under the contract to the detriment of the consumer."*

In determining the fairness of a contract term account must be taken of the nature of the goods or services supplied; the other terms of the contract and any related contract and all of the circumstances at the time the contract was made. Schedule 2 of the regulations sets out a number of factors to which the court shall have regard, including the strength of the bargaining positions of the parties, whether the consumer had an inducement to agree to the term and the extent to which the supplier has dealt fairly and equitably with the consumer.

Schedule 3 of the Regulations contains an indicative list of terms which may be regarded as unfair. The list is not exhaustive, and the following examples are drawn from it:

(a)   terms which make an agreement binding on the consumer when it is not binding on the seller or supplier;

(b)   terms requiring any consumer who fails to fulfil his obligations to pay a disproportionately high sum in compensation;

(c)   terms enabling the seller or supplier to alter the terms of the contract unilaterally without a valid reason which is specified in the contract;

(d)   terms authorising the seller or supplier to dissolve the contract on a discretionary basis where the same facility is not available to the consumer;

(e)   terms allowing the seller or supplier to increase the price without allowing the consumer the right to withdraw if the final price is too high as compared to the agreed price;

(f)   terms limiting the seller or suppliers' obligation to respect commitments undertaken by his agent; and

(g)   terms obliging the consumer to fulfil all his obligations where the seller or supplier does not perform his.

Where a term is found to be unfair it is not be binding upon the consumer although the contract will continue to be binding provided that it is capable of continuing in existence without the unfair term.

Where the supplier uses a standard form contract in relation to the transaction, it is clear that the terms are not individually negotiated. They have been drawn up in advance and the consumer has not been able to influence their content. Where the contract contains some terms which have been individually negotiated and others which are standard, the standard terms will be subject to challenge. Where the supplier claims that a particular term has been individually negotiated, the burden of proving this rests with him.

Certain contract terms, however, cannot be challenged as unfair even where they have not been individually negotiated. These are:

(a)   terms reflecting mandatory, statutory or regulatory provisions, for example terms which are implied by statute into particular types of contract. This means that the substance of such terms cannot be challenged as unfair;

(b)   terms reflecting the principles contained in international conventions, such as the Warsaw Convention which limits the liability of international air carriers for death or personal injury to passengers and for damage to or loss of luggage. There are a number of such conventions particularly in the area of international transport and travel;

(c)   terms defining the main subject matter of the contract and the price to be paid. This exception is in line with the common law rule relating to the adequacy of consideration, discussed in Chapter 8 in the context of the formation of contracts. Under this rule the courts will recognise a contract as valid where some element of consideration is provided by each contracting party to the other, but the court is not concerned to see that the value provided by each is equal or fair;

(d)   terms in insurance contracts which define the risks insured and the insurers liability.

Plain English

Where all or part of the terms of contract with a consumer are in writing, the Regulations provide that these terms must always be drafted in plain intelligible language. Where there is doubt about the meaning of a term, the interpretation most favourable to the consumer shall be given.

Preventing the continued use of unfair terms

Member states were required by the Directive to introduce adequate and effective means to prevent the continued use of unfair terms in contracts concluded with consumers by sellers and suppliers. This was to be achieved by the introduction of rules enabling consumer protection organisations to apply to the court for a declaration as to whether contractual terms drawn up for general use were unfair. The UK government has interpreted this provision narrowly in its implementation of the Directive, and the UK Regulations provide a power only to the Director General of Fair Trading to such action.

The Consumers Association is currently seeking a *judicial review* of the government's action, arguing that the Regulations do not adequately implement the provisions of art.7 of the Directive which require such a power to be given to *"persons or organisations having a legitimate interest under national law in protecting consumers"*.

Under the regulations as they are currently drawn, where the Director General of Fair Trading considers that a contract term is unfair, he may either seek an injunction to prevent its further use, or accept an undertaking that a supplier or trade organisation will not use or recommend the use of a particular term in the future.

Discharge of Contract

Since a contract gives rise to legally enforceable obligations, contracting parties need to know how and when these obligations have been discharged and cease to be binding on them. Discharge is this a technical term used to describe the ending of contractual liabilities. No legal claim will lie once a contract is discharged. Discharge can occur in any of the following ways:

Discharge by performance

The general rule is that complete performance, in which both parties comply precisely with the contractual terms they have agreed, is necessary to discharge the contract.

> This common law rule was applied in the case of *Sumpter v. Hedges* 1898, where the plaintiff builder had agreed to erect some houses for a lump sum of £565. Having carried out half the work to the value of £333 the builder was unable to complete the job because of financial difficulties. In an action by the builder to recover compensation for the value of the work he had already carried out, the Court of Appeal confirmed that he was not entitled to payment. The legal position was expressed by Smith, LJ who stated *"The law is that where there is a contract to do work for a lump sum, until the work is completed, the price of it cannot be recovered"*.

This appears to be a very harsh decision, for the builder was unable to recover for any work he had performed, whilst the purchaser obtained a half completed contract for nothing. The difficulty for the court in such a case is that a single sum has been arranged in consideration for the completion of specified works. If these works are not completed in their entirety the court would be varying the clearly expressed intentions of the parties if it was to award the builder payment of a proportionate part of the lump sum. In other words, by agreeing a lump sum the parties have impliedly excluded that possibility of part payment for partially fulfilled building work. Such a contract is said to be an *entire* contract.

The obligation on a contracting party to provide precise, complete performance of the contract before the contractual obligations can be treated as discharged can obviously produce injustice. There are however two exceptions that grant limited relief to the party obliged to perform. These are in cases where the contract is *divisible*, and where there has been *substantial performance*.

A divisible contract

In some circumstances the courts are prepared to accept that a contract is a divisible one so that partial performance of the contract can be set off against partial consideration to be given in return. Had the parties in *Sumpter v. Hedges* agreed a specified sum to be paid on completion of certain stages of the house building, then the builder could have recovered compensation for part of the work done. In practice it is usual in a building contract to provide for payment of parts of the total cost at various stages of completion.

It is not necessary for the parties to formally specify that the contract is a divisible one, although in contracts involving substantial work, such as civil engineering operations, it is standard practice to split the work, and hence the contract into stages, with payment falling due on completion of each stage. The courts seem willing to recognise a divisible contract wherever possible, and will, for example, regard an agreement based upon an estimate or quotation given in advance, which itemises the work to be performed and with a breakdown of the costs as a divisible contract.

Substantial performance

If a party to a contract has substantially performed his contractual obligations subject only to minor defects, the courts have recognised that it would be unjust to prevent him recovering any of the contractual price. Therefore under this exception the contractual price would be recoverable, less of course a sum representing the value of the defects. It must be stressed that the exception will only operate where the defects are of a trifling nature, an issue determined by considering not only the character of the defects but also the cost of rectifying them in relation to the total contract price.

> A claim of substantial performance of the contract was made in *Bolton v. Mahadeva* 1972. The plaintiff, a heating contractor, had agreed to install a central heating system in the defendant's house for £560. On completion of the work the system proved to be so defective that it would cost £174 to repair. The defendant refused to pay the plaintiff any of the cost of the work and the plaintiff sued. The County Court accepted the plaintiff's claim of substantial performance and awarded him the cost of the work less the cost of the repair. On appeal however, the Court of Appeal held that in the circumstances the plaintiff had not substantially performed the contract and he was not therefore entitled to recover any of the cost of the work. The substantial performance plea would not succeed where there were numerous defects requiring a relatively high cost of repair.

From the consumer's point of view it can be difficult to ascertain whether incomplete performance of the contract is nevertheless sufficient on the facts to amount to substantial performance. A refusal of payment may well be met with a legal action by the contractor to recover the debt owed. Further complications may be caused where the contractor offers to remedy the customer's complaint free of charge and the customer refuses to accept the offer. In the event of a dispute concerning the value of work performed, an offer of reduced payment by the debtor to the creditor will be binding on the creditor, an example of one of the exemptions to *Pinnel's case*.

> In *Lawson v. Supasink Ltd.* 1982 the plaintiff's employed the defendants to design, supply and install a fitted kitchen. The total cost was £1,200, and the plaintiffs had to pay a deposit. After the kitchen units had been fitted, but before work on the kitchen was completed, the plaintiffs informed the defendants of their dissatisfaction with the standard of workmanship. In response the defendants undertook to remedy the faults free of charge, but the plaintiffs later rejected this, asked for the units to be removed and for the return of their deposit. The defendants refused. The Court of Appeal, having accepted that the shoddy work did not amount to substantial performance, then considered the offer to remedy made by the defendants. The question was whether they had failed to mitigate their loss, that is minimise the damage they had suffered. In *Fayzu Ltd. v. Saunders* 1919 Scrutton LJ commented, *"... in commercial contracts it is generally reasonable to accept an offer from the party in default."* In *Lawson* the Court held that the plaintiffs had not acted unreasonably for, in the words of Shaw LJ *" I do not see how the plaintiffs could be required ... to afford the defendants a second opportunity of doing properly what they singularly failed to do adequately in the first instance."*

The acceptance of partial performance

If a party to a contract partially performs his obligations and the other party accepts the benefit, then he is obliged to pay a reasonable price for it. In such circumstances the courts allow an action on a quantum meruit basis an equitable principle literally meaning as much as he deserves. This exception however will only apply where the party receiving the benefit has the option of whether or not to accept or reject it. In *Sumpter v. Hedges* the owner had no choice but to accept the work done on the half completed houses and was therefore not obliged to pay for it. Compare that situation to the one in *Lawson v. Supasink* where the units were capable of being removed and returned.

Where performance is prevented

Obviously if a party to a contract is prevented from fulfilling his contractual obligations by the other party then he will not be in default. In a building contract if the owner should prevent the builder from completing, for example by locking him out of the site, the builder can recover a reasonable price for the work done on a *quantum meruit* basis.

As well as the above exceptions to the general rule that the performance of contractual obligations must be precise, it is important to note that if a party to a contract makes a valid tender (offer) of performance this may be regarded as equivalent to performance. The refusal of the other party to allow performance to take place will discharge any further obligations on the part of the tenderer. Thus if a seller of goods tries to deliver them at the agreed time and place and the goods meet contract description, the refusal of the buyer to accept them will,

- amount to a valid tender of performance; and
- entitle the seller to sue the buyer under s.50 Sale of Goods Act 1979 for damages for non-acceptance of the goods.

Despite the problems that can sometimes occur in performance, most contracts are nevertheless satisfactorily discharged in this way.

Discharge by agreement

This method of discharge occurs where the parties mutually agree to waive their rights and obligations under it. It is called bilateral discharge. To be an effective *waiver* the second agreement must be a contract, the consideration for which is the exchange of promises not to enforce the original contract.

Each party is agreeing to release the other from the original contractual promises and not to use on the grounds of non-performance. The situation however is more complex where one party to a contract has already executed or partly executed his consideration under it. Here for a waiver to be effective it must be embodied within a speciality contract or be supported by fresh consideration. This is called unilateral discharge and can only be achieved by *accord* and *satisfaction*. The accord is simply the agreement to discharge and the satisfaction is the consideration required to support it. An example occurs when a football manager with three years of a £100,000 per year contract still to run is asked by the club after a poor season to leave. If the two sides agree to a new deal (the accord) in which the manager will receive a £200,000 lump sum to go, both sides obtain a new benefit (satisfaction). The manager receives a substantial payment and the club can bring in a new manager. By contrast suppose X contracts to sell goods to Y for £50. X then delivers the goods to Y but hearing of Y's financial difficulties agrees to waive payment. Here the agreement of X to waive payment (the accord) is not enforceable unless supported by fresh consideration furnished by Y (the satisfaction). The fresh consideration of course must be of value but need not be adequate. As we saw in our examination of the principles of consideration, at common law the rule in *Pinnel's case* provides that there is no value in a creditor taking as satisfaction payment of a lesser sum than he was due under the original agreement.

A creditor's promise to accept a reduced amount may however be binding on him, through the operation of the equitable doctrine of *promissory estoppel*, established in *Hughes v. Metropolitan Railway Co.* 1877 by the House of Lords, and by Denning J as he then was in *Central London Property Trust Ltd. v. High Trees House Ltd.* 1947. In the High Trees case the defendant company took a 99-year lease on a block of flats from the plaintiff company at an annual rent of £2,500. The lease was granted in 1937. By 1940 the evacuation of large numbers of people out of London because of war meant that the defendant company was unable to let all the flats and could not meet the annual rent out of the profits it was making. As a result, the plaintiff company agreed to accept a reduced annual rent of £1,250. By the beginning of 1945 the flats were fully let again. An action was brought by the plaintiff company to recover the difference between the reduced rent and the full rent for the last two quarters of 1945. The action succeeded, for the court considered that the agreement of 1940 would continue only as long as wartime conditions prevailed. The Court also considered whether the plaintiffs could recover the remaining arrears from the defendants, relying on *Pinnel's case*. It took the view that such action would be inequitable, even though permissible at common law. In equity the creditor would be estopped, or denied the right of disowning his promise to accept the reduced amount, where the debtor had to the creditor's knowledge relied on the promise, and acted on it to his detriment. This rule is consequently referred to as promissory estoppel. It was said in the later case of *Combe v. Combe* 1951 that the doctrine is a shield rather than a sword, meaning that the person receiving the promise cannot sue on it, the *sword*, but can raise it as defence, the *shield*, if action is brought to recover the outstanding payment. The doctrine only arises within the context of a pre-existing contractual relationship, and does not remove consideration as a requirement of the simple contract.

In addition the *High Trees* decision is an authority which supports the view that a deed can be varied by a simple contract. Prior to 1947 it had always been considered that because a simple contract is inferior to the more formal deed, that only a deed could vary a deed.

Being a form of equitable relief, promissory estoppel can only be used as defence by those who have acted in an equitable manner themselves.

In *D & C Builders v. Rees* 1965 Mr. & Mrs Rees exacted a promise from D & C Builders to accept a reduced amount than that originally agreed, for building work carried out to the Rees's home. They claimed the building work was substandard, but in fact they were simply attempting to escape the full payment due, using their knowledge that the builders were in financial difficulties and desperate for cash. Sometime after the reduced payment had been made the company sued for the outstanding balance, and the defendants pleaded promissory estoppel. The court refused to allow Mr. & Mrs Rees the equitable defence, on the grounds of their own lack of equity.

As the earlier football example showed, a contract of employment can be terminated by the mutual agreement of the parties.

Such was the case in *Logan Salton v. Durham County Council* 1989. Here the complainant was a social worker who, as a result of disciplinary hearings, had been redeployed by his employer. In a statement to be considered at a further disciplinary hearing the complainant was given notice of a number of complaints against him and a recommendation that he be summarily dismissed. Prior to that meeting his union representative negotiated on his behalf a mutual agreement to terminate his employment with the Council. By that agreement the employment contract was to terminate in seven weeks' time and an outstanding car loan of £2,750 wiped out as a debt. Despite the fact that the agreement was signed by both parties, the complainant subsequently complained to an industrial tribunal that he had been unfairly dismissed. The Employment Appeal Tribunal thought that the agreement to terminate the contract was valid and that there was no dismissal. *"In the resolution of industrial disputes, it is in the best interests of all concerned that a contract made without duress, for good consideration, preferably after proper and sufficient advice and which has the effect of terminating a contract of employment by mutual agreement (whether at once or at some future date) should be effective between the contracting parties, in which case there probably will not have been a dismissal."*

Discharge by breach

A party to a contract who completely fails to perform his obligations under it or performs his obligations in a defective manner is in breach of contract. Generally, the remedy of an innocent party to a contract who has suffered as a result of a breach is to sue for damages. For some breaches of contract however, the innocent party is given the additional remedy of treating the contract as repudiated, in other words terminated, and thus discharging himself from any remaining obligations under it. Terms in a contract have different status and it is only when a condition has been broken that repudiatory breach can occur. If a breach of contract takes place before the time set for performance of the agreement it is called an *anticipatory breach*. This will occur where a party to a contract expressly declares that he will not perform his part of the bargain. Once an anticipatory breach has arisen the innocent party does not have to wait for the date set for performance but has the option of immediately suing for breach of contract.

In *Hochester v. De La Tour* 1853 the defendant agreed in April to engage the plaintiff for work to commence in June. The defendant told the plaintiff in May that he would not require his services. The court held that a cause of action for breach of contract arose on the anticipatory breach in May.

Thus in such circumstances the injured party has the choice of commencing legal action at the time of the anticipatory breach, or alternatively waiting until performance is due to see if it is in fact carried out, and if it is not, commence action thereafter. Crucially of course it has to be decided whether the words or actions that have given rise to the assumption of repudiation are in the circumstances sufficient. In *Woodar Investment Development Ltd. v. Wimpey Construction Ltd. 1980,* Lord Willberforce said the test was, "*whether, objectively speaking* (the defendants) *conduct showed an intention to abandon the contract.*"

Discharge by frustration or subsequent impossibility

A contract is discharged by frustration where as a result of an event subsequent to making the contract, its performance can no longer be carried out. The event must be subsequent to the contract for if the contract is impossible to perform at the time it is made there can be no contract. Originally the common law did not take such a lenient view of changes in circumstances and required that the parties to a contract should provide for all eventualities. If because of a subsequent event performance of an obligation became impossible, the party required to perform it would be liable to pay damages for non performance.

> In *Paradine v. Jane* 1647 the King's Bench Court held a tenant liable to pay three years' arrears of rent to a landlord despite the fact that the tenant had been dispossessed of his house by soldiers during the Civil War.

Today however the courts recognise that certain supervening events may frustrate a contract and thus release the parties from their obligation under it. Were the facts of *Paradine v. Jane* to come before a modern court, the outcome would probably be quite different.

> In *National Carriers Ltd. v. Panalpina (Northern) Ltd.* 1981 the plaintiffs leased a warehouse in Hull to the defendants. The lease was for ten years, however for a period of twenty months the only access road to the premises was closed by the local authority due to the poor state of a listed building nearby. The defendants refused to pay any further rent to the plaintiffs. The House of Lords accepted the defendant's argument that a lease could, in law, become frustrated, but felt that twenty months out of a ten year period, was not sufficiently substantial to frustrate the contract.

There are a number of grounds upon which a contract may become frustrated. They include:

- *Changes in the law*. If because of new legislation performance of the contract would become illegal this would be a supervening event to frustrate the contract.

In *Denny, Mott and Dickson Ltd. v. James B. Fraser Ltd.* 1944 the House of Lords held that a contract for the sale of timber was frustrated because of the subsequent passage of various Control of Timber Orders rendering performance of the contract illegal.

- *Destruction of subject matter*. If the subject matter or means of performance of the contract is destroyed this is an event which frustrates a contract.

In *Taylor v. Caldwell* 1863 the plaintiff agreed to hire the defendant's music hall to give some concerts. Prior to performance the hall was destroyed by fire and this event, the court held, released the parties from their obligations under the contract.

- *Inability to achieve main object*. If as a result of change in circumstances performance of the contract would be radically different from the performance envisaged by the parties then the contract is frustrated. It must be shown that the parties are no longer able to achieve their main object under the contract.

In *Krell v. Henry* 1903 the defendant hired a flat for two days to enable him to watch Edward VII's Coronation procession. Due to the King's illness the Coronation was cancelled and the defendant naturally refused to pay. The Court of Appeal held that as the main object of the contract was to view the procession, and this could no longer be achieved, the foundation of the contract had collapsed. The contract was thus frustrated and the parties released from their obligations under it.

A further claim of frustration as a consequence of the cancellation of the Coronation was brought in *Herne Bay Steamboat Co. v. Hutton* 1903. Here a steamboat had been chartered to watch the naval review as part of the Coronation celebrations and also for a day's cruise round the fleet. The Court of Appeal had to determine whether the cancellation of the naval review released the defendant from his obligation to pay the hire charge. The Court held that there has not been a sufficient change in circumstances to constitute a frustration of the contract. Here the defendant could have derived some benefit from the contract and was therefore liable to pay the hire charges. A further distinction between *Henry* and *Hutton* is that in *Henry* the claim was brought by a private individual whereas in *Hutton* the hirer was engaged in a commercial enterprise, using the hired boat to take trips of sightseers to Spithead. Frustration is not available in a commercial transaction merely because the contract turns out to be less profitable than one of the parties expected.

- *Death or illness*. In a contract for personal services the death or illness of the person required to perform will frustrate the contract. Temporary illness or incapacity will generally not release a party from his obligations. The illness must be such that it goes to the root of the contract.

Non frustrating events

The common law doctrine of frustration will not apply in the following circumstances:

(a)   If performance of the contract has become more onerous on one party or financially less rewarding.

In *Davis Contractors Ltd. v. Fareham UDC* 1956 the plaintiff building company claimed that a building contract should be regarded as discharged by frustration due to the shortage of available labour and resultant increased costs. The House of Lords rejected the arguments that frustration had discharged the contract. Performance of the contract had simply been made more onerous than originally envisaged by the plaintiffs.

(b)   If the parties to a contract have made express provision for the event which has occurred then the common law doctrine of frustration is inapplicable. The courts will simply give effect to the intention of the parties expressed in the contract.

(c)   If the frustrating event is self induced. If it can be shown that a party to the contract caused the supposed frustrating event by his own conduct then there will be no frustration however there may be a contractual breach.

In *Maritime National Fish Ltd. v. Ocean Trawlers Ltd.* 1935 the appellants had chartered a trawler from the respondents. The vessel was fitted with an otter trawl, which it was unlawful to use without a government licence from the Minister. The appellants used five vessels for fishing and applied for five licences, but were granted three and were allowed to nominate which vessel the licence would cover. They did not nominate the vessel chartered from the respondents, and refused to pay the charter fee. The court held that they were liable to pay it. They could not claim frustration since it was a self-induced situation which prevented them from using the vessel.

Consequences of frustration of contract

To determine the rights and duties of the parties following frustration it is necessary to consider the position at common law and under statute. As we have seen frustration will terminate a contract. However under common law it does not discharge the contract *ab initio* (from the outset) but only from the time of the frustrating event. Therefore, if before that date work had been done or money transferred, the common law rule is simply that losses lie where they fall. It is thus not possible to recover money due or paid prior to frustrating events, except if there is a total failure or consideration, for example if there has been performance of consideration by one party and non performance of consideration by the other.

The common law position has been altered to some extent by the Law Reform (Frustrated Contracts) Act 1943. The Act however does not apply to certain contracts such as insurance, charter-parties (shipping contracts) and contracts for the sale of specific goods, so the common law position is still relevant. Under the Act the following conditions apply:

* Money transferred prior to the frustrating event may be recovered.

* Money due prior to the frustrating event is no longer due.

* Expenses incurred prior to the frustrating event may be deducted from money to be returned.

* Compensation may be recovered on a quantum meruit basis where one of the parties has carried out an act of part performance prior to the frustrating event and thus conferred a benefit on the other party.

In *Gamero SA v. ICM/Fair Warmining (Agency) Ltd.* 1995 the plaintiffs had agreed with the defendants to promote the defendants rock concert. It was to be held in a Madrid stadium, however a few days before the concert the plaintiff's licence to hold it was taken away by the public authority following safety concerns about the stadium and the concert did not take place. Both the parties had incurred preliminary expenses, and the plaintiffs had made an advance payment to the defendants, which they sought to recover under the 1943 Act. The court found the contract to be frustrated because the stadium could not be used. The plaintiffs could recover the advance payment. The court decided not to deduct the defendants expenses from this sum, as the plaintiffs had also suffered loss and to make the deduction would be unfair.

Remedies for Breach of Contract

Whenever a breach of contract arises the innocent party is likely to seek a remedy against the contract breaker. We saw at the beginning of our study of contract law that the fundamental quality of contracts is their legally enforceability, and in the law on remedies that enforceability is realised. The options available are to claim damages and/or treat the contract as discharged under the common law, or to pursue an equitable discretionary remedy.

Damages

Damages is the technical term used to describe monetary compensation. The usual claim is for *unliquidated* damages under the common law. Unliquidated damages are damages whose level is determined by the court, exercising its own discretion. It is sometimes possible for a plaintiff to quantify the measure of damages being sought concisely, in which event the plaintiff will claim a *liquidated* amount e.g.: three weeks' loss of salary where the salary is of a fixed amount, or loss of profit on a sale.

The aim of awarding damages

Damages awarded under an unliquidated claim should amount to an amount which will put the innocent party in the position he would have been in had the contract been performed properly, that is the loss resulting from the breach directly and naturally. Consequently a plaintiff should not be awarded damages when the result would be to put him in a better position financially than would have been the case if the contract had not been broken. The aim of awarding contractual damages is not to punish the contract breaker.

> In *C & B Haulage v. Middleton* 1983 the Court of Appeal refused to grant damages to an engineer who was evicted from the business premises he occupied before the contractual licence he held had expired. The reason for the refusal was that he was working from home, and thus relieved from paying any further charges under the licence. Damages would make him better off.

> In *Paula Lee Ltd. v. Robert Zehil & Co. Ltd.* 1983, under an agreement made between the parties the defendants had undertaken to take 16,000 dresses from the plaintiff manufacturers each season, which they would sell in the Middle East. The dresses in question covered a range of prices. The defendants terminated the agreement with two seasons left, and were only willing to pay compensation representing loss of profit to the plaintiffs on the sale of 32,000 of their cheapest dresses. The Court took the view that for the purposes of determining the measure of damages a term could be implied into the original agreement that the 32,000 garments involved would have been selected in a reasonable manner from the various price ranges involved, thus increasing the damages beyond the minimum level suggested by the defendants.

Damages may be refused where the court is of the view that they are too speculative.

> On this basis the court awarded only nominal damages to the plaintiffs in *Entertainments Ltd. v. Great Yarmouth Borough Council* 1983. The council had repudiated an agreement under which the plaintiffs were to put on summer shows in the town. The judge, Cantley J took the view that as it had not been established as probable that the shows would have made the plaintiffs a profit, to award anything other than nominal damages would be speculative.

If as a result of a breach of contract the innocent party does not obtain what he expected under the contract, but the value of the performance is not affected, what is the level of damages that a court should award to compensate for the loss?

> This was the issue faced by the courts in *Ruxley Electronics and Construction Ltd. v. Forsyth* 1995 a case which was heard on final appeal by the House of Lords. The dispute arose over the building of a swimming pool. The builders had agreed to build a pool with a maximum depth of 7ft 6ins for £70,178. When the work was completed the owner discovered that the maximum depth was only 6ft 9 ins and only 6ft at the point that people would dive in. As is usual in this type of building contract certain sums had been paid by the owner towards the cost of the work during the construction and £39,072 remained outstanding. The builders claimed the balance and the owners counterclaimed for breach of contract. The High Court held that despite the builders breach of contract there had been no reduction in the value of the pool and ordered the owner to pay the balance less £2,500 for the loss of amenity. This decision was reversed by the Court of Appeal who decided that it was appropriate to award £21,560 damages to reflect the cost of replacing the pool to remedy the breach, even though the depth of the pool had not decreased its value. On final appeal the House of Lords held that in this type of case involving defective building work the court was entitled to take the view that it would be unreasonable to insist on reinstatement if the expense of the work involved would be out of all proportion to the benefit obtained. A relevant factor in determining reasonableness was the intention of the owner to rebuild. In this case as the owner did not intend to reinstate, his loss was restricted to the difference in value. The original judgment of £2,500 damages for the loss of amenity was restored and the decision of the Court of Appeal reversed.

Remoteness of damage

The consequences of a contractual breach can often extend well beyond the immediate, obvious losses. A failure to deliver goods may for example result in the buyer being unable to complete the work on a particular job, which will in turn put him in breach with the party who had contracted him to carry out the job. That party may in turn suffer further consequences, thus the original breach leads to a chain of events which become increasingly remote from it. Damages will only be awarded for losses which are *proximate*. The courts take the view that it is unfair to make a contract-breaker responsible for damage caused as a result of circumstances of which he was unaware.

> In *Hadley v. Baxendale* 1854 the plaintiff mill owner contracted with a defendant carrier who agreed to take a broken millshaft to a repairer and then return it. The carrier delayed in delivery of the shaft and as a result the plaintiff sought to recover the loss of profit he would have made during the period of delay. The court held that this loss was not recoverable as it was too remote. The possible loss of profit was a circumstance of which the carrier was unaware at the time of the contract. The result would have been different however had the plaintiff expressly made the defendant aware that this loss of profit was the probable result of a breach of contract.

The decision in *Hadley v. Baxendale* has been approved by the House of Lords on many occasions and knowledge of the circumstances which could produce the damage it still a crucial factor in determining the extent of the liability for the breach.

In *Czarnikow v. Koufos (The Heron II)* 1969 a shipowner delayed in delivering a cargo of sugar to Basrah. The sugar was to be sold by the cargo owners at Basrah, where there was an established sugar market. During the nine days the ship was delayed the market price fell. The cargo owners successfully sued for their loss. The House of Lords considered that the loss ought to have been within the reasonable contemplation of the shipowners as a consequence of the delay. It was felt that the shipowners should have appreciated that a market for goods is something which by its nature fluctuates over time.

In *Balfour Beatty Construction (Scotland) Ltd. v. Scottish Power plc* 1994 the defendants were supplying electricity to the plaintiffs under an agreement linked to a construction project the plaintiffs were carrying out. A break in the supply prevented the completion of a concrete pour. As a result prior construction work was rendered useless and had to be demolished, and then rebuilt. On the grounds that the defendants neither were aware, nor ought reasonably to have been aware of the full effect of interruption to a concrete pour, the House of Lords held the losses to be too remote.

Other principles applicable to a claim for damages

Where a breach has occurred the innocent party, if he accepts that the breach discharges the contract, must take all reasonable steps to mitigate the loss resulting from the breach. There is no requirement for the injured party to act immediately to take on a risky venture but rather act reasonably in order to minimise the loss rather than *sitting on the breach*. For instance an hotel would be expected to try and relet a room that a customer, in breach of contract, had failed to use.

In *Moore v. DER Ltd.* 1971 the plaintiff, a dentist, ordered a new Rover 2000 as a replacement for the one he had which was a total loss following an accident. He could have purchased a second-hand car. The Court of Appeal took the view that he had acted reasonably, for his practice was a busy one and he needed a car that was completely reliable. Nor did this arrangement prevent him from recovering the costs of hiring another vehicle during the period he was waiting for the new car, even though he could have bought a second-hand car much sooner.

By way of contrast in *Luker v. Chapman* 1970 the plaintiff lost his right leg below the knee following a motor accident partly caused by the negligence of the defendant. This injury prevented him from continuing his work as a telephone engineer, but he was offered clerical work as an alternative. He refused it, choosing instead to go into teacher training. It was held that he could not recover as damages the loss of income suffered whilst he underwent the teacher training.

Damages are not limited to the pure economic cost of the loss of the bargain but may also be recovered for inconvenience, discomfort, distress or anxiety caused by the breach.

In *Jarvis v. Swans Tours Ltd.* 1973 the Court of Appeal held that the plaintiff was entitled to damages for mental distress and disappointment due to loss of enjoyment caused by breach of a holiday contract.

In *Perry v. Sidney Phillips & Son* 1982 a surveyor negligently failed to notify his client of defects in a house which the client subsequently bought. The defects included problems with a septic tank which caused offensive smells and violated health legislation. Damages for the client's distress and upset were granted.

In substantial contracts involving large sums, such as building contracts, it is usual to attempt to liquidate damages payable in the event of a breach. This is achieved by the parties expressly inserting a clause into the contract providing for a sum of compensation to be payable on a breach. Generally, provided such clauses represent a genuine pre-estimate of the future possible loss rather than amounting to a penalty to ensure performance of contract, they are enforceable by the courts.

A term will generally be regarded as a *penalty clause* if

(i)   the amount involved is regarded as extravagant. In *Dunlop Pneumatic Tyre Co. Ltd. v. New Garage & Motor Co. Ltd.* 1915 the appellants supplied tyres to the respondents at a trade discount on terms that if the respondents sold the tyres below list price they would pay the appellants £5 per tyre. The House of Lords treated this as a genuine estimate of the harm which Dunlop would suffer by undercutting, and thus enforceable. However in *Ford Motor Co. v. Armstrong* 1915 Armstrong, a motor retailer, agreed to pay £250 to Fords for every car he sold below their list price. The Court of Appeal regarded this as an extravagant sum which was thus void as a penalty.

(ii)   A fixed sum is payable on the occurrence of any one of several events, some of which may be minor breaches and some of which may be more serious.

(iii)   The amount payable is greater than the maximum amount of loss that is likely to be sustained.

Once the court decides however that the sum stipulated represents a liquidated damages clause, rather than a penalty, it will be enforced, even though the actual loss sustained may be larger, or smaller, than damages specified.

Thus in *Cellulose Acetate Silk Co. Ltd. v. Widnes Foundry Ltd.* 1933 the foundry had agreed to pay £20 for every week of delay in completing the construction of premises for Cellulose Acetate. Delays amounted in total to 30 weeks, and Cellulose Acetate sought £6,000 compensation for the actual losses they had suffered. The court held that Widnes Foundry were only liable for damages of £600 (£20 x 30 weeks) as agreed.

Liquidated damage clauses are a common commercial device. In a holiday booking form you will find graduated cancellation charges inserted by the holiday company, which increase in amount the closer to the holiday the cancellation occurs. This reflects the anticipated difficulty the operator is likely to experience in reselling the holiday at short notice.

The right to treat a contract as discharged will depend upon the nature of the breach. For breaches of condition the innocent party may sue for damages and/or treat the contract as repudiated, whereas for less important terms the innocent party is limited to an action for damages.

Quantification of damages in relation to goods or land is essentially a question of assessing the market price and then determining the actual loss. The Sale of Goods Act 1979 provides for a number of remedies, including damages, available to an injured party to a sale of goods transaction.

Discretionary remedies

Historically these remedies became available through the intervention of the Court of Chancery. They include the injunction, specific performance and the remedy of quantum meruit.

Injunctions

An injunction is an order of the court which directs a person not to break his contract, and is an appropriate remedy where the contract contains a negative stipulation.

> This can be seen in *Warner Bros. Pictures v. Nelson* 1937. The defendant, the actress Bette Davis, had agreed to work for the plaintiff company for twelve months, and not to act or sing for anyone else or be otherwise employed for a period of two years, without the plaintiff's written consent. It was held that she could be restrained by injunction from breaking the negative aspects of her undertaking, thus preventing her from working under a new acting contract in England where she was earning more money. The injunction was however confined to her work as an actress, for it was recognised that if the negative terms in her contract were fully enforced it would have the effect of either forcing her to work for Warner Bros. or starve, and this would mean the injunction acting as a device for specific performance of the contract. Equity will not order specific performance of contracts of a personal kind which would involve constant supervision, and which, by their nature, depend upon the good faith of the parties. Similarly in *Page One Records Ltd. v. Britton* 1968 an injunction was applied for to prevent the Troggs pop group from engaging anyone as their manager other than the plaintiff. An injunction on these terms was refused, for to grant it would indirectly compel the pop group to continue to employ the plaintiff.

Types of injunction

There are three types of injunction which may be applied for:

(a) *an interlocutory injunction.* This is designed to regulate the position of the parties pending trial, the plaintiff undertaking to be responsible for any damage caused to the defendant through the use of the injunction if in the subsequent action the plaintiff is unsuccessful. In *American Cyanamid v. Ethicon* 1975 the House of Lords said that an interlocutory injunction should only be granted where the plaintiff can show that the matter to be tried is a serious one and that the balance of convenience is in his favour. One rarely used option for an employee who feels that his employer is unreasonably requiring him to do work which is not part of his contactual obligations is to seek an injunction to maintain the status quo at work.

> In certain circumstances a specialised kind of interlocutory injunction, known as a *Mareva injunction*, may be sought. The Mareva injunction takes its name from the case in which it was first successfully applied for, *Mareva Compania Naviera v. International Bulk Carriers* 1980, and it is used when the subject matter of a contract is in danger of being removed from the area of the courts jurisdiction. If the action which is to be heard involves a claim for damages and the sale of the subject matter is likely to be used to pay them, a Mareva injunction can be used to restrict the removal of these assets from

the courts' jurisdiction. This is a valuable protection in cases where the defendant is a foreign organisation. Section.37 of the Supreme Court Act 1981 grants the High Court the power to issue such injunctions.

(b) *a prohibitory injunction*. This orders a defendant not to do a particular thing. The injunction sought in the *Nelson* case (above) was of this kind. Much of the case law concerning prohibitory injunctions is concerned with employment contracts, and as we have seen such an injunction can only be used to enforce a negative stipulation. In addition the remedy of a prohibitory injunction will not be given where a court is of the opinion that damages would be anadequate remedy, although in the words of Sachs LJ in *Evans Marshall v. Bertola SA* 1973 *"The standard question in relation to the grant of an injunction, are damages an adequate remedy? might perhaps, in the light of the authorities of recent years, be rewritten: is it just, in all the circumstances, that a plaintiff should be confined to his remedy in damages."*

A prohibitory injunction was used in *Decro-Wall International v. Practitioners in Marketing* 1971 where a manufacturer was restrained from breaking a sole distributorship agreement by an order preventing him from disposing of the goods to which the agreement related in any other way. The Court was not however prepared to order him to fulfil the positive part of the agreement which was to maintain supplies of the goods to the distributor, for this would have amounted to specific performance of the contract (see below).

In cases involving land an injunction may be used where for example, the purchaser has undertaken contractually with the vendor not to build on the land, but after the contract has been made seeks to break the promise.

(c) *a mandatory injunction*. This is used to order that a positive act be done, for example that a fence blocking a right of way be taken down.

In *Sky Petroleum Ltd. v. VIP Petroleum Ltd.* 1974 the parties entered into a ten year agreement in 1970 under which VIP undertook to supply all Sky's petrol requirements. Following a dispute in 1973 VIP refused to continue its supplies to Sky, and because of an oil crisis at the time Sky found itself unable to secure any other source of supply. The Court granted a temporary injunction against VIP restraining it from withholding a reasonable level of supplies.

Specific performance

The decree of specific performance is an order of the court requiring a party who is in breach of contract to carry out his promises. Failure to comply amounts to a contempt of court. As an equitable remedy it will only be granted if certain conditions apply. These are:

- *Where damages would not provide an adequate remedy*. Usually in commercial transactions damages will be adequate, and will enable the injured party to purchase the property or obtain the services from some alternative source. However where the subject matter of the contract is unique, for example a painting, specific performance will lie. The item must however be unique, and in *Cohen v. Roche* 1927 specific performance was not ordered of a contract to sell some rare Hepplewhite chairs since it was difficult, but not impossible, to buy similar chairs on the open market.

Land is always regarded as unique, and it is in the enforcement of contracts for the sale of land that specific performance is most commonly used.

A contract for the purchase of shares or debentures can also be specifically enforced.

- *Where the court can properly supervise the performance.*

In *Ryan v. Mutual Tontine Association* 1893 the Court of Appeal held that despite the fact that a lessor of a service flat was in clear breach of his obligation to provide a porter who was to be *"constantly in attendance"*, an application for specific performance of the lease was refused. This was on the ground that to ensure compliance constant supervision by the court would be required. Damages only therefore should be awarded.

- *Where it is not just and equitable.*

In *Malins v. Freeman* 1837 the Court refused the remedy where a bidder at an auction erroneously and carelessly bought property believing he had put in a bid for an entirely different lot. Damages was felt to be an adequate remedy against the bidder, who refused to complete the contract.

Further the plaintiff must satisfy the various equitable maxims which demand high standards of behaviour if relief is to be granted. Thus for example it is said that *"he who comes to equity must come with clean hands"*, meaning that the plaintiff's behaviour must be beyond reproach.

Quantum meruit

A *quantum meruit* claim (for as much as is deserved) is available where:

- *damages is not an appropriate remedy*. This could occur where performance of a contract has begun, but the plaintiff is unable to complete the contract because the defendant has repudiated it, thus preventing the plaintiff from obtaining payment.

- *where work has been carried out under a void contract.*

In *British Steel Corporation v. Cleveland Bridge and Engineering Co. Ltd.* 1984 steel had been supplied to the defendants by the plaintiffs whilst the parties were still negotiating terms. The negotiations subsequently failed, and no contract was concluded between them. The court held that the plaintiffs were entitled to claim on a quantum meruit for the price of the steel supplied to the defendants and used by them.

Assignment An Incident at Ashburne Pool

Ashburne District Council owns and operates a sports complex in Ashburne town centre. A notice at the main entrance to the centre states:

> *"The Council can accept no responsibility for loss or damage to visitors personal possessions within this complex, howsoever arising."*

A notice at the bottom of the steps in the main pool leading to the high diving board states:

> *"Divers: you use the diving board at your own risk."*

Peter and his sister Mary visited the leisure complex in order to swim. They paid fifty pence each for keys to the cubicles in the changing rooms and locked the doors when they left. Whilst Mary swam in the pool Peter climbed the ladder to the diving board. The non-slip coating on the board had worn. Peter lost his footing and plunged into the pool injuring himself. He was rushed to hospital.

When Mary subsequently returned to collect their clothes from the cubicles she found the doors open and the clothes gone. She angrily complained to the changing room attendant who explained that he had left his desk to see what was happening when Peter had his accident, and could only assume that during this time someone had used the master keys from behind the desk to gain access to the cubicles. Changing room attendants are under strict instructions from the council never to leave the desk unattended.

Task

You work as a clerical assistant in Ashburne Leisure Services Department. The Director of Leisure Services is seeking your advice concerning the potential legal liability faced by his department for the injury suffered by Peter and the losses sustained by Peter and his sister. He has asked you to prepare a report which analyses the situation. Produce the report requested by the Director, and in it identify (a) the validity of the notices; and (b) the legal effect of the council's instructions to the changing room attendant.

Assignment A Bad Week at Britech

The Managing Director of Britech Systems Ltd., an electronics company for which you work, has asked you to look into two problems facing the company which have blown up over the last week and are causing him considerable anxiety. The company is based to the west of London. One of these problems concerns a major contract negotiated between the company and an international telecommunications organisation ITTB. The contract involves the construction, installation and maintenance by the company of a highly sophisticated computer monitoring system to control signals beamed to and from the United Kingdom and North America using ITTB's own satellite. The system was due to be installed and be fully operational by the beginning of December, eight months away, but work has been halted due to the commercial collapse of Modem plc, which is the only UK supplier of certain vital microelectronic components used by Britech in the construction of the monitoring system. Modem went into liquidation two weeks ago, and it is unclear whether there is any chance of receiving the components ordered by Britech from Modem. ITTB, aware of the problem, is arguing that its contract with Britech has been frustrated, and has indicated that it is seeking another company to supply the system as a matter of urgency.

Additionally one of Britech's senior employees, who left the company six months ago, has just set up his own business as a Microelectronics Consultant. In common with other senior staff the employee, Gerry McBain, had agreed to a clause in his contract of employment which stipulated, "The employee agrees and undertakes that in the event of the termination of his/her employment with the company, he/she will not compete in any way with the business of the company or so act as to cause damage to the interests of the company, for a period of five years, to run from the date of termination such undertaking to extend to the whole of England and Wales."

The managing director of Britech has arranged to meet you tomorrow ìto discuss the legal position in relation both to ITTB and to Mr McBain.

Tasks

Analyse the two situations described, and produce notes on them in which you seek to clarify the company's position, in order to advise the managing director (a) whether the company has a contractual claim against ITTB, and if it has what the measure of damages is likely to be, and (b) what the likelihood is of the company being able to successfully obtain an injunction to prevent the business operations of Mr. McBain.

Legal Terms found in Chapter 11

Ascertained goods	• goods which were unascertained at the time of contract and have been later singled out or identified
Dealing as a consumer	• a buyer who purchases for his private use from a business seller
Deliverable state	• goods which are in such a condition that the buyer would be bound to accept them in accordance with the terms of the contract
Delivery	• the voluntary transfer of physical possession of the goods from the seller to the buyer or his agent
Lien	• the unpaid seller's right to keep possession of goods against payment in the event of the buyer's insolvency
Nemo dat quod non habet	• a latin phrase meaning he cannot give what he does not have encapsulating the general principle that a buyer cannot acquire the ownership of goods from a seller who does not have the legal right to sell them
Passing off	• the transfer of ownership of goods from buyer to seller, sometimes also referred to as transfer of title
Price variation clause	• an express term of a contract which allows one of the parties to change the price in certain circumstances after the contract has been concluded
Property	• ownership
Retention of title clause	• an express term of a contract under which the seller retains the ownership of goods until certain conditions, such as full payment, have been met
Sale of goods	• a contract involving the exchange of the ownership of goods in return for money
Specific goods	• goods which have been identified and agreed upon at the time the contract is made
Supply of goods	• a wider term than sale of goods including for example contracts of hire and contracts of exchange or barter of goods
Transfer of risk	• the passing over from the seller to the buyer the risk of accidental loss or damage to goods
Unascertained goods	• goods which have been generally described but not specifically identified or singled out at the time the contract is made
Unconditional appropriation	• a final irrevocable setting aside of goods to be used in the performance of a contract, for example by the act of delivery

Chapter 11

Business Contracting

Sale of Goods and Related Transactions

This chapter aims to examine the contractual relationships arising between businesses and all those whom they supply. It is an area of critical importance in developing an understanding of business law, for it lies at the heart of commercial activity.

The primary objective of business activity is the provision of goods and services for consumers. Consumption of goods and services meets the private needs of individuals. All of us act as private consumers in this way. We make regular purchases of goods and services to satisfy our demand for a wide range of necessaries and luxuries, from food and clothing to motor cars, video recorders and holidays. Goods and services are also demanded by business organisations, who acquire them to meet their own internal requirements, as well as for the purpose of resale to other businesses in the chain of production or to consumers. The legal rules relating to inter business contracting are, in many cases, identical to those which apply where a business deals with a private consumer. However the law has increasingly sought to compensate for the relative economic weakness of individual consumers, by developing a framework of consumer protection. This framework is examined in relation to goods in Chapter 12 and in relation to services in Chapter 13.

Types and Nature of Business Agreements

In the previous two chapters we examined the legal rules relating to the formation of business contracts and the discharge of obligations arising under them. The remedies available in the event of non compliance by one of the contracting parties were also considered. We shall now examine in more detail the various types of contract which are encountered in business and identify the features which distinguish them. Some types of contract involving the supply of goods, for example, which appear very similar, are nevertheless governed by different rules. The distinction between them may depend upon the provisions in the contract relating to the transfer of ownership or the time for payment. It is particularly important to be able to distinguish between the various types of contract otherwise there is a danger of applying the wrong legal rules.

Contracts for the sale of goods

Contracts for the sale of goods are perhaps the most significant category of business agreement because they are the type which are most commonly encountered in the commercial world. A sale of goods contract is basically one in which goods are exchanged for money. Examples of this type of contract range from the sale of a loaf of bread for seventy pence to the purchase of an aircraft for tens of millions of pounds.

The law relating to contracts for the sale of goods is contained in the Sale of Goods Act 1979. As a general rule the principle of freedom of contract applies to them. Essentially therefore the buyer and seller are free to negotiate the terms of the contract and make whatever bargain suits their own purposes. Many of the rules contained in the 1979 Act apply only where the parties have not expressly made their intentions clear on the matter in the contract. Some of the provisions in the Act, however, cannot be overridden by agreement between the parties.

A contract for the sale of goods is defined in s.2(1) which states: *"A contract for the sale of goods is a contract by which the seller transfers or agrees to transfer the property in goods to the buyer for a money consideration, called the price".*

A closer consideration of the definition reveals the following:

   (a)   There must be *a contract*. The formation of the contract is governed by the ordinary principles of the law of contract. No special formalities are required. The 1979 Act in s.4 states; *"a contract of sale may be made in writing (either with or without seal), or by word of mouth, or partly in writing and partly by word of mouth, or may be implied from the conduct of the parties".*

   (b)   *the seller transfers or agrees to transfer*. The Act distinguishes between *a sale* in which property is transferred to the buyer on the making of the contract and thus the seller's consideration is executed, and *an agreement to sell* in which property is transferred to the buyer at some future time and thus the seller's consideration is executory.

   (c)   *property*. This means full legal ownership and is also sometimes referred to as title. This must be distinguished from mere physical possession of goods which does not necessarily signify ownership.

   (d)   *goods*. This includes any form of personal property which is tangible and moveable for example a motor vehicle, a computer or a ship. The definition does not extend to land or to intangible property rights such as intellectual property, shares or debts. It does however include an undivided share in goods, for example a 25% share in a racehorse

   (e)   *money consideration*. In order for a contract to come within the definition in s.2(1) the price for the goods must include an element of money consideration. For this reason contracts of exchange or barter are not covered by the 1979 Act. However where goods are exchanged for a combination of money and other goods, a part exchange, the contract will come within the definition.

   In *Aldridge v. Johnson* 1857 a contract for the exchange of 52 bullocks for a quantity of barley and a sum of money was held to be a contract for the sale of goods.

The importance of the definition in s.2(1) is that wherever there is a contract involving the exchange of ownership of goods for money the provisions of the Sale of Goods Act 1979 will apply to it.

Auction sales

Where goods are sold at auction the contract of sale will be governed by the Sale of Goods Act 1979. In relation to the formation of the contract of sale the auctioneer makes an invitation to treat when asking for bids. Each bid is a separate offer and no contract is concluded until a bid is accepted by the auctioneer. The 1979 Act provides in s.57 that: *"a sale by auction is complete when the auctioneer announces its completion by the fall of the hammer, or in other customary manner; and until the announcement is made any bidder may retract his bid"*.

This section also allows the seller to place a reserve price on the goods and instruct the auctioneer not to sell below that price. The seller may bid himself up to the reserve price against any buyer. In each situation the seller must expressly reserve his right before the auction sale and bidders must be notified.

In an auction sale there are in fact three separate contracts: between the seller and the buyer; the seller and the auctioneer; and the buyer and the auctioneer.

(a) The contract between the seller and the buyer

This is a contract for the sale of goods and the provisions of the Sale of Goods Act 1979 apply to it except to the extent that they may have been varied by the express terms of the contract. When we examine the law relating to exclusion clauses in contracts below it will be seen that the buyer of goods at an auction sale can never *deal as a consumer* for the purposes of the Unfair Contract Terms Act 1977. This means that the stronger legal protection afforded to consumers will not be available to the buyer at an auction, even if he is in fact buying consumer type goods for his personal use.

Under the Auctions (Bidding Agreements) Acts 1927 and 1969 where the person to whom goods have been sold at an auction sale is a party to a bidding ring the contract is voidable at the option of the seller. A bidding ring is an agreement between a person who attends auctions in the course of business for the purpose of buying goods to resell (a dealer) and any other person, in which it is agreed that the parties within the bidding ring will not try to outbid each other. The objective of the agreement is that the price of particular items are not forced up by competitive bidding. Its effect is that the seller loses money. Usually those involved in the bidding ring will meet after the auction to divide their spoils. Under these Acts it is also a criminal offence for a dealer to offer or agree to give an inducement or reward to another person in return for their abstaining from bidding at an auction.

(b) The contract between the auctioneer and the buyer

This contract is governed by the common law rather then the Sale of Goods Act 1979. The rights and obligations of the parties are a matter for agreement between the auctioneer and the buyer. In practice this usually means that the terms of the contract are laid down in the auctioneer's printed auction conditions. The common law implies the following terms into this contract unless the parties have expressly agreed on contrary terms:

    (i)   the auctioneer has the seller's authority to sell the goods;

(ii)   the auctioneer will give possession of the goods to the purchaser once the price is paid;

(iii)   the auctioneer may retain possession of the goods until the full price is paid or tendered;

(iv)   neither the auctioneer nor the seller will interrupt the buyer's quiet possession of the goods; and

(v)   the auctioneer knows of no reason by which the seller is legally unable to sell the goods.

(c) The contract between the auctioneer and the seller

This contract is also governed by the common law and its terms will be those which have been agreed between the auctioneer and the seller. Again these will usually be laid down in the auctioneer's printed conditions of contract. In the absence of agreed terms to the contrary, the common law implies a promise on the part of the auctioneer that he will not give the buyer possession of the goods without receiving payment. He will be personally liable to the seller for the price if the buyer takes the possession without making payment. The auctioneer has a common law lien on the proceeds of sale of the goods. This means that he is entitled to deduct his agreed fees from any sums which are due to the seller before making payment to him.

Contracts of barter

Barter is the method of trading used in the most primitive societies before the invention of money as a generally accepted medium of exchange. A contract of barter is one involving the exchange of goods or services for other goods or services in which no money actually changes hands. Such contracts are not governed by the Sale of Goods Act 1979 because of the absence of a money consideration.

A contract of barter or exchange is a *contract for the transfer of goods* as defined in Part I of the Supply of Goods and Services Act 1982.

Contracts of hire

The essence of a contract of hire is that the hirer, in return for some consideration, usually an agreed fee or the periodical payment of a sum of money, enjoys the possession and the use of goods belonging to someone else, the owner. It is never intended that the hirer shall become the owner of the goods himself under the terms of the contract. Contracts of hire are fairly common in the business world and the period of use by the hirer may range from hours to years. Examples of such contracts include the hire of a mobile crane for a specific task lasting two days; the rental of a household television set over a number of years; the hire of a car for a week whilst on holiday; and the hire of sports equipment at a sports centre. In recent times there has been a growth in the commercial leasing of plant and equipment, particularly motor vehicles, to businesses. Commercial leasing, which is a form of hiring, can be a tax efficient method of acquiring plant and equipment for use in a business.

Contracts of hire are governed partly by the Supply of Goods and Services Act 1982 and may also be regulated partly by the Consumer Credit Act 1974. In order to come within the 1974 Act the contract must be a `consumer hire agreement'. This is defined in s.15(1) of the 1974 Act as:

> "*an agreement made by a person (the owner) with an individual (the hirer) for the bailment of goods, which:*
>
> *(a)   is not a hire purchase agreement,*
>
> *(b)   is capable of subsisting for more than three months, and*
>
> *(c)   does not require the hirer to make payments exceeding £15,000".*

Some of the language of s.15(1) requires explanation:

(a)   An agreement made *by a person with an individual*. The Act distinguishes between a person and an individual. Whilst the owner may be a person, the hirer must be an individual before the agreement will be regulated by the Act. An individual is a flesh and blood person or an unincorporated association, such as a partnership. Persons, on the other hand, include, as well as individuals, legally created corporate entities such as limited companies or local authorities.

(b)   *for the bailment of goods*. The expression bailment describes a situation in which one person has possession of goods belonging to another. A contract of hire is one of several possible types of contract of bailment. Another example would be a contract under which goods are stored in a warehouse on behalf of a business.

(c)   *not a hire purchase agreement*. The nature of a hire purchase agreement is examined below. At this stage it is sufficient to note that an agreement will not be a consumer hire agreement if its real purpose is the eventual acquisition of ownership of the goods by the hirer. The basic idea of any contract of pure hire is that the hirer never becomes the owner of the goods. The goods revert to the possession of the true owner once the period of hire has expired.

Consumer hire agreements are regulated by the Consumer Credit Act 1974 which lays down strict rules as to their form and content. The agreement must be in writing and signed personally by the hirer. If either of these conditions are not fulfilled the owner has no right to sue the hirer under the agreement. The hirer must be given a copy of the agreement containing full information about his rights and duties and about the protection given to him by the 1974 Act. If any of these formalities are not complied with then no legal action can be taken against the hirer without the permission of the court.

Contracts for the supply of services

A contract for the supply of services (or contract for services) usually involves the exchange of an individual's time skill or effort in return for money. A person providing a service could do so by engaging in such diverse activities as surveying a house, tuning a car engine, transporting commodities, or providing legal advice. The contract for services is distinct from the contract of employment (or contract of service) which we consider in Chapter 14. The basic obligations owed by those who provide services in the course of a business are outlined in Part II of the Supply of Goods Act 1982.

Contracts for work done and materials supplied

Where services are provided and goods are supplied under the same contract, for example a contract to paint a portrait, to prepare and supply food or to service a motor vehicle, there may be some difficulty in classifying the contract. It could be a contract for the provision of services or a contract for the sale of goods. The court will decide into which category the contract falls by trying to identify the main purpose of the contract.

> In *Young and Marten v. McMannus Childs* 1968 the House of Lords held that a contract for the laying of tiles on the roof of a house was not a sale of goods contract even though the tiler supplied the tiles. The main purpose of the contract was the supply of services and so the contract was not within the Sale of Goods Act 1979.

> In *Robinson v. Graves* 1935 the Court of Appeal held that a contract under which an artist agreed to paint a client's portrait was not a contract for the sale of goods. The transfer of ownership of the canvas to the client was incidental to the main substance of the contract which was the provision by the artist of his skill, expertise and labour.

It may have been different if the client has selected a finished picture from the artist's studio and agreed to pay for it. Such an agreement is a contract for the sale of goods because the substance of the agreement is the transfer of ownership of a completed picture, not the provision of skill and labour by the artist. Parts I and II of the Supply of Goods and Services Act 1982 apply to contracts for work done and materials supplied.

Contracts for the sale or supply of goods on credit terms

There are various forms of credit transaction which provide ways of getting goods on tick, ranging from contracts of hire purchase, credit sale and conditional sale agreements, to the use of *plastic money*. Credit transactions were aptly characterised by one County Court Judge who complained that most of his time was taken up by: *"people who are persuaded by persons whom they do not know to enter into contracts that they do not understand to purchase goods that they do not want with money that they have not got"*.

Although this statement is somewhat exaggerated, it helps to highlight some of the problems with which the law has had to deal arising from such agreements, and we shall examine the ways in which the courts and parliament have sought to provide solutions to those problems in Chapter 9.

(a) Contracts of hire purchase

A contract of hire purchase, as its name suggests, combines elements of two types of contract. It is in effect a contract of hire which gives one party (the hirer or debtor) an option to purchase goods from the other (the owner or creditor) at the end of a period of hire. During the period of the agreement the debtor pays the creditor by instalments (usually monthly) and the ownership of the goods remains with the creditor. The agreement will contain a term giving the debtor an optional right to purchase the goods at a nominal price once all the instalments have been paid. Ownership of the goods will be transferred to the debtor if and when he exercises the option to purchase. He will invariably do this as soon as he has paid all of the instalments because the real point of the agreement, in practice, it to enable him to acquire ownership.

A hire purchase agreement is not a contract of sale falling within the Sale of Goods Act 1979. Many hire purchase agreements come within the definition of consumer credit agreements and these are regulated by the Consumer Credit Act 1974.

At first sight a hire purchase transaction appears to involve only two parties. In practice, however, the vast majority of hire purchase transactions involve a third party, a finance company. The person who supplies the goods may not be able to wait for his money and may require instant payment, while his customer wishes to have time for payment. The supplier will therefore sell the goods to a finance company, which will supply them to the customer on hire purchase terms under a separate contract.

The supplier will have in his possession a stock of hire purchase forms belonging to the finance company with whom he usually deals. A customer wishing to take goods on credit will be asked to complete one of these forms and thus make a contractual offer to the finance company to take the goods on hire purchase. The supplier will complete a different form which will constitute a contractual offer to sell the goods to the finance company for cash. The supplier will forward both these offers to the finance company which will either accept or reject them both. If accepted, the supplier will be paid immediately by the finance company. The finance company becomes the owner of the goods and the customer will be bound by a contract of hire purchase with the finance company. Usually the customer will take possession of the goods from the supplier at this stage.

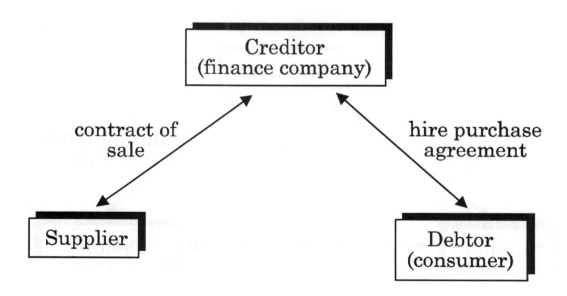

Figure 11.1   Hire purchase transaction

It would appear at first sight that there is no contract between the customer and the supplier where the finance company is involved in a credit transaction. If this were so, difficulties could arise for the customer, if, for example, he wished to sue the supplier for making false statements about the goods. The customer cannot at common law (though the position is different under the 1974 Act) rescind the contract with the finance company on the grounds that the supplier made a misrepresentation to him. However, the common law has recognised the existence of a contract between the customer and the supplier in these circumstances. The customer may sue the supplier for breach of this secondary or collateral contract.

> In *Andrews v. Hopkinson* 1956 the defendant car dealer showed a second hand car to the plaintiff and told him *"it's a good little bus. I would stake my life on it"*. As a result the plaintiff entered into a hire purchase contract with a finance company. Soon afterwards he was injured in a collision caused by a failure of the car steering mechanism. It was held that the defendant was liable in damages to the plaintiff for breach of a collateral contract between them. The court was satisfied that each of the parties had given consideration to support the contract. On the part of the defendant, this was his statement, which amounted to a promise that the car was in good condition and reasonably fit for use. On the part of the plaintiff, his entry into the contract with the finance company was the consideration. It had been of direct benefit to the defendant as he was able to sell the car to the finance company as a result.

As we shall see later, where the supplier and creditor have a business connection, the debtor will be able to sue the creditor as well as the supplier in these circumstances.

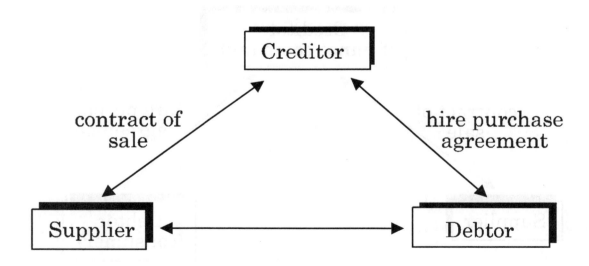

Figure 11.2   Collateral Contract

(b) Credit sale and conditional sale agreements

Credit sale and conditional sale agreements are credit transactions under which the price of goods is payable by instalments. They will often be financed by a finance company in exactly the same way as hire purchase agreements.

At common law the credit sale agreement is broadly similar to the conditional sale agreement. Each is a contract for the sale of goods under which the buyer commits himself at the outset to the purchase. Theoretically, this is not the case with a hire purchase agreement. Here the customer has an option to buy but is not legally bound to exercise that option.

The main difference at common law between credit sale and conditional sale agreements is that:

(i)   in a credit sale agreement ownership of the goods in transferred to the buyer as soon as the contract is made, whereas

(ii) in a conditional sale agreement ownership of the goods is not transferred to the buyer until some condition (usually the payment of the final instalment) is met.

While the instalments are being paid, the buyer is the owner of goods under a credit sale agreement; but the seller is the owner of goods under a conditional sale agreement. In this important respect a conditional sale agreement is similar to a hire purchase agreement. This is why many of the statutory rights of a consumer under a hire purchase agreement such as the right of termination and the protected goods provisions, examined later, also apply to a conditional sale agreement. These rights do not arise in relation to a credit sale agreement.

Inter-Business Contracting and Consumer Contracting

The rights of the business customer and the degree of consumer protection available to him will vary considerably depending upon whether one or both of the parties are entering into the contract in the course of their business. Generally a greater degree of legal protection is available to a private individual than to a business. It is possible to envisage a number of different situations:

(a)   private seller and private buyer or business buyer

(b)   business seller and business buyer

(c)   business seller and private buyer

Take as an example a contract for the sale of goods containing a clause excluding the seller's liability, where the buyer suffers loss because the goods are defective. On these facts the legal rules applicable in each of the above cases would be different, and the outcomes would vary accordingly. It is important then to be able to distinguish between a situation where someone is acting in the course of a trade or business on one hand, or dealing as a consumer on the other.

Dealing as a consumer

In a broad sense anyone to whom goods or services are supplied can be regarded as a consumer and, as we shall see later, the law gives protection to all consumers. However, the protection available is greater in the case of the private consumer. The Fair Trading Act 1973 defines a private consumer in s.137 as:

"the person to or for whom goods or services are, or are sought to be, supplied in the course of a business carried on by the supplier, and who does not receive or seek to receive the goods or services in the course of a business carried on by him".

The Unfair Contract Terms Act 1977 also provides a statutory definition of a private consumer. The Act states in s.12 that:

"a party to a contract deals as a consumer in relation to another party if:

(a)   *he neither makes the contract in the course of a business nor holds himself out as doing so; and*

(b)   *the other party does make the contract in the course of a business; and*

(c)   *where the contract involves the supply of goods, the goods are of a type ordinarily supplied for private use or consumption".*

Three aspects of the transaction must be examined in order to see whether the buyer deals as a consumer: the buyer, the seller and the goods themselves. If the buyer buys for his business or from a private seller or if the goods are of a type which would not usually be purchased for private use then the buyer cannot deal as a consumer. The courts have been prepared to give a fairly wide interpretation of s.12:

In *Peter Symmonds & Co. v. Cook* 1981 the plaintiffs were partners in a firm of surveyors and they bought a second-hand Rolls Royce in the partnership name with partnership money. The car was intended for use by one of the partners only. The High Court held that the plaintiffs were dealing as consumers in the purchase of the car even though it was to be used partly for business purposes.

A similar approach has been adopted more recently by the Court of Appeal in *R & B Customs Brokers Co. v. United Dominions Trust* 1988 which is considered more fully later in the context of s.6 of the Unfair Contract Terms Act. In this case it was held that, in order for a purchase to be made *in the course of a business* for the purposes of s.12, it must be established that such purchases are made with a degree of regularity. Where this is shown it can be said that the purchase is an integral part of the business (and therefore made in the course of the business) as opposed merely to being incidental to the carrying on of the business.

Where the contract is made at auction or by competitive tender, the customer can never be regarded as dealing as a consumer for the purposes of the Unfair Contract Terms Act.

Supplying in the course of a trade or business

Many of the legal rules which govern consumer protection apply only where goods or services are supplied in the course of a trade or business. There is no generally applicable precise definition of the expression `business', although there are a number of decided cases which give some guidance.

In *Havering London Borough v. Stevenson* 1970 a car hire firm regularly sold its cars after a period of use in the business. A sale in these circumstances was held to be in the course of its trade or business as a car hire firm.

On the other hand, in *Davies v. Sumner* 1984 the defendant was a self employed courier, who had a contract with a T.V. company to transport films and video tapes. He purchased a new car in June 1980, and travelled 118,000 miles in it before trading it in for another in July 1981. The mileometer had gone around the clock, and showed only 18,000 miles. The defendant did not disclose the true mileage, and was later charged with having applied a false trade description *"in the course of a trade or business"*. The House of Lords held that he was not guilty, as this was a one-off sale which could not be regarded as an integral part of his business.

In *Blakemore v. Bellamy* 1983 the defendant's spare time activity of buying, refurbishing and selling cars was held to be a hobby rather than a business. This was so even though he had sold eight different cars over a period of fifteen months and he had not driven them all himself or had them insured.

Business sellers may sometimes masquerade as private sellers for example by advertising in the small ad's in a newspaper. The purchaser may be mislead by this and think that his legal remedies are limited because he has purchased from a private seller. In order to prevent such disguised business sales the Business Advertisements (Disclosure) Order 1977 was made under s.22 of The Fair Trading Act 1973. Under this regulation it is a criminal offence for a trader or a businessman to advertise goods for sale without making it reasonably clear that the goods are being sold in the course of a business.

Where goods are sold by an agent in the course of his business for a private seller, the sale will be treated, for the purposes of the implied terms in s.14 of the Sale of Goods Act 1979, as a sale by a seller acting in the course of a business unless:

(a)   the buyer knows that he is purchasing from a private seller, or

(b)   reasonable steps are taken to bring it to his attention before the contract is made.

This could apply, for example, where goods are sold by a private seller at a public auction.

Inter-business contracting

Where a contract is made between a business seller and a business buyer, the parties are allowed greater freedom of contract to agree their respective obligations by negotiation. The courts will be reluctant to interfere with the terms of a bargain made between contracting parties of equal bargaining power. Business consumers should be better placed in terms of their experience knowledge and bargaining power to look after their own interests than the private consumer would be. If there is unequal bargaining power, however, the courts may be prepared to step in and protect the weaker party to the transaction by invalidating part of the agreement under the Unfair Contract Terms Act 1977.

Standard form contracts

Clearly it makes commercial sense to set out precisely and exhaustively the terms which are to apply to the contract, and the means used by the majority of organisations to achieve this is the *standard form* contract. A standard form contract is a printed document consisting of a uniform set of terms for use by an organisation as the basis upon which it trades. A standard form agreement is of advantage to a business in two ways:

- it helps to save time by removing the need for the regular negotiation of terms; and
- it will seek to provide the organisation with the maximum amount of commercial protection possible, by relying on terms which are favourable to it, for instance by enabling it to cancel the agreement in specified circumstances, to raise its price in line with increases in manufacturing costs, and so on.

We have already referred to the imbalance in trading strength that frequently occurs in contract making with the dominant party dictating terms to the weaker party. We have seen that contracts, usually of a standard form kind, in which this dominance is asserted are often referred to as contracts of adhesion, for the weaker party is unable to negotiate but must simply adhere to the stronger party's terms.

The danger of this type of economic oppression was pointed out by Lord Diplock in *Schroeder Music Publishing Co. Ltd. v. Macauley* 1974 when he stated *"The terms of this kind of standard form of contract have not been the subject of negotiation between the parties to it, or approved by any organisation representing the interests of the weaker party. They have been dictated by that party whose bargaining power, either exercised alone, or in conjunction with others providing similar goods or services, enables him to say: "If you want these goods or services at all, these are the only terms on which they are available. Take it or leave it"."*

Some of the more obvious abuses which were present at one time in this type of contract are now controlled by legislation; for example extortionate credit bargains by the Consumer Credit Act 1974, and exclusion or limitation of liability by the Unfair Contract Terms Act 1977.

The use of standard form agreements does not always indicate a situation of dominance by one party over the other. The standard agreement may be the basis upon which negotiations are conducted, or it may be that both sides have equal bargaining strength and both will try to insist on the use of their own form of agreement. In some areas of commercial and industrial activity standard terms are devised by organisations to represent the interests of the sector generally. For example local authorities may together produce sets of terms which they can all use in their dealings with suppliers of goods or services. In the building industry there are such arrangements. The present standard contract in use is the Joint Contracts Tribunal (JCT) form.

Where parties of relatively equal bargaining strength deal with each other over a long period of time, standard form agreements may evolve by negotiation. Far from being oppressive, this type of standard form contract provides a framework of certainty for business transactions and an appropriate division of rights and responsibilities between the parties. It may take into account possible occurrences and contingencies. The apportionment of risks under it can be linked with the insurance arrangements of the parties. Such an agreement will be designed to avoid the risk of litigation between the parties, for example by use of arbitration and liquidated damages clauses.

A standard form contract for the sale of goods is set out on the following pages.

1.   (a) THIS AGREEMENT is made the   day of   19

BETWEEN   of

(referred to in this agreement as "the seller") and

of

(referred to in this agreement as "the buyer")

WHEREBY IT IS AGREED that the seller shall sell and the buyer shall purchase the goods described in condition 2 in accordance with the terms of this contract.

(b) No amendments or modifications to these conditions and, in particular, no terms or conditions of purchase of the buyer shall form part of the contract or be binding upon the seller unless expressly agreed to in writing and signed by the seller.

2.   (a) Description of goods:

(b) The description of the goods in condition 2(a) above is believed to be correct as to weights, dimensions, capacity, composition, performance and otherwise. Any error, omission or mis-statement therein (whether or not it materially affects the description of the goods) shall not annul the sale nor entitle the buyer to be discharged from the contract or to claim any compensation in consequence thereof. Provided that nothing in this condition shall oblige the buyer to accept any goods which differ substantially in any of the above-mentioned respects from the goods agreed to be sold if the buyer would be prejudiced by reason of such difference. In that event the buyer shall be entitled to rescind the contract and to claim repayment of the price, but the seller shall incur no further liability in respect thereof.

3.   (a) In addition to the price of the goods, the buyer shall pay

(i) Vat or other taxes payable in respect of the goods;

(ii) the cost of insurance under condition 8; and

(iii) the cost of delivery under condition 4.

(b) The price of the goods is :

        add V.A.T :

        insurance :

        delivery :

        total amount due :

(c) Where the date of delivery specified in condition 4 is more than six months from the date of this agreement, the seller reserves the right to increase the price of the goods in proportion to any increase in costs to the seller of materials labour and other inputs between the date of this contract and the date of delivery.

(d) The buyer will pay the price of the goods and any other sums due to the seller under this contract within 30 days of the date of delivery. In the event of a failure to make payment by the due date interest at the rate of 10% per annum shall be payable on any sums outstanding.

4.   (a) The delivery date is   . This date is given as way of an estimate only and the seller shall not be liable for failure to deliver on time.

(b) Unless the seller is notified otherwise in writing at least seven days before the delivery date, the seller shall deliver the goods to the buyer's place of business. The cost of transportation and insurance up to the time of actual delivery will be paid by the buyer in accordance with condition 3.

(c) The seller shall be entitled at its sole discretion to make partial deliveries or deliveries by instalments.

(d) Deviations in quantity of the goods delivered (representing no more then 10% by value) from that stated in condition 2 shall not give the buyer any right to reject the goods or to claim damages. The buyer shall be obliged to accept and pay at the contract rate for the quantity of goods delivered.

5.   (a) The seller reserves the right to modify the specification or design of the goods in whole or in part without prior notification to the buyer. The buyer shall accept such modified goods in performance of the contract.

(b) The buyer shall be deemed to have accepted the goods unless within 14 days of delivery written notice is received by the seller to the contrary.

6.   (a) The property in the goods shall remain with the seller until the seller has received payment in full for the goods and all other sums owing to the seller on whatever grounds.

(b) If the buyer sells the goods prior to making payment in full for them, the rights of the seller under this condition shall attach to the proceeds of sale or to the claim for such proceeds. The buyer shall, if required to do so by the seller, formally assign any such rights.

(c) For so long as the property in goods remains with the seller, the buyer shall store the goods separately so that they may readily be identified as the property of the seller. The seller shall during this time have the right to retake possession of the goods. For this purpose the buyer hereby irrevocably authorises the seller of his agents to enter upon any premises occupied by the buyer.

(d) The seller may maintain an action for the price notwithstanding that property in the goods may not have passed to the buyer.

7.   The goods shall be at risk of the buyer in all respects from the date of this contract or, if later, the date of manufacture by the seller.

8.   Unless the buyer notifies the seller in writing to the contrary, the seller shall at the expense of the buyer insure the goods to the full replacement value thereof until the time of delivery.

9.   (a) In the event that the goods supplied to the buyer fail to comply with the terms of this contract, or prove to be defective, the liability of the seller is limited to the replacement of the goods or, at the seller's option, the refund of all payments made by the buyer in respect of the goods.

(b) Except as otherwise provided in condition 9(a), the seller shall be under no liability of whatsoever kind whether or not due to the negligence or wilful default of the seller or its servants or agents arising out of or in connection with any breach of the seller's obligations under this contract. All conditions, warranties or other terms, express or implied, statutory or otherwise, are hereby expressly excluded.

(c) Nothing in this condition shall exclude or restrict any liability of the seller for death or personal injury resulting from the negligence of the seller or its servants or agents.

(d) If it should be held in relation to any claim that the preceding provisions of this paragraph are ineffective, the buyer shall not be entitled to reject the goods and any damages recovered by the buyer shall be limited to the reasonable cost of remedying the breach of contract provided that the seller shall first be afforded the opportunity of itself carrying out such remedial work.

(e) Nothing in this condition or in conditions 2(b) or 4(d) shall exclude or restrict any liability of the seller for breach of its implied undertakings as to title; and, where the buyer deals as a consumer, any liability of the seller for breach of its implied undertakings as to description, quality, fitness for purpose, or correspondence with sample.

(f) In the case of transactions covered by paragraphs (4) and (5) of the Consumer Transactions (Restrictions on Statements) Order 1976 the provisions of this contract shall not affect the statutory rights of the consumer.

10. The seller shall not be liable for non-performance in whole or in part of its obligations under this contract due to causes beyond the control either of the seller or of the seller's suppliers including any Act of God, fire, flood, tempest, act of state, war, civil commotion, embargo, accident, plant breakdown, hindrance in or prevention from obtaining any raw materials or other supplies, interference by labour disputes, inability to obtain adequate labour, manufacturing facilities or energy, or any other like cause. If any such event continues for a period of more than 6 weeks, the seller may cancel this contract or vary condition 4(a) hereof by notice in writing to the buyer without liability on the part of the seller.

11. (a) The seller shall have the right to terminate this contract by notice in writing in the event of the buyer's insolvency and the buyer shall indemnify the seller against all losses and damage suffered by reason of such termination.

(b) Termination of the contract under this condition shall not affect the accrued rights of the parties arising in any way out of the contract as at the date of termination.

(c) In the event of termination under this condition the seller shall have the right to enter any business premises occupied by the buyer and recover any goods which are the seller's property.

12. In the event of cancellation of this contract by the buyer for whatever reason, the buyer agrees to pay 20% of the purchase price to the seller by way of liquidated damages.

13. The benefit of this contract shall not be assigned or transferred by the buyer without the prior written consent of the seller. The seller shall have the right to assign to any of its associated companies all of the rights, powers, duties and obligations under this contract without the consent of the buyer. In the event of any such assignment by the seller references in this contract to the seller shall be deemed to be references to any company taking under the assignment.

14. If any difference shall arise between the seller and the buyer upon the meaning of any part of this contract or the rights and liabilities of the parties hereto, the same shall be referred the arbitration of two persons (one named by each party) or their umpire in accordance with the provisions of the Arbitration Act 1950 or any amending or substituted legislation for the time being in force.

SIGNED for and on behalf)
of the SELLER:)
SIGNED for and on behalf)
of the BUYER:)

Standard Form Contract for the Sale of Goods

The terms of the standard form contract were drawn up by the seller, and it is clear that most of its contents are weighted in his favour. We shall now examine selected clauses of the agreement in order to see what they are attempting to achieve, and comment on any legal rules which may affect their validity.

It should be borne in mind that where the buyer is a consumer, the Unfair Terms in Consumer Contracts Regulations 1994 may be invoked to challenge the validity of any of the terms of the contract, other than those which define the consideration provided by each party i.e. the price and the goods supplied.

Clause 1(b) attempts to exclude any conflicting terms of business on which the buyer usually trades, or any other variation of the terms set out in the seller's standard form. As we noted in Chapter 8, where there is a battle of forms like the one which occurred in *Butler Machine Tool Co. Ltd. v. Ex-Cell-O Corporation Ltd.* 1979, the rules of offer and acceptance will determine whether clause 1(b) is actually effective.

Clause 2(b) is an attempt to deal with a problem posed by s.13 of the Sale of Goods Act 1979, which provides that compliance with description is a condition of the contract. Under s.13 anything less than strict compliance with the contract description used to give the buyer the right to reject the goods and rescind the contract, even if he suffered no loss as a result. This happened for example, in *Re Moore & Landauer* 1921 and *Arcos v. Ronnaasen* 1933. Since the coming into force of the Sale and Supply of Goods Act 1994, the position has changed. A buyer who does not deal as a consumer cannot reject goods where a beach of s.13, 14 or 15 by the seller is so slight that it would be unreasonable for him to do so. Where the buyer deals as a consumer however his right to reject for a minor breach of condition remains unaffected. Clause 2(b) is a limitation of liability and will be subject to the controls in s.6 of the Unfair Contract Terms Act 1977.

Clause 3(c) is a price variation clause. This type of clause is particularly significant when the rate of inflation is high. It allows the seller to pass onto the buyer any increase in costs between the date of the contract and the date of delivery. Increases cannot be passed on under clause 3(c) if delivery takes place within six months of the making of the contract. Obviously the longer the period of time between contract and delivery, the more the price will increase. A buyer faced with this type of term will usually try to negotiate an upper limit on any price increase if he cannot persuade the seller to withdraw it altogether.

Clause 3(d) provides for the payment of interest in the event of late payment of sums due to the seller from the buyer. This is an attempt by the seller to ensure a steady cash flow in his business. In the absence of a contractual right to interest:

(i)   no interest will be payable by the buyer in respect of late payments, unless the seller actually issues legal proceedings against him to recover the debt; and

(ii)   the buyer can avoid having to pay interest by paying the money at any time before legal proceedings are issued.

Clause 4(a) makes provision for the date of delivery. Under a commercial contract, the agreed delivery date is usually a condition rather than a warranty, unless the parties agree otherwise. This was established in the case *Hartley v. Hymans* 1920. Under clause 4 (a) the delivery date in any contract made by reference to these standard terms is a warranty only. The clause goes even further, however, and excludes the liability of the seller for failure to deliver on time. This exclusion of liability will be covered by s.3 of the Unfair Contract Terms Act 1977.

Clause 4(b) fixes the place of delivery. Where no provision is made for this in a contract, s.29 of the Sale of Goods Act 1979 provides that the place of delivery is the seller's place of business if he has one, and if not, his residence; except that, if the contract is for the sale of specific goods, which to the knowledge of the parties when the contract is made are in some other place, then that place is the place of delivery.

Clause 4(d) excludes the seller's liability for delivery of the wrong quantity if the amount delivered is within 10% of the amount ordered, and obliges the buyer to take and pay for the quantity actually delivered. Without this clause, and clause 2(b) with which it overlaps, the buyer would be entitled, under s.30 of the Sale of Goods Act 1979, to choose, in the event of delivery of the wrong quantity, between:

(i)   rejecting all of the goods delivered; or

(ii)   rejecting any excess over the contractual quantity; or

(iii)   accepting all of the goods delivered and paying for them at the contract rate.

Clause 5(b) limits the time during which the buyer can repudiate the contract by rejecting the goods for breach of condition. Once a buyer has accepted goods he is entitled to sue for damages only in the event of a breach of condition by the seller. Acceptance denies him the right of repudiation.

Clause 6 is a retention of title clause. This type of clause is examined later in this chapter.

Clause 7 transfers risk to the buyer on the making of the contract. The transfer of risk is examined later and at this stage we need only comment that the buyer should insure the goods once risk is transferred to him: a matter which is provided for in clause 8.

Clause 9 is an elaborate limitation of liability clause designed to minimise the seller's liability for breach of contract. As such it is covered by s.3 and s.6 of the Unfair Contract Terms Act 1977, and the particular wording is designed to give as much protection as possible to the seller at the same time as trying to satisfy the test of reasonableness.

Clause 10 is a force majeure clause which aims to make provision for events which otherwise could frustrate the contract.

Clause 12 is a liquidated damages clause. This type of clause aims to quantify the amount recoverable by one of the contracting parties where the other is in breach of contract. At common law a liquidated damages clause is valid if it represents a genuine pre-estimate of the amount of money which would be lost in the event of a breach of contract. If, however, it provides for a payment which is out of proportion to the actual losses which are likely, the clause will be void as a penalty. In *Dunlop Pneumatic Tyre Co. v. New Garage Motor Co.* 1915, Lord Dunedin stated that a liquidated damages clause:

> *"will be held to be a penalty if the sum stipulated for is extravagant and unconscionable in amount in comparison with the greatest loss that could conceivably be proved to have followed from the breach."*

Where the clause is held to be a penalty it is void and the innocent party can sue only for the loss actually sustained. On the other hand if the clause is valid and not a penalty, he can sue for the stipulated sum only, whether his actual loss is greater or smaller.

Clause 13 restricts the rights of the buyer to transfer the benefit of the contract. As we shall see in Chapter 17 the buyer's rights under the contract are a form of intangible business property (a chose in action) which can be sold or transferred to another person. Such a transfer would have to comply with the rules in s.136 of the Law of Property Act 1925.

Clause 14 is an arbitration clause. It enables either party to refer any dispute arising from the contract to arbitration. The process of arbitration is examined in Chapter 3, which also gives an assessment of the advantages and disadvantages of arbitration as compared to legal action in the courts. It will be recalled that under the Consumer Arbitration Agreements Act 1988, this type of clause can only be enforced as against a consumer in limited circumstances.

Delivery Acceptance and Payment

Delivery

Section 27 of the 1979 Act sets out the basic obligations of the buyer and seller under the contract for the sale of goods: *"It is the duty of the seller to deliver the goods, and of the buyer to accept and pay for them in accordance with the contract of sale".*

The rules relating to delivery and payment which are contained in the Act can be displaced by agreement between the parties, but where there is no such agreement the provisions of the Act apply. Section 28 provides: *"Unless otherwise agreed, delivery of the goods and payment of the price are concurrent conditions, that is to say, the seller must be ready and willing to give possession of the goods to the buyer in exchange for the price and the buyer must be ready and willing to pay the price in exchange for possession of the goods".*

The sellers duty to deliver the goods does not necessarily mean that he has to take them physically to the buyer, as delivery is defined in s.61 as *'the voluntary transfer of possession from one person to another'*. Where there is no agreement to the contrary, the place of delivery, by s.29(2), is the seller's place of business, if he has one, and if not his residence. However, where the contract is for the sale of specific goods, which to the knowledge of the parties when the contract is made are in some other place, then that place is the place of delivery. Where the seller has agreed to convey the goods to the buyer, he must do so within a reasonable time, to arrive at a reasonable hour.

In any event, as we have previously seen, time for delivery is normally a condition rather than a warranty in a commercial contract under the rule in *Hartley v. Hyams* 1920. Thus if a delivery date is agreed and the seller fails to deliver on that date the buyer will be entitled to repudiate the contract and sue for damages.

Delivery by the seller of the wrong quantity of goods is dealt with by s.30 which states:

> *"(1) where the seller delivers to the buyer a quantity of goods less than he contracted to sell, the buyer may reject them, but if the buyer accepts the goods so delivered he must pay for them at the contract rate.*

> (2) where the seller delivers to the buyer a quantity of goods larger than he contracted to sell, the buyer may accept the goods included in the contract and reject the rest, or he may reject the whole.

(3) where the seller delivers to the buyer a quantity of goods larger than he contracted to sell and the buyer accepts the whole of the goods so delivered he must pay for them at the contract rate."

Where the seller delivers goods of the contract description mixed with goods of a different description, s.30(4), which is now abolished, allowed the buyer to accept the goods which conformed to the contract and reject the rest, or reject all of the goods. This provision has been replaced with a new s.35A which is discussed below, and effectively provides the same choice of action for the buyer.

Damages for non delivery

Where the seller wrongfully neglects or refuses to deliver the goods to the buyer, the buyer can sue him for damages for non delivery under s.51. The measure of damages is the estimated loss directly and naturally resulting in the ordinary course of events from the seller's breach of contract. Under s.51(3) the measure of damages, where there is an available market for the goods in question, is prima facie the difference between the contract price and the market price at the time that the goods ought to have been delivered, or if no time for delivery was fixed, at the time of the refusal to deliver. It may be noted that under s.51 the amount of damages to which the buyer is entitled may be different to the actual losses which he has suffered.

Payment

It is the duty of the buyer to accept and pay for the goods, under s.28, and in the absence of contrary agreement the buyer is not bound to make payment until delivery is made. However, it is possible where the goods have been accidentally destroyed or stolen, and risk has been transferred to the buyer under the terms of the contract, that he will be liable to make payment even if delivery never takes place.

In the event of non payment by the buyer, the seller can sue him for the price under s.49 provided the buyer has wrongfully refused or neglected to pay according to the terms of the contract, and either property has passed to the buyer or the price is payable on a fixed date irrespective of delivery. In addition to an action for the price, the seller may be able to obtain damages under s.37(1), which provides: *"When the seller is ready and willing to deliver the goods, and requests the buyer to take delivery, and the buyer does not within a reasonable time after such request take delivery of the goods, he is liable to the seller for any loss occasioned by his neglect or refusal to take delivery, and also for a reasonable charge for the care and custody of the goods"*.

Damages for non acceptance

If the conditions of s.49 are not fulfilled, and the seller is unable to sue for the price, he may nonetheless be able to sue for damages for non-acceptance under s.50 where the buyer refuses to accept and pay for the goods. The measure of damages where the seller can resell the goods is the difference between the contract price and the market price at the time the goods ought to have been accepted.

The sellers rights in regard to non acceptance have been curtailed in a limited way by regulations made under the European Communities Act 1972. These are the Consumer Protection (Cancellation of Contracts) Regulations 1987 which apply where a consumer has purchased goods from a doorstep trader who has called on an unsolicited visit. Where the total payment for the goods exceeds £35, the consumer can cancel the contract within seven days. The regulations bring this type of sale into line with the provisions for cancellation of credit transactions under the Consumer Credit Act 1974, discussed below.

Rights of the unpaid seller

Where the seller is unpaid, either because the whole of the price has not been paid to him or because he has received a form of conditional payment, such as a cheque, which has been dishonoured, he may be able to exercise *real* remedies over the goods themselves. The first of these remedies is a lien, or a right to withhold delivery until payment is made. This arises under s.41 where either no credit was agreed, or an agreed credit period has expired, or the buyer has become insolvent; and the goods are still in the seller's possession. He may keep the goods until payment is made, and may ultimately be able to resell them under s.48.

The second is a right of stoppage in transit which arises under s.44 where the buyer becomes insolvent and the unpaid seller has parted with goods to a carrier. The seller may stop the goods at any time before they reach the buyer or his agent, and retain them pending payment of the price.

The unpaid seller may have a right of resale under s.48(3) which provides: *"Where the goods are of a perishable nature, or where the unpaid seller gives notice to the buyer of his intention to resell and the buyer does not within a reasonable time pay or tender the price, the unpaid seller may resell the goods and recover from the original buyer damages for any loss occasioned by his breach of contract."*

In addition to the unpaid seller's rights of lien, stoppage and resale, the seller may benefit from further valuable protection in the event of non payment, or the insolvency of the buyer, where there is a retention of title clause in the contract. As we have seen, this may enable the unpaid seller to reclaim goods, or the proceeds of sale of goods, in the hands of the buyer.

Rejection of the goods by the buyer

It was noted earlier that the remedy available to a buyer in the event of a breach of any term of a contract by the seller depends upon whether the term is classified as a condition or a warranty. Most of the implied terms by statute into contracts for the supply of goods are conditions, and the buyer's remedy for breach, in addition to damages, will be to reject the goods and recover the price. It is of course open to the buyer to choose to affirm the contract, thereby waiving his right to reject but retaining the right to sue for damages.

The Sale and Supply of Goods Act 1994, s.4, curtails the right of a buyer who does not deal as a consumer to reject goods for breach of the implied terms relating to quality and fitness for purpose and correspondence with description or sample. Where the breach is so slight that it would be unreasonable for him to reject goods, the buyer must treat the breach as a breach of warranty and is therefore restricted to making a claim for damages.

The right to reject may also be lost, in the case of a sale of goods contract, where there has been an acceptance of the goods by the buyer. This is provided for in s.11(4) of the Sale of Goods Act

1979, which states: *"Where a contract of sale is not severable, and the buyer has accepted the goods, or part of them, the breach of a condition to be fulfilled by the seller can only be treated as a breach of warranty, and not as a ground for rejecting the goods and treating the contract as repudiated, unless there is an express or implied term of the contract to that effect".*

Where the buyer has accepted the goods, then, he loses the right of rejection but still has a claim for damages, which is the normal remedy for breach of warranty. The buyer will be deemed to have accepted the goods under s.35, where:

- *he intimates to the seller (i.e. lets him know) that he has accepted them;*

- *after delivery he does any act in relation to them which is inconsistent with the ownership of the seller; or*

- *after a reasonable time has passed, he retains the goods without intimating to the seller that he has rejected them.*

However, where the buyer has not previously examined the goods, he is not deemed to have accepted them in the first or second situation indicated above until he has had a reasonable opportunity of examining them for the purpose of ascertaining whether they are in conformity with the contract. In the third situation the question whether the buyer has had a reasonable opportunity to examine the goods is a relevant consideration in determining whether a reasonable time has elapsed.

The right of the buyer to examine the goods is provided for in s.34 which states that the seller is bound, on request, to the buyer a reasonable opportunity to examine the goods for the purpose of ascertaining whether they are in conformity with the contract at the time the seller tendered delivery, unless otherwise agreed. Where the buyer deals as a consumer, the right of examination cannot be lost be agreement or otherwise.

Acceptance can take place where the buyer, after delivery, does something to the goods which is inconsistent with the ownership of the seller. This concept is potentially very wide, and has been held in *Perkins v. Bell* 1893 to include delivery of the goods to a second buyer under a sub-sale. It could also include the situation where a buyer has required a seller to repair defective goods, with the consequence that the buyer would have no right subsequently to reject them if they were still unsatisfactory. However the Sale and Supply of Goods Act 1994 amends s.35 so as to make clear that neither of these situations, of themselves, will amount to acceptance. A buyer will not now be deemed to have accepted the goods merely because he asks for or agrees to their repair by the seller.

Similarly the buyer will not be deemed to have accepted the goods merely because they are delivered to another under a sub-sale or other disposition. In any event this would not have amounted to acceptance unless the buyer had had a reasonable opportunity to examine them. In this connection the question arises as to where is the place of examination under the contract. It is normally the place of delivery unless it would not be reasonable to inspect at the place of delivery, or a different place of examination is within the contemplation of the parties.

In *Molling & Co. v. Dean & Son* 1901 the buyer ordered a large quantity of books to be produced by the plaintiffs intending, to the plaintiffs knowledge, to resell them directly to a sub-buyer abroad. The plaintiffs packed them for shipment to the sub-buyer and the buyer took delivery. Without inspection the buyer forwarded the goods to the sub-buyer, who rejected them for breach of condition. The buyer in turn rejected the goods and the plaintiffs sued for the price, arguing that the buyer had accepted the goods by shipping them to the sub-buyer. It was held that the buyer had not accepted the goods. As the goods had been packed for the sub-buyer by the plaintiffs, it was within the contemplation of the parties that the place of inspection was on delivery to the sub-buyer. The buyer had not therefore had a reasonable opportunity to examine the goods previously and were entitled to reject them.

A purchaser who retains goods for longer than a reasonable time without giving notice of rejection will be deemed to have accepted them under s.35(1)

In *Lee v. York Coach and Marine* 1977 a buyer purchased a second hand car which had defective brakes. The seller was therefore in breach of the implied condition that the car would be of merchantable quality. The buyer purported to reject the car some five months after taking delivery. It was held that she had accepted the car by retaining it beyond a reasonable time. Her only remedy was damages as she had lost the right of rejection.

Whilst it would be difficult to argue with the conclusion in the *Lee* case that retention of goods for five months was beyond a reasonable time, the decision in a more recent case that a period of three weeks is to be regarded in the same way is perhaps more surprising.

In *Bernstein v. Pamson Motors (Golders Green) Ltd.* 1987 the plaintiff purchased a new Nissan car from the defendant for £8,000. The plaintiff was ill at the time of the purchase and consequently did not use the car a great deal. Three weeks after delivery, when the car had done only 140 miles, the engine seized up. The plaintiff rejected the car on the grounds that it was not of merchantable quality, and demanded the return of the purchase price. The defendant repaired the car so that it was as good as new, but the plaintiff refused to take it back. Rougier J., in the High Court, held that the car was not of merchantable quality and that the plaintiff was entitled to damages, assessed at £250. He was not, however, entitled to reject the car because he had accepted it by retaining it for longer than a reasonable time without giving notice of rejection.

Partial rejection

Where a contract is not severable, or divisible, and part of the goods supplied are not in conformity with the contract for example because they do not correspond to the contract description or are not of satisfactory quality, the buyer has the choice under s.35A of rejecting all of the goods, accepting them all or rejecting some and accepting others so long as he accepts all of the goods which conform with the contract.

Where the goods in question form a commercial unit, the division of which would materially impair the value of the goods or character of the unit, a buyer who accepts part of the goods included in the unit is deemed to have accepted all of the goods within it. Thus a buyer could not for example accept one shoe out a pair and reject the other.

Where a contract is severable, for example a contract for the sale of goods to be delivered in instalments, the question of whether a breach of condition in relation to one instalment will entitle the buyer to reject all later instalments was held in *Maple Flock Co v. Universal Furniture Products* 1934 to depend on two main factors. These are first the quantitative ratio that the goods affected by the breach bears to the goods within the contract as a whole, and second the likelihood that the breach will be repeated in respect of later instalments. Where the breach affects a relatively small proportion of the contract as a whole and is unlikely to be repeated the buyer cannot reject all instalments, but is entitled to reject the instalment in question. Where the buyer is entitled to reject one instalment, he may choose under s.35A to accept part of the instalment provided it includes all of the goods which are in conformity with the contract, and to reject the rest.

Specific performance

Section 52 provides: *"In any action for breach of contract to deliver specific or ascertained goods the court may, if it thinks fit, by its judgment or decree direct that the contract shall be performed specifically, without giving the defendant the option of retaining the goods on payment of damages".*

The court will refuse to make an order of specific performance where damages would be an adequate remedy.

> In *Societe des Industries Metallurgiques SA v. Bronx Engineering Co. Ltd.* 1975 for example, the Court refused to make an order of specific performance in relation to a machine manufactured by the defendant even though another such machine was not available on the market immediately. The plaintiff was awarded damages for the defendant's breach of contract, including a sum for losses sustained while waiting for up to a year a new machine to be built.

Sale of Goods: Ownership and Risk

Transfer of ownership

The transfer of ownership, or passing of property, or title, must be distinguished from the transfer of physical possession of goods. As a general rule, s.28 of the Sale of Goods Act 1979 provides that, unless otherwise agreed, the buyer is entitled to delivery only upon payment for the goods. Ownership, on the other hand, can be transferred at any time depending upon the terms of the contract. It may be at the time of making the contract, or after the buyer has paid the price, or at some other time.

It is important to know exactly when ownership of goods is transferred under a contract of sale for a number of reasons:

- under s.20, the risk of accidental loss or damage is transferred to the buyer when property passes to him, unless otherwise agreed. The party which bears the risk of accidental loss or damage will probably wish to insure the goods;

- under s.49 the seller can normally only sue for the price after property has passed to the buyer;

- in considering whether the contract has been frustrated due to perishing of the goods. The contract cannot be frustrated if property has passed to the buyer before the goods perish;

- in the event of the insolvency of the buyer, the seller may be able to retake possession of the goods if property has not passed to the buyer; and

- if the buyer resells the goods immediately, as a general rule, the sub-buyer will get a good title only if property has previously passed to the buyer.

In order to determine when property passes in a contract for the sale of goods, it is of crucial importance to decide whether the goods are specific, unascertained, or ascertained.

Specific goods are defined in s.61 of the Act as: *"goods which are identified and agreed upon at the time the contract for sale is made".*

A contract is said to be for the sale of specific goods where the particular items being sold are conclusively identified at the time of the contract. An individual share, expressed as a fraction or percentage, of such goods also comes within the definition of specific goods. Examples include a contract for the sale of a half share in a particular sailing boat; a contract for the sale of the grandfather clock standing in the hallway of the seller's house; or for the sale of this particular copy of this book or for the sale of all of the oil in a given storage tank standing in the seller's yard.

Goods which are not singled out in this way at the time of contracting are unascertained goods. Ascertained goods are those which were unascertained and are subsequently set aside for the performance of the contract. Goods which were not identified and agreed upon at the time of the contract can never become specific goods.

> In *Kursell v. Timber Operators Limited* 1927 under a contract for the sale of uncut timber standing in a forest, the buyers were entitled to cut and remove, within 15 years, all timber above a certain minimum size. The forest was subsequently nationalised and the Court had to determine whether the ownership of trees fitting the contract specification had passed to the buyer. It was held that property had not passed because the trees were unascertained goods. They could not be specific goods because trees fitting the contract description were merely identifiable. They had not actually been identified.

At the time the contract is made, the goods can only be one of two types, specific or unascertained. If the particular goods to be used in performance of the contract are identified and agreed upon at that time, the goods are specific. If not the goods are unascertained. Unascertained goods cannot subsequently become specific goods. They will become ascertained goods after they have been identified.

Passing of property in specific goods

The general rule is contained in s.17 of the Act which provides:

> *"(1) Where there is a contract for the sale of specific or ascertained goods the property in them is transferred to the buyer at such time as the parties to the contract intend it to be transferred.*
>
> *(2) For the purpose of ascertaining the intention of the parties regard shall be had to the terms of the contract, the conduct of the parties and the circumstances of the case."*

This allows the parties to make whatever agreement they think fit in relation to the passing of property in the goods. Many standard form contracts include a retention of title clause under which property does not pass to the buyer until the purchase price has been paid. Such clauses, examined later, are permitted by s.17.

Where no provision is made in the contract and it is not clear from the circumstances what the parties' intentions are, s.18 provides a number of rules which can be applied in order to determine when property passes.

Rule 1:

> "Where there is an unconditional contract for the sale of specific goods in a deliverable state, the property in the goods passes to the buyer when the contract is made and it is immaterial whether the time of payment or the time of delivery, or both, be postponed".

Under this rule the ownership of goods may be transferred to the buyer even though they are still in the seller's possession.

In *Tarling v. Baxter* 1927 the seller sold a quantity of hay to the buyer, but the hay remained on the seller's land pending collection. Before it was collected it was destroyed by fire. It was held that property passed to the buyer when the contract was made. The loss was therefore his as he carried the risk of accidental destruction.

In *Dennant v. Skinner and Collom Ltd.* 1948 a rogue successfully bid for a car at auction and was allowed to take it away after paying by cheque. After the sale was complete, he signed a form agreeing that ownership of the vehicle would not pass to him until the cheque was cleared. He quickly resold the car to the defendant. When the cheque was dishonoured the original seller sued the defendant for the return of the car. It was held that the terms in the document signed by the rogue were introduced after the contract had been made at the auction. That contract was complete on the fall of the hammer. As no reference had been made to the retention of title clause prior to that moment, the clause was not part of the contract. Property therefore passed to the rogue on the making of the contract under s.18 r.1. He passed a good title to the defendant when he resold the vehicle. The plaintiff's claim therefore failed.

The goods must be in a deliverable state *before r.1 will apply. Under s.61(5): "goods are in a deliverable state ... when they are in such a state that the buyer would under the contract be bound to take delivery of them".*

In *Underwood v. Burgh Castle Brick and Cement Syndicate* 1922 the plaintiff sold a condensing engine to the defendants. The engine weighed over 30 tons and was cemented to the floor of the plaintiff's premises. It had to be dismantled and detached from the floor and the seller agreed to do this. The engine was damaged in the process. It was held that property had not passed to the buyer at the time it was damaged as the goods were not then in a deliverable state. The risk was therefore with the seller who had to bear the loss.

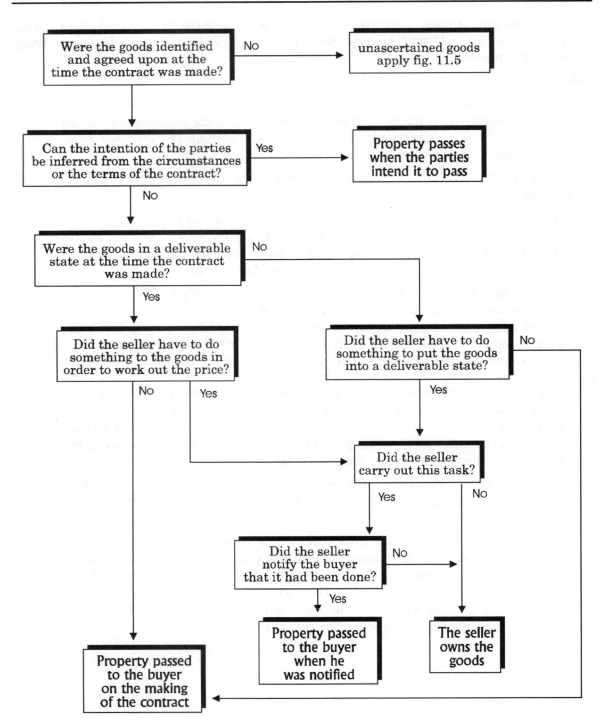

Figure 11.3   Passing of Property in Specific Goods

Goods are not in a deliverable state merely because they are transportable. Whether goods are in a deliverable state will depend in each case on the terms of the contract. Where specific goods are not in a deliverable state at the time the contract is made, r.2 may apply.

Rule 2:

> *"Where there is a contract for the sale of specific goods and the seller is bound to do something to the goods for the purpose of putting them into a deliverable state, the property does not pass until the thing is done and the buyer has notice that it has been done".*

This rule will apply if, for example, a contract for the sale of a motor vehicle contained a term that the seller would replace the exhaust system before delivery to the buyer. The ownership of the car would not be transferred until the work had been done and the buyer had been notified.

Rule 3:

> *"Where there is a contract for the sale of specific goods in a deliverable state but the seller is bound to weigh, measure, test or do some other act or thing with reference to the goods for the purpose of ascertaining the price, the property does not pass until the act or thing is done and the buyer has notice that it has been done".*

This rule, like r.2, only applies where it is the seller who must do something to the goods. If something must be done by the buyer rather than the seller, property will pass under s.18 r.1 on the making of the contract.

> In *Turley v. Bates* 1863 a contract for the sale of clay provided that the buyer had to weigh it in order to determine the price. It was held that property passed to the buyer when the contract was made.

Passing of property where goods are delivered on sale or return

Section 18 rule 4 applies where goods are delivered to the buyer on approval or on sale or return terms. It is unnecessary for the purposes of r.4 to decide whether the goods are specific or unascertained.

Rule 4:

> *"When goods are delivered to the buyer on approval or on sale or return or other similar terms, the property in the goods passes to the buyer:*
>
> *(a) when he signifies his approval or acceptance to the seller or does any other act adopting the transaction;*
>
> *(b) if he does not signify his approval or acceptance to the seller but retains the goods without giving notice of rejection, then, if a time has been fixed for the return of the goods, on the expiration of that time, and, if no time has been fixed, on the expiration of a reasonable time".*

Any act of the buyer, such as using or selling the goods, which is inconsistent with the ownership of the original seller, will be an act adopting the transaction *for the purposes of r.4(a).*

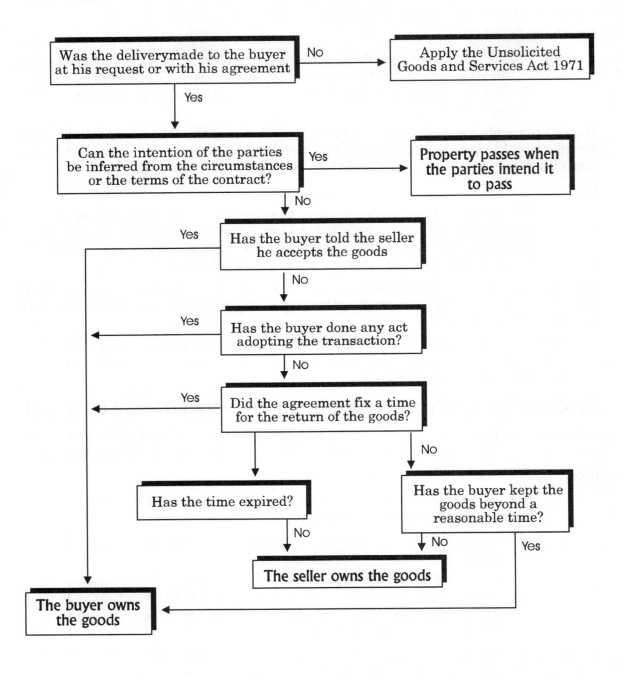

Figure 11.4   Passing of property where the goods are
delivered on approval or on sale or return

In *Kirkham v. Attenborough* 1897 the plaintiff gave goods to a customer on sale or return terms. He pawned the goods. The plaintiff was never paid and claimed the goods from the pawnbroker. It was held that he could not recover them because the pawning of the goods was *an act adopting the transaction*. Ownership passed to the customer as a result and he transferred it on to the pawnbroker.

In *Weiner v. Gill* 1906 the plaintiff delivered goods to his customer on sale or return under a standing contract which provided that "goods had on approbation or on sale or return remain the property of Samuel Weiner until such goods are settled for or charged". The goods were pawned with the defendant, from whom the plaintiff sought to recover them. It was held that s.18 r.4 did not apply. It was overridden by the express term in the contract, which, under s.17, governed the transfer of ownership. The rules in s.18 apply only where no intention has been made clear by the parties. Under the express terms of the contract the goods remained the property of the plaintiff. (Despite this, however, the defendant actually did get a good title under s.2 of the Factors Act 1889, discussed later in this chapter).

If the customer is unable to return goods within the approval period for a reason outside his control, for example because they have been stolen or accidentally destroyed without any fault on his part, he will not be deemed to have adopted the transaction and property will not pass to him.

If goods have been sent to the customer without his asking for them, the Unsolicited Goods and Services Act 1971 may apply. Under this Act the goods will become the property of the customer as an unconditional gift after the expiration of the time limit specified in the Act.

Passing of property in unascertained goods

Until the parties have identified which goods are the subject of the contract, property cannot pass from the seller to the buyer.

Section 16 provides:

> *"Subject to s.20A below, where there is a contract for the sale of unascertained goods no property in the goods is transferred to the buyer unless and until the goods are ascertained".*

This section cannot be used to determine when property passes to the buyer, it only tells us that property cannot pass until the goods have been ascertained. Once this has occurred s.17 will apply if there is evidence of the parties' contractual intention, otherwise rule 5 of s.18 must be applied. The following case provides an example of the application of s.16:

In *Healey v. Howlett & Sons* 1917 the defendant ordered twenty boxes of mackerel from the plaintiff, who was a fish merchant. One hundred and ninety boxes were dispatched by rail, and railway officials were instructed to set aside twenty boxes for the defendant. The train was delayed and, before twenty boxes were set aside, the fish deteriorated. It was held that property in the goods remained with the plaintiff at least until they were set apart. They were therefore at the seller's risk when they deteriorated.

The Sale of Goods (Amendment) Act 1995 has introduced an amendment to the operation of s.16, to overcome an inequity to which the section exposed the buyer. Under s.16 if a seller sells the buyer a quantity of goods from a larger specified source, for example 200 cases of wine from the stock of 1,000 cases of wine held at the seller's depot in Manchester, the 200 cases of wine cannot be treated as specific goods, because it is not yet clear which of 1,000 cases represent the buyer's 200 cases. The goods are unascertained. Property in them has not yet passed to the buyer. If however the buyer has already paid for them, and the seller becomes insolvent, the buyer is left in a vulnerable position as an unsecured creditor who has no property in the goods he has purchased.

The goods were still the property of the seller at the date of the insolvency, and so property in them will have passed automatically to the liquidator (if the seller is a company), or the trustee in bankruptcy (if the seller is an individual). The buyer may find it impossible to recover any of the price paid.

The 1995 Act seeks to overcome this difficulty. It provides that as soon as the buyer has paid for the goods (or for some part of them) the buyer acquires property in an undivided share of the total bulk of the goods. The share acquired is the share which, *"the quantity of goods paid for and due to the buyer out of the bulk bears to the quantity of goods in the bulk."* This means that in the above example as soon as the buyer has paid for the 200 cases of wine he obtains an undivided 20% share of the whole. If the seller subsequently disposes of some part of the bulk, for example by selling 500 cases, the buyer's undivided share automatically readjusts. He would now have a 40% share of the new bulk.

The 1995 Act makes further provision to cover the position where bulk reduces to less than the quantity the buyer has purchased. These amendments are introduced as s.20A to the Sale of Goods Act 1979.

Once goods are ascertained, it is a question of contractual intention under s.17 as to when ownership is transferred. If, for example, the contract contains a retention of title clause, this will govern the passing of property. Where no contractual intention appears, however, s.18 r.5 provides:

> *"Where there is a contract for the sale of unascertained or future goods by description, and goods of that description and in a deliverable state are uncondi-tionally appropriated to the contract, either by the seller with the assent of the buyer or by the buyer with the assent of the seller, the property in the goods then passes to the buyer; and the assent may be expressed or implied, and may be given either before or after the appropriation is made".*

Property cannot pass under s.18 r.5 unless the goods are in a deliverable state. It was noted earlier that goods are in a deliverable state when they are in such condition that the buyer would be bound to accept them under the terms of the contract.

> In *Philip Head and Sons Ltd. v. Showfronts Ltd.* 1970 the plaintiff sold carpeting under a contract which required them to lay it in the defendants' premises. Carpeting which was delivered for this purpose was stolen before it could be laid. The plaintiff sued for the price. It was held that the carpet was not in a deliverable state, as the seller was bound to lay it under the terms of the contract. The seller owned the carpet at the time it was stolen and had to bear the loss.

The expression *unconditional appropriation* is not defined in the Act. For an appropriation to be unconditional, the seller or the buyer must set goods aside irrevocably for the performance of the contract.

> In *Carlos Federspiel & Co. v. Charles Twigg and Co. Ltd.* 1957 the seller manufactured goods for the buyers. The goods were packed in containers with the buyers' name and address on them. The seller became insolvent. The buyers claimed that the ownership of a number of containers, still in the seller's possession, had passed to them under rule 5. It was held that there had not been an unconditional appropriation of the goods and therefore they were still in the seller's ownership. Pearson, J., stated that: *"a mere setting apart or selection by the seller of the goods which he expects to use in performance of the contract is not enough. If that is all, he can change his mind and use those goods in performance of some other contract and use some other goods in performance of this contact. To constitute an appropriation of the goods to the contract the parties must have had, or be reasonable supposed to have had, an intention to attach the contract irrevocably to those goods, so that those goods and no others are the subject of the sale and become the property of the buyer"*.

The act of delivery is the most usual form of unconditional appropriation and under s.18 rule 5(2) property in unascertained goods will pass to the buyer on delivery unless of course a different intention is evident in which case s.17(1) would apply to determine when property passes.

Section 18, rule 5(2) provides:

> *"where in pursuance of the contract, the seller delivers the goods to the buyer or to a carrier for the purpose of transmission to the buyer, he is deemed to have unconditionally appropriated the goods to the contract"*.

A less usual example of unconditional appropriation is provided for in s.18 rule 5(3). This is known as ascertainment by exhaustion. It occurs where a buyer contracts to purchase a quantity of unascertained goods forming part of an identified bulk, for example 200 of the 300 cases of brandy stored n the seller's bonded warehouse, and the remaining goods within the identified bulk (in this example the other 100 cases) are sold and delivered to another buyer. Property in the 200 cases passes to the buyer at the time the others are removed from the warehouse, as these are now the only goods which can be used to fulfil the seller's obligations under the contract.

There must be an assent to the appropriation before property will pass to the buyer. Rule 5 provides that an assent may be express or implied and may be given either before or after the appropriation is made.

> In *Pignatoro v. Gilroy and Son* 1919 there was a contract for the sale of rice, which the buyer had agreed to collect. The seller packaged the rice and informed the buyer that it was ready for collection. The buyer delayed for over three weeks before coming to collect. By this time the rice had been stolen. It was held that property had passed to the buyer under r.5 and he must bear the loss. His delay and the failure to object to the appropriation within a reasonable time was evidence of an implied assent.

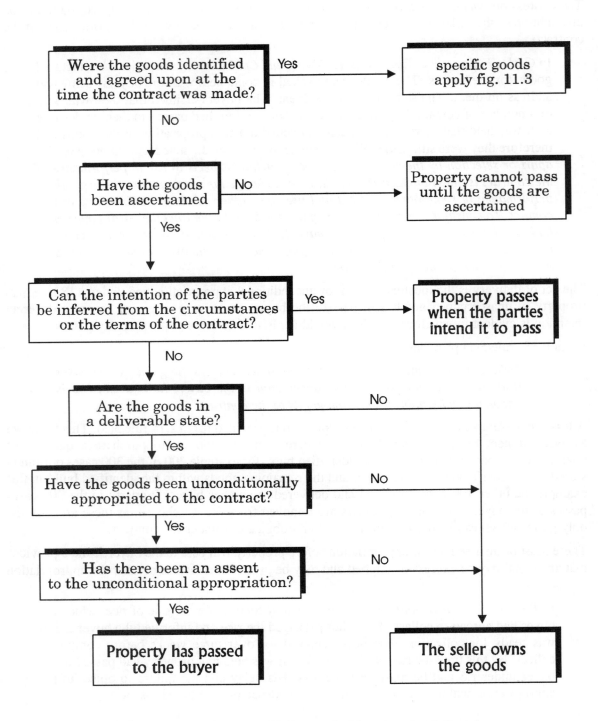

Figure 11.5   Passing of Property in Unascertained Goods

Retention of title

The 1979 Act in s.17 envisages that the parties may make express provision in the contract for the transfer of ownership. A retention (or reservation) of title clause is an express term which provides that ownership of goods will not be transferred to the buyer until payment has been made. The major advantage of retention of title, from the seller's point of view, is that the goods belong to him until he receives payment for them.

If the buyer becomes insolvent after delivery but before payment, the seller will be able to reclaim the goods because they belong to him. Without a retention of title clause the goods belong to the buyer. They will be available for distribution to the buyer's creditors on insolvency. The seller will be in the position of an unsecured trade creditor and therefore low down in the order of priority for repayment of debts. A retention of title clause effectively places the seller first in the order of priority in relation to goods which are still in the buyer's possession.

> In *Aluminium Industrie Vaassen BV v. Romalpa Aluminium Ltd.* 1976 the seller sold aluminium foil to Romalpa, an English company, for use in its manufacturing processes. At the time of manufacture the foil became mixed with other materials. The written contract contained a retention of title clause, under which ownership of the aluminium foil would be transferred to Romalpa when it had paid all sums owing to the seller. The clause went on to reserve ownership over any goods which were mixed with the aluminium foil. Romalpa became insolvent and a receiver was appointed. The seller claimed the ownership of aluminium foil still held by the company; and the proceeds of resale of unmixed foil sold by the receiver to third parties. No claim was made in respect of mixed goods or the proceeds of sale of mixed goods. The Court of Appeal held that the retention of title was valid and the seller's claim succeeded in full.

Transfer of risk

The party who carries risk must bear the loss where goods deteriorate or are stolen, damaged or destroyed in circumstances where no-on else can be made liable for the loss. The party who carries risk will usually protect himself by insurance.

Under a contract for the sale of goods risk can be transferred from the seller to the buyer at any time. If the parties make no express provision for the transfer of risk, it will take place at the same time as the transfer of ownership. The 1979 Act in s.20(1) provides: *"Unless otherwise agreed, the goods remain at the seller's risk until the property in them is transferred to the buyer but when the property in them is transferred to the buyer the goods are at the buyer's risk whether delivery has been made or not".*

Many standard form contracts transfer risk to the buyer on the making of the contract, or at the time of delivery.

It is possible that goods may be exposed to additional risks if one of the contracting parties does not comply with his obligations. To cover this possibility, the 1979 Act in s.20(2) provides: *"where delivery has been delayed through the fault of either the buyer or seller the goods are at the risk of the party at fault as regards any loss which might not have occurred but for such fault".*

In *Demby Hamilton v. Barden* 1949 there was a contract for the sale of thirty tons of apple juice by sample. The buyer agreed to take delivery in weekly loads. The seller crushed all thirty tons of juice at once in order to ensure correspondence with the sample. The buyer took delivery of the first few instalments and then took no further deliveries for a period of time, during which the juice went off. It was held that the buyer must bear the loss. Risk transferred to him under s.20(2) even though property remained with the seller.

Transfer of Title by a Non-Owner

Under a contract of sale, the principal obligation of the seller is to transfer the ownership of goods to the buyer. Clearly this presents no difficulty where the seller actually owns the goods or has the authority of the owner to sell them. However where the goods are stolen or where the seller holds them under the terms of a hire purchase agreement, in an attempted sale the seller does not have the legal right to transfer ownership. A person who buys such goods will not acquire a good title to them because the seller cannot pass on to the buyer that which he does not have. This rule is expressed in the latin maxim `nemo dat quod non habet'. This means no-one can give what he has not got.

The rule is embodied in s.21 of the Sale of Goods Act 1979, which provides: *"Where goods are sold by a person who is not their owner, the buyer acquires no better title to the goods than the seller had"*.

A thief has no legal title to goods and a purchaser from a thief acquires no better title. The thief could be prosecuted under s.1 of the Theft Act 1968 for the offence of theft. He could also be sued by the owner for damages, under the Torts (Interference with Goods) Act 1977.

If the purchaser knew that the goods were stolen at the time he bought them, he could be prosecuted under the Theft Act 1968 for the offence of handling stolen goods. He could also be sued by the owner for damages, or for an order of specific delivery, under the Torts (Interference with Goods) Act 1977. In turn, he could sue the thief for breach of the implied terms relating to title, under s.12 of the Sale of Goods Act 1979 provided he purchased the goods innocently.

Where the purchaser acts in complete innocence and the thief disappears with the purchase money, the owner and the purchaser are left in dispute about the ownership of the goods. Each has some justification for his claim. In these circumstances the law has recognised that some balance must be struck between the protection of the property rights of the original owner, and the protection of the legitimate claim of a purchaser acting in good faith.

In *Pearson v. Rose and Young Ltd.* 1951 Lord Denning summed up the difficulty of striking a fair balance between two innocent victims: *"In the early days of the common law the governing principle of our law of property was that no person could give a better title than he himself had got, but the needs of commerce have led to a progressive modification of this principle so as to protect innocent purchasers...the cases show how difficult it is to strike the right balance between the claims of true owners and the claims of innocent purchasers"*.

In an attempt to strike this balance, a number of exceptions to the general rule have been evolved. The principal exceptions are:

(a)   estoppel;

(b)   sale under common law or statutory powers, or by court order;

(c)   sale under a voidable title;

(d)   sale by a seller in possession;

(e)   sale by a mercantile agent;

(f)   sale by a buyer in possession; and

(g)   sale of a motor vehicle subject to a hire purchase agreement.

The former exception which related to the sale of goods in market overt was abolished by the Sale of Goods (Amendment) Act 1994.

Estoppel

This exception is contained in s.21 of the 1979 Act which, after stating the general rule that a buyer can acquire no better title to goods than the seller had, continues with the words: *"… unless the owner of the goods is by his conduct precluded from denying the seller's authority to sell"*.

An estoppel arises where the owner of goods, by his conduct, has allowed the purchaser to believe that the seller has a right to sell them. The true owner is prevented or estopped from denying to the purchaser that the seller had authority to sell.

> An example of conduct amounting to an estoppel can be seen in *Eastern Distributors Ltd. v. Goldring* 1967 where the owner of a van wished to raise a loan. He got together with a car dealer in order to deceive a finance company by making it appear that the dealer owned the van and the original owner wished to acquire it from him on hire purchase. The standard forms were forwarded to the plaintiff finance company who received them in good faith believing that the van belonged to the trader. The plaintiff bought the van and let it to the original owner on hire purchase. The original owner did not pay his instalments and subsequently sold the van to the defendant, an innocent purchaser. The finance company sued the ultimate purchaser of the van claiming ownership. It was held that the conduct of the original owner in making it appear that the car dealer owned the vehicle, acted as an estoppel. Thus he was prevented from denying that the finance company had the ownership of the van. This meant that the original owner could not transfer a good title to the ultimate purchaser. The van therefore belonged to the finance company.

Sale under common law or statutory powers, or under the order of a court

Such a sale will vest a good title in the purchaser, regardless of whether or not the original owner authorised or approved of it, so long as the power of sale exists and is properly exercised.

Sale under a voidable title

A contract may be voidable at the option of one of the contracting parties, for example where the buyer is induced by misrepresentation to make the agreement. The contract is binding until the buyer chooses to avoid it or set it aside. Similarly, where the buyer fraudulently persuades the seller to accept a cheque which is subsequently dishonoured, the contract is valid until the seller does some overt act evidencing an intention to avoid it.

Property may pass to a buyer under a voidable contract. His title to the goods is also voidable and will be lost if the seller avoids the contract. If the buyer resells the goods before the seller avoids the contract, the new buyer will obtain title. If the resale takes place after the seller avoids the first contract, the new buyer does not have title and the original seller can recover the goods from him.

This is provided for in s.23 of the 1979 Act, which states: *"When the seller of goods has a voidable title to them, but his title has not been avoided at the time of the sale, the buyer acquires a good title to the goods, provided he buys them in good faith and without notice of the seller's defect of title."*

> In *Phillips v. Brooks* 1919 a rogue obtained a ring worth £450 from a jeweller. The rogue had a voidable title to the ring and subsequently pawned it with the defendant pawnbroker. In an action by the jeweller to recover the ring from the pawnbroker, it was held that the pawnbroker had a good title to it. The jeweller had not avoided his contract with the rogue at the time the ring was pawned.

A contract can be avoided by informing the other party that the contract is at an end. This may not be possible however where the other party has made off with the goods dishonestly. In such a case the seller must do some other act evidencing his intention to avoid the contract, for example informing the police of the fraud.

> In *Car and Universal Finance Co. v. Caldwell* 1963 the plaintiff sold a car to a buyer, who fraudulently induced him to accept a cheque in payment. The cheque was dishonoured. The plaintiff contacted the police and the A.A. and asked them to recover the car for him. Subsequently the buyer resold the car to the defendant, from whom the plaintiff reclaimed it. It was held that the contract between the plaintiff and the buyer was voidable. The plaintiff's act of informing the police and the A.A. was sufficient to evidence an intention to avoid it. This had occurred before the buyer's resale to the defendant and therefore the car belonged to the plaintiff.

Where the original owner seeks to recover goods in the possession of someone who was not a party to the voidable transaction, and it is not clear whether the transaction was avoided before or after a resale by the purchaser from the original owner, the onus will be upon the person in possession of the goods to prove that he has a good title.

> In *Thomas v. Heelas* 1988 the defendant advertised his car for sale. After the banks had closed on Maundy Thursday a man came, inspected the car and agreed to buy it for £2,200. He gave the defendant a bankers draft in the sum of £2,200 and drove the car away. On Tuesday morning, when the banks re-opened after Easter weekend, the defendant discovered that the bankers draft was a forgery. He immediately reported the theft of the car to the police. Six months later the car was found in the possession of the plaintiff, having been bought and sold a number of times in between. There was no

evidence to indicate whether the first resale by the thief had taken place before or after the defendant avoided the contract on Easter Tuesday. The Court of Appeal held that the defendant was entitled to the return of his car, as the onus was on the plaintiff to demonstrate that the first resale had taken place before the contract was avoided and the plaintiff had been unable to do so.

Sale by a seller in possession

This exception, contained in s.24 of the 1979 Act, applies where a seller has sold goods to a buyer (B1) to whom property has passed. The seller, still in possession of the goods, resells them to a second buyer (B2). Applying the general principle, B2 would not obtain ownership because the seller has already transferred it to B1. However, if the conditions laid down in s.24 are satisfied, B2 will obtain a good title.

The 1979 Act, in s.24 provides: *"Where a person having sold goods continues or is in possession of the goods, or of the documents of title to the goods, the delivery or transfer by that person, or by a mercantile agent acting for him, of the goods or documents of title under any sale, pledge, or other disposition thereof, to any person receiving the same in good faith and without notice of the previous sale, has the same effect as if the person making the delivery or transfer were expressly authorised by the owner of the goods to make the same"*.

B2 will get a good title if he is acting honestly and does not know of the previous sale to B1. There must be an actual delivery of the goods or documents of title to him. B1 will be left with the right to sue the seller for damages for breach of contract. He will have no rights against B2 or against the goods.

> In *Pacific Motor Auctions Ltd. v. Motor Credits (Hire Finance) Ltd.* 1965 the seller, a car dealer, sold a number of cars to the plaintiffs (B1) under a `display agreement' whereby the seller remained in possession of the cars for display in his showroom. He was paid 90% of the purchase price and was authorised to sell the cars as the plaintiff's agent. The seller got into financial difficulties and the plaintiffs cancelled his authority to sell the cars. Disregarding their instructions, he sold a car to the defendant (B2) who took it in good faith and without notice of the previous sale. The Court held that the defendant, who had taken delivery of the car, obtained a good title to it by virtue of s.24.

Sale by a mercantile agent

A mercantile agent, or factor, is a person who, in the ordinary course of his business, buys, sells or otherwise deals with goods on behalf of others. A sale of goods by a mercantile agent will usually pass a good title to the purchaser under s.2 of the Factors Act 1889 even if the agent has no express authority to sell the goods.

The 1889 Act in s.2 (1) provides: *"Where a mercantile agent is, with the consent of the owner, in possession of goods or of the documents of title to goods, any sale, pledge, or other disposition of the goods, made by him when acting in the ordinary course of business of a mercantile agent, shall ... be valid as if he were expressly authorised by the owner of the goods to make the same; provided that the person taking under the disposition acts in good faith, and has not at the time of the disposition notice that the person making the disposition has not the authority to make the same"*.

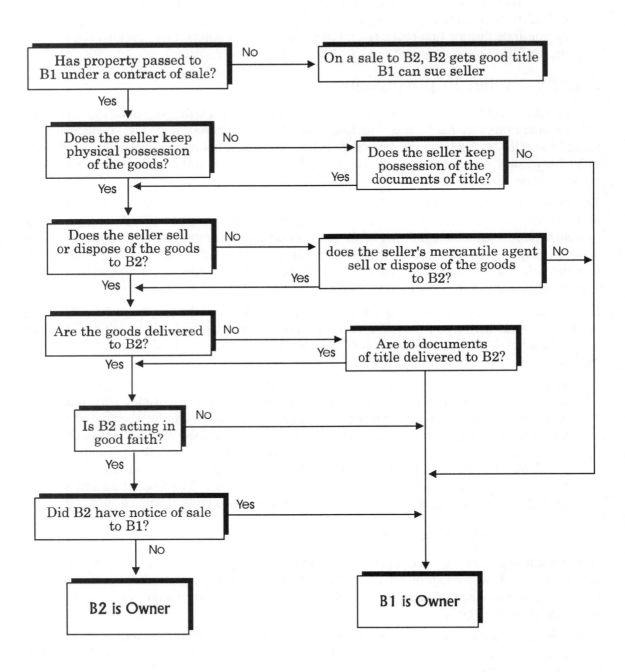

Figure 11.6   Sale by Seller in Possession
Section 24 Sale of Goods Act 1979

The purchaser will obtain a good title, even though the agent had no authority to sell, provided that:

(i)   the agent is in possession of the goods with the owner's consent;

(ii)   the sale is made within the ordinary course of business of a mercantile agent; and

(iii)   the purchaser did not know of the agent's lack of authority to sell the goods.

In *Folkes v. King* 1923 the plaintiff delivered his car to a car dealer with instructions to sell it for not less than £575. The car dealer sold it to the defendant for £340 and absconded with the proceeds. The plaintiff sued for the return of the car from the defendant. The Court held that the car dealer was a mercantile agent as he bought and sold goods in the ordinary course of his business. The defendant bought the car from him in good faith and therefore obtained a good title to it under s.2(1) of the Factors Act 1889.

Sale by a buyer in possession

This exception to the general rule applies where a buyer obtains possession of goods, but property has not passed to him under the terms of the contract. If the buyer resells the goods before the property passes to him, the sub-buyer may obtain a good title to the goods under s.25 of the 1979 Act.

Section 25 provides:

> *"Where a person having bought or agreed to buy goods obtains, with the consent of the seller, possession of the goods or the documents of title to the goods, the delivery or transfer by that person, or by a mercantile agent acting for him, of the goods or documents of title, under any sale, pledge or other disposition thereof, to any person receiving the same in good faith and without notice of any lien or other right of the original seller in respect of the goods, has the same effect as if the person making the delivery or transfer were a mercantile agent in possession of the goods or documents of title with the consent of the owner".*

The rule in s.25 will only apply where the seller retains ownership of goods which are in the buyer's possession after a contract of sale. This situation could occur under s.18 r.2 or r.3, although more usually it would be one in which there is a retention of title clause in the contract.

> In *Newtons of Wembley Ltd. v. Williams* 1964 the plaintiff sold a car to a rogue and was paid by cheque. The parties expressly agreed that ownership of the car would remain with the plaintiff until the cheque was cleared. The rogue took the car, with its registration book, and resold it to the defendant in Warren Street, London, a recognised second hand car market where dealers regularly operated. The defendant purchased the car in good faith and without notice. The rogue's cheque was dishonoured and the plaintiff claimed the car from the defendant. The Court of Appeal held that the rogue was a buyer in possession under s.25. The requirements of the section were satisfied and the defendant obtained a good title to the car.

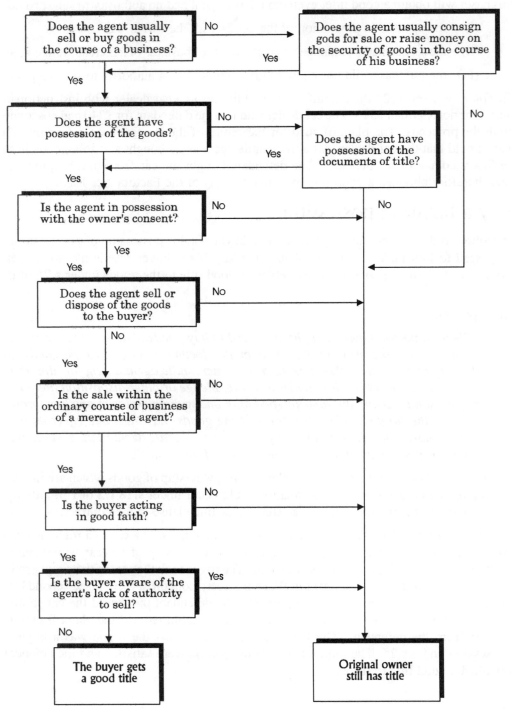

Figure 11.7   Sale by a Mercantile Agent in possession s.2(1) Factors Act 1889

In *Four Point Garage Ltd. v. Carter* 1985 the seller sold a car to B1, who resold it to B2, the defendant. Each contract contained a retention of title clause. The defendant paid B1 for the car. B1, who became insolvent, had not paid the plaintiff. It was held that, although property had not passed to B1, he was a buyer in possession and the defendant obtained good title to the car under s.25.

Where the original seller has a defective title to goods, it appears that B2, the sub-buyer from the buyer in possession, will not obtain title under s.25. The House of Lords has recently held that the section does not have the effect of perfecting the defective title.

In *National Employers Mutual Insurance Association Ltd. v. Jones* 1988 a car was stolen, and eventually, after passing through the hands of a number of dealers, it was bought in good faith by the defendant. The original owner sued for the return of the car, but the defendant claimed to have acquired a good title to it by virtue of s.25(1), because the previous purchaser, Mid Glamorgan Motors, had bought the car from an earlier purchaser, Autochoice, and obtained possession with the consent of Autochoice. The effect of this, the defendant argued, was as if Mid Glamorgan Motors were a mercantile agent in possession of the goods with the consent of the owner (ie the plaintiff). The defendants argument was consistent with a literal interpretation of s.25(1). The House of Lords, however, decided that the plaintiff was entitled to the return of the car, declining to give a literal interpretation to the word *owner* at the end of s.25(1), and preferring to interpret it as meaning the earlier non owning seller (ie Autochoice on the facts).

A bona fide purchaser was not able to override the true owner's title when the true owner had ceased to have possession of the goods because they were stolen.

Sale of a motor vehicle subject to a hire purchase agreement

This exception is contained in Part III of the Hire Purchase Act 1964. It applies where the debtor under a hire purchase or conditional sale agreement disposes of a motor vehicle before property passes to him under the terms of the credit agreement. The exception applies to motor vehicles only and not to goods of any other type.

The Hire Purchase Act 1964, in s.27 provides:

> *"Where a motor vehicle has been let under a hire purchase agreement, or has been agreed to be sold under a conditional sale agreement, and, at a time before the property in the vehicle has become vested in the hirer or buyer, he disposes of the vehicle*

Only a private purchaser of a motor vehicle is protected by s.27 A *trade or finance purchaser*, for example a garage or finance company, is not protected by the section because there are facilities, within these trades, to check up on the existence of an outstanding credit agreement relating to any motor vehicle. However, where a trade or finance purchaser buys a motor vehicle and then resells it, the first private purchaser to buy it will obtain the original creditor's title under s.27.

A private purchaser will be protected by s.27 so long as he acts in good faith and has no notice of the rights of the original creditor.

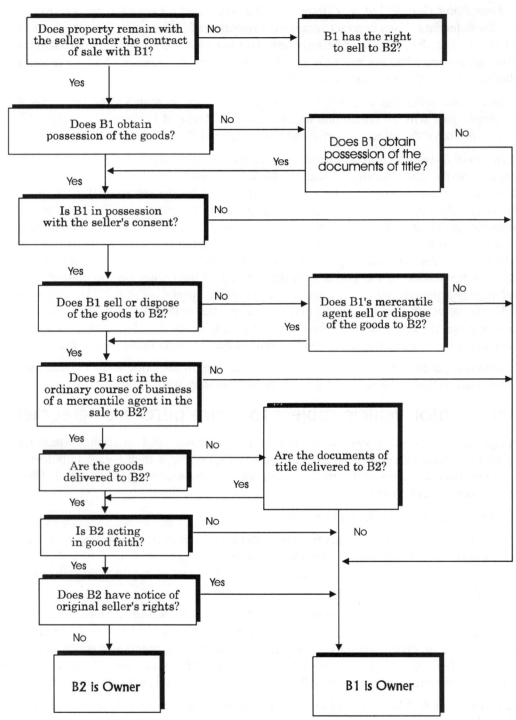

Figure 11.8   Sale by a buyer in possession s.25 Sale of Goods Act 1979

In *Barker v. Bell* 1971 the debtor had a car on hire purchase from a finance company. Before he paid off the sums due under the hire purchase agreement, he sold the car to an innocent private purchaser. He told the purchaser that the car had been subject to a hire purchase agreement which was paid off, and showed him a receipt marked with the words `final payment'. The Court of Appeal held that property passed to the purchaser by virtue of s.27 of the 1964 Act. The finance company's argument that the purchaser had notice of the hire purchase agreement was rejected. In his judgment, Lord Denning stated that: *"A purchaser is only affected by notice if he has actual notice that the car is on hire purchase. He is not affected merely by being told that it was previously on hire purchase which has now been paid off"*.

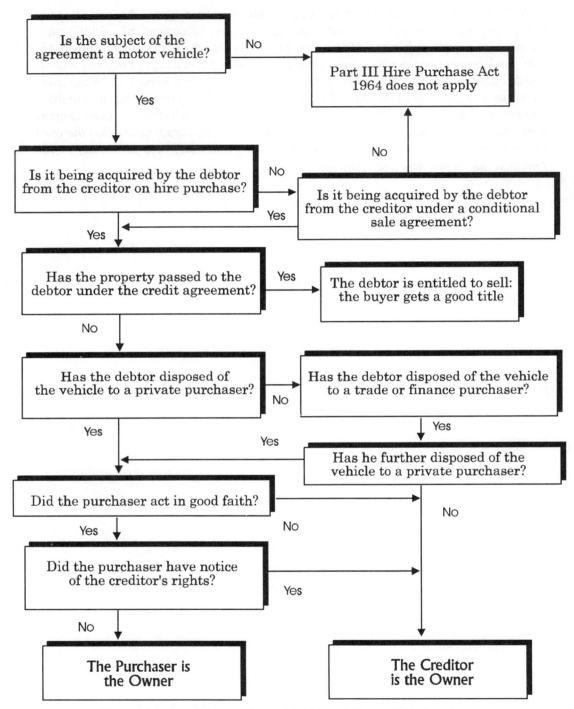

Figure 11.9   Sale of Motor Vehicle while on Hire Purchase
Part III Hire Purchase Act 1964

Assignment David and Christine Geary

Ian Trodd, who runs a smallholding, placed the following advertisement in the local newspaper:

> *FOR SALE: six Aberdeen Angus bull calves, four Hereford calves, up to five weeks old; quantity of hay and straw.*

David Geary, a local farmer, responded to the advertisement and agreed to buy the six Aberdeen Angus bull calves and two of the Hereford heifers at an inclusive price of £850. David noticed that none of the calves had ear tags and Ian subsequently agreed to tag them ready for collection by David the following morning.

David also agreed to buy 500 of the 2,000 bales of hay in Ian's barn for £750 and all of the straw bales in the same barn at a price of £40 per ton. The straw was to be loaded onto David's wagon the next day and weighed by him at a nearby public weighbridge. When David arrived the following morning he found that Ian's barn and all of its contents had been destroyed by a fire in which all of the Aberdeen Angus and Hereford calves have perished.

Tasks

1. David Geary is a member of the National Farmers Union (NFU), and has sought the Union's advice concerning his agreement with Mr. Trodd. You are an officer employed by the NFU, and have been asked to telephone Mr. Geary to explain to him his position in this matter. Prepare notes prior to making the telephone call, which identify clearly and precisely the legal issues raised by it. Bear in mind that Mr. Geary will wish to know exactly how he should proceed.

2. Following your telephone conversation with David Geary he raises a further issue with you, on which he seeks your help. His wife Christine runs a pottery business, supplying her products to sales outlets, usually craft shops, on a sale or return basis. Last month she supplied pottery to The Craft Corner, a shop in Bury St Edmunds, and to Flair, a specialist china and pottery shop in Exeter. She now learns that The Craft Corner has now closed down and sold all its stock to Suffolk Art Supplies, and that her pottery has been stolen from the shop in Exeter. David asks if you will write informing Christine of any rights she has to payment from Suffolk Arts Supplies, and from Flair, since she believes she will have to personally bear the loss. Write a suitable letter to Christine.

3. Draw up a set of standard trading terms for use by anyone operating a business which involves the supply of goods on sale or return. The terms should reflect the commercial protection necessary in such a trading activity, taking into account in particular (i) transfer of ownership, (ii) risk, (iii) insurance, and (iv) time limits for the return of goods.

Legal Terms found in Chapter 12

APR
(Annual percentage rate)

- statutory method for the calculation of credit costs which lenders must use in their advertising and quotations

Compensation order

- court order requiring a payment of money to the victim of a crime from the person convicted of the offence

Consumer goods

- goods which are ordinarily intended for private use or consumption

Consumer protection

- expression describing the legislative framework designed to grant rights to and generally protect the interests of consumers of goods and services

Cooling off

- a period provided for under statute within which a consumer who has entered into a credit transaction can cancel the agreement

Extortionate credit bargain

- a credit contract which requires repayments which are grossly exorbitant

Force majeure

- clause in a contract making provision for events which would otherwise frustrate the contract

Product liability

- legal basis upon which a person who suffers harm as a result of a defective product can be compensated

Prohibition notice

- a statutory notice served on a trader requiring him to stop trading in unsafe goods of a particular description

Protected goods

- statutory protection granted to debtors under consumer credit agreements preventing creditors from regaining lawful possession of goods once 1/3 of the total price has been paid

Satisfactory quality

- statutory standard of quality demanded of goods sold by a seller in the course of business

Tort of deceit

- a false statement made knowingly or recklessly intended to be acted upon and cause damage

Trade descriptions

- descriptions applied to goods or services by business sellers. If such descriptions are false or misleading they can give use to criminal liability

Consumer Protection: Goods

Consumer Protection

Although the statutory framework of consumer protection in respect of the sale of goods suggests this is an area of law which has only developed within the last twenty five years or so, dating perhaps from the introduction of the Trade Descriptions Act in 1968, the history of statutory intervention in contracts of sale is of far more ancient origin. This is perhaps not altogether surprising for the buying and selling of goods is the most basic form of trading activity, and regulation of trading to control the most fundamental abuses such as selling underweight or unfit goods can be regarded as an essential safeguard for buyers in any age. By the end of the nineteenth century the codification of important areas of commercial activity was largely completed, and probably the high watermark of this process was the introduction in 1893 of the Sale of Goods Act, a statute which sought to combine common law principles covering contracts of sale into a single comprehensive enactment. The present Act of 1979 is essentially the 1893 legislation with some minor alteration.

What has characterised the contemporary approach to consumer affairs has been the recognition by post-war governments of different political persuasions that ethical considerations concerning the rights of consumers, particularly private consumers, demand a comprehensive framework to safeguard consumers' interests and curb undesirable commercial practices. This is at least in part a reflection of the increasing economic importance of domestic consumers in the economy.

The result of these interventions is a battery of statutory provisions which grant rights to consumers by means of a combination of legal devices. These include:

(i) conferring remedies which are available by legal action in the civil courts, for example under the Sale of Goods Act 1979;

(ii) regulating certain types of trading activities, for instance through the licensing requirements of the Consumer Credit Act 1974 or registration under the Data Protection Act 1984; and

(iii) imposing criminal liability in respect of certain types of unacceptable trading practices, for example under the Trade Descriptions Act 1968.

	Civil Law	Criminal Law
Enforcement	Rescission of contract Sue for damages (or defence to an action for damages) in the County Court or High Court Arbitration	Local Authority: Trading Standards Department Prosecution in the Magistrates and Crown Courts Compensation orders under the Powers of Criminal Courts Act 1973 Director General of Fair Trading Data Protection Registrar
Defective Products	Sale of Goods Act 1979 Supply of Goods and Services Act 1982 Sale and Supply of Goods Act 1994 Tort of Negligence Consumer Protection Act 1987 Codes of Practice	Consumer Protection Act 1987 Food Safety Act 1990 Road Traffic Act 1988 and other specific legislation Health and Safety at Work Act 1974
Defective Services	Supply of Goods and Services Act 1982 Professional Negligence Regulation by trade or professional associations Codes of Practice Package Travel Regulations 1992	Trade Descriptions Act 1968 Consumer Credit Act 1974 Health and Safety at Work Act 1974 Package Travel Regulations 1992
False Statements	Misrepresentation Breach of Contract Negligent mis-statement Tort of Deceit Data Protection Act 1984	Trade Descriptions Act 1968 Consumer Protection Act 1987 Weights and Measures Act 1985 Fair Trading Act 1973 Data Protection Act 1984
Exclusion of Liability	Common Law rules of incorporation and interpretation Unfair Contract Terms Act 1977	Unfair Terms in Consumer Contracts Regulations 1994 Consumer Transactions (Restrictions on Statements) Order 1976 and (Amendment) Order 1978

Figure 12.1   Consumer Protection under the Civil Law and the Criminal Law

Consumer protection by means of statutory implied terms

Key consumer rights, for example in relation to faulty or shoddy goods or those which have been wrongly described or labelled, derive from the statutory implied terms contained in sections 12 to 15 of the Sale of Goods Act 1979 and equivalent provisions in other Acts. It should be appreciated that the statutory implied terms, in addition to providing protection for the consumer, will operate in situations where the buyer is not a consumer, for example where both the seller and buyer are contracting in the course of business.

We have seen that obligations may arise under a contract in two different ways. First because the law imposes them, for example by Act of Parliament, and second because the parties expressly agree to them. In a contract for the sale or supply of goods the law imposes obligations on the supplier by the legal mechanism of implied terms in the contract of supply. These statutory implied terms take the form of specific promises to the buyer in relation to such matters as, for example, the quality of the goods. Most of these terms are conditions, which, if broken, will give rise to the right to repudiate the contract, reject the goods and sue for damages. There are a small number of implied warranties also. The buyer's remedy in the event of a breach of warranty is damages. In the case of a breach of condition the buyer may lose the right to reject the goods where he has accepted them within the meaning of s.35 or where, in the case of a buyer dealing otherwise than as a consumer, the breach of condition is so slight that it would be unreasonable for him to reject them. The circumstances in which the buyers right of rejection for breach of condition may be lost are discussed more fully in the previous chapter.

The implied terms contained in sections 12 to 15 of the Sale of Goods Act 1979 automatically become part of any contract for the sale of goods. Equivalent terms have been introduced into most other types of contract involving the supply of goods. The Supply of Goods (Implied Terms) Act 1973 and the Supply of Goods and Services Act 1982 have followed the model originally laid down in the Sale of Goods Act with the result that the full range of contracts under which goods are supplied are now covered by the same terms. For convenience we shall refer to the 1979 Act for the purpose of examining the detailed content of the implied terms.

Consumer protection where the seller of goods has no right to sell

Under s.12 of the 1979 Act there is an implied condition that the seller has the right to sell the goods. If this is broken, for example because the goods belong to someone else, the buyer will be able to repudiate the contract and recover in full the price he paid.

> In *Rowland v. Divall* 1923 three months after buying a motor car the purchaser discovered that it had been stolen before it came into the seller's possession. The seller therefore had no right to sell it. The purchaser returned the car to its original owner and sued the seller under s.12. It was held that he was entitled to the return of the price because he had suffered *a total failure of consideration*. The fact that the buyer had used the car for over three months did not affect his right to recover the full purchase price.

Where the seller is the true owner of the goods he may nevertheless have no right to sell them if for example they infringe intellectual property rights held by another person.

In *Niblett v. Confectioners Materials Co.* 1921 the purchaser of a quantity of tins of preserved milk could not resell them without infringing the Nestle Company Trade Mark. This infringement arose because the labels placed on tins by the manufacturer bore the name *Nissly Brand*. The seller was held to be in breach of s.12.

Under s.12 there is also an implied warranty that the goods are free from any potential claims by any third parties which had not been disclosed to the buyer. There is also an implied warranty that the buyer will enjoy quiet possession of the goods.

In *Microbeads v. Vinhurst Road Markings* 1975 the seller sold road marking machines to the buyer. After the sale a third party obtained a patent on the machine. The continued use of the machine by the buyer was then in breach of the third party's patent rights. The buyer sued the seller under s.12 claiming that he was in breach of the implied condition that he had the right to sell, and of the implied warranty that the buyer would enjoy quiet possession. The Court of Appeal held that there was no breach of condition. At the time of the sale there was no infringement of the patent and therefore the seller had the right to sell. However, the seller was liable in damages for breach of the warranty that the buyer would enjoy quiet possession of the goods.

Consumer protection where goods are wrongly described or labelled

Where there is a contract for the sale of goods by description, s.13 of the 1979 Act implies a condition that the goods will correspond with the description. Whenever the buyer has not seen the goods before the contract is made the sale is obviously a sale by description. Also, if goods are packaged, for example food inside a tin or cardboard box, there is a sale by description. The buyer will only be able to see the goods after he has purchased them and opened the package. The vast majority of sales will be made by description. The 1979 Act provides in s.13(3) that a sale of goods is not prevented from being a sale by description by reason only that the goods are selected by the buyer after being exposed for sale, for example in a self-service store. The description can extend to such things as weight, size, quantity, composition and age.

In *Dick Bentley Productions Ltd. v. Harold Smith Motors Ltd.* 1965 a car dealer sold a second-hand car with a recorded mileage of 30,000. In fact the true mileage was nearer 100,000. The seller was held liable for a breach of s.13.

Similar conduct today could make the seller criminally liable under the Trade Descriptions Act 1968. One significant difference between the Sale of Goods Act and the Trade Descriptions Act is that the latter only applies where the sale is made in the course of a trade or business. Section 13 applies both to private and business sales.

In *Beale v. Taylor* 1967 the buyer purchased a car advertised as a 1961 Herald Convertible having had a trial run in it as a passenger. The buyer soon found the car to be unsatisfactory. On an examination by a garage it was discovered that the car had been made up of halves of two different cars. The rear portion was part of a 1961 Triumph Herald 1200 model while the front was part of a earlier 948 model. The two portions had been welded together unsatisfactorily into one structure, and the vehicle was unroadworthy and unsafe. The Court of Appeal held that the seller had broken the promise implied into the contract by s.13 and was liable in damages to the buyer.

Although extremely small deviations from the contractual specification may be disregarded under the de minimus not curat lex rule, the seller will be in breach of s.13 if he does not comply strictly with the contract description.

> In *Arcos Ltd. v. E.A. Ronaasen & Son* 1933 the buyer agreed to purchase a quantity of wooden staves, half an inch thick, for making cement barrels. When they were delivered only 5% of them were exactly half an inch and the vast majority were nine sixteenths of an inch in thickness. An arbitrator found that the staves were still reasonably fit for making cement barrels. The House of Lords held that the buyers were entitled to reject the goods because the seller had not strictly complied with the contract description. Lord Atkin observed: *"a ton does not mean about a ton, or a yard about a yard. Still less when you descend to minute measurements does half an inch mean about half an inch. If the seller wants a margin he must and in my experience does stipulate for it".*

Where the seller supplies goods which do not comply with the contract description he is in breach of an implied condition and in principle the buyer is entitled to reject the goods even though he suffers no damage.

> In *Re Moore & Co. Ltd. and Landauer & Co.* 1921 the buyer purchased a quantity of canned fruit. The contract stipulated that each case should contain thirty tins but on delivery about half the total quantity of tins were packed into cases of twenty four. The court held that the buyer was entitled to reject the goods, even though there was no evidence that the buyer would suffer any loss.

This principle now applies only where the buyer deals as a consumer. Under s.15A of the Sale of Goods Act 1979, which was introduced by the Sale and Supply of Goods Act 1994, a buyer who does not deal as a consumer will be unable to reject goods for trivial breaches of any of the conditions implied by sections 13, 14 or 15. Where the breach is so slight that it would be unreasonable for him to reject the goods, the buyer must treat it as a breach of warranty and not as a breach of condition. He may sue for damages if he is able to demonstrate that he has suffered financial loss.

Although the vast majority of sales will be made by description, it is possible even where the seller has applied a description to goods in the course of negotiations or in the contract itself, that the court may find that the sale is not made *by* description. This can occur where the buyer places no reliance on the description and the court imputes no common intention that the description is an essential part of the contract.

> In *Harlingdon & Leinster Enterprises Ltd. v. Christopher Hull Fine Art Ltd.* 1990 the plaintiffs were art dealers at a London gallery specialising in the German expressionist school. The defendants, who were dealers specialising in contemporary British artists, were asked to sell an oil painting described in an earlier auction catalogue as the work of Gabriele Munter, an artist of the German expressionist school. During the course of negotiations for the sale of the painting, it was made clear to the plaintiffs that the defendants did not know much about the painting and had no expertise in relation to it. It was described during negotiations and on the sales invoice as a Munter. Subsequent to the sale it was discovered to be a forgery and the plaintiffs sued to recover the purchase

price under s.13. The Court of Appeal held that the plaintiffs' claim failed because the sale was not made *by* description. The plaintiffs had not relied on the description but had bought the painting purely on their own assessment of it.

Consumer protection and faulty goods

Satisfactory quality

The expression *satisfactory quality* was introduced to replace the old fashioned and somewhat obscure expression, *merchantable quality*, by the Sale and Supply of Goods Act 1994, which put into effect the recommendations of a report of the Law Commission and the Scottish Law Commission in 1987 entitled *Sale and Supply of Goods*. The aim of this part of the 1994 Act was to clarify the obligations of a supplier of goods in relation to their quality and to express the consumers rights in a clear and accessible way using plain English. It was not intended to make dramatic changes to the substance of the buyers rights, and with minor exceptions the caselaw on merchantable quality remains relevant in the context of the changed wording.

Section 14(2) of the 1979 Act, as amended, provides:

> *"Where the seller sells goods in the course of a business there is an implied condition that the goods supplied under the contract are of satisfactory quality"*.

Under s.14(2)A, goods are of satisfactory quality if they *"meet the standard that a reasonable person would regard as satisfactory, taking account of any description of the goods, the price (if relevant) and all other relevant circumstances"*.

Before the passing of the 1994 Act, the statutory test as to whether goods were of merchantable quality was rather narrow in that it focused principally upon the question of their reasonable fitness for ordinary purposes. Following the publication of the Law Commission Report in 1987 however, the Court of Appeal began to widen its scope in line with the Report's recommendations.

> In *Rogers v. Parish (Scarborough) Ltd.* 1987 the plaintiff bought a new Range Rover from the defendant's garage. Although it was driveable and roadworthy the car had a number of defects in its engine, gearbox, oil seals and bodywork. The defendant argued that the car was of merchantable quality within the definition in s.14(6) as it could be driven in safety on a road and therefore was *"fit for the purpose for which goods of that kind are commonly bought"*. The Court of Appeal rejected the defendant's argument on the grounds that it was based upon too narrow an interpretation of s.14(6). Mustill LJ, declared that: *"the purpose for which goods of that kind are commonly bought would include not merely the purpose of driving the vehicle from one place to another but of doing so with the appropriate degree of comfort, ease of handling, reliability and pride in the vehicle's outward and interior appearance"*.

In two further cases, the Court of Appeal has made it clear that the principles laid down in *Rogers v. Parish* are equally applicable to sales of second hand cars.

> In *Business Applications Specialists v. Nationwide Credit Corporation Ltd.* 1988 the plaintiff purchased a second-hand Mercedes motor car for £14,850. It was two years old and had a recorded mileage of 37,000. The plaintiff drove the car for 800 miles when it

broke down due to burnt out valves and worn valve guides and guide seals. The cost of repairs was £635. The County Court judge dismissed the action on the grounds that the car was roadworthy despite the defects. The plaintiffs appeal was dismissed by the Court of Appeal which held that although judge had applied the wrong test he had reached the correct conclusion. He ought to have applied the test laid down in *Rogers v. Parish*.

In *Shine v. General Guarantee Corporation Ltd.* 1988 a second-hand Bertoni-bodied Fiat X19 had been advertised as *superb* and described verbally as *nice car, good runner, no problems*. In fact the car had been written off after having been submerged in water for 24 hours. The Court of Appeal held that, comparing the purchaser's reasonable expectations at the time of sale with the actual condition of the car, it was not of merchantable quality. In the words of Bush J: *"He was buying potentially a rogue car and irrespective of its condition it was in fact one which no member of the public, knowing the facts, would touch with a barge pole unless they could get it at a substantially reduced price to reflect the risk they were taking.... A car is not just a means of transport, it is a form also of investment (though a deteriorating one) and every purchaser of a car must have in mind the eventual saleability of the car as well as, in this particular case, his pride in it as a specialist car for the enthusiast"*.

The Act now provides, s.14(2)B, that:

"... the quality of goods includes their state and condition and the following (among others) are in appropriate cases aspects of the quality of goods:

(a) *fitness for all the purposes for which goods of the kind in question are commonly supplied;*

(b) *appearance and finish;*

(c) *freedom from minor defects;*

(d) *safety, and*

(e) *durability"*.

In *Bartlett v. Sydney Marcus Ltd.* 1965 the seller, who was a car dealer, warned the buyer that a second-hand car had a defective clutch. The buyer was given a choice of purchasing it for £550 as it was, or £575 after the seller had repaired it. The buyer opted to take the car as it was. The repairs cost more than the buyer expected. He sued the seller alleging that, for this reason, the car was not of merchantable quality. The Court of Appeal held that the seller was not liable as there was no breach of the implied term.

In *Crowther v. Shannon Motor Company* 1975 it was held that a second-hand car which needed a replacement engine after three weeks was not of merchantable quality. The car had been described as being in excellent condition.

The requirements of s.14(2) extend not only to the goods themselves but also to their packaging and any instructions supplied with them.

In *Wormell v. RHM Agriculture (East) Ltd.* 1987 the plaintiff was a farmer who purchased a chemical spray from the defendant in order to kill wild oats. The instructions provided with the spray indicated that its use outside a certain period carried the risk of injury to the crop. The plaintiff was aware of the warning and decided to take that risk. In fact, because of the late application, the spray was totally ineffective. The plaintiff claimed damages for the costs of the spray and the wasted labour in applying it. The Court of Appeal accepted that, as a matter of principle, any instructions supplied with goods would be treated as part of the goods themselves in assessing merchantability or fitness for purpose. On the facts, however, it was held that the seller was not liable as the instructions had clearly stated that spraying after a certain period of growth was not recommended. The seller was not bound to give full and exhaustive reasons for the instructions given.

The wording of s.14(2) makes it clear that the obligation applies to all goods which are supplied under the contract.

In *Geddling v. Marsh* 1920 mineral water was sold in bottles which were to remain the property of the manufacturer. The buyer was injured when a defective bottle burst. It was held that he was entitled to damages under s.14 even though the bottles were loaned rather than sold to him under the terms of the contract.

This rule applies even if the item which causes the harm was mistakenly supplied with the contract goods:

In *Wilson v. Rickett, Cockerell and Co. Ltd.* 1954 a delivery of *Coalite* included a detonator from the mine, which exploded when it was put onto a household fire. The Court of Appeal held that the sellers were liable for a breach of s.14(2).

The implied term may be broken even if the goods can easily be put right.

In *Grant v. Australian Knitting Mills Ltd.* 1936 the buyer purchased underpants which contained a chemical. This caused dermatitis, a skin disease, when the buyer wore them. The chemical would have been removed if the buyer had washed them before he wore them. It was held that the goods were not of merchantable quality, and the seller was liable.

The seller will not be liable, however, if the defect in the goods is caused by the way in which the buyer treats them.

In *Heil v. Hedges* 1951 the buyer was infected with tapeworms after eating a pork chop which had been undercooked. It was held that the seller was not liable because the meat would have been quite safe if it had been properly cooked.

The seller will not be liable under s.14(2) solely because there are no spare parts available to service the goods which he has supplied.

In *Gent v. Eastman Machine Co. Ltd.* 1985 the plaintiff purchased a knitting machine from the defendant. Not long afterwards spare parts were required and it took four months for the spares to be supplied. It was held that the knitting machine was not rendered unmerchantable by the seller's failure to be able to supply spare parts within a reasonable time.

There are a number of important features of s.14(2) which should be noted:

- the promise of satisfactory quality only arises where the sale is made by a seller in the course of his business. It does not apply for example to the sale of a second hand car by a private individual;

- the buyer may be either a private consumer or someone buying goods for business purposes, including resale;

- liability may pass along the chain of distribution. Thus a retailer who is successfully sued by a consumer for breach of s.14 may claim an indemnity from the wholesaler from whom he purchased the goods, and the wholesaler may in turn claim from the manufacturer. Each link in the chain is a separate contract containing the implied condition that the goods are of satisfactory quality;

- the implied term as to satisfactory quality is an extremely important aspect of consumer protection in relation to shoddy or defective goods, and is the legal basis of many consumer complaints for example where goods are taken back to a shop because they are damaged or not working properly;

- the consumer's remedy in the case of a breach of the promise that the goods are of satisfactory quality is damages and repudiation of the contract. This involves rejecting the goods and claiming your money back. As we have seen however the right to reject the goods may be lost in certain circumstances;

- only the buyer may use the remedies of repudiation and damages as a claim under s.14 is a claim based on a breach of contract and as we have seen the rule of privity of contract means that only a party to the contract can sue;

- there is no claim for breach of the implied term as to satisfactory quality either in respect of a defect drawn to the buyers attention before the contract is made, or where the buyer has examined the goods before buying them and ought to have discovered the defect;

- a business seller would be wise to maintain an insurance policy covering product liability risks in order to protect the business in the event of a claim under s.14; and a manufacturer will usually have a system of quality control in order to reduce the chances that such claims will arise;

- the seller's liability under s.14 is strict and it is therefore no defence to show that proper care has been taken.

In *Frost v. Aylesbury Dairies Ltd.* 1905 the dairy supplied milk contaminated with typhoid germs and was held liable despite establishing that it had used all reasonable care to prevent such contamination.

Fitness for notified purpose

Where the buyer requires the goods for a special or unusual purpose, the seller may be liable for a breach of s.14(3) if the goods are not fit for that purpose.

Under s.14(3):

> *"Where the seller sells goods in the course of a business and the buyer, expressly or by implication, makes known ... to the seller ... any particular purpose for which the goods are being bought, there is an implied condition that the goods supplied under the contract are reasonably for that purpose, whether or not that is a purpose for which such goods are commonly supplied, except where the circumstances show that the buyer does not rely, or that it is unreasonable for him to rely, on the skill or judgment of the seller".*

Consumers sometimes place reliance on the expertise of the seller, for example when a customer goes into a shop and asks whether the shop has something that will perform a particular task, say fixing a broken ornament or removing stains from a carpet. A business may describe its accounting procedures to a supplier of office equipment, relying on the supplier to provide a suitable system to cope with these procedures. In these cases the seller will be liable under s.14(3) if the goods, even though of merchantable quality, do not fulfil the purpose for which the buyer requires them.

> In *Cammell Laird & Co. Ltd. v. Manganese Bronze & Brass Co. Ltd.* 1934 the buyers supplied the sellers with a specification for ships' propellers which they were to manufacture for the buyers. Reliance was placed upon the sellers regarding matters outside the specification, including the thickness of metal to be used. The propellers were found on delivery to be too thin. The buyer's action was successful on the ground that the unfitness concerned a matter on which the buyers had relied upon the seller's skill.

There will be no liability under s.14(3) where the circumstances show that the buyer does not rely on the skill or judgment of the seller.

> In *Teheran-Europe Co. Ltd. v. ST Belton Tractors Ltd.* 1968 industrial equipment was sold to the plaintiff buyer for the purpose of exporting and resale in Persia. The seller knew this but was not familiar with the Persian market, unlike the buyer who carried on a business there. The equipment infringed Persian regulations and the plaintiff sued the seller for breach of s.14(3). The Court of Appeal held that the seller was not liable as the buyer had relied on his own skill and judgment as to whether the equipment was suitable for resale in Persia. There was no reliance on the skill or judgment of the seller.

When the product only has one purpose the buyer will be held to have impliedly made known to the seller the purpose for which he wants the goods.

> In *Priest v. Last* 1903 the buyer was held to have made known impliedly to the seller the purpose for which he required a hot water bottle. The seller was liable under s.14(3) when the bottle burst after a few days injuring the buyer.

The seller will not be liable however, where the buyer does not tell him of any particular requirements.

> In *Griffiths v. Peter Conway Ltd.* 1939 the buyer, who had particularly sensitive skin, developed dermatitis as a result of wearing a coat which she bought from the defendant. The coat would not have had this effect on a normal person and the buyer had not told the seller about her sensitivity. It was held that the seller was not liable under s.14(3).

Sometimes a claim based upon breach of s.14(3) will seek to make the seller liable for an external abnormality which causes the goods to be unfit.

> This was the case in *James Slater (A Firm) v. Finning Ltd.* 1996. Slaters had bought a camshaft from Finnings, which Finnings knew was to be fitted to a fishing boat belonging to Slaters. The camshaft failed due to tortional forces created by the boat. The House of Lords held that the sellers were not in breach of s.14(3). The tortional forces set up by the boat was a factor unknown to both parties, and so the seller could not be treated as having accepted any obligation that the camshaft would cope with them.

Consumer protection where goods are sold by sample

This is a form of protection which will apply mainly to the business customer, for example where raw materials or large quantities of goods are purchased after a sample has been examined and perhaps tested for its suitability for the customers purpose. It can also apply to consumer situations, for example, where a new carpet or a made to measure suit is purchased by an individual. The sample acts as a sort of three dimensional description of the final product which can be touched or tasted or in some other way give the potential buyer a fuller appreciation of the nature of the product on offer.

Under s.15 of the 1979 Act, where goods are sold according to a sample, there are implied conditions that:

(a)   the bulk of the consignment will correspond with the sample in terms of quality;

(b)   the buyer shall have a reasonable opportunity of comparing the bulk with the sample; and

(c)   the goods shall be free from any defect rendering them unmerchantable which would not be apparent on a reasonable examination of the sample.

The function of a sample was described by Lord MacNaghten in *Drummond v. Van Ingen* 1887 when he stated:

> *"The office of a sample is to present to the eye the real meaning and intention of the parties with regard to the subject matter of the contract which, owing to the imperfections of language, it may be difficult or impossible to express in words. The sample speaks for itself".*

Claims based on more than one ground

Where a person is injured by defective goods there may be a number of alternative grounds upon which he could sue. There is a considerable degree of overlap between s.14(2) and s.14(3), so that, for example the sellers in *Frost v. Aylesbury Dairies* 1905 and *Priest v. Last* 1903 were in breach of both implied conditions. The seller in *Beale v. Taylor* 1967 was found to be in breach of s.13, and would probably have been in breach of s.14 if he had sold the car in the course of a business. There is also a considerable overlap between the law of contract and the tort of negligence in this area. In *Grant v. Australian Knitting Mills* 1935 the retailer was liable because the goods were not of merchantable quality, and the manufacturer was liable in negligence.

Later in this chapter a number of cases are examined in the field of *product liability*, for example *Lambert v. Lewis* 1981, in which the injured party's claim is based both in negligence and in contract. Part 1 of the Consumer Protection Act 1987 gives additional remedies for injury by defective products. It is quite conceivable that an injured party would have a claim in contract, in negligence and under the 1987 Act. Figure 12.3 provides a comparison between these three alternatives. Of course the injured party can only recover damages once, but he may bring his claim under all of these headings by *pleading in the alternative*. If he fails in one aspect of his claim, he can still recover damages if another succeeds.

The rule of privity of contract means that only the buyer can claim for breach of the implied terms. If this claim against the seller succeeds then liability can be passed down the line through the chain of distribution. The seller can sue his supplier for an indemnity based upon the supplier's breach of contract. He is in effect trying to drop out of the picture by saying *"if I am liable then as my supplier you are liable on the same basis"*. This process, known as third party proceedings, continues until the manufacturer is sued. Only an effective exclusion of liability clause can break the chain of indemnity.

> In *Godley v. Perry (Burton & Sons Ltd., Third Party; Graham, Fourth Party)* 1960 a boy of six lost the sight of one eye when firing a catapult which he had bought for 6d from the defendant's shop. The catapult fractured below the point where the handle joined the fork. The evidence showed that is was made of cheap brittle polystyrene, indifferently moulded and containing internal voids. The retailer had purchased the catapult from a wholesaler who had purchased it from an importer. The importer had bought the goods from a manufacturer in Hong Kong. The plaintiff sued the defendant shopkeeper who issued third party proceedings against the wholesaler. The wholesaler in turn claimed against the importer. The court decided that the catapult was not of merchantable quality, and that the retailer was liable to the purchaser. Liability passed up the line so at the end of the day the importer (or his insurers) were left either to bear the loss or pursue the manufacturer in the Hong Kong courts.

Exclusion of liability for breach of statutory implied terms

In Chapter 10 we examined the legal framework which applies to control the use of exclusion or limitation of liability, both at common law and in statute. We considered a number of key aspects of the Unfair Contract Terms Act 1977, postponing examination of s.6 and s.7, which control the use of contract terms designed to exclude or limit liability for breach of the statutory implied terms in contracts for the sale or supply of goods, until we had dealt with the substance of those implied terms.

Section 6 of the 1977 Act applies to contracts for the sale of goods and hire purchase agreements, while s.7 applies to all other contracts under which the possession or ownership of goods passes to the customer. The rules contained in each section are very similar, although there are some minor differences between them. The extent of the protection given to a customer under these rules depends on whether or not he deals as a consumer.

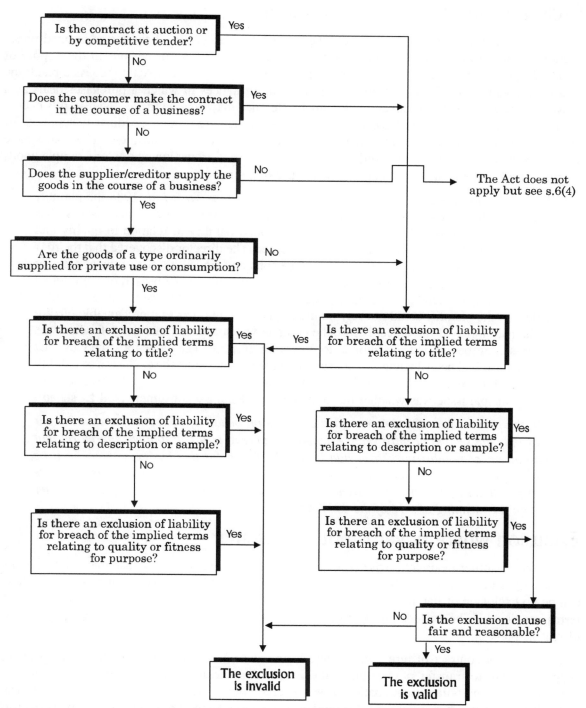

Figure 12.2   Exclusion of Liability for Breach of Statutory Implied Terms in Contract for the Sale and Supply of Goods: Section 6 and Section 7 Unfair Terms Act 1977

Exclusion where buyer is a consumer

Where the customer deals as a consumer, there can be no exclusion of the terms implied under Sections 12 to 15 of the Sale of Goods Act 1979 and the equivalent provisions in the Supply of Goods (Implied Terms) Act 1973 and the Supply of Goods and Services Act 1982. As a result the consumer obtains a high level of protection. The circumstances in which a purchaser deals as a consumer are examined in Chapter 11, to which reference may now be made. Briefly, this occurs where the seller sells goods in the course of a business which are of a type ordinarily supplied for private use to a purchaser who buys them other than in the course of a business. The courts have interpreted this concept broadly in order to extend the scope of protection where for example goods are purchased in the name of a company for the use of a director.

> In *R & B Customs Brokers Co. Ltd. v. United Dominions Trust Ltd.* 1988 the plaintiff company bought a second hand Colt Shogun car for the use of one of its directors, and signed a conditional sale agreement which excluded liability in relation to quality and fitness unless the buyer was dealing as a consumer. The director discovered that the roof of the car leaked before the defendant finance company signed its part of the agreement thereby concluding the contract. The plaintiff rejected the car for breach of the implied terms relating to merchantable quality and fitness for purpose. At first instance the judge held that the plaintiff could not rely on the implied condition as to merchantable quality as he had notice of the defect before the contract was made, but that the defendant was in breach of the implied condition as to fitness for purpose. The judge took the view that the plaintiff had been dealing as a consumer and accordingly that the exclusion of liability was invalid under s.6 of the 1977 Act. On appeal, the decision of the judge was upheld. The principal issue was whether the company was dealing a consumer. Neil LJ stated:

> *"In the present case the director gave evidence on behalf of the company that the car was only the second or third vehicle acquired on credit terms. It follows, therefore, that no pattern of regular purchases had been established for this business, nor can it be suggested that this transaction was an adventure in the nature of trade. I am therefore satisfied that in relation to the purchase of this car the company was dealing as consumer within the meaning of s.12 of the 1977 Act."*

Exclusion where buyer is not a consumer

Where the customer deals otherwise than as a consumer, for example because the supplier is not in business or because the goods are of a type which are not normally bought for private use, there can be no exclusion of liability for breach of the implied terms relating to title. The other implied terms can however be excluded as against such a customer, but only if the clause satisfies the test of reasonableness.

In the case of a contract of hire, where there is an exclusion of the implied terms relating to the supplier's right to transfer possession of the goods, this exclusion will be subject to the test of reasonableness and will not automatically be rendered void. This applies whether or not the hirer is dealing as a consumer. Figure 12.2 summarises the application of s.6 and s.7, except as regards the exclusion of the implied terms relating to the transfer of possession in hire contracts.

For the purpose of s.6 and s.7, the Act lays down guidelines which the court may take into account in determining whether an exclusion clause is reasonable. Strictly speaking, the Act does not apply these guidelines to determine reasonableness in relation to the other sections which apply the reasonableness test, but in practice the courts take them into account in those cases also. The factors to be taken into account under the guidelines are:

(a)   the relative bargaining strength of the parties;

(b)   whether there was an opportunity to purchase the product elsewhere without submitting to the clause;

(c)   whether any inducement was given to the buyer in return for accepting the clause;

(d)   whether the goods were made to the buyer's design or specification;

(e)   whether the customer knew or ought reasonably to have known of the existence of the clause;

(f)   the extent to which it was open for the parties to cover themselves by insurance; and

(g)   the particular circumstances of the case.

In *George Mitchell Ltd. v. Finney Lock Seeds Ltd.* 1983 the plaintiff was a farmer who purchased cabbage seed from the defendant. The seeds were described as those of a solid heading late winter cabbage. In fact they were of a different type, of inferior quality and unfit for human consumption. The plaintiff planted 63 acres of these cabbages. They proved to be of no value and had to be ploughed in. The seed had cost £192 but the plaintiff's loss was in excess of £61,000. The plaintiff was not insured for this loss and sued the seller for breach of the term implied by s.13 of the Sale of Goods Act 1979 that the goods would correspond with their description. The defence put forward by the sellers was an exclusion clause limiting liability to either the cost of the seed or its replacement value. The clause read *"in the event of any seeds or plants sold or agreed to be sold by us not complying with the express terms of the contract of sale or with a representation made by us or by any duly authorised agent or representative on our behalf prior to, at the time of, or in any such contract, or any seeds or plants proving defective in varietal purity we will, at our option, replace the defective seeds or plants, free of charge to the buyer or will refund all payments made to us by the buyer in respect of the defective seeds or plants and this shall be the limit of our obligation. We hereby exclude all liability for any loss or damage arising from the use of any seeds or plants supplied by us and for any consequential loss or damage arising out of such use or any failure in the performance of or any defect in any seeds or plants supplied by us or for any other loss or damage whatsoever save for, at our option, liability for any such replacement or refund as aforesaid"*.

The House of Lords affirmed the decision of the Court of Appeal that the clause was ineffective. In the Court of Appeal Lord Denning considered a number of questions relevant to the validity of the clause. The first was whether the clause was part of the agreement. He found that it was since such conditions were usual in the trade, and therefore well known, and in any event the clause was included on the back of the invoice.

The second was the wording of the clause, and whether as drafted it covered and effectively limited the supplier's liability. He found that the clause clearly did so. Finally the question arose as to whether the clause was a reasonable one. It had been imposed by the defendant without negotiation. The seedsmen could insure against the risk of crop failure without materially affecting the price of the seeds. The defendants could have tested the seeds but the plaintiffs had no opportunity of discovering the defectiveness of the seed until it was too late. In addition there was evidence that the defendants would usually negotiate a realistic settlement where a claim was justified in similar circumstances. Taking these factors into account the clause was held to be unreasonable and invalid.

In *R.W. Green Ltd. v. Cade Brothers Farms* 1978 the plaintiffs purchased a quantity of seed potatoes from the defendants under the terms of a written standard form contract which included a clause limiting liability of the defendants to a refund of the price. The potatoes were infected with a virus which could only be detected at harvest time. The crop failed and the plaintiffs sued the defendants for breach of the terms implied into the contract by s.14 of the Sale of Goods Act. It was held that the defendants were in breach of the implied terms, but were not liable because the exclusion clause was reasonable in the circumstances of the case. The seed had been sold cheaply because it was uncertified and the plaintiffs could have paid more and bought certified seed potato. The terms of the contract had not been imposed by the seller, rather they were the product of many years negotiation by trade associations and unions representing both sides of the industry.

Criminal liability for the use of invalid exclusion clauses

The Unfair Contract Terms Act 1977 invalidates many exclusion clauses so that they cannot be relied upon as a defence to an action for damages. The Act does not, however, prevent the trader from using invalid clauses. The clause may have no legal validity, but the consumer may be misled because of his lack of legal knowledge. The Consumer Transactions (Restrictions on Statements) Order 1976 (as amended in 1978) was made under the Fair Trading Act 1973 to prevent this unfair trading practice in a limited range of situations. The order applies to any clause in a consumer transaction which purports to exclude liability for breach of Sections 13, 14 or 15 of the Sale of Goods Act 1979. Under the order it is a criminal offence for a person, in the course of a business, to do any of the following:

(a) display a notice of such a clause at a place where consumer deals are likely to be made,

(b) publish any advertisement to supply goods which includes such a clause,

(c) provide the consumer with a written contract or other document containing such a clause, or

(d) supply goods bearing any statement about the seller's liability in relation to description quality or fitness for purpose, unless the statement makes it clear that it does not affect the statutory rights of the consumer.

Product Liability in Negligence

It was seen above that the right to make a product liability claim in contract is confined to an injured person who actually buys the goods himself. The contract claim can be brought against the supplier of the goods only. The supplier is strictly liable, even if he is not at fault. In negligence anyone injured by the product can sue anyone who has failed to take reasonable care in relation to it thereby causing the injury.

We shall now examine those elements of negligence liability which are particularly significant in defective product claims:

The duty of care

In relation to liability for manufactured products we have seen that it was not until as late as 1932 that it was recognised that a general duty of care was owed by manufacturers to consumers. This was established by the decision of the House of Lords in the case of *Donoghue v. Stevenson* the facts of which were described in Chapter 6. The importance of the decision in the field of product liability lies in the fact that, in his judgment, Lord Atkin described the duty of a manufacturer in the following terms *"... a manufacturer of products, which he sells in such a form as to show that he intends them to reach the ultimate consumer in the form in which they left him with no reasonable possibility of intermediate examination, and with the knowledge that the absence of reasonable care in the preparation or putting up of the products will result in an injury to the consumer's life or property, owes a duty to the consumer to take that reasonable care."*

Although this statement has been developed by subsequent interpretation it can still be regarded as the framework within which a court will decide whether a duty of care exists. Four elements within the framework require closer examination:

Who can be sued

Lord Atkin's reference to a manufacturer of products embraces everyone involved in the manufacturing enterprise from design to distribution. It also extends to others who have worked on the goods at any time.

> In *Stennet v. Hancock* 1939, for example, the plaintiff was a pedestrian who was injured when part of the wheel of a lorry broke away whilst the lorry was being driven. The defect in the wheel was the result of a repair which had not been carried out properly. The court held that the repairers were liable under Lord Atkin's manufacturing principle.

What type of defects will give rise to liability

Lord Atkin referred to products which the manufacturer sells in such a form as to show that he intends them to reach the ultimate consumer in the form in which they left him with no reasonable possibility of intermediate examination. This has been interpreted as limiting the application of the duty to products with latent defects. Latent defects are faults which are not apparent on an examination of the goods. Lord Wright in *Grant v. Australian Knitting Mills Ltd.* 1936 stated that:

> *"The principle of Donoghue's case can only be applied where the defect is hidden and unknown to the consumer ... the man who consumes or uses a thing which he knows to*

be noxious cannot complain in respect of whatever mischief follows, because it follows from his own conscious volition in choosing to incur the risk or certainty of mischance."

This interpretation of Lord Atkin's principle was followed in the case of *Crow v. Barford (Agricultural) Ltd. and H.B. Holttum & Co. Ltd.* 1963. The plaintiff bought a rotary lawn mower known as a Barford Rotomo from Holttum after it was demonstrated to him at home. The machine was designed in such a way that the guard for the blades had an opening to allow the grass to be expelled as it was being cut. To start the lawn mower the user's foot had to be placed on the casing containing the blade. While starting the Rotomo the plaintiff's foot slipped into the opening and two of his toes were cut off. The claim against the manufacturer was made on the basis of the principle in *Donoghue v. Stevenson* but the Court of Appeal decided that this did not apply because the danger was *"perfectly obvious"* and not hidden or unknown to the plaintiff. The claim in contract against the retailer was also unsuccessful because the plaintiff had inspected the lawn mower during the demonstration before he purchased it. This brought the case within the exception contained in s.14(2) of the Sale of Goods Act that the seller does not promise that the goods are of merchantable quality in relation to defects which ought to have been revealed by the buyer's prior examination of the goods.

To whom is the duty owed

Lord Atkin tells us that the duty of care is owed to the ultimate consumer of the product. This expression has been interpreted widely so as to include the purchaser, any person injured while using or consuming the product and any other person, such as the plaintiff in *Stennet v. Hancock,* who is injured by the product in circumstances where injury to him ought reasonably to have been foreseen.

For example, in *Lambert v. Lewis (Lexmead Ltd., third party; Dixon Bate Ltd., fourth party)* 1982 the driver of a car and his son were killed and the plaintiffs, his wife and daughter, were injured when their car was hit by a trailer which had become detached from a farmer's Land Rover and careered across the road into the path of their car. The accident was caused by a design defect in the towing hitch, which was unable to cope with the stresses to which it was subjected in normal use. The evidence showed that part of the towing hitch had been missing for a number of months before the accident and that the farmer should have realised this. The trial judge decided that the manufacturer was 75% to blame for the accident and that the farmer was 25% to blame and apportioned liability accordingly. The farmer issued third party proceedings against the retailer from whom he had purchased the towing hitch. He was seeking indemnity for the damages for which he was liable and basing his claim in contract on the retailer's breach of the implied terms in s.14 Sale of Goods Act. The retailer in turn issued fourth party proceedings against the manufacturer in contract and in negligence. On appeal the House of Lords decided that the retailer was not liable to the farmer because the farmer's own negligence, rather than the retailer's breach of contract, was the operative cause of his loss. The fourth party proceedings were consequently dismissed because the retailer had no liability to pass on to the manufacturer.

What type of damage is recoverable

In his statement of the duty of care owed by a manufacturer, Lord Atkin confines the scope of the duty to injury to the consumer's life or property. Within this damages are recoverable for death, personal injury or damage to property, excluding damage to the product itself.

One category of loss which cannot always be sued for in negligence is pure financial loss. A 1985 case provides a good illustration of this rule in the context of product liability.

> In *Muirhead v. Industrial Tank Specialities (ITT Marlow, third party; Leroy Somer Electric Motors Ltd., fourth party)* 1985, the plaintiff was a wholesale fish merchant who installed in his premises a large sea water tank in which to store lobsters. The sea water had to be filtered, oxygenated and recirculated. This was done by a series of pumps working 24 hours per day. The tank and pumps were installed by I.T.S. Ltd. The pumps were manufactured by Leroy Somer Electric Motors Ltd and supplied to the plaintiff by I.T.S. Ltd. through other suppliers in the chain of distribution. The pumps constantly broke down and on one occasion the recirculation of water was affected so that the plaintiff lost his entire stock of lobsters. The plaintiff successfully sued I.T.S. Ltd. in contract but the company went into liquidation unable to satisfy the judgment against it. The plaintiff then proceeded with action against the manufacturers claiming damages for all of the losses incurred as a result of the defects in the pumps. The vast bulk of the claim was for the loss of profits on intended sales but the Court of Appeal decided that this was pure financial loss and therefore not recoverable in a negligence action. The rest of the plaintiff's claim succeeded.

Breach of duty

Once it has been established that the manufacturer in a given case owes a duty of care to avoid injury to the plaintiff, the second major element of negligence liability which the plaintiff must prove is that the manufacturer was in breach of that duty. A breach of duty is a failure to take reasonable care and involves a finding of fault on the part of the manufacturer. In many cases the task of proving this may be a difficult one for the plaintiff, involving a detailed investigation of the defendant's processes of manufacture design and testing and a comparison with procedures adopted by other producers in the same field. The plaintiff will need to employ expert witnesses who can analyse these processes and procedures and pin-point any lack of care which may have caused the defect in the product and therefore caused the injury. If the plaintiff is unable to prove a breach of duty he may have to bear the loss himself without compensation, unless there is another available legal basis for his claim.

A breach of the duty of care may occur outside the process of development design and manufacture.

> In the case of *Vacwell Engineering v. BDH Chemicals Ltd.* 1971 for example, the manufacturer of a chemical produced for industrial use was held liable in negligence for a failure to give proper and adequate warnings that the chemical would explode when mixed with water. This should have been achieved by clear labelling of the product.

> In *Walton v. British Leyland (UK) Ltd.* 1978 the failure of British Leyland to recall the Austin Allegro car after a large number of 'wheel drift' faults had been reported to the

company was held to be a breach of the duty of care. Leyland were held liable to the plaintiffs who were severely injured when the wheel of their Allegro came off as the vehicle was travelling at 60 mph on a motorway. The Judge, Willis J., in the High Court stated *"The duty of care owed by Leyland to the public was to make a clean breast of the problem and recall all cars which they could in order that safety washers could be fitted ... The company seriously considered recall and made an estimate of the cost at a figure (£300,000 in 1974) which seems to me to be in no way out of proportion to the risks involved. It was decided not to follow this course for commercial reasons. I think this involved a failure to observe their duty of care for the safety of the many who were bound to remain at risk ..."*

Res ipsa loquitur

In the context of product liability the principle of res ipsa loquitur is of considerable significance. The tendency in recent times has been for the courts to allow the plaintiff to rely on the rule in many cases involving defective products. Res ipsa loquitur is considered in detail in Chapter 5. Here we may note its application in product liability cases.

In *Chaproniere v. Mason* 1905 the plaintiff broke a tooth when eating a bread bun which was found to contain a pebble. He pleaded res ipsa loquitur and the defendant baker was held to be liable because he was unable to prove that he had not been negligent.

Where the plaintiff pleads res ipsa loquitur, the manufacturer will need to produce strong evidence if he is to satisfy the court that the injuries were not caused by his negligence. It will not be sufficient for him to show that he has a good system of work and provides adequate supervision during the process of manufacture.

In *Grant v. Australian Knitting Mills* 1936 the plaintiff contracted dermatitis because of the presence in his underwear of excess sulphite after the process of manufacture by the defendant. The defendant's evidence was that he had manufactured over four and a half million pairs of underpants and had received no other complaints. Nevertheless he was held liable because the probability was that someone in his employment for whose acts he was legally responsible had failed to take care.

In *Hill v. James Crowe (Cases) Ltd.* 1978 the plaintiff, a lorry driver, was injured when he fell off a badly nailed wooden packing case on which he was standing in order to load his lorry. The manufacturer of the packing case gave evidence that the standards of workmanship and supervision in his factory were high and argued that he had not failed to fulfil his duty to the plaintiff to take reasonable care in producing the case. The Court held that the defendant was liable for the bad workmanship of one of his employees even though, in general terms, he had a good production system. He had not proved that the plaintiff's injuries were not due to the negligence of one of his employees.

This case provides an example of the manufacturer's liability for a foreseeable misuse of his product.

The extremely high standard of care which the courts are prepared to impose on a manufacturer can be seen in the following case.

In *Winward v. TVR Engineering* 1986 the defendants were in the business of producing specialist sports cars. They were responsible for the design and assembly of the vehicles using components bought in from other sources. The car in question incorporated a Ford engine which was supplied to the defendants fitted with a Weber carburettor. The carburettor had a basic design fault which ultimately caused petrol to leak from it. The plaintiff's wife was injured when leaking petrol came into contact with the hot engine. The defendants argued that it was reasonable for them to rely on the expertise of their supplier, particularly as the design fault had never previously manifested itself. The Court of Appeal held that the defendants were in breach of their duty through their failure to test the component and modify its design.

The Consumer Protection Act 1987: Strict liability for injury caused by defective products

Part I of the Consumer Protection Act 1987 provides a framework of strict liability for injury and damage caused by defective products. This part of the Act was introduced in order to give effect to the EC Directive on Product Liability (85/374/EEC) and represents a significant extension of consumer protection in this area by providing an additional basis upon which to obtain compensation for injury caused by unsafe or faulty goods.

Liability under s.2(1) of the Act arises *where any damage is caused wholly or partly by a defect in a product.* In order to succeed in a claim, the plaintiff must prove two things:

(a)   that the product was defective, and

(b)   that the defect caused the injury or damage.

If the plaintiff can prove these things, the defendant will be liable even though he took all possible care in relation to the product. This is the crucial difference between strict liability under the Act and liability based upon negligence which, as we have seen, depends upon proof of fault by the defendant.

Who is liable?

Liability falls upon all or any of the following persons:

(a)   the *producer* – this term is defined in s.1(2) and includes the manufacturer of the product, the producer of any raw materials or the manufacturer of a component part.

(b)   the *own brander* – any person who, by putting his name on the product or using a trade mark or other distinguishing marks in relation to it, has held himself out to be the producer of the product

(c)   the *importer into the EC* – a person importing the product into the Community from a non Community state for the purpose of supplying it in the course of his business.

(d)   *any supplier who cannot identify the person who produced the product, or supplied it to him.* In such circumstances that person will be liable, regardless of whether he was a business supplier, provided he supplied the product to someone else, and the following conditions are met:

(i)   he is requested by a person suffering any damage to identify any producer, own brander or importer into the EC;

(ii)   the request is made within a reasonable time after the damage occurs;

(iii) at the time of the request it is not reasonably practicable for the injured party to identify all of the potential defendants; and

(iv.) he fails, within a reasonable time, to comply with the request or to identify the person who supplied the product to him.

Thus it will be imperative, where litigation is threatened, for businesses to be able to identify the supplier of the products or component parts used in any goods sold by the business. It will be particularly important to differentiate, by product coding for example, between the products of two or more suppliers who are supplying identical components for incorporation into the same type of finished product. This will apply to all component parts ranging from electric motors to nuts and bolts.

Where two or more persons are liable for the injury each can be sued for the full amount of the damage. The party who is sued may be entitled to a contribution or indemnity from anyone else who is liable, under the Civil Liability (Contribution) Act 1978. Of course the injured person can only recover compensation once, regardless of the number of possible defendants or the legal basis of his claim. The injured person will usually choose to sue the defendant against whom liability can most easily be established and who is most likely to be able to afford to pay damages or to have insurance cover.

When is a product defective?

In order to succeed in a claim the plaintiff will have to prove that his injury was caused by a defect in the product. Section 3 tells us that a product will be regarded as defective *when the safety of the product is not such as persons generally are entitled to expect*. It is clear that the lawnmower in the *Crow v. Barford and Holttum* case mentioned earlier would be defective under this definition. The question of when a product is defective is likely to be central to much of the litigation under the Act. Section 3(2) gives us some guidance as to the factors which will be relevant in deciding whether a product is defective. It provides:

"In determining what persons generally are entitled to expect in relation to a product all the circumstances shall be taken into account, including:

(a)   *the manner in which, and purposes for which, the product has been marketed, its get-up, the use of any mark in relation to the product and any instructions for, or warnings with respect to, doing or refraining from doing anything with or in relation to the product;*

(b)   *what might reasonably be expected to be done with or in relation to the product; and*

(c)   *the time when the product was supplied by its producer to another person;*

and nothing in this section shall require a defect to be inferred from the fact alone that the safety of a product which is supplied after that time is greater than the safety of the product in question."

Clearly it is very important for any business to ensure that the packaging of their products is such that it does not suggest or imply that the product can be used in a manner or for a purpose which is unsafe. Appropriate warnings of the dangers associated with the use or foreseeable misuse of the product must be amply displayed on the packaging and, where necessary, on the goods themselves. A further precaution which may be taken by the producer of goods is the date coding of products in order to take advantage of the defence suggested by the final part of s.3(2). Thus if a safer product is subsequently developed and put onto the market, the level of safety provided by the original product cannot be judged solely by reference to improved safety features in the new product.

Defences

A number of specific defences are provided for in s.4 of the Consumer Protection Act. These are in addition to the obvious defences that the product was not defective or that it was not the cause of the plaintiff's loss. Thus it is a defence to show:

(a)   that the defect was attributable to the defendant's compliance with a legal requirement, or

(b)   that the defendant did not supply the goods to anyone.

In this connection it is interesting to notice s.1(3) which says that where a finished product incorporates component products or raw materials, the supplier of the finished product will not be treated as a supplier of the component products or raw materials by reason only of his supply of the finished product. Thus, for example, a builder using high alumina cement could argue that he was not a supplier of that cement for the purposes of the Act. He could invoke this defence if the building subsequently deteriorated due to defects in the cement.

(c)   Section 4 also enables the defendant to escape liability if he can show that he had not supplied the goods in the course of his business and that he had not own branded, imported into the EC, or produced the goods with a view to profit.

This defence could be invoked, for example, in relation to the sale of home made jam at a coffee morning in aid of charity.

(d)   The nature of the fourth defence under s.4 depends upon whether the defendant is a producer, own brander or importer into the EC. If he is, he can escape liability by proving that the defect was not present in the product at the time he supplied it. If he is not, he must show that the defect was not present in the product at the time it was last supplied by any person of that description.

(e)   Section 4 provides the development risks defence that, given the state of scientific and technical knowledge at the time the product was put into circulation, no producer of a product of that kind could have been expected to have discovered the defect if it had existed in his products while they were under his control.

The development risks defence has provoked much discussion. Its adoption was optional under the terms of the directive. It is argued that the defence reduces the strictness of liability by introducing considerations which are more relevant to negligence. Its main impact will be seen in those areas which are at the forefront of scientific and technical development. The pharmaceutical industry, for example, could benefit from it in relation to the development of new drugs. It may seem ironic that if an event like the Thalidomide tragedy were to re-occur the victims could be prevented from recovering compensation because of the operation of this defence. The tragedy was in fact a major cause of pressure for the introduction of strict product liability laws throughout Europe.

(f)   Where the defendant is a producer of a component product, he will have a defence under s.4 if he can show that the defect in the finished product is wholly attributable to its design or to compliance with instructions given by the producer of the finished product.

Damage

Assuming the plaintiff succeeds in his claim, the question arises as to the types of loss he will be compensated for. Under s.5 damages are recoverable for death or for personal injury. This includes any disease or other impairment of a person's physical or mental condition. The plaintiff will also be able to claim compensation for damage to his property. However, exceptions to this provide significant limitations on liability under the Act. There is no liability for loss of or damage to:

(a)   the product itself,

(b)   any property in respect of which the amount of the claim would be below £275,

(c)   any commercial property – property of a type which is not ordinarily intended for private use, occupation or consumption and which is not actually intended by the plaintiff for his own private use, occupation or consumption.

All of these categories of loss are recoverable in a contract claim, although the first category, loss or damage to the product itself, is not recoverable in negligence.Section 7 of the Consumer Protection Act provides for an absolute prohibition on the limitation or exclusion of liability arising under the Act.

Time limits for claims

The limitation period provided for in the Act, regardless of the type of damage, is three years from the date on which the right to take action arises, or, if later, three years from the date on which the plaintiff is aware:

(a)   that he has suffered significant damage,

(b)   that the damage is attributable to a defect in the product, and

(c)   of the identity of the defendant.

There is an overall cut off point 10 years after the product is put into circulation. After the 10 year period has elapsed no new claims can be made although any proceedings which have already been started may continue.

	Contract	Negligence	Consumer Protection Act
who is liable	seller; he may claim an indemnity from the previous seller in the chain of distribution	manufacturer; includes designer, repairer, processor and other persons working on goods	producer, own brander, importer into EC, supplier who refuses to identify previous supplier or producer
who can claim	buyer only	ultimate consumer provided injury to him is foreseeable	any person injured by a defect in the product
basis of liability	strict; if goods not reasonably fit for usual or notified special purposes	fault; failure to take reasonable care in relation to the product	strict; where the product does not provide the safety which persons are entitled to expect
types of loss	personal injury death damage to property financial loss	personal injury death damage to property other than the product financial loss in limited circumstances	personal injury death damage £275 + to consumer property other than product
exclusion of liability	prohibited if buyer dealing as consumer or for death or personal injury othrewise possible if exclusion is reasonable	prohibited if death or personal injury otherwise possible if exclusion is reasonable	prohibited in all cases
time limit for claims	personal injury; 3 years from the date on which the plaintiff had knowledge of the material facts giving rise to the claim Other claims; 6 years from the date on which cause of action arose; or in negligence cases only, (if later) 3 years from the date of plaintiff's knowledge of the material facts if within 15 years of the negligent act		3 years from the date on which the plaintiff was aware of the damage the defect and the identity of the defendant if no more than 10 years since the product was put into circulation

Figure 12.3   Comparison of Alternative Forms of Legal Liability:
Injuries caused by Defective Products

Criminal Liability for Unsafe Goods

Part II of the Consumer Protection Act 1987 replaces earlier legislation on consumer safety including the Consumer Safety Act 1978 and the Consumer Safety (Amendment) Act 1986.

Under s.10 of the 1987 Act it is a criminal offence to supply consumer goods which are not reasonably safe. An offence is also committed by offering or agreeing to supply unsafe goods or exposing or possessing them for supply.

In deciding whether goods are reasonably safe, the court must examine all the circumstances, including:

- the way in which the goods are marketed;
- the use of any mark, for example indicating compliance with safety standards;
- instructions or warnings as to the use of the goods;
- whether the goods comply with relevant published safety standards;
- whether there is a way in which the goods could reasonably have been made safer.

The offence in s.10 can be committed only in relation to *consumer goods*. Consumer goods are goods which are ordinarily intended for private use or consumption, with the exception of food, water, gas, motor vehicles, medical products and tobacco.

The Secretary of State has power, under s.11, to make regulations for the purpose of ensuring that goods of any particular type are safe. Safety regulations can cover the design, composition or finish of goods; and ensure that appropriate information is given in relation to them. They may also restrict the distribution of particular types of goods or prohibit their supply or exposure for supply.

A considerable number of regulations, made under previous legislation, are still in force. These relate for example to aerosols, babies' dummies, balloons, cosmetics, electrical goods, night-dresses, toys and many other types of product. Breach of safety regulations is an offence under s.12 of the 1987 Act.

Under s.41 of the 1987 Act any person who suffers injury or loss as a result of a breach of safety regulations has the right to sue the trader for damages for *breach of statutory duty*. This right cannot be restricted or excluded by any term or notice in any contract.

The Secretary of State also has a number of other powers under the 1987 Act. He may, for example, serve a *prohibition notice* on a trader requiring him to stop trading in unsafe goods of a particular description. Alternatively, where a trader has distributed goods which are unsafe, the Secretary of State may serve on him a notice to warn. This requires the trader, at his own expense, to publish warnings about the unsafe goods to persons to whom they have been supplied.

Power is also given to local authorities under the Act, to serve a *suspension notice* on any trader. This in effect freezes the goods in the hands of the trader for up to six months. The power to serve a suspension notice arises if the authority has reasonable grounds for suspecting that goods are not reasonably safe under s.10, or are in breach of safety regulations. A trader who fails to comply with a suspension notice is guilty of a criminal offence.

A Magistrates Court has power to order the forfeiture of goods where there has been a contravention of the safety provisions of the 1987 Act. Where goods are forfeit they must, under s.16, either be destroyed, or released for the purposes of being repaired, reconditioned or scrapped.

Consumer Credit

The Consumer Credit Act 1974 was introduced with the aim of ensuring *truth in lending*. The Act applies to a wide range of types of credit agreement and places strict controls upon persons who provide credit facilities in the course of their business. Overall responsibility for administering the Act lies with the Director General of Fair Trading. The Act creates many criminal offences and enforcement in relation to these is by local authority Trading Standards Officers.

Agreements regulated by the Act fall within two broad categories, consumer hire agreements and consumer credit agreements. Under s.8:

> *"A consumer credit agreement is an agreement between an individual (the debtor) and any other person (the creditor) by which the creditor provides the debtor with credit not exceeding £15,000".*

The agreement must be for the provision of credit. This is defined in wide terms by s.9(1) to include cash loans and any other form of financial accommodation. Hire purchase, conditional sale and credit sale agreements will all be consumer credit agreements if they satisfy the other elements of the definition. Certain types of credit agreement, particularly those concerned with the purchase and development of land and buildings, are excluded from the operation of the Act and are not consumer credit agreements.

An agreement will not be a consumer credit agreement where:

(a) the debtor is a limited company, and therefore not an individual (a flesh and blood person), or

(b) the amount of credit provided is in excess of £15,000.

In these cases most of the provisions of the Act will not apply and the agreement will be governed by common law principles.

Licensing of creditors

Any person who intends to carry on the business of providing credit cannot do so unless he first obtains a licence from the Director General of Fair Trading. The Director General must grant a licence to any person who makes an application, provided he is satisfied that:

(a) the name under which the business is operating is neither misleading nor undesirable, and

(b) the applicant is a fit person to engage in the activities covered by licence.

A consumer credit agreement made with an unlicensed creditor is not enforceable against the debtor without the consent of the Director General of Fair Trading.

Equal liability of the creditor and the supplier

Earlier in this chapter it was noted that many credit transactions involved three parties: debtor, creditor, and supplier. The policy of the 1974 Act is to make the creditor, in addition to the supplier, answerable to the debtor if anything goes wrong. This applies only where a business connection exists between the creditor and the supplier, for example where the supplier has an arrangement with a particular finance company under which the company provides credit for all suitable customers of the supplier. Because the creditor is responsible for the acts of the supplier, he will be careful to deal only with suppliers who are reputable. The long term aim of this policy is to raise general standards of trading and squeeze cowboy suppliers out of business. The policy is reflected in s.56 and s.75 of the Act.

Where there is a business connection between the supplier and the creditor, the supplier is deemed, by s.56, to be the agent of the creditor when he negotiates with the debtor before a consumer credit agreement is made. If the debtor is induced to enter an agreement by the supplier's misrepresentation, he is entitled under s.56 to exercise a right of rescission against the creditor.

Under s.75 the debtor can claim against the creditor, as well as the supplier, for any breach of contract or misrepresentation by the supplier. Again this applies only where there is a business connection between the creditor and the supplier. At common law the debtor could claim, under the rule in *Andrews v. Hopkinson* 1956, against the supplier only and had no claim against the creditor. The effect of s.75 can be far reaching, for example if goods are purchased with a credit card (such as Access or Barclaycard), the finance company behind the card can be sued for the retailer's breach of contract or misrepresentation.

Where the debtor sues the creditor under s.56 or s.75, the creditor in turn has a right of indemnity from the supplier.

Annual percentage rate (APR)

The Act introduces a uniform system which all lenders must use in quoting the cost of credit. This is the annual percentage rate or APR. It enables the consumer to make a true comparison between interest rates and other costs charged by one lender as against those charged by another.

Prior to the introduction of APR there was no standard method of calculating the percentage rate. At that time loans on identical terms in relation to interest and other costs could be advertised at widely varying rates, depending upon the statistical method used to calculate the rate. Consumers therefore had no reliable yardstick against which the different deals on offer could be measured.

All traders must now calculate the cost of credit using the statistical method laid down by the Act. The APR, arrived at in this way, must be shown on certain types of credit advertisement, for example in newspapers, catalogues or shop windows. In addition, the consumer has the right to ask for a written quotation of credit terms, which must specify the APR, where a trader advertises that credit is available.

Form and content of consumer credit agreements

The Consumer Credit Act lays down strict rules governing the form and content of agreements. The object of the rules is to protect the debtor by giving him the fullest possible information about his rights and obligations.

The agreement must be in a form which complies with regulations made under the Act. It must contain details of such things as:

(a)   the names and addresses of the parties

(b)   the APR

(c)   the cash price

(d)   any deposit

(e)   the amount of credit

(f)   the total amount payable

(g)   the amount of each payment

(h)   repayment dates

(i)   sums payable on default

(j)   certain rights and protections under the Act.

The agreement must be in writing and signed personally by the debtor. If either of these requirements is not met, the creditor will be unable to sue the debtor if he defaults, for example by stopping his payments.

The debtor must receive a copy of the agreement when he signs it, and a further copy as soon as it has been signed by the creditor. If this requirement is not complied with, the creditor cannot sue the debtor, or enforce the agreement in any other way, for example by repossession, unless he previously obtains the permission of the court.

Credit reference agencies

A credit reference agency is an organisation which collects financial information about individuals. This includes a person's record in paying off debts and previous credit agreements, and outstanding judgments recorded against them in the county court. Creditors will usually consult credit reference agencies before entering into agreements with new customers. There are two national credit reference agencies.

In addition there are a number of local agencies. Where an individual applies for credit he may require the trader to provide him with the name and address of any credit reference agency which has been consulted about him.

An individual has the right, under s.158 of the 1974 Act, to know what information is being held about him by a credit reference agency. He also has the right to correct any false information in the file kept by the agency. To exercise this right he must make a written request, containing sufficient particulars to enable the agency to identify the file and pay a fee.

The agency must supply the individual with a copy of any file which it keeps relating to him. The copy must be in plain English and accompanied by a notice of the individual's right to correct false information. If the agency does not keep a file relating to the individual, it must write informing him of that fact.

If any of the information in the file is incorrect, the individual can ask the agency to correct it. If the agency refuses to alter the file to the satisfaction of the individual, or if it does not reply within 28 days of a request, the individual can write a note of correction of up to 200 words. The agency must add the note of correction to the file. It also has a duty to send details of the correction to anyone who obtained information from the file within the previous 6 months.

An agency will be guilty of a criminal offence if it fails to comply with a duty imposed on it by the 1974 Act.

Cooling off and cancellation

It is a well established principle of the law of contract that once an agreement has been entered into, cancellation by one of the parties is a breach of contract which entitles the other to sue for damages. The Consumer Credit Act 1974 provides an important exception to this principle.

An agreement will be cancellable under the Act where:

> (a)   statements are made by the trader in the presence of the debtor prior to making the agreement, and

> (b)   the debtor signs the agreement at a place other than the trader's place of business, for example at home.

The right of cancellation typically applies to credit transactions entered into with doorstep salesmen, although the right exists whenever the above conditions are fulfilled. Where an agreement is cancellable, it must contain a notice informing the debtor of his right to cancel. The agreement can be cancelled at any time up to the end of the fifth full day after it has been signed by both parties.

Notice of cancellation must be given in writing. It can be expressed in any manner, so long as it indicates an intention to withdraw from the agreement. Where a debtor exercises the right to cancel, he ceases to be liable under the agreement and is entitled to the return of all sums paid by him.

Default by the debtor

Default notice

Where a debtor is in breach of a consumer credit agreement, the creditor cannot terminate the agreement or demand early payment or recover possession of goods until a default notice has been served on the debtor. The notice must in the form prescribed by the Act. It must specify the nature of the breach, the action required to remedy it, and the date (giving at least 7 days) by which remedial action must be taken.

The creditor cannot take any steps to enforce an agreement until the date specified in the notice has passed. If the debtor complies with a default notice within the required period, the breach of agreement by him is treated as not having occurred.

Protected goods

Where the debtor under a hire purchase or conditional sale agreement has paid at least one third of the total price, the goods are protected goods. If the debtor is in default of the agreement, the creditor at common law has an unrestricted right to repossess the goods because at this stage he still owns them. However, under s.90 of the 1974 Act, the creditor cannot retake possession of protected goods without either a court order or the debtor's permission. If he does so the agreement terminates. The debtor is released from all liability under it. In addition he is entitled to recover from the creditor all sums previously paid by him under the agreement.

> In *Capital Finance v. Bray* 1964 a finance company repossessed a car without a court order. As the debtor had repaid more than one third of the total price, the car was covered by the protected goods rules. The company, realising its mistake, returned the car to the debtor by leaving it outside his house. The debtor used the car for several months but refused to make any further payments. The finance company sued for payment. The debtor counterclaimed for the return of all money paid by him under the agreement. It was held that the finance company had wrongfully repossessed the car and could not correct the mistake by returning it to the debtor. The debtor was entitled to repayment of all sums which he had paid under the agreement.

Extortionate credit bargains

Under s.137 of the 1974 Act, the courts have power to re-open any credit agreement, whether or not it is a consumer credit agreement, which is part of an extortionate credit bargain, and relieve a debtor from payment of any sum in excess of that which is fair and reasonable. The courts have wide powers under this section and can order a creditor to repay all or part of any sum already paid; or set aside any obligation imposed on the debtor, or alter the agreement in any other way in order to do justice between the parties.

A credit bargain is extortionate under the Act if it requires the debtor to make payments which are grossly exorbitant or which otherwise grossly contravene the ordinary principles of fair dealing. In order to determine whether a credit bargain is extortionate a number of factors will be taken into account, including:

(a) interest rates prevailing at the time it was made;

(b) the age, experience, business capacity and state of health of the debtor;

(c) the degree and nature of any financial pressure on the debtor when the bargain was made;

(d) the degree of risk accepted by the creditor and his relationship to the debtor;

(e) whether or not a cash price was quoted;

(f) how far any linked transaction was reasonably required for the protection of the creditor, or was in the interest of the debtor.

> In *A. Ketley v. Scott* 1981 the defendant borrowed £20,500 in order to enable him to complete the purchase of a house. The money was released by the plaintiff on the same day that he was approached for the loan. The defendant did not tell him that his bank

account was £2,000 overdrawn, the bank had a first mortgage on the house, and he was also liable under a £5,000 guarantee. Nor did he disclose that the house had been valued at £24,000. The loan was for three months at an annual rate of interest of 48%. At the expiry of its term the plaintiff sued for repayment of capital and interest. The defendant counterclaimed for the re-opening of the agreement as an extortionate credit bargain. It was held that the plaintiff was entitled to enforce the agreement. This was not an extortionate credit bargain because the lender had taken a considerable risk; obtained little security; had been deceived by the defendant; had no time to check the defendant's financial position, and advanced the money with extraordinary speed.

Termination by the debtor

A debtor under a hire purchase or conditional sale agreement may terminate the agreement under s.99 at any time before the final payment falls due. He must give notice in writing to the creditor, or to any person authorised to receive payment on the creditor's behalf. The debtor must return the goods to the creditor.

Under s.100 the debtor's liability on termination is limited to:

(a)   any sums already due for payment before the date on which he exercises the right of termination; and

(b)   a further sum to bring his total payments up to one half of the total price (or less if the agreement so provides) or any lesser sum which in the opinion of the court represents the creditor's loss on termination; and

(c)   if he has broken an obligation to take reasonable care of the goods, compensation for this.

Contracting out

Under s.173 of the 1974 Act it is not possible to insert a term into a consumer credit agreement which takes away any of the protection given to the debtor by the Act. Contracting out is absolutely prohibited.

Administrative Machinery of Consumer Protection

Both central and local government have important roles to play in the field of consumer protection. The major role of central government is the promotion and implementation of legislation, whilst the enforcement of this legislation is mainly the responsibility of local government.

The role of central government in consumer protection

The consumer protection responsibilities of central government are spread across a number of departments, many of which have a junior minister with responsibility for consumer affairs.

The Home Office has responsibility for liquor licensing, dangerous drugs and poisons; as well as explosives and firearms.

The Department of Trade and Industry's responsibilities in the field of consumer protection include weights and measures, consumer credit, fair trading, consumer safety, trading standards, and monopolies, mergers and restrictive practices. The Department is also responsible for a number of national consumer protection bodies, including:

(a)   the Office of Fair Trading

(b)   the Monopolies and Mergers Commission

(c)   the British Hallmarking Council

(d)   the National Consumer Council

(e)   the Consumer Protection Advisory Committee

(f)   the Utilities Regulators

     and

(g)   the British Standards Institute.

The Ministry of Agriculture Fisheries and Food looks after food and drugs, food additives, pesticides, and public health standards in slaughterhouses. The Food Safety Directorate created in 1989, has specific responsibility for food safety matters.

The Office of Fair Trading

The Office of Fair Trading, created by the Fair Trading Act 1973, has a significant national role in relation to the broad task of protecting the interests of the consumer. The 1973 Act created the post of Director General of Fair Trading. The Director has wide powers under the 1973 Act and other legislation, notably the Consumer Credit Act 1974 and the Estate Agents Act 1979.

The duties of the Director are:

(a)   to review commercial activities and report to the Secretary of State;

(b)   to refer adverse trade practices to the Consumer Protection Advisory Committee;

(c)   to take action against traders who are persistently unfair to consumers;

(d)   to supervise the enforcement of the Consumer Credit Act 1974 and the administration of the licensing system under that Act;

(e)   to arrange for information and advice to be published for the benefit of consumers in relation to the supply of goods and services and consumer credit;

(f)   to encourage trade associations to produce voluntary Codes of Practice; and

(g)   to superintend the working and enforcement of the Estate Agents Act 1979.

Review of commercial practices

Under this general heading the Director has three functions:

(i)   to keep under review commercial activities in the U.K. relating to the supply of goods and services to consumers; and to collect information about these activities in order to become aware of practices which may adversely affect the *economic interests* of consumers;

(ii)   to receive and collect evidence of commercial activities which he thinks are adversely affecting the *general interests* of consumers, for example on economic, health or safety grounds;

(iii)   to supply information relating to adverse trade practices to the Secretary of State and make recommendations as to any action which the Director considers necessary to combat them.

Referral of adverse trade practices to the Consumer Protection Advisory Committee

The Director has power to refer to the Consumer Protection Advisory Committee any consumer trade practice which in his opinion adversely affects the economic interests of consumers. The type of activity which can give rise to such a reference include trade practices relating to:

(i)   the terms or conditions on which goods or services are supplied,

(ii)   the manner in which those terms or conditions are communicated to the consumer,

(iii)   promotion of goods or services by advertising, labelling or marking of goods, or canvassing,

(iv)   methods of salesmanship employed in dealing with consumers,

(v)   the way in which goods are packed, or

(vi)   methods of demanding or securing payments for goods or services supplied.

A reference by the Director may include proposals for the creation of delegated legislation by the Secretary of State. The Director has power to make such proposals where he considers that a consumer trade practice is likely to have any one of the following effects:

(i)   misleading consumers as to their rights and obligations under the transactions; or

(ii)   withholding adequate information on the rights and obligations of consumers; or

(iii)   subjecting consumers to undue pressure to enter into transactions; or

(iv)   causing the terms of the consumer transactions in question to be so adverse as to be oppressive.

The Consumer Protection Advisory Committee must report to the Secretary of State, usually within three months, indicating whether it agrees with the Director's proposals as they stand, or in a modified form. If so the Secretary of State may make regulations giving effect to the proposals. Under s.22 of the 1973 Act it is a criminal offence to contravene any such regulations.

Examples of regulations made under this procedure include the Consumer Transactions (Restrictions on Statements) Order 1976 and (Amendment) Order 1978, and the Business Advertisements (Disclosure) Order 1977, which were examined in the last chapter. Another example is the Mail Order Transactions (Information) Order 1976, which applies to goods sold by mail order which have to be paid for in advance. Under the regulations, any advertisement for such goods must state the true name or company name of the person carrying on the mail order business, as well as the true address of the business. Thus, for example, an advertiser giving only a P.O. Box number would be committing an offence if he required payment in advance.

Taking action against persistently unfair traders

The Director has power to bring proceedings in the Restrictive Practices Court against any person who persistently maintains a course of conduct which is unfair to consumers. Before making a reference to the Court, the Director must first attempt to obtain a written assurance from the trader that he will refrain from the unfair trade practice. If the trader refuses to give an assurance, or breaks an assurance once it has been given, the Director must apply for an order restraining the continuance of the unfair conduct. If the trader does not comply with the order, he will be in contempt of court and liable to imprisonment.

A course of conduct will be regarded as being unfair to consumers if it involves a breach of any legal obligations, either criminal or civil, by the trader. Examples of unfair conduct include persistently giving short measure or applying false trade descriptions, or repeatedly delivering unmerchantable goods.

Encouraging voluntary Codes of Practice

The Director has a duty to encourage trade associations and other organisations to prepare Codes of Practice. This aspect of his role is examined in Chapter 13.

The role of local authorities in consumer protection

Responsibility for the enforcement of most consumer protection legislation, other than that which gives the consumer a right to sue for damages, rests with local authorities. It is carried out by trading standards or consumer protection departments. In practice, these departments see their major role as one of giving guidance to traders. This is done by a combination of education and persuasion. Prosecution for criminal offences is seen as a last resort when other measures fail.

Another important aspect of the work of these departments is the verification of weights and measuring apparatus, and the analysis of samples. They also act as a channel of information from members of the public to the Office of Fair Trading about unfair trade practices.

Trading standards officers have wide investigatory powers to enable them to carry out their enforcement functions effectively. They can make sample purchases of goods or services; enter premises; require suppliers to produce documents; carry out tests on equipment; and seize and detain property. A person who obstructs a trading standards officer, or makes a false statements to him commits a criminal offence.

Many Acts of Parliament and regulations made under them are enforced by trading standards officers. A number of these are examined below, including the Consumer Credit Act 1974, the Food Safety Act 1990, parts of the Road Traffic Act 1988, the Trade Descriptions Act 1968, the Weights and Measures Act 1985, the Unsolicited Goods and Services Act 1971, and the Consumer Protection Act 1987. Before we consider this legislation in detail we shall examine the power of the criminal courts to award compensation to the consumer following the conviction of a trader for a criminal offence.

Consumer Protection by Means of the Criminal Law

Most, but not all, of the criminal offences designed to protect the consumer apply only to persons supplying goods or services in the course of a trade or business. Enforcement of the criminal law in this area is, as we have seen, primarily the function of trading standards departments. Traders who are charged with criminal offences will be prosecuted in the Magistrates or the Crown Court. If convicted, they will be liable to a fine or, in some cases, imprisonment. Following a conviction the criminal courts also have power to make a *compensation order* to the victim of the crime. In this context the victim will be the consumer who has suffered loss as a result of the offence.

The power to make a compensation order is contained in s.35 of the Powers of Criminal Courts Act 1973. This provides that any court convicting a person of an offence may, in addition to its sentencing power, make an order requiring the offender to pay compensation for any personal injury, loss or damage resulting from the offence or any other offence taken into consideration.

In deciding whether to make an order the court must take account of the ability of the defendant to pay. There is a limit of £5,000 compensation for each offence of which the accused is convicted. Under s.67 of the Criminal Justice Act 1982 the power to make compensation orders was extended. They may now be made *"instead of or in addition to"* a fine.

The power to make compensation orders is particularly useful from the point of view of the consumer. It saves him the trouble and expense of bringing proceedings in the civil courts. It will be used only in relatively straightforward cases, however. It is not designed to deal for example with complicated claims involving issues of causation or remoteness of damage.

The Food Safety Act 1990

The Food Safety Act 1990 is designed to strengthen consumer protection in relation to food safety, an area of increasing concern in recent years. The Act consolidates existing provision in this areas, adds a number of new regulatory powers and substantially increases the penalties for offences relating to the quality and safety of foods.

It is an offence, under s. 7, to process or treat food intended for sale for human consumption in any way which makes it injurious to health. Food is injurious to health if it causes any permanent or temporary impairment of health. The offence can be committed by food manufacturers, food handlers, retailers or restaurants. The offence may be committed, for example, by adding a harmful ingredient, or subjecting food to harmful treatment such as storing it at an incorrect temperature or storing cooked meat alongside uncooked meat.

Under s.8 of the Act, food intended for human consumption must satisfy the *food safety requirement*. It is an offence to sell, offer or have in one's possession for sale, prepare or deposit with another for sale any food which fails to meet this requirement. Food which is injurious to health, unfit for human consumption, or so contaminated that it is not reasonable to expect it to be eaten, will fail to satisfy the food safety requirement.

> In *David Greig Ltd. v. Goldfinch* 1961 a trader was convicted of selling food which was unfit for human consumption (under an equivalent provision in the Food and Drugs Act 1955). He sold a pork pie which had small patches of mould under the crust. The fact

that the mould was of a type which was not harmful to human beings was held to be no defence to the charge.

It is an offence, under s.14 of the Food Safety Act, for a supplier to sell, to the prejudice of the consumer, any food which is not of the nature, substance or quality demanded. This provision is a restatement of previous law and again can be illustrated by reference to earlier caselaw. It may be noted that the gist of s.14 is the supply of something which is different from that which the consumer has requested, and that an offence may be committed where no illness or injury results, although often it may.

In *Meah v. Roberts* 1978 an employee of a brewery cleaned the beer pumps and taps in a restaurant with caustic soda. He placed the remaining fluid in an empty lemonade bottle labelled 'cleaner' which he left for use by the restaurant. The caustic soda was mistakenly served to a customer who order lemonade. The customer became seriously ill as a result. It was held that the restaurant proprietor was guilty of the offence because the food was not of the nature demanded.

Liability under s.14 is strict and the trader may be guilty even though he has taken reasonable care.

In *Smedleys Ltd. v. Breed* 1974 a customer was supplied with a tin of peas which contained a small green caterpillar. The caterpillar had been sterilised in the defendants' processes and did not constitute a danger to health. The defendants had an extremely efficient system for eliminating foreign bodies from their products. They were found to have taken all reasonable care to avoid the presence of the caterpillar in the tin. Nevertheless, their conviction for supplying food which was not of the substance demanded was upheld by the House of Lords.

In *R. v. F & M Dobson* 1995 a manufacturer appealed against the severity of a fine of £25,000 and £7,834 prosecution costs when found guilty of supplying food which failed to comply with food safety standards. A consumer had been injured when she bit into the manufacturer's chocolate-covered nut crunch which contained the blade of a Stanley knife. The Court of Appeal stressed the very high duty of care imposed on manufacturers of foodstuffs, reduced the fine to £7,000, but affirmed the prosecutions high costs given that it was the defendant who had elected for jury trial in the Crown Court.

Section 15 of the Act creates a number of offences relating to the false description of food; including the publication of misleading advertisements, selling food which is falsely described, presenting food in a misleading way or selling food with a label which is likely to mislead the consumer as to its nature, substance or quality.

As with many other statutes creating criminal offences of strict liability, a number of defences are available, for example under s.20 it is a defence to a show that the commission of the offence was due to the act or default of another or, under s.21, that it was committed as a result of reliance on information supplied by another. Similarly, if the defendant can show that he exercised all due diligence and all reasonable precautions to avoid the commission of the offence, he will escape liability by virtue of s.21. These defences apply to charges for any offences brought under s.7, s.8, s.14 and s.15 of the Act.

The Ministry of Agriculture, Fisheries and Food has overall responsibility for food, and the Food Safety Directorate has particular responsibility for food safety matters. Under the Act the Minister has to make regulations in relation to food safety, governing such matters as the regulation of processes or treatments, the content and composition of food, presentation, labelling and packaging. The Minister also has powers to make *emergency control orders* where it appears that an imminent risk of injury to health arises from commercial activities concerned with food; and power to require minimum standards of training for food handlers.

Responsibility for enforcing the Act lies mainly with local authority trading standards officers and environmental health officers. They have wide powers of inspection, entry to premises, taking samples and preventing the sale or movement of food. The Act makes provision for the registration of all food premises with the local authority, which will assist in enforcement by giving the authority more information about food premises in its area, and the power to prohibit their use as such if they are not registered.

The Weights and Measures Act 1985

The 1985 Act provides for the inspection and testing of weighing and measuring equipment for use in trade. Under s.17 of the Act it is an offence to use for trade, or to have in one's possession for use in trade, any weighing or measuring equipment which is false or unjust. It is also an offence under s.28 to give short weight or short measure.

The Act restricts the units of measurement which can lawfully be used by a trader. It lays down detailed requirements as to the packing, marking and making up of certain types of goods; and provides that, in relation to pre-packed or containerised goods, a written statement must be marked on the container giving information about the net quantity of its contents.

Consumer Credit Act 1974

Schedule 1 of the Consumer Credit Act 1974 contains a list of over 35 criminal offences associated with contravention of the Act. These include, for example, trading without a licence; failure to supply copies of consumer credit agreements; refusal of a trader to give the name of a credit reference agency which he has consulted; failure by a credit reference agency to correct information on its files; and obstruction of enforcement authority officers.

Road Traffic Act 1988

The Road Traffic Acts, and regulations made under them, contain a large number of criminal offences relating to the construction and use of motor vehicles and the safe loading of vehicles. Under s.75 of the 1988 Act it is an offence for any person, whether or not he is a trader, to sell or supply a motor vehicle which is unroadworthy. This offence will be committed where, for example, a vehicle is sold with defects in its braking or steering system or in its tyres. It is also an offence under s.75 to fit defective or unsuitable parts to a motor vehicle; and under s.17(2) to sell a motor cycle crash helmet which does not comply with safety regulations.

The Unsolicited Goods and Services Act 1971

This Act was passed to impose criminal and civil liability on traders carrying on the practice of *inertia selling*. This involves sending goods or providing services which have not been ordered and demanding payment or threatening legal action if payment is not made. The Act provides that unsolicited goods or services need not to be paid for, and unordered goods may be retained by the recipient if they are not collected by the sender within six months of delivery. It is an offence for the sender to demand payment for unsolicited goods or services.

Trade Descriptions Legislation

We have previously examined the circumstances in which a person would be regarded as transacting in the course of a trade or business. An important application of this question arises in relation to criminal liability under the Trade Descriptions Act 1968 for false statements made in business transactions. There can be no liability under the 1968 Act unless the person applying the false description does so within the course of a trade or business rather than a private sale. This is one reason why the Business Advertisements (Disclosure) Order 1977 requires a trader to identify himself as such when he advertises in the classified advertisements in newspapers. The fact that a business organisation is the vendor or purchaser does not automatically mean that a sale is in the course of a trade. The transaction must be of a type that is a regular occurrence in that particular business, so that a sale of business assets would not normally qualify as a sale in the course of a trade or business.

> In *Roberts v. Leonard* 1995 veterinary surgeons were held to be carrying on a trade or business, the court deciding that there was no sufficient reason to exclude the professions from the scope of the Act.

Where there is a genuine private sale and, for example, the seller falsely describes the goods, the buyer's remedy will be rescission. He may also claim damages in a civil law action for misrepresentation or breach of the term implied into the contract by s.13 of the Sale of Goods Act 1979. A buyer from a business seller can also exercise these remedies, but in addition may report the trader to the trading standards department with a view to a prosecution for a breach of the criminal law under the 1968 Act. In all trade descriptions cases there is potentially liability under the civil law which illustrates the fact that here consumer protection law is founded upon the interrelationship between civil and criminal activities. Prosecutions for trade description offences are brought in the Magistrates Court and exceptionally in the Crown Court with the possibility of an appeal to the Divisional Court of the Queen's Bench Division of the High Court by way of case-stated on a point of law. There is no requirement for a re-hearing of the evidence, rather the appeal court is concerned with determining the validity of the legal reasoning upon which the decision to convict or acquit is based.

Two principal offences under the Trade Descriptions Act 1968 relate to false description of goods, and making misleading statements about services. A number of defences are also provided for. Further offences of giving misleading price indications were originally contained in s.11 of the Act, and the Price Marking (Bargain Offers) Order 1979 made under the Prices Act 1974. These offences have been replaced by others under Part III of the Consumer Protection Act 1987, and are considered separately below.

False Description of Goods

The 1968 Act provides, in s.1(1) that: *"Any person who, in the course of a trade or business:*

(a)   *applies a false trade description to any goods; or*

(b)   *supplies or offers to supply any goods to which a false trade description is applied;*

shall, subject to the provisions of this Act, be guilty of an offence".

Two different types of conduct will amount to offences under this section. The first is where the trader himself applies the false trade description contrary to s.1(1)(a). This offence could be committed, for example, by a trader who turns back the mileometer of a car to make it appear that the car has not travelled as many miles as it actually has. The second, under s.1(1)(b), involves supplying or offering to supply goods to which a false trade description has been applied by another person, for example where a retailer sells a garment to which the label *pure new wool* has been attached by the manufacturer, where the garment is partly composed of manmade fibres. There is a strict duty therefore not to pass on false trade descriptions applied by another subject to a defence which we will consider later.

In relation to the s.1(1)(b) offence, the trader will not be able to rely on a Fisher v. Bell type defence where he displays goods for sale.

> In *Fisher v. Bell* 1961, a shopkeeper who displayed flick knives for sale was acquitted of an offence of *offering to supply* them on the grounds that the display was an invitation to treat rather than a contractual offer.

The 1968 Act, in s.6, closes this loophole by providing that *"a person exposing goods for supply or having goods in his possession for supply shall be deemed to offer to supply them"*.

A false trade description may be applied verbally or in writing, for example in a label on goods or in an advertisement, communicated by pictorial representation or even by conduct.

> In *Yugotours Ltd. v. Wadsley* 1988 a photograph of a three-masted schooner and the words "the excitement of being under full sail on board this majestic schooner" in a tour operator's brochure was held to constitute a statement for the purpose of the Act. By providing customers who had booked a holiday relying on the brochure with only a two masted schooner without sails the tour operator was guilty of recklessly making a false statement contrary to the Trade Descriptions Act.

The meaning of the term *trade description* extends, by s.2, to statements relating to quantity, size, composition, method of manufacture, fitness for purpose, place or date of manufacture, approval by any person or other history including previous ownership of goods.

> In *Sherratt v. Geralds The American Jewellers Ltd.* 1970 the defendant sold a watch described by the maker as a diver's watch and inscribed with the word "waterproof". The watch filled with water and stopped after it had been immersed in water. It was held that the defendant was guilty of an offence under s.1(1)(b).

To constitute an offence under the Act the trade description must be false or misleading to a material degree.

In *Robertson v. Dicicco* 1972 a second-hand motor vehicle was advertised for sale by a dealer and described as *"a beautiful car"*. The car, although having a visually pleasing exterior was unroadworthy and not fit for use. The defendant was charged with an offence under s.1(1)(a). He argued that his statement was true as he had intended it to refer only to the visual appearance of the vehicle. It was held that he was guilty because the description was false to a material degree. A reasonable person would have taken the statement to refer to the mechanics of the car as well as its external appearance.

A similar approach was taken in *Kensington and Chelsea Borough Council v. Riley* 1973 where the trader was convicted of an offence under s.1(1)(a). It was held that the description *"in immaculate condition"* was false when applied to a car which required repairs costing £250 to make it roadworthy.

A trade description applied to goods for sale can be false for the purpose of s.1(1)(b) even when it is scientifically correct if it is likely to mislead a customer without specialist knowledge.

In *Dixon Ltd. v. Barnett* 1989 a customer was supplied with an Astral 500 telescope which was described as being capable of up to *"455 x magnification"*. The evidence showed that the maximum useful magnification was only 120 times, although scientifically 455 times magnification could be achieved. The Divisional Court held that the store was nevertheless guilty of an offence despite the fact that the statement was scientifically sound. An ordinary customer would have been misled by the statement because he would be interested in the maximum useful magnification rather than a blurred image produced at 455 times magnification.

A half truth is false for the purpose of the Act, so that while it was technically true to describe a vehicle as only having one previous owner in *R v. Inner London Justices and another* 1983 the fact that the owner was a leasing company and the car had had five different keepers meant that the statement was grossly misleading and false.

In *Routledge v. Ansa Motors (Chester-le-Street) Limited* 1980 a Ford Escort motor car which was manufactured in 1972 was first registered in 1975. Subsequently it was advertised by the defendant as *"a used 1975 Ford Escort"*. It was held that the defendant had applied a false trade description to the car, contrary to s. 1(1)(a).

In *Denard v. Smith and another* 1990 the Divisonal Court considered whether it is a false trade description to advertise goods in a shop at the point of sale as items offered for sale when they are temporarily out of stock and are not immediately available. The court held that unless customers are informed of the non-availability of the goods at the time of purchase the advertisement constituted a false trade description of offering to supply goods.

In order to be guilty of an offence under s.1, the trader must make the statement in connection with a sale or supply of goods.

In *Wickens Motors (Gloucester) Ltd. v. Hall* 1972 the purchaser of a car from the defendant complained about its performance. The complaint was made 40 days after the car had been supplied to him. The defendant told him that there was nothing wrong with the car, although this was untrue. It was held that the defendant was not guilty of an offence under s.1(1)(a) because there was insufficient connection between the false description and the sale.

An offence under s.1 may be committed by *any person*. This is not limited to the seller, but may include the buyer, particularly where he is an expert in relation to the subject matter of the contract.

> In *Fletcher v. Budgen* 1974 a car dealer bought an old car from a customer for £2 saying that it was only fit to be scrapped. In fact the dealer repaired the car and advertised it for a resale for £135. It was held that he was guilty of an offence under s.1(1)(a) because he applied a false trade description to the car when he bought it in the course of his business.

Where defects in goods are disguised and the trader has no reason to realise or suspect that they are present, he will not be guilty of an offence under s.1(1)(b).

> In *Cottee v. Douglas Seaton Ltd.* 1972 the bodywork of a car which had been in very poor condition was repaired using plastic body filler. This was smoothed down and the car repainted before it was sold to the defendant. The defendant was unaware of the fact that the bodywork was defective. He resold the car to a purchaser who subsequently discovered the defect. It was held that the disguised defects amounted to a false trade description as the goods, in effect, told a lie about themselves. The defendant was not guilty of an offence, however, because he was unaware that the description had been applied to the goods.

A person may be guilty of an offence under s.1(1)(b), even though he does not know the description is false, provided he knows that the description has been applied to the goods by another person. This situation may arise for example where a car dealer sells a car which records an incorrectly low mileage on its mileometer. If a dealer is uncertain as to the accuracy of the recorded mileage, he may try to ensure that a false trade description is not applied by displaying a notice disclaiming the accuracy of the mileage reading.

> In *Norman v. Bennett* 1974 a customer bought a second-hand car with a recorded mileage of 23,000 miles. In fact the true mileage was about 68,000 miles. He signed an agreement containing a clause which said that the reading was not guaranteed. It was held that this was not an effective disclaimer. Lord Widgery, the Lord Chief Justice, stated that, in order to be effective, a disclaimer: *"must be as bold, precise and compelling as the trade description itself and must be as effectively brought to the notice of any person to whom the goods may be supplied. In other words, the disclaimer must equal the trade description in the extent to which it is likely to get home to anyone interested in receiving the goods".*

The use of a disclaimer will be an effective defence provided it complies with the test laid down in *Norman v. Bennett*. The Motor Trade Code of Practice, approved by Director General of Fair Trading in 1976, recommends the use of the following form of wording in these circumstances:

> *"We do not guarantee the accuracy of the recorded mileage. To the best of our knowledge and belief, however the recording is correct/incorrect".*

Clearly a disclaimer will only be an effective defence to a charge under s.1(1)(b). If the trader himself has turned back the mileage he will be unable to rely on this defence.

A disclaimer cannot exclude liability once it has arisen and is only effective to the extent that it prevents the commission of a criminal offence. The disclaimer could:

- prevent an indication being regarded as a trade description; or
- qualify a description so that it does not mislead; or
- qualify a description so that it is not false to a material degree.

Certainly it would be pointless to attempt to disclaim liability after an offence has already been committed.

> In *Doble v. David Greig Ltd.* 1972 the defendants displayed bottles of Ribena for sale in their self service store at a particular price with an indication that a deposit on each bottle was refundable on its return. At the cash till however, a different notice stated that in fact no deposit would be charged because in the interest of hygiene the store would not accept the return of empty bottles. The retailer was convicted of the offence of offering to supply goods with a false price indication. The court held that the offence of offering to supply was committed when the goods were displayed and the subsequent notice at the cash till was ineffective in disclaiming liability.

While a disclaimer may prevent the commission of an offence of offering to supply goods, it will not apply to an offence of applying a false trade description.

> In *Newham LBC v. Singh* 1988 as the defendant car dealer had not been aware that a car mileometer had been altered and had not been the person applying the false trade description to the car, he could successfully rely on a disclaimer when charged under s.1.

Finally, an important feature of disclaimers is that it is for the prosecution to establish the offence and prove that the disclaimer is ineffective whereas the specific defences under the Act must be established by the defendant.

Defences under the Trade Descriptions Act 1968

It is a defence to any charge under the 1968 Act that the defendant innocently published a misleading advertisement received by him for publication in the ordinary course of his business. This defence, available for example to newspapers, is provided by s.25.

A number of separate defences are contained in s.24. These are available to a defendant who can prove

> " *(a) That the commission of the offence was due to a mistake or to reliance on information supplied to him or to the act or default of another person, an accident, or some other cause beyond his control; and*
>
> (b) *that he took all reasonable precautions and exercised all due diligence to avoid the commission of such an offence by himself or any person under his control".*

In order to have an effective defence under s.24, the onus is on the defendant to prove any one of the reasons listed in paragraph (a) above and all of the elements in (b). He must also supply to the prosecution, at least 7 days before the hearing, a written notice giving such information as he has to enable the other person to be identified.

In *Baxters (Butchers) v. Manley* 1985 the defendant was accused of offences under the 1968 Act in relation to the pricing and weight of meat exposed for sale in his butcher's shop. He claimed that the offences were due to the act or default of the shop manager. This claim was accepted by the court, but the defence under s.24 failed because he was unable to prove that he had taken reasonable precautions to avoid the commission of the offence by his manager. In particular he had failed to give the manager any detailed instructions or guidelines on the requirements of the Act; there was no staff training; and the standard of supervision by a district manager was inadequate.

In *Lewin v. Rothersthorpe Road Garage* 1984 the s.24 defence was raised in response to a prosecution for selling a motor car to which a false trade description had been applied. The defendant was a member of the Motor Agents Association, and had adopted the code of practice drawn up by the Association in consultation with the Office of Fair Trading. Staff had been instructed in the contents of the code of practice. The court held that he had taken reasonable precautions to avoid the commission of an offence by his employee.

Alternatively in *Gale v. Dixon Stores Group* 1994 the defendant committed a s.1 offence when he supplied as new a computer that had already been returned by another customer as defective. This constituted a s.1 offence. The Magistrates accepted that the statutory defence under s.24 had been established on the basis that the defendants intended to introduce a procedure that would prevent such an occurrence in the future. On appeal it was held that the new procedure was a reasonable precaution but the fact that it was not in place at the time of the incident meant that the statutory defence could not stand.

To establish that he took all reasonable precautions and exercised all due diligence the defendant needs to show that he has an effective system of operation. A court should also bear in mind the size and resources of the organisation in determining the steps you would expect a reasonable business to take.

In *Denard v. Smith* 1990 the defendant attempted to establish a s.24 defence when charged with falsely advertising at the point of sale that particular goods were offered for sale when in fact they were out of stock and not available. The court found that an elementary requirement of due diligence would have been to issue some instructions that some amendment should be made to the point of sale literature. A simple notice hung over or beside the advertising placard would have been sufficient to show reasonable precautions and due diligence for the purposes of s.24.

Where an offence has been committed under the 1968 Act due to the act or default of another person, the other person may be prosecuted under s.23. This is the only situation under the Act where a person can be guilty of an offence even though he is not acting in the course of a trade of business.

In *Olgeirsson v. Kitching* 1986 the defendant was a private individual who had owned a Ford Granada car. It had previously belonged to Humberside police and whilst in their ownership required a new mileometer. At that stage the car had travelled 64,000 miles. When the police sold it to the defendant the recorded mileage was 10,500 miles, although the true mileage was disclosed. The defendant later sold the car to a garage, telling them that it had only travelled 38,000 miles. The car was resold on that basis. Later the truth was discovered and the defendant was charged under s.23. It was held that he was guilty and the fact that he was not a trader did not bring him outside the scope of the offence.

In relation to enforcement of the 1968 Act, as we have seen, wide investigatory powers are conferred on local authority trading standards officers. Before a prosecution is brought, however, the local authority is required to inform the Department of Trade. This is to prevent numerous unnecessary prosecutions for the same false trade description.

The legality of bringing a second prosecution where there are a number of complaints in relation to the same false statement was at issue in *R. v. Thomson Holidays Limited* 1973. In this case a misleading statement in a travel brochure constituted an offence under s.14. The Court of Appeal held that a separate offence was committed every time someone read the brochure, and that it was not necessarily improper to bring more than one prosecution in these circumstances.

Misleading price indications:

Part III of the Consumer Protection Act 1987

The provisions of the Consumer Protection Act 1987, s.20 to s.26, replace both s.11 of the Trade Descriptions Act 1968 and the Price Marking (Bargain Offers) Order 1979. The previous provisions had proved to be badly drafted and difficult to enforce.

The offence of giving a misleading price indication is contained in s.20 of the 1987 Act, which provides: *"A person shall be guilty of an offence if, in the course of any business of his, he gives (by any means whatever) to any consumers an indication which is misleading as to the price at which any goods, services, accommodation or facilities are available"*.

The types of statements which would be caught by s.20 include:

- false comparisons with recommended prices, for example a false claim that goods are £20 less than the recommended price; or

- indications that the price is less than the real price, for example where hidden extras are added to an advertised price; or

- false comparisons with a previous price, for example a false statement that goods were £50 and are now £30; or

- where the stated method of determining the price is different to the method actually used.

Failure to correct a price indication which initially was true, but has become untrue, is also an offence under s.20.

The Secretary of State, after consulting the Director General of Fair Trading, has issued a code of practice designed to give practical guidance on the requirements of s.20. It aims to promote good practice in relation to giving price indications. Breach of the code will not, of itself, give rise to criminal or civil liability, but may be used as evidence to establish either that an offence had been committed under s.20, or that a trader has a defence to such a charge.

The following cases, decided under previous legislation, illustrate the type of behaviour which will be contrary to s.20.

In *Richards v. Westminster Motors Ltd.* 1975 the defendant advertised a commercial vehicle for sale at a price of £1,350. When the buyer purchased the vehicle he was required to pay the asking price plus VAT, which made a total price of £1,534. It was held that the defendant was guilty of giving a misleading indication as to the price at which he was prepared to sell goods.

In *Read Bros. Cycles (Leyton) v. Waltham Forest London Borough* 1978 the defendant advertised a motor cycle for sale at a reduced price of £540, £40 below the list price. A customer agreed to purchase the motor cycle and negotiated a £90 part exchange allowance on his old vehicle. The defendant charged him the full list price for the new cycle, and stated that the reduced price did not apply where goods were given in part exchange. It was held that the defendant was guilty of giving a misleading price indication.

In one significant respect the offence under s.20 is narrower than the offences which it replaced. This is that s.20 only applies to consumer transactions. For the purpose of s.20, the expression *consumer* means:

(a)   in relation to any goods, any person who might wish to be supplied with the goods for his own private use or consumption;

(b)   in relation to any services or facilities, any person who might wish to be provided with the services or facilities otherwise than for the purposes of any business of his; and

(c)   in relation to any accommodation, any person who might wish to occupy the accommodation otherwise than for the purposes of any business of his.

A consequence of the narrowing down of the offence is that misleading price indications to business customers will not be caught by it. On the facts of *Richards v. Westminster Motors*, for example, the defendant would not now be guilty of an offence under s.20 because the customer was not a consumer.

Assignment Spicer and Sharp

Spicer and Sharp plc is a company based in the West Midlands. The company is engaged in the production of power tools, D.I.Y. equipment and accessories. Most of its products are actually manufactured by subcontractors and supplied to Spicer and Sharp's main works in Kings Norton, where they are assembled and packaged in the style of the company under their brand name. The company's expansion is based on an aggressive marketing strategy which aims to establish strong product identity and brand loyalty in order to capture a major share of the UK market.

Having been in post as a legal assistant in Spicer and Sharp's legal department for three years, you have been appointed to run the consumer complaints department. Your first task is to deal with a complaint which has recently been received relating to injuries sustained by Andrew Tucker while using a circular saw fitted with a Spicer and Sharp circular saw blade and belonging to his brother Alan. Alan purchased the new blade for his Spicer and Sharp Circular saw from Home Handyman Stores and loaned it to Andrew who was constructing built-in wardrobes in his daughter's bedroom.

While Andrew was using the saw, the blade shattered when it was applied to a piece of second hand timber which contained a number of old nails. Part of the blade flew up hitting Andrew who suffered facial injuries and may be disfigured permanently as a result. It appears likely that the steel used in the blade had been subjected to excessive hardening in the process of production with the result that it was unusually brittle and more likely to shatter in these circumstances.

Home Handyman Stores purchased the saw blade from Spicer and Sharp as part of a larger consignment of the company's products. Unfortunately there is no certain means of establishing the identity of the supplier of the defective saw blade to Spicer and Sharp because three separate suppliers are under contract to supply identical blades to the company. However, records of the initial testing and subsequent random testing of each of the three supplier's products are on file in the quality control department at Kings Norton. Examination of the records gives no indication that this type of defect had ever come to light in respect of any of the blades which had previously been tested.

Task

Prepare a report for circulation to the legal department in which you indicate:

1. whether Andrew would have a viable claim against the company in the tort of negligence or under part 1 of the Consumer Protection Act 1987;

2. the nature of any defences which may be available to the company in the event of any claim;

3. whether any steps should be taken in relation to circular saw blades still in the possession of the company or its retails customers, given that three further complaints have been received involving circular saw blades within a month of the complaint by Andrew Tucker.

Assignment A Swift Exhaust

Task

You work for Swift Exhaust plc and have been assigned to Jane Princetown's office in the Legal Services department for a period of three months as part of your management training programme. Your task is to prepare for her a report setting out the legal basis of the company's claim against Exhaust Systems Supplies Ltd. in relation to the defective exhaust systems, and dealing with the validity of the limitation of liability clause in the standard terms and conditions. In your report you should make reference to decided cases and/or statutes as appropriate. On the basis of the conclusions in your report prepare a draft memo to send from Jane Princetown to Charles Carver, and append it to the report. The memo should be clear and precise, but written in non technical language.

MEMORANDUM

To:	Charles Carver Senior Purchasing Officer	***Date:*** *15 October 1996*
From:	Bob Paisley Quality Manager, Western Division	
Copy to:	Jane Princetown Legal Services	
Subject:	Consignment No. SE92/4752/JB/VAE	

I have received complaints from a number of Western Division Centres relating to replacement exhaust systems for Vauxhall Astras. The complaints indicate a weakness in the soldered joints between the main exhaust pipe and the rear silencer unit. One of the major fleet customers of the Hereford Centre had replacement exhausts fitted on twenty vehicles during April and May 1995, and eight of these systems are now showing an unacceptable degree of deterioration, two having sheered completely.

It appears that the systems in question were all part of consignment No. SE92/4752/JB/VAE. Of the consignment, comprising 500 systems supplied to Western Division in August 1995, the records show that 280 have been fitted to customers' vehicles and 220 are still in stock. Tests which have just been completed in the quality assurance centre in Birmingham confirmed an inherent weakness in the relevant joints in three of the eight systems which were tested.

In these circumstances I have withdrawn the remainder of the consignment from stock. I have also spoken to Jane Princetown in Legal Services in Head Office in Manchester. She has requested me to refer the matter to you for investigation with a view to legal action against the supplier. Please let her know details of the name and address of the supplier and of any written contract terms or other relevant information in your possession.

Clearly the costs to the Company as a whole, and Western Division in particular, arising from this situation will be high both in financial terms and in terms of customer goodwill. In accordance with our Swift Exhaust customer satisfaction charter, the owners of all vehicles fitted with exhaust systems from this consignment are being invited to attend at their nearest Swift Exhaust Centre for a free quality check. I anticipate that we will ultimately have to replace a very substantial number of these systems, free of charge to the customer, if the results of the Birmingham tests prove to be representative.

I have undertaken to supply details of costs incurred in this connection directly to Jane Princetown, and will copy details to yourself as they become available. Quality Assurance in Birmingham will do likewise in relation to test results etc.

If you require any further information I will be pleased to assist in any way I can. Otherwise please respond directly to Jane Princetown when you have gathered the relevant information.

MEMORANDUM

To:	Jane Princetown Legal Services	*Date:* *28 October 1996*
From:	Charles Carver Senior Purchasing Officer	
Copy to:	Bob Paisley Quality Manager, Western Division	
Subject:	Consignment No. SE92/4752/JB/VAE	

I have now established the position with regard to this consignment as requested. It was supplied by Exhaust Systems Supplies Ltd., 104 Western Way, Kings Norton, Birmingham, BH1 4JX in June 1994. It appears to have been supplied under the terms of their standard form contract, a copy of which is enclosed herewith.

The company is a relatively new supplier to Swift Exhaust, and extremely price competitive. Prior to the consignment in question the company had supplied three previous batches of exhaust systems. No problems were reported with the earlier batches.

John Blakeson, the purchasing assistant who handles this account, informs me that when he places an order with this supplier, a simple acknowledgement and acceptance is faxed to him within a few days. When a delivery takes place, a couple of weeks later, an invoice is forwarded to us together with a copy of the standard form contract terms and conditions.

I am concerned to note that the `Claims' clause in that contract seems to limit our ability to recover the full losses that we suffer as a result of the defective exhaust systems, and I await with interest your opinion on the legal validity of this clause.

Exhaust System Supplies Ltd.
Terms and Conditions of Contract

Prices

All prices are subject to change without notice.
Unless stated otherwise prices quoted are for individual items.
Prices are quoted in £ Sterling.
Recommended retail prices are shown were available.

All prices quoted are exclusive of Value Added Tax which will be charged at the rate in force at the time of dispatch.

All prices quoted exclude carriage.

Settlement Terms

30 days from the date of invoice. We reserve the right to apply a levy of 3% over bank base rate on all overdue balances.

Damage or Non-delivery

Should damage occur to goods in transit this must be notified to us in writing within 3 days of delivery, non-delivery within 7 days of the date of invoice. Should these conditions not be met we reserve the right to ask for payment in full.

Bulk Discounts

Bulk discounts are available for large orders.

Acceptance of Orders

We reserve the right to accept orders subject to:

   (i)   Our minimum order value of £120.

   (ii)   Availability of raw materials.

   (iii) Product specification are subject to constant improvement and may alter without prior notice.

   (iv)   Prices ruling at date of dispatch.

   (v)   Correction of errors/omissions on invoices or credit notes.

Claims

If any goods supplied by Exhaust System Supplies Ltd. (the Company) prove on inspection to be defective in material or workmanship the Company undertakes at its option to replace the same or refund to the buyer the price of the goods and in no circumstances will liability exceed the cost of replacement or (at the Company's option) the price paid by the buyer for such goods.

The Company shall not under any circumstances whatsoever be liable for damages whether consequential or otherwise, howsoever caused or occasioned and this undertaking is given in place of and excludes all other warranties and conditions whatsoever whether implied by statute or otherwise.

Retention of Title

   (i)   The risk in respect of any goods supplied under this contract shall pass to the customer on the invoice date, but the property in the goods shall not pass to the customer until the customer has paid all monies due and owing to Exhaust System Supplies Ltd. whether under this contract or otherwise.

(ii) Until the date of full payment of all monies due and owing to us, you shall keep the goods as bailee in such a manner that they can clearly be identified as being the property of Exhaust System Supplies Ltd.

(iii) The customer shall be entitled to sell the goods in the ordinary course of business, subject to the conditions that until the date of full payment of all monies due and owing to Exhaust System Supplies Ltd., the customer shall account to us for all monies obtained therefrom. Such account shall be in a form which clearly identifies what money has derived from the sale of our goods as a separate element from any monies derived from the sale of any other products whether the goods are sold separately or mixed with any other products. Such monies are to be held by the customer on trust for the benefit of Exhaust System Supplies Ltd.

(iv) In the event of any default by the customer in complying with any of the conditions of this agreement including failure to pay to Exhaust System Supplies Ltd. all monies owed to us on the due date, or if a receiver of the customers assets be appointed, or if a petition be presented to wind up the customer or the customer becomes otherwise incapable of trading for whatever reason, the entire sum of money remaining unpaid shall become immediately due and owing to use and we shall be entitled forthwith to stop further delivery of goods and to enter upon the premises of the customer with such transport as may be necessary to remove all property the ownership whereof is retained by us under this or any other contract with the customer without prejudice to our right to claim further monies as remains due and owing to us, nor shall the customer construe this or any other conditions of this agreement as entitling the customer to return the goods or refuse or delay payment therefor.

(v) The right to recover the possession of goods the ownership whereof is retained by Exhaust System Supplies Ltd. pursuant to the foregoing provisions of this Condition, shall include the right to detach and remove those goods from any other goods to which they may be attached whilst those goods still remain on the premises of the customer.

Removal of the Goods

All goods delivered to the buyer or agent, or person on behalf of the buyer, may be removed from the buyer's premises by the seller at any time after the due date of payment has been passed.

Force Majeur

Exhaust System Supplies Ltd. shall not be liable to any loss or damage caused by non performance due to act of God, war, civil disturbance, government action, strike, lock out, trade dispute, fire accidents, or other causes beyond our control.

Variation of Condition

All quotations and contracts are subject to the above conditions and may only be varied by express permission in writing from the company.

Legal Construction

The contracts shall in all respects be construed and operate as an English Contract and in conformity with English Law. Each individual delivery and invoice is to be regarded as the satisfaction of a separate order.

Legal Terms found in Chapter 13

Code of practice	• a statement of trading behaviour produced by a trade association which it expects its members to observe. Such a code is self regulating
Data protection	• legal protection granted to individuals in relation the collection, storage and distribution of personal data about them, using computers
Data protection principles	• set of eight statutory principles which data users are required to observe in their use of personal data
Data users	• individuals and organisations who hold and use personal data and who must be registered with the Data Protection Registrar
Negligent statement	• a statement made without reasonable grounds for belief in its truth
Package holidays	• combination of specific holiday components, such as accommodation and transport, sold or offered for sale on a pre-arranged basis, at an inclusive price, and which are subject to legislative control designed to protect the consumer
Professional negligence	• principles upon which damages can be claimed against a professional person in the tort of negligence
Property misdescription	• expression used to describe the making of false misleading statements by estate agents or property development businesses regarding the sale of land and buildings
Reckless statement	• a statement made regardless of whether it is true or false
Tour operator	• business specialising in putting together and selling holiday packages

Chapter 13

Consumer Protection: Services

Consumer Protection in Relation to Services

Consumer protection in relation to services is achieved in a number of ways. One important method is the regulation of those who provide services. This may be done by a statutory system of licensing, for example the licensing of those who sell alcoholic liquor; or the licensing of those who provide credit in the course of a business under the Consumer Credit Act 1974.

Regulation by professional bodies

Many professional service providers such as lawyers, doctors, architects, surveyors and accountants are regulated by professional associations. These associations often have the power to authorise the individual professional to practice his profession, or indeed to withdraw or refuse to give such authorisation. This may be done by the issue of annual practising certificates to those who have demonstrated their fitness to practice and who comply with conditions laid down by the association, for example by providing evidence of adequate professional indemnity insurance cover. Providing professional services without a current practising certificate is usually a criminal offence.

Professional associations are almost invariably authorised, through contractual conditions of membership or by Act of Parliament, to exercise disciplinary powers over members of the profession. These disciplinary powers are usually exercised, in the more serious cases, by a domestic tribunal. The tribunal will act rather like a court and will hear formal complaints against members of the profession. If a complaint is proven, the tribunal will have power to impose punishments ranging from a simple reprimand to the imposition of a fine or the suspension or withdrawal of the right to practise as a member of the profession.

In addition to disciplinary tribunals, many professional bodies sponsor arbitration schemes which provide a means by which compensation claims can be adjudicated without reference to the courts. One example is the *Solicitors Arbitration Scheme* set up by the Law Society in 1986. The scheme is run by the *Chartered Institute of Arbitrators*. In order to use the scheme both the solicitor and the claimant must agree. They will be bound by the decision of the arbitrator and neither party can subsequently take the matter to court. The arbitrator will look at written submissions by the parties and other supporting documents. He will decide whether the claim is valid and fix the amount of compensation to be awarded. In exceptional cases, where it appears that a decision cannot be made on the examination of documents alone, there is provision for a verbal hearing with the agreement of both parties. Each party must pay a registration fee in advance but the fee will be refunded to the successful party. The remaining costs of the scheme are paid by the Law Society itself.

Codes of practice under the Fair Trading Act 1973

In those parts of the service sector which fall outside the sphere of the traditional professions, many service providers are members of trade associations. These bodies tend not to have legal powers of the type possessed by professional bodies to regulate the conduct of their members. The *Director General of Fair Trading* has a duty under the Fair Trading Act 1973 to encourage trade associations and other similar organisations to prepare Codes of Practice and circulate them to their members. The codes should be designed to give guidance to traders relating to the safeguarding and protection of the interests of consumers.

A code of practice is a statement by a trade association which aims to establish and define the standards of trading which it expects from its members. Voluntary codes of this type have been introduced, following consultation with the *Office of Fair Trading*, to cover many areas of business. Such codes often provide a mechanism for the arbitration of consumer complaints as an alternative to legal proceedings in the courts.

Codes of practice provide a means whereby, in effect, a sector of industry or commerce can regulate itself. There are a number of costs and benefits to this. The main advantages are:

- a code can encourage a positive approach to trading standards and set high standards in excess of the legal minimum;

- a code can be changed fairly quickly in order to meet changing circumstances;

- a code can be expressed in non-technical language and interpreted positively according to its spirit;

- a code normally deals with one type of business or product. It can be drawn up to meet particular problems which are likely to arise in the limited area which it covers. Legislation, on the other hand, usually applies to all sectors of business;

- a code can clarify the rights and obligations of the trader and the customer in simple language;

- a code can often provide procedures and remedies which are appropriate to its subject matter in a more flexible way than legislation.

There are, however, a number of drawbacks associated with self regulation by Codes of Practice. The main disadvantages are:

- limited sanctions are available in the event that a trader does not comply with the provisions of a code. The ultimate penalty is usually expulsion from the trade association. In some sectors at least, this is not a very real punishment;

- the trade association may be in a position of conflict of interests when drawing up a code. Its principal function is the protection of the interests of its members;

- the consumer may not be aware of the existence of a code or the remedies which it offers;

- a code will not apply to a trader who is not a member of the trade association. In some sectors, particularly where the trade association has a high profile, for example ABTA in the travel trade, most traders are members. In other sectors, however, only a minority of traders belong to a trade association.

Contractual liability for defective services

Where services are provided in a manner which is inconsistent with the express terms of the contract, the consumer will be able to sue for damages for breach of contract, and in some cases will be able to withdraw from the contract on the grounds of a breach of condition by the service provider. This will depend upon the exact wording of the express terms of the contract, and the seriousness of the breach. Where the consumer has suffered loss or damage but there has been no breach of an express term, the service provider may still be liable for breach of an implied term in the contract.

The Supply of Goods and Services Act 1982 sets out terms which will be implied both into contracts for the supply of services and into contracts for work done and materials supplied. These terms will apply, for example, to contracts for dry cleaning, entertainment and professional services, home improvements and motor vehicle maintenance. The major areas of concern in relation to this type of contract were identified in a report of the National Consumer Council in 1981 entitled *Services Please*. These concerns were quality, delay in performance and cost. They are all dealt with by the 1982 Act. The aim of this part of the 1982 Act is simply to codify the common law without changing it. The NCC believed that this was necessary for three reasons: certainty and clarity; ease of reference, and in order to focus attention on the existence of the obligations owed by those who supply services.

Implied duty to use reasonable care and skill

The 1982 Act in s.13 provides: *"In a contract for the supply of a service where the supplier is acting in the course of a business, there is an implied term that the supplier will carry out the service with reasonable care and skill"*.

The nature of the duty was explained by Lord Denning in *Greaves & Co. (Contractors) Ltd. v. Baynham Meikle and Partners* 1975 in the following terms *"The law does not usually imply a warranty that the professional man will achieve the desired result, but only a term that he will use reasonable care and skill. The surgeon does not warrant that he will cure the patient. Nor does the solicitor warrant that he will win the case .... whether it is a medical man, a lawyer, or an accountant, an architect or an engineer, his duty is to use reasonable care and skill"*.

The section has wide ranging application embracing most situations where a client or customer is paying for services. In addition to those professions mentioned by Lord Denning, it applies to *builders, hairdressers, dry cleaners, surveyors, auctioneers, tour operators, bankers, car repairers and many others* who provide services in the course of their business.

The following cases illustrate the scope of the duty:

In *Curtis v. Chemical Cleaning and Dyeing Company* 1951 the plaintiff took a wedding dress to the defendant dry cleaners for cleaning. When she came to collect the dress she found that it had been stained. It was held that the company were liable for the damage to the dress which had been caused by their failure to take care of it.

In *Lawson v. Supasink Ltd.* 1984 the plaintiffs employed the company to design, supply and install a fitted kitchen at a price of £1,200. Plans were drawn up and agreed but the company did not follow them when installing the units. The plaintiffs complained about the standard of work before the installation was complete. After taking independent expert advice the plaintiffs demanded the return of their deposit and asked the defendants to remove the kitchen units. The defendants refused and the plaintiffs sued. The judge found that the kitchen was installed in *"a shocking and shoddy manner"* and that the work was *beyond redemptio*n. He awarded damages of £500 for inconvenience and loss of the use of the kitchen; damages of the difference between the cost of equivalent units and the contract price; and the return of the deposit. On appeal the defendants argued that they had substantially performed the contract and were therefore entitled to the contract price less the cost of remedying any defects. This was rejected by the Court of Appeal on the grounds that the standard of workmanship and design was so poor that the doctrine of substantial performance could not be applied, having regard to the large sums which would have to be spent to remedy the defects.

The contract in the *Supasink* case was a contract for work and materials. Section 13 of the 1982 Act applies to the work element in such a contract. In some cases it may be important to know whether the defect complained of is due to fault in the materials themselves or the supplier's failure to take care in doing the work. This is because the nature of the liability for each of the two elements of the contract is different. In relation to the supply of materials, the supplier will be strictly liable, even if he is not at fault (like the defendant in *Frost v. Aylesbury Dairies* 1905 above). If the work is defective the supplier will only be liable if he has failed to take reasonable care. Another reason why the distinction may be important is that different controls on the use of exclusion clauses are applied by the Unfair Contract Terms Act 1977 to each element of contracts of this type.

Where services, or goods and services, are supplied by any person taking on work in connection with the provision of a dwelling house, s.1(1) of the Defective Premises Act 1972 imposes a duty of care on that person. He has a duty to see that the work is done in a workmanlike or professional manner with proper materials so that, in relation to the work he has taken on, the dwelling will be fit for habitation when it is completed.

Exemptions from the operation of s.13 of the 1982 Act have been made for company directors who have a duty to use such care as they would use in relation to their own personal affairs in performance of their duties as directors.

A solicitor acting as an advocate before a court is also exempted from the section because of the rule that advocates cannot be made liable for professional negligence. The potential liability of lawyers for professional negligence is examined later in the chapter.

Implied terms relating to time for performance

Section 14 of the 1982 Act provides: *"Where, under a contract for the supply of a service by a supplier acting in the course of a business, the time for the service to be carried out is not fixed by the contract,....there is an implied term that the supplier will carry out the service within a reasonable time. What is a reasonable time is a question of fact".*

> In *Charnock v. Liverpool Corporation* 1968 the plaintiff recovered damages for the defendant's unreasonable delay in performing a contract. The defendant took eight weeks to repair the plaintiff's car when a reasonably competent repairer would have completed the repair within five weeks.

If a reasonable time has elapsed within which the contract should have been performed, the customer is entitled unilaterally to serve a notice fixing a time for the performance of the contract.

The new time limit must be reasonable. If the supplier fails to meet it, the Court of Appeal held in *Charles Rickards Ltd. v. Oppenheim* 1950 that the customer is entitled to withdraw from the contract without penalty.

If the time for performance of the contract has been agreed then s.14 does not add an additional requirement that the services should be provided within a reasonable time.

Implied terms relating to the cost of the service

Section 15 of the 1982 Act deals with the cost of services supplied. It provides: *"Where under a contract for the supply of a service, the consideration for the service is not determined by the contract,....there is an implied term that the party contracting with the supplier will pay a reasonable charge. What is a reasonable charge is a question of fact".*

Section 15 does not enable a customer to reopen an agreement on the grounds that the charge for the service is unreasonably high, if the customer originally agreed to pay that charge. It applies only where there is no mechanism in the contract for determining the price and limits the amount recoverable to a reasonable sum.

Non-contractual Liability for Defective Services

The vast majority of claims for injury or loss caused by defective services are made by customers of the service provider rather than by third parties who have no contractual relationship with him. Most claims will therefore be based on an allegation of breach of contract, often on a breach of the implied duty to use reasonable skill and care in the performance of the contract. This is usually referred to as *contractual negligence*. Where the plaintiff has no contractual relationship with the service provider, he will have to establish that the service provider owes him a duty of care under the general principles of the law of negligence examined in Chapter 6. Without a contract he will obviously be unable to rely on s.13 of the 1982 Act. The term *third party negligence* may be used to distinguish this situation from one of contractual negligence.

In either case the term professional negligence may be used where the defendant has failed to take care in providing professional services.

	CONTRACT	TORT
who can sue	client only	client or third party
type of loss recoverable if not too remote	all types of loss	all types except that pure financial loss is recoverable only in very limited circumstances
test for remoteness of damage	*Hadley v. Baxendale* (i) damage arising in the ordinary course of events (ii) unusual loses if known to be likely at time of contract	*The Wagon Mound* damage of a type which was reasonably foreseeable at the time of the breach of duty
time limits for claims	(i) time runs from breach (ii) Latent Damage Act 1986 does not apply (iii) see Figure 10.3 for time limits	(i) time runs from damage (ii) Latent Damage Act 1986 does apply (iii) see Figure 10.3 for time limits
exclusion of liability	s.2 and s.3 Unfair Contract Terms Act 1977	s.2 Unfair Contract Terms Act 1977

Figure 13.1   Main differences between contractual and third party negligence

One important difference between contractual negligence and third party negligence lies in the range of types of loss or damages which may be sued for. It is well settled law that the contractual duty of care is owed in respect of the full range of losses, including personal injury, death, damage to property and financial loss. Whilst these are all recoverable in a contractual negligence claim, the rules governing third party negligence cases are more restrictive. Where the plaintiff suffers personal injury or damage to property, the neighbour principle laid down by Lord Atkin in *Donoghue v. Stevenson* 1932 will be applied by the court to determine whether a duty of care is owed by the service provider in a third party negligence claim. Many claims against members of the medical profession, for example, arise as a result of personal injuries suffered by patients in their care. In the case of NHS patients, where there is no contract with the practitioner, third party negligence will be the basis of any such claim. In such cases the existence of a duty of care can readily be shown. Applying the neighbour principle, the practitioner can reasonably foresee that carelessness on his part is likely to injure the patient. The patient is clearly a neighbour as he is closely and directly affected by the practitioner's acts or omissions.

Where the claim is based upon third party negligence, the plaintiff may have more difficulty in establishing that the defendant owed a duty of care to avoid causing financial loss. A claim for financial or economic loss usually relates to the loss of profits which the plaintiff would have made but for the defendant's negligence, or the loss of money invested as a result of advice or information given by the defendant. It is possible to distinguish two broad categories of claim for financial loss:

- financial loss caused by negligent statements
- financial loss caused by negligent acts.

The basis and scope of the duty of care will vary according to which of these categories the plaintiff's claim comes within. We shall examine the basic ground rules for each category, returning to them later when we consider the liability of members of particular professions for negligence.

Financial loss caused by negligent statements

Prior to the decision of the House of Lords in *Hedley Byrne v. Heller* 1964 it was well settled law that there could be no liability in tort for financial loss caused by negligently made statements. In *Candler v. Crane, Christmas & Co.* 1951, for example, the Court of Appeal by a majority held that a false statement, carelessly made, was not actionable in the tort of negligence. Lord Denning dissented and was prepared to recognise the existence of a duty of care where the defendant had some special knowledge or skill upon which the plaintiff relied. He stated *"From early times it has been held that persons who engage in a calling which requires special knowledge and skill owe a duty of care to those who are closely and directly affected by their work, apart altogether from any contract or undertaking in that behalf."*

The judgment of Lord Denning was approved by the house of Lords in *Hedley Byrne v. Heller*, and the decision of the majority in the *Candler* case was overruled.

> In *Hedley Byrne & Co. v. Heller and Partners Ltd.* 1964 the plaintiffs were advertising agents whose clients, Easipower Ltd, were customers of the defendant merchant bank. The plaintiffs had been instructed to buy advertising space for Easipower's products on television and in the newspapers. This involved them in the expenditure of large sums of money. Never having dealt with Easipower before, the plaintiffs sought a reference as to their credit worthiness to the extent of £100,000 from the defendant. The reference was given `without responsibility on the part of the bank' and stated with reference to Easipower: *"Respectably constituted company, considered good for its ordinary business engagements. Your figures are larger than we are accustomed to see"*. In fact Easipower had an overdraft with the bank, which ought to have known that the company would have difficulty meeting payments to the plaintiff. Within one week of giving the reference the bank was pressing Easipower to reduce its overdraft. Relying on the reference the plaintiffs incurred personal liability by placing advertising contracts. Easipower then went into liquidation due to insolvency and as a result the plaintiffs lost over £17,500. The actual decision in the case was that the defendant was not liable as the disclaimer of responsibility was effective to prevent the bank from assuming a duty of care.

The principal importance of the decision, however, is that the House of Lords recognised the existence, in certain circumstances, of a duty of care in relation to financial loss caused by negligently made statements. Lord Morris stated:

> *"if someone possessed of a special skill undertakes, quite irrespective of contract, to apply that skill for the assistance of another person who relies upon such skill, a duty of care will arise."*

Lord Pearce expressed the view that the duty would only arise in relation to a statement about *"a business or professional transaction whose nature makes clear the gravity of the inquiry and the importance and influence attached to the answer"*.

For reasons of public policy, the scope of the duty and the class of persons to whom it is owed was restricted by the House of Lords. The main policy reason for this was a reluctance to create open ended liability by exposing a defendant to claims by numerous plaintiffs for a single instance of negligence. In Lord Reid's view the danger of 'opening the floodgates' in this way was particularly acute for a number of reasons: *"I would think that the law must treat negligent words differently from negligent acts… Quite careful people often express definite opinions on social or informal occasions even when they see that others are likely to be influenced by them; and they often do so without taking that care which they would take if asked for their opinion professionally or in a business connection… But it is at least unusual casually to put into circulation negligently made articles which are dangerous… Another obvious difference is that a negligently made article will only cause one accident and so it is not very difficult to find the necessary degree of proximity or neighbourhood between the negligent manufacturer and the person injured. But words can be broadcast with or without the consent or the foresight of the speaker or writer. It would be one thing to say that the speaker owes a duty to a limited class, but it would be going very far to say that he owes a duty to every ultimate 'consumer' who acts on those words to his detriment."*

For these reasons the House of Lords held that in order for a duty to arise there must be a *special relationship of reliance* between the parties. It was characterised by Lord Devlin as *a relationship equivalent to a contract* (albeit lacking the essential ingredient of consideration). A useful definition of the special relationship of reliance was given by Lord Reid who said that it included: *"… all those relationships where it is plain that the party seeking information or advice was trusting the other to exercise such a degree of care as the circumstances required, where it is reasonable for him to do that, and where the other gave the information or advice when he knew or ought to have known that the inquirer was relying on him."*

Clearly there would be no special relationship of reliance in respect of casual remarks in the course of conversation on a social or informal occasion. In any event the person who is asked for information or an opinion could refuse to give it; make clear that it was given without careful consideration, or, as happened in the *Hedley Byrne* case, disclaim responsibility for it. In Lord Reid's opinion: *"A reasonable man, knowing that he was being trusted or that his skill and judgement were being relied on, would, I think, have three courses open to him. He could keep silent or decline to give the information or advice sought: or he could give an answer with a clear qualification that he accepted no responsibility for it or that it was given without that reflection or inquiry which a careful answer would require: or he could simply answer without any such qualification. If he chooses to adopt the last course he must, I think, be held to have accepted some responsibility for his answer being given carefully, or to have accepted a relationship with the inquirer which requires him to exercise such care as the circumstances require."*

Where the person making the statement excludes liability for it or states that it is given without responsibility, the Unfair Contract Terms Act 1977 applies with the result that the disclaimer will be invalid unless the person who made the statement proves that it is fair and reasonable in the circumstances to allow reliance on the disclaimer. It may be then that a case with similar facts to those of *Hedley Byrne v. Heller* would be decided differently if it came before the courts today.

The test for determining whether a duty of care exists outside a contract in relation to careless statements causing financial loss is whether a special relationship of reliance exists between the parties. This is narrower in its scope than the neighbour principle and under it the duty will be established if the plaintiff can prove:

(i)   that the defendant possessed special skill or knowledge,

(ii)   that the plaintiff relied on the defendant to exercise care,

(iii) that the defendant knew or ought to have know that the plaintiff was relying on him, and

(iv) that reliance by the plaintiff was reasonable in the circumstances.

We have already seen in Chapter 9 that damages for loss caused by a careless statement may be recovered under the Misrepresentation Act 1967 where the statement is a negligent misrepresentation which induces a person to enter a contract. When we considered liability for negligent misrepresentation many of the cases which we examined were argued on the basis both of the Misrepresentation Act and of the *Hedley Byrne* principle. It may be useful to refer in particular to *Esso Petroleum Co. Ltd. v. Mardon* 1976 and *Howard Marine and Dredging Co. v. Ogden (A.) & Sons (Excavations)* 1978.

Financial loss caused by negligent acts

It has been a long-standing principle of law of negligence that pure financial loss caused by a negligent act rather than a statement is not recoverable.

> Thus for example in *Weller Co. v. Foot & Mouth Disease Research Institute* 1965 the defendants carried out research into foot and mouth disease, a highly infectious disease affecting cattle. The virus escaped from their premises and affected cattle in the surrounding area. As a result restrictions on the movement of cattle were introduced and two cattle markets belonging to the plaintiff auctioneers had to be closed. The plaintiffs sued for loss caused to their business. It was held that, because the loss was purely financial and not connected with any physical harm caused to the plaintiffs or their property, no duty of care was owed by the defendants to the plaintiffs, and the claim failed.

The major policy reason for refusing to recognise a duty of care for pure financial loss is that it could lead to open ended liability. In the *Weller* case, for example, the closure of the markets would have affected the businesses of all those who transported cattle to and from the markets; of the shops, cafes and public houses in the vicinity of the markets; of the banks which would have handled the money in the sale and purchase of cattle; and the destruction of cattle caused by the escape of the virus could have adversely affected the economic interests of cattle feed suppliers, agricultural workers and milkmen, with substantial knock-on effects throughout the local economy. If the defendants were not to be liable for all of these consequences, the line of legal liability has to be drawn restrictively. Thus claims can be brought for injury to the person and damage to property, and for financial losses which are closely associated with such injury or damage. However, with one exception discussed below, claims for pure financial loss caused by the defendant's negligent act are not allowed. The extent of a plaintiff's financial loss may not readily be foreseen by the defendant before the negligent act occurs and the plaintiff will be in the best position to assess the extent and insure against the risk of financial loss.

Financial loss directly associated with physical injury may be referred to as consequential rather than pure financial loss. Here the defendant may owe a duty to the plaintiff under the neighbour principle. An example of the distinction between these types of financial loss can be seen in the following case:.

> In *Spartan Steel & Alloys Ltd. v. Martin & Co. (Contractors) Ltd.* 1972 the defendant's employee, while digging up a road with a mechanical excavator, carelessly damaged an electricity supply cable and cut off the power to the plaintiff's factory. In order to prevent damage to a furnace, the molten metal in it had to be poured off before it solidified. The melt was damaged to the value of £368, and the plaintiffs lost the profit of £400 which they would have made had the process been completed. The electricity supply was cut off for 14 hours during which four additional melts could have been processed. The profit on the additional melts would have been £1,767. The Court of Appeal held that the first two items claimed were recoverable - these were damage to property and consequential financial loss. The loss of profits on additional melts, however, was a pure financial loss not sufficiently connected with the physical damage and therefore not recoverable.

A 1982 decision of the House of Lords has created an exception to the rule that no duty can be owed in respect of pure financial loss unassociated with physical damage.

> In *Junior Books Ltd. v. Veitchi Co. Ltd.* 1982 the plaintiff engaged a main contractor to build a new factory. The main contractor, at the request of the plaintiff, engaged the defendant to lay the floor of the building. The defendant was therefore a nominated sub-contractor and had no contractual relationship with the plaintiff. Due to the defendant's failure to mix and lay the floor with reasonable care, the floor began to crack up leaving the plaintiff with an unserviceable building bearing high maintenance costs. The plaintiff ceased production, had the floor relaid and sued the defendant for all the costs and losses incurred by him. The defendant denied that he owed a duty to the plaintiff in respect of that part of the claim which represented pure financial loss. The House of Lords, by a majority, held the defendant liable for the full claim, including the element of pure financial loss. The duty of care was thus extended beyond one of preventing physical harm being done by faulty work to a duty to avoid the presence of defects in the work itself and to avoid the resultant financial losses. Lord Fraser, in his judgement, stressed that he was deciding the case *"strictly on its own facts. I rely particularly on the very close proximity between the parties."* After discussing the floodgates argument Lord Fraser continued: *"The proximity between the parties is extremely close, falling only just short of a direct contractual relationship. The injury to the plaintiff was a direct and foreseeable result of negligence by the defendants. The plaintiffs nominated the defendants as specialist sub-contractors and they must therefore have relied on their skill and knowledge."*

The *Junior Books* case has been treated in subsequent cases as laying down a narrow exception to a general principle, rather than as a springboard for the extension of liability. Thus in *Muirhead v.*

Industrial Tank Specialities 1985, discussed in Chapter 12 in the context of product liability, the Court of Appeal refused to extend the duty to a manufacturer of defective electric motors which caused financial loss to the ultimate consumer. The decision was made on the grounds that there was not a sufficient degree of close proximity between the plaintiff and the defendant to give rise to a duty of care to avoid causing financial loss.

> In *D & F Estates Ltd. v. Church Commissioners for England* 1988 the third defendants, who were builders, had been employed to erect flats on land owned by the Church Commissioners. The plaintiff, a tenant of one of the flats, found that the plaster on the wall of its flat was loose, and sued the builders for the cost of replastering the flat. The basis of the claim was that the plastering was defective in quality. There was no allegation that it had caused damage to other property of the plaintiff or that it had caused personal injury. The claim was therefore to recover damages for pure economic loss in the tort of negligence. The House of Lords held that the builders were not liable as such losses are irrecoverable. The decision in *Junior Books v. Veitchi* was treated as *"not laying down any principle of general application"*, and as being dependent upon the finding of a *"unique, albeit non-contractual relationship"* and the ratio of *Junior Books* was effectively confined to its own particular facts.

In any case in which a plaintiff claims damages for economic loss resulting from damage to property caused by a negligent act, it should be noted that the plaintiff cannot succeed unless he has a proprietary or possessory interest in the property at the time the damage occurs.

> In *Leigh & Sillavan Ltd. v. Aliakmon Shipping Co. Ltd. The Aliakmon* 1986 the House of Lords held that the buyer under an export contract, to whom the ownership of the goods had not passed, but to whom the risk of accidental destruction had been transferred by the terms of the contract, could not sue the shipowner in negligence for pure financial loss caused to him by the fact that the goods were damaged whilst in transit on board ship, as he had no proprietary or possessory interest in the goods at the time they were damaged.

Exclusion of liability for negligence in providing services

Section 2 of the Unfair Contract Terms Act 1977 provides

(1) *"A person cannot by reference to any contract term or to a notice given to persons generally or to particular persons exclude or restrict his liability for death or personal injury resulting from negligence.*

(2) *In the case of other loss or damage, a person cannot so exclude or restrict his liability for negligence except insofar as the term or notice satisfies the requirement of reasonableness".*

This gives us two important basic rules. First that it is not possible to exclude liability for death or personal injury resulting from negligence.

The second rule is that liability for loss or damage other than death or personal injury cannot be excluded unless the exclusion is reasonable. This would apply, for example, to clauses which excluded liability for damage to property or financial loss caused by negligence. The application of the rule in situations involving contractual negligence and in providing services can be seen in the following case.

In *Spriggs v. Sotheby Parke Bernet and Co. Ltd.* 1984 the plaintiff, who was a businessman, deposited a diamond with Sotheby's to be auctioned. He signed a document which, among other things, excluded Sotheby's liability for negligence. He was given the opportunity to insure the diamond but did not do so. Whilst the diamond was on view prior to the auction, it was stolen despite the defendant's fairly comprehensive security system. The plaintiff sued for negligence and the defendants relied on the exclusion clause. Under s.2(2) the clause is only valid if the defendant can show that it is reasonable. The court held that the clause in this case was reasonable and valid. The plaintiff was a successful and experienced businessman and no doubt was used to contracts containing exclusion clauses. He could not be regarded as having unequal bargaining power. The risk was one which could have been covered by insurance but the plaintiff turned down the opportunity to take this precaution.

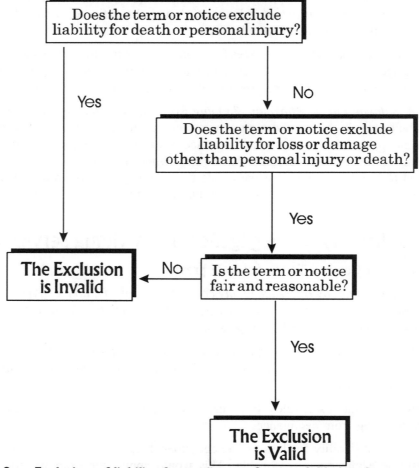

Figure 13.2   Exclusion of liability for negligence:Section 2 Unfair Contract Terms Act 1977

Professional Negligence Liability for Lawyers and Accountants

We shall now consider the way in which the courts have applied the principles outlined above in a variety of circumstances involving allegations of negligence against members of two specific professions lawyers and accountants. In doing so we should bear in mind that the rules laid down in relation to one profession can often be applied to other professions. You may find it useful, in relation to each case, to attempt to identify the essential elements of each negligence action as they arise, and to analyse each decision so as to pinpoint the element which is at the centre of the dispute. A famous case involving an allegation of medical negligence provides us with some guidance as to the standard of care required of a professional person.

> In *Whitehouse v. Jordan* 1981 a senior hospital registrar in charge of a difficult birth used forceps to assist in the birth. The use of forceps was unsuccessful and the baby was eventually delivered by Caesarean section. The baby was born with brain damage. It was alleged that this resulted from the defendant's negligence in pulling too hard and too long with the forceps. The Court of Appeal held that the defendant was not liable in negligence even though he had made an error of judgement. Lord Denning, M.R., in a statement which was not accepted as valid by the House of Lords, stated: *"we must say, and say firmly, that, in a professional man an error of judgement is not negligent"*

> The House of Lords, whilst confirming the decision of the Court of Appeal, disagreed with the statement by Lord Denning. Lord Fraser stated " *I think that Lord Denning M.R. must have meant to say that an error of judgement 'is not necessarily negligent' ... Merely to describe something as an error of judgement tells us nothing about whether it is negligent or not. The true position is that an error of judgement may, or may not, be negligent; it depends on the nature of the error. If it is one that would not have been made by a reasonably competent professional man professing to have the standard and type of skill that the defendant held himself out as having, and acting with ordinary care, then it is negligent. If, on the other hand, it is an error that a man, acting with ordinary care, might have made, then it is not negligence.* "

Accountants

In recent years there has been some uncertainty as to the precise extent of the accountant's liability in negligence. The uncertainty has centred around the situation in which the accountant, acting as auditor of a limited company, negligently paints too rosy a financial picture of the company in its accounts, and a third party loses money in a transaction entered into on the strength of that financial picture. A limited company's accounts are widely circulated. They are filed with the annual report at the Companies Registry and are available for public inspection. Consequently a wide range of people may use them for a variety of purposes. Many such people will have no contractual relationship with the auditor. After a period of uncertainty, the legal principles governing the auditor's liability to such people have now been settled by the House of Lords in *Caparo Industries plc v. Dickman* 1990. Before examining some of the relevant caselaw, it may be useful to remind ourselves of the position of auditors of a plc under the Companies Act 1985. This was summarised by Bingham L.J. in the *Caparo* case as follows:

> *"The members, or shareholders, of the company are its owners. But they are too numerous, and in most cases too unskilled, to undertake the day-to-day management of that which they own. So responsibility for day-to-day management of the company is delegated to directors. The shareholders, despite their overall powers of control, are in most companies for most of the time investors and little more. But it would, of course, be unsatisfactory and open to abuse if the shareholders received no report on the financial stewardship of their investment save from those to whom the stewardship had been entrusted. So provision is made for the company in general meeting to appoint an auditor whose duty is to investigate and form an opinion on the adequacy of the company's accounting records and returns and the correspondence between the company's accounting records and returns and its accounts . The auditor has then to report to the company's members (among other things) whether in his opinion the company's accounts give a true and fair view of the company's financial position . In carrying out his investigation and in forming his opinion the auditor necessarily works very closely with the directors and officers of the company. He receives his remuneration from the company. He naturally, and rightly, regards the company as his client. But he is employed by the company to exercise his professional skill and judgement for the purpose of giving the shareholders an independent report on the reliability of the company's accounts and thus on their investment.*

There are a large number of claims for professional negligence against accountants in the UK. Such claims are invariably for financial loss and are governed by the rules of contractual negligence or by the principles laid down by the House of Lords in *Hedley Byrne v. Heller* 1964 and *Caparo Industries plc v. Dickman* 1990. In the discussion of the *Hedley Byrne* case earlier in this chapter, reference was made to the dissenting judgement of Lord Denning in *Candler v. Crane Christmas* 1951, which has been approved by the House of Lords on a number of occasions.

> In *Candler v. Crane Christmas & Co*. 1951 the plaintiff proposed to invest £2,000 in a company, but before making the investment he wished to examine the company's accounts. The defendant accountants were in the course of preparing the accounts. They were instructed by the managing director of the company to complete their work quickly and to show the accounts to the plaintiff. On the strength of the accounts the plaintiff invested his money in the company. The accounts were carelessly prepared and gave a wholly misleading picture of the state of the company, which was wound up within a year. The plaintiff lost his investment and sued the accountants for professional negligence. In a majority decision which has since been overruled by the House of Lords, the Court of Appeal held that the defendant owed no duty of care to the plaintiff. The dissenting judgement of Lord Denning was described in the *Caparo* case by Lord Bridge as a *"masterly analysis, requiring little, if any, amplification or modification in the light of later authority."* Lord Denning stated that a duty to use care in making statements is owed by: *"those persons such as accountants, surveyors, valuers and analysts, whose profession and occupation is to examine books, accounts, and other things, and to make reports on which other people - other than their clients - rely in the ordinary course of*

business. Their duty is not merely a duty to use care in their reports. They also have a duty to use care in their work which results in their reports. " and he continued *"to whom do these professional people owe this duty? I will take accountants, but the same reasoning applies to the others. They owe the duty, of course to their employer or client; and also I think to any third person to whom they themselves show the accounts, or to whom they know their employer is going to show the accounts, so as to induce him to invest money or take some other action on them. But I do not think the duty can be extended still further so as to include strangers of whom they have heard nothing and to whom their employer without their knowledge may choose to show their accounts. Once the accountants have handed their accounts to their employer they are not, as a rule, responsible for what he does with them without their knowledge or consent..... I can well understand that it would be going too far to make an accountant liable to any person in the land who chooses to rely on the accounts in matters of business, for that would expose him to liability in an indeterminate amount for an indeterminate time to an indeterminate class".*

Candler v. Crane Christmas was followed in 1964 by the decision of the House of Lords in *Hedley Byrne v. Heller* which, in addition to approving Lord Denning's judgement in *Candler*, established the *special relationship of reliance* as the test to be applied in determining whether a duty of care is owed by a person making a careless statement, including an accountant carelessly preparing misleading accounts, and causing financial loss.

Subsequently, however, the Court of Appeal in *JEB Fasteners Ltd. v. Marks Bloom & Co.* 1983 appeared to have abandoned the special relationship test preferring to follow the less restrictive approach outlined by Lord Wilberforce in *Anns v. Merton* 1977.

In *JEB Fasteners Ltd. v. Marks Bloom & Co.* 1983 the plaintiff proposed to take over another company called B.G. Fasteners Ltd. The principal reason for the take-over was that the plaintiff wished to acquire the services of the two directors of the target company. A copy of the audited accounts of the target company had been certified by the defendant accountants, without qualification, as giving atrue and fair view of the state of the company. The accounts were relied upon by the plaintiff, which acquired the entire share capital of B.G. Fasteners. The accounts had been carelessly prepared and gave a misleading picture as to the value of the company. At the time the accounts were audited the defendants had no knowledge of the plaintiff or its intentions, and were not aware that a take-over from any source was contemplated. The Court of Appeal held that the defendants owed a duty of care to the plaintiff even though it was a complete stranger to them at the time of the audit. The defendants ought to have foreseen that B.G. Fasteners would require funds from money lenders or investors in the short term and that such persons were likely to rely on the audited accounts; secondly that the defendants were in breach of the duty of care as the accounts did not provide a true and fair view of the company. In particular there was a gross overvaluation of stock which caused the profit and loss account to show a profit when in reality the company had made a loss in excess of £13,000; and thirdly that the plaintiff's claim failed on the issue of causation of loss. The evidence clearly indicated that, even if the plaintiff had known the true financial position of the target company, it would nonetheless have gone ahead with the take-over. This was because the plaintiff's overriding object was to acquire the services of the two directors of B.G. Fasteners. Therefore the defendant's negligence was not the operative cause of the plaintiff's loss.

This decision caused a good deal of uncertainty because the Court of Appeal approached the question of duty by applying the broad test of reasonable foresight of harm - the neighbour principle - rather than the more restrictive test of whether there was a special relationship of reliance between the parties. The Court of Appeal felt able to do this, despite the considerable authority of the *Hedley Byrne* decision, by applying the two-stage test laid down by Lord Wilberforce in *Anns v. Merton* 1977. This uncertainty persisted until the House of Lords in *Caparo Industries plc v. Dickman* 1990 disapproved the approach adopted in the *JEB Fastners* case, and reaffirmed *Hedley Byrne v. Heller* 1964.

> In *Caparo Industries plc v. Dickman* 1990 the plaintiff owned shares in a public company, Fidelity plc, whose accounts for the year ending 31 March 1984 showed profits far short of the predicted figure. This resulted in a substantial drop in the quoted share price. After receiving the accounts for the year, which had been audited by the third defendant, Touche Ross & Co, the plaintiff purchased further shares in Fidelity plc and shortly afterward made a successful take-over bid. The plaintiff sued the auditors in negligence, claiming that the accounts were inaccurate and misleading in that they showed a profit of £1,200,000, when in fact there had been a loss of over £400,000. The plaintiff argued that the auditors owed it a duty of care either as a potential bidder for Fidelity plc because they ought to have foreseen that the 1984 results made Fidelity plc vulnerable to a take-over bid, or as an existing shareholder of Fidelity plc interested in buying more shares. The House of Lords held that a duty of care in making a statement arises only where there is a relationship of proximity between the maker of the statement (in this case the auditors) and the person relying on it (the plaintiff). A relationship of proximity is created where the maker of the statement knows that the statement will be communicated to the person relying on it specifically in connection with a particular transaction and that person would be very likely to rely on it for the purpose of deciding whether to enter into the transaction. Applying this principle to the case, the House of Lords held that no duty of care was owed by the auditors to the plaintiff as there was no relationship of proximity on the facts as the auditors were not aware of the plaintiff or its intentions at the time the statement was made. Although auditors owe a statutory duty to shareholders, this is owed to them as a class rather than as individuals. The nature of this duty was explained by Lord Jauncey who stated: *"the purpose of the annual accounts, so far as members are concerned, is to enable them to question the past management of the company, to exercise their voting rights, and to influence future policy and management. Advice to individual shareholders in relation to present or future investment in the company is no part of this purpose."*

The principles laid down by the House of Lords in the *Caparo* case have been applied by the Court of Appeal in two further cases within a very short period of time. In the first of the two, *Caparo* was distinguished.

In *Morgan Crucible Co. Plc v. Hill Samuel Bank Ltd. and Others* 1991 the plaintiff announced a take-over bid for a company called First Castle Electronics plc. First Castle recommended it shareholders not to accept the bid, and issued a number of documents to its shareholders intended to encourage them to retain their shares in order to defend the company from the proposed take-over. One of the defence documents forecast an increase in profits of 38% for the financial year and included a letter from the accountants stating that the profit forecast had been properly compiled. Shortly afterwards the plaintiff increased its bid and succeeded in acquiring First Castle. Subsequently the plaintiff sued claiming that the accounting policies adopted in the profit forecast were negligently misleading and grossly overstated the profits. On an appeal relating to the preliminary issue of whether a duty of care could arise in these circumstances, the Court of Appeal held that it could on the basis that if during a contested take-over bid the directors and financial advisers of the target company made express representations after an identified bidder had emerged, intending that the bidder would rely on those representations, they owed the bidder a duty of care not to mislead him.

In the second of the two cases, the *Caparo* decision was applied.

In *James McNaughton Papers Group Ltd. v. Hicks Anderson & Co.* 1991 the plaintiff was negotiating an agreed take-over of a loss making rival company, MK Papers. The defendants were accountants for MK. At MK's request draft accounts were quickly prepared for use in the negotiations. During a meeting between the plaintiff and MK, a representative of the defendants stated, in answer to a question, that as a result of rationalisation MK was breaking even or doing marginally worse. After the take-over was completed the plaintiff discovered discrepancies in the draft accounts and sued the defendants in negligence. The Court of Appeal, applying principles laid down in *Caparo*, held that the defendants did not owe a duty of care to the plaintiff, in particular because the accounts were produced for use by MK and not the plaintiff, they were merely draft accounts and the defendants could not reasonably have foreseen that the plaintiff would treat them as final accounts. The defendants did not take part in the negotiations, and the plaintiff was aware that MK was in a poor state and could be expected to consult their own accountant. Further it could not reasonably be foreseen that the plaintiff would rely on the answer given to the question without further inquiry or advice, particularly because the answer was in very general terms.

The legal profession

The legal profession in the UK is divided into two distinct branches with solicitors and barristers having different but overlapping roles within in the legal process. In relation to that part of their work which involves the presentation of cases before a court, members of both branches of the legal profession enjoy an immunity from liability for professional negligence, for reasons which we will consider below. This immunity is of particular significance for the barrister, as most of his work will involve advocacy in the courts.

Barristers

In *Rondel v. Worsley* 1967 the plaintiff, who had been convicted of causing grievous bodily harm, sued his barrister for professional negligence. He claimed that the defendant barrister had failed to take reasonable care in the conduct of his criminal defence and that he would have been acquitted if the case had been properly handled. The House of Lords held that the plaintiff's claim failed. A barrister's conduct of a case in court could never give rise to a claim in negligence.

The decision was made on the grounds of public policy. It would be contrary to the public interest to allow such a claim for the following reasons:

(a)   A barrister owes a duty not only to his client but also to the court, for example he has a duty not to mislead the court. These twin duties could, on occasion, conflict with each other. He should not be placed, under the pressure of a potential negligence claim, in a position in which he might be tempted to disregard his duty to the court.

(b)   A finding of negligence would necessarily involve a finding that the case in question had been wrongly decided. Thus the negligence proceedings would amount to a retrial of the original case and cast uncertainty on the finality of the previous decision.

(c)   The judge in the original case has a duty to ensure a fair trial and will intervene if necessary to ensure that all of the relevant issues are properly considered.

(d)   Barristers operate under the so-called cab rank principle which means that they have no choice but to accept a client provided the proper fee is paid.

The immunity of the barrister in these circumstances was said by the majority of the Law Lords in *Rondel's* case to extend to solicitors engaged in litigation before the courts.

The scope of the barrister's immunity was further considered by the House of Lords in *Saif Ali v. Sydney Mitchell & Co*. 1978. A barrister failed to advise the plaintiff to bring proceedings against the correct defendant in a personal injuries claim within the three year limitation period. The House of Lords held that the barrister was not immune from proceedings in negligence in these circumstances because the immunity only extends to matters of pre-trial work which are intimately connected with the conduct of the case in court.

In relation to work carried out by a barrister which is not connected with litigation, for example giving opinions and drawing up wills, he may be liable for professional negligence under the principles laid down by the House of Lords in *Hedley Byrne v. Heller* 1964. However he cannot be sued for breach of contract as he has no contractual relationship with his client.

Solicitors

The extent of the solicitor's immunity under the principles laid down in *Saif Ali* was considered by the Court of Appeal in *Somasundaram v. Julius Melchior & Co*. 1989. The plaintiff claimed that the defendant solicitors had been negligent in over persuading him to plead guilty to the malicious wounding of his wife whom he had stabbed during an argument. The defendant argued that advice as to plea of guilty or not guilty in a criminal case is so intimately connected with the conduct of the case in court as to be covered by immunity. The Court of Appeal accepted this argument and recognised that the immunity applied both to barristers and to solicitors when acting as advocates. However the court did not accept that the immunity applied to a solicitor when a barrister had also been engaged to advise. Despite this finding, the plaintiff did not succeed in his action, as the court also held, as a matter of causation, that the barrister's advice as to plea breaks the chain of causation between the solicitor's advice and the client's plea; and in any event an action for negligence against a barrister or a solicitor could not be brought where its effect would be to challenge the decision of a court of competent jurisdiction.

A solicitors may be liable in negligence to a third party with whom he has no contract:

In *Ross v. Caunters* 1979, for example, a solicitor drew up a will and sent it out for his client to sign. The solicitor gave instructions for the signing and witnessing of the will but forgot to warn his client that if the will was witnessed by a beneficiary or the spouse of a beneficiary then the gift would be invalidated. The will was witnessed by the husband of the plaintiff and the mistake was not discovered until after the client's death. The plaintiff, who was a beneficiary under the will, lost her gift and sued the solicitor for the financial loss caused by his negligence. It was held that the solicitor owed a duty of care to the plaintiff and was liable as his failure to take care had caused her loss.

Whether the courts will recognise the existence of a duty of care in tort where there is a contract between the parties is now an open point.

In *Midland Bank Trust Co. Ltd v. Hett, Stubbs and Kemp* 1979 the defendant solicitors carelessly failed to register as a land charge an option to purchase a farm granted to their client. The client's right to exercise the option to purchase was defeated, because of the failure to register, on the sale of the farm to a third party. The client sued in negligence and the court held that the solicitors were in breach of their duty of care to the client both in contract and in tort under the *Hedley Byrne* principle. It was essential to the success of the claim that the court recognised the existence of a duty in tort in addition to the contractual duty. This is because the plaintiff's claim in contract was statute-barred under the Limitation Act as more than six years had elapsed since the breach of contract by the solicitors. The limitation period in the tort of negligence, however, does not begin to run until the damage has occurred, in this case the date on which the farm was sold to the third party. As this was within six years of the commencement of proceedings in this case, the claim in negligence was not time-barred.

It appears that the approach taken by the High Court in the *Midland Bank Trust* case may no longer be sustainable. Although there has not been a further decision specifically on the point, a number of recent cases strongly suggest that the courts are unwilling to recognise the existence of liability in tort where the relationship between the parties is based on contract.

In *Tai Hing Cotton Mills v. Liu Chong Hing Bank Ltd.* 1986, a decision of the Privy Council, Lord Scarman stated *"Their Lordships do not believe that there is anything to the advantage of the law's development in searching for a liability in tort where the parties are in a contractual relationship."*

A similar approach was adopted more recently by the Court of Appeal in *National Bank of Greece SA v. Pinios Shipping Co. The Maria* 1989 where the court took the view that, in the words of Lloyd, L.J *"if the plaintiff fails in contract, he must necessarily fail in tort"*.

The important decision of the House of Lords in *White and another v. Jones and others* 1995 considered the potential liability of the defendant solicitors who caused the plaintiff's financial loss as a result of a negligent omission. The plaintiffs had originally been cut out of their father's (the testator) will but then reinstated on the testator's instructions to the defendant solicitors. The solicitors had delayed in carrying out the instructions to change the will for over six weeks and unfortunately, meanwhile, the testator died. As there was no contractual relationship between the plaintiffs and the defendants the action for financial loss could only be based on the tort of negligence. The central issue in the dispute was whether a solicitor in drafting a will owes a legal duty of care in the tort of negligence to a potential beneficiary. The High Court thought not. This decision was reversed on appeal and the solicitors then made a final appeal to the House of Lords. By a three to two majority decision their Lordships held that the potential loss to the plaintiffs in these circumstances was reasonably foreseeable and the relationship of a solicitor, called upon to draft a will, and the potential beneficiary, should be brought within the established categories of relationship under which a duty of care arises. This duty of care had been broken by the solicitor's negligence causing financial loss for which the defendants were liable.

Consumer Protection in relation to Package Holidays

The Package Travel, Package Holidays and Package Tours Regulations 1992, which we shall call the Package Travel Regulations came into force in December 1992 and are designed to implement the EC directive on Package Travel, Package Holidays and Package Tours (90/314/EEC). The regulations introduce a fairly comprehensive set of rules covering package travel and package holidays which are designed to protect the consumer. A number of the matters covered by the regulations were previously dealt with in the ABTA codes of practice for travel agents and tour operators, although the new regulations go much further in protecting the consumer.

The regulations apply to packages sold or offered for sale in the United Kingdom and, unlike the ABTA codes, apply to domestic packages as well as overseas travel arrangements. The concept of a package is central to the application of the regulations. Only if the travel arrangements fall within the definition of a package will the many elements of consumer protection contained within the regulations apply. A package is defined as:

"The pre-arranged combination of at least two of the following components when sold or offered for sale at an inclusive price and when the service covers a period of more than 24 hours or includes overnight accommodation:

a.   transport

b.   accommodation

c.   other tourist services not ancillary to transport or accommodation and accounting for a significant proportion of the package, and

i.   the submission of separate accounts for different components shall not cause the arrangements to be other than a package,

ii.   the fact that a combination is arranged at the request of the consumer and in accordance with his specific instructions (whether modified or not) shall not of itself cause it to be treated as other than pre-arranged"

In order to come within the regulations, the travel arrangements must be *pre-arranged*. This would obviously include the packages which can be bought off-the-shelf, for example a fortnight in Majorca selected from a tour operators brochure. It also includes tailor made travel arrangements put together to meet the needs of a particular client, provided that the arrangements are put together before the conclusion of the contract. The package must be sold at an *inclusive price*. If a customer books travel and accommodation through a travel agent, for example, and pays the travel agent for his air ticket, but pays the hotel direct at the end of his stay, this is not a package and the regulations do not apply. As an anti-avoidance measure, the definition makes clear that the separate invoicing of the individual elements does not of itself prevent the creation of a package. Where transport and accommodation are combined, then provided that the arrangements last for at least 24 hours or include overnight accommodation, a package will come into being. However, if one of these elements is missing, the arrangements must include *other tourist services* which are not ancillary to transport or accommodation and which account for a significant proportion of the package. The other services provided here must be tourist services and not, for example, educational services. If a language summer school is advertised including accommodation and modern language tuition, but excluding transport, this combination is not of itself enough to create a package. The other tourist services must account for a significant proportion of the package. This would not be the case, for example, where a guest could use a swimming pool at a hotel as this is a facility which goes with the use of the hotel and not another tourist service. Neither would it usually be significant.

The person or organisation who puts together the package is known as the *organiser*. This will usually be a tour operator, although the travel agent will come within the definition of organiser where he puts together a package for his customers. This will be so even though the customer may end up with individual direct contracts with the providers of the components that make up the package. The expression *consumer* within the regulations includes the person who takes or agrees to take the package, any person on whose behalf the package is purchased, and any person to whom the package is transferred. This third category of consumer arises because the regulations introduce a new *right to transfer a booking* where the original consumer is *prevented* from proceeding with the package. This may occur for example, due to illness or jury service although the consumer will not be regarded as being prevented from proceeding if he simply changes his mind. The person to whom the package is transferred must satisfy all the conditions applicable to the package, and reasonable notice must be given of the intention to transfer.

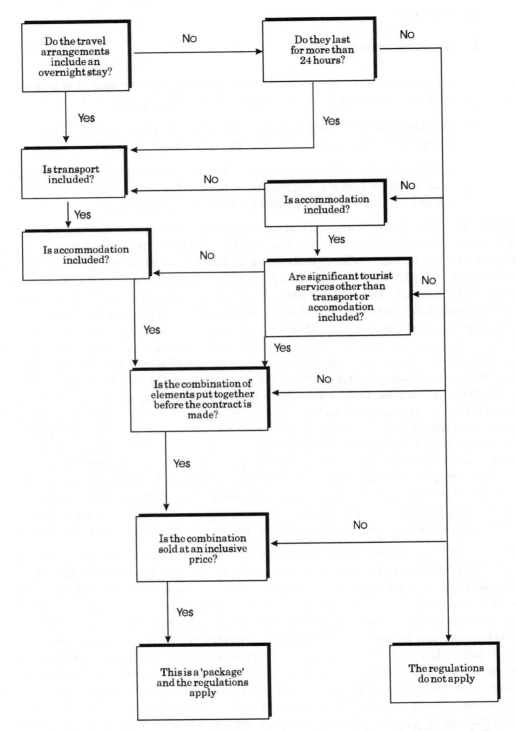

Figure 13.3   The Package Travel Regulations - When do they apply?

Consumer rights contained in the regulations

Regulation 4 gives the consumer the right to sue for compensation where he suffers loss as a result of any misleading description relating to a package or misleading information as to its price. This new right arises in circumstances where an offence would be committed by a trader under s.14 of the Trade Descriptions Act 1968 or s.20 of the Consumer Protection Act 1987, although r.4 is wider in its scope as it applies both to those operating in the course of business and to those who are not. The criminal offences only apply to misleading information which is supplied knowingly or recklessly whereas the regulation applies to information which is misleading even if it is not applied knowingly or recklessly.

Under r.5 it is a criminal offence for an organiser or retailer to make a brochure available to a prospective consumer unless the description of the package in the brochure indicates in an understandable and accurate manner both the price and certain key information relating to the package. This would include:

- the destination and the type of transport used;
- the type of accommodation, its location, degree of comfort and main features;
- the meals which are included;
- the itinerary;
- general information about passports, visas and health formalities;
- when the deposit and balance of the price is due, and
- the arrangements for security for money paid and for repatriation of the consumer in the event of insolvency.

Under r.6 the particulars in a brochure constitute implied warranties for the purposes of any contract to which they relate. Where the brochure states that the information in it may change and the changes are clearly communicated before the contract is made then these will override inconsistent statements in the brochure. Under r.7 a retailer or organiser will be guilty of a criminal offence if they do not provide the intending customer with information in writing or in some other appropriate form about passport and visa requirements, health formalities and the arrangements for the security of money paid over and for the repatriation of the consumer in the event of insolvency. This information must be supplied before the contract is concluded.

It is also a criminal offence, under r.8, to fail to provide the consumer in good time before the start of the journey with written information about the journey and the arrangements for assistance from representatives of the organiser and contact names in the event of difficulties on the tour.

It is an implied condition of the contract that all of its terms should be communicated to the consumer before the contract is made. This does not apply where circumstances make it impracticable, for example in the case of last minute bookings. In any event a written copy of the contract must be supplied to the consumer. The written terms must comply with the regulations and contain certain minimum information. This is similar to, but more detailed than, the information which must be included in a brochure under r.5.

The regulations limit the organiser's ability to increase the price of the package by way of a surcharge. If the contract contains such a clause, it will be void unless the contract allows for the possibility of a price reduction as well as an increase. The contract must state precisely how the revised price is to be calculated. Price changes can only be made to reflect changes in transport or fuel costs, exchange rates, taxes or fees. In any event no price increase may be made in the period of 30 days before departure and the tour operator must always absorb the first 2% of an increase.

If where the organiser, within the terms of the contract, wishes to make a significant alteration to an important term, such as the price, he must notify the consumer as quickly as possible. The consumer will have the option to withdraw from the contract without penalty or to accept the change. If the consumer does withdraw then he is entitled to take an available substitute package of the equivalent quality; a full refund or a lower quality substitute package coupled with a rebate.

Where the organiser is in breach of contract because a significant proportion of the services contracted for are not provided he must make suitable alternative arrangements at no extra cost to the consumer for the continuation of the package. If it is not possible to make such arrangements or if the consumer validly refuses to accept them the organiser must provide the consumer with equivalent transport home or to another destination with the consumers agreement. The organiser may still be liable to compensate the consumer for the difference between the services contracted for and those supplied.

The regulations also make detailed provision for the protection of the consumer in the event of the insolvency of the tour operator or organiser. He is required at all times to be able to provide sufficient evidence of security for the refund of money paid in advance and for the repatriation of the consumer in the event of insolvency. This is important as booking conditions for package holidays will almost invariably require full payment by the consumer eight weeks before departure, and because it provides protection for the holiday maker who would otherwise be stranded abroad if the tour operator becomes insolvent while they are on holiday. This protection is further enhanced by the licensing and bonding requirements in the regulations.

Tour operator's liability

When booking a package holiday, the consumer makes a contract with a tour operator. This contract is usually made through a travel agent, though in the case of direct sell operators the contract may be made without the use of an intermediary. Where a travel agent is involved he will bring together the parties to the contract in return for a commission paid by the tour operator. In accordance with the ordinary principles of the law of agency, the travel agent will not himself be a party to the contract. The tour operator puts together the various elements of the package such as flights, transfers from airport to hotel, hotel accommodation and food; and sells them together as one product. The tour operator will enter into separate contracts with the suppliers of the component parts of the package. In addition to the elements already noted, the package may include other items such as car hire, excursions, tickets for events and holiday insurance, although these may be optional extras.

Where the consumer books a package holiday he is contracting only with the tour operator and has no direct contract with the suppliers of individual components of the holiday. The terms of the contract with the tour operator are set out in the brochure, though not necessarily all on the same page. There will usually be at least one page of general booking conditions, sometimes referred to as a fair trading charter, often towards the back of the brochure. These must be read in conjunction with the information on the booking form itself, and the information in the main body of the brochure about the particular hotel and resort chosen by the consumer which is entered onto the booking form with the holiday dates and the price.

The tour operator may be liable to pay damages to a dissatisfied consumer if facilities described in the brochure are not available, for example where the consumer books a room in a particular hotel which is specified as having a balcony overlooking the sea and bathroom facilities en suite and this turns out not to be the case. The tour operator may incur criminal liability under s.14 Trade Descriptions Act 1968 in these circumstances. The tour operator's civil liability for damages will be based upon the breach of an express term of the contract.

> In *Jackson v. Horizon Holidays* 1975 the plaintiff had booked a month's holiday in Ceylon staying in an hotel. The defendant's brochure described the hotel facilities. These included a swimming pool, a mini golf course and a hair-dressing salon. The hotel in fact had none of these facilities and the food was poor. The plaintiff's children's room was unusable due to mildew and fungus on the walls, and the sanitary facilities were dirty. The Court of Appeal awarded damages of £1,100 to the plaintiff for breach of contract. This was made up of £600 for the reduction in the value of the holiday and £500 damages for mental distress, vexation and disappointment.

> In *Jarvis v. Swans Tours Ltd.* 1973 the plaintiff booked a skiing holiday which was described in the defendant's brochure as a house party in Morlialp. The price included a number of house party arrangements, a welcome party on arrival, afternoon tea and cake, Swiss dinner by candle-light, fondue party, yodel evening, and a farewell party. The brochure also stated that ski packs could be hired in Morlialp, the hotel owner spoke English and the hotel bar would be open several evenings a week. In the first week of the holiday the house party comprised only 13 people, and in the second week the plaintiff was the only guest at the hotel. The hotel owner did not speak English, the bar was only open on one evening, and the plaintiff was unable to hire full length skis except for two days during the second week. The Court of Appeal held that the quality of holiday provided fell far short of that which was promised in the brochure and awarded damages to the plaintiff. This included damages representing the difference between what the plaintiff had paid for the holiday and what he had been supplied with; as well as damages for mental distress, frustration, annoyance and disappointment.

The tour operator may also be liable for breach of an implied term in the contract. As a provider of services in the course of a business, s.13 of the Supply of Goods and Services Act 1982 applies to the tour operator, and implies a term in the contract between him and the consumer that he will use reasonable care and skill in carrying out the contract.

> In *Davey v. Cosmos Air Holidays* 1989 the plaintiff booked a two weeks' package holiday in the Algarve for himself and his family. During the holiday the entire family suffered diarrhoea and the plaintiff's wife and son both contracted dysentery. The evidence showed that the illness was caused by a general lack of hygiene at the resort and the fact that raw sewage was being pumped into the sea just fifty yards from the beach. The defendant tour operators had resident representatives at the resort who knew of the dangers. It was

held that the defendants were liable for breach of the implied duty in the contract to take reasonable care to avoid exposing their clients to a significant risk of injury to their health.

The tour operator will not be liable merely because the consumer has suffered injury, provided the tour operator has taken reasonable care. In the Davey case, for example, Cosmos would not have been liable had they warned the plaintiffs of the risks and advised them as to the steps to take to avoid injury.

A tour operator has a duty to exercise reasonable care and skill in selecting the suppliers of components of the package. In order to fulfil this duty he should, for example, undertake thorough inspections of the hotels, not only to verify the availability of facilities for inclusion in the brochure but also to satisfy himself as to the standards of kitchen hygiene, general safety, sanitary conditions and such things as fire escapes.

In *Wilson v. Best Travel Ltd.* 1993 the plaintiff suffered serious injuries after tripping and falling through glass patio doors at an hotel in Greece. The glass doors were fitted with 4mm glass which complied with Greek safety standards but would not have met equivalent British standards. The plaintiff claimed damages against the defendant tour operators, arguing that the hotel was not reasonably safe for use by the defendants' customers and that they were in breach of their duty of care under s.13 of the Supply and Goods and Services Act 1982. It was held that the tour operators were not liable. They had discharged their contractual duty of care by checking that local safety regulations had been complied with. It was not necessary for them to ensure that the Greek hotel came up to English safety standards provided that the absence of a relevant safety feature was not such that a reasonable holiday maker might decline to take a holiday at the hotel in question. This could be the case, for example, if the hotel had no fire precautions at all even though they were not required under local law.

In *Wall v. Silver Wing Surface Arrangements Ltd. (trading as Enterprise Holidays)* 1981 the plaintiff holiday maker was injured as a result of the fact that the management at his hotel had locked the fire exit. The evidence showed that the fire escape had not been locked when it was inspected by the defendants. It was locked on the occasion in question for security reasons to prevent unauthorised access into the hotel. It was held that the defendants were not liable as they had exercised reasonable care in selecting a suitable hotel and checking that the safety arrangements were satisfactory. The court rejected the plaintiff's argument that the tour operator had an implied contractual duty to ensure that the plaintiff would be reasonably safe in the hotel. The duty to take reasonable care in selecting the hotel had been fulfilled and the tour operator was not liable.

In *Wan (Wong Mee) v. K Wan Kin Travel Services Ltd* 1994 the Privy Council considered the scope of the responsibility of a tour operator who puts a package holiday together by arranging services for the client. Here a tour was arranged of mainland China by a Hong Kong travel company the price to include *"transportation"* as specified in the itinerary. An employee of another travel company engaged as a contractor organised a speedboat to ferry the tour group across a lake and as a result of negligent driving the speedboat crashed and the plaintiff's daughter was drowned. The Hong Kong Court of

Appeal agreed with the lower court that the second travel company as contractor and the speedboats owner were liable in negligence, but not the tour operator. The court said that to impose liability for a non-delegatable primary contractual duty would be an intolerable burden on a company putting a package tour together. On further appeal however the Privy Council held that the tour operator was liable. The court drew a distinction between situations where a person agrees as an agent to arrange for services to be provided by some third party and those in which he undertakes to supply the services and then arranges for another to do the work. This was the position here and *"the fact that the supplier of services may under the contract arrange for some or all of them to be performed by others does not absolve the supplier from his contractual obligation"*. He may be liable if the service is performed without the exercise of due care and skill on the part of the subcontractor just as he would be liable if the sub-contractor failed to provide the service or failed to provide it in accordance with the terms of the contract. If a person undertaking to supply the services performs them himself, that he must do so with reasonable skill and care, and if, where the contract permits him to do so, he arranges for others to supply the services, that they should be supplied with reasonable skill and care.

The above decision is a reflection of the Package Tours Regulations 1992 which of course do not apply in Hong Kong. A tour operator who puts together a package by arranging services should require an indemnity from the supplier and/or rely on insurance cover.

In circumstances where the tour operator is not shown to have been negligent, the consumer may be left with the difficult task of suing the hotel. As we have seen there is no contract between the consumer and the hotel. The claim could not therefore be based in contract. A major problem for the consumer is that the hotelier's liability will depend on the national law of the country in which the hotel is situated, and whether an equivalent of the English law of third party negligence exists there. There is the additional expense and inconvenience of having to take legal action in a foreign country with an unfamiliar legal system and perhaps in a foreign language.

The consumer's rights in this situation have been greatly improved as a result of the implementation of the Package Travel Directive by the Package Travel Regulations 1992. Under r.15 the tour operator is legally responsible to the consumer for the proper performance of the obligations arising under the contract, and it does not matter whether the obligations are to be performed by the tour operator or by other suppliers of services. The tour operator is liable to the consumer for any damage caused by the improper performance of the contract by any of his suppliers. This new right to sue the tour operator where, for example, the consumer is injured by the negligence of the hotelier means that the consumer's position is made much easier as he does not have to face the problems involved in suing abroad. If the consumer is successful in his claim, the tour operator will be able to seek an indemnity from his supplier and unlike the consumer who has no contract with the supplier, the tour operator will be able to base his claim on a breach of contract. Thus in a case such as *Wall v. Silver Wing* the tour operator would be liable to the plaintiff, and in turn would seek an indemnity from the hotel. In *Wilson v. Best*, however, it is probable that the consumer's claim would still fail on the grounds that the supplier had properly performed the contract.

The tour operator will have a defence to a claim by a consumer under r.15 if he can show that the failures in the performance of the contract are attributable to the consumer himself or are unforeseeable or unavoidable and caused by a third party. In such circumstances, except where the problems are entirely due to the consumer, the tour operator still has a duty to render prompt assistance to the consumer.

The tour operator is permitted to limit his liability in line with the levels of compensation provided for in international conventions such as the Warsaw Convention in respect of international flights.

He is also permitted to limit his contractual liability to the consumer for damage other than personal injury, provided that the limitation is not unreasonable. This is in line with the provisions of s.2 Unfair Contract Terms Act 1977, except that the regulations only permit a limitation and not a total exclusion of this liability.

Where the consumer experiences problems when he is actually on the package holiday or tour, he has a duty under r.15 to communicate his complaint to the organiser where he considers that it arises from defective performance of the contract by a component supplier, for example where the hotel room which has been allocated to him is unsatisfactory or is significantly inferior to that which was described in the brochure. The organiser, or his local representative, must then make prompt efforts to resolve the problems in an appropriate way.

Trade Descriptions Offences in relation to Services

In Chapter 12 we examined the scope of a trader's criminal liability for false descriptions of goods and misleading price indications, the statutory defences available to a person charged with a Trade Descriptions Act offence, and the mechanisms for enforcement of this legislation. We shall now consider the issue of criminal liability for false or misleading statements relating to the supply of services. This is provided for in s.14 Trade Descriptions Act 1968. Before examining this important provision we may note firstly that the offence in s.20 Consumer Protection Act 1987 of giving a misleading price indication applies in the same way to services as it does to goods; and secondly that the statutory defences referred to in Chapter 12 are available to a trader charged with an offence under s.14.

False statements relating to the provision of services, accommodation or facilities

Suppliers of services, such as holiday tour operators, hairdressers and dry cleaners will be liable to prosecution under s.14 of the Trade Descriptions Act 1968 if they make false statements knowingly or recklessly in the course of their business.

> In *Ashley v. Sutton LBC* 1995 the supply of a betting strategy contained in a book was held to be the provision of a service rather than a supply of goods so that a false statement in relation to a refund guarantee fell within s.14 of the Act.

Under s.14(1):

"It shall be an offence for any person in the course of any trade or business:

> (a)   *to make a statements which he knows to be false; or*

> (b)   *recklessly to make a statement which is false;as to any of the following matters:*

(i)   *the provision ... of any services, accommodation or facilities;*

(ii)   *the nature of any services, accommodation or facilities*

(iii) *the time at which, the manner in which or persons by whom any services, accommodation or facilities are provided;*

(iv)   *the examination, approval or evaluation by any person of any services, accommodation or facilities;or*

(v)   *the location or amenities of any accommodation*

In order to obtain a conviction under s.14, the prosecution must show *mens rea,* (guilty mind) either that the trader knew that the statement was false, or that he was *reckless* as to its truth or falsity. A statement is made recklessly if it is made regardless of whether it is true or false. It need not necessarily be dishonest. The knowledge or recklessness must be present at the time the statement is made.

In *Sunair Holidays Ltd. v. Dodd* 1970 the defendant's travel brochure described a package holiday in a hotel with *"all twin bedded rooms with bath, shower and terrace"*. The defendant had a contract with the hotel owners under which they were obliged to provide accommodation of that description. A customer who booked the package was given a room without a terrace. The defendant had not checked with the hotel to make sure that its customers were given the correct accommodation of that description. It was held however, that the statement was not false when it was made, and therefore the defendant was not guilty of an offence under s.14.

It must be shown that the trader, at the time the statement is made, either knows that it is false or is reckless as to its truth or falsity; and that the statement actually *is* false. Subsequent developments are irrelevant if these elements are present at the time the statement is made.

In *Cowburn v. Focus Television Rentals Ltd.* 1983 the defendant's advertisement stated: *"Hire 20 feature films absolutely free when you rent a video recorder"*. In response to the advertisement a customer rented a video recorder. The documentation supplied with it indicated that he was entitled only to 6 films, and that they were not absolutely free because he had to pay postage and packing. When he complained, the defendant refunded his postage and packing and supplied 20 free films to him. It was held that the defendant was guilty of an offence under s.14 because the statement in his advertisement was false and recklessly made. The fact that he subsequently honoured the advertisement provided no defence, as this was done after the offence had been committed.

Conduct of the defendant subsequent to the false statement is relevant however to determine whether an inference of recklessness can be maintained.

In *Yugotours Ltd. v. Wadsley* 1988 the fact that statements in a holiday brochure were clearly false and known to be so by the company meant that when the company failed to correct the statement, it was guilty of an offence. The court stated that there was sufficient material before the court to infer recklessness on the part of the maker of the statement. *"If a statement is false and known to be false, and nothing whatever is done to correct it, then the company making the statement can properly be found guilty of recklessness notwithstanding the absence of specific evidence of recklessness".*

In *Wings Ltd. v. Ellis* 1984 the false nature of a statement in their travel brochure was not known by a tour operator when its brochure was published. Some 250,000 copies of the brochure contained an inaccurate statement that rooms in a hotel in Sri Lanka were air conditioned. The brochure also contained a photograph purporting to be a room in the same hotel which was of a room in a different hotel. When the mistake was discovered, reasonable steps were taken to remedy it by informing agents and customers who had already booked by letter. Despite this, a holiday was booked by a customer on the basis of the false information. It was held by the House of Lords that the tour operator was guilty of an offence under s.14 because the statement was made when the brochure was read by the customer, and at the time the defendant knew that it was false. The fact that the tour operator was unaware that the uncorrected statement was being made to the customer did not prevent the offence being committed. As a result of this judgment the offence under s.1(1)(a) has been described rather crudely as a *"half mens rea offence"*. Knowledge that a statement is false is necessary but there is no need to show mens rea as to the making of the statement.

For corporate liability under s.14 the prosecution must establish that a high ranking official of the company had the necessary mens rea. The Chairman of a company would certainly suffice but not the *"Contracts Manager"* in *Wings Ltd. v. Ellis* who had approved the photograph of the hotel which gave a wrong impression.

The Property Misdescriptions Act 1991

The Property Misdescriptions Act was passed in 1991 although it did not come into force until April 1993. The Act, which imposes criminal liability for making false statements in relation to the sale of residential and commercial land and buildings, is similar in many respects of the Trade Descriptions Act 1968, although there are several significant differences.

The main offence is set out in s.1(1) which states:

> *"Where a false or misleading statement about a prescribed matter is made in the course of an estate agency business or a property development business... the person by whom the business is carried on shall be guilty of an offence".*

The offence only applies to statements made in the course of an estate agency business or a property development business. Those made by a private seller or a seller in a different line of business are not caught by the Act. Statements made in the course of providing conveyancing services, for example by solicitors or licensed conveyancers, are also outside the scope of the offence. The offence covers statements made by estate agents in advertisements or in written particulars describing a property for sale. It also applies to statements made in the course of a property development business. This covers builders of new commercial and residential premises and those who renovate old properties to sell. The Act does not apply, however, where property is being advertised for rent rather than for sale.

In order for an offence to be committed, the false or misleading statement must be about a prescribed matter. The Property Misdescriptions (Specified Matters) Order 1993 sets out a long list of prescribed matters, including the price, structural characteristics, accommodation, size, outlook or environment, view, proximity to any services, or the results of any survey. The expression *statement* covers pictures as well as written and spoken words. Statements will be regarded false under the Act if they are *false to a material degree*. It will be a question of fact in the circumstances of each case as to whether a statement is materially false. A statement which is not false may nevertheless be misleading if a reasonable person would be likely to draw a false conclusion as a result of it, for example where a half truth is told.

The offence will be committed by the person who carries on the estate agency or property development business. Where the business is carried on by a limited company, the company's senior officers are liable where the offence was committed with their consent or connivance or was attributable to neglect on their part. Where the making of the statement is due to the act of default of an employee the employee is guilty of an offence and may be prosecuted independently of the employer.

It will be a defence under s.2(1) for any defendant to show that he took all reasonable steps and exercised all due diligence to avoid committing the offence. This is similar to the defence available under s.24 of the Trade Descriptions Act 1968. The defendant needs to show that he has an effective system in place which is designed to ensure that offences are not committed.

Where the defendant seeks to rely on information given by another person in his defence, s.2(1) provides that he can only do so if it was reasonable in all the circumstances for him to have relied on that other person. In this context regard shall be had to the steps which the defendant took or might reasonably had taken in order to verify the information; and whether he had any reason to disbelieve the information. Thus an estate agent can not safely take at face value statements which are made by his client about the property where he ought reasonably to take steps to verify the information. Where the defendant is found guilty he may be punished by a fine of up to £5,000 in the Magistrates Court, or an unlimited fine in the Crown Court. In 1993 Mr. Ian Sinclair, an estate agent in Great Yarmouth, was the first person to be prosecuted under the Property Misdescriptions Act. He was fined £500 with costs of £570 after advertising a property for sale in both a newspaper advertisement and his window at a lower price than that actually quoted in the sales particulars.

Data Protection Act 1984

The widespread use of computers in modern society has meant than an increasing amount of information, much of it about individuals, is collected and stored in computer files by business, the public sector and other organisations. This has given rise to concern about issues such as individual privacy, the possible damage that can arise if errors are made and incorrect information is held about someone, and the use to which information may be put.

The Data Protection Act 1984 provides a legal framework governing the collection, storage and distribution of *personal data,* information relating to identifiable living individuals where this is done using computers. The Act does not, however, apply to records or information held in paper files; or to information about a company or any other body which is not an individual.

The Act provides for the registration and supervision by the Data Protection Registrar of *data users*, that is people and organisations who hold and use personal data; and of *computer bureaux*, people or organisations who process personal data for others or who allow others to use their equipment for this purpose. Certain categories of information, however, are exempt from the workings of the Act, for example, data held by a club about its members in certain circumstances. Other categories of information are subject to a partial exemption, for example, information which is held by the police in relation to crime detection. These are examined below. The Act gives a number of important rights to *data subjects*, the individuals about whom the information is processed. They have the right to know what information is held by the data user relating to themselves and to a copy of that information, a right to have inaccurate information corrected or erased, and a right to sue for compensation for loss or damage caused by the inaccuracy of personal data, or by its loss or unauthorised destruction or disclosure. More generally the individual has the right to complain to the Data Protection Registrar if he feels that the Act has not been complied with in some way as the Registrar has a duty to enforce the Act as a whole. A complaint may be based, for example, upon a failure by a data user to observe the *data protection principles* which are set out in the Act and which are central to its operation. The principles give a guide to good practice in the processing of personal data and are designed to safeguard the rights of data subjects. The Registrar has a number of powers available to him to secure compliance with the data protection principles.

Registration

The Registrar maintains a registrar of data users and computer bureaux. Under the Act every data user who holds personal data is required to register unless all of the personal data which he holds is exempt. The information which is contained in the registration will include:

    a.   the name and address of the data user;

    b.   a description of the personal data to be held by him and the purposes for which they are to be held or used;

    c.   a description of the sources from which he intends or may wish to obtain the information contained in the data;

    d.   a description of any person to whom he intends to disclose the information;

    e.   the names of the countries outside the U.K. to which he may wish to transfer the data; and

    f.   the address for the receipt of requests from data subjects for access to the data.

Once the registration is made the data user must operate strictly within its terms. He will commit a criminal offence if he holds personal data of a type or for a purpose which is not specified in the registration, or if he obtains data from unregistered sources. Similarly if he discloses personal data to any person not described in the registration or transfers it to another country which has not been specified. The data user may alter the terms of the registration if this becomes necessary. This could occur, for example, if he finds that he wishes to disclose information to people or organisations which are not specified in the original registration. In any event the registration lasts only for three years after which is must be renewed and alterations can be made on renewal.

A computer bureau must also be registered if it provides services relating to the processing of personal data, although no registration is necessary if all of the data is exempt. The register entry will comprise only the name and address of the computer bureau.

The Registrar must provide facilities for making the information contained in the register available for public inspection by anyone at all reasonable hours and free of charge, and must supply a copy of the particulars contained in an entry on the register, although he may charge a fee for this.

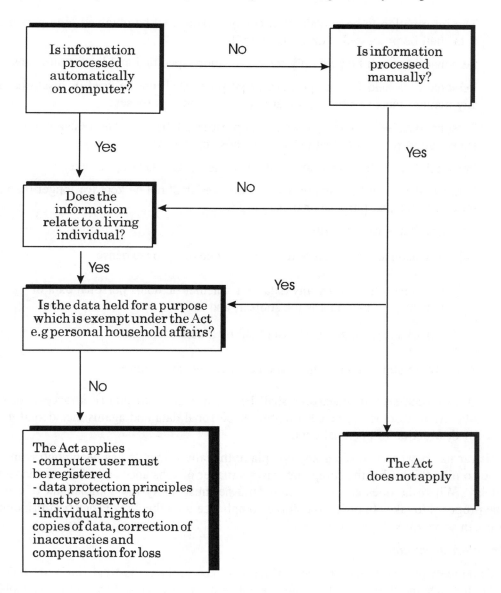

Figure 13.4   Data Protection Act 1984: when does it apply?

The Data Protection Principles

The Act lays down eight Data Protection Principles which are intended to govern the way in which data users deal with personal data. Data users are required to observe all of the principles, but only the eighth principle, relating to security, applies to computer bureaux. The Data Protection Principles set out a framework of good practice which computer users must follow. They are as follows:

1. The information to be contained in personal data shall be obtained, and personal data shall be processed, fairly and lawfully.

2. Personal data shall be held only for one or more specified and lawful purposes.

3. Personal data held for any purpose or purposes shall not be used or disclosed in any manner incompatible with that purpose or those purposes.

4. Personal data held for any purpose or purposes shall be adequate, relevant, and not excessive in relation to that purpose or those purposes.

5. Personal data shall be accurate, and where necessary, kept up to date.

6. Personal data held for any purpose or purposes shall not be kept for longer than is necessary for that purpose or those purposes.

7. An individual shall be entitled:

    (a) at reasonable intervals and without undue delay or expense

        (i) to be informed by any data user whether he holds personal data of which that individual is the subject; and

        (ii) to access to any such data held by a data user; and

    (b) where appropriate to have such data corrected or erased.

8. Appropriate security measures shall be taken against unauthorised access to, or alteration, disclosure, or destruction of, personal data and against accidental loss or destruction of personal data.

The Registrar has power to consider any complaint that any principle has been contravened and a duty to do so if he thinks that the complaint raises a matter of substance and has been made without undue delay. Where he does consider a complaint he must notify the complainant of any action which he proposes to take. In order to enforce compliance with the Data Protection Principles, the Registrar can serve three types of notice:

An enforcement notice.

This notice will specify the principle which has been broken, the Registrar's grounds for believing this and the steps which must be taken in order to comply with the principle. The notice will give a time limit within which action must be taken. This will usually be at least

28 days, though in cases of urgency it can be as little as 7 days. Failure to comply with an enforcement notice is a criminal offence.

A de-registration notice.

This will be served where the Registrar is satisfied that an enforcement notice will not be effective to secure compliance with the principle or principles in question. The effect of a de-registration notice is to cancel the whole or a part of the data user's register entry. The effect of de-registration is that the data user will be committing a criminal offence if he continues to undertake the activities which were previously covered by the register entry before it was removed.

A transfer prohibition notice.

This has the effect of prohibiting the transfer of personal data to a place outside the United Kingdom and can be served where the Registrar is satisfied that a proposed transfer is likely to lead to a breach of any of the Data Protection Principles. Failure to comply with a transfer prohibition notice is a criminal offence.

There is a right of appeal to the Data Protection Tribunal against the issue of any of the notices described above. The Tribunal may allow an appeal completely or substitute another decision or notice on the grounds of an error in law or on the grounds that the Registrar ought to have exercised his discretion differently.

The Registrar has power to prosecute in the criminal courts where he considers that an offence has been committee under the Act. Where an offender is found guilty, a Magistrates Court may impose a fine not exceeding £2,000 whilst the Crown Court may impose a fine of any amount.

The Individual's right of access

If an individual wishes to know whether a particular data user holds information on computer about him, he must make a request in writing to the data user at the address given in the entry on the register. The individual is entitled to be informed by the data user whether he holds any such personal data and to be supplied with a copy of all of the information which comprises the personal data. The data user may charge a fee of up to £10 for dealing with the request. He has a duty to respond within 40 days of receiving it. However, he need not comply until the fee is paid, although the 40 day period starts to run as soon as the request is made. In certain circumstances the 40 day period does not begin until the data user receives further information from the individual. This includes any information he reasonably requires to satisfy himself as to the identity of the person making the request, any information reasonably required to enable him to locate the data, and/or any consent required from another person where this is necessary. Consent may be required where the nature of the data is such that the data user cannot disclose it without also disclosing information relating to another person who can be identified from the information.

In complying with a request, the data user must supply any data which was held by him at the time the request was received, although amendments or deletions which would normally have been made regardless of the request may still be made by the data user prior to supplying the information. If any of the information is not intelligible without explanation, the data subject must be given an explanation of the information, for example where it is in a coded form.

If the data user fails to reply to a request for access the individual may complain to the Registrar that there has been a breach of the seventh Data Protection Principle. The Registrar may then issue an enforcement notice requiring the data user to give access. If the data user does not comply with the notice he commits a criminal offence. Alternatively, the Registrar could issue a de-registration notice. Rather than complaining to the Registrar, the individual may apply to the court, which has power to order the data user to comply with the request for access and supply the information to the individual. The court will not use this power if it considers that in all the circumstances it would be unreasonable to do so, for example, because of the frequency with which the applicant has made requests for information to the data user.

Where an individual suffers damage due to the inaccuracy of data held by a data user, he is entitled to compensation from the data user for that damage and for any distress which he has suffered as a result. Data are inaccurate if they are incorrect or misleading as to any matter of fact. A statement of opinion cannot give rise to a claim for compensation for inaccuracy even where the individual does not agree with the opinion which is recorded about him. The Registrar does not have the power to award compensation and the individual must take action in the court. It will be a defence for the data user to show that all reasonable care was taken to ensure the accuracy of the data. It will also be a defence to show that the data accurately records information received or obtained from a third party where the data indicates the source of the information and also records any challenge which has been made by the data subject as to the accuracy of the information.

Where an individual has suffered damage because of a loss of personal data by a data user or a computer bureau he can claim compensation against them. It will be a defence to show that all reasonable care was taken to prevent the loss. Similarly if damage has been caused by the unauthorised destruction or disclosure of personal data or because someone has obtained unauthorised access to it, the individual can claim compensation. The defence that all reasonable care was taken also applies in such a case.

In an individual thinks that personal data held about him by a data user is inaccurate he may apply to the court for an order that the data be corrected or erased. The court also has power to order the erasure of data where the individual is entitled to compensation for unauthorised disclosure of the data or unauthorised access to it if it can be shown that there is a substantial risk of further unauthorised disclosure or access. The Registrar also has power to order the correction or erasure of inaccurate personal data.

Exemptions from the Act

Certain types of personal data are totally exempt from the workings of the Act. The computer user is not required to register, for example, nor is he required to give access to the data. Within this category are included personal data held for domestic or recreational purposes; and personal data held by a club and relating only to members of the club where the members are asked and have no objection to the data being held Other categories of personal data have partial exemption. Disclosures made to people or organisations outside the terms of the data user's registration may be exempt, for example where they are made for the purpose of preventing or detecting crime, the assessment or collection of tax or in order to safeguard national security. Other exemptions have the effect of restricting or removing the data subject's right of access, for example, data held by the police for the purpose of crime prevention.

Assignment Les Trois Vallées

Calder Travel plc is a large tour operator specialising in Winter Ski-ing holidays which are sold by retail travel agents throughout the United Kingdom. The company resolves to attempt to increase its share of the market for ski-ing holidays in France, in particular the Trois Vallées. To enable the company to achieve this, a decision is taken to make an offer of a financial inducement to prospective clients. Accordingly in their Winter Holiday 1996 brochure, of which 200,000 are distributed, Calder Travel make the following offer:

Throughout the 1996 winter season for every individual package ski-ing holiday booked at a resort in the Trois Vallées at a cost of £800 or more:

(a) ski equipment and ski lessons will be provided absolutely free for the duration of the holiday; and

(b) a voucher will be issued which will entitle the holder to a 20% discount on any ski clothing purchased at *"Sherrats Ski Wear"*, a retailer with outlets all over the UK.

Three weeks after the brochure containing this offer has been circulated to travel agents, Geoffery Swift, the company secretary of Calder Travel, despite having given prior approval for the offer, decided that after a closer consideration the offer should be amended due to its ambiguity. All company staff and sales agents are therefore instructed to inform travel agents that the offer of free ski equipment hire relates to down-hill skis and sticks only and does not extend to ski boots or cross country equipment. The offer of free ski lessons applies to beginners only and not to intermediate or advanced skiers. Travel agents are told to give the information to clients at the time of booking and inform those who had already booked by letter. Unfortunately some travel agents are never informed of the new instructions and a small proportion who are informed fail to pass it on to the clients. Consequently a large number of complaints are made both to Calder Travel, Travel Agents and local authorities by disappointed clients throughout the 1996 season. The main grievances are the fact that ski boots are not provided on free hire to clients who had booked relevant holidays and that lessons are only free for beginners. Also despite the fact that Sherrats Ski Wear shops display notices stating that they accept Calder discount vouchers, the available discount does not extend to clothing which is advertised as *on sale*.

Task

You are employed as a trading standards officer in the South East of England. Numerous complaints have been made to your office regarding the various *'free offers'* made by Calder Travel plc. You are required to present an informal report to your senior officer in which you advise whether any trade descriptions offences have been committed and assess the chances of bringing a successful prosecution.

Assignment   An Arabian Tale

Thompsons Importers was owned and managed by Michael Thompson. Michael had decided to sell the business, having reached an age at which he felt he ought to be taking life more easily. The major activity carried on by Thompsons was the import into the United Kingdom of luxury goods from the Middle East and India.

The business was put on the market, and one of Michael's trading competitors, Arabian Exportex Ltd. expressed an interest in acquiring it. The managing director of the company, Alan Naseem, indicated to Michael that the company would require a report on the condition and future prospects of the business and Michael agreed to this.

The report was prepared by Rupert Gray, an accountant with Frayne and Company a reputable firm of accountants in Birmingham. Alan Naseem happened to know Rupert Gray, and encouraged him to make the report, "as pessimistic in assessing the future prospects of Thompsons as you feel truth will permit."

Rupert Gray's report contained a number of reasons for doubting the future viability of Thompsons. In particular it contained statements that: "the business is unlikely to withstand competition from foreign competitors whose profit margins and overheads are lower, and who are attracting and increasing share of the market"; and "import duties on luxury goods from outside the EEC are to be increased from next year."

Rupert Gray actually had no knowledge or information about foreign competition either for the present of the future, but had relied on observations made by Alan Naseem during a conversation with him. He had however read an article in Accountancy World in which it was stated that *"import duties on some luxury items brought into the United Kingdom from outside the EEC are to be revised."* Arabia Exportex Ltd. sent a copy of the report to Michael Thompson, who in consequence dropped his price by £100,000. Arabia Exportex Ltd. purchased at the lower price.

Two years after selling out to Arabia Exportex Ltd., Michael happened to meet a former business colleague who knows the import business well. Michael discovered that no changes had been made to import duties since he sold the business, and the foreign competition referred to in the report had not materialised. Following an angry phone call to Alan Naseem, Mr. Naseem has revealed the instruction he gave to Rupert Gray regarding the report, and says his company cannot be held responsible for a report produced by an independent professional.

Task

You are employed by a large firm of accountants who handle Michael Thompson's affairs. You are called upon to provide legal advice from time to time, and the senior partner has passed on to you the situations described above. The senior partner has asked you to arrange to meet Mr. Thompson to discuss the matter when he calls in to the office next week, or alternatively to write advising him. Prepare notes on the issues involved as a preliminary to meeting and discussing the matter with Mr. Thompson.

Assignment   A Really Brilliant Holiday

John Sayburn booked a two week package holiday in Portugal for himself, his wife Linda and their two young children with Really Brilliant Holidays Ltd. The booking included a suite in a three star hotel with full board and the total price was £1,870.

The brochure stated that there was a good beach at the resort, and that there was a swimming pool and nanny service. It also stated that the resort and hotel were ideal for children. Upon arrival the Sayburns found the suite to be cramped with one double and only one single bed. The children shared a bed for the first two nights after which a further mattress with some bedding was provided. The swimming pool contained dirty untreated water and was unsuitable for children. The nanny service had been discontinued two years previously. Meals were of poor quality and there was little choice on the menu. The beach was small and overcrowded and the water depth shelved away steeply close to the shoreline.

On day ten of the holiday a fire broke out in the hotel affecting a large part of the floor close to the main entrance. The Sayburns were in their room at the time and followed the sign indicating the emergency exit in case of fire. Linda Sayburn suffered serious injuries, including broken ribs, when she was caught up in a crush against a locked fire exit. It appears that the fire exit had been open when the hotel was inspected three years ago by the Really Brilliant's representative. During the current season, however, due to a number of intrusions into the hotel through unlocked fire doors, the management had decided to leave the doors locked.

Task

Following the return home of the Sayburn family after doctors in Portugal considered Linda to be fit to travel, friends advised John that he should bring a claim against Really Brilliant Holidays Ltd. John needs advice on how he should proceed with such a claim, and the legal basis upon which the claim can be founded. As a friend of the family with some legal knowledge in this field, produce a written summary for John identifying those matters in respect of which he and Linda may bring legal proceedings regarding their holidays, and specifying the legal basis upon which their claim can be made. This should be produced in a form which John can use in his preliminary dealings with Really Brilliant Holidays Ltd.

Legal Terms found in Chapter 14

Casual labour	• workers who are hired only for a short period
Contract for services	• a contract between an employer and a self employed contractor for the supply of work services
Contract of service/employment	• a contract between an employer and an employee containing employment terms
Direct discrimination	• less favourable treatment against a particular group
Disability	• a physical or mental impairment which has a substantial long term affect on the person's ability to carry out normal day to day activities
Indirect discrimination	• less favourable treatment against a particular group by requiring compliance with an unjustifiable condition which is more difficult to satisfy for a member of that group
Prima facie case	• "on the face of it" a case to answer
Race discrimination	• discrimination based upon colour, race, nationality, or ethnic or national origin
Sex discrimination	• discrimination based on gender
Statutory statement	• written notification of terms and conditions of employment required by statute
The balance of probabilities	• standard of proof, "more likely than not"
Trust and confidence	• implied term in a contract of employment signifying mutual respect
Uberrimae fidei	• a state of utmost good faith which applies to certain types of contractual relationship such as partnership or insurance
Victimisation	• less favourable treatment because a person has given evidence or information or brought proceedings under the discrimination legislation

Chapter 14

Law Relating to the Recruitment of Staff

An employment relationship exists where one person, an employer, who may be an individual, partnership, corporate body or unincorporate association, employs another person or persons under a contract of service as an employee or a contract for services as a contractor. In the Employment Rights Act 1996 s.230 an employee is defined as *an individual who has entered into or works under a contract of employment* and it is to employees that the bulk of individual employment rights apply. Some employees, for instance civil servants, the police, prison officers and health services employees, are regarded as special categories and their legal position tends to differ from employees generally. Also while an apprentice is not regarded strictly as an employee, in practice both the common law and statutory rights available to such a person are very similar to those of any full-time worker under a contract of service. Expiration of the apprenticeship contract however does not carry with it a right to a redundancy payment or the right to claim unfair dismissal in the case where there is no offer of full time employment.

> In *Wallace v. C A Roofing Services Ltd.* 1996 the plaintiff was employed as an *"apprentice sheet metal worker"* for four years and in his statutory statement it provided that *"at the end of your apprenticeship your employer will terminate unless there is a suitable vacancy that we can offer you at the time"*. When the plaintiff was dismissed prematurely by reason of redundancy he claimed that his apprenticeship contract could not be terminated on that ground and he sued for damages. The High Court held that the oral agreement entered into was a contract of apprenticeship rather than a contract of employment and it could not be terminated by redundancy other than closure of the business or a fundamental change in the character of the work. The plaintiff was therefore entitled to damages for breach of his apprenticeship contract. *"Although modern legislation has assimilated apprenticeships to contract of employment the contract of apprenticeship remain a distinct entity at common law. Its first purpose is training, the execution of work for the employer is secondary. In such a relationship, the ordinary law as to dismissal does not apply. The contract is for a fixed term and is not terminable at will as a contract of employment is at common law."*

Where full time employment is offered, but only on a temporary basis, perhaps to cover for an employee on maternity leave or secondment, the fact that there is an undertaking as to the temporary nature of the work is important in determining the rights of the parties when the contract is terminated. Certainly the dismissal of a temporary worker eligible to present a claim for unfair dismissal is not automatically *fair*, but it could be regarded as such if the employer has acted reasonably in the circumstances in reaching his decision to dismiss. This would be the same for an employee who is required to serve out a probationary period and is dismissed having worked for the necessary period of continuous employment to qualify to present a claim for unfair dismissal.

Employees and Contractors

There are an infinite variety of terms and conditions under which one person may do work for another. The requirements of employers will range from the need to engage full-time employees where a long standing relationship with their workers is envisaged, characterised by mutual trust and confidence between the parties, to the use of temporary workers engaged to complete a particular task. It may be that the temporary worker, such as the accountant or solicitor, provides a specialist skill which is required by the employer only on an intermittent basis. Alternatively temporary and casual employment only may be offered, because of economic necessity or the expansion or contraction of the size of the workforce in line with demand. Independent contractors (or self employed workers) are now well established as a substantial proportion of the workforce of some industries, for instance, the media, catering and construction. Of the million or so construction workers, well over half a million are self employed. The changing face of employment patterns in Britain is shown by official figures which reveal that while 62.3% of household income is earned from wages and salaries, over 10% is now derived from self-employment. This form of employment has many advantages for both sides. The employer *gets the job done* and the contractor is normally well paid in return. A criticism of the system is that it provides no support for the older or infirm worker, no security of employment, and may lead to a general reduction in health and safety standards. The increasing use of the self employed in business to execute work and provide services both in the public and private sectors makes the basic division between the employed and self employed a matter of considerable importance.

A large number of legal and economic consequences stem from the distinction between employed and self employed status. For this reason it is necessary to be able to identify the status of the employment relationship that has been entered into. Employment legislation and the common law both recognise the distinction between employment under a *contract of service* and self employment under a *contract for services*. The distinction is a relatively straightforward one to make in the majority of cases. It is only in a small proportion of cases that difficulties arise, often where employers, or those they employ are seeking to achieve contractor status for economic advantage or in order to evade legal responsibilities. The table on the following page provides a summary of the major legal and economic consequences of the employment classification.

Legal and Economic Consequences of Employment Classification

Contract of Service (Employed Persons)

Contract for Services (Self-employed)

Liability

An employer may be made vicariously liable for the wrongful acts of employees committed during the course of their employment.

As a general principle an employer may not be made liable for the wrongful acts of contractors he employs other than in exceptional cases.

Common Law Employment Terms

Numerous terms are implied into a contract of employment by the common law to regulate the relationship of employer and employee e.g. trust and confidence.

The common law is much less likely to intervene in the relationship of employer and contractor.

Health and Safety

A high standard of care is owed by an employer both under statute and the common law with regard to the health and safety of his employees.

While both the common law and statute recognise the existence of a duty of care by an employer in relation to the contractors he employs, at common law it is of a lesser standard than the duty owed to employees.

Statutory Employment Rights

A large number of individual employment rights are conferred on employees by statute which generally arise after a period of service e.g. the right to unfair dismissal protection; to redundancy payments; to belong to a trade union and take part in trade union activities; to protection in the event of the employer's insolvency; to guarantee payments, to security of employment after maternity leave; to statutory maternity pay; to a written statement of the main terms and conditions of employment and the right not to be discriminated against on the grounds of sex, race or marital status.

Contractors are effectively excluded from the mass of individual employment rights conferred by statute. One notable exception however is the legislation in relation to sex and race discrimination, which protects the self-employed when they are providing personal services.

Income Tax

The income tax payable by an employee is deducted at source by the employer under the PAYE (pay as you earn) scheme. An employee is referred to as a Schedule E tax payer.

The income tax of a self employed person is payable by the taxpayer and not his employer, on a lump sum preceding year basis (Schedule D). From 1994 however the self employed are gradually being moved to a 'current year basis' of assessment. They do however retain more favourable treatment in claiming reasonable expenses when assessed for tax. Furthermore an independent sub-contractor may have to charge VAT on services.

Welfare Benefits

Under the Social Security Act 1975 both employer and employee must contribute to the payment of Class 1 National Insurance contributions assessed on an earnings related basis, entitling the employee to claim all the available welfare benefits e.g. Job Seekers Allowance, statutory sick pay, industrial disablement benefit, state retirement pension.

Under the Social Security Act 1975 a self-employed person is individually responsible for the payment of lower Class 2 National Insurance contributions and has only limited rights to claim welfare benefits e.g. statutory sick pay.

Distinguishing between the Employed and Self Employed

Once again while it should be stressed that in the vast majority of cases it is easy to recognise a contract service and a contract for services the distinction between the contracts in borderline cases is not so straightforward. It does seem that all legal systems find the distinction between the two contracts a difficult one to make.

In the final analysis the determination of whether an individual is an employee or a contractor is a question of law for the courts rather than a question of fact involving placing sole reliance on the description of the contract given by the parties to it. Over the years a number of tests have been formulated by the courts to attempt to determine any given worker's status. Originally the courts would only consider the level of control over a worker by an employer. In *Performing Rights Society Ltd. v. Mitchell and Booker* 1924, McCardie J. said that *"the final test, if there is to be a final test, and certainly the test to be generally applied, lies in the nature and degree of detailed control over the person alleged to be a servant"*. If an employer could tell his workers not only *what* to do, but also *how* and *when* to do it, then the workers would be regarded as employees, employed under a contract of service. Today the courts adopt a much wider approach and take account of all the circumstances to determine a worker's status. This is not to say that control is no longer a significant factor, for it would be difficult to imagine a contract of service where the employer did not have the ultimate authority to control the work performed by the employee.

Control is of course a less obvious feature the more specialised, skilled or trusted the workers become, for example a surgeon. This was why in the 1950s and 60s it was thought necessary to move away from a test based solely on control over the worker. The integration or organisational test favoured by the Court of Appeal at this time was expressed by Denning L J in *Stevenson, Jordan and Harrison v. MacDonald and Evans* 1952. Here he said that *"under a contract of service a man is employed as part of the business and his work is done as an integral part of the business, whereas, under a contract for service, his work, although done for the business, is not integrated into it, but is only accessory to it"*. Adopting this approach the Court of Appeal was able to determine that medical staff in a hospital were employees and that a trapeze artist in a circus who also helped out with general duties was also an employee. In both cases their work was regarded as an integral part of the organisation.

The present approach of the courts, which involves viewing all of the circumstances of the case to determine status, has been described in various ways as the mixed, multiple or economic reality test. It has its origins in the following case.

> In *Ready Mixed Concrete Ltd. v. Ministry of Pensions* 1968 under a peculiar procedure laid down in National Insurance legislation MacKenna J, a single judge of the Queens Bench Division of the High Court, sat as the final appellate court to decide the employment status of a driver for the plaintiff company. This was in order to determine the employer's responsibility in relation to the National Insurance contributions of its drivers. The Ministry of Pensions had rejected the employer's contention that its drivers were self employed, despite the existence of written contracts of employment (30 pages long) which had attempted to create a contract for services rather than contracts of service. The declaration that the driver was self employed was not decisive and all aspects of his job were considered, for instance the fact that the driver purchased the lorry from the

company; had to maintain it; that pay was calculated on the basis of the driving work performed. All these factors pointed to the driver being a contractor. Others pointed to his status as an employee. He had to paint the lorry in the company colours, he had to use it exclusively for company business and he was required to obey reasonable orders. McKenna J stated that there is a contract of service if an individual agrees to provide his own work, submits to his employer's control and in addition the majority of the contractual provisions are consistent with a contract of service. This approach has since been referred to as the mixed or multiple test. On the facts the power to delegate work was regarded as a decisive indication that the drivers were self employed under a contract for services.

The status of self employment cannot be achieved simply by including an express provision in a contract. The courts will look to the substance of an employment relationship rather than the label applied by the parties in order to decide a worker's status.

In *Ferguson v. John Dawson Ltd.* 1976 the plaintiff, a builder's labourer agreed to work as a *self employed labour only sub contractor* an arrangement commonly known as the *lump*. When working on a flat roof he fell and suffered injuries. No guard rail had been provided, in breach of the duty to employees owed under the Construction (Working Places) Regulations 1966. The High Court decided that the employer was in breach of this statutory duty towards the plaintiff and damages of over £30,000 were awarded. On appeal the employer argued that as the plaintiff was self employed the statutory duty was not owed to him. It was the plaintiff's responsibility to ensure that the guard rail was in place. The Court of Appeal held, by a majority, that the plaintiff was in reality an employee and so entitled to the compensation awarded. The *lump* was no more than a device to attempt to gain tax advantages and whilst a declaration as to employment status may be relevant, it is not the conclusive factor to determine the true nature of the employment relationship.

A difficult case to reconcile with the decision in *Ferguson* 1976 is *Massey v. Crown Life Insurance Company* 1978. Here a branch manager of an insurance company, who also acted as a general agent, decided to become *self employed* on his accountant's advice, despite the fact that his duties remained unchanged. The Court of Appeal concluded that a change of employment status had in fact taken place so that he was unable to bring a claim for unfair dismissal. Lord Denning M R stated that if there is ambiguity in the relationship then this can be resolved with a declaration one way or the other.

Whilst there was a degree of ambiguity in the above case in the branch manager's original position as manager/agent, it was significant that here was a *professional man*, having considered independent advice, making a declaration which he believed would be to his benefit. This is in contrast to the labourer in *Ferguson* 1976 who was unadvised and could not be said to have consciously chosen to be a contractor with the legal consequences that this involved.

Despite the existence of a clear agreement between the employer and the worker that he should be treated as self employed this may nevertheless be regarded by the courts as a false designation and overturned.

In *Young & Wood Ltd. v. West* 1980 the complainant, a sheet metal worker, asked his employer if he could be treated as self employed. This was accepted and despite the fact that there was no difference between his working conditions and those of PAYE workers, he was paid without deductions of tax and was not given holiday entitlement or sick pay. Furthermore the Inland Revenue had accepted the change, resulting in an estimated tax advantage of about £500 over five years because of assessment under Schedule D rather than Schedule E. Stephenson L J seemed to cast doubt on Lord Denning M R's approach in *Massey* 1978 by stating that *"It must be the court's duty to see whether the label correctly represents the true legal relationship between the parties"*. The Court of Appeal found that as it was impossible to regard the complainant as in `business on his own account' he was not self employed but remained an employee. Consequently the tribunal had jurisdiction to hear his complaint of unfair dismissal.

In *Duke v. Martin Retail Group plc* 1993 a large number of newsagent shop managers called contract managers were employed under an agreement which referred to them as independent contractors. They could employ staff and were paid commission with no holidays sick pay or pension. A tribunal decided that such a manager was self employed and the Employment Appeal Tribunal (EAT) agreed despite the large degree of control over the company's property the opening hours and the lack of financial investment. Features which pointed to self employed included the freedom on managers to employ staff, insure, delegate managerial work and carry on other business not in close competition with the employer.

The growth of employment agencies who recruit potential staff and supply them to organisations as temporary workers has led to a debate as to the status of workers when placed with employers.

In *Pertemps Group plc v. Nixon* 1993 the applicant, a fitter machinist, entered into a contract with an employment agency under which he was described as a `temporary worker' engaged under a contract `for services'. The object of the contract was to offer the applicant opportunities to work for clients of the agency. The applicant could refuse such work but if he accepted it, he would be paid an hourly rate by the agency subject to deductions of national insurance and PAYE. Under such an arrangement the applicant worked for three years continuously for a particular client and when this work terminated, and no alternative work was available, the applicant terminated his contract with the agency and claimed a redundancy payment. The tribunal found that he was entitled to such a payment concluding that when he worked for the client a contract of employment existed between himself and the agency. This contract of service existed under the `umbrella' of the contract for services. On appeal however the EAT disagreed and found that the applicant's contract with the agency was a contract for services and there was no authority to support the implication of a second contract when work with a client was accepted.

By asking the question whether the worker is *in business on his own account* or under the control of an employer under a continuing business relationship, the courts have found it possible to conclude that a relationship traditionally regarded as self employment, namely that of a homeworker, was in reality a contract of service. Questions posed in applying this entrepreneurial test would include whether the individual was in business on his own, provides his own equipment, employs other workers and has a financial stake in the business.

Reliance on a pool of casual workers has long been a tradition in some sectors of business including the catering industry.

> The legal status of so called `regular casuals` was put to the test in *O'Kelly and Others v. Trusthouse Forte plc* 1983. Here a banqueting department run by the employer was staffed in part by full time employees but mainly by so called `casuals'`. Among the casuals were `regulars'` who were given preference when work was available, were often expected to work very long hours and consequently had no other employment. The applicants in this case were *regulars* but when they became trade union shop stewards they were told by the employer that their services would no longer be required. In a claim for unfair dismissal brought by the applicants, the first issue the industrial tribunal had to deal with was whether they were employed under a contract of service and so protected by the law relating to unfair dismissal. In determining their employment status the tribunal acknowledged that its role was to *"consider all aspects of the relationship, no feature being itself decisive, each of which may vary in weight and direction and, having given such a balance to the factors as seem appropriate determine whether the person was carrying on business on his own account"*. Applying this mixed or multiple test the tribunal isolated factors consistent with a contract of service including the lack of mutual obligations on the part of the employer to provide work and on the part of the worker to offer services (referred to as *mutuality of obligation*). In addition there was the custom and practice of the catering industry to employ large numbers on a casual basis. By placing most emphasis on the inconsistent factors the tribunal found that the applicants were not employees and therefore not entitled to statutory protection. The Court of Appeal later found it unable to interfere with the tribunal's decision given that the correct legal approach has been adopted.

While there is no doubt that the decision in *O'Kelly* supports the custom and practice of the hotel and catering industry and confirms the fact that a fundamental feature of the contract of employment is the requirement to provide work and offer services, it is nevertheless difficult to reconcile with previous decisions, in particular *Ferguson* 1976. The reality of *O'Kelly* is that the regular casuals were subject to the same control as full time employees. They often worked longer hours than full time staff and a failure to work when required had the dramatic consequences of removal from the regular casual lists. Having no alternative employment, capital equipment or profit sharing, it would be difficult to describe them as business people working on their *"own account"*.

In the final analysis in a borderline case the determination of a worker's status can only be made by asking a number of questions relating to the main features of the relationship such as the extent to which the employee is:

- providing personal services;
- under the employer's control;
- regarded as an integral part of the organisation;
- in business on his own account;

- providing tools and equipment;

- sharing in the profit and contributing towards the losses;

- able to delegate work;

- in agreement as to his status.

An example of the approach of the Court of Appeal to the issue is provided by the decision in *Hall (HM Inspector of Taxes) v. Lorimer* 1994. Here the Inland Revenue claimed that a free-lance vision-mixer who worked for a number of production companies should be charged to income tax under Schedule E as an employee rather than Schedule D as a self employed person. The reasoning behind the claim was that the vision-mixer provided no equipment for his work and had no financial status in the programmes upon which he worked. On his behalf it was argued that he took a financial risk in relation to payment for his work, he could also delegate work and had had a large number of different employers. The Court of Appeal agreed with the High Court that he was a self employed person employed under a contract for services. The court stated that *"there is no single path in determining whether or not the contracts from which a person derives his earnings are contracts of service or contracts for services. An approach which suits the facts and arguments of one case may be unhelpful in another"*. The earlier decision of the High Court was approved of in particular the approach to this type of analysis that *"it is not a mechanical exercise of running through items on a check list to see whether they are present in, or absent from a given situation. The object of the exercise is to paint a picture from the accumulation of the detail. The overall effect can only be appreciated by standing back from the detailed picture which has been painted, by viewing it from a distance and by making an informed, considered, qualitative appreciation of the whole. It is a matter of evaluation of the overall effect of the detail which is not necessarily the same as the sum total of the individual details. Not all details are of equal weight or importance in any given situation. The details may also vary from one situation to another"*.

In *Lane v. Shire Roofing Company (Oxford) Ltd* 1995, the Court of Appeal considered the issue of employment status in the context of a personal injury scenario. The complainant was Mr Lane a general builder who traded under the name of PJ Building as a one man business. He was categorised as *"self employed"* for tax purposes working directly for clients and sometimes for other contractors. Shire Roofing was a roofing contractor whose owner Mr Whittaker often hired men for individual jobs.In 1986 Mr Lane was hired by Shire Roofing to work on a large roofing sub-contract. When that work was near completion Mr Whittaker asked Mr Lane to re-roof a porch in a private house. The job was agreed an they both visited the house to decide the fee and the equipment that was necessary to do the work. Because the cost of hiring scaffolding would have made the job unprofitable it was decided that Mr Lane should use his own ladder to do the work. When carrying out the work Mr Lane fell from the ladder and suffered severe head injuries. In an action claiming damages from Shire Roofing the High Court held that as Mr Lane was a contractor he was owed no duty of care. Factors that the court thought were significant in reaching that conclusion included the fact that Mr Lane had his own business, he was recognised as self employed for tax purposes and he was working on a single job without supervision. In addition the court concluded that there was no evidence to support the finding of a breach of duty. The Court of Appeal disagreed with the High Court on both of the main issues and held that Mr Lane as an employee was owed a duty of care by Shire Roofing which they had broken. As a consequence Mr Lane was awarded £102,100 in damages. The court confirmed that in determining whether a worker is an employee or a contractor control is an important factor *"Whose business was it?"* – was the workman carrying on his own business, or was he carrying on that of his employers? The answer to this question may cover much of the same ground as the control test, such as whether he provides his own equipment and hires his own helpers, but may involve looking to see where the financial risk lies, and whether and how far the workman has an opportunity of profiting from sound management in the performance of his task. These questions must be asked in the context of who is responsible for the overall safety of those doing the work in question. The court felt that there are good policy reasons in the safety at work field to ensure that the law properly categorises between employees and independent contractors and recognises the employer/employee relationship when it exists because of the responsibilities that the common law and statutes place on the employer. Despite the fact that Mr Lane was self-employed for tax purposes, his relationship with the employer was much closer to the "lump", where workmen are engaged only for their labour and are clearly employees as in *Ferguson v. John Dawson Ltd.* 1976

The significance of this case is that it illustrates the contemporary approach of the higher courts to the issue of employment status. By emphasising the importance of public policy in deciding a workers' status in the health and safety context, the court found it possible to categorise the worker as an employee and so owed a duty of care by his employer. This was despite the fact that a strict analysis of his contract might have produced a different conclusion. Certainly if the issue had been one of security in employment such as in the *O'Kelly v. Trust House Forte* scenario, the result might well have been different.

The fact that there has been such litigation on the employed/self employed distinction suggests that in the borderline cases in particular, decisions are by no means clear cut. The courts are faced with the difficult task of maintaining a balance between the freedom of employers to offer employment on the terms that best suit their interest and the rights of workers, for the most part in an unequal bargaining position, to obtain the benefits of status as an employee. Under European Union employment law rights and duties tend to be conferred and imposed on 'workers' which would include employees or contractors providing personal services.

Formation of the Contract of Employment

Having identified the two main employment relationships it is now possible to focus attention on the process by which an employer recruits his staff, both full-time and part-time. A significant trend of employment over the last decade has been the growth of reliance on part-time workers. While as a general rule self employed workers tend to work longer hours than employees, there are nevertheless over a half a million (9.5% of the total workforce) self employed part-timers in Britain.

Full-time and part-time employees

A full-time worker is anyone who works under a contract of employment for sixteen hours a week or more and as an employee such a person will enjoy the full range of statutory employment rights, generally after two years continuous employment. In relation to part-time workers the position was that statutory rights could be acquired after five years continuous service for those employed under a contract for between 8 and 16 hours per week.

Following the momentous decision of the House of Lords in *R v. Secretary of State for Employment ex parte EOC and Another* 1994 the legal position of part-time workers has changed dramatically. Their lordships ruled that UK legislation conferring statutory rights on full-time workers and not part-timers in relation to redundancy and unfair dismissal was indirectly discriminatory against women and incompatible with European Union Law.

Now part-time workers with two years service are eligible to bring a complaint of unfair dismissal regardless of the hours they work. The government has now confirmed this position in legislation. This was achieved by the Employment Protection (Part-time Employees) Regulations 1995 made under s2(2) of the European Communities Act 1972 and in force on the 6th of February 1995. Under these regulations the hours thresholds are abolished so that all distinctions in statutory employment rights based on the number of hours worked no longer apply. This means that part-time workers can rely on the same amount of continuous service as a full time employee to qualify for rights relating to redundancy pay, unfair dismissal, written reason for dismissal, notice and maternity absence. Other statutory rights such as time off for trade union duties and a statement of employment terms and conditions will also apply to part-time employees regardless of the number of hours worked.

All part-time employees are protected by discrimination law, and to comply with European Community law all part-time women are now entitled to 14 weeks maternity leave under the Trade Union Reform and Employment Rights Act 1993. Following the 1995 regulations all part-time employees with two years continuous service will also qualify for extended maternity absence.

Employers across the full range of occupational categories offer part-time employment but there are particular concentrations of part-time workers in;

- sales and services (check out operators, cleaners, catering assistants, porters)
- teaching and health professionals (school teachers, lecturers, nurses, physiotherapists)
- personal services (cooks, bar staff, hairdressers, domestic staff)
- clerical and secretarial (clerks, typists, computer operators)

Clearly while a number of part-time workers would prefer the opportunity to enter full-time employment a significant proportion of part-time workers choose to work part-time because of the impracticably of full-time hours, given their other responsibilities. Both full-time and part-time staff are recruited by means of entering into a contract of employment. Despite the unique nature of such a contract the common law rules relating to formation, construction and discharge of contracts are largely applicable. The formation of an employment contract is the culmination of a recruitment process which will normally involve advertising for staff, submission of application forms, job interviews, negotiating terms of employment and selection of staff.

The Recruitment Process

The recruitment process will normally begin when the employer places an advertisement indicating that staff are required. Statements of fact in the advertisement may be classified as representations and if they prove to be false and having induced a contract of employment an innocent employee could seek a remedy for misrepresentation. In rare cases statements in the advertisement maybe given the status of contractual terms or at least used as evidence to determine the express terms of employment.

> In *Holliday Concrete v. Woods* 1979 the job advertisement indicated that a fifteen month contract was available. This was regarded as the period of employment rather than the employer's view that there was an understanding that the job would last as long on the project continued.

> In *Joseph Steinfeld v. Reypert* 1979 the EAT held that the fact that the job advertised *"sales manager"* bore no relation to the actual job which was mainly clerical, amounted to a repudiatory breach of the contract of employment.

A job advertisement may also place clear obligations on an employee so that if they are not fulfilled this will be a factor in determining the reasonableness of the employer's decision to dismiss as a result.

The Application form

Advertisements for job applications normally indicate that a prospective employee should complete an application form to assist in the selection process. While a significant feature of the employment contract is that it involves a relationship of trust and confidence it is not a contract uberrimae fidei (utmost good faith) such as partnership or insurance. This means that there is no duty on an applicant to volunteer information which is not requested during the recruitment process, which includes the completion of the application form.

> In *Walton v. TAC Construction Materials Ltd.* 1981 the complainant was dismissed after working for thirteen months when the employer discovered that he was a heroin addict. During a medical inspection prior to employment the employee had answered "none" when asked to give details of serious illnesses and failed to reveal that he was injecting himself with heroin. Both the tribunal and the EAT held that it was fair to dismiss the applicant firstly because of his deception and secondly in accordance with their policy not to employ anyone who was addicted to drugs. Although not relevant for the case the EAT considered whether the complainant should have disclosed his addiction for the purposes of employment and decided that *"it could not be said that there is any duty on the employee in the ordinary case, though there may be exceptions, to volunteer information about himself or otherwise than in response to a direct question"*.

If a job applicant is deliberately dishonest on an application form this will normally make any subsequent decision to dismiss fair.

> In *Torr v. British Railways Board* 1977 the EAT held that the employers *"were justified in deciding to dismiss the employee as soon as they appreciated that he had obtained*

employment as a guard by dishonest concealment of a criminal conviction carrying a sentence of three years imprisonment, even though the conviction was as far back as 1958 and the employee had apparently been working satisfactorily as a guard for sixteen months". The sentence was of such a duration not to be covered by the Rehabilitation of Offenders Act 1974 and neither could the philosophy behind that Act be extended to render a dismissal in the circumstances unfair *"It is of utmost importance that an employer seeking an employee to hold a position of responsibility and trust should be able to select for employment a candidate in whom he can have confidence. It is fundamental to that confidence that the employee should truthfully disclose his history so far as it is sought by the intending employer"*.

In determining the fairness of an employer's decision to dismiss after discovering an employees mis-statement on an application form all the circumstances must be considered including the significance of the mis-statement, the length of employment and whether the work was satisfactory.

Job interviews

The primary objective of the job interview from the employer's viewpoint is to assist in the selection process. It should be stressed however if a decision to employ an applicant is made it may be at this point that a formal offer is made and accepted and a contract concluded. Even in cases where an understanding is reached, subject to a formal written offer at a later stage, statements or promises made during the interview may be used to interpret the contractual terms or constitute express terms of the contract in themselves. Certainly it makes sense to ensure at the interview stage that a prospective employee is given a realistic picture of the terms and conditions of employment and what the job entails. Even statements such as promotion prospects could be regarded as a term of employment if they later prove to be unrealistic. Certainly a clearly worded job offer will override conflicting statements made in the job advertisement. In the event of conflict between oral statements and writing the writing will normally have primacy but it is the intention of the parties which must be determined.

> In *Hawker Siddeley Power Engineering Ltd. v. Rump* 1979 the complainant was employed as a heavy goods vehicle driver in 1973 and signed a contract of employment which stated that he would be liable to travel all over the country. This obligation was confirmed in a later statement of terms of employment issued in 1976 and signed by the employee. In fact the complainant had made it clear when he took the job that because of his wife's illness he would not travel beyond the south of England and that had been orally agreed by a manager when he signed the contract. When finally in 1978 the complainant refused to obey an instruction to travel to Scotland and this led to his dismissal, one issue before the EAT was whether he was contractually obliged to do so. The EAT held that the promise to work only in the south was an oral contractual term. Here *"there was a direct promise by the employers which must have become part of the contract of employment because it was following upon the promise that the employee signed the contract"*. Even the subsequent written statement which included a mobility clause signed by the employer was insufficient to exclude the oral term previously agreed. Here the employee *"had no notice that the oral term he had secured was going to form no part of his new contract. The mere putting in front of him a document and invitation for him to sign it could not*

be held to be a variation by agreement so as to exclude the important oral term which he had previously secured. Rather if there was a variation at all to the contract, it was a unilateral variation which was not binding upon the employee".

Quite often an offer of employment is made *conditional,* for instance *"subject to the receipt of satisfactory written references"* or the *" passing of a medical examination".*

> In *Wishart v. National Association of Citizens Advice Bureaux Ltd.* 1990 The Court of Appeal considered a case where the plaintiff had been offered the post of information officer "subject to satisfactory references" and then when the employer discovered his past attendance record withdrew the job offer. The issue before the Court of Appeal was whether the employer's decision to treat the references as unsatisfactory could be viewed objectively and tested by the standard of the reasonable person in the position of the employer. In fact the court decided that unlike medical opinion as to the employee's fitness which could be tested objectively, there was no obligation in law on the employer other than to decide in good faith whether the references were satisfactory. *"The natural reading of a communication, the purpose of which is to tell the prospective employee that part of the decision on whether he is firmly offered the post has yet to be made, is that the employer is reserving the right to make up his own mind when the references have been received and studied. "*

If the acceptance of the job offer is *conditional* the normal contractual rules apply and it will be taken as a rejection and amount to a counter offer capable of acceptance or rejection.

It is in the interests of both the employer and the employee that the express terms of employment are precise and clearly understood. It is then less likely that legal problems will arise in the future when contractual terms are possibly subject to change or it becomes necessary to bring the employment relationship to an end.

Once a contract of employment is concluded there is legal redress available if either party decides to back out of the contract in breach. The unilateral withdrawal by an employer of an offer of employment, once accepted, will constitute the breach of a collateral contract, a contract to employ. Here the damages awarded could in exceptional cases exceed the wages due under the contractual notice period.

It should be stressed however that the above scenario is rare and damages available against an employer in breach will normally be restricted to the wages due under the notice period Also the courts will not, other than in exceptional cases, order specific performance of a contract of employment. The remedy for breach by the employee is damages. In practice unless an employer has incurred substantial recruitment costs the cost of litigation would make an action against an employee in breach unwise. There is no right to bring a potential unfair dismissal claim without two years continuous employment unless the reason for dismissal is shown to be inadmissible such as related to trade union membership, statutory rights or health and safety.

Equal Opportunities

As a general principle, employers are free to pick and choose to whom they offer employment and can reject an applicant for all manner of reasons including qualifications, attitude, references or suitability. A limitation on the freedom to employ is embodied within the Disabled Persons (Employment) Act 1958 which provides that an employer with twenty or more employees must in the absence of an exemption certificate, have a minimum of three percent of the workforce registered as disabled persons. Indeed in certain jobs, disabled persons must be given priority. Furthermore, rather than stigmatising an individual for life because of his past conduct, the Rehabilitation of Offenders Act 1974 allows past offenders who have criminal convictions to regard them as 'spent' in certain circumstances. Imprisonment for 30 months or more can never be spent and in a number of professions even spent offences must be disclosed for instance medicine, the law and teaching. If the offence is spent then on a job application the past conviction need not be mentioned and the failure to disclose it is no ground for an employer to discriminate against individuals by refusing to employ them or by dismissing them for past offences. It is reasonable of course for an employer to expect full disclosure of information on a job application and this would most certainly include a prospective employee providing details of criminal convictions which were not spent. A failure to fully disclose details of previous employment or trade union activities however may not be regarded as fatal to the validity of the contract of employment.

> In *Fitzpatrick v. British Railways Board* 1991 the complainant obtained a job with British Railways Board and deliberately failed to provide full details of her previous employment and participation in trade union activities. When it became obvious to the employer that the complainant was, and had been a union activist, they dismissed her on the ground that she had obtained the job by deceit. The complainant then claimed that her dismissal was unfair as it was on the ground of trade union activities contrary to s.152 of the Trade Union and Labour Relations (Consolidation) Act 1992). If the reason for a dismissal is trade union membership or activities then the requirement of two years continuous employment to qualify for protection does not apply. The Court of Appeal held that the true reason for the complainant's dismissal was her union activities in previous employment and the fear that these activities will be repeated in her present employment. Here the Court of Appeal felt that the reason for dismissal here was a fear of a repetition of the same conduct and in the circumstances it was therefore unfair.

Under the Trade Union and Labour Relations (Consolidation) Act 1992 s.137 it is unlawful to refuse employment because a person is or is not a trade union member. Also under the Act if a job advertisement indicates that trade union membership is a requirement and, then employment is refused it will be presumed to be for that reason if the applicant is not a trade union member.

Unfortunately you should appreciate that despite the superficial emphasis given to equal opportunities in business, industry and the professions, numerous studies have shown that discriminatory practices are still widespread in staff recruitment in the UK. Prospective employees are discriminated against for various reasons including racial origin, sex, sexuality, religion, age and disability. In an attempt to reduce and hopefully eradicate these practices, legislation has been passed in the UK to make sex, race and disability discrimination unlawful in employment.

As yet there is no legislation covering age and sexuality while there has been increasing pressure to make discrimination against the disabled unlawful. It became the government's intention to introduce a bill to tackle discrimination against people with disabilities in recruitment and employment following the demise of the Civil Rights (Disabled Persons) Bill in 1994. The Disability Discrimination Act was passed in 1995.

As a consequence of discriminatory recruitment practices we have a workforce in the UK divided by sex and race. Members of racial and ethnic minority groups generally occupy a low position in the occupational structure, concentrated in unskilled manual jobs and unrepresented in skilled manual jobs, managerial and professional occupations. They are found mainly in low paying industries such as clothing and textiles, in service sector jobs and in hospitals, shops and catering. Furthermore male black workers earn considerably less than male white workers and suffer a much higher rate of unemployment. Female workers are similarly concentrated in low paid unskilled jobs in a relatively small number of occupations including mainly clerical and related jobs and industries such as cleaning, catering and manufacturing. Because of child care responsibilities many women take part-time or casual work, often unskilled with poor pay and conditions. Economic trends in the labour market indicate an increase in the use of wage payment systems which encourage overtime, shift work and bonus payments, which necessarily discriminate against women. In addition to UK legislation on discrimination there is also European Community law which is directly applicable in UK Courts and also incorporated into United Kingdom law by Statute and by Statutory Instruments.

The right not to be discriminated against on the grounds of sex, race or marital status is one of the few individual employment rights that has not been weakened but rather strengthened over recent years. This has been mainly due to the impact of Community law and judgments of the European Court of Justice particularly in relation to gender.

The tendency to stereotype sexes and races and also perceive jobs to have male or female characteristics means that discrimination in Britain is still widespread. Nevertheless there are still relatively few complaints brought and success rates are consistently low. Studies have shown that there are numerous reasons for this, ranging from ignorance as to legal rights, insufficient support for complainants, difficulties of proof, low levels of compensation, and fear of victimisation. On the positive side however, there have been some notable successes recently which have caused change in employment practices. Unlawful discrimination has been found in a number of important equal pay cases, in relation to part-time workers, in unnecessary demands for British qualifications, in maximum age limits and in stringent language tests. There is no doubt that there is a change in attitude, for there is increasing evidence that employers are adopting equal opportunity employment practices. Equal opportunity is an important issue in industrial relations, and the law can act as an important stimulus to ensure that organisations adopt employment practices designed to combat discrimination. There is increasing pressure in Britain to extend the law to protect those in our society who are less favourably treated in employment because of their age, religion, sexuality or disability.

Sex and Race Discrimination

The *Race Relations Act* 1976 and the *Sex Discrimination Act* 1975 as amended, identify similar categories of unlawful acts in relation to discrimination, namely direct discrimination, indirect discrimination, and victimisation. It is convenient to set out these unlawful acts of discrimination in tabular form as a means of comparison. See the table on the following page.

Race Relations Act, 1976	Sex Discrimination Act, 1975

Direct Discrimination

This occurs where one person: Treats another less favourably on racial grounds e.g. by segregating workers by race. s.1(1)(a)	This occurs when one person: Treats another less favourably on the grounds of sex or marital status e.g. by providing women with different working conditions or selecting married women first for redundancy. s.1(1)(a) s.3(1)(b)

Indirect Discrimination

This occurs where one person: Requires another to meet a condition which as a member of a racial group is less easily satisfied because: (a)the proportion of that group who can comply with it is smaller; and (b)the condition is to the complainant's detriment and is not justified., There would therefore be indirect discrimination if an employer required young job applicants to have been educated only in Britain. s.1(1)(b)	This occurs where one person: Requires another to meet a condition which as a member of a particular sex or as a married person is less easily satisfied because: (a) the proportion of that sex or married persons who can comply with it is smaller; and (b)the condition is to the complainant's detriment and is not justified. There would therefore be indirect discrimination if an employer advertised for a clerk who is at least six feet tall. s.1(1)(b) s.3(1)(b)

Victimisation

This occurs where one person: Treats another less favourably because the other has given evidence or information in connection with, brought proceedings under, or made allegations under the Act against the discriminator. s.2	This occurs where one person: Treats another less favourably because the other has given evidence or information in connection with, brought proceedings under, or made allegations under the Act or the Equal Pay Act, 1970, against the discriminator. s.4

The fact that both pieces of legislation are drafted in a largely similar fashion means that case-law involving the *Sex Discrimination Act* will also serve as an aid to the interpretation of the provision of The *Race Relations Act*. It is proposed to consider the provisions of both Acts in unison.

The *Sex Discrimination Act* 1975 is concerned with discrimination on grounds of gender either by males against females, or vice versa, and on grounds of marital status by treating a married person less favourably than an unmarried person.

In *Nemes v. Allen* 1977 an employer in an attempt to cope with a redundancy situation dismissed female workers when they married. This was held to be unlawful direct discrimination on the grounds of sex and marital status.

The *Race Relations Act* 1976 is more complex in relation to those it protects and under s.3 is concerned with discrimination on racial grounds which, is based upon colour, race, nationality, or ethnic or national origin.

> In *Race Relations Board v. Mecca* 1976 an individual telephoned to apply for a job but when the employer discovered the applicant was black, he put the telephone down. This was held to be unlawful direct discrimination as the applicant had been denied the opportunity to apply for a job on racial grounds.

While the definition of racial grounds is wide there is no reference to discrimination based on religion. It does seem however that some religions would normally be covered by the definition *colour, race, nationality, or ethnic or national origins*.

> In *Seide v. Gillette Industries* 1980 the EAT held that the term *"Jewish"* can mean membership of a particular race or ethnic group as well as a religion. Also in *Mandla v. Dowell Lee* 1983 the House of Lords held that Sikhs were a racial group within the meaning of the Act.

> In *Crown Supplies PGA v. Dawkins* 1993 the Court of Appeal held that Rastafarianism is no more than a religious sect and not an ethnic group for the purposes of the Race Relations Act. As a consequence when a Rastafarian is refused employment because of the way in which he wears his hair that does not amount to discrimination under the 1976 Act.

In relation to employment, any discriminatory practice which comes within any of the three categories (direct, indirect or victimisation) is unlawful. Section 6 of the *Sex Discrimination Act* and section 4 of the Race Relations Act are similar in format and relate to discrimination by employers in the recruitment process, at the workplace and in relation to the termination of employment.

It is therefore unlawful for a person in relation to employment by him to discriminate in the arrangements he makes for the purposes of deciding whom should be offered employment, the terms on which it is offered or by refusing to offer employment. Also where there is an existing employment relationship it is unlawful for an employer to discriminate in the way he gives access to opportunities for promotion, transfer, training or any other benefits, or refuses to afford such access. Furthermore, it is unlawful to discriminate by dismissing the complainant or subject him to any other detriment.

> In *Blaik v. The Post Office* 1994 the complaint was based on the fact that postwomen were not required to wear a tie and this it was alleged discriminated against men who were required to wear a tie as part of their dress code. Applying *Schmidt v. Austicks Bookshops* 1977 it was held that the requirement to wear a tie was not to be regarded as *serious* so as to amount to a detriment. In Schmidt *"the employers treated both female and male staff alike in that there were in force rules restricting wearing apparel and governing appearance which applied to women, although the rule in the two cases were not the same given the differences in sex"*.

The Equal Treatment Directive has had considerable impact on UK discrimination law and in *Johnston v. Chief Constable of the RUC* 1987 it was confirmed that the Directive was unconditional and sufficiently precise to be used by an individual against a member state or in a national court. An individual could not enforce the Directive against a private employer however.

While it is clear that UK domestic law, particularly the *Sex Discrimination Act*, provides no redress to a person who suffers discrimination in employment because of sexual orientation there is a possibility that European Union law may provide a remedy.

> In *P v. S* 1996 the European Court of Justice considered whether the Equal Treatment Directive applied to the case where a transsexual had been dismissed for a reason related to a sex change. Following the complainant's announcement that he intended to undertake gender reassignment, and the commencement of initial surgery, he had been dismissed. The European Court held that the Directive's principle of equal treatment required no discrimination on the grounds of sex and its scope should not be confined to a person's gender status but also to gender reassignment. A comparison should be drawn in such a case with the treatment the applicant received before undergoing the reassignment and after.

The anti-discrimination legislation provides redress for those who *"contract personally to execute any work or labour"*.

> The EAT in *Hill Samuel Investment Services Group Ltd. v. Nwauzu* 1994 held that an insurance agent employed on a commission only basis as a self employed person offering personal services was protected by the Race Relations legislation. The employer was found to be guilty of discrimination when the issue of the complainant's race influenced the decision to terminate his contract.

Disability Discrimination

Disability discrimination legislation was introduced in 1995 in the form of the Disability Discrimination Act in force from December 1996 in relation to employment.

The extent of the Act has been the subject of much criticism particularly from groups representing the disabled.The Act applies to employers who have 20 or more employees,making it unlawful to discriminate against someone who has or who had a disability in recruitment or at the workplace.Disability is defined as *"a physical or mental impairment which has a substantial and long term adverse affect on the persons ability to carry out normal day to day activities"*. The unlawful forms of discrimination created under the legislation are *less favourable treatment* and *failure to make adjustments* both of which are potentially justifiable.

Less favourable treatment is equivalent to direct discrimination with which we are already familiar.

An employer discriminates against a disabled person

For a reason which relates to the disabled person's disability;

- *the employer treats that person less favourably than he treats or would treat others to whom that reason does not or would not apply; and*
- *if, and only if, the employer cannot justify the less favourable treatment.*

An employer also discriminates against a disabled person if:

- *the employer fails to comply with any duty to make adjustments imposed by the 1995 Act; and*

- *if, and only if, the employer cannot justify the failure to comply with the duty.*

A significant feature of both forms of unlawful discrimination is that they may be justified. Justification must however be by reference to a reason which is both substantial and material to the circumstances of the particular case.

There would be a prima facie case if failure to make adjustments when an employer makes arrangements or his premises have a feature which places the disabled person at a substantial disadvantage in comparison with non-disabled persons. In such circumstances the employer is under a duty to take such steps as are reasonable to stop the arrangements or remove the feature, for instance adjust the premises or alter terms and conditions of employment. In deciding whether it is reasonable for the employer to make the adjustments all the circumstances including cost and disruption should be taken account of.

Time limits

Complaints of unlawful discrimination are made to the industrial tribunal and the time limit for presenting a complaint is three months from the act or last act of discrimination. The tribunal has power to permit a claim presented out of time if it is just and equitable in the circumstances. While time begins to run from the date of the last act complained of, the statutes also provide that *"any act extending over a period shall be treated as done at the end of the period"*.

> In *Barclays Bank v. Kapur* 1991 an employer's refusal to give its Asian employees the same favourable pension terms as its European employees was held to be a continuing discriminatory act extending over the period of employment until the employment terminated.

If the complainant is out of time the tribunal still has jurisdiction to hear the complaint if it is *"just and equitable in the circumstances"*.

> In *Forster v. South Glamorgan Health Authority* 1988 the failure to present the complaint within the time limits was found to be understandable as it was due to a change in the law. In such circumstances the EAT held that whether or not it is *"suitable"* to hear a complaint out of time is a *"question of fact and degree for the tribunal to determine in each case"*.

A copy of a complaint of unlawful discrimination must be sent to ACAS who will pass it on to a conciliation officer. It is the duty of the conciliation officer to attempt to resolve the conflict between the parties, if requested by them to do so, or if he feels that he has a reasonable prospect of success. If there is no settlement and the tribunal finds that there has been discrimination it can declare the rights of the parties, award compensation up to the unfair discrimination limits, and recommend action to be taken by the guilty party to reduce the adverse affects of the discrimination. A failure to respond to a recommendation without good reason could lead to an award of increased compensation.

Both the *Commission for Racial Equality* and the *Equal Opportunities Commission* have a role to play in encouraging, advising and providing financial assistance to prospective litigants. Furthermore only the Commissions may bring proceedings in respect of certain unlawful acts including discriminatory advertising, unlawful instruction to discriminate and unlawful inducements to discriminate.

Direct discrimination in recruitment

Direct discrimination occurs where one person treats another less favourably on the grounds of sex, race or marital status. In an allegation of direct discrimination in recruitment the formal burden of proof is on the complainant. The difficulty is of course that often direct evidence of discrimination is not available and consequently it is sufficient if the complainant can establish primary facts from which inferences of discrimination can be drawn. Evidence is necessary therefore to draw comparison with some person, actual or hypothetical who falls outside the relevant racial group or gender who was or would be treated differently by the employer.

> A good example of this approach is provided by *Humphreys v. St. Georges School* 1978. Here a complainant woman teacher established the following primary facts. As an experienced teacher along with two less experienced and less well qualified male applicants, she had applied for two vacant posts within a school. These facts, along with the fact that both male applicants were appointed, were sufficient to raise a prima facie (on the face of it) case of sex discrimination. The Court of Appeal stressed that it is only in an "exceptional or frivolous case" that the complainant will fail to establish a prima facie case.

Once the primary facts indicate a prima facie case of discrimination therefore *"the employer is called on to give an explanation and, failing a clear and specific explanation being given by the employer to the satisfaction of the industrial tribunal, an inference of unlawful discrimination from the primary facts will mean the complaint succeeds".*

Certainly there is no burden on an employer to disprove discrimination but once a prime facie case has been made out a tribunal is entitled to turn to an employer for an explanation of the facts.

> In *King v. The Great Britain–China Centre* 1991 the applicant who was Chinese and educated in Britain, failed to secure the post of deputy director of the China Centre despite her obvious qualifications for the job. She was not one of the eight candidates short-listed who were all white and no other ethnic Chinese person had ever been employed at the Centre. The Court of Appeal held that the tribunal was entitled to conclude that it was legitimate for them to draw an inference of discrimination on racial grounds in the absence of a satisfactory explanation by the employer

While there is no legal obligation as a employer to give reasons for not selecting a candidate for a job the legislation provides that an employer could be required to complete a questionnaire in which reason for decision making are asked. The questionnaire is admissible in evidence and evasive responses by the employer in the questionnaire will influence the tribunal's findings.

> In *Brighton Borough Council and Bishop v. Richards* 1993 the fact that the employer had delayed for two and half months in completing the questionnaire without good reason was thought to be significant by the EAT. In looking to the council for an answer to a

prima facie case of discrimination the tribunal was entitled to take account of the delay with the questionnaire, the failure to provide an explanation as to why the successful candidate had been selected, the fact that no notes had been made of the significant stages of the selection process and the failure to monitor the equal opportunities policy.

Direct discrimination extends not only to acts based on sex but also decisions made on gender-based criteria. The intention of the alleged discriminator is immaterial and tribunals should focus simply on whether the act or decision satisfies the *"but for"* test. Would the complainant have received the same treatment but for his or her sex?

In *Ace Mini Cars Ltd. and Loy v. Albertie* 1990 the EAT held that there was unlawful direct discrimination by an employer who refused to employ a black female minicab driver because he believed that she would be the subject of racial attacks.

If the employer puts forward a number of reasons for his conduct, some valid and some discriminatory, then provided the discriminatory reason was an important factor, there is unlawful discrimination.

In *Owen & Briggs v. James* 1982 a case involving race discrimination, the complainant was a young black girl who had applied for a job as a shorthand typist with a firm of solicitors. She was interviewed for the job but rejected. When the post was re-advertised some months later she re-applied, but when she arrived for her interview the employer refused to see her. The same day a young white girl was appointed to the post despite the fact that her shorthand speed (35 words per minute) was far inferior to the complainant's (80 words per minute). It was also established that one of the partners of the firm had said to the successful candidate *"why take on a coloured girl when English girls were available"*. The applicant's unlawful direct discrimination on the grounds of race was upheld in the industrial tribunal and on appeal in the Employment Appeal Tribunal. On further appeal to the Court of Appeal by the employer, it was argued that there could be no unlawful discrimination unless the sole reason for the conduct was the racial factor. This argument was rejected, the court deciding that it is sufficient if race is an important factor in the employer's decision and accordingly the appeal was unsuccessful.

One major difficulty facing a complainant is that proving discrimination may be impossible without access to documents which the employer holds. Since they may be confidential the applicant cannot have access to them unless the industrial tribunal chairman believes that they are relevant.

The Court of Appeal in *Nassè v. SRC* 1979 held that an industrial tribunal should not order or permit the disclosure of a report or reference, given and received in confidence, except in rare cases where, after inspection of the document, the chairman decides that it is essential in the interests of justice that the confidence should be overridden.

The words *on the grounds of sex, race or marital status* in the statutes would cover the situation where the reason for discrimination was a *generalised assumption* that men, women, married persons, or persons of a particular race, possess or lack certain characteristics.

In *Skyrail Oceanic Ltd. v. Coleman* 1981 two rival firms employed a man and woman who were subsequently married and for reasons of confidentiality, the woman was dismissed. The Court of Appeal held by a majority that, as the reason for dismissing the woman rather than the man was based on a general assumption that the man in a marriage is the breadwinner, and this is an assumption based on sex, this amounted to unlawful discrimination.

A useful tool to attack the credibility of the employer's denial of discrimination is statistical evidence. This is particularly so when the management decisions on matters such as promotion or access to benefits are based upon subjective criteria such as *excellence*, *potential* or *efficiency*. In *Owen & Briggs v. James* 1982 if the firm of solicitors could have shown that they had other black employees, this could have gone a long way towards enabling the tribunal to reach a contrary decision.

In *West Midlands Passenger Transport Executive v. Singh* 1988 the Court of Appeal ruled that statistical evidence of the employer's record of appointing ethnic minority applicants in the past, is material as to whether he has discriminated on racial grounds against a particular complainant. This enables a tribunal to scrutinise the employer's stated reason for rejecting the complainant and test it against comparative evidence of the employer's overall record.

The types of questions asked in interviews may be of relevance to determine whether there has been discrimination.

In *Saunders v. Richmond on Thames LBC* 1978 the EAT confirmed that it is not in itself unlawful to ask a question of a woman which would not be asked of a man. Here in an interview for a job as a golf professional, the female applicant was asked whether there were other female golf professionals and whether she thought that men would respond as well to a woman golf professional as to a man. Her claim of unlawful discrimination when she was not appointed did not succeed. The existence of direct discrimination depended upon whether she was treated less favourably on the grounds of sex than a man. Here, while the questions demonstrated an out of date attitude, the industrial tribunal was entitled to find that they were not asked with the intention of discriminating.

Asking questions about domestic circumstances would not necessarily be discriminating particularly when they could be asked of both male and female candidates.

In *Adams v. Strathclyde Regional Council* 1989 an applicant for a post as senior lecturer was asked at her interview how many children she had and their ages. This question was held not to constitute unlawful discrimination given that it could have equally have been asked of a male candidate and had been asked simply to help put her at her ease in the interview despite having the very opposite affect.

It is also unlawful to show an intention to commit an act of discrimination in relation to employment. Therefore the publication of an advertisement which invites applicants for the post of salesman or barmaids would constitute unlawful discrimination.

Under the EC *"Equal Treatment Directive"* the UK is required to implement the principle of *"equal treatment for men and women as regards access to employment"*. *The directive also provides that "there shall be no discrimination whatsoever on grounds of sex in the conditions, including selection criteria, for access to all jobs or posts"*.

In *Dekker v. Stichting Vormingscentrum voor Jonge Volwassenen Plus* 1991 the European Court of Justice held that it is a breach of the directive to refuse to employ a woman because she is pregnant despite the fact that this could mean grave financial consequences for the employer. If a woman receives less favourable treatment because she is pregnant this is direct discrimination and there is no need to establish that a man in comparable circumstances would not have been treated better.

EC law does not refer specifically to race discrimination but does provide that there should be no discrimination based on nationality within the Community in Article 48 of the Treaty of Rome Nationality is under the Race Relations Act 1976 included within the protection against discrimination on racial grounds.

Indirect discrimination in recruitment

Indirect discrimination, a more subtle form of discrimination than direct discrimination, is designed to cover overt yet not blatant acts of discrimination. A complaint of indirect discrimination could be brought under the UK legislation or the Equal Treatment Directive if applicable. Indirect discrimination occurs where a person requires another to meet a requirement or condition which as a member of a particular sex, race or marital status is less easily satisfied. This is because the proportion of those of that type who can comply with the requirement or condition is smaller, and it is to the complainant's detriment and not justifiable. It was held in *Perera v. Civil Service Commission* 1981 that in an allegation of indirect discrimination it is necessary to show that the requirement or condition is mandatory rather than one of a number of criteria which the employer would take into account.

> In *Meer v. London Borough of Tower Hamlets* 1988 the requirement was alleged to be job selection criteria, one of which was to have experience working in Tower Hamlets. The fact that this particular criteria was not mandatory meant that it could not constitute a requirement for the purposes of indirect discrimination.

For the purposes of showing that the proportion of the complainant's type who can comply with the condition is smaller there is no need to produce elaborate statistical evidence, but rather a common sense approach is to be encouraged. Nevertheless to succeed it is necessary to show that the proportion who can comply is considerably smaller.

> In *Price v. Civil Service Commission* 1978 the complainant alleged indirect discrimination on the grounds of sex because far fewer women than men could comply with the age limits of seventeen and a half to twenty eight to qualify as an eligible candidate for the executive officer grade. By comparing the proportion of qualified women with the proportion of qualified men, it is obvious that as a larger number of women of that age group will be likely to be having or bringing up children, then the proportion who can comply with the age requirement is less. The EAT held that as the proportion who can comply in practice is less and the requirement was not justifiable, there was unlawful indirect discrimination.

Even where indirect discrimination is established there are no damages payable if it is shown to be unintentional. Where the fundamental purpose of the claim is to secure compensation for the victim there is little point in presenting a complaint where there was no intention to discriminate.

In *Tickle v. Governors of Riverview CE School and Surrey County Council* 1994 the tribunal held that damages are available for unintentional indirect discrimination if the claim is brought under the Equal Treatment Directive. Here as the teacher involved was employed by a local authority, an emanation of the state, the Directive was applicable.

It is a question of fact in each case to determine the proportion of the complainant's group who can comply with the requirement or condition in practice. By deciding what proportion of the complainant's group can comply and comparing that figure with the proportion of qualified persons who can comply but fall outside the group, it is possible to decide whether it is considerably smaller.

In *Fulton v. Strathclyde Regional Council* 1986 the employer decided that certain social work posts should be exclusively for full-time staff. Of the basic grade social workers the statistics showed that 90% of the women could comply with the full-time requirement and all of the men. It was held on a complaint of indirect discrimination that 90% is not *"considerably smaller"* than 100% and so the claim must fail.

The definition of indirect discrimination also requires the complainant to have suffered a detriment and the requirement or condition must not be justifiable. The fact that the complainant has been adversely affected by the condition is sufficient to establish a detriment. It is open however for the defendant to show as a question of fact that in all the circumstances the requirement is justifiable.

In *Singh v. Rowntree Mackintosh* 1979 the complainant objected to a *no beard rule* operated by confectioners, which was alleged to be indirectly discriminatory against Sikhs. Here the EAT held that while the rule was discriminatory, it was a justifiable requirement on the grounds of hygiene, supported by medical advice, and therefore not unlawful. The burden of proof was on the employer to justify the requirement or condition and here the tribunal recognised that in adopting standards the employer must be allowed that independence of judgment as to what he believes is a common expedient in the conduct of his business. Certainly the requirement must be more than convenient but need not be necessarily essential.

If a person produces reasons for doing something which would be acceptable to right thinking people as sound and tolerable reasons for so doing, then he has justified his conduct.

In *Hampson v. Department of Education and Science* 1989 Balcombe L J held that to determine whether a condition is justifiable or not, an objective standard is required in each case. Justifiable *"requires an objective balance to be struck between the discriminatory effect of the condition and the reasonable needs of the party who applies that condition"*.

The fact that a claim of indirect sex discrimination may also be founded upon Article 119 of the Treaty of Rome and the Equal Treatment Directive is no better illustrated than by a direct challenge to national legislation brought by the Equal Opportunities Commission in 1994. In a momentous judgment in March 1994 the House of Lords ruled by a majority of four to one that UK legislation that gives part-time workers, predominantly women, less protection than full-time workers, predominantly men, is incompatible with European Union law as to equality between employees.

In *R v. Secretary of State for Employment, ex parte the Equal Opportunities Commission* 1994 the House of Lords considered the Employment Protection (Consolidation) Act 1978 which confers statutory rights relating to unfair dismissal and redundancy on full-time employees who have been continuously employed for two years. When compared with the position of part-time employees (employed between eight and sixteen hours) who qualify for such statutory rights after five years employment, the Lords held that such provisions indirectly discriminate against women.

Both the *Equal Opportunities Commission* and the *Commission for Racial Equality* have issued Codes of Practice to provide guidance to employers as to how to avoid sex and race discrimination particularly in recruitment. While the Codes are not law they are admissible in evidence in any proceedings under the legislation. An employer who complies with the Codes is more likely to avoid liability. One recommendation that employers should adopt is to monitor their recruitment processes, for resultant statistics could be used to overturn an inference of discrimination. Certainly this would be useful information to enable an employer to comply with the questionnaire procedures available to an individual considering or having brought proceedings under the discrimination legislation.

It is of course much more difficult to challenge recruitment decisions as discriminatory when informal recruitment methods are used because of the secrecy attached to them. Quite often jobs are filled without advertising or interviewing with staff appointed on the basis of personal recommendations. In these circumstances if ethnic minorities or a particular gender do not have access to these informal networks then they will continue to be under represented. In 1990 an enquiry by the Commission for Racial Equality into the London Underground revealed that following a reorganisation none of the numerous managers appointed were from the organisation's substantial ethnic minority staff.

Lawful discrimination in recruitment

Both the *Sex Discrimination Act* 1975 and the *Race Relations Act* 1976 identify circumstances where it is lawful to discriminate in the recruitment of staff. They are referred to as instances of *genuine occupational qualification (goq)*. It should be stressed from the outset that goq defence only applies to the making of a job offer or access to promotional, training or other benefits.

If a job applicant shows on the balance of probabilities that an act of direct or indirect discrimination has occurred it is open to an employer to establish as a defence that being of a particular sex or racial group is a genuine occupational requirement. To do this the employer must establish that the job falls within a number of identified categories. It would not be sufficient to argue that the employer was simply motivated to recruit from a particular sex or race to achieve a more balanced workforce.

> In *Etam plc v. Rowan* 1989 the complainant was refused a job as a sales assistant because the employer argued he could not carry out all the duties of the post because as a man he could not enter the fitting rooms in a shop which sold female clothing. The EAT agreed with the tribunal's finding that the complainant could have performed the majority of the job functions and there were plenty of female sales assistants who could enter the fitting rooms should that prove necessary. The complainant had suffered sex discrimination and the goq provided no defence.

The categories of genuine occupational requirements under the Sex Discrimination Act are as follows.

- where the job requires a man or woman for physiological reasons other than physical strength, or in dramatic performances or other entertainment for reasons of authenticity, e.g. female stripper or male model;

- where there are considerations of decency or privacy because the job is likely to involve physical contact with men in circumstances where they might reasonably object to it being carried out by a woman, e.g. male toilet attendant;

- where there are statutory requirements, e.g. woman may not work underground in coal mines. Following the *Sex Discrimination Act* 1986 there are few statutory restrictions that survive;

- where the work location makes it impracticable to live elsewhere than the employer's premises and it is unreasonable to expect the employer to provide separate facilities for sleeping or sanitation;

- where the personal service is most effectively provided by a man or woman, e.g. a female social worker dealing with unmarried mothers;

- where the nature of the establishment within which the work is done requires the job to be held by a man because it is a hospital, prison or other establishment for males, requiring special care, and it is reasonable that the job should not be held by a woman;

- where the job needs to be held by a man because it is likely to involve the performance of duties outside the United Kingdom, in a country whose law and customs are such that the duties could not be effectively performed by a woman, e.g. Saudi Arabia;

- where the job is one of two to be held by a married couple.

The decency or privacy genuine occupational can only be raised if in the circumstances it is not practical to employ a man or a woman.

In *Secretary of State for Scotland v. Henley* 1983 the decency or privacy goq was raised as a defence to recruit a male as a hall governor in a men's prison on the grounds that the job holder might have to be present in the toilet areas or where the men might be in a state of undress. The fact that no objection had been raised by the men helped the tribunal decide that the goq did not apply.

The categories of genuine occupational requirement in race discrimination set out in the Race Relations Act 1976 are

- drama and entertainment where the person of that racial group is required for reasons of authenticity, e.g. employing only a black actor to play the part of Martin Luther King;

- artist's or photographic models in order to achieve authenticity, e.g. a photograph depicting a national scene;

- bar or restaurant work where the setting requires an employee from a particular race, again for reasons of authenticity, e.g. Chinese Restaurant;

- the holder of the job provides persons of that racial group with personal services promoting their welfare and those services can most effectively be provided by a person of that racial group, e.g. a Bangladeshi social worker.

In *London Borough of Lambeth v. Commission for Racial Equality* 1990 the EAT held that this GOQ exception provides a defence only if the post advertised is for the provision of personal services, and the particular racial groups of the holder of the post and persons to whom the services are provided are sufficiently identified so as to establish that they are both of the same racial group. Here the fact that the local authority's advertisement related to posts which were of a managerial and administrative nature which involved very little contact with the public meant that they should not be confined to applicants of Afro-Caribbean or Asian origin. The intention of this exception under the 1976 Act *"envisaged circumstances where there was direct contact, mainly face to face or where there could be physical contact, and where language, cultural understanding and religious backgrounds were of material importance"*. Subsequently the Court of Appeal agreed with the EAT that the holders of the jobs advertised, being managerial positions, did not provide personal services promoting the welfare of persons of a particular racial group.

Enforcement and remedies

Discrimination law in employment may be enforced by individual complaint to an industrial tribunal. Also both the *Commission for Racial Equality* and the *Equal Opportunities Commission* have a role to play in the enforcement of the law and where certain unlawful acts are alleged, their role is an exclusive one. The process and time limits relating to the presentation of a complaint were considered earlier. If despite the attempts at conciliation the complainant decides to go ahead, there is a special pre-tribunal procedure to assist in the effective presentation of the complaint and access to information.

The remedies available to a tribunal who felt that a complaint has been made out are:

- an order declaring the rights of the parties;
- an order requiring the respondent to pay the complainant damages subject to the upper limit for unlawful dismissal claims;
- a recommendation of action to be taken by the respondent to reduce the adverse effect of discrimination.

A failure by the respondent without reasonable justification to comply with a recommendation may lead to an award of increased compensation. In the case of indirect discrimination if the respondent proves that the requirement or condition was applied without any intention to discriminate then no compensation will be awarded.

In *Noone v. North West Thames Regional Health Authority* 1988 the Court of Appeal confirmed that awards for incidents of racial discrimination were subject to the same rules as awards for damages for personal injury in respect of any other breach of statutory duty. Here the complainant was devastated by the discriminatory act and suffered a severe injury to feelings which should be acknowledged by the award of damages.

Nevertheless bearing in mind that she suffered no actual loss, the award of £5,000 was too high and should be reduced to £3,000.

The *Sex Discrimination and Equal Pay (Remedies) Regulations* 1993 formally removed the ceiling on compensation for unlawful sex discrimination and set out the method of calculating the interest. In 1993 it was also recognised that thousands of women who had been dismissed from the armed forces because they were pregnant can claim sex discrimination. The fact that the ceiling on compensation was lifted dramatically increased the significance of the potential claims and tens of thousands of pounds have been awarded. Tribunals have recognised that injury to feelings in such cases can include the emotional effect of discharge from the services evidenced by feelings of humiliation, isolation, loss of status and career aspirations and personal hurt.

The statutory ceiling of £11,000 on a compensatory award for race discrimination has also been lifted under the *Race Relations (Remedies) Act* 1994. If a complaint is well founded then the tribunal must decide whether it is *"just and equitable"* to award damages. The damages should reflect a sum of injury to feelings and the pecuniary loss subject to the ceiling. Damages for injury to feelings should compensate the complainant for the insult and humiliation suffered. In *Browne v. Cassell* 1972 Ld Diplock said that *"where salt is rubbed into the wound by high handed malicious insulting or offensive conduct additional compensation may be awarded by way of aggravated damages"*.

Pecuniary loss which is quantifiable includes the loss of wages, the loss of opportunity to work and the loss of advantage on the labour market.

> In *British Gas Plc v. Shama* 1991 the Employment Appeal Tribunal confirmed that there are limits to the extent that tribunals have power to make recommendations to reduce the adverse affects of unlawful discrimination. While the tribunal had found that the complainant had been the victim of direct racial discrimination when she was not promoted, the tribunal had no power to recommend that she should be promoted to the next suitable vacancy.

Enforcement of the legislation is also the role of the Commissions who having instituted a formal investigation and, being satisfied that unlawful discriminatory acts or practices have taken place, may issue a non-discrimination notice on any person. Such a notice will require the person on whom it is served not to commit the acts complained of and also comply with any required changes in conduct. The Commissions may seek an injunction to prevent repeated discrimination within five years of the non-discrimination notice becoming final.

Only the CRC or EOC can initiate proceedings under the legislation alleging discriminatory advertising which indicates an intention to discriminate. A job advertisement which indicates a racial or sexual preference such as *"steward"* or *"waitress"* would contravene the legislation without further explanation. Both the publisher and the advertiser could be made liable for a discriminatory advertisement but the publisher would have a defence if he can establish that he reasonably relied on a statement by the advertiser that the advertisement was not unlawful.

> In *Cardiff Women's Aid v. Hartup* 1994 it was confirmed that only the Commission for Racial Equality can bring proceedings for racially discriminating advertising. The important point was made however that it is still possible for an individual complainant to use a discriminatory advertisement as evidence of direct discrimination in the recruitment process.

Where an unlawful act is committed by an employee in the course of his employment, the principles of vicarious liability apply and the employer is also made liable for the act whether or not it is done with his approval. It is a defence for an employer to prove that he took such steps as were reasonably practicable to prevent the employees from doing that act or from doing, in the course of his employment, acts of that description. Such steps would certainly include full implementation of the Commission for Racial Equality Code of Practice on discrimination. Furthermore an employer is not liable unless the discriminatory act is done in the course of employment. Vicarious liability for discrimination in the workplace is considered in more detail in the next Chapter.

> In *Irving & Irving v. Post Office* 1987 the complaint of race discrimination was based on the conduct of an employee of the post office who when sorting the mail had written a racially insulting comment on a letter addressed to his neighbours who were of Jamaican origin. The issue before the Court of Appeal was whether the employee was acting in the course of his employment so that the Post Office could be made vicariously liable for the discriminatory act. The employee's act of writing on the mail was clearly unauthorised so the question was whether the act was an unauthorised mode of doing an authorised act. Here the misconduct formed no part of the postman's duties and could not be regarded as an unauthorised way of performing his work. *"An employer is not to be held liable merely because the opportunity to commit the wrongful act had been created by the employee's employment, or because the act in question had been committed during the period of that particular employment."*

If it does little else, discrimination law should stimulate equality of opportunity and act as a framework within which to identify barriers facing women and ethnic minority workers at work. As was suggested earlier, there is a view that there should be similar laws to protect people who are discriminated against because of their disability, sexuality or age. Ethically, job applicants should be judged on the basis of their ability rather than their gender or racial origin.

Legal Formalities and the Contract of Employment

Contrary to popular belief, apart from merchant seamen and apprentices, there is no legal requirement that a contract of employment be in writing. While there are problems associated with identifying the terms of an oral agreement, nevertheless given the fluid nature of a contract of employment there is no guarantee that a requirement to reduce the original contract to writing would solve all the problems of interpreting its content. A contract of employment is unenforceable if it is illegal under statute or its objects are contrary to public policy at common law. *Illegality* can arise in the formation or during the continuance of the contract.

> In *Napier v. National Business Agency* 1951 the plaintiff was employed on a salary of thirteen pounds per week with six pounds a week expenses. Both parties were aware that genuine expenses would never exceed one pound. Following her dismissal the plaintiff claimed damages for wrongful dismissal. The Court held that the contract was unenforceable as contrary to public policy. By contracting as they had *"the parties to it were doing that which they must be taken to know would be liable to defeat the proper claim of the Inland Revenue and to avoid altogether, or at least to postpone, the proper payment of income tax"*.

Statutory statement of terms and conditions of employment

Under s1 of the *Employment Rights Act* 1996 there is a statutory requirement on employers to provide their employees within two months of the commencement of employment with a written statement of the main terms of employment. The section originally applied to full-time employees (those engaged under an employment contract for sixteen hours or more a week) or part-time workers (engaged between eight and sixteen hours) after five years employment. Under the *Employment Protection (Part-time Employees) Regulations* 1995 the hours threshold has been removed and part-time employees are entitled to a statutory statement. Certain classes of employees are excluded from s.1 including registered dock workers, Crown employees and employees who work wholly or mainly outside Great Britain. The objective of s.1 is to ensure that employees have written confirmation and a source to scrutinise at least the main terms of their employment contracts. Employers can issue the statement in instalments but within the two months limit and the principal statement should contain certain information prescribed by section 1.

Particulars which must be included in the statutory statement include:

- reference to the parties and the dates on which the period of continuous employment began (stating whether a previous period of employment is included as part of continuous employment);
- the scale of remuneration and the method of calculation;
- the intervals at which remuneration is paid (whether weekly or monthly or some other period);
- the terms and conditions relating to hours of work;
- the terms and conditions relating to holidays and holiday pay (sufficient to enable the employee's entitlement to accrued holiday pay on the termination of employment to be precisely calculated);
- the terms and conditions relating to sickness or injury and sickness pay;
- the terms and conditions relating to pension and pension scheme;
- the length of notice which the employee is obliged to give and entitled to receive;
- the title of the job which the employee is employed to do or a brief description of the work;
- in addition every statement given shall include a note containing a specification of any disciplinary rules or reference to an accessible document containing such rules;
- the name of the person to whom the employee can apply if he is dissatisfied with any disciplinary decision relating to him;
- the name of the person to whom the employer can apply to seek the redress of any grievance;
- any collective agreement which directly affects terms and conditions of employment.

A section 1 statement may refer to other documents such as a staff handbook or written policy for the purposes of sickness provisions and pensions and a collective agreement for the purposes of notice provisions provided the employee has either a reasonable opportunity of reading such documents during the course of employment or they are readily accessible. It would also be permissible to include a disciplinary and grievance procedure in separate documents provided they are reasonably accessible.

There is no requirement to include a note on disciplinary proceedings in the written statement where the employer (together with any associated employer) has less than twenty employees on the date when the employee's employment began.

To satisfy the requirements of s.1 it is not sufficient simply to be told or shown the above particulars of employment. The employer must present the employee with a document containing the information or at least make such a document available for inspection (e.g. a collective agreement and a rule book). It should be stressed that a statutory statement is not the contract of employment but rather strong prima facie evidence of its terms. Certainly the mere acknowledgment of its receipt does not turn the statement into a contract.

> In *System Floors (UK) Ltd. v. Daniel* 1982, Browne-Wilkinson J said in relation to the statement that *"It provides very strong prima facie evidence of what were the terms of the contract between the parties. Nor are the statements of the terms finally conclusive: at most, they place a heavy burden on the employer to show that the actual terms of the contract are different from those which he had set out in the statutory statement"*. This view of the status of the statutory statement was subsequently approved by the Court of Appeal in *Robertson v. British Gas Company* 1983 where it was held that if the written statement does not accurately reflect the agreed terms then the agreed terms prevail.

Contractual terms we shall discover, are often the subject of change, in which case an employer is obliged to notify the employee of changes in the statement within one month of the change. An employer who fails to comply with obligations in relation to the statutory statement could be the subject of a complaint to the industrial tribunal. With no effective sanction available for employers who fail to comply with s.1, complaints to tribunals are rare, and only arise usually in connection with other complaints, for instance in relation to unfair dismissal. Finally it should be mentioned that those employers who provide their employees with a written contract of employment which covers all the matters which must be referred to in the statutory statement, do not have to supply their employees with a separate statutory statement. The writing should of course reflect what has been orally agreed by the parties.

> In *Discount Tobacco and Confectionery Ltd. v. Armitage* 1990 the complainant was a shop manageress with only a short period of continuous employment who enlisted the help of her trade union official to secure a written contract of employment from her employer. When finally such a contract was issued, and she felt that it contained discrepancies, the complainant attempted to raise them with her employer. The response of the employer was to dismiss her, giving the reason for dismissal as lack of suitability or capability. This led to a complaint of unfair dismissal, the complainant alleging that the true reason for dismissal was her trade union membership which was unfair under s.152 of the *Trade Union Labour Relations (Consolidation) Act* 1992. If trade union membership or activities is the reason for dismissal there is no need to qualify with two years continuous employment for protection against unfair dismissal. Both the industrial

tribunal and the Employment Appeal Tribunal thought that there was no genuine distinction between trade union membership and making use of the essential services of a union officer and as a consequence the dismissal in this case was unfair.

The Contents of a Contract of Employment

A contract of employment is composed of its *terms,* the mutual promises and obligations of the parties to it. Contractual terms may be `express' and become part of the contract through the express agreement of the parties. Usually of course, there is simply agreement by the prospective employee to the standard terms dictated by the prospective employer or terms previously agreed between the employer and a trade union. Alternatively, contractual terms may be implied into the contract of employment by an external source. The major sources for implication we shall discover, are the courts and tribunals but occasionally terms are implied into contracts of employment by statutory provisions or through custom. Such mutual obligations have legal significance and a failure to comply with the requirement of a term of the contract could provide the innocent party with the option of securing legal redress. An action for breach of contract may be brought to secure damages against the party in breach of a contractual term. If damages would not suffice to provide a remedy, an injunction could be sought to restrain the breach of contract. In such circumstances an interlocutory (temporary) injunction is often sought as a remedy. One rarely used option for an employee who feels that his employer is unreasonably requiring him to do work which is not part of his contractual obligations is to seek an injunction to maintain the status quo at work. A further option for an employee in these circumstances is to apply to the High Court for a declaration as to the legal position.

Later in Chapter 16 we shall see that if a breach of contract is regarded as so serious as to be repudiatory, then the innocent party has the option of accepting the breach and terminating the contract. A repudiatory breach by an employer could, if accepted by the employee, entitle him to regard himself as constructively dismissed if he walks out as a result. Alternatively, a repudiatory breach by the employee could in some circumstances justify summary dismissal by the employer.

In the majority of cases of conflict or dispute between the employer and employee, the true legal position can only be assessed by identifying and analysing the express terms of employment and any implied terms which have become incorporated into the contract.

Express Terms

Earlier in the chapter we saw that the express terms of a contract of employment are those expressly agreed by the employer and employee, and may be in writing or may be purely oral. The statutory statement of the main terms and conditions of employment will normally provide sound evidence of the express terms. Even a job advertisement, an application form or a letter of appointment could contain contractual terms, as well as matters orally agreed in the interview. Express terms relate to matters such as *wages, hours, holidays, sick pay, job description, restraints, etc.* Of course, what has expressly been agreed by the parties may often require interpretation in the courts and industrial tribunals.

It is the ordinary courts that generally but now not exclusively deal with disputes surrounding the interpretation of the terms of a contract of employment based upon an action for breach of contract.

The majority of employment disputes however relate to statutory employment rights such as unfair dismissal, redundancy and discrimination and they are heard by industrial tribunals and on appeal by the Employment Appeal Tribunal.

A court or tribunal may be called on to determine the rights of the parties by interpreting the exact wording of the express terms of a contract of employment.

> In *Cole v. Midland Display Ltd.* 1973 the tribunal was faced with the problem of determining the meaning of the term, *"employed on a staff basis"* when it was applied to a manager. The tribunal held that the phrase meant that the employee was entitled to wages during periods of sickness or no work but in return the employee could be required to work overtime with out pay.

> An employee whose job title was described as carrying out *"general duties"* in *Peter Carnie & Son Ltd. v. Paton* 1979 was held to be required to be very flexible in relation to the needs of his employer for the type of work to be carried out.

> In *Securicor Ltd. v. Reid and others* 1992 the EAT construed the express term that an employee was *"based at"* a certain location to mean that he could be required to work at any site within the area administered from that location. The employee could be required therefore, under the express terms of his contract to move from one site to another and if the employee refuses to move and is dismissed, he would not be entitled to a redundancy payment.

Express terms must not be drafted so widely that all eventualities are covered and they become meaningless. An appropriate form of words should be used in order to achieve a realistic expectation of the employer's requirements. Express terms covering matters such as a staff mobility should be activated in a reasonable and humane way.

Work rules

It is common practice in many spheres of employment for the employer to issue work rules by printing notices or handing out rule books. Such rule books often contain instructions as to time-keeping, meal breaks, disciplinary offences and grievance procedure, sickness and pension rights, job descriptions, and the employer's safety policy. Although there is still some doubt as to the legal status of work rules, the present view is that such documents are unlikely to contain contractual terms. One school of thought is that work rules should be regarded as `conditions' rather than `terms' of employment, hence the expression, *"terms and conditions of employment"* and as such they should be subject to unilateral change by the employer. For example, while the number of hours worked would normally be the subject of express agreement and constitute a contractual `term', instructions as to when these hours should be worked will normally be contained in a rule book and as a *condition* be liable to unilateral change.

> In *Dryden v. Greater Glasgow Health Board* 1992 the EAT held that an employer was entitled to introduce a rule imposing a smoking ban at the workplace and the staff has no implied right to smoke. *"An employer is entitled to make rules for the conduct of employees in their place of work within the scope of the contract and once it was held that there was no implied term in the contract which entitled the employee to facilities for smoking, the rule against smoking was a lawful rule"*.

Where, however, a rule book is given or referred to by the employer at the time the contract of employment is formed, the fact that the employee has agreed that it is to be part of the contract and acknowledges that fact by his signature would more than likely give the rule book contractual effect. Certainly there is case law authority which suggests that by posting a notice of the fact that the rule book has contractual effect, an employer would ensure that the rules become incorporated into individual contracts of employment.

Implied Terms

A contract of employment is composed of contractual terms which have been expressly agreed or incorporated into the contract by an extraneous source such as a collective agreement, the custom and practice of a particular trade or business, or the common law. To have a full appreciation of the content of a contract of employment you should be aware of the role of the common law in defining rights and duties of employers and employees. In addition to a large number of common law rights and duties relating to such matters as good faith, confidentiality, health and safety, and obedience, there is an increased willingness of the courts and tribunals to imply terms into employment contracts to deal with issues such as trust and confidence, mutual respect and sexual harassment. Later when we consider the termination of employment, you will discover that the need to point to a clear breach of the contract of employment to establish a constructive dismissal has encouraged judicial ingenuity in incorporating implied terms which the court then declares that the employer has broken.

Apart from one notable exception in relation to equal pay, statute is not a major source of implied terms of employment. On the creation of a contract of employment, however, a number of statutory rights arise immediately, most of which are non-excludable and further rights attach to the contract after a period of continuous employment.

The fact that common law implied terms confer rights and impose duties on both parties to the employment relationship, suggests that they can be more meaningfully examined by considering each of them in turn in relation to both the employer and the employee. Most of the implied terms can be categorised under broad headings such as the wage/work bargain, health and safety, good faith, confidentiality, fidelity, and trust and confidence.

The courts are careful to stress that terms are implied into contracts of employment by applying one of a number of tests. A term maybe implied if it is either:

- *necessary to the functioning of the contract or;*
- *reflecting the obvious intention of the parties at the time the contract was concluded or;*
- *an inevitable incidence of the employment relationship.*

It does seem however that the courts and tribunals find it possible to imply a term wherever it is thought necessary.

In *Mears v. Safecar Security* 1983 the Court of Appeal held that if there is no express agreement on a matter, the courts are entitled to consider all the facts and circumstances of the relationship, including the parties' conduct, to determine whether a term should be implied into the contract of employment.

In *Courtaulds Northern Spinning Ltd. v. Sibson* 1988 the Court of Appeal was called on to determine the nature and extent of an implied term in a contract of employment in relation to the place of work. Slade L J said that *"in cases ... where it is essential to imply some term into the contract of employment as to place of work, the court does not have to be satisfied that the parties, if asked, would in fact have agreed the term before entering the contract. The court merely has to be satisfied that the implied term is one which the parties would probably have agreed if they were being reasonable."*

In *Jones v. Associated Tunnelling Ltd.* 1981 the EAT held a contract of employment cannot simply be silent on the place of work. If there is no express term, it is necessary to imply some terms into each contract of employment laying down the place of work in order to give the contract *business efficacy*. The term to be implied in that which in all the circumstances the parties, if reasonable, would probably have agreed if they had directed their minds to the problem.

The role of the courts and tribunals in implying contractual obligations into contracts of employment is a fundamental feature of employment law. Employment conflicts sometime occur in determining whether a particular job function carries the status of a contractual duty even where job descriptions have been agreed by the parties. This conflict often arises during industrial action.

In *Sim v. Rotherham Metropolitan Borough Council* 1986 the High Court had to decide whether the requirement of school teachers to provide cover for absent colleagues during normal school hours was an implied contractual obligation or merely a matter of goodwill. Refusing to provide such cover during a period of industrial action had led the employer to deduct an appropriate sum from the teacher's monthly salary. The High Court recognised that school teachers are a member of a profession and as such you would not expect their contracts to detail the professional obligations under their contracts. *"The contractual obligations of persons employed in a profession are defined largely by the nature of their profession and the obligations incumbent upon those who follow that profession. Teachers have a contractual obligation to discharge their professional obligations towards their pupils and their school. Cover arrangements, the court decided, are part of a teacher's professional obligations and the refusal of teachers to comply with them was a breach of contract".*

The wage/work bargain

In a contract of employment there is an implied duty on the employee to provide personal service for which the employer is obliged to provide a wage. At the appointed time therefore, an employee is required to present himself for work and be ready and willing to perform at the direction of the employer. Absence from work without good reason would clearly constitute a breach of contract which would entitle the employer to adjust the wage accordingly. If the absence is due to industrial action there is an increasing tendency for the courts and tribunals to deal with conflict over entitlement to a wage or a partial wage by applying strict contractual principles.

The principle of *no work no pay* was reaffirmed by the House of Lords in *Miles v. Wakefield MBC* 1987. Here industrial action taken by Registrars involved them in refusing to carry out a proportion of their work, that of performing marriages, on Saturday mornings. While the Registrars attended for work on Saturdays and performed other duties the employer made it clear that wages would be deducted for Saturday morning hours if the employees were unwilling to perform the full range of their duties. The House of Lords upheld the employer's position that they were entitled to withhold the Saturday wage despite the fact that a substantial part of the work was performed. Lord Templeman said that *"in a contract of employment, wages and work go together, in an action by an employee to recover his pay he must allege and be ready to prove that he worked or was willing to work".*

The Court of Appeal has also expressed the view that limited industrial action which involves non-performance of a part of an employee's contractual duties will prejudice an employee's claim for wages or even partial wages during the relevant period. This is certainly the case where the employer makes it clear that he does not condone part performance of the contract by the employee, so that he can regard any contractual duties performed as purely voluntary. By allowing the employee to come to work and carry out less than his full contractual duties the employer is not accepting a partial performance of the contract, and there is no requirement to prevent the employee working.

In *Wiluszynski v. London Borough of Tower Hamlets* 1989 an estates officer in the Council's Housing Department, as a result of an industrial dispute between NALGO and the Council, took part in limited industrial action which involved boycotting enquiries from council members. While the contractual duty was only a small but important part of the officer's workload, the response of the employer was to warn the officer by letter that if he carried on limited work it would be regarded as unauthorised and purely voluntary and wages would not be paid. The industrial action lasted five weeks, during which the officer was not paid and when it ended it took him two and a half to three hours to deal with the members' enquiries which had built up. The officer's claim for salary during the relevant period was upheld by the High Court on the basis that he had substantially performed his contract and higher management were aware of that, acquiesced in it and took the benefit of the work. On appeal, however, a totally different view was expressed by the Court of Appeal. In these circumstances, the court held, an employee is entitled to dismiss an employer in repudiatory breach of his contract of employment or decline to accept the partial performance of the contract. Here the employer had made it clear that any work undertaken would be voluntary, so that the employee could not reasonably have been confused or misled by this statement. There was no question, therefore of the employer waiving the right not to pay by accepting the services rendered and no obligation to prevent the employee from working, particularly where there is a large workforce. In this case partial performance of the contract had not been condoned by the employer so that no wages were payable.

While it seems that there is an obligation to pay the contractual wage, this does not carry with it a duty to provide the employees with work. The general proposition was illustrated by Asquith LJ in *Collier v. Sunday Referee Publishing Company Ltd.* 1940 when he said, *"Provided I pay my cook her wages regularly she cannot complain if I choose to take any or all of my meals out."*

If an employee's pay depends upon work being provided, for instance piece work, or commission, the court in *Devonald v. Rosser and Sons* 1906 held that the employer is under an implied obligation to provide sufficient work to enable a reasonable wage to be earned. The obligation to provide work would also apply where the employee's occupation is such that the opportunity to work is an essential feature of the contract because of the possibility of loss of reputation due to inactivity such as an entertainer in *Herbert Clayton v. Oliver* 1930.

Health and safety

At common law an employer is obliged to provide his workers with a safe system of work. This common law duty encompasses an obligation to ensure that workers are provided with safe plant and appliances, appropriate safety equipment, safe work methods and safe fellow workers.

> In *British Aircraft Corporation v. Austin* 1978 the employer was held to be in breach of his implied duty of safety when he failed to investigate a complaint relating to the suitability of protective glasses for an employee. This conduct was held to be a repudiatory breach of the contract of employment sufficient to entitle the employee to terminate the contract and regard himself as constructively dismissed.

Employees themselves are under a duty to co-operate in relation to their own safety and that of their work colleagues. An employee who is unduly negligent in the performance of his work will be in breach of his employment contract and while he is unlikely to be sued by his employer, this could be used as a justifiable reason for dismissal.

> In *Lister v. Romford Ice and Cold Storage Co. Ltd.* 1957 the House of Lords held that an employee who caused injury by negligently reversing his lorry, was in breach of an implied term of his contract of employment.

The law relating to health and safety at work is examined in the next chapter.

Good faith (mutual trust and confidence)

Of all the implied duties, the duty of good faith and mutual respect is the most difficult to define precisely. This is because good faith is such a wide ranging concept and involves an obligation on the employee to respect confidences, obey reasonable instructions, take care of the employer's property, account for money received in the performance of duties and not disrupt the employer's business. An employer on the other hand must treat his workforce with respect, indemnify them for expenses incurred in the performance of their duties and when providing a reference, ensure that it is accurate and fair.

Employee's duty of faithful service

Any attempt by an employee to use his position for undisclosed personal gain, for instance by accepting bribes or making a secret commission, will constitute a breach of the employment contract. The origins of this implied duty can be traced back to nineteenth century case-law.

> In *Boston Deep Sea Fishing and Ice Company v. Ansell* 1889 an employee who received secret commissions from other companies for placing orders with them was held to be in breach of this implied duty of his contract of employment.

Reasonable Instructions

Part of the obligation of good faith requires an employee to submit to his employer's control and this involves obeying reasonable orders. What would constitute a reasonable instruction depends upon an objective interpretation of the employee's contractual duties both express and implied.

> In *Pepper v. Webb* 1969 the head gardener who responded to the request to plant some flowers with the words, *"I couldn't care less about your bloody greenhouse or your sodding garden"* was held to be in breach of the implied duty to obey reasonable instructions.

Even if an instruction is within the scope of an employee's duties, it may not be reasonable if it involves a risk of serious injury such as *Robson v. Sykes* 1938 or a breach of the criminal law. Certainly the duty of good faith would require an employee to be flexible and move with the times, so that an instruction to adopt work techniques involving new technology, after proper training has been given, would normally be regarded as reasonable.

> In *Cresswell v. Board of Inland Revenue* 1984, Walton J said that *"there can really be no doubt as to the fact that an employee is expected to adapt himself to new methods and techniques introduced in the course of employment"*.

It is important to distinguish however, between a change in work methods and change in the job itself which if not authorised or agreed to, could not be unilaterally imposed without a possible claim for a redundancy payment or compensation for unfair dismissal. A wilful refusal to obey a reasonable order could lead ultimately to a dismissal so we will return to the problem of reasonable instructions in Chapters 16.

Employees have an implied obligation to take care of their employer's property. An employee who negligently allows his employer's property to be stolen or causes it wilful damage will be in breach of his employment contract and liable to dismissal.

> In *Adamson v. B & L Cleaning Services Ltd.* 1995 the complainant employee tendered for a contract which his employers were attempting to renew. It was held that his subsequent dismissal was fair, for he had acted in breach of the implied duty of faithful service to his employer.

Industrial Action

Given that the objective of industrial action is normally to cause disruption to the employer's business, an employee who takes part in a strike, go-slow, partial performance or even a *work to rule* will be in breach of his contract of employment. Industrial action of itself involves a withdrawal of good faith so it is arguable that even an overtime ban, where there is no contractual obligation to work overtime, could be regarded as a breach of contract.

> In *Secretary of State for Employment v. ASLEF* 1972, the Court of Appeal held that wilful disruption of the employer's undertaking would amount to breach of this implied duty of good faith. Here the railwaymen were disrupting British Rail services by working to the letter of the British Rail rule book, but nevertheless were held to be in breach of contract.

In *Ticehurst and Thompson v. British Telecommunications Plc* 1992 the Court of Appeal considered the legality of the employer's act of withholding wages during a period of industrial action when staff refused to work normally. The Court held that wages could be withheld if employees are not ready and willing to perform in full their obligations under their contracts of employment and withdraw goodwill. *" There is an implied term to serve the employer faithfully within the requirements of the contract. This term must be implied into the contract if a manager is given charge of the work of other employees and who, therefore, must necessarily be entrusted to exercise her judgment and discretion in giving instructions to others and in supervising their work. Such a direction, if the contract is to work properly, must be exercised faithfully in the interests of the employer. There is a breach of the implied term of faithful service when the employee does an act or omit to do an act, which would be within her contract ... and the employee so acts or omits to do the act not in the honest exercise of choice or discretion for the faithful performance of her work but in order to disrupt the employer's business or to cause the most inconvenience that can be caused. "*

One tactic often employed by trade unions is an industrial dispute is to call for members to participate in half day or one day strikes over a period of time. Clearly by taking strike action an employee is in breach of contract and the appropriate sum could be deducted from his wage. If however the employee in question is otherwise working normally during the dispute the employer would not be entitled to refuse to accept work or refuse to pay wages. Again in *Ticehurst and Thompson v. British Telecommunications plc* 1992 the Court of Appeal held that *"the plaintiffs evinced intention to take part in future in a rolling campaign of strike action would not be a sufficient ground, by itself, for the employers to refuse to let her continue to work during the dispute. If the only intention evinced by the plaintiff was to continue to respond to a strike call if and when called upon by the union to strike, then she would, in effect, have been saying to the employers that she was intending to perform the full range of her contractual duties until sometime in the future, which might not happen at all, when she would break her contract by going on strike. If, during the time that her services would be rendered, the employers would receive full value from those services, there was no reason why they should not perform their part of the contract. "*

Misconduct

While there is no implied obligation on an employee to reveal to an employer his own misconduct or deficiencies, the relationship of trust and confidence may demand that an employee in a managerial capacity should report the misconduct of others in the organisation.

In *Sybron Corporation v. Rochem Ltd. and Others* 1983 the Court of Appeal held that an employee may be so placed in the hierarchy of an organisation so as to have a duty to report either his *superior's* or *inferior's* misconduct.

Confidentiality

Good faith most certainly includes respecting confidences so there would be a clear breach of the contract of employment if the employee revealed confidential information relating to any aspect of his employer's business to a competitor, or made use of such information for his own purposes.

Business goodwill revealed in customer lists and accounts or trade secrets such as manufacturing processes or designs, are in the nature of rights in property which the employer is entitled to protect during the employment relationship and to some degree even after its termination. It is a question of fact in each case whether information could be classified or confidential but some guidance was provided in *Marshall Thomas (Exports) Ltd. v. Guinle* 1978 where relevant factors were identified:

- the owner of the information must reasonably believe that its release would benefit a competitor or cause detriment to himself;

- the owner must reasonably believe that the information is confidential and not already public knowledge;

- the information must be judged bearing in mind the practice of the particular trade or industry.

By relying on the duty of fidelity an employer could obtain an injunction to prevent an employee working for a competitor in his spare time or revealing confidential information to a competitor. Breach of confidence could also be a reason relied on by an employer to convince an industrial tribunal that in the circumstances the decision to dismiss an employee was fair.

Further guidance in relation to the implied duty on an employee to respect confidential information even on the termination of employment was provided in *Universal Thermosensors Ltd. v. Hibben* 1992. The court concluded that *"The contracts of employment between the plaintiff and the three defendants did not include any provision restraining their activities after their employment had ended. So when they left they were free to set up at once a directly competing business in the same locality. Further, they were entitled to approach the plaintiff's customers and seek and accept orders from them. Still further they were entitled to use for their own purposes any information they carried in their heads regarding the identity of the plaintiff's customers or the plaintiff's pricing policies, provided they had acquired the information honestly in the course of their employment and had not for instance, deliberately sought to memorise lists of names for the purposes of their own business. What the defendants were not entitled to do was to steal documents belonging to the plaintiff, or to use for their own purposes information which can sensibly be regarded as confidential information contained in such documents regarding the plaintiff's customers or customer contacts or customer requirements or the prices charged. Nor were they entitled to copy such information onto scraps of paper and take these away and use the information in their own business".*

Employer's duty of good faith

It is only relatively recently that the courts and tribunals have recognised that an employee's duty to trust and respect his employer is in fact a mutual obligation in an employment relationship.

Trust and Confidence

In *Woods v. W H Car Services (Peterborough) Ltd.* 1982 the EAT recognised that in every employment contract there is an implied term of great importance, that of trust and confidence between the parties. Such a term requires that employers *"will not, without reasonable and proper cause, conduct themselves in a manner calculated or likely to destroy or damage the relationship of trust and confidence between employer and employee".*

Employers who have been guilty of conduct such as verbal or physical abuse of their employees or unilateral attempts to impose unreasonable changes in employment terms have found themselves in breach of this implied term.

In *Hilton International Hotels (UK) Ltd. v. Protopapa* 1990 the complainant resigned from her job as a telephone supervisor in one of her employer's hotels when she was severely reprimanded by her manager. The reason for the reprimand was her failure to obtain permission before making a dental appointment and the fact that it was *"officious and insensitive"* constituted a repudiatory breach of her contract of employment. The EAT confirmed that she was *"humiliated, intimidated and degraded to such an extent that there was a breach of trust and confidence which went to the root of the contract".*

The notion that an employee is under the control of his employer carries with it an obligation to indemnify the employee for expenses incurred in the performance of his duties. Furthermore an employer may be made vicariously liable for the wrongs committed by an employee during the course of his employment.

The Right to Information

In *Scally v. Southern Health and Social Services Board* 1991 the House of Lords held that there is an implied term in a contract of employment imposing a duty on the employer to take reasonable steps to provide an employee with certain information. Here the information in question related to pension rights which had been negotiated on the employee's behalf but they had not been informed of the benefits they conferred. Four junior doctors sued their employer for loss sustained by them because of the failure of their employer to give them notice of the right to purchase added years of pension entitlement. *"It is necessary to imply an obligation on the employer to take reasonable steps to bring a term of the contract of employment to the employee's attention so that he may be in a position to enjoy its benefit where the terms of the contract have not been negotiated with the individual employee but result from negotiation with a representative body".*

The Right to a Reference

While there is no duty to provide one, if an employee decides to supply his employee with a reference the employer should ensure that it is a fair and accurate assessment of the employee in question. If it is alleged that the reference supplied contains a *defamatory statement,* the employee is entitled to raise the defence of *qualified privilege* which is effective, provided that the employer can show that the statements were made without malicious intent.(see Chapter 17).

In *Spring v. Guardian Assurance Plc* 1994 the Court of Appeal held that the giver of a reference owes no duty of care in negligence to the person who is the subject of the reference or in obtaining the information upon which it is based. On appeal to the House of Lords however in 1994 their Lordships took a different view. The case surrounded a reference which had been supplied for the plaintiff in which he was described as a man of *"little or no integrity and could not be regarded as honest"* and that there was evidence of negligence in his work. Not surprisingly the plaintiff found it difficult to find employment and claimed damages against his ex-employer for the economic loss he had suffered as a result of the bad reference. His claim based on malicious falsehood failed because of the lack of malice and the failure to establish a contractual term which required references to be supplied with reasonable care. His claim in negligence succeeded in the High Court however and despite being reversed in the Court of Appeal has now been affirmed on final appeal to the House of Lords. By a majority of four to one their Lordships held that an employer giving a reference is under a duty to the subject of the reference to take reasonable care in compiling it or in obtaining the information on which it was based. If the subject of the reference suffers economic loss as a result of an employer's failure to meet this duty he can claim damages. Liability based on negligent misstatement could be established if:

1. the damage was foreseeable and it occurred. An employer who gives a careless reference can foresee economic loss;

2. there was a certain proximity between the nature of the misstatement and the subject so as to create a duty situation. The relationship of employer and employee was sufficiently closer to give rise to a duty; and

3. the situation was one where it was fair just and reasonable to impose a duty of care. This was the case with the giver of a reference who should take reasonable care in compiling it

Assignment The Hotel Union

The Hotel, Catering and Allied Workers Union (HCAW) is an independent Trade Union with a membership of approximately three hundred thousand. Its members are mainly classified as ancillary staff working within the Hotel and Catering Industry, including cleaners, bar staff, reception staff and waiters/waitresses.

Oliver Kingston plc is a large company having, as its main activity, the operation of a chain of hotels throughout the United Kingdom. Despite the fact that the majority of full-time ancillary staff are members of the HCAW, Oliver Kingston refuses to recognise the union for collective bargaining purposes.

Oliver Kingston plc operates the practice of employing ancillary staff as either *full-time employees*, or *regular casuals* or *casuals*. The casual workers are regarded by the company as having self-employed status and are responsible for paying their own tax and National Insurance contributions. The distinction between regular casuals and *casuals* is that the regulars are given the first opportunity to work when required, but if they refuse to work, which they are entitled to do at any time then they become mere casuals .

Mrs Ruby Marshall has worked as a regular casual in the banqueting suite of an Oliver Kingston hotel for the past five years as a waitress. She has worked on average 45 hours per week, 50 weeks per year, which is well in excess of the hours worked by full-time waiters. Having been accepted as a member of the HCAW, Mrs Marshall is then informed by the management of Oliver Kingston that they no longer require her services and her contract is instantly terminated. When Marshall asked why her contract was terminated, she was given a written statement which identified *general incompetence* and *sloppy work* as the reasons for dismissal. She believes that she was dismissed because she joined the Union.

Recently the company interviewed for the full-time post of senior barman, After the interviews one of the interviewees, Roger Shields, was invited back before the interview panel and formally offered the post subject to the receipt of appropriate references. Roger immediately accepted the offer. Some days later the company contacted Roger and informed him that they were no longer willing to proceed with his post having received an unsatisfactory reference from his last employer. Angry and upset, Roger telephoned the Personnel Manager of his ex-employer. He was told that the reference given described him as *"conscientious and efficient employee who had been an active HCAW union member"*.

Tasks

For the purpose of the these tasks you are an officer of the HCAW employed at the union's National Headquarters who has been required to prepare a report in which you advise as to the legal position of Marshall and Shields and the legal status of *regular casuals*.

Legal Terms found in Chapter 15

Collective agreement	• the product of collective bargaining
Collective bargaining	• negotiation between employer and workers representatives about terms and conditions of employment and industrial relations
Contributory fault	• a partial defence where the plaintiff has contributed to the harm caused
Improvement notice	• an order served by a health and safety inspector requiring a contravention of safety law to be remedied within a specified time
Legal declaration (Declaratory judgment)	• a statement of the court as to the legal position
Maternity absence	• statutory right to a period of absence in the event of pregnancy dependent upon two years continuous service
Maternity leave	• statutory right to fourteen weeks leave in the event of pregnancy regardless of the length of service
Mobility clause	• a term in a contract of employment which authorises the employer to transfer the employee from one workplace to another
Negligence	• breach of a legal duty to take care
Prohibition notice	• an order served by a health and safety inspector requiring that an activity that contravenes safety law should be terminated
Repudiatory breach	• serious breach of contract giving the innocent party the right to accept the breach and terminate the contract
Risk assessment	• a comprehensive survey of organisational, job, workplace and individual factors that affect health and safety at work
Sexual harassment	• conduct of a sexual nature that is unwanted, unreasonable and offensive to the recipient
Strict liability	• liability imposed without fault
Unilateral action	• an act done by one party only
Volenti non fit injuria	• a legal defence where the plaintiff has consented to the harm caused
Working environment	• arrangements of a workplace including physical and psychological conditions of work

Chapter 15

Law Relating to the Workplace

In the previous chapter we considered the legal process under which a business organisation recruits its staff. Here it is proposed to consider the rights and responsibilities of employers and employees during the substance of the employment relationship. This will involve a consideration of the legal position relating to changing contractual arrangements, equal opportunities, health and safety and some of the statutory rights and responsibilities which apply to the parties to a subsisting contract of employment.

Changing Contractual Arrangements

In practice, the process of negotiating and varying terms and conditions of employment is not carried on by employees individually bargaining with their employers but in the majority of cases, by employers and trade unions engaging in *collective bargaining* on their behalf. The product of collective bargaining is called a collective agreement which will normally contain, along with a number of other matters, specific reference to individual terms and conditions of employment. Over seventy five percent of workers are still covered by *collective agreements* so that it is crucial to appreciate their legal standing and those parts of a collective agreement that are suitable for incorporation into individual contracts of employment. The legal status of collective agreements is referred to in the Trade Union and Labour Relations (Consolidation) Act 1992 which provides that such agreements are *conclusively presumed not to be legally enforceable unless in writing and expressed to be so*. As between the parties to a collective agreement therefore, (the trade union or unions and the employer or employer's association), collective agreements while in writing are not usually expressed to be legally enforceable and are consequently not legally binding. Those parts of the collective agreement that are incorporated into individual contracts of employment will become legally enforceable however between the employer and employee.

It is inevitable that the success and in some cases the survival of any business organisation in the public or private sector will depend on its ability to respond positively to legal, economic or social change. Here we will consider the legal position relating to changing contractual arrangements. Human nature dictates that there will be a degree of opposition to change so it makes sense for an employer to attempt to manage the change process sensitively. This will involve supplying affected employees with information, engaging in consultation and seeking their acceptance of the proposed change. A contemporary feature of present day employment is the attempt by employers to introduce new contracts which in some spheres of employment represent a move away from collectively bargained terms and conditions of employment to individual or *personal* contracts.

In the last chapter we considered the expression terms and conditions of employment and said that conditions of employment cover numerous matters under the control of the employer such as disciplinary procedures, safety policy, meal breaks which are ultimately subject to unilateral change.

> In *Dryden v. Greater Glasgow Health Board* 1992 the EAT held that an employer was entitled to introduce a rule imposing a smoking ban at the workplace and the staff had no implied right to smoke *"An employer is entitled to make rules for the conduct of employees in their place of work within the scope of the contract and once it was held that there was no implied term in the contract which entitled the employee to facilities for smoking, the rule against smoking was a lawful rule".*

While it would be prudent to consult before changing working rules obviously substantial alterations to the working environment can nevertheless be achieved unilaterally by an employer in this way.

More significantly as a result of a change process in any organisation, an employer may wish that members of the workforce should accept an increase or decrease in hours or pay, different contractual duties or responsibilities, a change in job location or different job functions or work practices. A sensitive employer would usually seek their consent even where the workforce may be legally required to accept the change within their terms of employment. If express terms of employment authorise the employer to implement the change, then an employee is legally obliged to accept it provided the term is interpreted reasonably.

> In *McCaffery v. A.E. Jeavons Ltd.* 1967 an employee employed expressly as a *travelling man* in the building trade was held to be bound to move anywhere in the country.

Even where there is a well drafted *mobility clause* in a contract of employment an employer must act reasonably when relying upon it. It is perfectly proper for a tribunal to imply a term into a contract which has the effect of controlling the exercise of a discretion expressly conferred in the contract.

> In *United Bank Ltd. v. Akhtar* 1989 the employer was in repudiatory breach of an implied term of the contract of employment requiring reasonable notice when he sought to rely on the above mobility clause to require a junior bank employee to move from the Leeds branch to Birmingham after giving only six days notice. As a consequence the employee who refused to move without more notice could regard himself as being constructively dismissed. The EAT held that *" the tribunal were entitled therefore to imply a term that the employer's discretion under the mobility clause was one which they were bound to exercise in such a way as not to render it impossible for an employee to comply with his contractual obligation to move. It was necessary to imply that requirement into the contract in order to avoid impossibility of performance".* Furthermore the employer's conduct in relation to the transfer could also be said to be in breach of the general implied contractual duty of trust and confidence.

Previously we saw that courts and tribunals have a wide discretion to imply terms into contracts of employment to give effect to the parties' intentions by more fully expressing the contractual bargain.

By implying a term into employment contracts that employees should be flexible and adaptable and react positively to change, an employer is authorised to implement quite sweeping changes in job functions provided staff are given sufficient training to enable them to cope with the different demands placed upon them.

> In *Cresswell v. Board of Inland Revenue* 1984, employees sought a legal declaration that their employers had broken the terms of their contract of employment by introducing new technology and expecting them to adapt to it. The High Court declared, however, that, provided they received adequate training, employees were expected to adapt to new methods and new techniques. There is a general contractual duty on employees to adapt to changing working methods. There was also a right for the employer to withhold pay for those employees who refused to conform to the new methods, for they are in breach of their contractual obligations.

The legal position is much more complex if the changing contractual arrangements are not expressly or impliedly authorised by the contract of employment. An obvious example would be the situation where an employer requires his staff to move from full-time to part-time work or accept a reduction in wages. Here the employer must seek the express or implied assent of his workforce or their trade union to the change and he cannot legally impose the change unilaterally.

If there is no agreement to a proposed change and the employer attempts to unilaterally impose a more onerous term on an employee, for example a wage cut, then the employee has a number of options. He could:

- accept the variation as a repudiatory breach of the contract, walk out and claim constructive dismissal;
- remain passive without protest and eventually be taken to have accepted the varied contract;
- continue to work under protest and sue for damages for breach of contract.

> In *Rigby v. Ferodo Ltd.* 1988 the employee, in response to a unilateral wage cut, took the final option and sued for damages representing the unpaid wages. Both the High Court and the Court of Appeal agreed that there had been no mutual variation of the contract of employment so that the unreduced wage was payable and, further, that the damages should not be limited to the twelve week notice period under which the employee could have been dismissed. The House of Lords agreed and held that a repudiatory breach does not automatically terminate a contract of employment unless the breach is accepted by the employee as a repudiation. Damages were not limited therefore to the notice period of twelve weeks and the primary contractual obligation to pay the full wage survived.

It seems therefore that provided the correct notice is given, an employee could be contractually bound to accept a change in terms of employment. There must be an unequivocal termination of existing contracts however by the employer for the courts would be unlikely to imply a dismissal from a notice of variation. An attempt by an employer to vary existing contracts unilaterally could be restrained by court action.

Termination of employment

In the absence of agreement therefore it seems that an employer who wishes to impose change must proceed by way of notice of termination with the offer of a new contract. An employee who is faced with a dismissal notice however, if qualified to do so, having two years continuous employment, would have the right to pursue a claim for unfair dismissal.

By requiring such an employee to accept more onerous terms of employment an employer will be in repudiatory breach and if accepted by the employee this could constitute constructive dismissal and potentially an unfair dismissal.

> In *Greenaway Harrison Ltd. v. Wiles* 1994 a telephonist who worked a split shift to fit in with her child care responsibilities was told to work a new shift pattern which was not compatible. Her employer warned her that unless she accepted the new shift pattern she would be dismissed with one month's notice. The complainant left claiming constructive dismissal which was unfair. The EAT upheld the finding that the case fell within a constructive dismissal because the decision to dismiss had already been taken before she left and this was a fundamental breach of contract.

In the present employment climate the potential redress for a successful complaint of unfair dismissal will hardly compensate for the loss of secure employment. Rights in relation to unfair dismissal are considered later in Chapter 16

Health and Safety at Work

Any treatment of the law relating to the workplace should involve an examination of health and safety law. Here the topic is given detailed consideration in an attempt to minimise its complexity and reflect the high priority that should be given to the aim of securing a safe working environment. In addition while health and safety law is embodied within the UK legislation and common law it is an area of business law that has been subjected to dramatic change due to our membership of the European Union.

In the United Kingdom legal intervention in the field of health and safety has a long history and the earliest examples of employment legislation, the nineteenth century Factories Acts, were designed to ensure that a slender cushion of legislative protection was provided for those categories of workers at particular risk. The criminal codes in relation to health and safety law were contained in numerous statutes and statutory instruments e.g. the Factories Act 1961, the Office Shops and Railway Premises Act 1963. Eventually in 1972 the Robens Committee on Safety and Health at work criticised this fragmented state of the law. As a result of the Robens Committee recommendations the Health and Safety at Work Act 1974 was passed.

The aims of the Act were to:

- lay down general duties applicable across the industrial spectrum;
- provide a unified system of enforcement under the control of the Health and Safety Executive and local authorities;
- create the Health and Safety Commission to assist in the process of changing attitudes and producing detailed regulations applicable to each industrial sector backed up by

codes of practice designed to give guidance as to how general duties and specific regulations could be satisfied.

By imposing legal duties on employers, employees, contractors, manufacturers and others backed up by criminal sanctions, the 1974 Act is designed to achieve minimum standards of conduct and so minimising the risk of injury and enhancing the welfare of those at the workplace. In addition to criminal sanctions however the possibility of civil redress must also be considered so that those injured at the workplace have a further avenue of redress to secure compensation by relying on common law principles.

European Community Law

As previously stated UK businesses also operate in a European legal framework and health and safety issues are an established part of European Community social policy. Since the adoption of the Single European Act 1986 the regulation of Health and Safety at work in the UK as been refined by European Community law initiatives. In 1990 the Chairman of the Health and Safety Commission said that *"the European Community has now to be regarded as the principal engine of health and safety law affecting the UK not just in worker safety but also major hazards and most environmental hazards"*. Article 22 of the Single European Act 1986 added a new Article 118A to the Treaty of Rome and so introduced a new concept *"the working environment"*.

Article 118A provides that *"Member States shall pay particular attention to encouraging improvements especially in the working environment, as regards the health and safety of workers and shall set as their objective the harmonisation of conditions in this area, while maintaining the improvements made"*.

The significance of Article 118A is that it incorporates the qualified majority procedure rather than unanimity procedure for the adoption of health and safety provisions by the Council of Ministers. (See Chapter 2).

This means that despite the objection of individual member states the majority view as to setting health and safety standards throughout the European Community will prevail. Furthermore the European Parliament has suggested that the expression *"working environment"* in Article 118A should be given a wide definition so that it could embrace matters such as the arrangement of a workplace as well as physical and psychological conditions at work. The working environment provisions were also acknowledged by the acceptance of the Charter of Fundamental Rights of Workers in December 1989 as an integral part of the development of the internal market.

In Chapter 1 in the section on change, reference was made to the controversial Working Time Directive which introduces the concept of the 48 hour working week subject to a number of exceptions. The directive had been passed under the qualified majority procedure as a health and safety measure and this was challenged by the UK government which had voted against it. In November 1996 the European Court of Justice ruled that the directive was lawfully introduced and should be incorporated into UK law. (The time limit is November 23 1996.)

There is no doubt that recently there has been a dramatic acceleration in the pace of the community legislation on health and safety compared with the minimal achievement of the previous two decades.

Health and Safety Regulations

In order to implement numerous directives a number of regulations have been produced clarifying new law and repealing out of date law. In addition, practical guidance in the form of codes of practice have also been produced to ensure compliance with the regulations which have been in force from the beginning of 1993.

The new regulations apply to virtually all work activities and place duties on employers in relation to their employees and in some circumstances to the public and self employed contractors in relation to themselves and others who may be affected by their acts or omissions. The regulations are very comprehensive however it should be stressed that the main focus is initially to promote awareness and enforcement is not likely unless:

- *the risks to health and safety are immediate and evident, or*
- *employers appear deliberately unwilling to recognise their responsibilities to ensure the long term health, safety and welfare of employees and others affected by their activities.*

Management of health and safety at work regulations 1992

These regulations are aimed at improving health and safety management and apply to almost all work activities in Great Britain and offshore. Under them employers are required to adopt a well organised and systematic approach to comply with their statutory duties in relation to health and safety. In pursuing this objective employers are required to:

- carry out a risk assessment of health and safety so that preventive and protective measures can be identified. While there is an existing obligation in the Health and Safety at Work Act for employers of five or more employees to prepare a written health and safety policy there is now an additional obligation on them to record the findings of the risk assessment.

- make arrangements for putting into practice the health and safety measures that follow from the risk assessment. These arrangements will include planning, organisation, control, monitoring and review and must be recorded by employers with five or more employees.

- appoint competent people to help devise and implement the appropriate measures and ensure that employees including temporary workers are given appropriate health and safety training and understandable information.

- provide appropriate health surveillance for employees and set up emergency procedures where the risk assessment shows it to be necessary.

- consult employees safety representatives, provide facilities for them and co-operate with other employers sharing the same working environment.

Risk assessments should identify hazards and then evaluate risks which should be remedied as soon as possible. The assessment should be carried out by health and safety personnel or suitably qualified line managers. It should be comprehensive covering organisational, job, workplace and individual factors and where sible include the participation of individual employees and safety representatives.

In relation to employees the regulations require them to follow health and safety instructions and report dangers. Finally as far as the management of health and safety is concerned it should be recognised that there is an overlap between the new regulation and some existing requirements contained in duties and regulations. A specific regulation will replace a general duty but there is no requirement to for instance carry out two risk assessments for the purposes of different regulations.

Provision and use of work equipment regulations 1992

Under the regulations general duties are placed upon employers in relation to equipment used at work and minimum requirements are identified to apply to all industries.

The expression *"work equipment"* is given a very wide definition and covers machinery of all kinds ranging from a hand tool to a complete plant. The *'use'* of such equipment includes all activities ranging from installing and repairing to transporting and dismantling.

It should be stressed that employers who already use 'good practice' in the use of work equipment will find themselves in compliance with the new regulations.

The general duties will require an employer to:

- assess working conditions in particular risks and hazards when selecting work equipment.
- ensure that equipment is suitable for its use and that it conforms with EC product safety directives.
- give staff adequate information, instruction and training and maintaining equipment in efficient working order and a good state of repair.
- In addition to the general duties the regulations also contain specific requirements in relation to equipment which will replace existing regulations. They include:
- guarding of the dangerous parts of machines.
- protection against specific hazards such as articles or substances, fire risks and explosion.
- ensuring adequate lighting, maintenance, warnings, stability, control systems and control devices.

The regulations apply to existing work equipment in use and further regulations will be made to implement EC directives requiring that new work equipment sold in member states should satisfy specific requirements.

Manual handling operations regulations 1992

These regulations are aimed at preventing injuries which occur at the workplace due to the mishandling of loads by incorrect lifting, lowering, pushing, pulling, carrying or simply moving them about. Such operations should have been identified in the risk assessment. The regulations require an employer to ensure that:

- there is a genuine need to move a load and that manual handling is necessary rather than mechanical means

- the weight size and shape of the load is assessed along with the working environment and the handler's capabilities

- in so far as is reasonably practicable the risk of injury is reduced by for example reducing the load, employing mechanical means or training the handler.

Workplace (health safety and welfare) regulations 1992

The aim of these regulations is to replace numerous parts of existing legislation including the Factories Act 1961 and the Office Shops and Railway Premises Act 1963. They cover many aspects of health safety and welfare at the workplace in particular the working environment which includes temperature, ventilation, lighting, room size, work stations and seating. Facilities at the workplace are covered which includes toilets, washing, eating and changing facilities, drinking water, clothing storage, rest areas and facilities along with the need for cleanliness and effective removal of waste. Specific aspects of safety are included in particular relating to safe passage of pedestrians and vehicles, windows and skylights, doors, gates and escalators and floors.

Personal protective equipment at work regulations 1992

By these regulations some old law relating to PPE is replaced but more recent legal rules, in particular the Control of Substances Hazardous to Health or Noise at Work Regulations, remain in force. Personal protective equipment includes protective clothing, eye foot and head protection, harnesses, life jackets and high visibility clothing. Where risks are not adequately controlled by other means there is a duty to provide PPE free of charge for employees exposed to risks. The PPE provided must provide effective protection as appropriate to the risks and working conditions, take account of the worker's needs and fit properly. Further regulations are necessary to comply with a separate EC directive on the design certification and testing of PPE. The present regulations require an assessment of risks to determine the suitability of PPE; the provision of storage facilities; adequate training information and instruction; appropriate methods of cleansing maintenance and replacement and effective supervision to ensure its proper use.

Heath and safety (display screen equipment) regulations 1992

These regulations apply where an individual habitually uses display screen equipment as a significant part of normal work. Duties are imposed on employers if equipment is used for the display of text, numbers and graphics but some systems are excluded including transport systems for public use, cash registers, window typewriters and portable systems not in prolonged use. The duties require employers to:

- assess display screen work stations and reduce risks revealed.

- ensure that minimum requirements are satisfied in relation to the display screen, keyboard, desk and chair, working environments and task design and software

- plan the work so that there are changes of activity and appropriate breaks and

- provide information and training for display screen users, eye testing and special spectacles if needed.

There is no doubt that under these regulations in particular, employers will have to incur considerable expense to ensure that equipment meets the basic minimum requirements. Existing work stations must be brought up to standard by the end of 1996 and the costs of eye testing spectacles and insurance must all be borne by the employer.

Enforcement of Health and Safety Law

Enforcement of the safety legislation is in the hands of the *Health and Safety Executive* and local authorities which have a number of powers at their disposal. The main power is to appoint inspectors who have authority to enter premises, take samples and require information to be given. The breach of a general duty or a specific regulation under the Health and Safety legislation is a criminal offence. This can lead to a prosecution in the criminal courts. Less serious offences are dealt with summarily in the Magistrates Court and those of a more serious nature are tried on indictment in the Crown Court. Conviction in *summary* proceedings carries a fine of up to £5000, or for an *indictable* offence, an unlimited fine and/or up to two years imprisonment. The fundamental aim of those enforcing the law is to encourage a positive attitude to health and safety at the workplace rather than to take numerous employers through the criminal courts. There is no doubt however that some employers resent the economic cost of health and safety and it may only be the threat of criminal prosecution, that will cause the more recalcitrant employers to respond. There is no doubt however that enforcement remains inadequate due to under resourcing of the inspectorate.

One of the major innovations of the Health and Safety at Work Act was the introduction of *constructive sanctions*. A Health and Safety Inspector who believes that an employer is contravening one of the statutory provisions may serve on that person an *improvement notice* requiring that the contravention be remedied within a specific period of not less than twenty one days. The notice will specify the provision which is contravened and state how it is being broken. In cases where the contravention involves an immediate risk of serious injury, the inspector may serve a *prohibition notice* which will direct that the particular activity is terminated until the contravention is rectified. Such a notice may take immediate effect or be deferred for a specified time. Failure to comply with a prohibition notice, for example by using a machine which has been identified as a serious source of danger, is an offence triable on indictment in the Crown Court.

While liability is generally associated with fault the courts have recently confirmed that even where there was little evidence of personal blame, an occupier of factory premises may still be held liable under the Factories Act 1961 if he fails to make his premises as safe as is reasonably practicable for all persons who may work there, even if they are not employees.

> In *Dexter v. Tenby Electrical Accessories Ltd.* 1991 contractors were employed by the defendants to install fresh air fans at their factory premises and for this purpose an employee of the contractor was required to work for a period on the factory roof. Despite the fact that the defendants were unaware that the employee was working on the roof they were nevertheless liable as occupiers of the factory when he suffered injuries after falling through it. The Health and Safety Executive charged the defendant with a contravention of s29(1) of the Factories Act 1961 which provides *"there shall, so far as is reasonably practicable, be provided and maintained safe means of access to every place which any person has at anytime to work, and every such place shall, so far as is*

reasonably practicable, be made and kept safe for any person working there". While the Magistrates accepted the argument that the defendants had no control over the employee's place of work and so there was no case to answer, this was rejected in an appeal by the prosecution to the Queen's Bench Divisional Court. The appeal court held that lack of knowledge was no defence and if a person is ordered by his employer, a contractor, to work on a factory roof, the occupier of the factory is liable under the Act if the roof is in an unsafe condition.

General duties

Most of the general duties contained in the 1974 Act impose on a number of different categories of person, a standard of care based on the idea of reasonable practicability. The most important general duty is that contained in s.2(1). Section 2(2) identifies matters to which the duty extends:

> *Under s.2(1) It shall be the duty of every employer to ensure, so far as is reasonably practicable, the health, safety and welfare at work of all his employees.*
>
> (2)   *Without prejudice to the generality of an employee's duty under the preceding subsection, the matters to which that duty extends includes in particular-*
>
>> (a)   *the provision and maintenance of plant and systems of work that are, so far as is reasonably practicable, safe and without risks to health;*
>>
>> (b)   *arrangements for ensuring, so far as is reasonably practicable, safety and absence of risks to health in connection with the use, handling, storage and transport of articles and substances;*
>>
>> (c)   *the provision of such information, instruction, training and supervision as is necessary to ensure, so far as is reasonably practicable, the health and safety at work of his employees;*
>>
>> (d)   *so far as is reasonably practicable as regards any place of work under the employer's control, the maintenance of it in a condition that is safe and without risks to health and the provision and maintenance of means of access to and egress from it that are safe and without such risks;*
>>
>> (e)   *the provision and maintenance of a working environment for his employees that is, so far as is reasonably practicable, safe, without risks to health, and adequate as regards facilities and arrangements for their welfare at work.*

The scope of the general duty, contained in s.2, qualified by the words *"reasonably practicable"* is difficult to determine and little guidance has been provided by the courts. However the meaning of this phrase is obviously crucial in determining the scope of an employer's duty. It would be wrong to assume that it imposes a standard of care comparable with the duty to take reasonable care at common law. The statutory duty requires the employer to take action to ensure health and safety unless, on the facts, it is impracticable in the circumstances. This has been taken to mean that in determining the scope of general duties cost-benefit considerations must be taken account of.

In *Associated Dairies v. Hartley* 1979 the employer supplied his workers with safety shoes which they could pay for at £1 per week. An employee who had not purchased the shoes suffered a fractured toe when the wheel of a roller truck ran over it. There was an obvious risk to workers from roller trucks in the employer's warehouse. Accordingly an improvement notice was served on the employer requiring him to provide his employers with safety shoes free of charge (estimated cost £20,000 in the first year and £10,000 per annum thereafter). The Court of Appeal held that while such a requirement was practicable in all the circumstances of the case, it was not reasonably so, bearing in mind the cost in relation to the risk of injury. The improvement notice was therefore cancelled, the court confirming that in relation to the general duty, practicability alone is not the test, for it is qualified by the term *"reasonable"*.

More recently there is evidence that the courts have adopted a more positive approach to the interpretation of the general duties under s.2(1) and s.2(2).

In *Bolton Metropolitan Borough Council v. Malrod Insulation Ltd.* 1993 a prosecution was brought against the defendant contractors under the general duty in s.2(1) and for failing to provide and maintain safe plant under s.2(2)(a). Following an inspection, an electrically driven decontamination unit, used by the contractors, was found to have defects which could cause electric shocks to those who used it. Following a conviction the defendants appealed on the grounds that the duties owed under s.2 only applied when the employee is at work and at the time of the alleged offences work had yet to begin. The Crown Court, upheld the appeal agreeing with the defendant's interpretation of the section. On further appeal the Divisional Court rejected this interpretation and held that the use of the *"at work"* in s.2(1) could not on any common sense basis mean that the duty to provide safe plant only arises when men are actually at work. This would mean that the health and safety inspectorate would be powerless to act if they discovered unsafe machines on an inspection at the end of the working day. The duty is to *"provide plant"* which is safe, subject to the question of reasonable practicability.

In *R. v. Associated Octel Co. Ltd.* 1994 (considered later in the chapter) the Court of Appeal gave further guidance as to reasonable practicability stressing the subjective nature of the concept *"what is reasonably practicable for a large organisation employing safety officers or engineers contracting for the services of a small contractor on routine operations may differ markedly from what is reasonably practicable for a small shopkeeper employing a local builder on activities on which he has no expertise"*

Safety representatives

A further requirement of s.2 for employers other than those with less than five employees is the obligation to prepare and revise a written statement of their general policy on health and safety and bring this statement to the notice of their employees. The statement should be more than a bland statement of responsibilities but rather a genuine attempt to identify specific health and safety problems of the employer in question and the arrangements that have been made to deal with them. Matters to be included would cover inspection procedures, emergency arrangements, safety precautions, consultative arrangements and training. Under the Safety Representatives and Safety Committee Regulations 1977 it is only recognised trade unions who have the exclusive right to appoint safety representatives and request the creation of safety committees. The functions of safety representatives are laid down in the 1977 regulations and include:

(a)   *to investigate potential hazards and dangerous occurrences at the work-place;*

(b)   *to investigate complaints by any employee he represents relating to that employee's health, safety or welfare at work;*

(c)   *to make representations to the employer on general matters affecting the health, safety or welfare at work of the employees at the workplace;*

(d)   *to carry out inspections;*

(e)   *to represent the employees he was appointed to represent in consultations at the workplace with inspectors of the Health and Safety Executive and of any other enforcing authority;*

(f)   *to receive information from inspectors in accordance with the 1974 Act; and*

(g)   *to attend meetings of safety committees where he attends in his capacity as a safety representative in connection with any of the above functions.*

If safety representatives are appointed under s.2 then it is the duty of an employer to consult with such representatives in order to promote health and safety at the workplace. In many cases this will involve consultations with safety committees which have the function of reviewing measures taken to ensure health and safety at work. Safety representatives have a number of powers, including the right to inspect the workplace and require the establishment of a safety committee. The Trade Union Reform and Employment Rights Act 1993 inserted a new right on safety representatives which is included in the Employment Rights Act 1996. Under s.44 safety representatives have the right not so suffer a detriment for carrying out their health and safety functions.

Duty to non-employees

Both employers and those who are self employed are required, in the words of s.3(1), to *"conduct their undertakings in such a way, in so far as is reasonably practicable, to protect persons other than their own employees from risks to their health and safety."* This would require an employer to give anyone who may be affected, information relating to health and safety risks arising from the way in which the business is run.

In *Carmichael v. Rosehall Engineering Works Ltd.* 1983 an employer was found to be in breach of his duty under s.3(1) when he failed to provide two youths on a work experience programme with suitable clothing for carrying out a cleaning operation using flammable liquid. The failure to give proper instruction and information, as to the possible risks to their health and safety, was a factor which led to the death of one of the boys when his paraffin soaked overalls burst into flames.

Those to whom an employer owes a duty under s.3(1) include contractors and employees of independent contractors.

> In *R v. Associated Octel Co. Ltd.* 1994 the defendant employer was convicted of an offence under s.3(1) when an employee of a contractor engaged to carry out maintenance and repair work suffered severe injury when working at the defendant's chemical plant. On appeal the employer argued that under s.3(1) an employer is not liable for the acts of independent contractors over whom he has no control. The Court of Appeal held that the employer had been correctly convicted. *"The cleaning, repair and maintenance necessary for carrying on the employer's business or enterprise is part of the employee's conduct of its undertaking within the meaning of s.3(1) so as to impose a duty of care with regard to persons not in its employment, whether it is done by the employer's own employees or by independent contractors. The ingredients of an offence under s.3(1) are that the accused is (i) an employer (ii) who so conducts his undertaking (iii) as to expose to risk of health and safety (iv) a person not employed by him (v) who may be affected by such conduct of the accused's undertaking .... if there is actual injury as a result of the conduct of that operation, there is prima facie liability subject to the defence of reasonable practicability".*

In determining reasonable practicability under s.3(1) it is necessary to consider the extent of control over the contractor, the requirement of instruction as to work methods and safety measures, the degree of risk and the competence and experience of the workmen.

Under the Act proceedings may be taken against a director of a company which, with his consent or due to his negligence committed an offence. In a prosecution brought against Mr Chapman in 1992 whose company had contravened a *prohibition notice*, the Crown Court used its powers under the Company Directors Disqualification Act 1986 to ban him from being a company director for two years in addition to a £5,000 fine and a £5,000 fine on the company.

Duty for premises and machinery

By virtue of s.4 a general duty is imposed on those who control work premises to ensure *so far as is reasonably practicable the safety of the premises, any means of access and exit from the place of work, and of any plant or substance provided for use on the premises.*

The duty extends to persons in control of non-domestic premises which are made available as a place of work and is owed to those who are not their employees.

> Under s.4(2) *"It shall be the duty of each person who has control of non-domestic premises or of the means of access thereto or therefrom or any plant or equipment in such premises, to take such measures as is reasonable for a person in his position to take to ensure, so far as is reasonably practicable, that the premises, all means of access available for use by persons using the premises and any plant or equipment in such premises is safe and without risk to health."*

> In *H M Inspector of Factories v. Austin Rover Group Ltd.* 1989 the defendants were prosecuted for a breach of s.4(2) when the employee of a contractor working on the defendants' premises was killed following a sudden flash fire where he was working. A combination of breaches of safety instructions had contributed to the cause of the fire

and at the original trial the defendants were convicted of a s.4(2) offence for failing to take precautions which would have constituted *"reasonable measures"* and been *"reasonably practicable"* for a person in the position of Austin Rover. On appeal and then further appeal to the House of Lords however, it was held that in determining the reasonableness of the measures to be taken under s.4(2) account must be taken of the extent of control and knowledge of the occupier in relation to the actual use to which the premises are put. *"If the premises are not a reasonably foreseeable cause of danger, to anyone acting in a way which a person reasonably may be expected to act, in circumstances which reasonably may be expected to occur during the carrying out of the work, or the use of the plant or substance for the purpose of which the premises were made available, it would not be reasonable to require an individual to take further measures against unknown and unexpected risks."*

A successful prosecution under s.4(2) requires the proof of:

- unsafe premises and a risk to health;
- the identity of the individual having control of the premises; and
- the fact that the person in control ought reasonably to have taken measures to ensure safety.

A further general duty imposed on those who control work premises is to *use the best practicable means to prevent the emission of offensive substances and to render harmless and inoffensive those substances emitted.*

Those who design, manufacture, import or supply any article for use at work are required under s.6 in so far as is reasonably practicable to ensure the article's safety, to carry out necessary testing and examining and provide sufficient information about the use of the article at work to render it safe and without risks to health.

Finally there is a general duty on every employee while at work under s.7 to take reasonable care for the health and safety of himself and of other persons who may be affected by his acts or omissions at work and to cooperate with employers in the discharge of their health and safety duties. Those employees who act in disregard of health and safety should be counselled but in the end dismissed if they are a danger to themselves or others. Wilful breaches of a safety rule, for instance a no smoking policy was has been held to be a justifiable reason for dismissal.

Certainly there is no room to be complacent about compliance with health and safety law for of the 5000 or so deaths at the workplace over the last ten years in the UK, the Health and Safety Executive estimated that over 70% are due to the failure of companies to provide workers with adequate safety equipment, training, supervision and instruction as they are bound to do under the legislation. Lack of enforcement, particularly against individual directors or managers is a particular cause for concern and the small number of prosecutions that are brought against companies only result in a limited fine in the Magistrates Court.

Civil Redress

A further major objective of the law relating to health and safety at the workplace is to provide a means by which those who have suffered injury may recover compensation. Since the mid 1960s, state benefit has been available for employees who suffer injury from accidents arising out of and in the course of employment or contract prescribed industrial diseases. If injury is caused through fault however, whether of the employer or a fellow worker, an injured person can bring a claim for damages through the courts. If it can be shown that injury has occurred as a result of a failure to comply with a regulation under the Health and Safety at Work Act 1974 or some other statutory obligation, for instance under the Factories Act 1961, then a claim could be brought for damages under a civil action for breach of statutory duty. This action has the status of a separate tort and can provide a means of redress for persons who suffer harm as a result of a breach of a duty imposed by statute.

The Tort of Breach of Statutory Duty

To succeed in an action based upon breach of statutory duty it is necessary to prove:

- that the statute in question imposes a statutory duty on the defendant which is owed to the plaintiff;

- that the defendant is in breach of the statutory duty; and

- that the plaintiff suffered injury as a result and the harm caused was of a kind contemplated by the statute.

In cases where the duty imposed by statute is a strict one, then the burden on the plaintiff is to prove that it has been broken without the need to show any fault on the part of the defendant. In applying s.14(1) of the Factories Act 1961 therefore, *"Every dangerous part of any machinery ... shall be securely fenced unless it is in such a position or of such construction as to be as safe to every person employed or working on the premises as it would be if securely fenced"* , it is necessary to show:

- that the Factories Act applies to the premises in question and that the s.14(1) duty is imposed on the employer and is owed to the employee;

- that the machine in question is a source of danger and that it was not securely fenced;

- that the employee suffered injury as a result of the failure to securely fence and the harm was a type contemplated by the section.

In *H Wearing v. Pirelli Ltd.* 1977 the plaintiff suffered a broken wrist when his hand came into contact with a rubber coating around a revolving metal drum which had not been securely fenced. The House of Lords held that the employers were liable for breach of their statutory duty under s.14(1) to fence securely dangerous parts of machinery despite the fact that the employee's hand had come in contact with the rubber coating only, rather than the machinery itself.

The Factories Act 1961 s.29(1) provides that there shall so far as is reasonably practicable, be provided and maintained safe means of access to every place at which any person has at any time to work and every such place shall, so far as is reasonably practicable, be made and kept safe for any person working there.

> In *Larner v. British Steel plc* 1993 the Court of Appeal confirmed that in relation to s.29(1) the burden of proof lies with the employer to show what was or was not reasonably practicable. Also the argument by the employer that `safe' means safe from reasonably foreseeable danger was also rejected. The word `safe' the court said is to be applied as a question of fact and indicates a higher duty of care than that imposed under the common law.

There are of course new health and safety regulations (see earlier in the chapter) which are replacing the factory legislation. Section s.29 is now superseded by the *Workplace (Health, Safety and Welfare) Regulation* 1992 and now new issues of interpretation such as the burden of proof will arise.

Common Law Negligence

An alternative course of action for an employee who has suffered harm due to the fault of his employer or a fellow employee is to base a claim on common law negligence. Under the common law, an employer owes a legal duty of care to ensure the health and safety of his employees and this duty takes effect on an implied term of the contract of employment. An employer is required to take reasonable care with regard to the safety of his employees by providing a safe system of work. The provision of a safe system of work involves an obligation to provide safe fellow employees, safe plant and equipment, safe working premises and safe working methods. If an employer is in breach of his common law duty to take reasonable care, and damage in the form of injury is caused as a result, he will be liable.

It should be stressed that in civil proceedings it is often the case that a claim is based upon both the breach of a common law duty and for breach of statutory duty if relevant.

> In *Smith v. Vange Scaffolding & Engineering Company Ltd. and Another* 1970 the plaintiff scaffolder suffered injury when he fell over a welding cable when walking back from his place of work. The High Court held that the employee's immediate employers were liable for breach of their common law duty of care because they were aware of the dangerous state of the site where their employees worked. In addition the employers were in breach of their statutory duty imposed, by regulation 6 of the *Construction (working places) Regulations* 1966, to provide a suitable and sufficient access to an egress from the plaintiff's place of work.

Certainly there is no intention that statutory regulation is designed to supersede the common law so that even if an employer has complied with a regulation, for instance to supply his workers with safety equipment, an employee is still entitled to pursue a claim under the common law if he is injured due to a failure to wear it.

> In *Bux v. Slough Metals* 1973 the plaintiff lost the sight of one eye as a result of a splash from molten metal when he was pouring it into a die. While safety goggles had been supplied, the plaintiff refused to wear them because they misted up, and no attempt was made to persuade him otherwise. The Court of Appeal held that while the employer had provided suitable goggles for the purpose of safety regulations, they were nevertheless

negligent under the common law. The evidence suggested that the plaintiff would have followed clear instructions to wear the goggles, and that the question whether or not an employer's common law duty of care extended to instructing, persuading or insisting on the use of protective equipment depended on the facts. By failing to make use of the goggles the plaintiff was guilty of contributory fault and damages were reduced by forty percent.

As far as safety equipment is concerned, the contemporary view seems to be that the common law duty to make it available and ensure that employees are aware of it does not necessarily carry with it any further obligation to inspect it or insist that it is worn. Obviously there is some obligation on the employee to take some responsibility for his own safety by ensuring that safety equipment is renewed when necessary.

In *Smith v. Scott Bowyers Ltd.* 1986 the plaintiff, who was just twenty years of age, and employed by the company for nineteen months, suffered injury when he slipped on the greasy factory floor. To help minimise the risk the employer provided the workers with wellington boots with diamond ridge soles and they were renewed on request. Having already replaced one pair of boots the accident was due to the plaintiff's failure to renew the replacement pair which had also worn out and were a danger. In an action for damages for breach of the employer's duty of care, the High Court found that the failure of the employers to emphasise the danger and carry out checks of the safety equipment made them in breach of the legal duty of care they owed to the plaintiff. Damages were to be reduced by one third however, due to the plaintiff's contributory fault. On appeal however, the Court of Appeal reversed the decision and held that there was no breach of the employer's duty to take reasonable care. The failure of the employee to renew the boots was due to his own lack of care and could not be taken as the fault of the employer. *"The employer's duty to provide employees with properly designed Wellington boots would not be filled out with any further obligation to instruct them to wear them or to inspect the condition of the soles from time to time."*

In *Pape v. Cumbria County Council* 1991 the plaintiff had been employed as a cleaner by the council for many years and her job involved the use of chemical cleaning materials and detergents. While rubber gloves were supplied they were rarely used the employer failing to point out the dangers of frequent contact of the skin with cleaners or encouraging the use of gloves. In 1982 the plaintiff was diagnosed as suffering from dermatitis and told by a consultant to protect her skin at work. This she did but her medical condition deteriorated so that all her skin became infected and in 1989 she gave up her job as a result. Mrs Pape claimed damages against her employer for negligence in that her dermatitis resulted from exposure to chemicals in the course of her employment and the employer was in breach of a clear duty to warn of the dangers and persuade staff to take preventative measures. The High Court awarded her £58,000 in damages stating that *"there is a duty on an employer to warn cleaners of the dangers of handling chemical cleaning materials with unprotected hands and to instruct them as to the need to wear gloves all the time. The argument on behalf of the defendant that an employer's duty to his office cleaners is fully discharged when he provides them with gloves could not be accepted."* The risk of dermatitis was not an obvious risk to the cleaners but should be appreciated by a reasonable employer.

The common law duty encompasses an obligation to provide safe plant and appliances. If an employer was aware that machinery or tools are not reasonably safe, and an employee is injured as a result, the employer will be in breach of his duty under the common law.

> In *Bradford v. Robinson Rentals* 1967 the employer provided an unheated van for the employee, a 57 year old, to make a 400 mile journey during the winter, which would involve him in at least 20 hours driving. The court held that the employer was liable for the employee's frost bite, which was the type of injury that was reasonably foreseeable from prolonged exposure to severe cold and fatigue. The court also confirmed that even if the plaintiff had been abnormally susceptible to frost bite he would still be entitled to succeed under the rule that the defendant must take his victim as he finds him.

In the past an employer could satisfy his duty to provide safe equipment by showing that he purchased the equipment from a reputable supplier and that he had no knowledge of any defect. Now however, following the Employers Liability (Defective Equipment) Act 1969, injury occurring to an employee under those circumstances may be attributed to the deemed negligence of the employer. If damages are awarded against the employer then it is up to him to seek a remedy from the supplier of the defective equipment. A good example is provided by *Knowles v. Liverpool City Council* 1993 covered in Chapter 1.

The obligation to provide a safe system of work also encompasses a requirement to provide safe fellow employees. If there are untrained or unskilled people employed at the workplace then a higher standard of care is owed by the employer to ensure their safety and the safety of those who work with them.

> In *Hawkins v. Ross Castings Ltd.* 1970 the plaintiff was injured following a spillage of molten metal, due partly to the employer's failure to comply with safety regulations in relation to the maintenance of a safe pouring systems. An additional contributing factor was the fact that the plaintiff was working closely with a seventeen year old untrained Indian who spoke little English and yet was required to carry and pour molten metal with the plaintiff. This factor contributed to the employer's liability.

The conduct of fellow employees of contributing to an unhealthy working environment by smoking could be the responsibility of the employer in relation to an employee who suffers damage to health through passive smoking.

The duty to provide safe fellow employees exists irrespective of any issue of the employer's vicarious liability for the actions of his employees. Vicarious liability is considered in Chapter 6. If an employee is injured through the negligence of some third party then the court must decide in the circumstances whether this constitutes a breach of the employer's duty of care and so imposing liability.

> In *Reid v. Rush & Tompkins Group* 1989 the plaintiff driver claimed that his employer was in breach of their duty of care in failing to insure him or advising him to obtain insurance cover when driving abroad. The plaintiff had suffered severe injuries as a result of an accident which occurred in Ethiopia resulting from the negligence of another driver.

Both the High Court and the Court of Appeal were reluctant to impose liability on the employer for the loss sustained by the employee. *"It was impossible to imply into the plaintiff's contract of service any term a breach of which would entitle him to recover damages from the defendants for the loss he sustained. There was no basis on the facts as pleaded for holding that the defendants gave an implied undertaking to insure his plaintiff against the risk of uncompensated injury caused to him, while acting in the course of his employment in Ethiopia, by third party drivers."*

The employer's common law duty also imposes an obligation to provide safe working methods and safe working premises. To determine whether an employer is providing safe working methods, it is necessary to consider a number of factors including:

- the layout of the work place;
- training and supervision;
- warnings; and
- whether protective equipment is provided.

It should be stressed that the common law duty on an employer is to take reasonable care, and if he gives proper instructions which the employee fails to observe then the employer will not be liable if the employee is then injured. The common law duty is not one of strict liability but rather a duty to take reasonable care in the circumstances.

In *Latimer v. AEC* 1953 after a factory was flooded, the employer asked his workforce to return, warning them of the dangerous state of the factory floor. Sawdust had been used to cover most of the damp areas but not enough was available, and the plaintiff slipped, and was injured. To determine whether the employer had broken the common law duty of care he owed his employees the court weighed the cost of avoiding the injury against the risk of injury and held that the employer had acted reasonably in the circumstances.

More recently in *Dixon v. London Fire and Civil Defence* 1993 the fire authority was held not to be in breach of its common law duty of care to an officer who slipped and fell as a result of a wet floor. The fact that water had leaked on to the floor of the fire station from an appliance did not constitute negligence for such an occurrence was endemic in the fire service and appeared to be insoluble.

If the plaintiff is a trained professional it may be reasonable to allow the employer to rely on the plaintiff's expertise without the need for warnings or instruction.

In *Woolgar v. West Surrey and Hampshire Health Authority* 1993 the Court of Appeal held that the defendant was not in breach of duty when it failed to warn a nurse against the use of a method of lifting a patient which caused the nurse back injury. The nurse should have realised the likely consequences of her action and used her own reasonable skill and judgment.

The courts have recognised that to require an employee to work long hours, which is related to health problems, could put an employer in breach of his common law duty.

In *Johnstone v. Bloomsbury Health Authority* 1991 the plaintiff, a senior house officer, was required to work forty hours by his contract with an additional average of forty eight hours per week on call. He alleged that some weeks he had been required to work for one hundred hours with inadequate sleep and as a consequence he suffered from stress, depression, diminished appetite, exhaustion and suicidal feelings. It was claimed that the employers were in breach of the legal duty to take reasonable care for the safety and well being of their employee by requiring him to work intolerable hours with deprivation of sleep. The majority of the Court of Appeal held that an employer's express contractual rights had to be exercised in the light of their duty to take care of the employee's safety and if the employer knew that they were exposing an employee to the risk of injury to health by requiring him to work such long hours, then they should not require him to work more hours than he safely could have done.

Although only a majority decision, the Court of Appeal by this judgment is recognising that the implied objective of health and safety in an employment contract may override a clear express contractual right in relation to the hours of work.

There is an increased recognition that individual employees may suffer stress as a direct result of their work. If an employer has reason to believe that this is the case and takes no steps to alleviate the problem there is now authority to suggest he could be in breach of duty.

In *Walker v. Northumberland CC* 1995 the High Court held that a local authority was in breach of duty if care to a senior social worker who was required to cope with an increased workload despite the fact the employer was aware of his susceptibility to mental breakdown. Mr Justice Coleman said that *"An employer owes a duty to his employees not to cause them psychiatric damage by the volume or character of the work which they are required to perform. Although the law on the extent of the duty on an employer to provide an employee with a safe system of work and to take reasonable steps to protect him from risks which are reasonably foreseeable has developed almost exclusively in cases involving physical injury to the employee, there is no logical reason why risk of injury to an employee's mental health should be excluded from the scope of the employer's duty. The standard of care required for performance of that duty must be measured against the yardstick of reasonable conduct on the part of a person in the employer's position. What is reasonable depends on the nature of the relationship, the magnitude of the risk of injury which was reasonably foreseeable, the seriousness of the consequences for the person to whom the duty is owed of the risk eventuating, and the cost and practicability of preventing the risk. The practicability of remedial measures must take into account the resources and facilities at the disposal of the person or body who owes the duty of care, and purpose of the activity which has given rise to the risk of injury"*.

It should be noted that a material fact in deciding liability in the Walker case was that the plaintiff complained of his employers breach of duty in relation to a second nervous breakdown which was reasonably forseeable.Previously Mr Walker had suffered a breakdown due to the stress caused by his heavy workload which was not reasonably foreseeable and for which there would have been no breach of duty.By allowing Mr Walker to be exposed to the same workload as before however the employer should have appreciated that he was as a result of the first breakdown more vulnerable to psychiatric damage.

In *Pickford v. Imperial Chemical Industries* 1996 a secretary who suffered *repetitive strain injury* due to her secretarial duties claimed that her employer had been negligent in failing to instruct her about the need for rest breaks and work organisation to alleviate the need for long periods of typing. By a majority decision the Court of Appeal reversed the decision of the High Court and found that the employer was in breach of the duty of care he owed to his employee. The court stated that *"It is plainly reasonably foreseeable that typists might suffer from a repetitive strain condition if they type for prolonged periods without a break. Accordingly, employees who are likely to do a great deal of typing should be told that they must take breaks and rest pauses. It is advisable to explain why that is necessary, especially if the employee asks or there is any risk that the instruction will not be obeyed. Employers are not entitled to assume that employees understand the importance of taking rest pauses or breaks in typing without being told. In the present case, the defendants were guilty of negligence in failing to instruct the plaintiff to break up long periods of typing with her other secretarial work. It could not be accepted that since it was rare for employees to contract repetitive strain injury as a result of typing, the risk of the plaintiff doing so was not reasonably foreseeable and the defendants were therefore not negligent in failing to warn her of the need to take breaks from typing."*

The standard of care owed by an employer will vary with regard to each individual employee. A young apprentice should be provided with effective supervision while this may not be required for an experienced employee.

In *Paris v. Stepney BC* 1951 the plaintiff, a one-eyed motor mechanic, lost the sight of his good eye while working at chipping rust from under a bus. Despite there being no usual practice to provide mechanics with safety goggles, the court decided that they should have been provided to the plaintiff. The defendants were liable as they could foresee serious consequences for the plaintiff if he suffered eye injury. *"The special risk of injury is a relevant consideration in determining the precautions which the employer should take in the fulfilment of the duty of care which he owes to the workman."*

Defences available to the employer

In very exceptional cases the plaintiff may be taken to have consented to the risk of injury and the defence of *"volenti non fit injuria"* (no wrong is done to one who consents) established.

In *Imperial Chemical Industries v. Shatwell* 1965 two employees, both experienced shot firers, in contravention of specific safety instructions, fired a shot causing injury to both of them. The House of Lords held that the employer could rely on volenti as an absolute defence to the action, due to the act of gross disobedience.

It is more likely that the employer will be able to rely on the Law Reform (Contributory Negligence) Act 1945 which provides a partial defence. If the employer can show that the injured employee contributed to his injury by his own fault then damages may be reduced to *"such extent as the court thinks just and equitable having regard to the claimants share in the responsibility for the damage"*.

If the employer can show that the injured employee contributed to his injury by his own fault then damages may be reduced to *"such extent as the court thinks just and equitable having regard to the claimants share in the responsibility for the damage"*.

Unfair dismissal

By s.28 of the Trade Union Reform and Employment Rights Act 1993 a new category of automatically unfair dismissal was introduced (now s.100 Employment Rights Act 1996). The new right applies irrespective of an employee's length of service. It covers the situation where an employee is dismissed for acting as a safety representative or bringing health and safety matters to the employers attention.

A new right on employees not to suffer a detriment by an employer for carrying out health and safety activities is included as s.44 Employment Rights Act 1996.

This right not to suffer a detriment for carrying out health and safety functions applies to safety representatives and individual employees who raise health and safety matters with the employer where there is no safety committee. If a health and safety risk is perceived to be a serious danger the section also purports to confer protection on employees who refuse to work. The right under s.44 is enforceable by means of a complaint to the industrial tribunal.

Equal Opportunities at the Workplace

In the previous chapter we considered discrimination law relating to staff recruitment, in particular s.6 of the Sex Discrimination Act 1975 and s.4 of the Race Relations Act 1976 which make it unlawful for a person in relation to employment by him to discriminate in the arrangements he makes for the purpose of deciding who should be offered employment, the terms on which it is offered or by refusing to offer employment. Here we are concerned with subsisting employment relationships which are also covered by s.6 and s.4 making it unlawful for an employer to discriminate in the way he gives access to opportunities for promotion, transfer, training or other benefits, or refuses to afford such access. They further provide that it is unlawful to discriminate by dismissing an individual or subjecting him to any other detriment. Once again an allegation of discrimination at work must be categorised as either direct discrimination, indirect discrimination or victimisation.

Discrimination at Work

Unlawful discrimination in the form of victimisation is rarely alleged but is intended to protect employees at the work place who are given less favourable treatment by the employer for bringing a complaint under the legislation or giving evidence on behalf of a complainant. It is of course the fear of victimisation that often prevents employees from taking or supporting legal action against an employer. Possible victimisation and sensational reporting are reasons why many employees who suffer sexual harassment from a superior decide not to seek legal redress.

> In *Northampton County Council v. Dattani* 1994 the complainant's employers promised to investigate a complaint that she has not been selected for a period of paid study leave. When the employer received notification of her claim under the Race Relations Act the investigation was dropped. The EAT upheld the tribunal's ruling of unlawful victimisation.

For the purposes of direct discrimination the intention of the alleged discriminator is immaterial, rather tribunals should focus simply on whether the act or decision satisfies the "but for" test. Would the complainant have received the same treatment but for his or her sex or race.

> In *Horsey v. Dyfed CC* 1982 the act complained of was a refusal by the employer to recommend a married female social worker for secondment in London. The reason for the refusal was the fact that the wife's husband was already working in London and the employer believed that on completion of her secondment she would not return. This assumption the EAT held was one based on sex and in the circumstances constituted direct discrimination.

It is still necessary to establish for a successful claim of sex discrimination that the complainant was subjected to a detriment on the grounds of his or gender. It is entirely permissible for a tribunal to decided that while the act complained of may be offensive and a detriment it may be equally so for a man or woman.

> This was the decision of the EAT in *Stewart v. Cleveland Guest (Engineering) Ltd.* 1994 when the substance of a female worker's complaint was the practice of the male dominated workforce in a factory displaying pin ups and calendars featuring naked and semi naked women. The management of the factory thought the complaint trivial and it was only following union intervention that the pictures were removed. Nevertheless when the complainant suffered hostility from fellow workers for her action she resigned and complained of unlawful sex discrimination. The EAT agreed with the tribunal that even though it was possible to find that the complainant suffered a detriment there may be no sex discrimination. The display of the pictures could be equally offensive to men so that there was no less favourable treatment on the grounds of sex for the purpose of direct discrimination. The tribunal, as the industrial jury, was best placed to decide whether the employer had discriminated against the complainant.

> In *Smith v. Safeways plc* 1996 the Court of Appeal provided guidance as to the circumstances in which an employer's dress and appearance code would constitute sex discrimination. Here the employer had adopted an appearance code which applied to delicatessen staff but which operated differently for men and women particularly in relation to length of hair. The complainant was dismissed for refusing to have his ponytail shortened claiming that a woman in a comparable position would surely be required to keep her hair clipped back. The majority of the EAT thought that the hair length rule was discriminatory and unlike a dress code it was a rule which extended beyond working hours. In an important judgment the Court of Appeal disagreed with EAT and emphasised that *"there is an important distinction between discrimination between the sexes and discrimination against one or the other of the sexes. Discrimination is not failing to treat men and women the same. If discrimination is to be established, it is necessary to show not merely that the sexes are treated differently, but that the treatment accorded to one is less favourable than the treatment accorded to another"*. Appearance codes should be even handed and will not be discriminatory if their content is different *"if they enforce a common principle of smartness or conventionality, and takes as a whole and not garment for garment or item by item, neither gender is treated less favourably in enforcing*

that principle." The guide provided by the court therefore is that there should be a package approach to the effect of an appearance code in deciding whether it is discriminatory.

A useful tool to attack the credibility of the employer's denial of discrimination is statistical evidence. This is particularly so when the management decisions on matters such as promotion or access to benefits are based upon subjective criteria such as *excellence*, *potential* or *efficiency*.

> In *Clymo v. Wandsworth LBC* 1989 the issue before the EAT was whether the failure to extend job sharing to managerial positions within the respondent council constituted indirect sex discrimination. Both the complainant and her husband were employed as librarians by the defendant council. The complainant had a more senior position with managerial responsibilities and following maternity leave she applied to share her job with her husband so that they could share child care between them. The council's job sharing policy covered non-managerial positions. Her request was consequently refused, and she resigned and presented a claim for unlawful indirect discrimination. Both the industrial tribunal and the EAT rejected the claim. The EAT held that the unavailability of job sharing was not a denial of access to a facility since no such facility was currently available. Neither was the complainant subjected to a detriment by being refused access to a facility which was not available and the provision of an advantage which is not available to others is not a detriment.

A different attitude was expressed in April 1995 by the Court of Appeal in a claim brought on behalf of Mrs Meade-Hill against her employer the British Council. The court ruled that a mobility clause in her contract was indirectly discriminatory in that a higher proportion of women than men are secondary earners and so find it more difficult in practice to comply with a direction to move

Sexual harassment

Sexual harassment while not referred to specifically in the Sex Discrimination Act has been held to constitute unlawful direct discrimination for which an employer could be made vicariously responsible. The EC Resolution on the Protection of the Dignity of Men and Women at Work defines sexual harassment as conduct of a sexual nature, or other conduct based on sex affecting the dignity of men and women at work which is

- unwanted, unreasonable and offensive to the recipient;
- used as a basis for employment decisions; or
- such as to create an intimidating, hostile or humiliating work environment for the recipient.

The code recommends that employers should facilitate a climate of opinion at work which inhibits sexual harassment. This could involve the issuing of a policy statement which is communicated and promoted through training. Also employers should adopt clear and precise procedures for dealing with complaints including sympathetic counsellors and incorporating independent and objective investigations.

A range of conduct which could constitute sexual harassment emerges from the case-law including:

- physical attacks;
- brushing against the victim;
- making suggestive statements or telephone calls;
- pressurising the victim to enter into a sexual relationship;
- sending the victim suggestive material.

An employer may be made vicariously liable for the action of his employees committed during the course of employment and this would include sexual harassment constituting unlawful discrimination. Sexual harassment constitutes less favourable treatment for the purpose of direct discrimination and also amounts to a detriment. Liability for sexual harassment is imposed vicariously on the employer. An action against the harasser could of course be brought in tort and if his conduct constitutes a criminal offence there could be a prosecution. Under the Sex Discrimination Act however he may only be made liable as a secondary party. This means that if the harasser is acting outside the course of employment the victim could not claim against him under the Sex Discrimination Act. Alternative actions in tort for the victim include assault and battery and more significantly the increasing recognition of a separate tort of harassment. The victim of sexual harassment at the workplace has a potential claim for unlawful direct sex discrimination, victimisation or even unfair dismissal where appropriate.

To succeed in such a claim the complainant would need to establish that she suffered less favourable treatment on the grounds of her sex which caused her a detriment.

> In *Porcelli v. Strathclyde Council* 1985 the complainant, a science laboratory technician working in a school claimed that she was sexually harassed by two male technicians. The men's conduct, which was clearly sexual harassment, actually led to her request for a transfer to another school. Nevertheless her complaint of sexual discrimination was rejected by the tribunal on the ground that the men's treatment of her was not related to her sex, but they would have acted in a similar unpleasant way to any male colleague that they had disliked. This surprising decision was thankfully reversed by the EAT who found that the men's conduct, having sexual overtones, constituted to unlawful direct discrimination for which their employer, Strathclyde Regional Council, could be made vicariously liable. The Appeal tribunal stressed however that sexual harassment at work does not of itself amount to unlawful discrimination and it is necessary that the victim should point to a detriment related to her employment such as dismissal, non promotion, or access to training, etc. Here the fact that the complainant was obliged to seek a transfer was a sufficient employment detriment for the purpose of the Act.

Now, following *Snowball v. Gardner* 1987 the tribunals are more willing to accept that suffering sexual harassment is of itself detrimental to the person concerned and capable of constituting unlawful direct discrimination.

> In *Bracebridge Engineering Ltd. v. Derby* 1990 the EAT held that a single act of sexual harassment was a `*detriment*' to the complainant within the meaning of s.6 of the Sex Discrimination Act. *"A single incident of sexual harassment, provided it is sufficiently*

serious, clearly falls within the proper intention and meaning of the statute as it is an act of discrimination against a woman because she is a woman". When the act of sexual harassment took place the perpetrators were supposedly engaged in exercising their disciplinary and supervisory function and were consequently within the course of their employment for the purpose of vicarious liability. Here when the employee had left her job because of the treatment she received and her employers failure to treat her allegations seriously, this also amounted to a constructive dismissal which was unfair.

In *Insitu Cleaning Co Ltd. v. Heads* 1995 the EAT considered whether a single act of verbal sexual harassment is sufficient to found a complaint of direct sex discrimination. Here the complaint related to a derogatory remark made by a young male manager in a meeting and directed at the complainant, a female area supervisor. Despite the fact that the remark referred to complainant's breasts the employer argued that it was not sex related and therefore could not amount to direct discrimination. The EAT agreed with the tribunal that the employer was vicariously liable for the sexual harassment which constituted direct sex discrimination. *"The appellant's argument that the remark was not sex-related in that a similar remark could have been made to a man, for example, in relation to a balding head or beard, was absurd. A remark by a man about a woman's breasts cannot sensibly be equated with a remark by a woman about a bald head or a beard. One is sexual, the other is not. The industrial tribunal was entitled to find that the respondent suffered a detriment as a result of the remark."* The EAT confirmed that one incident of verbal sexual harassment can constitute direct discrimination depending on its seriousness.

It is inevitable that in a claim for sexual harassment the industrial tribunal will award compensation for hurt feelings and decide the level that is appropriate whether or not compensation is payable under any other head. In *Sharifi v. Strathclyde DC* 1992 the EAT held that £500 was at or near the minimum for hurt feelings. Certainly conduct which causes distress should be reflected in the level of compensation and substantial awards should be made if the harassment leads to depression, resignation or transfer. In *Cobbold v. Sawyer t/a Immigrants Advisory Bureau* 1993 the complainant was a seventeen year old who walked out of her first job as a result of sexual harassment by her manager. Her claim off sex discrimination was upheld and the meagre award of £150 for hurt feelings was increased by the EAT on appeal to £750.

In *Burton and Rhule v. De Vere Hotels* 1996 the EAT held that two black waitresses who were employees at a hotel had suffered sexual and racial harassment when they were required to work in a banqueting hall during Bernard Manning's performance as guest speaker. Their employer, the hotel, could be held vicariously liable for subjecting the staff to racial abuse and sexual harassment by a third party if the employer had sufficient control to minimise the harm by adopting *good employment practice*. *"An employer subjects an employee to the detriment of racial harassment if he causes or permits harassment serious enough to amount to a detriment to occur in circumstances in which he can control whether it happens or not. A persons subjects another to something if he causes or allows that thing to happen in circumstances where he can control whether it happens or not. Foresight of the events, or the lack of it, is not determinative of whether the events were under the employer's control."*

Equal Pay

Equal opportunity legislation relating to the sexes was originally contained in the Sex Discrimination Act 1975 and the Equal Pay Act 1970 and while both Acts have been considerably amended, not least because of the UK's membership of the European Community, they still remain the corner stones of equal opportunity law. While the Equal Pay Act is concerned with pay and related matters arising from the contract of employment, as we have seen the sex discrimination legislation covers non financial matters from the contract or any other matter not dealt with in the contract of employment. In cases of doubt a decision as to the relevant legislation must be left to the industrial tribunal.

At present there is still widespread inequality in the way men and women are financially rewarded for the work that they do and general agreement that the status of women must be improved. A conservative interpretation of the equal pay legislation in the courts and a tendency to employ women exclusively in low paid jobs so that comparisons are difficult to make, has meant that the law has provided little assistance in redressing the balance. By restricting the right to equal pay under the Equal Pay Act 1970 to cases where `like work' or `work rated as equivalent' can be shown, many women in low paid jobs were effectively excluded from a remedy. Despite the introduction of the Equal Pay Amendment Regulations 1983 applicants have still found it necessary to turn to European Community law to maintain a successful claim. Certainly the Treaty of Rome and various European Community Directives have had considerable impact in the field of equal pay.

European Community Law

Article 119 of the Treaty of Rome imposes a requirement of equal pay for equal work and by virtue of the European Communities Act 1972 this Article is directly applicable to the UK. As early as 1976 the European Court of Justice in *Defrenne v. Sabena* ruled that Article 119, which lays down the principle of equal pay for equal work, is directly enforceable by every employee and against every employer throughout the Member States. *Macarthys v. Smith* 1981 also confirmed that Article 119 is directly enforceable in domestic courts who in theory should apply the law of the national state first. In *Pickstone v. Freemans plc* 1988 the House of Lords held that a complainant could rely on domestic or European law in attempting to secure a remedy. There is no doubt that a wide interpretation of equal pay rights is achievable by applying Article 119 rather than the Equal Pay Act (see later in the chapter).

In addition to the Treaty of Rome each member state of the European Community is required to bring its domestic law into line with Community law. As we saw in Chapter 2 this is achieved mainly by Directives from the European Community outlining the law which member states should then adopt. An example is the Equal Pay Directive which expands the principle of equal pay in Article 119. A failure to incorporate a Directive into domestic law could be pointed out by the European Court of Justice.

> In *Commission for the European Communities v. The United Kingdom* 1982 the Commission successfully argued that UK law had not adopted *"the necessary measures"* to adopt the Equal Pay Directive. Under existing British law a worker's claim that work is of equal value would have to be dropped if the employer refused to cooperate by not

introducing a job classification system. This decision led to an amendment in UK Equal Pay law by the 1983 Equal Pay Amendment Regulations.

This whole process of effecting change on a reluctant member state by means of EC Directives laying down the law and the state being left with the form and method of implementation can be very drawn out. Attempts have been made therefore to enforce European Directives directly in national courts. The European Court of Justice has ruled that a Directive may be relied on by an individual before a national court where the Directive is *"sufficiently precise and unconditional"*. Such actions however are limited to where the respondent is a government authority acting *"as an employer"*. The rationale for restricting the direct enforcement of European law to government authorities is that it is the member states' responsibility to bring its own domestic law into line and private employers should not be made responsible for that failure.

The Equal Pay legislation is not just concerned with pay discrimination but covers discrimination in all aspects of an employees' contract of employment including holiday entitlement and sick leave provision. The definition of *"pay"* under Article 119 is even wider and covers *"the ordinary basic or minimum wage or salary and any other consideration whether in cash or kind, which the worker receives."*

> In an extremely important decision the European Court of Justice in *Barber v. Guardian Royal Exchange Assurance Group* 1990 held that pensions are pay within the meaning of the directly enforceable provisions of Article 119 of the Treaty of Rome. This means that an occupational pensions scheme that discriminates on the grounds of sex and offends Article 119 may be declared unlawful.

The dramatic impact of the above ruling therefore is that pension benefits cannot discriminate on the grounds of sex, and any condition differing according to sex contravenes Article 119. Pensions must now be equated with pay and if rates are determined by gender criteria they are now unlawful. People must be treated as individuals rather than members of gender groupings so that in determining pay and pensions the fact that statistically women live longer, or take more sick leave than men, should be disregarded in determining levels of sick pay or pension benefits. Also despite the present difference in the State pension age, as a result of this case, pension ages under occupational schemes must be equalised. The court further confirmed that the Treaty takes precedence over Directives so that Social Security Directives which permitted the implementation of equal treatment in occupational pension schemes to be deferred, are consequently overridden by the decision. Finally the court has decided that the principle of equal pay applies to each element of remuneration and is not satisfied by a comprehensive assessment of overall pay. This means that differences in contractual terms between men and women employed on equal work cannot be offset against each other. Applying the equality clause therefore, each aspect of the contract of employment must be equalised.

Equal Pay Act Claims

The main objective of the Equal Pay Act 1970 is to secure equal treatment for men and women in the same employment in relation to terms and conditions of employment. Originally certain terms were excluded from the operation of the Act including those affected by laws relating to the employment of women. In fact such laws are gradually being removed for example by the Sex Discrimination Act 1986 and the Employment Act 1989. Terms *"affording special treatment to women in connection with pregnancy or childbirth"* are still outside the province of the Act and so a man has no right to paternity leave in circumstances where a woman is entitled to maternity leave. Also, terms *"related to death or retirement, or to any provision made in connection with death or retirement"* are also excluded. This would not cover terms related to the *"membership of an occupational pension scheme"*.

The mechanism by which the Equal Pay Act attempts to achieve its objectives is the `equality clause'. The Equal Pay Act is one of the few employment law statutes that actually implies a term into a contract of employment. Under the Act if *the terms of a contract under which a woman is employed at an establishment in Great Britain do not include (directly or by reference to a collective agreement or otherwise) an equality clause they shall be deemed to include one.*

Under the equality clause a woman has the right to equal pay with a man if either:

- she is employed on *'like work'* with a man in the same employment;
- she is employed doing *'work rated as equivalent'* with a man following a job evaluation study; or
- she is employed to do work of *'equal value'* with a man in the same employment in terms of the demand placed upon her.

There are therefore three avenues upon which a claim could be based, *'like work'*, *'work related or equivalent'* or *'equal value'*. Equal value was introduced by the *Equal Pay Amendment Regulations* 1983. A claim based on equal value can only be considered where there is no basis for a claim on *'like work'* or *'work rated as equivalent'*. The starting point for a claimant under the Equal Pay Act is to identify an individual male *comparator* with whom she wishes to claim equal pay. This man must be employed on work which is the same or broadly similar to her own (like work or work rated as equivalent).

The problem of using the concept *like work* as a criterion for achieving fair treatment for women at the workplace, is that in fact large numbers of women workers are often at establishments where there are no male employees upon which to draw comparisons. Accordingly, the definition of *like work* has been given a *'broad brush approach'* interpretation by courts and tribunals. Section 1(4) provides that a "woman is to be regarded as employed in like work with men if, but only if, her work and theirs is of the same or a broadly similar nature and the differences (if any) between the things she does and the things they do are not of practical importance in relation to terms and conditions of employment: and accordingly in comparing her work and theirs regard shall be had to the frequency or otherwise with which any such differences occur in practice as well as to the nature and extent of the differences".

Insignificant differences in work and vague or unrealistic responsibilities are to be ignored therefore, in deciding whether individuals are engaged in like work.

> In *Electrolux v. Hutchinson* 1977 female workers engaged in broadly similar work to their male counterparts were held to be entitled to equal pay, despite that the men alone would be required to work overtime, at weekends or at night. The fact that the men were rarely called on to do extra work was a major consideration.

The decision as to whether similar work is being carried on demands not a comparison between the contractual obligations of the parties, but rather a consideration of the things actually done and the frequency with which they are done.

> In *Coomes (Holdings) Ltd. v. Shields* 1978 the female counter clerks in bookmakers shops were paid a lesser rate of pay than their male counterparts. The employers sought to justify the differences on the grounds that the male employees had extra duties, including acting as a deterrent to unruly customers and transporting cash between branches. The Court of Appeal held that, in deciding the question as to `like work', it was necessary to consider the differences between the things the men and women were required to do. Furthermore, it was necessary to consider the frequency with which such differences occur in practice. Finally, the court must consider whether the differences are of any practical importance. This approach should enable the court to place a value on each job in terms of demands placed upon the worker, and if the value of the man's job is higher he should be paid an increased rate for the job. In the present case the differences were not of sufficient importance to justify a different rate of pay.

> In *Thomas v. National Coal Board* 1987 the EAT held that for the purposes of determining `like work' there was no implicit requirement that a selected male comparator should be representative of a group. It was possible therefore to compare the terms and conditions of female canteen assistants with the only male canteen attendant. The EAT also held however that the tribunal was entitled to find that the additional responsibility of the male attendant in working permanently at night alone, and without supervision, was a *"difference of practical importance in relation to terms and conditions of employment"* and so not 'like work' for the purposes of the Act.

The second means by which an equality clause will operate is if the employer has carried out a job evaluation study or work rating exercise and the women's work is rated as equivalent to that of a man employed at the same establishment. The study must be carried out in accordance with the Act which provides in s.1(5) that *"a woman is to be regarded as employed on work rated as equivalent with that of any men, if but only if, her job and their job have been given an equal value in terms of the demands made on a worker under various headings (effort, skill, decision making etc.) on a study undertaken with a view to evaluating in those terms the jobs to be done by all or any of the employees in an undertaking or group of undertakings"*.

To maintain an equal pay claim based upon job evaluation therefore it is necessary that a valid study has been carried out adopting one of the principal job evaluation methods laid down by ACAS. The fact that both trade unions generally and a number of employers are wary of job evaluation studies and there is still doubt as to whether an employer is bound to implement a scheme which has been carried out, means that equal pay claims based on work rated as equivalent are relatively rare.

The Comparison

For both `like work' and `work rated as equivalent' it is left to the woman rather than her employer, to choose the male comparator but such a person must be typical and cannot be a hypothetical person. The comparison could even be with the man whom the woman replaced provided there was only a short break between this occurring. Both the applicant and the comparator must be employed which includes employees and contractors providing personal services.

A further requirement is that the comparison must be between the applicant and another in the `same employment' which would include the same establishment. Comparison with an individual employed by the same or associated employer at a different establishment is also permissible provided common terms and conditions of employment are observed at both establishments.

> In *Leverton v. Clwyd County Council* 1988 the complainant, a nursery nurse, sought to compare herself with higher paid clerical staff employed at different establishments by the council. To prevent a comparison the employers argued that common terms and conditions of employment were not observed for the relevant employees despite the fact that they were covered by the same collective agreement. In particular the nurses worked a 32.5 hour week and had 70 days annual holiday compared with the comparator's 37 hour week and 20 days basic holiday. Both the tribunal and the EAT felt that these differences were sufficient to defeat the contention that there were common terms of employment observed at the different establishments and so the claim failed. By a majority the Court of Appeal agreed. *"Although common terms and conditions of employment does not mean 'identical' terms and conditions, as that would defeat the whole purpose of the legislation, there must be a sufficient element of common identity to enable a proper comparison to be made".*

The above case gives considerable support to the notion of cross establishment comparison where the applicant and the comparator are covered by the same collective agreement. This is particularly significant in the public sector where national agreements prevail and even in the private sector where employers have multi-site operations and employees with standard terms and conditions of employment.

Earlier we said that an equal pay claim based on Article 119 may be easier to establish then relying on the Equal Pay Act. Certainly a claim based on the Act relies heavily on the complainant identifying an appropriate male comparator. A claim under Article 119 can have a broader basis however and the European Court in *Handels-og Kontorfunktion-aerenes Forbund i Danmark v. Dansk Arbejdsgiverforening (acting for Danfoss)* 1989 said that the complainant must establish a prima facie case of discrimination and usually reliable statistical evidence of average pay differences will suffice. It is then left to the employer to explain the differences on non discriminatory grounds. It is the industrial tribunal which must determine the validity and reliability of the statistical evidence and whether a good explanation is put forward by the employer. The onus under Article 119 falls on the employer to provide employees with as much information as possible about their pay systems showing how pay increments are obtained and how job evaluation and performance related pay schemes operate.

> In *British Coal Corporation v. Smith and Others* 1996 the House of Lords held that the expression *"common terms and conditions of employment"* for the purposes of comparisons between different establishments should be given a wide interpretation and mean terms and conditions which are substantially comparable on a broad basis rather than the same terms and conditions. It is sufficient therefore to show that the comparator would be employed on broadly similar terms as the applicant. In this case therefore it was valid

to compare the work of female canteen workers and cleaners with male surface mineworkers at a different establishment, when their terms and conditions were covered by national agreements and conclude that they were in the *"same employment"* for the purposes of the legislation.

In cases where the provisions of `like work' and `work rated as equivalent' do not apply, a further option is to rely on an equality clause based on work of equal value added by the Equal Pay (Amendment) Regulations 1983. The equal value route is crucial in achieving the goal of equal pay for there are numerous areas of work even of a professional nature, which tend to be female dominated with relatively low rates of pay. Under the regulations a woman is employed on work, which is, in terms of the demands made on her (for instance under such headings as effort, skill and decision making), of equal value to that of a man in the same employment. In such circumstances the equality clause has the effect of modifying less favourable terms in the woman's contract to bring them in line with the man's contract and inserting any beneficial terms in a man's contract into the woman's contract of employment. If a complaint is presented, the tribunal has no jurisdiction to hear the case unless it is satisfied either that there are no reasonable grounds for determining that the work is of equal value or it has required a member of the panel of independent experts to prepare a report with respect to that question and has received that report. The panel is designated by the Advisory, Conciliation and Arbitration Service (ACAS) but must not comprise officers or members of that body.

There would be no reasonable grounds for determining that the work is of equal value if different values have been given to the work and that of the male comparator following a study and there is no evidence that the evaluation was made on a system which discriminated on the grounds of sex.

An important decision of the European Court of Justice in *Enderby v. Frenchay Health Authority* 1993 has gone some way to remove some of the obstacles facing women seeking equal pay for equal value. The claim was brought by the complainant, a NHS speech therapist, a profession dominated by women, who sought pay comparable with NHS clinical psychologists and principal pharmacists, professions which were male dominated. The EAT struck out the claim finding no direct discrimination and holding that the level of pay was dictated by collective bargaining arrangements. The European Court rejected this view however and proposed a more realistic burden of proof for those attempting to establish equal value claims. The complainant is required to establish a prima facie case and can do this by showing that the work is of equal value, that there is a significant pay differential, and that the lower paid workers are almost exclusively women and the higher paid are men. The burden then shifts to the employer to show that the pay differential is based on objectively justified factors unrelated to sex discrimination.

At this point it is convenient to consider the main defence to an equal pay claim. An equality clause shall not operate in relation to a variation between the woman's contract if the employer proves that the variation is genuinely due to a material factor which is not the difference of sex. If the claim is based on an equality clause relying on `like work' or `work rated as equivalent' then there must be a material difference between the woman's case and the man's for the defence to operate. For claims based on equal value however, it is slightly different and the factor may be a material difference.

In *Snoxell and Davies v. Vauxhall Motors* 1977 the EAT held that an employer cannot establish a defence, that the variation between the woman's contract and the man's contract was genuinely due to a material difference between her case and his, when it can be seen that past discrimination has contributed to the variation. Even if the original discrimination occurred before the effective date of the Act *"it cannot have been the intention of the legislation to permit the perpetuation of the effect of the earlier discrimination"*.

Genuine material differences would include a consideration of factors such as the place of employment or academic qualifications of the individual involved.

In *Rainey v. Greater Glasgow Health Board* 1987 the House of Lords held that the word `material' means `significant and relevant' and the difference had to be between the woman's case and the man's. The decision involves a consideration of all the relevant circumstances and they might go beyond personal qualifications, skill, experience or training. It could be that the difference was reasonably necessary to achieve some result such as economic necessity or administrative efficiency and was not directly related to the personal characteristics of the individual involved.

A complaint in relation to equal pay may be presented to a tribunal by an individual, an employer and in certain circumstances, by the Secretary of State for Employment. If the tribunal finds that a claim has been established, it can make a declaration to that effect and award up to two years' back pay to the successful applicant. The burden of proof rests with the complainant and it is for the employer to an establish a defence.

Maternity Rights

A pregnant employee has four statutory rights:

- the right not to be dismissed for pregnancy or a reason connected with it;
- the right to maternity pay;
- the right to return to work after her pregnancy or childbirth;
- the right to time off for ante-natal care.

The right not to be unfairly dismissed under s.99 of the Employment Rights Act 1996 is considered in chapter 16. In the UK while we have the longest maternity leave period in the European Community our Statutory Maternity Pay Scheme is one of the least generous. There is no provision for paternity rights under UK law and existing European Community law cannot be used to establish one.

The right to maternity leave and pay was first introduced in the Employment Protection Act 1975 and the law is now contained in the Employment Rights Act 1996.

Despite the very basic nature of the right to maternity pay and leave, legislative provisions governing the right are difficult to interpret and were described by Browne-Wilkinson J as of *"inordinate complexity, exceeding the worst excesses of a taxing statute"*. He further observed that this was especially regrettable bearing in mind that they are regulating the rights of ordinary employers and employees.

The Employment Rights Act 1996 provides that if a woman has a contractual right to maternity leave in addition to the statutory right, then it is the most favourable right that should be exercised.

Maternity leave and maternity absence

Prior to 1993 to qualify for maternity pay and leave with the right to return to work, the employee must have been continuously employed for two years as at the beginning of the eleventh week before the date of her expected confinement. Now all pregnant women are given the right to fourteen weeks maternity leave regardless of the length of service but dependent on compliance with strict notice provisions. For those employees with two years continuous service however they also retain the right to up to forty weeks maternity absence, eleven weeks before the expected week of confinement and twenty nine weeks following the birth. The contract of employment does not continue automatically during this period of absence. An employee relying on the new fourteen week maternity leave period, however, has her contract of employment continue automatically. The expression `maternity leave' refers to the fourteen week period and the expression `maternity absence' to the longer period which depends upon having two years continuous service. Following the *Employment Protection (Part-Time Employees) Regulations* 1995 the right to maternity absence now extends to part-time as well as full-time employees.

The maternity leave period will start when the employee chooses subject to the qualification that she cannot under start earlier than the beginning of the eleventh week before the expected week of childbirth. The period of leave is fourteen weeks subject to other statutory provisions prohibiting working after childbirth such as the restriction on women working in a factory within four weeks of childbirth.

An employee who has the right to maternity leave and also a contractual right to maternity leave under her contract of employment should take advantage of the most beneficial right.

It must be stressed that the right to maternity leave is conditional upon strict compliance with notice requirements. The Act requires the applicant to give at least three weeks notice of the commencement of maternity leave. The expected week of childbirth and if required verification by a medical certificate. While the new maternity leave does not carry with it a right to return to work this is not really necessary given the fact that the contract of employment continues to exist during the leave period.

For those employees who qualify for the longer period of maternity absence, the right to return to work is also included. Employment up to the eleventh week before the expected week of childbirth is crucial for the purposes of the right. The statutory right to return is lost if there is a resignation before that date.

The right to maternity leave includes the right to return to work with your original employer or successor at any time before the end of the period of twenty nine weeks beginning with the week in which the date of confinement falls. The right is to return to the original job on terms and conditions which are not less favourable than those which would have been applicable to the applicant had she not been absent. If the employer can show that it is not practicable by reason of redundancy to permit the applicant to return to work, she is entitled, where there is a suitable available vacancy, to be offered alternative employment. This alternative employment must be suitable and appropriate with provisions which are not substantially less favourable than the original contract.

This then is a significant limitation on the right to return to work, for if there is a redundancy situation and no suitable available employment or suitable alternative work which is unreasonably rejected, then the right to return is lost. Some protection is provided however where the employer fails to make an offer of suitable alternative work.

> In *Community Task Force v. Rimmer* 1986 the EAT held that the test of availability of employment is not qualified by considerations of what is economic or reasonable, so that despite the difficulties involved in offering an employee alternative employment in these circumstances, failure to do so made her dismissal automatically unfair.

The right to return to work was also amended to accommodate small employers so that the Act now provides that if immediately before the absence, the employer had five or less employees, and it is not reasonably practicable for the employer to permit a return to work, the right to return does not apply.

Failure to comply strictly with the notice requirements may also prejudice the right to return. Having served the original notice, the employer is entitled to confirm the position by sending the employee an intermediate enquiry in writing not earlier than twenty one days before the end of the maternity leave period with the purpose of asking whether the employee still intends to return to work. The letter of enquiry must notify the employee of her obligation to reply within fourteen days.

To exercise the right to return the employee must notify her original employer (or his successor) in writing at least twenty one days before the date on which she proposes to return. The employer may postpone the return for not more than four weeks from the notified date provided he informs the employee before that notified date and gives specified reasons for the postponement. The employee may also postpone the return to work by four weeks if she notifies the employer of her ill health supported by a medical certificate before the notified day of return. Such a postponement can only be exercised once. If there has been an interruption of work (due to industrial action or some other reason) which would make it unreasonable to expect the employee to return to work on the notified day, she may return when work resumes after the interruption or as soon as is reasonably practicable.

> In *Hilton International Hotels (UK) Ltd. v. Kaissi* 1994 the EAT confirmed the *"failure to comply with the maternity leave procedure does not in itself terminate the contract of employment although it means that the employee has no statutory right to return to work."* Whether the contract comes to an end or not depends on the agreement and actions of the parties which may differ from case to case.

It should be noted that there may also be a contractual right to return to work following maternity leave which an employee could rely on in preference to the statutory right. Whether relying on the statutory or contractual right to return, if an employer refuses to allow the employee to return in breach of this right, then this is deemed to be a dismissal and the employee is entitled to present a claim for unfair dismissal. The period of maternity leave will count towards continuous employment for the purpose of qualifying to present an unfair dismissal claim.

In the case of *maternity pay*, it is also necessary for the woman to notify the employer, in writing if requested, at least twenty one days before the absence begins or as soon as is reasonably practicable that she will be absent from work because of the pregnancy. The same notice could be used to inform the employer that she intends to return to work after the birth of the child. A further requirement for the woman is that if requested by her employer she must produce a certificate from a registered medical practitioner or a certified midwife indicating the expected number of weeks of her confinement.Statutory maternity pay is paid by the employer at the moment at two levels depending on the length of service, the lower rate and the higher rate. The lower rate for those qualified under the Social Security Contributions and Benefits Act 1992 is a fixed amount whereas the higher rate, for those with two years continuous employment, depends on the claimant's average weeks pay.

Assignment   The Accident

David Hall has been employed as a machine operator by Fitters and Turners at their Stockport factory for the past six years. He is a member of the JMB, the largest trade union representing machine operators in Great Britain. As part of safety equipment supplied to him on the commencement of his employment David was supplied with a pair of work boots with a steel toe cap and heavy tread. It was explained to David by his supervisor that all safety equipment supplied was renewable on request.

Last Tuesday afternoon a drum of oil thinner was accidently split onto the factory floor near to David's work station. While cleaning up operations were put into effect almost immediately, part of the factory floor was still in a highly dangerous state on the Wednesday morning. Last thing on Tuesday afternoon David had heard the works manager warn, over the firm's tannoy, of the increased risk of injury caused by the spillage and the need for increased vigilance when walking across the factory floor. Despite the warning however, when making his way to his machine on Wednesday morning, David slipped on a mixture of oil thinner and grease and landed on the base of his spine. As he was in severe pain David was immediately taken by ambulance to the local hospital. The initial medical opinion is that while the fall was not of itself serious it has further exacerbated a back condition from which David already suffered and as a consequence David may be unfit for work for a considerable period. David has an appointment to be examined by a back consultant in three weeks time.

Task

You are also employed by the JMB at their headquarters in Sheffield and specialise in advising on members legal problems. You have been called to a meeting in Stockport to discuss the legal position relating to the accident with David and his safety representative. You should be prepared to advise as to any civil or criminal proceedings that may be brought as a result of the accident and the likely outcomes.

Prepare a set of briefing notes to assist you in the meeting.

Legal Terms found in Chapter 16

Conciliation	• bringing together the parties to a dispute in an attempt to settle it
Constructive dismissal	• a contract of employment terminated by the employee because of the employer's repudiatory conduct
Express dismissal	• a contract of employment terminated by the employer with or without notice
Frustration	• a change in circumstances making contractual performance radically different from that envisaged
Gross misconduct	• grave misconduct which constitutes a repudiatory breach of the contract of employment
Implied dismissal	• a contract of employment for a fixed term which terminates when the term expires
Mutual termination	• a contractual agreement to terminate a contract of employment
Redundancy situation	• an employer's requirement for workers of a particular kind have ceased or diminished
Re-engagement	• to re-employ an employee following a dismissal in the same or similar job
Reinstatement	• to re-employ an employee following a dismissal and treat him as if there had been no dismissal
Repudiatory breach	• a serious breach of contract which allows the innocent party to accept the breach and regard the contract terminated
Summary dismissal	• instant dismissal without notice
Unfair dismissal	• dismissal without good reason contrary to statute
Wrongful dismissal	• dismissal in a wrongful manner by contravening notice requirements in breach of contract

Chapter 16

The Law Relating to the Termination of Employment

Legal conflict between employer and employee arises most usually when the employment relationship comes to an end. Important statutory rights, such as unfair dismissal and redundancy, and common law rights, such as a wrongful dismissal all depend upon showing that the employment relationship was terminated by means of a dismissal. For this purpose therefore, it is necessary to explore the various modes of termination of the employment relationship and identify when a dismissal, whether express or implied has occurred.

Dismissal and Notice

If an employer or an employee wishes to terminate a contract of employment they are required to comply with the employee's contractual requirements in relation to notice. Generally the length of the notice period will depend upon the nature of the employment and may increase in relation to the number of years' service. In addition, the Contract of Employment Act 1963 introduced statutory minimum periods of notice that apply where the contract is silent or provides for less favourable periods. The statutory statement of the main terms and conditions of employment supplied under s.1 of the Employment Rights Act 1996 will stipulate the minimum notice period to which the employee is entitled.

After continuous employment for:	Minimum notice required:
4 weeks up to 2 years	1 week
2 years up to 12 years	1 week for each year
12 years or more	12 weeks

If the contractual notice period is less than the statutory minimum period then the statutory minimum period will apply. Following the Employment Protection (Part-Time Employees) Regulations 1995, the right to a statutory minimum period of notice extends to part-time employees regardless of their hours of work.

One further complication is that if the contract is silent as to the notice period, there is an implied term under the common law that the notice given will be reasonable and such a notice period may, in exceptional cases, exceed the statutory minimum. Certainly the seniority of the employee, the nature of his job, and the length of service could dictate that a relatively long period of notice is required.

> In *Hill v. Parsons & Company Ltd.* 1972 a senior engineer was held to be entitled to notice of six months under the common law, well in excess of the statutory rights.

There is nothing to prevent an employee from waiving his right to notice or, in fact, accepting a lump sum payment in lieu of the notice period to which he is entitled. Failure by the employer to comply with notice requirements would entitle the employee to bring an action for damages in the ordinary courts based on breach of contract. Such a claim is known as 'wrongful dismissal' referring to the wrongful manner in which the contract of employment has been terminated.

Wrongful Dismissal

Summary dismissal occurs when the contract of employment is terminated instantly without notice and it is prima facie wrongful. Such a dismissal is justifiable under the common law, however, if it can be shown that the employee is in repudiatory breach of the contract of employment because of his 'gross misconduct'. By summarily dismissing, the employer is accepting the repudiatory breach of the employee and treating the contract as discharged. Whether the alleged misconduct may be classified as gross is a question of fact and degree, but it would normally include conduct such as disobedience, neglect, dishonesty, or misbehaviour. Certainly early cases must now be viewed with caution. The summary dismissal of a housemaid in *Turner v. Mason* 1854 because she went to visit her sick mother in contravention of her employer's instructions was held not to be wrongful but would be unlikely to constitute gross misconduct in the present day. Until recently an action for wrongful dismissal was a common law claim for breach of contract and could only be dealt with in the ordinary courts. Now industrial tribunals also have jurisdiction to hear an action for wrongful dismissal.

A fundamental question that is often asked is whether the employment relationship can survive the nature of the misconduct.

> In *Pepper v. Webb* 1969 the action of the head gardener in wilfully disobeying a reasonable order was sufficient to amount to gross misconduct and provide grounds for summary dismissal, despite the contract of employment providing for three months' notice. It should be stressed, however, that the reaction of the gardener in this case represented the culmination of a long period of insolence, and the isolated use of choice obscenities by an employee to an employer may not amount to gross misconduct if there is provocation.

More recently in *Denco Ltd. v. Joinson* 1991 the EAT felt that if an employee uses an unauthorised password in order to enter a computer known to contain information to which he is not entitled that of itself is gross misconduct which could attract summary dismissal. In such cases the EAT thought it desirable that the management should stress that such dishonesty will carry with it severe penalties.

The remedy for a successful claim of wrongful dismissal is an action for damages amounting to the loss of wages payable during the notice period.It seems therefore that if an employer pays the employee an appropriate lump sum on summary dismissal, which represents a full payment of pay in lieu of notice, there would be little point in bringing a claim for breach of contract as no further damages would be payable.Of course since 1971 an aggrieved employee who is qualified has the further option of complaining to a tribunal that the instant dismissal is unfair.

In cases where a fixed term contract is prematurely brought to an end by the employer's repudiatory breach, a claim for damages for breach of contract may be the more appropriate avenue for redress, for the sum due under the unexpired term of the contract may be well in excess of the possible compensation available for unfair dismissal

Dismissal

For the purposes of unfair dismissal the meaning of `*dismissal*' is defined in s.95(1) of the Employment Rights Act 1996

> Section 95(1) provides that: *subject to sub-section (2) an employee shall be treated as dismissed by his employer if, but only if;*
>
> (a)   *the contract under which he is employed is terminated by the employer, whether it is so terminated by notice or without notice, or*
>
> (b)   *where under the contract he is employed for a fixed term, that term expires without being renewed under the same contract, or*
>
> (c)   *the employer terminates the contract, with or without notice, in circumstances such that he is entitled to terminate it without notice by reason of the employer's contract.*

The section envisages a dismissal arising expressly, impliedly on the expiration of a fixed term contract of employment and constructively in response to the employers conduct.

Express dismissal

Under s.95(1)(a) an express dismissal occurs where the employer terminates the contract of employment with or without notice.

We have already said that an employer is normally required to give the employee notice in accordance with the terms of the contract or least the statutory or common law minimum period. For a dismissal with notice, therefore, there is normally no room for any misunderstanding in relation to the employer's intentions. In cases of alleged summary dismissal, however, where there is no notice, there have been claims by the employer that it was not his intention to dismiss but rather merely to discipline. While the words, "you're dismissed, fired, sacked", etc. leave little doubt as to the employer's intentions, if he uses more ambiguous language, perhaps to register his discontent with the employee, the argument that there has been no express dismissal could have some merit.

In *Futty v. Brekkes Ltd.* 1974 the tribunal was called on to place an interpretation on the quaint language used on the Hull dock. During an altercation with his foreman the complainant fish filleter was told, *"If you do not like the job, fuck off"*. The complainant took this as a dismissal, left, and found a job elsewhere. For the purposes of an unfair dismissal claim the employer argued in his defence that there had been no dismissal. Here the words were to be considered in the context of the fish trade, and in these circumstances were taken to mean that if you do not like the work you are doing, clock off and come back tomorrow. The custom of the fish trade was that, for a dismissal, the language used was clear and formal. The tribunal agreed with the employer's view and held that the complainant had terminated his own employment by deciding on this occasion that he would leave and subsequently find himself alternative employment.

It should be noted, of course, that a failure to treat employees with respect could indicate a breakdown in trust and confidence so as to entitle an employee to walk out and regard himself as constructively dismissed.

Implied dismissal

Previously we said that if a fixed term contract is terminated by either party prematurely without good reason or authorisation under the contract then an action may lie for damages for breach of contract. If the contract runs its course however there is an implied dismissal of the employee when the term expires. Potentially therefore if the fixed term contract is not renewed the employee is entitled to present a complaint of unfair dismissal. In practice however the Employment Rights Act provides that an employer under a fixed term contract of one year or more can expressly exclude unfair dismissal and redundancy rights.

It is usual under a fixed term contracts of a year or more to exclude unfair dismissal rights and to exclude the right to a redundancy payment if the term of the contract is two years or more.

In *Mulrine v. University of Ulster* 1993 the Northern Ireland Court of Appeal held that if the parties to a two year fixed term contract of employment agree to waiver statutory rights to claim unfair dismissal and/or redundancy on the contracts' termination then this waiver will apply if the parties agree and the contract is extended for a further term of four months. As its only possible to waive statutory rights in a fixed term contract of one year or more, here it was argued that if the four months extension constitutes a new contract, the waiver should not apply. The Court of Appeal held however that the second shorter term was clearly an extension of the first and as the fixed term was now two years and four months, statutory rights were validly excluded by the waiver.

Constructive dismissal

In a large number of cases it may seem superficially that the contract of employment has been terminated by the employee's conduct in *walking out* and treating the contract as at an end. Where however, the reason for leaving was due to the conduct of the employer or those under his control, it may be that the employee could show that the employer is responsible for the contractual termination. In such circumstances an employee could argue implied dismissal . Such a dismissal is commonly referred to as a constructive dismissal.

Originally the test for determining whether a constructive dismissal had taken place was to judge the reasonableness of the employer's conduct. Since *Western Excavating (ECC) Ltd. v. Sharp* 1978 however, the Courts have rejected that approach as being too vague and now the so called 'conduct test' is to be applied based upon strict contractual principles. The aim of the conduct test is to bring some degree of certainty to the law by requiring the employee to justify his leaving as a response to the employer's repudiatory conduct. *"If the employer is guilty of conduct which is a significant breach going to the root of the contract of employment, or which shows that the employer no longer intends to be bound by one or more of the essential terms of the contract then the employee is entitled to treat himself as discharged from any further performance."*

A breach by the employer of the express terms of the contract of employment covering such matters as wages, job location, contractual duties and job description, normally comes about when the employer unilaterally attempts to impose a change on the employee without his consent.

By demoting an employee and failing to provide him with suitable office accommodation an employer could be held to be in fundamental breach of the contract of employment. Such an employee could accept the repudiatory breach and regard himself as constructively dismissed.

> This was the case in *Wadham Stringer Commercials (London) Ltd. & Wadham Stringer Vehicles Ltd. v. Brown* 1983 where a fleet sales director was effectively demoted to no more than a retail salesman. At the same time he was moved from reasonable accommodation to an office 8ft x 6ft with no ventilation, next to the gentleman's lavatory. As a consequence the employee eventually resigned and claimed a constructive dismissal which was unfair. The EAT agreed that there had been a fundamental breach of contract, accepted by the employee, and following *Western Excavating (ECC) Ltd. v. Sharp*, a constructive dismissal. The employer's argument that their actions were the result of economic necessity were relevant, but only in deciding the reasonableness of their conduct for the purposes of the test of fairness or for the purpose of assessing the level of compensation in an unfair dismissal claim.

The need to look for a clear breach of contractual term in applying the conduct test has encouraged both tribunals and courts in the absence of relevant express terms to imply terms into a contract of employment. It is the need therefore to accommodate the doctrine of constructive dismissal that has encouraged judicial ingenuity in applying the business efficacy test to find implied obligations in employment contracts. An excellent example is provided by the need to maintain trust and confidence in the employment relationship.

> In *Courtaulds Northern Textiles Ltd. v. Andrew* 1979 the EAT stated that *"there is an implied term in a contract of employment that the employers will not, without reasonable and proper cause, conduct themselves in a manner calculated or likely to destroy or seriously damage the relationship of confidence and trust between the parties"*. Here a comment made to the complainant by his assistant manager that *"you can't do the bloody job anyway"* which was not a true expression of his opinion was held to justify the complainant in resigning and treating himself as constructively dismissed. While criticism of a worker's performance would not necessarily amount to repudiatory conduct so as to lead to constructive dismissal, here telling the employee that he could not do his job, when that was not a true expression of opinion, was conduct which was *"likely to destroy*

> *the trust relationship which was a necessary element in the relationship between the supervisory employee and his employers".*

Failing to treat an employee fairly in relation to a disciplinary matter could constitute repudiatory conduct for the purposes of constructive dismissal.

> In *Greenaway Harrison Ltd. v. Wiles* 1994 the EAT held that a telephonist who refused to accept a radical change in her shift pattern and was threatened with dismissal was entitled to leave and regard herself as constructively dismissed. The threat of dismissal constituted an anticipatory breach of contract by the employer.

An employer is of course vicariously responsible for the actions of his employees within the scope of their employment so that if a supervisor in reprimanding an employee does so in a reprehensible manner this can be taken to be the *employers' conduct* for the purpose of constructive dismissal.

> In *Hilton International Hotels (UK) Ltd. v. Protopapa* 1990 an employee resigned when she was subjected to an officious and insensitive reprimand not justified by her conduct. The industrial tribunal held that she was *"humiliated intimidated and degraded to such an extent that there was breach of trust and confidence which went to the root of the contract".* The employer nevertheless appealed against the finding of constructive dismissal arguing that the person who had carried out the reprimand, while a supervisor, had no authority to effect a dismissal. This the EAT found was an irrelevant consideration and restated the general principle that an employer is bound by acts done in the course of a supervisory employee's employment. *"Therefore, if the supervisor is doing what he or she is employed to do and in the course of doing it behaves in a way which if done by the employer would constitute a fundamental breach of the contract between the employer and employee, the employer is bound by the supervisor's misdeeds."*

Frustration

There is no dismissal if it can be shown that the contract of employment has been brought to an end through the operation of the common law doctrine of frustration. Frustration occurs where, due to a change in circumstances, performance of the contract becomes impossible or radically different than the performance envisaged by the parties when they made the contract. The specified events upon which a claim of frustration could be based are limited generally to long illness, and imprisonment. Certainly the distinction between the termination of a contract of employment by dismissal and termination by frustration is of critical importance.

> In *Shepherd & Company Ltd. v. Jerrom* 1986 the Court of Appeal considered the position of an apprentice plumber who was sentenced to Borstal training for a minimum period of six months. Failure to dismiss him in accordance with standard procedures for apprentices led the tribunal and the EAT to find that he had been constructively dismissed unfairly and so entitled to compensation. The Court of Appeal disagreed however and held that the four year apprenticeship contract had been frustrated by the six month sentence.

It is difficult in any given case to say whether the circumstances of an illness are such that it is no longer practical to regard the contract of employment as surviving. Obviously the seriousness and length of the illness are crucial factors but generally all the circumstances are relevant, including the nature of the job, the length of employment, the needs of the employer and obligations in relation to replacement, and the conduct of the employer.

Resignation

There is no dismissal if the employee expressly terminates the contract of employment by resigning.

> In *Kwik-Fit v. Lineham* 1992 as a direct consequence of issuing a written warning to a depot manager in accordance with the company's disciplinary procedure, he walked out in protest. While the employer took the view that the manager had resigned he nevertheless presents a complaint of unfair dismissal. The EAT held that where words or action of resignation are unambiguous an employer can accept them as such unless there are `special circumstances'. *"Words spoken or action expressed in temper or in the heat of the moment or under extreme pressure, or the intellectual make-up of an employee may be such special circumstances"*. In a case such as this, where there are special circumstances, an employer is required to allow a reasonable period to elapse, perhaps a matter of days, before accepting a resignation to determine an employee's true intention. The correct question to ask in deciding whether a resignation constitutes a dismissal is *"Who really terminated the contract of employment"*.

There will normally be a contractual provision as to the length of notice to be given and, in addition, there is a statutory minimum period of one week where the employee has at least one month of continuous employment. Failure to comply with notice requirements is a breach of contract for which the employee could be made liable in damages. Employers rarely sue in these cases due mainly to the problem of quantifying their loss which would include the additional cost of advertising for and hiring a replacement during the notice period.

The unilateral act of resigning must be distinguished from the consensual termination of employment which normally involves an exchange of consideration

Mutual termination

If the parties to a contract of employment, without duress and after taking proper advice, enter into a separate contract, supported by good consideration, with the objective of terminating the employment relationship by mutual consent, the contract will be valid and enforceable.

> Such was the case in *Logan Salton v. Durham County Council* 1989. Here the complainant was a social worker who, as a result of disciplinary hearings, had been redeployed by his employer. The complainant was given notice of a number of complaints against him and a recommendation that he be summarily dismissed. Prior to that meeting his union representative negotiated on his behalf a mutual agreement to terminate his employment with the Council. By that agreement the employment contract was to terminate in seven weeks' time and an outstanding car loan of £2,750 wiped out as a debt. Despite the fact that the agreement was signed by both parties, the complainant subsequently complained to an industrial tribunal that he had been unfairly dismissed. It was argued that a dismissal had occurred in law, for the mutual agreement to terminate was either void as an agreement entered into under duress, or void because it offended the EPCA 1978 because

its effect was to remove statutory protection. The EAT held that the fact that the appellant was aware of the employer's recommendation of dismissal did not constitute duress, bearing in mind the financial inducement. *"In the resolution of industrial disputes, it is in the best interests of all concerned that a contract made without duress, for good consideration, preferably after proper and sufficient advice and which has the effect of terminating a contract of employment by mutual agreement (whether at once or at some future date) should be effective between the contracting parties, in which case there probably will not have been a dismissal."*

Unfair Dismissal

The introduction of the right not to be dismissed without good reason in the Industrial Relations Act 1971 was a recognition that an employee has a stake in his job which cannot be extinguished simply by serving contractual notice. In the same way that a tenant may acquire security of tenure in his home and resist the enforcement of a notice to quit unless it is reasonable in the circumstances, an employee, through continuous employment, can acquire security in his job. The right not to be unfairly dismissed is intended to act as a constraint on employers who feel they have the authority to hire and fire as they please. The extent to which the law of unfair dismissal achieves the objective of constraining management prerogative is arguable. Over the last twenty years unfair dismissal has developed into a highly complex area of law recognised as such as early as 1977 by Philips J in *Devis & Sons Ltd. v. Atkins* 1977, when he said, *"the expression 'unfair dismissal' is in no sense a common-sense expression capable of being understood by the man in the street"*. The present unfair dismissal law is contained in the Employment Rights Act 1996 which is the main source of statutory employment rights. Under s.94(1) in every employment to which the section applies, every employee shall have the right not to be unfairly dismissed by his employer.

Qualifications

The Act identifies the qualifying period and the upper age limit for the purpose of unfair dismissal.

On the 6th February 1995 the Employment Protection (Part-Time Employees) Regulations came into force which formally abolish the thresholds distinguishing between full-time and part-time employment. All part-time workers, regardless of the number of hours that they work, enjoy the same statutory rights as full-time workers.

To fall within the provisions of s.94 then an employee had to show full-time continuous employment in a job which is not an excluded category of work. The minimum period of continuous employment is not less than two years ending with the effective date of termination. This is the date that the contract of employment actually comes to an end and if a summary dismissal is unjustified it may be necessary to add the statutory period of notice onto the date of dismissal.

In *R v. Secretary of State for Employment ex parte Seymour Smith and Perez* 1995 the Court of Appeal held that the two year qualifying period for bringing a complaint of unfair dismissal indirectly discriminated against women and was incompatible with the Equal Treatment Directive during the period from 1985 to 1991. This case has gone on appeal to the House of Lords and in November

1996 we await the court's judgment. It does seem unlikely however that the House of Lords will quash the Order containing the present qualifying period.

A further requirement is that if on, or before, the effective date of termination, the employee has reached the 'normal retiring age' or, if more than the age of 65 (whether male or female), then there is no right to present a claim.

In addition to qualifying through service, an employee must not fall within one of the excluded categories of employment.

- Persons employed in the police force.
- Share fishermen e.g. members and crew paid by a share of the profits.
- Employees who work ordinarily outside Great Britain.
- Employees who are employed on fixed term contracts of one year or more and have agreed in writing to exclude their rights.
- Employees covered by a designated dismissal procedure agreement.
- Certain registered dock-workers.
- Members of the armed forces. Following the Trade Union Reform and Employment Rights Act 1993 members of the armed forces can claim unfair dismissal if they have exhausted the internal service procedures.

Procedure

The procedure involved in presenting a complaint of unfair dismissal is considered in chapter 3 The Act provides that a tribunal will not have jurisdiction to hear a complaint unless it is presented within three months "*beginning with*" the "*effective date of termination*".The expression "*effective date of termination*" means for most purposes the date that the employment actually terminates.It seems that for a summary dismissal, whether or not in breach of contract, the effective date of termination is the date of dismissal.

> In *Stapp v. The Shaftesbury Society 1982* the Court of Appeal held that the '*effective date of termination*' means the actual date of termination of the employment whether or not the employee was wrongfully dismissed. Here the effect of a summary dismissal with wages paid in lieu of one month's notice was to make the effective date of dismissal the date of termination of employment and so the employee had insufficient continuous employment to bring a claim for unfair dismissal.

An industrial tribunal may hear a complaint presented outside the time limits if it is satisfied that it was not reasonably practicable to present the claim in time.

> In *Palmer and Saunders v. Southend on Sea Borough Council* 1984 the Court of Appeal held that in construing the expression `*reasonably practicable*`, the best approach is to read `*practicable*' as the equivalent of `*feasible*' and to ask "*was it reasonably feasible to present the complaint to the industrial tribunal within the relevant three months*". Also the court stressed that the issue is one of fact for the industrial tribunal and it is seldom that an appeal from its decision will lie.

Conciliation

A copy of the IT1 having been sent to ACAS, a conciliation officer is appointed to get in touch with both parties in an attempt to resolve the conflict and reach an amicable settlement. It should be stressed that in many cases an agreement is reached because of the intervention of the conciliation officer. While he is under a statutory duty to endeavour to promote a voluntary settlement of the complaint by encouraging an agreement to reinstate the employee, or make a payment of compensation, there is no requirement for the parties to co-operate or even communicate with him. If the complaint proceeds to a full hearing, the burden of proof is on the complainant to show that he has been dismissed unless that is conceded.

Having established that a dismissal has occurred, it then falls to the tribunal to determine the reason for dismissal, whether it is a reason categorised in the statute and, if so, whether the dismissal is fair or unfair and redress where appropriate.

Reason for dismissal

To assist the complainant in a claim for unfair dismissal the complainant is entitled to be provided with a written statement of the reason or reasons for dismissal within fourteen days of a written request.

The written statement provided under this section is important evidence of the employer's reason or reasons for dismissal. The period of continuous employment to qualify for this statutory right was increased from six months to two years by the Employment Act 1989. Following the Employment Protection (Part-Time Employees) Regulations 1995 the right applies to part-time employees regardless of their hours of work. The right to a statement of the reason or reasons applies where the dismissal is express or the non-renewal of a fixed term contract, but not if the complaint is based on a constructive dismissal. If an employer unreasonably fails to comply with a request the employee may present a complaint to the tribunal who may declare what it finds the reasons for dismissal are and also compensate the employee with an award of two weeks' wages.

The purpose of the statutory right to compel the employer to supply the employee with the reason or reasons relied on for dismissal is to enable the employee to scrutinise them in advance of the proceedings and also to tie the employer down to that reason in any subsequent proceedings. The Act requires an employer to state truthfully the reason that he was relying on in dismissing the employee so that the employee does not start with the disadvantage of not knowing the reason for dismissal if he wishes to pursue a claim for unfair dismissal.

Statutory reasons for dismissal

The heart of unfair dismissal law is contained in s.98 and it is to this section we must devote attention.

Under the section therefore it clearly states that it is the employer who must show the reason or principal reason for the dismissal, and that the reason falls within one of the four categories of reasons identified in s.98(2) or is a substantial reason under s.98(1) of a kind such as to justify the dismissal of an employee holding the position which that employee held. If the employee establishes the true reason for dismissal, and that it falls within one of the five statutory reasons identified in s.98, then the dismissal is prima facie fair. The final determination of fairness is achieved by applying the test of reasonableness contained in s.98(3).

Guidance in relation to the section was provided by Lord Bridge in *West Midlands Cooperatives Society v. Tipton* 1986, who said that there are three questions which must be asked in determining whether a dismissal is fair or unfair.

- What was the reason (or principal reason) for the dismissal?

- Was that a reason falling within s.98(2) or some other substantial reason of a kind such as to justify the dismissal of an employee holding the position which that employee held?

- Did the employer act reasonably or unreasonably in treating that reason as a sufficient reason for dismissing the employees for the purpose of s.98(3)?

The burden of proving, on the balance of probabilities, the real reason for dismissal, and that it is a statutory reason falling within s.98, is upon the employer. Failure to establish this true reason will make the decision to dismiss automatically unfair. We will now consider the four reasons in s.98(2) and the "*some other substantial reason*" in s.98(1).

Capability or qualification

For the purposes of this reason *capability' is assessed by reference to skill, aptitude, health or any other physical or mental quality*. The majority of cases where capability is the reason relied upon relate to incompetence or ill health. Where an allegation of incompetence is established through evidence, in determining the reasonableness of the employer's decision to dismiss it is also necessary to examine the reasons for the alleged incompetence. This could involve a consideration of the employer's appraisal processes, the amount of training and supervision required, and the extent to which employees are given the opportunity to improve their performance. Obviously there are degrees of incompetence, but even one serious lapse could be sufficient to justify a dismissal.

> In *Taylor v. Alidair Ltd.* 1978 the applicant pilot was dismissed when as a result of an error of judgment, the passenger plane he was flying landed so hard that serious damage was caused to the plane. The Court of Appeal held that *"the company has reasonable grounds for honestly believing that the applicant was not competent"*. As a result of this serious act of incompetence the belief was reasonably held, and the dismissal was consequently a fair one.

If incapability is alleged, due to the ill health of the employee, once again reasonableness of the employer's decision to dismiss must be viewed by the extent to which it is an informed judgment bearing in mind the various options available. Earlier in the chapter we considered the extent to which a long illness can amount to a frustration of the contract of employment.

If the reason for dismissal is related to 'qualifications' of the employee this is taken to mean *"any degree, diploma or other academic, technical or professional qualification relevant to the position which the employee held."*

Misconduct

Misconduct as a reason for dismissal covers a wide range of circumstances including such matters as lateness, absenteeism, insubordination, breach of safety rules and immorality. Of course the gravity of the misconduct, and the steps taken by the employer to address it, are crucial factors in determining whether the decision to dismiss for misconduct is a reasonable one or not. Misconduct at work has been held to include:

- stealing from the employer;
- a breach of safety instructions;
- refusal to obey reasonable instructions;
- immorality;
- drunkenness ; and
- absenteeism.

If the misconduct of the employee is of a sufficiently serious nature it may be reasonable for the employer to dismiss the employee with immediate effect.

> In *Hamilton v. Argyll & Clyde Health Board* 1993 the complainant was a chief hospital technician who was dismissed following an allegation that she had torn up a request card for a respiratory test on a patient so that the test was not carried out. Following an investigation the employer concluded that she had committed the guilty act and dismissed her for gross misconduct. The misconduct complained of, the employer believed, fell within the definition of misconduct set out in the employer's disciplinary procedure. The finding of a fair dismissal in the tribunal was challenged on appeal on the grounds that the employer had, in response to a union request, considered the employee for employment within some other sphere within the organisation. As the employment relationship had not been destroyed by the misconduct, the misconduct could not be classified as "gross" within the definition. This argument was rejected by the EAT which upheld the tribunal's decision. *"Willingness by an employer to offer re-employment is not inconsistent with a conclusion that an employee has been guilty of gross misconduct. What is gross misconduct must be considered in relation to the particular employment and the particular employee".*

Redundancy

The employer may show that the reason for dismissal was that the employee was redundant. Essentially a redundancy situation arises when an employer closes part or all of his business operation, the purposes for which the employee was employed, or alternatively the requirements of the business for workers of a particular kind have ceased or diminished. For the purposes of unfair dismissal however, not only must the dismissal be by reason of redundancy but the selection of the employee in question must also be fair. A separate section devoted to unfair selection for redundancy is included later in the chapter.

Employment in contravention of the law

For the purposes of this limited category it must be shown that it would be illegal to continue to employ the employee in question. A good example is where driving is an integral part of the employee's work and he is disqualified from driving. As usual the reasonableness of the employer's decision to dismiss must be viewed in the light of the particular circumstance, not least the availability of alternative work.

> In *Gill v. Walls Meat Company Ltd.* 1971 to have continued to employ the complainant, who worked on an open meat counter would have infringed Food Regulations, for he had grown a beard. After refusing to shave it off and also an offer of alternative work, the tribunal held that the decision to dismiss was a fair one.

Some other substantial reason

This final category of reason is used to include reasons for dismissal which do not fall neatly into the previous categories.

> A clash of personalities in the office was held to be a substantial reason of a kind to justify dismissal in *Treganowan v. Robert Knee & Company Ltd.* 1975. Here the complainant was dismissed because the atmosphere in the office where she worked had become so hostile that it was seriously affecting the employer's business. The prime cause of the trouble was the complainant, whose constant reference to her private life seriously upset her colleagues who felt that they could not work with her.

If the reason for dismissal is related to unacceptable periods of absence because of illness then it could fall into this category as the reason for dismissal.Certainly the refusal of an employee to accept an alteration in terms of employment has been held to fall within this category.

In rare cases the pressure on an employer to dismiss an employee comes from some third party source such as a trade union, customers or clients and even fellow employees. They may claim that the employee has been guilty of some objectionable conduct, that there is an insoluble personality conflict, or that the reason for the pressure is based upon some rational or irrational fear of HIV contagion. In this type of case the employer could rely on some other substantial reason as the reason for dismissal. The fairness of a dismissal in these circumstances will depend largely on the conduct of the employer who should have made practical and genuine efforts to resolve the conflict. The circumstances should be investigated and there should be consultation with the parties concerned with a view to reaching a solution. The employers should consider solutions other than dismissal, for instance, a relocation of work. Dismissal under third party pressure is only fair if after investigation there is a valid and serious complaint or the goodwill of a third party is so important that dismissal is the only sensible commercial decision.

The Test of Fairness

Once the employer has shown that the principal reason for dismissal is on the face of it fair it is then necessary for the industrial tribunal to determine the heart of the issue, whether the employer acted reasonably in the circumstances.

> The test of fairness is contained in s.98(3) which provides that the *determination of the question of whether the dismissal was fair or unfair, having regard to the reason shown by the employer, shall depend on whether in the circumstances (including the size and adminis-trative resources of the employer's undertaking) the employer acted reasonably or unreasonably in treating it as a sufficient reason for dismissing the employee, and that question shall be determined in accordance with equity and the substantial merits of the case.*

Where there are multiple reasons for dismissal it must be determined which is the principal one for the purposes of applying s.98(3).*Fairness* then has to be judged by the industrial tribunal acting as an industrial jury applying the words of s.98(3). The tribunal is not an arbitrator and has no jurisdiction to substitute its own views of reasonableness for the employer's but must adjudicate upon what a reasonable employer would have done in the circumstances.

Useful guidelines in relation to the approach to be adopted in applying s.57(3) were provided by the EAT in *Iceland Frozen Foods v. Jones* 1982. Here Brown Wilkinson J. suggested that the approach which should be adopted by tribunals was to start by considering the words of the section and then determine the reasonableness of the employer's conduct, not whether they believe the conduct to be fair. The tribunal must resist the temptation to substitute its own views as to the right course for the employer to adopt and recognise that there is a *band of reasonable responses* to the employer's conduct. Within this `band' reasonable employers could take different views. The role of the tribunal is to decide whether the decision of the employer in the case before it comes within the band of reasonable responses which the employer might have adopted. If the dismissal is within the band of reasonable responses which the employer might have adopted it is fair, otherwise it is unfair. This approach has been widely adopted.

 As the test of fairness is based upon the actions of a reasonable employer it is possible to find an employer acting within his contractual authority nevertheless acting unfairly for the purposes of unfair dismissal. A decision to dismiss based purely on economic considerations may fall within the band of reasonable responses of a reasonable employer.

> In *Saunders v. Scottish National Camps* 1980 the complainant, a handyman employed at a children's holiday camp, was dismissed when the employer discovered that he was a homosexual. The reason for dismissal was that the employee indulged in homosexuality and it was unsuitable to employ someone of that tendency in children's camps. Both the industrial tribunal and the EAT found the dismissal to be fair. They decided that a large proportion of employers in this situation would perceive that the employment of a homosexual should be restricted where there is close contact with children. This is despite the fact that such a view may not be rational or supported by evidence which is scientifically sound. There is no doubt however that the continued employment could have proved to be an economic liability for the employer, bearing in mind the views of certain parents.

If the reason for dismissal is connected with the employer's belief in the culpability of an employee, then to act reasonably the employer must have made due investigation and enquiry in order to equip himself with sufficient information to arrive at an *"honest belief"* in the employee's guilt.

In *British Railways Board v. Jackson* 1994 the complainant, a buffet car steward, who had fourteen years service with British Rail, was summarily dismissed when he was discovered to have bread and bacon in his possession at the beginning of his early morning shift without a satisfactory explanation. The reason for dismissal was contravening the BR rule relating to the possession of goods for the purposes of engaging in trade or business for his own benefit. Following a disciplinary hearing the complainant was summarily dismissed for gross misconduct. Both the tribunal and the EAT felt that the employer had "jumped the gun" in that the complainant was challenged in the locker room and had not taken the food onto the train. This conclusion was held to be flawed by the Court of Appeal who stated that the *"question which the tribunal had to determine was whether it was reasonable for the employers to find that the employee intended, in breach of the rules, to trade for his own advantage in the goods found in his possession. It was the wrong approach to adopt a legalistic stance and ask whether technically the BR rule had been infringed and conclude: that the employer had 'jumped the gun'."* To determine whether dismissal was a reasonable response the employer was entitled to take into account:

- the prevalence of this type of conduct among stewards;

- the need to deal with it severely as a deterrent;

- the conduct of the employee in not owning up and put forward unconvincing explanations.

Despite the facts that there was no completed act of dishonesty and the complainant had a long period of service with a good record, there was no basis that the tribunal could conclude that the decision to dismiss was not a reasonable response to the misconduct.

If an employee is dismissed for alleged misconduct the employer is normally obliged to investigate the circumstances and this is the case even where an employee is already under a final written warning.

In *Harrow LB v. Cunningham* 1996 the EAT confirmed that it could be reasonable for an employer to give two employees, guilty of the same misconduct, disparate treatment given their different disciplinary records. Here two employees of the cleansing department had wrongfully undertaken a private job of refuse disposal and given the fact that one of them was on a final written warning he was dismissed. The EAT held that *"a reasonable employer can respond to misconduct by taking disciplinary decisions which takes account of mitigating as well as aggravating factors"*.

Procedural fairness

In addition to examining the reason relied upon, the process of determining the reasonableness of the employer's decision to dismiss necessarily involves a consideration of the procedure implemented by the employer in relation to the dismissal. There exists a Code of Practice drawn up by ACAS on *"Disciplinary Practice and Procedures in Employment"*. The Code provides that employees should be fully informed of disciplinary rules and procedures and the likely consequences if the rules are broken. Also the Code identifies the essential features of a disciplinary procedure so that in cases of misconduct, the procedure should have built in a process involving formal and informal, oral and written warnings. In particular, at some point, the employee should be given the opportunity of putting his side of the case accompanied by a representative from a trade union or otherwise.

A second source of procedural standards is the increasing tendency of tribunals to require that the process of dismissal adheres to the rules of natural justice developed and refined in administrative law.

One important point in relation to procedures is that the graver the misconduct the less requirement there would be to implement a system of warnings. Also, where warnings are given for less serious matters they should be recorded but then after a period of satisfactory conduct eventually disregarded.

> In the important case of *Polkey v. A E Dayton Services Ltd.* 1987 the complainant, a van driver, employed by the defendants for over four years, was without warning or consultation, handed a letter of redundancy. His claim of unfair dismissal was based on the employer's failure to observe the statutory code of practice which provides for warning and consultation in a redundancy situation. Despite there being a *"heartless disregard"* of the code, the tribunal, EAT and the Court of Appeal all found that the dismissal was fair. Applying the *"no difference principle"*, if a fair procedure had been adopted, the employer could still have reasonably decided to dismiss. This approach was rejected by the House of lords who held that the employer's decision to dismiss had to be judged by applying the test of reasonableness. There was no scope for deciding what the employer might have done had he adopted a different procedure. Where the employer fails to observe the code, he will only be acting fairly if the tribunal is satisfied that *"the employer could reasonably have concluded in the light of circumstances known at the time of dismissal that consultation or warning would be utterly useless"*.

The House of Lords held in Polkey therefore that a failure to follow an agreed procedure in dismissing an employee is likely to result in a finding of unfair dismissal. This is subject to the exception where it is obvious that use of the proper procedure would be futile. The Court of Appeal has recently provided guidance as to when as employer can rely on this exception.

> In *Duffy v. Yeomans & Partners Ltd.* 1994 the Court of Appeal held that to come within the Polkey exception there was no need for an employer to have actually considered and rejected the possibility of going through a consultative process required by a disciplinary procedure. Rather the test is an objective one, for the industrial tribunal must ask itself whether an employer acting reasonably could have failed to consult in the circumstances.

It is now established that in assessing the fairness of the employers decision to dismiss or otherwise it is necessary to consider whether the disciplinary code was fully adhered to.

> In *Cabaj v. Westminster City Council* 1996 following the dismissal of a senior computer programmer for poor attendance, the appeal tribunal which considered his appeal against the decision to dismiss, was attended by the Chief Executive of the council and two members, rather than three members required by the disciplinary code. The EAT disagreed with the tribunal and found that this significant error rendered the dismissal unfair. The EAT stated that *"where an employee has a contractual right to have an*

appeal against dismissal heard and decided by an appeals panel constituted in a particular way, as a matter of law a defect in the composition of such a body is a significant contractual and jurisdictional failure, not simply a matter of procedural error... The absence of the third member meant that the decision on appeal was not taken by the appeal tribunal at all but by two members of the council who did not have the power to hear and determine the employee's appeal against dismissal... The denial to the employee of his contractual entitlement was so fundamental a defect in the dismissal procedure that the only conclusion could be that the dismissal was unfair." On further appeal to the Court of Appeal the court agreed that the employee had a contractual entitlement to have his dismissal determined by an appeals panel of three members and that here there had been a breach of contract. The court disagreed however with the decision of the EAT that such a failure to observe the contractual appeals procedure made the dismissal necessarily unfair. Failure by an employer to observe its own contractually enforceable disciplinary procedure does not inevitably require an industrial tribunal to conclude that a dismissal was unfair. The question which the industrial tribunal has to determine is not whether the employer acted reasonably in dismissing the employee, but whether the employer acted reasonably or unreasonably in treating the reason shown as a sufficient reason for dismissal. The relevance to that question of a failure to entertain an appeal to which the employee was contractually entitled, as Lord Bridge pointed out in *West Midlands* Co-operative Society v Tipton, is whether the employee was *"thereby"* denied the opportunity of showing that the real reason for dismissal was not sufficient. As Lord Mackay and Lord Bridge indicated in *Polkey v A E Dayton Services Ltd*, *"it is also relevant to consider whether the employer acted reasonably if he actually considered or a reasonable employer would have considered at the time of dismissal that to follow the agreed procedure would in the circumstances of the case be futile."* The question that the tribunal was bound to consider in the case was whether the appeals tribunal as constituted prevented the employer showing the the reason for dismissal was insufficient and why the employer carried out the dismissal without observing the disciplinary code. These questions the Court of Appeal held should be considered by a new industrial tribunal.

In *Securicor Guarding Ltd. v. R* 1994 the complainant was dismissed from his post as a security guard with an important customer when his employer discovered that he had been charged with sex offences against children. The decision to dismiss was reached after holding a disciplinary hearing. The employer concluded that the reputation of the business could suffer if they continued to employ the complainant. Both the tribunal and the EAT found the dismissal to be unfair. The EAT held that the tribunal *"was entitled to find that although the employers were unable to carry out any inquiries into the truth of the allegations, before deciding how to deal with the employee, any reasonable employer would have enquired of the customer concerned to see what they thought of the situation and what they wished to be done. The mere fact that an employee in a sensitive position has been charged with an offence will not justify the employer in dismissing him rather than suspending him or moving him away from the sensitive position until the truth of the matter is determined."*

Unfair selection for redundancy

In cases where the reason for dismissal is redundancy then the dismissal will be prima facie fair. If however the circumstances of the dismissal show that the employer failed to act reasonably then a redundancy dismissal would be found to be unfair and a remedy awarded.

Consequently if in a redundancy selection the employer failed to observe agreed industrial practice, this could render a decision to dismiss on grounds of redundancy unfair.

> Guidance in relation to the approach to be adopted by industrial tribunals in determining the fairness of redundancy selections was provided by the Employment Appeal Tribunal in *Williams v. Compair Maxim Ltd.*. 1982. Here the complainants had been dismissed for redundancy, the employer having failed to consult with the recognised trade union. Selection had been left to departmental managers, one of whom gave evidence that he had retained those employees whom he considered would be best to retain in the interests of the company in the long run. Length of service was not a factor taken into account. The industrial tribunal's finding of fair dismissal was reversed by the EAT which held the decision to be perverse. Measuring the conduct of the employer in question with that of a reasonable employer, a tribunal taken to be aware of good industrial practice, could not have reached the decision that the dismissals were fair. The employer's decision to dismiss was not within the range of conduct which a reasonable employer could have adopted in these circumstances. While accepting that it was impossible to lay down detailed procedures for a selection process, the EAT felt that reasonable employers would attempt to act in accordance with five basic principles and should depart from them only with good reason.
>
> * As much warning as possible should be given of impending redundancies to enable the union and employees to inform themselves of the facts, seek alternative solutions and find alternative employment.
>
> * The employer will consult with the union as to the best means of achieving the objective as fairly and with as little hardship as possible. Criteria should be agreed to be applied in selection and the selection monitored.
>
> * The criteria agreed should not depend upon subjective opinion of the person selecting but it must be capable of objective scrutiny and include such matters as attendance record, job efficiency, experience or length of service.
>
> * The employer must seek to ensure that the selection is made fairly in accordance with these criteria and consider union representations.
>
> * The employer should examine the possibility of finding suitable alternative employment.

It is not good industrial practice for an employer to abrogate his decision making in relation to redundancy selection.

> In *Boulton & Paul Ltd. v. Arnold* 1994 the complaint of unfair dismissal arose from the selection of the complainant for dismissal by reason of redundancy. The selection was made by applying a number of criteria one of which was attendance and the complaint

of unfairness arose from the fact that in the complainant's case no distinction had been made between authorised and unauthorised absences. When the complainant appealed against her selection for redundancy the employer offered to retain her but on terms that another employee would be dismissed in her place. The complainant rejected the offer and presented a complaint of unfair dismissal. On appeal the EAT upheld the tribunal's finding of unfair dismissal *"An offer to retain an employee under notice at the expense of another employee cannot be held to prevent a finding of unfair dismissal on the basis that the employee has had the opportunity of staying employed. It is unfair to put the onus on an employee to decide whether she or another employee is to be selected for dismissal. That is effectively an abrogation of the employer's responsibility to manage the business."*

Certainly the need for consultation in a redundancy situation is one of the fundamentals of fairness and it is only in exceptional cases that a failure to consult can be overlooked.

Automatically Unfair

Under the 1996 Act certain reasons for dismissal are categorised as automatically unfair

Such reasons would include the employee asserting a statutory right, raising health and safety issues or on the grounds of pregnancy or childbirth.

Dismissal on the grounds of pregnancy or childbirth

It is automatically unfair to dismiss an employee because she is pregnant or has given birth or has taken maternity leave. This is contained in s.99 of the Employment Rights Act 1996 and it applies regardless of the length of service.

The European Court of Justice in *Webb v. EMO Air Cargo (UK) Ltd.* 1994 adopted the approach that as pregnancy can only affect women a pregnancy dismissal is unlawful sex discrimination under the Equal Treatment Directive. Here the applicant had been engaged on a permanent contract, but in the first place to cover for an employee on maternity leave. She had been dismissed when she then become pregnant and having insufficient continuous employment to qualify for unfair dismissal protection she had relied on discrimination law. By adopting the comparator approach the tribunals and appellate courts had dismissed her claim. In the light of this ruling by the European Court however the House of Lords finally decided in her favour in *Webb v. EMO Air Cargo (UK) Ltd.* (No 2) 1995. A decision to dismiss by reason of pregnancy therefore will constitute direct discrimination and given that the maximum level of compensation has been removed in sex discrimination cases it could provide a more significant remedy than unfair dismissal.

Recently the EAT in *O'Neill v. Governors of St Thomas More RCVA Upper School* 1996 upheld a complaint of unfair discrimination against a school which had dismissed a religious instruction teacher during her maternity leave when it became known that the father of her child was the local Roman Catholic priest. The EAT rejected the contention that the motive for the dismissal was the paternity of the child and the applicants position at the school. These reasons it was held were all related to the pregnancy which was the dominant reason for the dismissal.

The EAT also held in *Caruana v. Manchester Airport* 1996 that the failure to renew a fixed term contract on the grounds that the applicant would not be available for work due to her pregnancy constituted sex discrimination. Here the new contract was an extension of a continuing employment relationship and to disqualify it from the protection of discrimination law *"would be a positive encouragement to employers to impose a series of short term contracts to avoid the impact of discrimination law, rather than offer a continuous and stable employment relationship"*. The applicant in this case was self employed and did not therefore qualify for protection under unfair dismissal law.

Dismissal in connection with union activities

For dismissals in relation to trade union activities there is no requirement for the complainant to show continuous employment to qualify to present a claim or be within the prescribed age limits.

Under s.152 of the Trade Union and Labour Relations (Consolidation) Act 1992 *a dismissal shall be regarded as unfair if the reason for it was that the employee:*

(a)   *was, or proposed to become, a member of an independent trade union, or*

(b)   *had taken part, or proposed to take part, in the activities of an independent trade union at an appropriate time. or*

(c)   *was not a member of any trade union, or of a particular trade union, or of one of a number of particular trade unions, or had refused or proposed to refuse to become or remain a member.*

Previously a dismissal for non-membership of a trade union could, in certain circumstances, be fair if it was to prevent the contravention of a closed shop agreement supported by a ballot. Following the Employment Act 1988, all dismissals for non-membership of a trade union are automatically unfair irrespective of whether there is a closed shop agreement. Section 152 then is concerned with dismissals connected with membership or non-membership of trade union or for taking part in trade union activities. For claims based on membership, the union in question must be independent and so not under the control or domination of an employer or a group of employers.

For claims based on union activities carried on at an *appropriate time,* further guidance is needed to determine whether a dismissal falls within this category. The Act deals with the question of *appropriate time* by limiting it to a time outside working hours or within working hours with the employer's consent.

In *Marley Tile v. Shaw 1980,* the Court of Appeal confirmed that in a proper case the consent of an employer to trade union activities could be implied. Here however, where a union meeting was held without express permission, causing more than *"a mere trifling inconvenience",* to the employer's business, it was not carried out at an *"appropriate time",* for it was carried out during working hours and was not in accordance with arrangements made or consent given.

It seems that distributing union material, recruiting and advising members and attending meetings are all types of conduct which could be described as *" trade union activities "*.

The section confers protection on an employee who is proposing to take part in union activities and dismissed as a result.

In *Fitzpatrick v. British Railways Board 1991* an employee with a reputation as a union activist was dismissed because it was felt she would be a disruptive influence. This dismissal was unfair as contrary to the section.

Dismissal in connection with health and safety and statutory rights

Under s.100 of the Employment Rights Act 1996 all employees, irrespective of hours and service have the right not to be dismissed or subjected to any detriment for engaging in activities such as:

- acting as a safety representative;

- bringing a health and safety matter to the employer's attention where the employee reasonably believed there was potential harm;

- carrying out designated activities in connection with preventing or reducing risks to health and safety;

- leaving or refusing to return to the place of work because of a reasonable belief in a serious or imminent danger;

- in circumstances of danger taking steps to protect himself or his colleague;

In an unfair dismissal claim which succeeds for this reason the dismissed employee is entitled to a special award in addition to the compensatory and basic award.

Under s.104 of the 1996 Act it is automatically unfair to dismiss an employee for alleging that the employer had infringed a statutory right or for bringing proceedings to enforce such a right. Once again employees are entitled to make a complaint regardless of their length of service

In *Mennell v. Newell & Wright (Transport Contractors) Ltd.* 1996 the complainant Mr Mennell an HGV driver, refused to sign a new contract of employment because one of the clauses in the draft contract provided that the employers would recover certain training costs by way of a deduction from payment of final salary due to the employee on termination of employment. He maintained that any such deduction from his wages would amount to a breach of the Wages Act. Eventually Mr Mennell was dismissed and he claimed that he had been dismissed for asserting a statutory right. The industrial tribunal, accepted the employers argument that because no deduction had in fact been made from Mr Mennell's wages, there had been no infringement of any right under the Wages Act in respect of which a complaint could be made to an industrial tribunal and, therefore, no infringement of a relevant statutory right. The Employment Appeal Tribunal held that the industrial tribunal had wrongly interpreted the section. "*A threat of dismissal in order to impose a variation of the contract of employment so as to enable the employer to make deductions from wages may amount to an infringement, at the time the threat is made, of the employee's statutory right under the Wages Act not to have deductions made from wages without his freely given written consent.*"

In *Lopez v. Maison Bouquillon Ltd* 1996 the complainant, a counter assistant in a cake shop, left her workplace and complained to the police that she had been assaulted by the chef who was married to the shop manageress. Subsequently the complainant was told by her employer that she no longer worked for the company. Claiming unfair dismissal she said that the reason she was dismissed was that she left the workplace, but in the circumstances that was perfectly reasonable, given the assault. The tribunal found that the dismissal was unfair. In this type of scenario a complainant who can show that a dismissal is related to the fact that she raised health and safety issues or had taken appropriate steps to protect herself form imminent danger can rely on section 100(1) ERA 1996. A dismissal in these circumstances is automatically unfair and no qualifying period of employment is required.

Remedies for unfair dismissal

If a complaint of unfair dismissal is successful, the tribunal has authority to make an order for *reinstatement or re-engagement* or make an award of *compensation*. Irrespective of whether he has requested the remedies on his IT1, the tribunal is obliged to explain the remedies of reinstatement and re-engagement to a successful complainant and discover whether he wishes to apply for such an order.

An order for reinstatement requires the employer to treat the complainant in all respects as if he had not been dismissed. By such an order, the employer would be required to make good any arrears of pay or any rights or privileges which would have accrued but for the dismissal. If the employee would have benefited from improvements in terms and conditions but for the dismissal, then the order must reflect the improvement from the date it was agreed. In exercising its discretion to make an order of reinstatement the tribunal must take account of:

- the wishes of the complainant;
- whether it is practicable for an employer to comply with such an order; and
- whether the complainant contributed to the dismissal and whether it would be just to make such an order.

If the tribunal decides not to make an order for reinstatement it must then consider the possibility of re-engagement. An order of re-engagement requires the employer, his successor, or an associate to employ the complainant in comparable work or other suitable employment and on making such an order the tribunal must specify the terms upon which the re-engagement is to take place. Such would include the identity of the parties, the nature of the employment remuneration. An amount payable for arrears if pay rights and privileges restored and the date the order must be complied with.

For re-engagement the tribunal must take account of the following considerations:

- the wishes of the employee;
- whether it is practicable for the employer to comply with an order for re-engagement; and

- where the employee contributed to some extent to the dismissal and whether it would be just to order re-engagement and if so, on what terms.

If a tribunal decides not to make either order it must make an award of compensation. But even if either order is made, a tribunal has no power to ensure that it is complied with. Failure to comply or fully comply with an order of reinstatement or re-engagement can only lead to an award of compensation subject to the maximum limit.

Regardless of the loss which could include substantial arrears of wages, if the employer refuses to re-employ, the complainant's compensation was limited to the statutory compensation in force at the time, the basic compensatory and additional awards. Now following the Trade Union Reform and Employment Rights Act 1993 there is no longer a limit on the extent of compensation for non compliance with an order.

Compensation

The most common form of redress for unfair dismissal is compensation.

An order for compensation as redress for unfair dismissal may consist of a *basic award*, a *compensatory award*, an *additional award* and where the dismissal related to the membership or non-membership of a trade union, a *special award*.

Basic award

The basic award is payable in all cases of unfair dismissal irrespective of loss and is calculated with reference to the complainant's continuous employment and average week's wage. It should be noted however that if it can be shown that the complainant contributed to the dismissal through his own fault, or has unreasonably refused an offer of reinstatement, the amount of the basic award can be reduced by a just and equitable proportion. The computation of the basic award is the same as for a redundancy payment, so the present maximum is £6,300.

The amount of the basic award is calculated by reference to the period the employee has been continuously employed, ending with the effective date of termination. By reckoning backwards from the effective date of termination the number of years employment can be determined allowing:

> *one and a half weeks' pay for each year of employment in which the employee was not below 41 years of age;*
>
> *one week's pay for each year the employee was not below 22 years of age;*
>
> *a half week's pay for each year of employment between 18 and 21 years of age.*

To calculate the basic award therefore it is necessary to determine the employee's gross pay up to a maximum of £210, his length of service up to a maximum of 20 years and his age. The maximum award payable therefore is for an employee who is dismissed after 20 years' service, over the age of 41, with a gross wage in excess of £210. He will be entitled to a basic award of 20 x 11/2 x £210 = £6,300.

614   Chapter 16   The Law Relating to the Termination of Employment

In many cases the employee's period of continuous service will cover more than one age rate barrier. In such circumstances it is necessary to calculate the entitlement at the relevant rate, e.g. for an employee who is made redundant at the age of 44 who, after 15 years' service has a gross wage of £160, is entitled to:

$$3 \text{ years } \times 1\tfrac{1}{2} \times £160 \quad = \quad £620$$
plus
$$12 \text{ years } \times 1 \times £160 \quad = \quad \underline{£1,920}$$
$$\overline{£2,540}$$

Compensatory award

In assessing the amount of the compensatory award, up to the present maximum of £11,400 a tribunal must have regard to the loss sustained by the complainant in consequence of the dismissal.

The amount of a compensatory award should take account of any failure by the employee to mitigate his loss, for instance by refusing an offer of suitable alternative employment. The Court of Appeal held in *Babcock Fata v. Addison* 1987 that any money paid in lieu of notice should be deducted from a compensatory award as should any ex gratia payment made. Heads of compensation that are assessable include the loss of fringe benefits attached to the job, expense incurred in seeking alternative work, net wages lost up to the hearing, estimated future earnings, the termination of continuous employment which necessarily limits future rights and the loss of pension rights.

As a general rule the compensatory award is limited to financial loss and cannot extend to hurt feelings. Although unfair dismissal may be traumatic, no damages are available for the distress caused by the employer's action. It would be possible however to compensate for financial loss resulting from the manner of the dismissal, rather than injury to feelings, particularly when it affects future prospects of employment. Injury to feelings are recognised for the purposes of compensation in discrimination legislation so that if a dismissal is proved to be sex or race discrimination then the distress suffered by the applicant can be compensated.

The compensatory award, like the basic award, may be reduced because of the complainant's contributory fault.

Additional award

If the tribunal makes a reinstatement or re-engagement order with which the employer fails to comply, the tribunal will make an additional award unless it was not practicable to comply with the order. Previously this award was restricted to the compensatory award limit but this limit has been removed by the Trade Union Reform and Employment Rights Act 1993.

Special award

The special award may be payable if the dismissal is in connection with membership or non-membership of a trade union or health and safety following the Trade Union Reform and Employment Rights Act 1993. *The amount of a special award is one week's pay multiplied by 104 or £13,400 whichever is greater, up to a maximum of £26,800.*

Assignment Unfair Dismissal

For the purpose of this assignment you are to assume the role of Sarah Maxwell, a newly appointed legal advisor employed at the regional office of ACAS in the North East of England. One of the main functions of your job is to assess the legal position when complaints of unfair treatment are presented to the Industrial Tribunal. Complaints of unfair dismissal have been presented in relation to the following two areas of conflict.

The first dispute involves a Mr. Simmonds who was employed by Hennessy, a transport company from 1984 to May 1996 as a HGV driver at their Gateshead depot. All drivers at the Gateshead depot are members of the Transport and General Workers Union. Mr. Simmonds, unhappy at the attitude of the TGWU shop steward of the depot, left the union in March 1996. Although there is no closed shop at the depot the other drivers threatened to strike if Mr. Simmonds was not sacked or moved elsewhere. In April 1996 the Transport Manager at the company's head office instructed Mr. Simmonds by letter that he must either rejoin the TGWU or work from the Middlesbrough depot where union membership is not an issue. Mr. Simmonds replied by letter in late April stating that the company had no right to move his place of work, particularly to pacify militant trade unionists, and that he was left with no option but to tender his resignation. His employment terminated at the end of May and in early June he started proceedings alleging unfair dismissal.

Major Homes Ltd. is a large construction company specialising in private housing developments mainly in the north of England. On 5 May 1996 the company's personnel manager for the North East reported to the management that David Allgood the site manager on a development in Durham has been charged with assault occasioning actual bodily harm for which he is to be prosecuted in the near future. It is alleged that following a heated argument between Mr. Allgood and Jimmy Power, a labourer, in a public house, Allgood attacked Power and physically assaulted him. The argument concerned Mr. Power's entitlement to overtime pay from the company. Foreseeing the possibility of further conflict, the management decide to transfer Mr. Allgood to a new site in South Wales and they inform him of their decision to take effect from 1 June 1996. Allgood objected to the transfer and failed to report for work on 1 June 1996 despite having nine years loyal service with the company. His request for a hearing was rejected by the company on the grounds that this procedure only applies where there has been a dismissal rather than a resignation. A further request on 7 July 1996 by Allgood's solicitor for a hearing to deal with the issue, is also rejected by letter on 26 August 1996 following Allgood's conviction for assault on 20 August 1996. On 3 September 1996 Allgood's solicitor presents a complaint on his behalf alleging unfair dismissal.

Task

In the role of Sarah Maxwell your task is to prepare reports on the above scenarios in which you assess the legal position.

Legal Terms found in Chapter 17

Assignment	• legal transfer of property
Copyright	• an intellectual property right arises automatically without registration in favour of the author of original literary, musical, artistic or other work
Chose in action	• intangible property such as debts, patents and business goodwill
Chose in possession	• items of property which are tangible and moveable
Covenant	• an undertaking found in a deed
Conveyance	• legal document which transfers the ownership of land from the vendor to the purchaser
Defamation	• a tort which involves damaging a person's reputation by way of statements made about them
Freehold	• absolute right to hold land for an unlimited time without payment
Intellectual property	• property rights designed to protect ideas, information and other outcomes of human intellectual creation such as copyrights, patents and designs
Leasehold	• right to hold land for a fixed or periodic term subject to the payment of rent
Moral rights	• rights of an author of copyright work to be identified as such (paternity) and not to have the work subjected to derogatory treatment (integrity)
Passing off	• a legal action in tort available where a business represents its goods or services as those of another business
Patent	• an intellectual property right which arises on registration of a new invention capable of use in an industrial context
Punitive damages	• damages awarded to punish the defendant for the losses caused
Security of tenure	• right to retain leasehold premises subject to certain conditions
Trade mark	• an emblem, symbol or other sign designed to establish a connection in the mind of a customer between goods or services and their product or supplier

Chapter 17

Business Property

The Nature of Property

All businesses own property of some kind and most will own a wide range of property. This property is likely to take many different forms and perform a variety of functions. A glance at the balance sheet of any business will reveal the major types of property – or assets – commonly used by the trading organisation.

Under the heading of *fixed assets* come items of property of a relatively permanent character which are acquired for use in the business. These may be tangible assets such as plant and machinery, vehicles and premises, or intangible assets such as patents, trade marks and goodwill. The balance sheet will also show the *current assets* of the business such as raw materials, work in progress, stock, debtors and cash.

The legal rules which regulate the ownership, use and disposal of these different forms of business property vary according to the nature of the property itself and hence the legal category into which it is placed.

The ownership of property brings with it certain legal rights and duties. Rights include the right to use and enjoy physical possession of the property, to consume it, destroy it or dispose of it by transferring ownership of it to another person by way of gift or sale. An owner must also bear the risk of loss or damage to the property by accident or liability arising because of the use to which the property is put. Prudent owners will usually safeguard against these risks by taking out adequate insurance. In this chapter it is proposed to consider some of the main rights and duties which arise in relation to business property. A useful starting point is to set out a formal classification of property under English law. From this model it is possible to identify the types of property which are of significance in the business world. You must appreciate however that English property law has developed over hundreds of years so that the legal terminology may well be unfamiliar to you.

The Classification of Property

Most legal systems distinguish between two main types of property, movable and immovable. This distinction is based upon the nature and characteristics of the property itself. Movable property includes goods and chattels, shares, debts and cheques; while immovable property is land and the things which go with land such as buildings and rights of way.

The English legal system unfortunately does not adopt this approach and, for historical reasons, makes a primary distinction between *real* and *personal property*. Real property is simply freehold land and we all will consider the rights of the freeholder later. All forms of property other than freehold land are categorised as personal property.

The historical reason for the distinction between real and personal property is that, in the early days of the common law, a form of legal action known as a *real* action could be used by an owner of freehold land if he had been wrongfully dispossessed of the land. If the real action was successful the common law courts could order that the true owner be entitled to physically recover the land wrongfully taken. This remedy was not available to an owner of any other type of property, not even to a holder of leasehold land, and such owners could only take an action in court to recover damages or financial compensation from the person who had taken their property, because the court had no power to order the restoration of their property to them. Thus real property was that property which could be recovered by taking a *real* action in the courts and all other property was classified as personal property. The classification survives today even though the powers of the courts have long since evolved so that it is now perfectly possible for a court to make an order restoring personal property to its true owner.

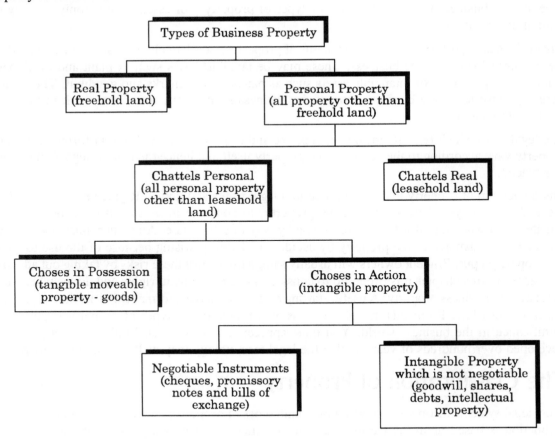

Figure 17.1   Classification of Business Property

All types of personal property are known as chattels. *Chattels* is an old English word meaning goods, derived from the word for cattle, which were in early times one of the most valuable forms of personal property. Land and buildings held under the terms of a lease are classified as *chattels real*. They are the form of personal property (chattels) most closely resembling freehold land (real property) and derive their name accordingly. Technically therefore the holder of leasehold land has a form of personal property, despite the fact that it may be a valuable interest in land.

All other forms of personal property are known as *chattels personal*. Chattels personal, a term covering forms of property, whether tangible or intangible, which other systems would classify as movable property, such as plant and equipment, vehicles, patents and debts.

A further division or classification of chattels personal is made between *choses in possession* and *choses in action* depending on whether they are tangible or intangible.

Choses is a French word meaning things. Choses in possession or things in possession therefore are items of physical movable property for instance *goods* within the meaning of the Sale of Goods Act 1979 such as books, machinery, cars or desks.

Choses in action or things in action differ from choses in possession in that they have no physical existence. Choses in action are intangible forms of personal property such as goodwill, patents and debts, the rights in which can only be asserted by taking legal action. There may be some physical or tangible evidence of the existence of the property rights in question but the rights themselves are intangible. For example, a share certificate is a tangible piece of paper, but its value lies in the legal rights which it represents such as rights to vote at meetings of the company, rights to receive dividends and rights to share in the ultimate division of the property of the company on winding up once prior claims have been met.

Negotiable instruments such as cheques, bills of exchange and promissory notes are choses in action which represent the right to receive the payment of sums of money. Among the tangible assets of a business what is often regarded as the most significant, is the land from which it operates.

Land

Land is the most permanent and often the most valuable asset which a business can own. For legal purposes the buildings and other permanent structures like trees and fences are treated as being part of it, and thus the ownership of business premises is regarded by the law as the same thing as the ownership of the land on which those premises stand. The airspace above and the soil below the land are also treated as being part of the land, so the owner has rights to them as well.

The premises from which businesses operate may be owned by the business outright. This is referred to as freehold ownership. On the other hand the premises may be rented from some other person or organisation. This is referred to as *leasehold* ownership. Technically all land in England and Wales is owned by the Crown and individuals or business organisations may hold an *estate* in land. The expression *estate in land* refers to the measure of a person's interest in land from the point of view of time.

Under s.1 of the Law of Property Act 1925, only two legal estates can exist in land: the fee simple absolute in possession (the freehold estate); and the term of years absolute (the leasehold estate).

Freehold Land

The *fee simple absolute in possession* is the freehold estate in land which effectively represents absolute ownership. The expression *fee* refers to the fact that the estate is inheritable; *simple* means that there are no restrictions on who may inherit; *absolute* refers to the fact that the grant is unconditional and *in possession* means that the grant is to take effect immediately.

A freehold owner is entitled to immediate possession of the land and this entitlement cannot be brought to an end except by the owner himself. He is entitled to pass on his ownership by sale to another or by inheritance to any of his heirs.

The only practical effect of the Crown's technical ownership of land is that the land will pass to the Crown as *bona vacantia* in the unlikely event that the freehold owner dies without any next of kin whatsoever, and without a will giving the property to a named beneficiary.

For all practical purposes the freeholder is the absolute owner of the land and consequently the purchase of the freehold estate will normally necessitate the payment of a substantial sum of money to the vendor. The money can of course be raised by using the land as security to negotiate a business mortgage and repaying the capital sum plus interest to a lender, *the mortgagee*, over a number of years. Nevertheless a lender will still require that a significant proportion of the cost must be funded by the prospective purchaser. The acquisition of the freehold of business property therefore, if it is available, will represent a substantial investment and should only be considered in the light of the prevailing property market.

Additionally, while it is usual to equate a freehold with absolute ownership, you should also appreciate that even a freeholder is subject to many common law and statutory restrictions in relation to his freedom to use the land for his own purposes. Some of the following restrictions apply equally to the holder of leasehold land (considered later in the chapter.)

The right to develop the land

A landowner is subject to the control of the local planning authority in relation to any proposed *development* of the land. *Planning permission* is required for any material alterations to buildings on land or the use to which they are put. If an individual is considering acquiring a piece of land, there is a means by which he can obtain outline planning permission for any proposed development to ascertain whether full planning permission is likely to be granted.

If an owner carries out development without permission, the local planning authority may serve an *enforcement notice* on him requiring the works to be removed or the new use to be discontinued. If the enforcement notice is not complied with the authority may enter the land and restore it, charging the cost to the owner and alternatively, or in addition, may take proceedings in the Magistrates' Court against the owner. The Magistrates may impose a fine and a further penalty for each day that the contravention continues.

Under the Building Act 1984, formerly the Building Regulations 1965 and 1976, plans for the construction of new buildings or for the structural alteration of existing buildings must be approved by the local authority. The purpose of the Building Regulations is to ensure that building construction is carried out in accordance with good building and design principles. Building inspectors may inspect the building works as they continue in order to see that the approved plans are adhered to.

The right to retain ownership

Wide powers are conferred on local authorities and other bodies with regard to the compulsory purchase of land. A freeholder can be required to sell his interests in the land to a body exercising compulsory purchase powers, usually in order to facilitate some development scheme such as new road construction. An owner can, of course, object to a compulsory purchase order and then a public local inquiry will have to be held to consider the views of those affected. Such inquiries are conducted by an inspector who will recommend a course of action to the appropriate Minister (the Secretary of State for the Environment) whose decision is final.

The right to water and natural resources

An owner has certain mineral rights in relation to natural resources on his land. An owner will also enjoy certain rights if his land adjoins a river. These riparian rights as they are known, allow him to take water for ordinary purposes connected with the land. The right however is subject to a licensing system in relation to the extraction of water.

Rights in relation to the use of land

As a general proposition a landowner, subject to planning control, can use the land as he likes. However the ability of the businessman to operate any business he chooses is subject to a number of restrictions. Such restrictions may arise by means of express or implied agreement. An individual occupying premises either as a freeholder business or a business tenant may be subject to some restriction on his rights to use the property for business purposes contained in the agreement under which the land was acquired.

Whether a freehold or leasehold estate is acquired the deed conveying the property will contain a number of covenants. A covenant is simply a contractual term contained in a deed. One such covenant will normally restrict business use, and this could come in a positive or negative form. In a business lease the covenant may restrict the tenant from carrying on a particular business or using the property for a particular purpose, for instance carrying on the business of a retail travel agent. Alternatively the covenant could prevent the tenant from carrying on a particular form of trade or any activity causing a nuisance or annoyance, such as a public house. Both the landlord and tenant have bound themselves personally by the covenants in the lease and will retain this contractual liability throughout its term. A covenant restricting business use will also be enforceable against a sub tenant or an assignee of the business lease, by the original landlord or even a new landlord who has purchased the freehold estate.

Restrictive covenants may also apply to a freeholder. Usually restrictive covenants could originate from a transaction under which one landowner, Smith sold part of his land to a purchaser, Jones. In the deed conveying the land to Jones, Smith may for the benefit of land retained by him, have extracted a promise from Jones not to use the land for anything except residential purposes. Thus if Jones now attempts to break the covenant by setting up a business, Smith can seek an injunction to prevent him. Of course it is not always the seller who abstracts the promise, it could be the purchaser who imposes a restriction on the seller. A major feature of such covenants is that they will become attached to the land which carries the burden and enjoys the benefit so that successive holders of the land may be bound by them.

In *C & G Homes Ltd. v. Secretary of State for Health* 1990 the issue before the Court of Appeal was whether the acquisition and use by the Health Secretary of two adjoining houses on a private housing estate in Bath as accommodation for four former mental patients contravened a restrictive covenant to use the houses as private dwellings. The court held that while the houses were being used as dwellings they were not *"private dwelling houses"* within the terms of the covenant for the occupiers were neither owners, tenants or members of the Health Secretary's, family but remained patients in NHS care. *"the use of these houses seemed to be that of a hospital annex or mental health hostel. Praiseworthy though that no doubt was, it was not a use which would be regarded as a normal use of a private dwelling house."*

Where the character of a neighbourhood changes or it becomes obvious that the covenant impedes some reasonable use of the land it is possible to apply to the Lands Tribunal which has power to modify or discharge the covenant.

The freedom to use premises for business purposes is also subject to constraints imposed by the criminal and civil law. An occupier of land may be restrained by injunction from using his property in such a way as to cause a nuisance to his neighbours, adjoining occupiers or to the public as a whole.

In *Halsey v. Esso Petroleum* 1961 the plaintiff was the owner of a house on a residential estate and the defendant owned and occupied an oil storage depot on the river bank nearby. On various occasions noxious acid smuts were emitted from metal chimney stacks at the depot which caused damage to the plaintiff's washing, and the paint work of his car. There was also a particularly pungent oily smell from the depot of a nauseating character but which was not a health risk. Further cause for complaint was the noise emitted from the boilers during night shift which varied in intensity but at its peak reached 63 decibels causing the plaintiff's windows and doors to vibrate. The noise was exacerbated by the arrival of heavy tankers at the depot, sometimes in convoy and as many as fifteen in one night. It was on the basis of these complaints that the plaintiff brought an action alleging nuisance and claiming damages and injunctions to restrain the activity. The court held that:

- The acid smuts emitted from the chimneys constituted the crime of *public nuisance* for they affected a class of people, and as the plaintiff had suffered special damage in relation to his motor car he could recover damages for the tort of *private nuisance*.

- Acid smuts which arise from a non natural use of land and then escape to adjoining land and cause damage will also give rise to strict liability in tort based on the principles laid down in the case of *Rylands v. Fletcher 1868*

- Injury to health is not a necessary ingredient in the cause of action and since the particularly pungent smell from time to time emitted from the depot went far beyond a triviality, and was more than would effect a sensitive person, it was an actionable nuisance.

- The noise from the boilers at night disturbed the resident's ordinary comfort and use of their property as did the noise from the vehicles and both would constitute a private nuisance.

- Injunctions and damages were awarded to restrain the unlawful activities to the extent that they constituted an actionable nuisance.

The question that arose in *Wheeler v. J J Saunders Ltd.* 1995 was whether an activity on land authorised by planning permission could prevent an actionable nuisance action by an adjoining occupier. Here an action was brought for damages and an injunction against the defendant pig farmer in respect of the nuisance caused by additional pig housing units built following the grant of planning permission. The plaintiff claimed that the smell from the units made his life intolerable and constituted a nuisance in respect of holiday cottages on his land close by. The Court of Appeal held that while planning permission could not authorise a nuisance the issue of liability had to be considered in the light of the change in the neighbourhood effected by the planning permission. Here there was no change in the character of the neighbourhood, rather the change of use of a small piece of land for the benefit of the defendant and at the plaintiff's expense. The interference constituted an actionable nuisance and the decision of the High Court that the farmer was liable was upheld

Activities on land have also been made unlawful by statute and may constitute a statutory nuisance. Under the Environmental Health Act 1990 s.79(1) a list of circumstances may amount to a statutory nuisance including emissions of smoke, gas, fumes, dust, steam, smells or other effluvia and noise from premises which are prejudicial to health or a nuisance. Detection and enforcement of the law is in the hands of local authorities, in particular environmental health officers. They are charged with the duty of inspecting their areas and also investigating complaints with the aim of preventing and eliminating statutory nuisances. Their powers extend to serving *abatement notices* on individuals or organisations requiring the abatement, prohibition or restriction of the nuisance and the execution of works or the taking of other necessary steps. Contravention of a notice or failure to comply with its terms is a criminal offence and could lead to a prosecution in the Magistrates Court and a fine for each offence.

The right to freedom from unlawful interference

Interference with the right of an owner of land to enjoy quiet possession of his land may be actionable under the civil law as the tort of trespass. Any person who, without lawful authority, enters or remains upon the land of another, or places or throws any physical object on to such land, is a trespasser. An occupier of land may use reasonable force, if necessary, to eject a trespasser, but only after asking him to leave and allowing him a reasonable opportunity to do so. An occupier of land may also sue a trespasser for damages and does not have to prove that he suffered any loss as a result of the trespass. He may apply for an injunction in order to prevent the continuation or repetition of the trespass. As previously illustrated in *Halsey v. Esso Petroleum* 1961 an owner or occupier of land may also be able to sue in the torts of nuisance or *Rylands v. Fletcher* either for *a*n injunction or for damages in circumstances where his enjoyment of his own land is interfered with as a result of activities carried on by his neighbours which amount to an unreasonable or unlawful use by his neighbours of their land.

Acquisition of Land

The acquisition of land involves the transfer of property rights in land which is usually achieved by the formal process of conveyancing. Contracts for the sale or other disposition of land are governed by the Law of Property (Miscellaneous Provisions) Act 1989. Under s.2 of the 1989 Act a contract for the sale or other disposition of an interest in land can only be made in writing, signed by the parties and incorporating all the terms which the parties have expressly agreed in one document or, where contracts are exchanged, in each. It is no longer possible therefore to have an oral contract for the sale of land simply evidenced in writing and a failure to comply with s.2 will make the contract invalid.

> The Court of Appeal applied s.2 in *Firstpost Homes Ltd v. Johnson* 1995 Here an oral agreement for the sale of land was supported by a letter prepared by the purchaser with the vendors name on it which both parties were expected to sign. In fact the vendor did not sign the letter but merely the enclosed plan of the land she agreed to sell. The purchaser signed both the letter and the plan. The court concluded that the requirements of s.2 had not been complied with for the typing of a name could not amount to a signature and while one document could incorporate another, here the plan was not the principal document for that purpose.

The process of conveyancing

The process of conveyancing is concerned with the legal mechanism for the sale or purchase of land or of an interest in land. The process is basically the same for all land regardless of the purpose for which it is used, be it a private house, an office, a factory or farmland. There may be some variation in the detail of the process, however, depending upon (a) whether the freehold or the leasehold estate is being transferred and (b) whether the title to the land is registered at the Land Registry, or is unregistered. We need not examine the detail of these variations and shall simply consider the basic process in outline.

This process is divided into two stages - the periods before *and* after *an exchange of contracts*.

Prior to exchange of contracts

A person who wishes to sell land may either advertise the property himself or employ an estate agent to act on his behalf in negotiating the sale. When a purchaser is found, an agreement will be made in principle for the sale of the property at an agreed price, and it is then that the vendor and the purchaser will instruct their respective legal representatives, who may be either solicitors or licensed conveyancers. At this stage the transaction is *subject to contract*.

A contract for the sale of land is only valid if it complies with s.2 of the Law of Property (Miscellaneous Provisions) Act 1989. In fact both the purchaser and vendor will not usually wish to be legally bound until a formal exchange of contracts has been made. This is because the purchaser will have to conclude his financial arrangements and fully investigate the property before he commits himself, and the vendor may wish to arrange the purchase of a new property to take effect at the same time as his sale is completed. All correspondence passing between the parties or their representatives will be marked with the words *subject to contract* but following s.2 of the 1989 Act this expression is of less significance.

The following matters will need to be dealt with before an exchange of contracts can take place.

(a) **Draft contracts**

The vendor's solicitor will obtain the title deeds relating to the property and, using information gathered from the deeds and from the vendor himself, will draw up a draft contract with an identical counterpart which will be submitted to the purchaser's solicitor for approval.

(b) **Enquiries and searches**

The purchaser's solicitor will make investigations about the property by:

- visiting the property and inspecting it;

- sending a standard form of preliminary enquiries containing questions about physical and legal aspects of the property to the vendor's solicitor;

- making enquiries to the Local Authority to discover what information it has relating to it or to proposals which may affect it, for example demolition orders or road improvement schemes;

- making a search in the Register of Local Land Charges to determine whether any matter registered there affects the property.

(c) **Finance**

Prior to an exchange of contracts the purchaser will wish to conclude his financial arrangements so that he can satisfy himself that once he is legally bound he is able to raise the full amount of the purchase price. The majority of domestic purchases are made with the aid of a building society mortgage, and it is at this stage in the process that confirmation is required from the mortgagee that the necessary funding will be available to finance the purchase. The purchase of business premises is often funded, at least partly, by a mortgage also, but from a commercial bank rather than a building society. The nature of a mortgage, and the rights and obligations of the mortgagor and the mortgagee are considered later in the chapter. Before lending money on the security of a mortgage, the mortgagee will wish to be satisfied firstly that the borrower has the ability to repay. He will do this by enquiring of the employer of a private individual borrower, or assessing the accounts of a business borrower covering the last three financial years. Secondly he will wish to be sure that the property itself is sufficiently valuable to provide full security in the event of default by the borrower. This will usually be done by instructing an independent surveyor to give a valuation of the property.

(d)   *Survey*

A contract for the sale of land is governed by the common law principle *caveat emptor* or *let the buyer beware*! There are no statutory implied terms of quality or fitness for purpose. The purchaser takes the property as he finds it and must therefore satisfy himself about its physical condition and the state of any buildings before an exchange of contracts with the vendor.

Therefore a purchaser will usually employ a surveyor to act on his behalf to inspect the property in order to find out whether there are any structural defects or other problems such as dry or wet rot, rising damp or woodworm. If any problems of this nature are detected while the purchase is subject to contract, the purchaser is free to look for another property, or to re-negotiate the price. If the defects become manifest after he has purchased, he will not usually be able to sue the vendor because of the *caveat emptor* rule.

Where the purchaser is financing the purchase with a loan on the security of a mortgage of the property, the mortgagee will usually arrange a survey himself, at the purchaser's expense, before agreeing to advance the money. If the mortgagee is a building society, then under the Building Societies Act 1986, it must arrange a survey for the purposes of valuation. A surveyor, acting for a building society in these circumstances owes a duty to the borrower to take reasonable care in carrying out a visual inspection of the property.

In *Yianni v. Edwin Evans & Sons* 1981 the plaintiffs were buying a house for £15,000 with the aid of a £12,000 building society mortgage. The building society instructed the defendant surveyors to carry out a valuation of the property. After an inspection of the house the defendants reported to the building society that in their opinion the house was adequate security for a loan of £12,000. The plaintiffs completed the purchase of the property and soon afterwards discovered serious cracks in the foundations. They sued the defendants for £18,000 which was the estimated cost of repairing the foundations. The court held that the defendants owed a duty of care to the plaintiffs and that they were liable to pay the £18,000 damages in the tort of negligence for a breach of that duty of care.

Exchange of contracts to completion

Once the parties are satisfied that all the preliminary matters outlined above have been satisfactorily sorted out, they will be clear to enter into a legally binding contract. They will sign identical counterparts of the formal contract and the purchaser's solicitor will deliver his client's signed part along with a deposit representing 10% of the purchase price to the vendor's solicitor. In exchange he will receive the vendor's signed part of the contract. At this point the parties become legally bound. It will usually be a matter of three or four weeks before the sale is finally completed. The 10% deposit paid by the purchaser on exchange is a sign of his good faith and will be forfeited if he subsequently withdraws from the contract without justification.

Once contracts have been exchanged, the purchaser has an insurable interest in the property and should take out a policy of insurance immediately. He will not however, be in full possession of the property until completion takes place.

In the time before completion, the purchaser's solicitor will examine the title deeds to the property and investigate the vendor's title in order to be absolutely certain that the vendor is able to give full ownership to the purchaser without any possibility of a claim by any other person. For this purpose the purchaser's solicitor also makes further searches in central registers. It is possible for a person with legal rights over the property, such as a second mortgage, to protect his rights by registering them in a central register. The effect of such a registration is that the person to whom the property is conveyed will take subject to those rights unless they are discharged before completion by the vendor, for example by redeeming the second mortgage out of the proceeds of sale.

The purchaser's solicitor prepares the formal deed of conveyance in readiness for completion. Following the Law of Property (Miscellaneous Provisions) Act 1989 certain formalities for the creation and execution of deeds have been abolished. Under s.1 there is no longer a requirement that a deed made by an individual must be made by sealing the document. A valid deed must be signed and witnessed and make it clear that it is intended to be a deed.

Where the vendor conveys the land to the purchaser as a *beneficial owner* the following covenants are implied by s.76 the Law of Property Act 1925:

(i)   that the vendor has a good right to convey the property;

(ii)   that the purchaser will enjoy quiet possession of the property;

(iii) that the property will be free from claims or demands by any other person;

(iv)   that the vendor will, if necessary, at a future date, remedy any defect in the present conveyance.

Completion of the transaction

On the day of completion the purchaser will pay the balance of the purchase price (90%) to the vendor in return for the title deeds to the land, including the conveyance to himself, and the keys to the property. The property now fully belongs to the purchaser and he may take up possession.

Leasehold Land

Where a business operates from premises which are rented, the occupier will be a tenant and own a leasehold estate in the land. The landlord will be the owner of the freehold estate. A leasehold estate, or *term of years absolute* is created when a freeholder grants a lease to a tenant for a certain term. This will include a lease for a time period which is fixed, for example a seven year lease. Alternatively the lease may be periodic, where rent is paid on a weekly, monthly, or quarterly basis. Either side can terminate a periodic lease by serving the appropriate notice. The lease gives the business tenant the right to occupy the land and premises to the exclusion of all others (including the landlord) in return for the payment of rent. When the period of the lease comes to an end the landlord is entitled, at common law, to regain possession of his property. By Act of Parliament, however, the tenant will usually have the right of *security of tenure*. This right to stay in possession will override the landlord's common law right to regain possession, and will enable the tenant to extend his period of occupation by virtue of a new lease on terms which are reasonably equivalent to the terms contained in the original lease.

The terms of a business lease

A business lease will normally be granted by deed and will contain the rights and obligations of the landlord and the tenant in the form of covenants. A covenant is simply a contractual promise made in a deed.

Leases of business premises will usually contain the following covenants:

(a) **By the tenant**

    (i)   to pay rent and rates (there may also be a rent review clause under which the amount of the rent may be increased from time to time);

    (ii) to keep the premises in a good state of decorative repair;

    (iii) to permit the landlord to enter the premises from time to time in order to view the state of repair;

    (iv) not to carry out alterations to the premises without the landlord's consent;

    (v) not to assign, sublet or otherwise part with possession of the premises;

    (vi) not to use the premises for any purpose other than that stated in the lease.

(b) **By the landlord**

    (i)   not to interfere with the tenant's quiet enjoyment of the property;

    (ii) to insure the premises;

    (iii) to keep the main structure and exterior of the premises in good repair.

The covenants of a business lease may be positive, for instance to pay rent or negative for example not to sublet. They are enforceable by means of an action for damages, or in some cases an injunction to prevent a breach or specific performance, for instance to require a landlord to fulfil a repair obligation. A business tenant may also have a number of important rights conferred by statute. Under the Landlord and Tenant Act 1927 the right of a tenant to claim compensation for improvements made to the premises was first introduced and under the Landlord and Tenant Act 1954 Part II security of tenure was first recognised. It is of crucial importance therefore in determining the rights of a business tenant to ensure that the tenancy in question falls within the protection of the 1954 Act.

The Act applies to tenancies where the property comprised in the tenancy is or includes premises occupied by the tenant for the purposes of his business. It must be emphasised that the Act is limited to tenancies only and would not cover a mere licence.

    In *Addiscombe Garden Estates Ltd. v. Crabbe* 1958 following the analysis of a document which was referred to as a licence, the court concluded that it was in fact a lease. This conclusion was reached on the basis that the content of the document was written in the form of a lease rather than a licence. Included in the document were terms referring to repair, quiet enjoyment, and re-entry. The court held that the relationship of the parties was determined by the law and not by the label which the parties chose to put on the document.

Alternatively in *Shell-Mex and B.P. Ltd. v. Manchester Garages Ltd.* 1971 the plaintiffs allowed the defendant garage company occupation of a filling station under a licence agreement. One clause of the licence required the defendants not to impede the plaintiffs rights of possession and control of the premises. The court held that this clause showed that the transaction constituted a licence and not a tenancy and represented a genuine management agreement not covered by the 1954 Act.

A business tenant must also show that the occupation of the premises is for the purpose of a business carried out by the tenant.

In *Nozari - Zadeh v. Pearl Assurance* 1987 the landlord claimed that a business tenancy of restaurant premises in London was not protected by the 1954 Act because the business was not carried out by the tenant but rather by a number of companies controlled by him. As a consequence the tenant failed to satisfy the requirement of occupying the premises for the purposes of a business carried out by him. The argument by the tenant that the companies were his *alter ego* and occupation by them was equivalent to occupation by him was rejected by the Court of Appeal which held that the tenancy did not come within the protection of the 1954 Act.

In *Graysim Holdings Ltd v P & O Property Holdings Ltd* 1995 the House of Lords unanimously reversed the Court of Appeal on the issue of occupation for the purposes of the 1954 Act. The case concerned the tenant of a covered market hall who had granted subtenancies of individual stalls to market traders. The stalls were exclusively occupied by the traders with the tenant having overall control of the common parts. The question faced by the court was whether the tenant occupied the hall for the purposes of a business carried on by him and so entitling him under the 1954 Act to security of tenure. The view of the Court of Appeal that the tenant did occupy the hall because of the control he exercised over the stall holders was rejected by the House of Lords. Their Lordships held that even though a business tenancy could include property not occupied by the tenant, that is not property in respect of which the tenant is entitled to a new tenancy. The purpose of the 1954 Act was not to afford protection to non occupying intermediate landlords relying on rental income. As a consequence the tenancy fell outside the protection of the Act and when it terminated the tenant had no right to a new tenancy.

Additionally, the occupation of premises must be for business purposes. Business is defined as to include a *trade, profession or employment or any activity carried on by a body of persons whether corporate or unincorporate*. For a body of persons therefore, corporate or unincorporate, *any activity* may be regarded as a business for the purposes of the Act.

In *Westminster Roman Catholic Diocese Trustee v. Parkes* 1978 occupation of premises as a community centre in connection with a church was held to be a business and come within the Act's protection. This was in accordance with the decision in *Addiscombe Garden Estates Ltd. v. Crabbe* 1958 where the activity of a member's tennis club was held to be within the Act.

As far as operating a business from home is concerned, the question as to business purposes is decided by examining the extent of business activity.

> In *Royal Life Saving Society v. Page* 1978 a partner in a firm of seafood importers who interviewed business clients at home, kept business documents and a business phone there, was held to operate a business for the purposes of the Act.

If the business is being operated in breach of a use covenant then the Act does not apply unless the immediate landlord or his predecessor in title has consented to the breach or the immediate landlord has acquiesced in its continuance.

> In *Bell v. Alfred Franks and Bartlett Company Ltd.* 1980 the tenant used a garage for business purposes in contravention of a covenant that it was to be used for a car only. As there was no evidence of consent or acquiescence on the part of the immediate landlord then the 1954 Act was inapplicable and a notice to quit which had been served was valid and effective.

If a tenancy is protected by the 1954 Act then it can only be terminated by the landlord in accordance with the provisions of the Act and will not end automatically on the expiration of the term. The procedure for termination involves the service of a statutory notice by the landlord which if countered by the tenant could lead in the absence of agreement to a final determination by the County Court. As a general rule the tenant is entitled to a new tenancy, on fair terms, unless the landlord establishes a statutory ground of opposition.

Landlord's grounds for opposing a new tenancy

The alternative grounds upon which a landlord can rely to oppose a tenant's application to the court for a new tenancy are set out in s.30 of the 1954 Act.

S.30(1) (a) Breach of a repairing obligation

Relying on this ground the landlord must prove that in view of the state of repair of the premises resulting from the tenant's failure to observe a repairing obligation under the current tenancy, a new tenancy ought not to be granted. To grant possession on this ground the court must be satisfied that the breach of the repairing covenant is a serious one. This was the case in *Lyons v. Central Commercial Properties Ltd.* 1958 where the court held that the breach of a repairing covenant was of such a serious nature that the tenant ought not to be granted a new tenancy.

S. 30(1) (b) Persistent delay in paying rent

Here the landlord must prove that in view of the tenant's persistent delay in paying rent due under the current tenancy, a new tenancy ought not to be granted. Here again the court must be satisfied that the delay is a serious one, either over an extended time period or consist of a number of separate delays.

S. 30(1) (c) Other substantial breaches

In this case the landlord must prove that the tenant ought not to be granted a new tenancy in view of other substantial breaches of obligation under the current tenancy or for any other reason connected with the tenant's use or management of the holding.

Again the important question for the court to determine is the seriousness of the breach and whether the tenant has any proposals for its remedy. In relation to *"any other reason connected with the tenant's use or management of the holding"* an illegal use of the premises would certainly amount to such a reason.

> In *Turner & Bell v. Searles Ltd.* 1977 the tenants were found to be using the premises unlawfully by parking coaches in breach of planning law, having had an enforcement notice served upon them. As the tenants intended to continue the illegal use under a new tenancy, the landlord was held to be entitled to possession under s.30(1) (c).

S. 30(1) (d) Provision of suitable alternative accommodation

Relying on this ground the landlord must prove that the tenant ought not to be granted a new tenancy as the landlord is willing to provide him with suitable alternative accommodation. The question of deciding whether the alternative accommodation offered is suitable is to be determined by reference to all the circumstances, and in particular whether any goodwill attaching to the premises will be preserved.

S. 30(1) (e) Letting or disposing of the property as a whole

Here the landlord may object to the granting of a new tenancy in a case where the current tenancy was created by a sub-letting of only part of the premises let under a superior tenancy, and the interest of the tenant's immediate landlord is to terminate in the near future. The ground relied on is that the superior landlord requires possession of the premises as he might reasonably be expected to re-let the property as a whole or dispose of the property as a whole. To succeed on this ground the superior landlord would have to show that the re-letting value of the property as one unit is much higher than if re-let in separate parts.

S. 30(1) (f) Demolishing or reconstructing the premises

The objection of the landlord in this case is that the tenant ought not to be granted possession because the landlord intends, on the termination of the tenancy, to demolish or reconstruct the premises, or a substantial part of them, or to carry out substantial work of construction on them and he could not reasonably do this work without obtaining possession of the premises.

> In *Betty's Cafe v. Phillips Furnishing Stores* 1959 it was held that the relevant intention of the landlord has to be established at the date of the court application. This intention must be proved to be a fixed one evidenced by positive steps to secure its implementation, e.g. planning applications, building contracts and building plans.

Certainly the expression *"reconstruction"* envisages rebuilding work and a demolition of part so that reconstruction as opposed to construction can take place.

> In *Botterill and Another v. Bedfordshire C.C.* 1984 the council landlord opposed the renewal of a lease of four acres of land to a gun club by relying on s.30(1)(f). The substantial work of reconstruction planned by the council was to remove top soil, deposit waste and then plant some trees. The Court of Appeal held that landscaping of this nature could not constitute a substantial work of reconstruction under the Act and a new tenancy was ordered.

In *Peter Goddard & Sons v. Hounslow BC* 1992 the Court of Appeal held that if the court is convinced of the landlord's intention to develop a site despite the fact that there may be obstacles to the development it may still be a sufficient ground to oppose a new tenancy.

S.30(1)(g) The landlord intends to occupy for his own purposes

Here the ground is that the tenant ought not to be granted a new tenancy because the landlord intends to occupy the premises for the purpose of a business to be carried on by him therein or as his residence. For the purpose of showing intention the same factors to establish proof applicable to s.30(1)(f) are relevant.

> In *Lightcliffe & District Cricket and Lawn Tennis Club v. Walton* 1978 the landlord, a farmer, relied on s.30(1)(g) to resist the tenant's application for a new tenancy of a piece of land. However the fact that the farmer failed to show through clear evidence his plans for making use of the land convinced the court that his application should be rejected, and a new tenancy was granted to the tenant.

A statutory limitation on the landlord relying on the s.30(1)(g) ground is that it cannot be relied on if the landlord's interest was purchased or created within the five years previous to the termination of the tenancy and throughout that five year period there had been a tenancy or succession of tenancies of the holding.

Proof of any of the seven alternative statutory grounds may be sufficient to enable the landlord to recover possession of the business premises and successfully oppose the tenant's application for a new tenancy. It should be stressed however that grounds 30(1) (d), (f) and (g) are *absolute* in that if they are proved by the landlord then the court must grant him possession. The remaining grounds 30(1) (a), (b), (c) and (e) are *discretionary* and even if proved by the landlord the court nevertheless has a final discretion to determine whether a new tenancy is granted.

The court application and the new tenancy

It should be stressed that in the majority of cases and usually as the result of a compromise, agreement is reached as to the grant and/or terms of the new tenancy without the need for court intervention. In the event of failure to reach agreement however, a court application will proceed. The court must determine two distinct issues. Firstly, whether the tenant is to be granted a new tenancy and if this is so, then to determine its content.

The first issue of course is determined by the court deciding whether the landlord has satisfied the particular s.30 ground relied on.

Having decided that a new tenancy is to be ordered, the court is faced with the second issue, its content. In the absence of agreement the Act confers a wide discretion on the courts in this matter. The subject matter of the new tenancy is generally that part of the premises occupied by the tenant for the purpose of the business under the original tenancy. So far as the length of the new tenancy is concerned, its duration is to be such, up to a maximum of 14 years, as the court considers reasonable in all the circumstances. It is unlikely that the new tenancy will be granted for a term which exceeds the original tenancy and factors such as the landlord's intention to demolish or redevelop in the future are relevant to decide its length. In *Betty's Cafe v. Phillips Furnishing Stores*

1959 the renewed lease with a fourteen year term was reduced to five years on appeal after considering the length of the original lease.

The rent payable under the new tenancy is that amount, having regard to the terms of the tenancy, that a willing lessor might reasonably expect to let the property at, on the open market.

> In *O'May v. City of London Real Property* 1982 the court confirmed that the onus is on the party seeking a departure from the status quo. Here the landlord attempted to insert a service charge into a three year term in return for a rent reduction. The court held that the charge was an unacceptable burden in comparison with the reduced rent and should not be permitted. The attempt to impose a service charge for common parts, lifts, etc., was an attempt to shift a burden which normally fell on the landlord.

The courts are concerned to ensure that if there is a variation in the lease there is a sufficient reason for it and that any change in rent will adequately compensate the tenant for any variation in the lease. The objective is simply to achieve a fair and reasonable balance between the parties.

Compensation for improvements

During the term of a business tenancy it is likely that the tenant, or his predecessors in title will carry out improvements to the property. These improvements will ultimately benefit the landlord, since they will increase the potential letting value of the property when the letting under which they were carried out comes to an end. The Landlord and Tenant Act 1927 provides for compensation to be paid to the tenant by the landlord in such circumstances, subject to certain requirements being satisfied, and certain conditions being fulfilled.

In order to obtain compensation it is not enough that the tenant has simply carried out the improvements. He must in addition have followed the statutory procedure laid down in the 1927 Act. Under this procedure the tenant must first have served notice on the landlord of his intention to carry out improvements, accompanied by a specification and plan of the works to be carried out. The landlord then has 3 months to serve a notice of objection. If he fails to do so then the improvement is regarded as being authorised. In any event no objection can be served if the improvement is being carried out in pursuance of a statutory obligation. If the landlord does serve a notice of objection during the statutory time period the tenant can apply to the court for a certificate that the improvement is a proper one. Once the certificate is granted, and the court may in granting it impose conditions and modify the specification or plans, the improvement becomes an authorised one. The claim must be served on the landlord within strict time limits on the termination of the tenancy. The Act provides for a further payment of compensation for disturbance where the landlord has been given possession because of reconstruction or carrying on a business himself. The amount of compensation is three times the rateable value, and six times if the tenancy has lasted for fourteen years or more.

> In *Department of the Environment v. Royal Insurance* 1987 the fact that the tenant had occupied the premises one day short of the fourteen years meant that there was no entitlement to the larger sum. The practical difference for the tenant was £161,665 compensation rather than £333,330.

Land as Security

The value to a business of its freehold or leasehold land extends beyond the intrinsic value of such property as a place from which the business is conducted, or a resource in the production process. The business may also use the land as a means of raising finance by obtaining a loan secured by a mortgage of the land. Land is generally regarded as the most valuable security available to a lender.

A mortgage is simply a transaction under which a borrower, the mortgagor, in return for a loan from the lender, the mortgagee, gives security in the form of property which is usually land. Domestic mortgages are most commonly created when a building society, bank, insurance company or local authority lends money towards the purchase of a home. For business premises a commercial mortgage will usually be arranged through a mortgage broker with a bank or finance company. In the business context the mortgage transaction can provide the means by which either:

(a) commercial premises are acquired from which the business activity is carried on, or

(b) additional funds are raised to finance business activity.

To create a formal or *legal* mortgage of a freehold or leasehold two methods are available under the Law of Property Act 1925. The first method involves the transfer of a lease (usually for 3000 years) from the mortgagor to the mortgagee subject to a clause that the lease is to terminate when the loan is repaid. This is called a provision for *cesser on redemption*. If the property to be mortgaged is leasehold then a sub lease is granted for a shorter period than the original lease. While the lease is merely notional and no rent is payable under it, it does provide a means by which the mortgagee can if necessary enforced his security. The second method available is simpler, more popular with institutional lenders and is known as the *charge* method. Here the mortgagor charges his land with the repayment of the debt by the means of a short deed expressed to be a charge by way of legal mortgage. The main difference between a charge and a mortgage is that under the charge the borrower retains ownership in the property and the lender is given certain rights over it. Under the mortgage however ownership of the property is transferred to the lender for the purposes of providing security for the loan.

An alternative to the legal mortgage is the less formal *equitable* mortgage. An equitable mortgage arises where no mortgage deed is executed and the borrower merely deposits the title deeds of the property with the lender. While there is no transfer of ownership to the lender under such an arrangement the borrower is effectively prevented from selling or remortgaging the land. A weakness of the equitable mortgage is that if a subsequent legal mortgage were to be created over the land, that mortgage would take preference if the mortgagee had no knowledge of the equitable mortgage.

Where a legal mortgage is created, this must be done by deed. The deed must comply with the Law of Property Act 1925 and the Law of Property (Miscellaneous Provisions) Act 1989. The mortgage deed will set out the rights and obligations of the mortgagor and mortgagee, which will usually include the following:

The rights of the mortgagor

   (a)   *The right to redeem the mortgage* - the mortgage deed will provide for the repayment of the amount borrowed (the capital sum) with interest by instalments over a definite period of time which is usually a number of years. The mortgagor has the right to be discharged from his obligations under the mortgage deed once the capital sum has been repaid with interest; and he has the right to make a full repayment at any time, even before the date specified in the mortgage, and thereby redeem his property. Generally the courts have sought to protect the right of the mortgagor and have not allowed mortgage terms which unreasonably prevent or postpone the mortgagor's right to redeem the mortgage.

In *Fairclough v. Swan Brewery Co. Ltd.* 1912 a twenty year mortgage term postponed the right to redeem for nineteen years and forty six weeks. This postponement was held to make the mortgage virtually unredeemable and so declared void.

   (b)   *The right to enjoy the use of his land* during the repayment period, without any interference by the mortgagee, so long the mortgagor is fulfilling his obligations under the mortgage and repaying the instalments as they fall due. In these circumstances the mortgagor has full use of his property though there may be some restrictions, for example on structural alterations or leasing without the consent of the mortgagee since these could affect the value of the security.

The rights of the mortgagee

The principal right of the mortgagee is to the repayment of the capital sum with interest in accordance with the terms of the mortgage. If the mortgagor defaults in his obligation to repay, the mortgagee can rely on one or more of the following rights.

   (a)   *The right to sue the mortgagor.* The mortgagor is under a contractual obligation to repay the full amount of the loan with interest. If he is in arrears he may be sued personally by the mortgagee for the full amount and not merely for the outstanding instalments. Usually however, the mortgagee will prefer to enforce his rights against the property because the mortgagor is not likely to be able to satisfy a judgment debt if he is in such financial difficulty as to be unable to repay the mortgage instalments.

   (b)   *The right to take possession of the property if the mortgagor defaults in the repayment of the loan.* This right will be contained in the mortgage deed and will usually be exercised by the mortgagee as a preliminary step, prior to exercising a power of sale, in order to obtain vacant possession of the property.

   (c)   *The power of sale.* This power may be exercised by the mortgagee where at least two months' interest is overdue and where he has served notice on the mortgagor requiring him to repay the mortgage debt in full and the mortgagor has failed to do so within three months. The mortgagee may then sell the property over the head of the mortgagor, take out all sums due to him from the proceeds of sale and pay any remaining monies back to the mortgagor.

(d)   *Foreclosure.* This amounts to the transfer of the mortgaged property to the mortgagee absolutely and may only be done by an order of the court, which is obtained in two stages.

The first stage involves an application to the court, where the mortgagor is substantially in arrears, for an order requiring him, within a specified time, to repay the loan and redeem the mortgage.

If the mortgagor fails to redeem the mortgage, the second stage involves a further application to the court for a final order of foreclosure terminating the mortgagor's right of redemption and transferring the ownership of the land absolutely to the mortgagee.

Tangible Property other than Land

Choses in possession

Earlier in this chapter it was noted that choses in possession are items of personal property which have a physical existence and can be touched or moved. In other words they are goods. Chapter 11 deals with the legal rules relating to contracts for the sale of goods and other contracts involving the transfer of ownership of goods from one party to another. The detailed regulation of such transactions simply reflects the fact that the production and distribution of goods is the lifeblood of the majority of business organisations in the commercial world.

We shall now consider the legal consequences, both under the criminal law and under the civil law, of the unlawful interference by one person with the goods of another.

Criminal liability for interference with goods

A person who interferes with the property of another may be liable, under the criminal law, to punishment in the form of a fine, or imprisonment, or both. The main offences relating to such interference are contained in the Theft Act 1968 and the Criminal Damage Act 1971.

Theft

By section 1 of the Theft Act 1968 a person is guilty of theft if he dishonestly appropriates property belonging to another with the intention of permanently depriving the other of it.

Property, for the purposes of this offence, is defined in s.4 of the Act to include *"money and all other property, real and personal, including things in action and other intangible property"*, although the section goes on to exclude land from the definition except in one or two specified instances. Theft, like most other criminal offences, contains two main elements:

(a)   the mental element or guilty mind, called *mens rea*.

(b)   the physical element or guilty act, called *actus reus*.

The guilty act is the *appropriation* . This involves taking or otherwise assuming the rights of an owner of property belonging to another. The mental element of the offence is the dishonesty of the accused, and his intention to permanently deprive the owner of his property. Without an intention to permanently deprive the owner of his property the offence is not committed. The dishonest borrowing of property belonging to another is not theft, but a separate offence is created by the Theft Act 1968, s.12, of taking a conveyance such as a motor car without lawful authority and this offence may be committed without an intention to permanently deprive the owner of his conveyance.

Criminal damage to property

By section 1 of the Criminal Damage Act 1971 a person who without lawful excuse destroys or damages any property belonging to another, intending to destroy or damage such property or being reckless as to whether any such property would be destroyed or damaged is guilty of an offence.

Property, for the purposes of this offence, is defined by the Act as *"property of a tangible nature, whether real or personal, including money"*. Because of the nature of the offence, choses in action are not included in the definition, although clearly land and buildings are included as well as goods and money. The guilty act which constitutes the offence is the damage or destruction caused to another's property. If this is done by fire then the offence is known as arson. The mental element is the intention of the accused or his recklessness as to whether the property is damaged or destroyed.

Civil liability for interference with goods

The civil law remedies available to a person whose goods have been wrongfully interfered with are contained in the Torts (Interference with Goods) Act 1977. The Act applies to goods, which are defined by s.14 to include *"all chattels personal other than things in action and money"*. The Act therefore applies to choses in possession but not to choses in action.

Section 1 of the Act defines *"wrongful interference with goods"* to mean conversion of goods, trespass to goods, negligence so far as it results in damage to goods and any other tort so far as it results in damage to goods.

Conversion of goods

Conversion of goods is the denial of an owner's title to goods. Such a denial may take the form of wrongfully taking them away from the owner, keeping them, destroying them or disposing of them to a third party.

Trespass to goods

Trespass to goods is denying the owner of goods the right to possession of them by wrongfully removing them or damaging them without depriving the owner of them completely.

Negligence

Negligence involves a failure to take reasonable care which results in foreseeable damage to the goods.

The remedies available under the Act are contained in s.3 which provides for

(a)   damages alone; or

(b)   damages in addition to an order for specific delivery of the goods. An order for specific delivery is discretionary and may be refused, or if granted, may be subject to conditions imposed by the court; or

(c)   an order that the defendant pay the value of the goods to the plaintiff instead of specific delivery.

Earlier in the chapter we stated that choses in action are forms of personal property which have no physical existence, although they may be evidenced by some physical thing such as a share certificate or a mortgage deed. The essential characteristic of a chose in action is that it is a property right which can, if necessary, be asserted by taking legal action in the courts.

Examples of choses in action which are important in a business context include the following.

Debts owed to a business

A debt is a legal right to receive payment. In a business context this will usually involve the right to payment for goods and services provided to a customer. The business owns the right to payment. This creates an asset, which appears in the balance sheet. As an item of business property a debt can be sold. Some organisations actually specialise in purchasing debts, at a discount. Unless they are in need of immediate funds businesses will not usually sell their debts. However where a debtor is in financial difficulties, and the chances of enforcing the debt through court action are small the business may be glad to cut its losses and sell the debt at a heavy discount. Debt recovery presents a major problem for all businesses, especially small businesses which have limited funds available to them, and can easily experience cash flow difficulties. It is not unusual for small organisations with a full order book but with many outstanding debts to go under as a result of such difficulties.

Shares held in a business

Shares are issued to members of a company according to their capital contributions, and represent their stake in the ownership of the company. Shares usually carry voting rights as well as the right to share in the profits of the company by way of dividends. The characteristics of shares are more fully examined in Chapter 4.

Business goodwill

Business goodwill is the term used to describe perhaps the most fundamental asset of any business organisation, its reputation. The reputation of any business operating in a market is measured by the extent to which its goods or services have achieved public respect. This respect is normally built up over a number of years so that a regular custom develops to ensure a steady level of business. To obtain a good reputation it is necessary for a business to recruit a skilled and loyal workforce and in many cases maintain a high level of research and development into its products. A number of factors contribute to establishing and maintaining the goodwill of a business including its marketing strategy, custom, workforce and future plans for the goods and services it provides. The torts of defamation and passing off, discussed below, are the legal means by which a business can protect its goodwill. Defamation is available to protect business reputation and passing off to protect businesses whose goods or services are misrepresented.

There is normally no need to place a monetary value on businesses goodwill and therefore it will not usually appear in the assets column of the balance sheet when yearly accounts of a business are drawn up. Unlike tangible assets however, if it is lost it cannot be easily replaced. The necessity to value goodwill arises when there is a change in the ownership of the business. On the introduction of a new partner into a partnership it may be necessary to value the goodwill to determine his or her capital contribution. If a business is sold as a going concern then the amount by which the purchase price exceeds the value of the tangible assets of the business represents the value of the goodwill.

Defamation

The tort of defamation is a civil wrong providing redress for an individual or organisation which has suffered damage to its reputation due to the defamatory statements of another. To the extent that it provides for the protection of business reputation it can be regarded as a *business tort*. As we have seen reputation is the goodwill of a business, an important element of business property. Any business is entitled therefore to seek a remedy to protect this property if defamatory statements are made about it by another. While there are many examples of litigants recovering substantial damages in defamation actions, particularly when compared with victims of serious personal injuries, a prospective plaintiff should commence proceedings with caution, for defamation is not legally aided and costs are likely to be substantial. Defamation lawyers tend to be highly paid specialists and the costs of the trial have the added burden of the costs of a jury.

Libel and slander

As you are probably aware there are two forms of defamation, *libel* and *slander*. An action is based upon libel where the defamation is contained in a medium which has a degree of *permanence* such as writing, recordings, paintings, films etc. The less serious form of defamation and more difficult to prove is slander which is usually an oral statement alleged to be defamatory. By statute oral statements broadcast on the radio or television or on the stage fall into the category of libel. Unlike slander, libel may also constitute a crime, but prosecutions for *criminal* libel are extremely rare. Also libel is actionable *per se* (that is without proof of damage) while in an action for slander the plaintiff must prove actual loss resulting from the slanderous statement. For serious forms of slander this is not the case and for our purposes the relevant exception is defamatory statements about an individual's *office, profession, calling, trade or business*.

Defamatory statements

The essence of the tort of defamation is lies in establishing that the defendant has made a defamatory statement about the plaintiff. An untrue statement is not necessarily defamatory and neither is a mere insult or a derogatory comment. What must be established is a loss of reputation which necessarily involves a publication of the statement to some third party. The courts still rely on the test devised by Lord Atkin in *Sim v. Stretch* 1936. He said that *"the conventional phrase exposing the plaintiff to hatred, ridicule and contempt is probably too narrow. The question is complicated by having to consider the person or class of persons whose reaction to the publication is the test of the wrongful character of the words used.... I propose in the present case the test: would the words tend to lower the plaintiff in the estimation of right-thinking members of society generally?"*

It is crucial to consider the words used in the context in which they appear. To say that an Australian rugby player is too fat as in *Boyd v. Mirror Newspapers* 1980 could constitute an attack on professional competence of a professional player. Similarly to remark of a company during the course of the first World War that it was a German company could also be treated as defamatory; *Slazengers Ltd. v. Gibbs & Co.* 1919.

The intention of the defendant is irrelevant in deciding whether a statement is defamatory. What is significant is the effect it has on those to whom it is published. An unintended innuendo could therefore be defamatory.

> In *Tolley v. Fry* 1931 a prominent amateur golfer was depicted in a caricature advertising chocolate. The House of Lords held that the advertisement was capable of defamatory meaning by innuendo for it suggested that the golfer had accepted money for the advertisement and so offended his amateur status.

> In defamation cases it is for the court to determine as a matter of law whether the words used are capable of being defamatory but then it is a matter for the jury to decide whether in fact they are. In *Mitchell v. Faber & Faber* 1994 Hurst LJ said that *"it is well settled that the question whether the words which are complained of are capable of conveying a defamatory meaning is a question of law and therefore one calling for decision by the court. If the words are so capable then it is a question for the jury to decide whether the words do in fact convey a defamatory meaning"*.

In the highly competitive travel industry there have been a number of recent examples of airlines and tour operators describing their competitor's products in a manner which is capable of being defamatory. Certainly if representatives of a tour operator tell travel agents and hoteliers that a particular competitor is *"going bust"* or will be *"bankrupt in a few days"* such words are clearly defamatory.

> The Court of Appeal in *Aspro Travel Ltd. v. Owners Abroad* 1995 thought that such words were also capable of meaning that a travel company was insolvent and the directors continued to trade, knowing of the insolvency. The fact that a company is insolvent could be due to market forces some misfortune or the actions of third parties and all these reasons would have no impact on the reputation of the director and so would not be defamatory. However *"to say of a director of a family company that he permitted the company to trade knowing that it was insolvent, without making .... extra comments, could be defamatory in the sense that the director standing in the community could be injured because even a fair minded member of the community might .... hold it against the director that he permitted an insolvent company to continue trading"*.

A shameful practice occasionally adopted by the tabloid press is to represent public figures in unusual situations in the guise of so-called news. If a full story is factually correct it is nevertheless defamatory when it is obvious that a large number of readers will have only read part of the material which is capable of being defamatory.

> In *Charleston and another v. News Group Newspapers* 1995 the defendant newspaper published images of a computer game in which the plaintiff's faces were superimposed onto the bodies of pornographic film action engaged in sexual activity. An accompanying headline made it appear that the images were of the plaintiffs, actors in the television

soap Neighbours, but the rest of the article made it clear that the material had been produced without the plaintiff's consent. The House of Lords had to decide whether an action for defamation could succeed because a number of readers would only read the part capable of a defamatory meaning. Their Lordships upheld the traditional view that the meaning to be given to an article must be gathered by considering the article as a whole. Despite the fact therefore that many readers would not have read the full article and merely glanced at the headline and the photograph the article was not capable of conveying a defamatory meaning to the reasonable and fair minded reader.

The tort of defamation is concerned with the loss of reputation of an individual or organisation in the minds of third parties. A crucial element of the tort is that the statement has been brought to the attention of a third party referred to in legal terms as being *published*. Usually there is no question that a statement has been published because it is included in a newspaper story or a book and in such circumstances every organisation involved in the publication process is a potential defendant. However a defamatory statement made face to face and not in the presence of a third party is not actionable and neither is a letter containing defamatory material sent to the potential plaintiff. Also for the purposes of publication a husband and wife are regarded as one.

Beyond these limited exceptions prima facie liability in defamation is established if the plaintiff proves that the defendant has published a defamatory statement which refers to him, subject to the defendant establishing one of the many defences to the tort.

Defences

The primary defence to an action in defamation is to establish that the statement made is true or substantially true. This defence is called *justification* and while there is at present a continuing debate about the right to privacy, for the purposes of defamation even a *malicious publication* is not actionable if it is proved to be true. While it is the task of the plaintiff to show that a statement is defamatory it is for the defendant to establish, on the *balance of probabilities,* that the statement is true or substantially so. It may be that the defendant fails to establish the truth of every one of a number of allegations. In such circumstances s.5 of the Defamation Act 1952 provides that he may still rely on the defence of justification.

Absolute privilege attaches to defamatory statements that are made by a judge in the course of legal proceedings, in Parliament by an MP or between husband and wife. Even if such statements are made with a malicious motive absolute privilege provides a complete defence. Of more relevance to business is the defence of *qualified privilege* which attaches to statements made in the performance of a legal or moral duty. Not only must the maker of the statement have a duty in publishing it, the recipient must have a corresponding interest in receiving it.

Qualified privilege can be destroyed as a defence if the plaintiff establishes that the defendant made the defamatory statement with a *malicious motive*. In business qualified privilege could apply to such matters as external and internal communications within business organisations, employee references and professional advice.

The defence of *fair comment* embodies the notion that in a democratic society everyone including broadcasters and the press, has the right to make outspoken comment on matters of public interest. What then constitutes *public interest* is a dilemma often faced by the courts and in *London Artists*

Ltd. v. Littler 1969 Lord Denning expressed the view that *"whenever a matter is such as to affect people at large so that they may be legitimately interested in, or concerned at, what is going on; or what may happen to them or to others; then it is a matter of public interest on which everyone is entitled to make fair comment."*

Whereas the defence of justification is concerned with establishing that a defamatory statement is factually true, fair comment is concerned with statements of opinion, for example that a particular tour operator, firm of accountants, manufacturer, retail outlet, or business entrepreneur is not reliable. Once again the defence of fair comment may be destroyed by *malice* so the crux of the defence is that the opinion expressed is one that is honestly held. Once again Lord Denning has provided some guidance when he said in *Slim v. Daily Telegraph* 1968 that *"the important thing is to determine whether or not the writer was activated by malice. If he was an honest man expressing his genuine opinion on a subject of public interest, then no matter that his words conveyed derogatory imputations: no matter that his opinion was wrong or exaggerated or prejudiced; and no matter that it was badly expressed so that other people read all sorts of innuendoes into it; nevertheless he has a good defence of fair comment"*.

If there is a case of *unintentional* defamation the Defamation Act 1952 provides that the publishers can make an *offer of amends* which is an offer to publish a suitable correction with a suitable apology. Usually the publisher will also have to pay the plaintiff's costs. If such an offer is made but not accepted it may nevertheless provide the publisher with a defence.

Remedies

If the plaintiff can establish a prima facie case of libel he will be entitled to an *injunction* to prevent further publication. If in the face of an injunction the publication goes ahead then this will constitute contempt of court. The main remedy for defamation is of course an award of damages, and for a number of successful litigants in the past quite often a substantial sum awarded by the jury. A sum should be awarded to reflect the extent to which the defamatory statement has an impact on the plaintiff's good name. In rare cases the sum is a *nominal* amount or the damages awarded are *contemptuous*. More usually however the defendant, perhaps a large media corporation, has acted so badly that the damages awarded have a punitive element and *exemplary* damages are added to compensatory damages awarded.

Under s.8 of the Court of Legal Services Act 1990 the Court of Appeal is empowered where the damages awarded are excessive, in place of ordering a new trial, to substitute for the sum awarded by the jury such sum as appears to the court to be reasonable. In *Rantzen v. Mirror Group Newspapers (1988) Ltd.* 1993 the Court of Appeal held that the appellate court should ask *"whether a reasonable jury could have thought that this award was necessary to compensate the plaintiff and to re-establish his reputation"*.

Intellectual Property

The law of intellectual property is concerned with the protection of ideas, information and other outcomes of human intellectual creation. IPR, or Intellectual Property Rights, is a general term which embraces a number of specific rights including patents, authors rights, copyright, moral rights, trade marks and design rights. The protection conferred on the owner of intellectual property usually takes the form of an exclusive right to exploit the ideas or information in the market place, in most cases for a limited period of time, coupled with a range of remedies to enable him to enforce his right in the event of infringement. This enables him, in effect, to curtail the activities of competitors who are unable to engage in specific types of conduct relating to the subject matter of his rights without his consent. The effective monopoly conferred by the ownership of intellectual property can clearly be an extremely valuable business asset. This asset may be exploited directly by the business as part of its ordinary commercial activity or by licensing others to use it in their business in return for licence fees or royalties.

In order to gain legal protection, some forms of intellectual property need to be registered. Patents, registered trade and service marks and registered designs come within this category. Others, such as copyright and the unregistered design right automatically qualify for protection without the need for registration. Where registration is required, this can be a time consuming and costly exercise involving the services of specialist agents, and in some cases substantial renewal fees are payable in order to maintain the registration.

At this point it may be noted that there is an inherent tension between the monopoly of exploitation conferred by intellectual property rights on the one hand, and the aims of competition policy, as embodied in competition law on the other, so that for example in cases relating to trade within the European Community, the provision in the Treaty of Rome governing the free movement of goods (articles 30-36) and competition (articles 85-90), have been used in some situations to limit the effect of national intellectual property rights.

In this context, whilst intellectual property law is relevant to the question of whether particular rights exist, competition law may be applied to control the way in which such rights are exercised. The granting of exclusive rights under intellectual property law is aimed at creating incentives for authors, software developers, designers and creative professionals to ensure investment in new products and promote technical progress in the public interest. Competition law aims to ensure that competition is not distorted by IPR owners exercising their exclusive rights in a way which goes beyond the intended purpose of those rights.

One feature of UK law which attempts to deal with the possible abuse of monopoly power in this context is the availability in some cases of compulsory licences as of right to competitors. Under the Patent Act 1977, for example, licences as of right are available during the last four years of the twenty year term, and compulsory licences may be granted by the Comptroller General of Patents Designs and Trademarks on grounds set out in s.48. These are broadly based on the unreasonable underuse of the patent by the patentee. Under the Copyright, Designs and Patents Act 1988, anti competitive licensing conduct in relation to copyright, or the unregistered design rights, may give rise to compulsory licensing powers. This can occur where the Monopolies and Mergers Commission have reported that the conduct is operating against the public interest, following a reference made under the Fair Trading Act 1973 or the Competition Act 1980. Similar powers arise under the Registered Designs Act 1949 and the Patents Act 1977.

A comparison of some of the features of the major forms of intellectual property is contained in Figure 17.2.

	Copyright	Patents	Registered design	Unregistered design right	Products (protection of topography) Regulations 1987	Registered trade marks	Common law trade marks and service marks: passing off
Rights protected	literary dramatic musical and artistic work, sound recordings, films, broadcasts, cable programmes, published editions, computer software	inventions: processes or products with industrial application	features of shape configuration pattern or ornament applied to an article by an industrial process to give visual appeal	any aspect of the shape configuration of all or part of an article other than surface decoration – includes purely functional design	computer chips layout of semiconductors	any sign capable of being represented graphically which is capable of distinguishing goods or services of one undertaking from those of others	goodwill of a business
Need for registration	no	yes	yes	no	no	yes	no
Duration of protection	lifetime of author plus 70 years	20 years	renewable five year periods, maximum 25 years after 1.8.89 maximum 15 years Before 1.8.89	lesser of 15 years from creation or 10 years from marketing	lesser of 15 years from creation or 10 years from marketing	unlimited where mark is in use in trade	unlimited
Availability of licence as of right to competitor	no	licence as of right during last four years except for pharmaceutical patents compulsory licence where patent unreasonably underused	compulsory licence where design unreasonably underused	licence as of right during last five years	no	no	no
First ownership	author or his employer	inventor or his employer	designer or commissioner or designer's employer	designer or commissioner or designer's employer	designer or commissioner or designer's employer	registered proprietor	owner of the business

Figure 17.2   Comparison of major forms of intellectual property

Patents

The grant of a patent gives to the patentee a twenty year monopoly in the exploitation of a process or a product, in return for clear and complete disclosure of the invention.

The principal objectives of the patent system are threefold. Firstly, to reward the creative effort of the inventor. This aim was made clear in the judgment of the European Court of Justice in *Centrafarm v. Sterling Drugs* 1974 *"the patentee, to reward the creative effort of the inventor, has the exclusive right to use an invention with a view to manufacturing industrial products and putting them into circulation for the first time, either directly of by the grant of licences to third parties; as well as the right to oppose infringements."*

Secondly, as an incentive to innovation and increased economic activity; and thirdly as a means of making known to others in industry full information about the latest technical advances.

A patent for the UK may be registered either at the British Patent Office in London or at the European Patent Office in Munich. An application to the European Office, which was created by the European Patent Convention 1973, may result in the grant of identical patents covering each of the signatory states. It is also possible to obtain a single priority date for patents covering a number of other countries worldwide under the Patent Co-operation Treaty 1970, although separate applications must then be pursued in each country. The Patent Act 1977 was introduced in order to bring the UK system for granting patents into line with the European system as contained in the 1973 Convention.

In order to qualify for the grant of a patent, s.1 of the Patent Act 1977 provides that an invention must:

(a) *be novel,*

(b) *involve an inventive step,*

(c) *be capable of industrial application, and*

(d) *fall outside the categories of excluded subject matter.*

In order to satisfy the requirement of novelty under s.2 the invention must not be part of the *"state of the art"* at the time at which the patent application is made. The state of the art includes *"any matter (whether a product, a process, information about either, or anything else) which has at any time been made available to the public (whether in the United Kingdom or elsewhere) by written or oral description, by use, or in any other way."* Prior public disclosure by the inventor or any other person, for example by publication of an article in a periodical, will therefore defeat an application for a patent.

> In *Windsurfing International v. Tabur Marine* 1985 an application relating to a windsurfer included a feature described as *"a pair of circuate booms"*. This referred to the wishbone shaped grip which is held by the user whilst windsurfing. Evidence showed that prior to the application an amateur had used in public a model which he had made with a pair of straight booms which flexed into arc shapes when used. The Court of Appeal held that the wishbone feature was part of the state of the art, and the requirement of novelty was not satisfied.

An invention will be taken to involve an inventive step, under s.3, if, having regard to the state of the art, it is not *"obvious to a person skilled in the art."* Obviousness will defeat the requirement of an inventive step. Obviousness is judged by the standards of the notional skilled technician who is familiar with the state of the art but is himself lacking in inventive ability.

The invention will be taken to be capable of industrial application, under s.4, if it can be made or used in any kind of industry, including agriculture. If it has no known practical application, or if it doesn't actually work, then no matter how interesting it is, it is probably not patentable. Methods of treatment of the human or animal body by surgery or therapy, or of diagnosis practised on the human or animal body are deemed to be incapable of industrial application by s.4(2). Clearly it would be against the public interest if new medical techniques were not available for the benefit of all.

Certain things are specifically excluded from patent protection under s.1(2) and s.1(3). These include discoveries, scientific theories or mathematical methods not associated with practical applications; literary, dramatic, musical or artistic works or computer programs which attract copyright protection; plant and animal varieties and essentially biological processes for the production of plants and animals although some protection is given in the case of plant varieties by the Plant Varieties and Seeds Act 1964; and inventions which encourage offensive, immoral or anti-social behaviour.

Where an invention is made by an employee at the workplace, the approach of the common law was that it is the property of his employer. Thus in *Patchett v. Sterling* 1955 Lord Simonds stated *"It is an implied term of the contract of service of any workman that what he produces by the strength of his arms or the skill of his hand or the exercise of his inventive faculty shall become the property of the employer."*

The scope of this principle has been limited by s.39 of the Patent Act 1977, under which the employee is entitled to the rights in his own invention unless either the invention might reasonably be expected to result from the carrying out of his duties or at the time of the invention he has a special obligation to further the interests of the employers undertaking because of the nature of his duties and the particular responsibilities which flow from them. The employer will be entitled to the patent rights where the employee is employed to use his skills to solve technical problems or is employed in a research and development capacity or in a senior managerial position. Otherwise they will belong to the employee.

> In *Reiss Engineering Co. v. Harris* 1985 the defendant was employed to sell valves and deal with customer problems in the first instance. He was not required to deal with serious technical problems as these were referred to the Swiss company who supplied the technology to the plaintiff. After receiving notice of redundancy but before his employment had terminated, the defendant invented a new valve. His employers claim that they owned the invention was rejected because the defendant was not employed to design or invent, nor could an invention reasonably be expected to result from his normal duties.

Where an invention made by an employee belongs to an employer, the inventor may have a statutory right to compensation under. This arises where the patent is of *"outstanding benefit"* to the employer and it is just that compensation should be awarded. Where the patent belongs to the employee the employer is entitled to use it only if he has a licence from the employee or where it has been assigned to him by the employee. In such cases the employer will have paid for the licence or assignment, but nonetheless, the employee may be entitled to compensation where the consideration which he received is inadequate compared to the benefit derived by the employer from the patent, and where it is just that compensation should be paid. This is an example of a statutory exception to the normal rules relating to consideration in the law of contract.

The protection conferred by the grant of a patent lasts, subject to the payment of renewal fees, for twenty years from the date of filing the application. The process of registration can be lengthy - up to four and a half years from application. The exclusive rights of exploitation vesting in the patentee may of course be assigned or licensed to others contractually, or exercised by the patentee himself. In any event, during the last four years, licenses as of right may be obtained by competitors on terms as to payment or otherwise which will be settled by the comptroller general of patents, or by the courts. In addition, once a patent has been granted for three years, the comptroller has power to grant compulsory licences on grounds set out in s.48 of the 1977 Act, again on terms which will be settled by him. The grounds are broadly based on underuse of the invention, for example resulting in an undersupply to the UK market or to export markets of the product.

Infringement of a patent may arise directly, for example where the infringer produces or uses a patented product, or indirectly, for example where the infringer supplies another person with the means of putting the invention into effect, in each case without lawful authority. Remedies for infringement, include an injunction; an order for delivery up and destruction of any infringing product; damages; an account of profits and a declaration.

Trade Marks and Passing Off

A trade mark is an emblem symbol logo or other sign which is designed to establish a connection between goods or services and their producer or supplier. The use of such a mark is one of the means whereby a business establishes product identity with the aim of encouraging brand loyalty among consumers and enhancing business goodwill.

English law recognises two types of trade or service marks, those which are registered under the Trade Marks Act 1994 and those which, although unregistered, are recognised at common law. The former are protected by legal action for infringement under the 1994 Act and by the common law tort of passing off. The latter are protected by a passing off action only. Other significant differences between common law and registered trade marks are that a distinctive trade mark may be registered prior to the acquisition of a reputation connected with it whereas at common law the mark is protected only on evidence of an established reputation, and a registered mark may be assigned or licensed to another and thereby become divorced from the goodwill of the business in respect of which it was acquired. Unregistered marks are inseparable from the goodwill of the business which they represent.

Registered trade marks

The Trade Marks Act 1994 was passed partly in order to implement EC Directive 89/104/EEC of 21 December 1988 on the approximation of the laws of the Member States relating to trade marks and it has the effect of harmonising the rules governing the conditions under which a trade mark may be registered and the rights which arise following registration.

The 1994 Act came into force on 31 October 1994, replacing the Trade Marks Act 1938 and bringing substantial changes to the law relating to registered trade marks. The distinction between trade marks and service marks, present in the previous law, has been removed by the 1994 Act, so that a mark designed to establish a connection between services and their supplier now comes within the definition of a trade mark. Under s.1 of the 1994 Act a trade mark is defined as:

> *"...any sign capable of being represented graphically which is capable of distinguishing goods or services of one undertaking from those of other undertakings.*

In order to be registerable, a trade mark must firstly be a *"sign capable of being registered graphically"*. The section goes on to say that this may consist of *"words (including personal names), designs, letters, numerals or the shape of goods or their packaging."*

Under the previous law it had not been possible to register the shape of goods or their packaging as a trade mark.

> In *Re: Coca-Cola Co's Applications* 1986 the House of Lords held that the Coca-Cola Company was not entitled to register as a trade mark the distinctively shaped bottle in which their products had been marketed worldwide since the early 1920s on the grounds that a mark must be something distinct from the thing being marked, and a bottle is a container and not a mark.

Such a container will now be registerable. However there are restrictions in s.3(2) on the registration of certain shapes as trade marks, so that signs which consist exclusively of the shape which results from the nature of the goods themselves or the shape of goods which is necessary to obtain a technical result will not be registerable.

The second requirement is that the proposed trade mark must be *"capable of distinguishing goods or services of one undertaking from those of other undertakings"*. It must have the capacity to distinguish. A trade mark which is devoid of any distinctive character cannot be registered. The same applies to a trade mark which is simply descriptive unless, in either case, it has achieved a distinctive character in fact as a result of the use made of it.

Certain marks will be excluded from registration, including those inappropriately containing Royal symbols or certain flags or national emblems and those which are deceptive or contrary to public policy or accepted principles of morality.

A register of trade and service marks is maintained at the Patent Office by the Registrar of Patents Designs and Trade Marks. The register is open to public inspection and is being computerised following the Patents, Designs and Marks Act 1986 so as to make the process of searching and obtaining copies of entries quicker and less costly.

The Registrar will refuse to register a mark which is deceptive at the time of the application because for example there has been prior registration of the same or a confusingly similar mark for the same goods or services. In this respect the 1994 Act goes further than the earlier legislation which restricted the protection of registration to the use of the mark in relation to the same goods or services. Now the trade mark owner can prevent the registration of the same mark for similar goods or services, a similar mark for the same goods or services or a similar mark for similar goods or services.

Where a trade mark has an established reputation the protection afforded by registration is wider again. An identical or similar trade mark will not be registerable even for goods or services which are dissimilar where the use of the mark would be detrimental or take unfair advantage of the registered trade mark. Where there has been prior use of an unregistered mark, registration will be refused if it would give rise to reasonable doubt as to the source of the product, leading to a real and tangible danger of confusion.

> In *Mitsubishi v. Fiat* 1987 the plaintiffs manufactured cars and used the word *Lancia* as a trade mark. They sought to prevent the defendants from registering *Lancer* as a name for one of their cars. While the words sounded similar the two trade marks looked completely different. The Court of Appeal, which took the view that in the case of important or expensive purchases the sound of the words is likely not to play a significant role, held that there was no risk of confusion between the two trade marks and that the defendants could register *Lancer* as a trade mark.

Infringement of a registered trade mark or service mark occurs where a similar or identical mark is used by another trader without authority in relation to similar or identical goods or services; or where the trade mark has a reputation in relation to goods or services which are not similar. Remedies for infringement include an injunction and an account of profits or damages. Delivery-up or destruction of infringing goods may also be ordered by the court. It is a criminal offence to represent that a mark is registered when in fact it is not, and fraudulently to apply a mark to goods, labels, packaging or advertising materials where the mark is identical or similar to a registered trade mark.

Passing off

The tort of passing off is designed to protect the goodwill of a business and to enable it to defend its common law rights in respect of unregistered trade or service marks. Goodwill, which is a type of intangible property, was defined by Lord Macnaghten in *I.R.C. v. Muller & Co. Margarine Ltd.* 1901 as *"the benefit and advantage of the good name, reputation and connection of a business. It is the attractive force which brings in the custom."* In *Star Industrial Co. Ltd. v. Yap Kwee Kor* 1976 Lord Diplock stated:

> *"A passing off action is a remedy for the invasion of a right of property … in the business or goodwill likely to be injured by the misrepresentation made by passing-off one person's goods as the goods of another. Goodwill, as the subject of proprietary rights, is incapable of subsisting by itself. It has no independent existence apart from the business to which it is attached."*

The tort of passing off is committed where one business represents its goods or services, either innocently or intentionally, to be those of another. The basic principle was stated in *Perry v. Truefitt* 1842 by Lord Langdale:

> *"A man is not to sell his own goods under the pretence that they are the goods of another man."*

This may occur, for example, where the defendant simply lies about the origin of his product.

In *Lord Byron v. Johnson* 1816 the defendant advertised that certain poems which he had published were written by the plaintiff. In fact they were written by someone else. It was held that he was liable in the tort of passing off.

Liability extends well beyond this, so that for example, the use by a trader of a term which accurately describes the composition of his own goods might nevertheless amount to passing off if that term is understood in the market in which the goods are sold to denote the goods of a rival trader.

In *Reddaway v. Banham* 1896 the plaintiffs manufactured camel hair belting bearing a design consisting of an image of a camel and the words *Camel Hair Belting*. The defendants also manufactured camel hair belting bearing the words *camel hair belting* for sale in the same market in which the plaintiff's product was well established. The defendants were held to have passed off their goods as the goods of the plaintiff because, although camel hair belting was accurately descriptive of the goods, the words had acquired a secondary meaning under which customers within that market understood them to be goods of the plaintiff.

The essential elements of an action in passing off were identified by Lord Diplock in *Erven Warnink B.V. v. J. Townend & Co. (Hull) Ltd.* 1979. He said that there are:

"five characteristics which must be present in order to create a valid course of action for passing off: (1) a misrepresentation (2) made by a trader in the course of trade, (3) to prospective customers of his or ultimate consumers of goods or services supplied by him, (4) which is calculated to injure the business or goodwill of another trader (in the sense that this is a reasonably foreseeable consequence) and (5) which causes actual damage to a business or goodwill of the trader by whom the action is brought or will probably do so."

The facts of *Warnink v. Townend* were that the Dutch plaintiffs manufactured a drink called *advocaat* which had acquired a substantial reputation in Britain as a distinct and recognisable beverage, having been marketed here for many years. The essential ingredients of advocaat were spirits, egg yolks and sugar. From 1974 a drink called *"Keeling's Old English Advocaat"*, which was a mixture of dried egg powder and Cyprus sherry, was made and marketed by the defendants in England, where it captured a substantial share of the plaintiffs market. The House of Lords held that the plaintiffs were entitled to protection from the deceptive use of the name advocaat by the defendants, and granted an injunction preventing its use by them.

In order to show that there has been a misrepresentation by the defendant, the plaintiff must establish that his goods have acquired a reputation in the market and are known by some distinguishing feature. This feature may be a name, such as advocaat or camel hair belting, a symbol or logo in the nature of a common law or registered trade mark, or some other feature, such as the appearance or packaging of the goods. The misrepresentation occurs when the distinctive feature is adopted in relation to the product of the defendant and as a result customers in the market are deceived or are likely to be deceived into buying the product believing it to be the plaintiffs. As to the degree of likelihood of deception, the requirement will not be fulfilled if, in the words of one judge, *"only a moron in a hurry would be misled"*. On the other hand, in a case where it is demonstrable that the public has been or will be deceived, it is no defence to argue that they would not be deceived if they were *"more careful, more literate or more perspicacious."*

> In *Reckitt & Colman Products Ltd. v. Borden Inc.* 1990 the plaintiffs had, since 1956, sold lemon juice under the brand name *Jif* in plastic squeeze containers made in the shape, colour and size of natural lemons. No other trader in the UK sold lemon juice in a similar container until the defendants launched such a product. The trial judge found that although a careful shopper would realise the defendants lemon was not that of the plaintiffs, since it was merely a question of reading the label, the evidence nevertheless established conclusively that the introduction of the defendants lemons would result in many shoppers buying them in the belief that they were purchasing the plaintiffs' lemons, as the lemon shape was the crucial point of reference for the shopper who paid little attention to the labels. Accordingly, the judge granted an injunction to restrain the defendants from marketing their product *"in any container so nearly resembling the plaintiffs' Jif lemon shaped container as to be likely to deceive without making it clear to the ultimate purchaser that it is not of the goods of the plaintiffs"*. The defendants appealed and the House of Lords held, on the basis of the judge's finding of fact, that the elements of passing off had been established and the injunction should remain in place.

> In *McDonald's Hamburgers v. Burgerking (UK)* 1986 the defendants advertised their *"whopper"* hamburger stating *"It's Not Just Big, Mac"* and *"Unlike some Burgers, its 100 per cent, pure beef, flame grilled, never fried, with a unique choice of toppings."* The plaintiffs were granted an injunction on the grounds that, reading the advertisement, the public would be likely to be deceived into thinking that the burger was an improvement of their *Big Mac* burger, available at the defendants premises.

The element of damage will usually be proved by evidence that the plaintiff's potential customers have been or are likely to be diverted to the defendant. Where there is no damage, actual or anticipated, the action will fail.

> In *Wombles v. Womble Skips* 1977 the owners of the copyright in the Wombles books and children's television series were unable to obtain an injunction against a company that hired out Wombles rubbish skips because the essential elements of passing off had not been established. They were unable to demonstrate that they had suffered or were likely to suffer, any damage as a result of the defendant's activities.

The remedies available in a passing off action are damages for the loss which the plaintiff has suffered, or an account of the profits which the defendant has made as a result of the passing off. In addition the court may grant an injunction to restrain the defendant from continuing his unlawful activities.

Designs

The protection of industrial designs, since the coming into force of the Copyright, Designs and Patents Act 1988, arises either by registration under the Registered Designs Act 1949, (as amended by the 1988 Act), or without registration by virtue either of the *unregistered design right* created by the 1988 Act or, in the case of computer microchips, by the Products (Protection of Topography)

Regulations 1987. The unregistered design right in effect replaces the protection previously conferred by the Copyright Act 1956 on industrial drawings, and thereby reduces the scope of protection available for industrial designs.

Registered designs

A design which gives visual appeal to mass produced goods may be registered under the Registered Designs Act 1949. This gives protection for a period of five years, renewable on payment of renewal fees for further five year periods up to a maximum of 25 years in total if registered after the 1988 Act, or 15 years in total if registered before.

A design is not registrable under the 1949 Act where the ultimate appearance of the article is not material to the consumer, for example in the case of a waste disposal unit which, when installed, will be hidden from view. An unregistered design right may however arise in respect of purely functional articles of this nature, where aesthetic considerations are not normally taken into account by a purchaser.

In order to qualify for registration, the design must come within the definition of a design in s.1(1) of the 1949 Act, which states:

> *"In this Act "design" means features of shape, configuration, pattern or ornament applied to an article by any industrial process, being features which in the finished article appeal to and are judged by the eye, but does not include -*
>
> *(a)   a method or principle of construction, or*
>
> *(b)   features of shape or configuration of an article which*
>
> > *(i)   are dictated solely by the function which the article has to perform, or*
> >
> > *(ii) are dependent upon the appearance of another article of which the article is intended by the author of the design to form an integral part".*

In *Interlego AG v. Tyco Industries Inc.* 1988 the Privy Council had to rule upon a case governed by the pre 1988 Act law, under which the plaintiff claimed copyright protection for the design drawings of Lego bricks. Copyright could be claimed pre 1988 if the artistic work in question as not a design capable of registration under the 1949 Act. The plaintiff argued that the design of the bricks was purely functional and therefore incapable of registration due to the wording of s.1(1)(b)(i). The Privy Council held that the designs were capable of registration under the 1949 Act and consequently were not protected by copyright. The design of the bricks was not purely functional as they clearly had eye-appeal as well as significant features in terms of outline and proportion which were not dictated by function.

The so called *must match* exception contained in S.1(1)(b)(ii) was newly introduced by the 1988 Act, and applies to situations where the design of the article must match that of another article of which it is intended to form an integral part. This covers such items as replacement body panels for motor vehicles, the designs of which are not capable of registration. As we shall see such articles are also outside the protection of the unregistered design right.

In order to be registrable, the design must be new. This requirement of novelty will not be satisfied if a substantially similar design is registered in pursuance of a prior application or has already been published in the UK.

The original ownership of a design is vested in its author under s.2, except in two cases. First, where the design is created pursuant to a commission for money or money's worth, in which case the person commissioning it is treated as the original owner. Second, where the design is created by an employee in the course of his employment, his employer is treated as the original owner. Under s.2(4), where a design is generated by computer in circumstances where there is no human author, the person by whom the arrangements necessary for the creation of the design are made is taken to be the author.

The registration of a design gives the registered proprietor the exclusive right, to make or import articles of that design for sale, hire or business use and to sell, hire or offer to sell or hire them. Any person who does any such act without the authority of the proprietor, or makes anything to enable such articles to be made will be liable for infringement. This liability is strict and arises without the need to prove copying. Remedies for infringement of a registered design include an injunction and damages, although damages cannot be awarded against a defendant who neither knew nor had reasonable grounds for supposing that the design was registered. The Act further provides that merely marking the article *"registered"* will not constitute reasonable grounds unless this is accompanied by the design number.

Unregistered design right

The unregistered design right was created by Part III of the Copyright, Designs and Patents Act 1988. The 1988 Act, in s.51, withdrew copyright protection from most functional industrial designs. Prior to this, although artistic copyright could not subsist in manufactured articles as such, prior drawings of such articles had copyright protection as artistic works provided they were not registerable under the Registered Designs Act 1949.

As we saw in the case of *Interlego AG v. Tyco Industries Inc.* 1988 this put design owners into a surprising position of having to argue that their designs did not qualify for registration under the 1949 Act, in order to claim the considerably better protection offered by the law of copyright. This anomalous situation was the subject of much criticism, not least by the House of Lords in *British Leyland Motor Corporation v. Armstrong*, a decision which took away that protection in relation to the design of spare parts for cars.

> In *British Leyland Motor Corp. Ltd. v. Armstrong Patents Co. Ltd.* 1986 the defendant, without having seen the plaintiff's design drawings, copied spare parts for its cars by a process of reverse engineering, which simply involved copying the shape and dimensions of the original articles. The House of Lords held that this infringed the plaintiffs copyright in the design drawings since, by s.48(1) of the Copyright Act 1956, *reproduction* of the artistic work included converting it into three dimensional form. However, the plaintiff's rights were, in their lordships' opinion, subordinate to the competing entitlement of car owners to access to a free market in spare parts in order to keep their cars in working order. Accordingly the plaintiff was not entitled to enforce its copyright in a manner so

as to maintain a monopoly in the supply of spare parts for its vehicles, and the defendant was free to manufacture without licence.

Copyright as a means of protecting functional industrial designs was, as previously noted, substantially withdrawn by s.51 of the 1988 Act. and replaced by the unregistered design right.

The unregistered design right arises in respect of an *original design* under s.213 of the 1988 Act. Designs covered by the section are defined in s.213(2) and (3) which state:

> *"(2)   In this Part "design" means the design of any aspect of the shape or configuration (whether internal or external) of the whole or part of an article.*
>
> *(3)   Design right does not subsist in -*
>
> *(a) a method or principle of construction,*
>
> *(b)   features of shape or configuration of an article which -*
>
> > *(i)   enable the article to be connected to, or placed in, around or against, another article so that either article may perform its function, or*
> >
> > *(ii)   are dependent upon the appearance of another article of which the article is intended by the designer to form an integral part, or*
>
> *(c)   surface decoration."*

The exceptions contained in s.213(3)(b), the so-called *must-fit* and *must-match* exceptions, are a significant extension of the consequences of the decision in *British Leyland v. Armstrong* 1986. The *must-fit* exception in s.213(3)(b)(i) clearly applies to spare parts, such as exhaust systems, engine parts etc., and probably goes a good deal further. For example it could apply to fixing devices, or accessories for an electric drill. The *must-match* exception in s.213(3)(b)(ii) applies to spare parts such as vehicle body panels, the shape of which is integral to the appearance of the vehicle as a whole.

An unregistered design right does not subsist, by s.213(3)(c), in surface decoration. This is not excluded from copyright protection by s.51, and may also be protected by registration as *"features of pattern or ornament"* under the 1949 Act.

The unregistered design right arises when the design has been recorded in a design document or when an article has been made to the design. A design document, by s.263(1), means any record of a design, whether in the form of a drawing, a written description, a photograph, data stored in a computer or otherwise. The right belongs to the designer unless it was created in pursuance of a commission, in which case it belongs to the person who commissioned it. Where the design was created in the course of the designer's employment, the right belongs to the employer.

The design right expires fifteen years from the end of the calendar year in which the right arose, or, if sooner, ten years from the end of the calendar year in which articles made to the design were first available for sale or hire. During the last five years of the design right term, any person is entitled to a licence as of right upon terms which, in the absence of agreement, will be settled by the comptroller.

The owner of the unregistered design right has, by s.226, the exclusive right to reproduce the design for commercial purposes, either by making articles exactly or substantially to the design, or by making a design document for the purpose of enabling such articles to be made. Any person who, without authority, engages in any of these activities is liable for primary infringement. Secondary infringement arises where an infringer who knows or has reason to believe that an article is an infringing article, imports it into the UK, has it in his possession for commercial purposes, sells or hires it, or offers or exposes it for sale or hire in the course of a business.

Remedies for infringement include an injunction, an order for delivery up of infringing articles or moulds or tools for making them, an account of profits, or damages. Additional damages may be awarded for flagrant infringement under s.229(3). No damages, however, will be awarded for innocent primary infringement, although the other remedies are available. In a case where a licence as of right would have been available at the time of infringement, a defendant who undertakes to take such a licence will not be subjected to an injunction, an order for delivery up, or an award of damages in excess of double the amount of royalties which would have been payable if such a licence had been granted.

Products (Protection of Topography) Regulations 1987

The 1987 regulations were introduced under the enabling provisions of the European Communities Act 1972 in order to implement an EC directive. Their purpose is to confer protection, which bears some of the features of the unregistered design right, upon the creator of the patterns of circuitry and layout of semiconductor products such as the computer microchip. A semiconductor product is defined in r.2(1) as:

> *"an article the purpose of which is the performance of an electronic function and which consists of two or more layers, at least one of which is composed of semiconducting material and in or upon one or more of which is fixed a pattern appertaining to that or another function."*

The *topography right* subsists in the arrangements of the layers of a semiconductor product, and in the pattern on the surface of the layers. Under r.3, the topography must be original in order to qualify for protection. Like the unregistered design right, the duration of protection is the lesser of fifteen years from the end of the calendar year in which the topography is created, or ten years from the end of the calendar year in which it is first marketed.

Ownership of the topography right, which arises automatically without the need for registration, confers a monopoly in the commercial exploitation of the semiconductor product. This vests in the designer unless it was created in pursuance of a commission, in which case it belongs to the person who commissioned it. Where the topography was created in the course of the designer's employment, the right belongs to the employer. There is no provision for the grant of licences as of right in the topography regulations.

Copyright

Copyright is an important form of intellectual property, the ownership of which gives rise to a range of exclusive rights in relation to the copyright work. The effect of these rights is to enable their owner to prevent others from using the copyright work in a number of different ways. The Copyright Designs and Patents Act 1988, which came into effect on 1st August 1989, applies to all copyright works made on or after that date. Works made prior to that date are governed by previous legislation, such as the Copyright Act 1956 or earlier Acts, which will continue to have practical importance for many years to come having regard to the duration of copyright protection. In this text, however, it is proposed to deal only with the main features of the 1988 Act.

Copyright arises automatically without the need for registration or other formality. It is, however, common to see published work carrying the copyright symbol ©. Whilst this is not necessary in order to obtain copyright protection in the UK, the use of the symbol in conjunction with the name of the copyright owner and the year of first publication has three purposes. First it confers protection under the terms of Universal Copyright Convention 1952 in a number of other countries, including the USA, without the need for any other formality. Second, it raises a number of presumptions under s.104, s.105 and s.106 as to the authorship of the work, ownership of the copyright and date of first publication. These presumptions may of course be rebutted by appropriate evidence to the contrary. Third, it serves as a reminder of the rights of the copyright owner, and a warning against infringement.

Copyright work

The range of subject matter which attracts copyright is set out in s.1 of the 1988 Act, which states:

> *"1(1)Copyright is a property right which subsists in ... -*
>
> *(a) original literary, dramatic, musical or artistic works,*
>
> *(b) sound recordings, films, broadcasts or cable programmes, and*
>
> *(c) the typographical arrangements of published editions."*

It may be noted that in order at attract copyright there must actually be a work. The law of copyright does not protect ideas as such, rather the embodiment or expression of the ideas in a work.

> In *Green v. Broadcasting Corp of New Zealand* 1989 the plaintiff, Hughie Green, claimed for damages from the defendant for infringement of his copyright in the scripts and dramatic format of the television show, Opportunity Knocks. The defendant had broadcast a similar show in New Zealand with the same title and without the authority of the plaintiff. Although no scripts were produced in evidence, the plaintiff's evidence was that he wrote the scripts of the show, such as they were, by having the same form of introduction for each competitor, using the same catch phrases throughout the show like *"For so-and-so, Opportunity Knocks", "This is your show, folks, and I do mean you", "make your mind up time"* and using the *clapometer* to measure audience reaction to competitors' performances. The Privy Council accepted that the evidence established the existence of scripts, but concluded, in the absence of precise evidence as to what they contained, that they did no more than express a general idea or concept for a talent quest and therefore were not the subject of copyright.

A general idea or concept will not of itself attract copyright protection. A book or article containing the original expression of an idea or concept will be protected by copyright. This will not prevent the creation of other books or articles based on the same concept or idea provided that the expression of the concept or idea is not copied from the earlier work.

A work must be original in order to attract copyright protection.

	Literary work	Dramatic and musical work	Artistic work	Sound recording	Film	Broadcasts and cable programmes	Published editions
Nature of work	any work which is written, spoken or sung (other than dramatic and musical work) including tables, compilations and computer programmes	dramatic work includes dance and mime (recorded in any form) musical work consists of music without words (literary work) or actions (dramatic work)	graphic work (painting, diagram, chart etc) photograph, sculpture, collage (all irrespective of artistic quality) architectural work and works of artistic craftsmanship	recording of sounds or of literary dramatic or musical work from which the sounds may be reproduced	recording on any medium from which a moving image may by any means be produced	transmission of information (eg tv or radio programme or teletext) by wireless telegraphy (broadcast) or by non-wireless cable programme service (cable programme)	typographic arrangement (layout) of published edition of literary, dramatic or musical work
First ownership	author (creator of the work), or, if made in the course of employment, the author's employer			person undertaking arrangements necessary for making sound recording or film		person making broadcast or providing cable programme service	publisher
Duration of protection	70 years from end of year of author's death, or 70 years from end of year of death of last surviving joint author, or, where author unknown, 70 years from end of year in which first made available to the public, or, where computer generated, 70 years from end of year in which the work was made. Parliamentary copyright: 70 years for Acts and Measures Crown Copyright 125 years or 70 years from first commercial publication			end of 70th year from making, or end of 70th year from release if release within 70 years of making		end of 70th year from first transmission	end of 25th year from first publication

Figure 17.3 Copyright: subject matter, first ownership and duration

The requirement of originality in s.1(1)(a) in relation to literary, dramatic, musical or artistic works was explained in *London University Press v. University Tutorial Press* 1916 by Peterson J as follows:

> *"The word original does not in this connection mean that the work must be the expression of original or inventive thought. Copyright Acts are not concerned with the originality of ideas, but with the expression of thought, and, in the case of literary work, with the expression of thought in print or writing. The originality which is required relates to the expression of the thought. But the Act does not require that the expression must be in an original or novel form, but that the work must not be copied from another work - that it should originate from the author."*

Literary work is defined in s.3(1) as:

> *"any work, other than dramatic or musical work, which is written, spoken or sung, and accordingly includes:*
>
> *(a)   a table or compilation,*
>
> *(b)   a computer programme, and*
>
> *(c)   preparatory design material for a computer programme."*

Literary work is one of the most important categories of copyright work, embracing a wide range of subject matter such as textbooks, novels, newspaper articles, poems, plays, song lyrics, letters, essays, scripts, speeches, bus timetables, instructions, databases and computer programs. Where the work consists of the spoken word, copyright does not arise unless and until the work is recorded. The recording, which may be by writing, tape, film or any other means, will trigger the creation of copyright in favour of the speaker, or his employer, whether or not the speaker has authorised the recording. This also applies in the case of original dramatic or musical work which is spoken or sung.

Dramatic work encompasses not only drama but also works of dance and mime. In *Green v. Broadcasting Corp of New Zealand* 1989, discussed above, the plaintiff's argument that his use of a number of catch phrases in the presentation of each Opportunity Knocks show gave rise to the subsistence of copyright in the format of the show as a dramatic work, was rejected by the Privy Council. Lord Bridge stated that *"a dramatic work must have sufficient unity to be capable of performance and ... the features claimed as constituting the format of [the plaintiff's] show, being unrelated to each other except as accessories to be used in the presentation of some other dramatic or musical performance, lack that essential characteristic."*

Musical work is defined in s.3(1) as:

> *"a work consisting of music, exclusive of any words or action intended to be sung, spoken or performed with the music".*

This refers to the music only; song lyrics being literary work and accompanying action being dramatic work. Where these three elements are the creation of different authors, the duration of copyright in each will vary according to the lifespan of the individuals concerned.

Artistic work is widely defined in s.4 and falls into two categories. The first includes graphics, paintings, drawings, diagrams, maps, charts, plans, engravings, etchings, lithographs, woodcuts, photographs, sculptures and collages, all of which attract copyright regardless of artistic quality. In the second category come architectural structures, buildings or models and works of artistic craftsmanship, all of which must display some degree of artistic merit in order to come within the definition.

In addition to literary, dramatic, musical and artistic works, copyright subsists in sound recordings, including records cassettes and compact disks; films and videos; broadcasts; cable programmes and the typographical layout of published editions.

Copyright in computer programs and databases

Computer programs

Copyright for computer programs has been harmonised within the European Union by the laws which were introduced by member states following the adoption of the Directive 91/250 of 14 May 1991 on the legal protection of computer programs. In the UK the Copyright (Computer Programs) Regulations 1992 were introduced to give effect to the directive by making amendments to the Copyright Designs and Patents Act 1988.

Thus provides that the exclusive rights of the copyright owner of a computer program shall include the right to do or authorise:

- the permanent or temporary reproduction of a computer program by any means and in any form, in part or in whole. In so far as loading, displaying, running, transmission or storage of the computer program necessitates such reproduction, these acts shall be subject to authorisation by the copyright owner;

- the translation, adaptation, arrangement and any other alteration of the computer program; and

- the distribution of a computer program by means of sale, licensing or rental.

By way of exemption from these exclusive rights, a person who lawfully acquires a computer program is allowed to reproduce, translate, adapt, rearrange or alter the program in so far as this is necessary to enable him to use the program in accordance with its intended purpose, including for the correction of errors, without the authorisation of the copyright owner. The right may, however, be excluded by the terms of a contract.

The lawful user is also allowed to study how the program functions in order to determine the ideas principles which underlie any element of the program, provided he does so while performing any of the acts of loading, displaying, running, transmitting or storing the program which he is entitled to do.

Additionally it is not an infringement of copyright for a lawful user of a copy of a computer program to make any back up copy of it which it is necessary for him to have for the purposes of his lawful use. Where the lawful user has the right to make a back up copy, this may not be taken away by contract.

Under the provisions introduced by the EC directive, the decompilation or reverse engineering of a computer program will not be an infringement of copyright where the process is indispensable to obtain the information necessary to achieve the inter-operability of an independently created computer program with other programs. The authorisation of the copyright owner will not be required where a number of conditions are met:

- the information necessary to achieve inter-operability has not previously been readily available;

- decompilation is confined to the parts of the original program which are necessary to achieve inter-operability;

- the information obtained is not used for any purpose other than to achieve inter-operability of an independently created program;

- the information obtained is not given to any other person except where this is necessary for the inter-operability of the programs; and

- the information is not used to create a program which is substantially similar in its expression to the program decompiled, or to do any other act restricted by copyright.

These rules are designed to prevent major companies with a dominant position in the computer software supply market using the law of copyright to gain an unfair advantage over competitors by restricting their ability to produce compatible programs and software.

Databases

Directive 96/9/EC on the legal protection of databases was adopted on 11 March 1996 and requires member states to bring it provisions into force before the 1 January 1998. Implementation of the directive will harmonise the legal protection of databases within the countries of the European Union, although certain aspects of the directive are already reflected in the national law of a number of member states.

The objectives of the database directive are:

- to harmonise elements of copyright law which are applicable to the structure of databases, and

- to introduce a new *sui generis* (unique) right to prevent unauthorised extraction from a database, whether or not the database itself qualifies for copyright protection.

For the purposes of the directive a database is a collection of independent works, data or other material arranged in a systematic or methodical way and individually accessible by electronic or other means. This includes both electronic and paper based databases. The directive does not affect the rights of those copyright owners whose works are incorporated into the contents of a database.

A database which, by reason of the selection or arrangement of its contents, is original in so far as it constitutes the author's own intellectual creation shall be protected by copyright. The protection will endure for the same time period as is the case with literary work, i.e. the life of the author plus seventy years.

The author of a copyright database has the exclusive right to carry out or authorise reproduction, adaptation and distribution of the database and its communication to the public. There will be no infringement where a lawful user does an act such as copying during normal use of the database or where this is necessary for the purpose of obtaining access to its contents.

Authorship and ownership of copyright

The first ownership of copyright in a work is the author of it, under s.11(1). Where a literary, dramatic, musical or artistic work is made by an employee in the course of his employment, however, his employer is the first owner of the copyright, subject to any agreement to the contrary.

In the case of literary, dramatic, musical or artistic work, the author, under s.9(1), is the person who creates the work. Where such work is computer generated, the author is taken to be the person by whom the arrangements necessary for the creation of the work are undertaken.

In relation to other types of copyright work, s.9(2) provides that the author shall be taken to be:

"*(a) in the case of a sound recording or film, the person by whom the arrangements necessary for the making of the recording or film are undertaken;*

(b) in the case of a broadcast, the person making the broadcast ...;

(c) in the case of a cable programme, the person providing the cable programme service in which the programme is included;

(d) in the case of the typographical arrangements of a published edition, the publisher."

Like any other form of property, copyright can be dealt with by way of sale purchase or gift, or devolve as part of a deceased person's estate on death. The copyright owner has, in effect, a number of separate rights. These rights can be divided up, and dealt with separately. Take, for example, the case of an author who has written a novel. A number of different rights in his original literary work could be assigned to separate purchasers. Thus he could sell the right to publish in hardback to A, in paperback to B, the French translation rights to C, electronic publishing rights to D, the film rights to E and the right to publish in comic strip form to F. Further subdivision along these lines, or in terms of time period, or geographical area, are also possible. Such possibilities are recognised by s.90(2) which states:

"*(2) An assignment or other transmission of copyright may be partial, that is, limited to apply -*

(a) to one or more, but not all, of the things the copyright owner has the exclusive right to do;

(b) to part, but not the whole, of the period for which the copyright is to subsist."

Under s.91, future copyright can be assigned in whole or in part before the work comes into existence. Where this is done, for example as part of an agreement to publish work which has not yet been written, copyright vests in the assignee as soon as it comes into being.

Any assignment of copyright, in whole or in part, existing or future, will not be effective unless the assignment is in writing, and signed by or on behalf of the assignor.

Duration of copyright

Copyright in literary, dramatic, musical or artistic work expires, under s.12, seventy years from the end of the calendar year in which the author dies. In the case of joint authorship the seventy year period is counted from the end of the year in which the last of the joint authors dies. Where the work is of unknown authorship, copyright expires seventy years from the end of the year in which it is first made available to the public. In the case of computer generated work, the seventy year period begins at the end of the year in which the work is made.

Copyright in a sound recording or a film expires, under s.13, seventy years from the end of the year in which it is made, unless it is released during that time, in which case copyright expires seventy years from the end of the year in which it is released. In the case of broadcasts and cable programmes, copyright expires seventy years from the end of the year of first transmission, while copyright in the typographical arrangement of a published edition expires twenty five years from the end of the year in which the edition was published.

Infringement of copyright

Infringement of copyright occurs where a person does something in relation to a copyright work, without the authority of the copyright owner, which is an *"act restricted by copyright"* under s.16(1), and which falls outside the scope of *"acts permitted in relation to copyright works"* within sections 28-76 of the 1988 Act. In defining acts restricted by copyright, the performance of which will amount to primary infringement, s.16(1) sets out the rights associated with copyright ownership. These are, in effect, two sides of the same coin. Section 16(1) states:

> *"The owner of the copyright in a work has ... the exclusive right to do the following acts in the UK -*
>
> *(a)   to copy the work;*
>
> *(b)   to issue copies of the work to the public;*
>
> *(c)   to perform, show or play the work in public;*
>
> *(d)   to broadcast the work or include it in a cable programme service;*
>
> *(e)   to make an adaptation of the work or do any of the above in relation to an adaptation;*
>
> *and those acts are referred to as the 'acts restricted by the copyright'."*

Infringement may take the form of doing an act restricted by the copyright, or authorising another person to do such an act.

> In *CBS Songs Ltd. v. Amstrad Consumer Electronics plc* 1988 the plaintiff sued for damages and an injunction to prevent the sale of twin deck tape recording machines by the defendant, on the grounds that the tape to tape facility on the machines was likely to encourage home taping and copying of copyright material. The House of Lords dismissed the plaintiff's argument that the defendant had authorised infringement, or was a joint infringer with any person who used the machines for taping copyright material, and the claim failed as the machines were perfectly capable of lawful use.

The Act takes a broad view of the scope of primary infringement.

This is reflected in s.16(3) which states:

> *"References to the doing of an act restricted by the copyright in a work are to the doing of it -*
>
> *(a) in relation to the work as a whole or any substantial part of it, and*
>
> *(b) either directly or indirectly"*

Whether the defendant has copied a *substantial part* of the plaintiff's work is a question of degree depending on the particular facts of the case. In *Ladbroke v. William Hill* 1964, Lord Reid stated that the question *"depends much more on the quality than on the quantity of what he has taken"*. Where the plaintiff's work is highly original, the taking of a fairly small part of it may be held to be substantial. On the other hand where the plaintiff's work, although original, is rather common-place, the taking of a greater part of it quantitatively may still not be substantial.

Where there is a claim of infringement based on copying, the plaintiff must prove that the defendant's work is taken from the work of which he is the copyright owner. The claim will fail, therefore, if the defendant can show either that both pieces of work were derived from a common source, or that he produced his work independently. Where the two works are substantially similar, and it is shown that the defendant had access to the plaintiff's work or the opportunity to become familiar with it, the court will infer copying in the absence of evidence to the contrary.

> In *Francis Day & Hunter Ltd. v. Bron* 1963 the plaintiff owned the copyright in a musical work *In a Little Spanish Town*, composed in 1926 and exploited extensively by way of sheet music, broadcasting and gramophone records. The song retained its popularity over the years and a number of recordings of it were made. In 1959 the defendant published a song *Why,* which, the plaintiff alleged, reproduced a substantial part of its work. The plaintiff claimed that the first eight bars of the chorus of Spanish Town had been reproduced consciously or unconsciously in the first eight bars of Why. The judge, Wilberforce J, accepted the defendant's evidence that he had not consciously copied the plaintiff's work. He found that the first eight bars of the chorus of Spanish Town constituted a substantial part of the whole tune and that there was a considerable degree of similarity between those eight bars and the first eight bars of Why, though there were differences enough to take into account when considering whether Why could be an independent creation. In considering whether there had been unconscious copying, he stated: *"The final question to be resolved is whether the plaintiff's work has been copied or reproduced, and it seems to me that the answer can only be reached by a judgment of fact upon a number of composite elements: The degree of familiarity (if proved at all, or properly inferred) with the plaintiff's work, the character of the work, particularly its qualities of impressing the mind and memory, the objective similarity of the defendant's work, the inherent probability that such similarity as is found could be due to coincidence, the existence of other influences upon the defendant composer, and not least the quality of the defendant's own evidence on the presence or otherwise in his mind of the plaintiff's work."* In a decision which was subsequently confirmed by the Court of Appeal, the judge held that there was insufficient evidence upon which to find unconscious copying, and the plaintiff's claim failed.

It may be noted that in addition to a range of civil remedies for infringement, including damages, an injunction, an order for delivery up and a right in limited circumstances to seize infringing copies and other associated articles, the 1988 Act creates a number of criminal offences, under s.107, for activities in the course of a business, which amount to infringement.

In any action for infringement of copyright, it is a defence to show that the activities of the defendant come within the scope of acts permitted in relation to copyright works. These are contained in s.28 to s.76 of the 1988 Act, and include, for example, fair dealing with a literary dramatic musical or artistic work for the purposes of research or private study under s.29, fair dealing for the purposes of criticism or review of the work under s.30, non reprographic copying for the purpose of instruction or any copying for the purpose of examinations under s.32, things done for the purposes of parliamentary or judicial proceedings under s.45 and a range of other acts.

Moral rights

The 1988 Act created, for the first time in UK copyright law, the so called rights of *paternity* and *integrity* in favour of the author of copyright work, and a right of *privacy* in favour of a person commissioning a film or photograph for private and domestic purposes. The rights of paternity, integrity and privacy all subsist for the duration of the copyright under s.86, and can be enforced by an action for breach of statutory duty under s.103. They are personal to the author and cannot be assigned, although they may be waived either by contract or in a signed document, and they devolve as part of the author's estate after his death.

The right of paternity is a right to be identified as the author of a literary, dramatic, musical or artistic work or the director of a film whenever the work is being published commercially, performed in public or broadcast. The right of paternity does not come into effect unless it is asserted either by a term in the assignment of copyright, or in a signed written notice.

The right of integrity is a right which arises, without the need to assert it, in favour again of an author or film director. It is a right not to have the work subjected to derogatory treatment. For these purposes, under s.80(2):

"*(a)   treatment of a work means any addition to, deletion from or alteration to or adaption of the work, other than -*

    (i)   a translation of a literary or dramatic work, or

    (ii)   an arrangement or transcription of a musical work involving no more than a change of key or register; and

(b)   the treatment of a work is derogatory if it amounts to distortion or mutilation of the work or is otherwise prejudicial to the honour or reputation of the author or director".

The right of privacy was introduced in the 1988 Act to counterbalance the abolition of the rule previously contained in s.4(3) of the Copyright Act 1956 that copyright in commissioned photographs belonged to the person who commissioned them. Under the 1988 Act copyright in such works belongs to the photographer. However, where a person commissions a film or a photograph for private and domestic purposes, he has the right, under s.85(1), not to have the work exhibited in public or broadcast, and not to have copies of the work issued to the public.

Assignment What's in a Name?

In the last fifteen years Ricca has become a household name in fabrics and furniture design. To have Ricca furnishings in your home is for many people the mark of success.

When the young designers Richard and Catherine Bratton formed their Ricca company in 1979 they had no idea that their up-market products would become the basis of a £50 million business by the mid nineteen nineties, or that their distinctive style and Ricca logo would become internationally known.

In 1989 when the company went public, it was already an organisation employing four hundred staff at its main premises in Derby. You work in its small legal department at Derby, as an assistant to one of the two company lawyers, Michael Richardson. Your department deals with a wide range of legal matters, and at the moment you are working on three separate issues which Michael has asked you to look over, prior to discussing them with him. These issues are briefly described below.

The Ricca name and logo. A newly formed company that is competing in the same market as Ricca, is regarded by the Ricca board of directors has having unreasonably infringed Ricca's business interests, by incorporating in the name of Reeca Ltd., and selling a range of furniture described as the *Celeste range*. Ricca produces a range called *Celestial* a term which the company has registered as a trade mark. The two furniture ranges are of a different style however, and whilst the logo of each company is a design based upon the letter *R*, which incorporates a similar typeface, the Ricca logo is circular, whereas the Reeca logo is triangular.

The design director. Following an internal disagreement with other members of the board, the design director, Milos Kasna left the company earlier this year and set up his own business designing and printing fabrics. His company is already selling fabrics which are based upon a design started by Mr. Kasna after he resigned from the company, while he was still working out his notice. Additionally he is selling a fabric which he designed for Ricca four years ago, but which the company stopped producing after one year because of poor sales.

The lease. Part of the Derby premises, housing the furniture division of the company, is held on a ten year lease which is due to expire in eight months time. There is evidence that the landlord, wishes to expand his business, which adjoins the furniture division and may oppose the renewal of the lease.

Tasks

1. Examine the situations involving the competition from Reeca Ltd. and Milos Kasna's new company, and produce a brief report for Michael Richardson which advises him of Ricca's legal rights, and how the company should proceed.

2. Produce a paper to be tabled at the next meeting of the board of directors which outlines the rights of the company in relation to the renewal of its business lease.

Index

C